PRAISE FOR *SUSTAINABLE PROCUREMENT*

"An essential and highly practi_____ _____ving responsible purchasing practices – helps make sense of t___ _omplex topic of transforming buying through the lens of sustainability."
Anke Ehlers, Managing Director CRI, ALDI SÜD KG

"Jonathan addresses procurement's need to work with the supply networks on how they think about environmental sustainability. Our need to build our supply networks to be robust to support the environmental challenges is critical."
Chris Shanahan, VP Global Sustainability – Supply Chain Operations, Thermo Fisher Scientific

"Rethinking business practices with corporate social responsibility in mind has become an imperative for all organizations. This provides a huge opportunity for procurement teams to demonstrate new sources of value by managing the business' consumption habits and rebuilding supply chains in line with business CSR strategy. But how? Jonathan O'Brien's *Sustainable Procurement* provides comprehensive insights into the tools, tactics and strategies procurement teams can put into practice to drive CSR best practices and measure their results."
Philip Ideson, Founder and Managing Director, Art of Procurement

"As concerns about anthropogenic climate change, biodiversity loss, pollution and social impacts have become more common, global organizations both in the public and private sectors have shifted to embrace sustainable practices and policies. However, many organizations have no or under-developed sustainable procurement programmes and thus are ill-equipped to achieve these ambitions. Jonathan O'Brien has provided the much-needed insights and practical tools to help organizations and procurement professionals define and implement sustainable procurement programmes that yield desired outcomes for all stakeholders, whilst simultaneously uplifting the mission of procurement as an enabler of strategic intents."
Vusi Fele, Group Chief Procurement Officer, Absa Group

"Talk of sustainability is not new, but operational progress continues to lag behind aspiration and vision. In this passionately written book, Jonathan O'Brien makes the case for the sustainability imperative, demonstrates why progress cannot be made without coordinated efforts from procurement and supply chain professionals, and turns previously abstract guidance into an actionable, achievable mission."
Kelly Barner, Head of Content and Operations, Art of Procurement

"Sustainability is an era-defining opportunity for procurement. It is the strategic imperative that will turn failed SRM initiatives into successful programmes and will cement action and transformation for the betterment of the function and for the future of our planet. This book acts as a practical roadmap that translates greenwashing and greenwishing into evidence-based action. A must-read for all procurement and sustainability professionals today."
Mark Perera, CEO & Founder, Vizibl

"This is the most insightful and – perhaps more importantly – the most useful book on sustainable procurement. Jonathan O´Brien shows us how to weave category management and SRM together and use it as leverage to enable sustainable supply chains. *Sustainable Procurement* is undoubtedly one of the most important sources of knowledge for our own transformation to sustainable sourcing."
Andreas Takacs, Chief Procurement Officer, Green Cargo AB

"Sustainable procurement is a topic on every procurement leader's agenda, but the path forward is often unclear. Jonathan O'Brien provides the information needed to understand the options and create a compelling path forward."
Erik Stavrand, Partner, SEAK LLC

Sustainable Procurement

A practical guide to corporate social responsibility in the supply chain

Jonathan O'Brien

KoganPage

Publisher's note
Every possible effort has been made to ensure that the information contained in this book is accurate at the time of going to press, and the publishers and authors cannot accept responsibility for any errors or omissions, however caused. No responsibility for loss or damage occasioned to any person acting, or refraining from action, as a result of the material in this publication can be accepted by the editor, the publisher or the author.

First published in Great Britain and the United States in 2023 by Kogan Page Limited

Apart from any fair dealing for the purposes of research or private study, or criticism or review, as permitted under the Copyright, Designs and Patents Act 1988, this publication may only be reproduced, stored or transmitted, in any form or by any means, with the prior permission in writing of the publishers, or in the case of reprographic reproduction in accordance with the terms and licences issued by the CLA. Enquiries concerning reproduction outside these terms should be sent to the publishers at the undermentioned addresses:

2nd Floor, 45 Gee Street	8 W 38th Street, Suite 902	4737/23 Ansari Road
London	New York, NY 10018	Daryaganj
EC1V 3RS	USA	New Delhi 110002
United Kingdom		India
www.koganpage.com		

© Jonathan O'Brien 2023

The right of Jonathan O'Brien to be identified as the author of this work has been asserted by him in accordance with the Copyright, Designs and Patents Act 1988.

ISBNs
Hardback   9781398604704
Paperback 9781398604681
Ebook   9781398604698

British Library Cataloguing-in-Publication Data
A CIP record for this book is available from the British Library.

Typeset by Hong Kong FIVE Workshop
Print production managed by Jellyfish
Printed and bound by CPI Group (UK) Ltd, Croydon CR0 4YY

Kogan Page books are printed on paper from sustainable forests.

CONTENTS

Introduction 1

PART 1 Our current situation 5

01 **Situation planet Earth, part 1: The planet** 7
Six areas of critical threat and detrimental impact 10

02 **Situation planet Earth, part 2: People and communities** 48
Impacts on people 48
Impacts on communities 76
Digital world impacts on people 81

03 *Homo sapiens*: **extinct in 100 years?** 91
Future planet – with or without people? 91
How unsustainable are we? 97
Everybody wants to change the world 100

PART 2 The sustainability imperative 107

04 **Introducing sustainable procurement** 109
The ability to exist constantly 110
Sustainable procurement 112

05 **The business case for sustainable procurement** 123
The business of business is business 123
Selling the business case 156

06 Setting the direction for sustainability 162
Defining the vision for sustainability 163
Frameworks for sustainability 176
Setting the sustainable procurement strategy, goals and targets 204

PART 3 Sustainable procurement 213

07 Assessing the supply base 215
Where to start with assessment 215
Hot spot analysis 224
GHG emissions analysis 257

08 Prioritizing risks, impacts and opportunities 270
Prioritization 272

09 Evaluating potential sustainable procurement projects 285
Fact finding 289
Driving new sustainable value 298

10 Making what we buy sustainable 307
A completely new approach 308
Analysing what we buy 315

11 Driving sustainability in our suppliers 338
A new dimension to SRM 340
Redefining relationship requirements 347
Contracting for sustainability 352
Driving supplier improvements 355

12 Audit and assessment of suppliers 366
First-hand understanding 366
Defining the minimum 370
Supplier assessment 374
Auditing a supplier 384

13 Driving sustainability in the supply chain 402
Understanding supply chains 402
Supply chain/SVCN mapping 410
Driving supply chain improvements 420

14 Making it happen, measuring outcomes and driving success 438
Implementing sustainable procurement 439
Measuring outcomes and sharing success 450
The future is (possibly) bright 469

Appendix 479
Glossary 496
References 497
Index 511

ABOUT THE AUTHOR

Jonathan O'Brien is the CEO of the global procurement and negotiation digital platform, consultancy and training provider Positive Purchasing Ltd (positivepurchasing.com). Jonathan has over 30 years' experience working in procurement and negotiation. He has worked all over the world to help global organizations increase their capability through training, education, working directly with practitioners and executive teams, and equipping teams with the digital tools to enable the adoption of category management, supplier relationship management, negotiation, and other strategic procurement and supply chain methodologies.

Jonathan is an electronics engineer who ended up in procurement. His career in engineering soon moved into supplier quality assurance, and it was the hundreds of supplier audits undertaken involving detailed examination of business practice and process that provided a sound understanding of how organizations work, and thus began the process of working with companies to help them improve. A move to a senior buying role in a large utility company shifted the focus to the commercial aspects of purchasing and this career path culminated in a global category director role for an airline business. Jonathan moved to an internal consultant role and helped lead a series of major organizational change programmes. A subsequent move into consultancy, initially with a large global strategic purchasing consultancy and later with his own business, provided Jonathan the opportunity to work with some of the biggest and most well-known companies in the world to help improve procurement and negotiation capability, and gain a rich experience along the way.

Jonathan holds an MBA from Plymouth University Business School, a Diploma in Marketing and an HNC in electronics, is an NLP Master

Practitioner and a former registered Lead Assessor of quality management systems.

Jonathan and his team at Positive Purchasing Ltd have developed and created the 5i® Category Management process, the 5S and 5A™ Supplier Relationship Management process and the Buyer's Toolkit. They have also created the OMEIA® Sustainable Procurement methodology featured in this book and also Red Sheet® negotiation tool that has become the way many individuals and corporations approach negotiation.

Jonathan has published five books so far. He is also an accomplished broadcaster and artist and lives with his family in Plymouth, UK.

You can email Jonathan at jonathan@jonathanobrien.co.uk

PREFACE

This book provides everything organizations need to do to make sustainable procurement a reality. The need for sustainability is now well recognized and crucially there is now a groundswell among individuals, organizations and some nations towards action. And where action is lacking, the criticality of some issues we now face, coupled with emerging legislation, means change is inevitable. Whether the motivation is 'want to' or 'need to', sustainability is now firmly on the boardroom agenda. Policies abound and the new shoots of widespread change are all around, yet the main focus by organizations is on that which can be readily influenced. Realizing sustainability on the supply side presents perhaps the biggest challenge and is one where traditional procurement and supply chain approaches won't do. Instead we need to rethink the role of procurement as a strategic contributor to business success and sustainability, and equip the function with new tools and new ways of thinking.

Sustainable procurement is about augmenting existing good strategic practice and process with the necessary components that drive in sustainable procurement. This book is designed to build on and complement the existing titles I have published that form the 'strategic procurement trilogy' (*Category Management in Purchasing*, *Supplier Relationship Management* and *Negotiation for Procurement and Supply Chain Professionals*). It provides new tools and methodologies as well as the means to extend the use of existing tools and approaches to deliver a complete sustainable procurement assessment and improvement programme. The book explores the global imperative to act and why organizations need new approaches now. It includes a step-by-step approach to determining and implementing sustainable procurement as well as the key success factors.

If you want to understand sustainability and sustainable procurement some more, or if you are seeking to implement improvements in how you source or even drive in a full sustainable procurement programme, then you need to read this book.

I am interested to learn of your experiences of making sustainable procurement a reality and how the approaches outlined in this book may have helped. Please feel free to connect with me on LinkedIn or email me at jonathan@jonathanobrien.co.uk and share.

ACKNOWLEDGEMENTS

This is the book I have always wanted to write. It is my fifth title and has been written to help procurement practitioners to place sustainability at the centre of strategic procurement. It complements and integrates with all my other titles to provide the complete strategic procurement approach organizations need for the future.

I have been a fierce advocate for sustainability in organizations for many years and have long since recognized the crucial role of procurement to enable this. Sadly though, until recently there has been little corporate interest for such things. Back in 2003 when I co-founded Positive Purchasing Ltd, the business was created with the aim of helping global companies achieve what we then called corporate social responsibility in their supply chains. Clients were interested to hear what we had to say, but not ready to commit. Instead they wanted help to reduce cost, better manage key suppliers, negotiate more effectively with suppliers and so on. And so I ended up being CEO of a world-leading business that became known for helping global companies do these things well and I wrote four books covering these topics. I'm proud to say these have become seminal texts in this space. One has even won an award. Yet for sustainability, the idea got shelved. Despite my belief it was critical, it seemed that with the exception of a handful of other advocates, no one was really interested. Perhaps I had got it wrong.

With my previous research and work now long since archived, and the idea of helping organizations figure out sustainable procurement abandoned, in recent years I increasingly found myself despairing over the very real, and increasingly critical, issues that threaten our planet and everyone and everything on it. My despair grew watching the inability or reluctance of nations, organizations and people to do something about it. Yet it was in 2018 when I saw the then 15-year-old Greta Thunberg protesting outside the Swedish parliament holding a sign saying 'School Strike for Climate' in an attempt to compel the Swedish government to take its carbon emissions targets seriously that made me realize I had to do something too. I dusted off my previous work, started researching again and decided it was time to get serious about sustainable procurement. We can all make personal changes to our lives to make a contribution in the right direction – such things are tiny but still worthwhile. Governments hold the potential to drive highly effective change but typically lack the ability to do so, let alone do it in concert with other nations to create a global effort. The greatest positive impact is possible if organizations can change what they do and how they do it to drive sustainability, with the supply base typically holding the greatest potential. Such effort can influence and drive both governmental and consumer changes also.

Therefore, the contribution I can make is to take the 30+ years' experience I have of working with, and building procurement and negotiation capability in, hundreds of the biggest-name organizations on the planet and combine this with my passion, knowledge and insight on sustainability to create a practical approach for sustainable procurement. That is why I am so excited about this book more than any other I have written, and it is my hope that what you will find in the pages in this publication will enable, equip and drive meaningful change in companies all over the world. Small as it is, that is my contribution to try to help change the world.

So thank you Greta Thunberg! A remarkable woman who started a movement. I've not met her, and she will have no idea who I am, but she helped me to decide to write this book.

Thank you too to the many people who have contributed directly, shaped my thinking or freely shared examples with me. I have the privilege of working with many very clever people pioneering leading-edge programmes in this space around the world. Thank you to three guests on my podcast who shaped my thinking – Chris Holmes for insight into the circular economy in practice, Dr Deborah Hemming, one of the world's leading authorities on climate change, for helping me make sense of a gargantuan topic and Andy Martyr-Icke for insight on the future of energy supply. Thanks to Catarina Brito, Frank Rietdijk and Giulia Martinetti from whom I learnt a lot about practical application of many sustainability topics. Thanks also to Brian Houlihan and a special thanks to Katherina Wortmann for taking the time to help me straighten out the complexities of legislation in this area and sharing such important thinking in this area. Thanks to Glen Duncanson for helping me with the peanut butter supply chain. Thank you also to the many people who have shaped my thinking on this over the years, too many to mention or remember. If I have ever had a conversation with you about sustainability, then you have shaped this book. Thank you to you all.

Thank you to the United Nations for permission to use SDGs and thanks also to the incredibly patient team at Kogan Page, especially Anne-Marie Heeney and Nick Hoar for actually reading what I wrote and providing some really great feedback.

The biggest thank you, as ever, is once again to my wife Elaine for putting up with me writing yet another book.

Finally thank you to you for buying this book. I hope it equips you with something worthwhile. Sustainability is a huge topic, and one that I cannot begin to do justice to in this book; however, I hope that this publication adequately focuses on the relevant elements and what procurement and supply chain functions can do to drive change.

Most of the models and concepts in this book are new and original work; many are ground breaking. I have made every effort to properly research, reference and duly credit all work of others, however I apologize in advance for any omissions.

The OMEIA® process and many of the graphics and tables included in this book are © Positive Purchasing Ltd, reproduced here with permission.

Introduction

Using this book

This is a book about sustainable procurement and how to implement a sustainable procurement programme within an organization. Sustainability has come to mean all manner of things and is the generic label that seems to be applied in response to a plethora of modern-day problems that need fixing. It can be difficult to hold a common understanding of precisely what the most pressing issues are, and what exactly we should do and in what order. Is it the climate crisis or plastic bottles in the ocean, child labour making the goods we buy or loss of habitat? It is of course all these things and many more. However, the all-encompassing nature of the 'sustainability zeitgeist' risks diluting the underlying need and urgency the sustainability movement seek to address, and it is hard to be precise about what we need to do. This is particularly relevant when we consider our supply base. As we move through this book I will provide clarity here and describe approaches to assess where procurement is today and form and implement a programme to move forward.

This book includes a process and methodology for sustainable procurement to help practitioners, yet sustainable procurement is not really a linear process. There are some clear steps we follow but to be truly successful at implementing sustainable procurement it needs to be regarded as a new way of applying the existing, well-developed strategic procurement approaches through the lens of sustainability. It is like doing really great strategic procurement with a new sustainability hat on (more on the sustainability hat later). Therefore, to really get the most from this book it should be read together with the strategic purchasing trilogy.

A strategic purchasing trilogy

This is my fifth book and is designed to enhance, complement and integrate with the frameworks and approaches defined within three of my other titles that make up the 'strategic purchasing trilogy' – *Category Management in Purchasing*, *Supplier Relationship Management* and *Negotiation for Procurement and Supply Chain Professionals*. It will also enhance the effective buying approach outlined in *The Buyer's Toolkit* (all titles also published by Kogan Page). Sustainable procurement uses many of the strategic tools found within the strategic trilogy and therefore this book has been written so as to be used together with these three titles. Where a tool has already been expanded in one of these previous works it is not repeated again in this book but referenced at a high level. It is recommended all four publications are used together to provide the complete sustainable procurement approach.

Sustainable procurement pathway questions

This book is organized so as to explore each component or section of an overall sustainable procurement approach and show how these fit together. It seeks to provide answers and practical steps for 15 key or 'pathway' questions. If you can answer all of these questions with confidence then you're in great shape. However, for many organizations these are difficult questions that represent the gap between aspiration and reality. They also help reveal the pathway to move towards making sustainable procurement a reality. This book will help not only to form answers to these questions but will help to develop real actions that enable the firm to progress and take significant steps to being more sustainable.

SUSTAINABLE PROCUREMENT PATHWAY QUESTIONS

1 What is sustainability?
2 Why is sustainability important?
3 What is sustainable procurement?
4 What is the business case for sustainable procurement?
5 How do we determine sustainability goals for the organization?
6 How do we determine goals for sustainable procurement?
7 How can we assess sustainability within our procurement?
8 What improvement areas should we focus on first?
9 How do we build a strategy and road map for sustainable procurement?

10 How can we make 'what we buy' sustainable?

11 How can we drive sustainability in our suppliers?

12 How can we make our supply chains more sustainable?

13 How can we ensure our sustainable procurement programme is a success?

14 How do we measure sustainable procurement outcomes?

15 What should we be thinking about for the future?

A book of three parts

Sustainable procurement and supply chains change everything we know in procurement and supply chain functions. They need new skills, new processes, new ways of thinking, and we need to work even more closely and be more integrated with the wider business than ever before. In short, procurement and supply chain functions that have sustainability at their heart are different now. To help grasp this, and before we get to how we will do sustainable procurement, we will explore everything a procurement or supply chain practitioner needs to know about the broader topic of sustainability. This book is therefore in three parts:

- **Part 1: Our current situation** – Everything you need to know about our planet and its people and the risks and detrimental impacts we face.
- **Part 2: The sustainability imperative** – What it is, why we need it and how this relates to procurement and the supply chain.
- **Part 3: Sustainable procurement** – What it is and how to be good at it.

PART 1
Our current situation

Situation planet Earth, part 1   01
The planet

> This chapter begins to explore our current 'situation planet Earth' and some of the biggest threats and challenges we now face. We explore our current situation in terms of the planet and environment and what this means for us and future generations. The implications for organizations are examined and the chapter sets the scene to consider our current situation in terms of people and communities.
>
> *Pathway questions addressed in this chapter*
>
> 1 What is sustainability?
> 2 Why is sustainability important?

The air was still and very cold. The kind where you can see your every breath. The kind that fascinates a seven-year-old boy. But on this particular January morning in 1974 there was a new thing as my mother walked me to school. On any other day there would be a steady stream of cars passing us by along the road we walked, but not on this morning. On this morning all the cars were stopped. There was some hold-up. The drivers had all kept their engines idling, presumably to keep the heaters inside going. It was a very cold morning. The cold had made the exhaust plumes of cars become clouds of fluffy white hanging in the air. Each car had its own cloud attached, each growing bigger with every stroke of the engine. I had never seen this before. It was beautiful. With my hand held tightly in my mother's, we crossed the road and passed between two cars. As we did, I leaned in towards the white cloud to experience how it felt but mostly to smell it. I didn't get that far and was pulled back sharply by my mother who told me strongly that I should not breathe it. She told me it was harmful. This made no sense to that seven-year-old boy. It sparked a succession of questions. If it was harmful why had we just walked so close? Why are cars allowed to drive near to people? Where does all the white stuff go and if all the cars kept producing it what would happen when the world filled up? I didn't get satisfactory answers from my mother on that walk to school. Later I asked my father the same questions and he replied with something about it containing lead (which exhaust fumes did back then) and that the world was very big, and I think a word I didn't understand at the time like 'dispersed' might have been used but that it was all all right and I didn't need to worry. Whatever he said, I was equally dissatisfied with his response yet none of the grown-ups around me were concerned. I resigned myself to not needing to be concerned.

Today car exhaust gases no longer contain high levels of lead, yet that seven-year-old me back in 1974 had every reason to be concerned for as we now know they are one of the significant contributors to the climate change crises we now face. The threat of climate change did not exist in 1974. Today, however, we have a new understanding. What's more, climate change is not our only threat, in fact we now face many significant interrelated threats of our own creation and of a magnitude we cannot ignore that will, at best, cause significant disruption and difficulty to our generation, and more so to future generations. At worst they will bring about the end of the human race. Human advancement has brought about seismic social, technical, demographic and economic development in ever-growing societies and the resultant changes in lifestyles, consumption, production and waste now threaten our very existence.

There is still time and irrespective of where we and the scientists might sit between holding an optimistic or apocalyptic view of the future there is widespread agreement that the 'do nothing' option is no longer available to us.

The term 'Sustainability' is used interchangeably to mean a response to all manner of adverse impacts, either individually or collectively. Because of this there is no clarity on what precisely sustainability relates to; is it climate change or plastic bottles in the ocean? Is it employees not receiving a fair wage or overuse of resources, social inequality or pollution and so on? It is, in fact, each of these things and all of these things and many others besides. Sustainability, put simply, is *the ability to exist constantly*. Making sense of this means considering the ability to exist constantly in the context of the key threats and adverse impacts on our world while recognizing in doing so we cannot fix everything immediately, so focusing our efforts is essential.

In order to understand sustainable procurement, we must first understand sustainability and have a deep understanding of all the factors that are making our world unsustainable. Therefore, as we move through this book, we will explore sustainability, what this means for organizations, and in particular procurement and supply chain functions and the critical role these functions will play in driving sustainability in organizations in coming years. I will outline frameworks and approaches to help here. We will begin in Part 1 with the first three chapters considering our current situation – a fact-based exploration of the critical threats we face that carry the potential of grave impact on our world and our lives within it, along with the other significant detrimental impacts and the drivers behind these. Efforts towards sustainability therefore centre around these. I have grouped these under six key themes (Figure 1.1). They are the loss of biodiversity, ocean degradation, climate change, depletion of resources and waste mismanagement, social injustice and mistreatment of people and communities, and finally the growing threat and impacts from another world; that of data, digital and the internet. I will set the scene for the rest of this book by exploring each in turn. It may seem overwhelming to devote such a large section at the start of the book to this; however, the reason for this will become clear as a

Figure 1.1 The six planet and people impact areas

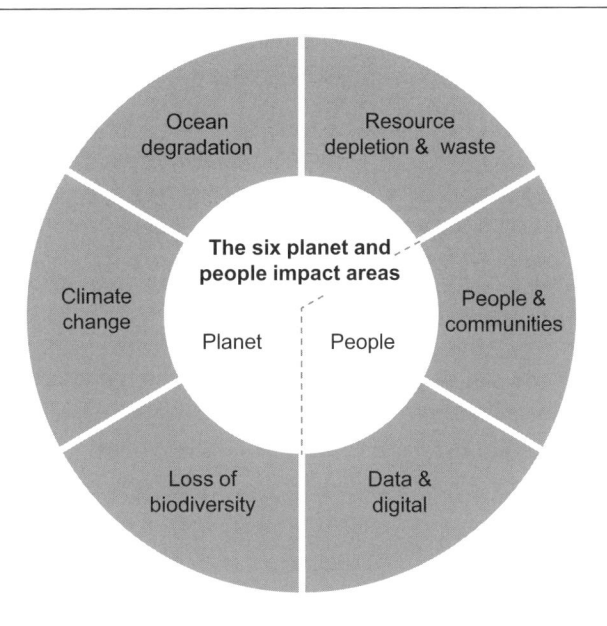

Six areas of critical threat and detrimental impact

Biodiversity loss

Our world is a complex interconnected global ecosystem that we are part of and depend upon. This system works and sustains life on this planet because of the way all life on our planet exists, interacts with and depends upon each other within this system. If parts of the system get removed or stop working it can have a significant impact on part or all of the system and threaten food and water supply, the environment and ultimately life (including ours) on this planet. The variety and variability of life on earth is called biodiversity and is, in essence, the living fabric of our planet.

Biodiversity loss is the reduction in the number of genes, organisms, species and ecosystems. Biodiversity across the earth is currently being lost hundreds of times faster than the natural rate with 1 million of the 8 million species on the planet now facing extinction. One in four plant or animal species are threatened (IPBES, 2019) and an estimated 10 per cent or greater of the world's insects are also threatened, which will impact the 75 per cent of the world's food crops that rely on pollination by insects (Attenborough, 2020a). As varieties and breeds of plants, animals and insects disappear, the risk to global food security heightens as agriculture becomes less able to withstand threats such as pests, disease and the impacts of climate change.

Almost all biodiversity loss is a result of human activity and there are a number of contributors (Figure 1.2). By far the biggest is the destruction of habitat by humans to clear land for agricultural use (such as beef and other livestock, palm oil, paper products, soya or cocoa plantations). Between 1990 and 2016 nearly half of the earth's trees were felled, which equates to an area larger than South Africa (Nunez, 2019). In the Amazon, 17 per cent of the forest has been lost in the past 50 years and (WWF, nd). Today 31 per cent of the earth remains covered by forests and they continue to be lost at a rate of an area equivalent to the size of Italy every year despite commitments by governments to reduce deforestation and some reduction in recent years.

Figure 1.2 The major contributors to biodiversity loss

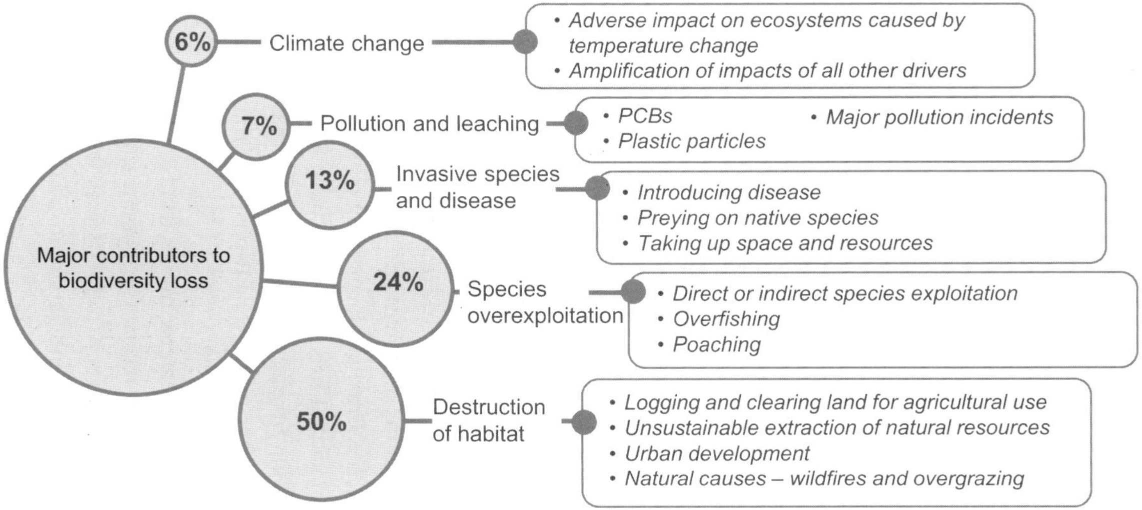

- Climate change — 6%
  - Adverse impact on ecosystems caused by temperature change
  - Amplification of impacts of all other drivers

- Pollution and leaching — 7%
  - PCBs
  - Plastic particles
  - Major pollution incidents

- Invasive species and disease — 13%
  - Introducing disease
  - Preying on native species
  - Taking up space and resources

- Species overexploitation — 24%
  - Direct or indirect species exploitation
  - Overfishing
  - Poaching

- Destruction of habitat — 50%
  - Logging and clearing land for agricultural use
  - Unsustainable extraction of natural resources
  - Urban development
  - Natural causes – wildfires and overgrazing

SOURCE Adapted from Ang (2020)

Deforestation upsets our ecosystem because 80 per cent of the earth's land-based species live in forests and these forests supply and purify water, provide homes and livelihoods for millions of people, and they are essential for sustainable food production (Nunez, 2019). They play a vital role in maintaining our environment and mitigating climate change by soaking up CO_2, so as they diminish climate change is accelerated.

Biodiversity loss also arises from the extraction of natural resources, urban development, species overexploitation (overfishing, poaching, direct species exploitation, or indirect where species are lost as a consequence of other human activities), unsustainable agricultural practices, overgrazing, invasive species and disease (increased due to human activity), pollution and climate change. Biodiversity loss happens above ground and also below ground for many of these same reasons, where it manifests as soil degradation. Here the quality of soil declines or diminishes and with it its capability to support plants and animals, which accelerates biodiversity loss above ground. In addition, as soil degrades it loses its cohesive properties, and turns to dust that gets swept up by winds creating the increasing modern phenomena of regular large dust clouds and poor air quality in some regions.

It seems biodiversity loss has gone largely unnoticed until now, or at best we regarded it as a problem that existed somewhere else in the world and wondered why no one was doing anything. Awareness is stronger today and we better understand how wealthier nations have been importing biodiversity loss; creating demand for the resources that drive agricultural prosperity in developing nations and, with it, deforestation. Without any other economic stimulus, if a Brazilian farmer can make a living cutting down forests on their land or setting fire to them to burn them away in order to create a palm oil plantation or grazing land for cattle that satisfy demand in the UK, Europe, US and other wealthier nations, then that is what they will do, thus this perpetuates the problem.

Biodiversity loss threatens future food and fresh water security for a growing population. It accelerates climate change and the changes to ecosystems bring new threats. Covid-19 was widely regarded as a 'once in a 100-year pandemic' yet biodiversity loss brings the threat of more frequent pandemics. The most widely held science-based view regarding the SARS-CoV-2 pathogenic coronavirus that caused Covid-19 is that it originated from bats, passed directly or most likely via another animal (such as a cat, mink or pangolin) to humans. While the food market in Wuhan is credited in playing a part in the original outbreak, and some have even hypothesized that the virus emerged from the nearby Wuhan Institute of Virology, both of these ideas have little standing (Kunzmann, 2021). What is clear is SARS-CoV-2 was passed to humans originally from bats. Similar viruses exist in the animal world, typically contained in species far removed from us in remote parts of the world. However, as we encroach more and more into nature and as species decline or become extinct, other species that no longer have predators gain new dominance and become more prevalent. This moves us closer and closer to new viruses which, with the potential to jump to humans, creates a new threat of a pandemic as often as one in every ten years, and worse, those in the future could be more dangerous.

Our ailing oceans

Loss of biodiversity is not confined to land. Loss of marine biodiversity, the degradation of our oceans and all the species that live in them and the associated loss of habitat for marine life presents another gargantuan threat to the future of human life on this planet. Once again, the drivers behind this are almost entirely as a result of human activity (Figure 1.3).

Our oceans cover 70 per cent of the planet, made up of 1.3 billion cubic kilometres of water and are, on average, about 4,000 meters deep. There are approximately 8 billion people on the planet; this means that each one of us has about one-sixth of a cubic kilometre of ocean as our proportion. We each rely upon this one-sixth of a cubic kilometre to generate half of the oxygen each of us breathes, to provide us with all the fish and seafood each of us eats and to be the original source of all the water we need (UN, 2016). Yet human activity has degraded our oceans to such an extent that the ability of our proportion of ocean to support our needs is threatened and sadly, despite the increased awareness of the threats we face, the situation has not improved in recent years and our oceans and the many benefits the oceans provide are at risk (UN, 2021).

Changes in our oceans drive weather systems and influence all ecosystems (both marine and on land). Our oceans provide a vital food source, yet we have long since exceeded what is termed the maximum sustainable yield as defined in international law, which relates to the balance of extraction of fish and the ability for the remaining fish stocks to compensate for the extraction and recover. We are overfishing on a global scale. We extract 80 million tonnes of fish from the world's oceans each year as part of a $127 billion industry. Fish accounts for about 17 per cent of all protein consumed by humans and supports about 12 per cent of human livelihoods.

Figure 1.3 The main contributors to ocean degradation

Major contributors to ocean degradation

- Noise
  - Includes
    - *Anthropogenic noise from shipping, gas exploration, extraction of resources and other heavy industry*

- Climate change
  - *Diminished ocean movement due to overfishing*
  - *Acidification of oceans*
  - *Rising sea levels*

- Destruction of habitat
  - *Bottom or near-bottom trawling*
  - *Submarine cables*
  - *Anchoring*

- Pollution and microparticles
  - *Pollution events*
  - *POPS, metals, radioactive substances, PPCPs*
  - *Marine litter – plastics, waste and microparticles*

- Overfishing
  - *Fishing of stocks currently at unsustainable levels*
  - *Fishing of stocks at maximum sustainable yields*
  - *By-catch kills of marine mammals, marine reptiles and sea birds*

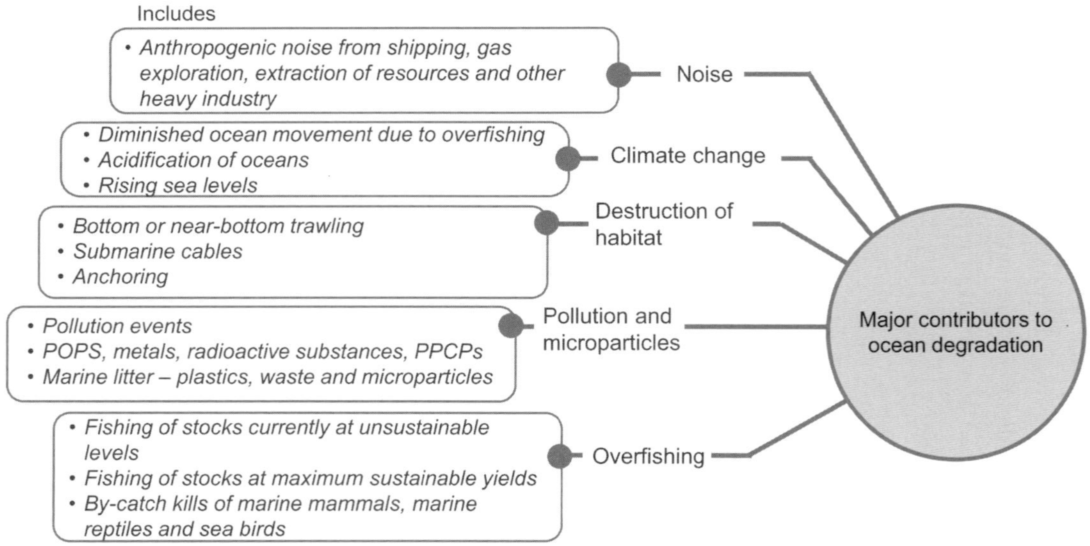

Currently, about 33 per cent of the world's fish stocks are being overfished at biologically unsustainable levels and more are still recovering from past overfishing. Furthermore, about 60 per cent of world fish stocks are currently being extracted at the maximum sustainable level (UN, 2021). Overfishing compromises food security and this is without counting that which gets caught by accident as part of the fishing process. While some fishing methods have changed in recent times, the incidental by-catch still includes large numbers of dolphins, resulting in a significant reduction of certain dolphin species, together with sea birds, marine reptiles (fishery by-catch is now the highest threat across the marine turtle population), endangered species and other marine mammals. Each year commercial long-net fishing kills an estimated 160,000 albatrosses and petrels as by-catch of commercial fishing. In addition, further loss of marine biodiversity is caused because many commercial fishing methods cause long-term damage to the ocean seabed and habitats; the most notable of these is bottom trawling.

Bottom trawling is where either a single trawler or two trawlers acting together drag a net behind or between the vessel(s) collecting up everything on the seabed or just above it. While the concept of drag net fishing has been sustainable practice for millennia, modern large-scale methods have made it unsustainable. Nets close to the seabed stir up sediment and those that drag across the seabed destroy all habitat. Each seabed pass of a bottom net trawl removes between 6 and 41 per cent of the organisms on the seabed and the recovery time can exceed six years (Hiddink et al, 2017). Despite some countries seeking to ban bottom trawling in certain areas, the practice remains legal and where it is not enforcement can be absent or difficult.

Destruction of habitat by damage to the ocean seabed also occurs from the laying and movement of submarine cables, anchoring and deep-sea mining.

A further impact to oceans results from climate change. Climate change impacts the oceans and degradation of our oceans accelerates climate change because the ocean plays a key role in maintaining our climate. Our oceans absorb about one-third of the CO_2 we produce (Le Quéré et al, 2016) and help regulate the world's temperate by absorbing heat. This happens through ocean movement, which acts to transport carbon and heat as well as oxygen and nutrients around the ocean. Good ocean circulation is crucial in keeping the global ecosystem in balance. The circulation of ocean water occurs as a result of surface winds, changes in water density as ocean temperature or salinity varies around the world, and the movement of fish and marine mammals. Ocean movement, and therefore the ocean's ability to extract

CO_2 from the atmosphere and help regulate the earth's temperature, is reducing and there are many factors behind this, including:

1. As species of fish and marine mammals diminish due to overfishing, the circulation they bring by their movement is reduced.
2. The rising ocean temperature, together with the resultant rise in sea levels due to melting of the polar ice caps along with thermal expansion, reduce the temperate gradients across the world's oceans and slow circulation.
3. Rising ocean temperatures also change the chemical balance and the salinity of the ocean, reducing salinity gradients and slowing circulation.

In addition, increased CO_2 in the atmosphere means more is dissolved into oceans, which lowers pH making oceans more acidic and this, together with the rising ocean temperature, stresses and kills ecosystems. The higher acidity makes it more difficult for marine calcifying organisms such as coral and plankton to form, which then extends up the food chain to threaten all other marine species. Ocean acidity levels at the surface have increased by nearly 30 per cent since the Industrial Revolution, ten times faster than at any time in the last 55 million years (CoastAdapt, 2017). This is predicted to continue to rise unless emissions are reduced.

As if this wasn't enough to upset the balance of our oceans, human activity has used the world's oceans as a convenient sink and garbage can to take away waste. All this has happened in plain sight, and most of it has been legal, presuming ocean vastness would support this practice. Where this is not so, governments are either unconcerned or unable to drive enforcement. Yet the impacts of the many decades of this practice have taken their toll and caused dangerous damage to many fragile ocean ecosystems. This includes (based upon and adapted from UN, 2021):

- **Pollution events** – Oil spills, shipping and industrial discharges, offshore oil and gas platform discharges, atmospheric fallout and run-off from agricultural land.
- **Persistent organic pollutants (POPs)** – A varied and complex list of pollutants that originate from industrial chemicals, by-products and use of pesticides including such nasties as polychlorinated biphenyls (PCBs) and dichlorodiphenyltrichloroethane (DDT). Today legislation prohibits production of many POPs – the problem is these chemicals endure and do not degrade. Legacy pollution means our oceans contain some concerning concentrations in some 'hot spot' areas. POPs cause adverse biological effects to marine and human life and these chemicals are now found in

plankton, fish and shellfish in small amounts in these areas. However, the greatest impact happens further down the food chain where there is a cumulative effect of all the small concentrations, which build to concerning levels in larger sea mammals causing biological impacts such as birth defects in the whale population.

- **Metals** – High concentration of metals, especially highly toxic metals such as mercury, cadmium, lead and tributyltin that hold the potential to adversely impact human life. Metals are mainly absorbed from airborne pollution originating from coal-burning plants.
- **Radioactive substances,** largely from historical events, remain in our oceans. These have resulted from discharges from the world's 450 nuclear power reactors, historical weapons testing and reprocessing plants, including a relatively small impact from world nuclear accidents including Chernobyl and Fukushima. Levels today do not present cause for concern; however, social changes and a move to more nuclear energy could cause future concerns.
- **Pharmaceuticals and personal care products (PPCPs)** – Chemicals used for healthcare, cosmetics and medical purposes (both human and animal) discharged in waste water from households, from agriculture or through recreational activities. Waste-water treatment facilities are ineffective in removing PPCPs and so they end up in freshwater systems and oceans. PPCPs typically don't or only slowly degrade and are concerning because many degrade and transform to more toxic products.
- **Deliberate dumping at sea** – Domestic and industrial waste, sewage, garbage from ships, aircraft, platforms and dumping of scrap vessels.
- **Marine litter** – Plastics in the ocean have perhaps become the most obvious and visible on or in the ocean or left on the coastline; however, marine litter also includes metal, glass, rubber, wood and other materials, and enters the oceans by being blown from land sources, washed into storm drains, accidental release or deliberately dumped. Marine litter has an adverse impact on the marine environment as it leads to entanglement, especially of larger marine species, and is ingested by marine mammals, turtles, birds and fish. Marine litter can travel great distances and can carry non-indigenous pests, pathogens, algae, bacteria and other organisms that cause infestations and damage to marine ecosystems. Marine litter is now present in all marine habitats and can now be found in remote regions and even at the bottom of deep-ocean trenches and includes:

- Single-use plastic items (the biggest contributor to marine litter) such as plastic bottles, plastic bags (estimated at 1–5 trillion bags worldwide each year (UNEP, 2018)), straws, cutlery, cigarette butts, caps and lids, and food trays. Today, we produce about 400 million tonnes of plastic waste every year (UNEP, 2022), of which it is estimated between 4.8 and 12.7 million tonnes entered the ocean (Jambeck et al, 2015).
- Discarded plastic fishing gear.
- Loss and purposeful disposal of cargo, shipping pallets and containers.
- **Microparticles** – Small mainly plastic particles (and some other materials) ranging from less than a micron to a few millimetres in size. Over time single-use plastics in the ocean break up into smaller and smaller particles and these, together with microbeads or other industrial pellets entering via waste streams, as well as particles such those created from vehicle tyres through breaking, being washed into drains is creating concerning levels of microparticle pollution. Waste-water treatment processes are largely ineffective against microparticles, so they flow into rivers and oceans and enter the food chain. Microplastics and the chemical additives they might contain present a risk to the health of organisms in high concentrations. Such particles are now in the human food chain when we eat fish or shellfish, which brings human health concerns, the level of which is not yet understood.

In addition to the above, ocean ecosystems are increasingly under threat from an impact least heard about, which is noise. Anthropogenic noise (noise from human activity) is that which is transmitted through the ocean and comes from sources such as shipping, oil and gas exploration, extraction of resources and other heavy industry. Noise has an impact on many marine species.

The outlook for our oceans

It is a sobering thought to realize that by 2050 there will be an estimated 9.7 billion people on the planet, which means that our portion of the ocean, which will then be our children's portion, will have shrunk to one-eighth of a cubic kilometre and will still need to provide oxygen, food and water (UN, 2016).

Ocean degradation, acidification and warming accelerate climate change and loss of biodiversity, and climate change accelerates ocean degradation.

Climate change

It is unequivocal that human influence has warmed the atmosphere, ocean and land. Widespread and rapid changes in the atmosphere, ocean, cryosphere and biosphere have occurred.

(IPCC, 2021)

Climate change is the global warming of the earth caused by human emissions of greenhouse gases, the main ones being carbon dioxide, methane and nitrous oxide, and the resulting large-scale weather changes across the planet. Today the world adds 51 billion tonnes of greenhouse gases (of which 38 billion tonnes is CO_2) into the atmosphere every year; this figure is increasing and with it the temperature of the earth. If nothing changes this could triple by the end of the century. There are many contributors to climate change (Figure 1.4) with the largest being energy production and use in all its forms accounting for 74 per cent of all emissions produced. Of this energy, use for transportation accounts contributes 17 per cent of all emissions with the remainder being energy production for industrial use, commercial and residential buildings and other general energy production.

Since preindustrial times the temperature of the earth has already increased by around 1.1°C with each of the last four decades being successively warmer than any decade that preceded it since 1850 (IPCC, 2021). The seven-year period from 2015 to 2022 was the warmest on record and that included a drop of 4 per cent of global emissions due to Covid-19 lockdowns (World Meteorological Organization, 2022). The scale of recent changes and present state of the climate are unprecedented, even looking back over many thousands of years (IPCC, 2021).

If we can halt the increase so that the earth's temperate does not rise by more than 1.5°C we can avert what is nothing short of a climate catastrophe that will impact all life on this planet and the future of the human race (more on that shortly).

By 2015 the world was on track for a possible 4°C rise. In 2016 global leaders met in Paris and agreed a climate deal to hold the average temperature increase to 'well below' 2°C. However, by 2020 it was clear that progress towards this target was lacking. Based upon the policies and pledges from nations of the world, the predicted increase was set to be between 2.8°C and 3.2°C by the end of the century. In 2021 nations of the world made pledges at the COP26 summit to work to keep rises to 1.5 °C yet since that time action by nations has fallen short that needed to realize this

Figure 1.4 The contributors to climate change

Includes

- Emissions from landfill — Waste — 3%

- Cement processing
- Chemical production
- Other industrial processes
— Industrial processes — 5%

- Digestive emissions from livestock (5.8%)
- Nitrogen-based fertilizers
- Crop burning
- Cutting down trees (releasing carbon)
— Agriculture, forestry and land use — 18%

- Energy production and use – for general use — General energy — 15%

- Road transport (12%)
- Aviation (1.9%)
- Shipping (1.7%)
— Transportation — 17%

- Commercial buildings (6.6%)
- Residential buildings (11%)
— Energy use in buildings — 18%

- Iron and steel production (7.2%)
- Chemical and petrochemical (3.6%)
- Food production (1%)
— Energy use in industry — 24%

Major contributors to climate change

Total from energy 74%

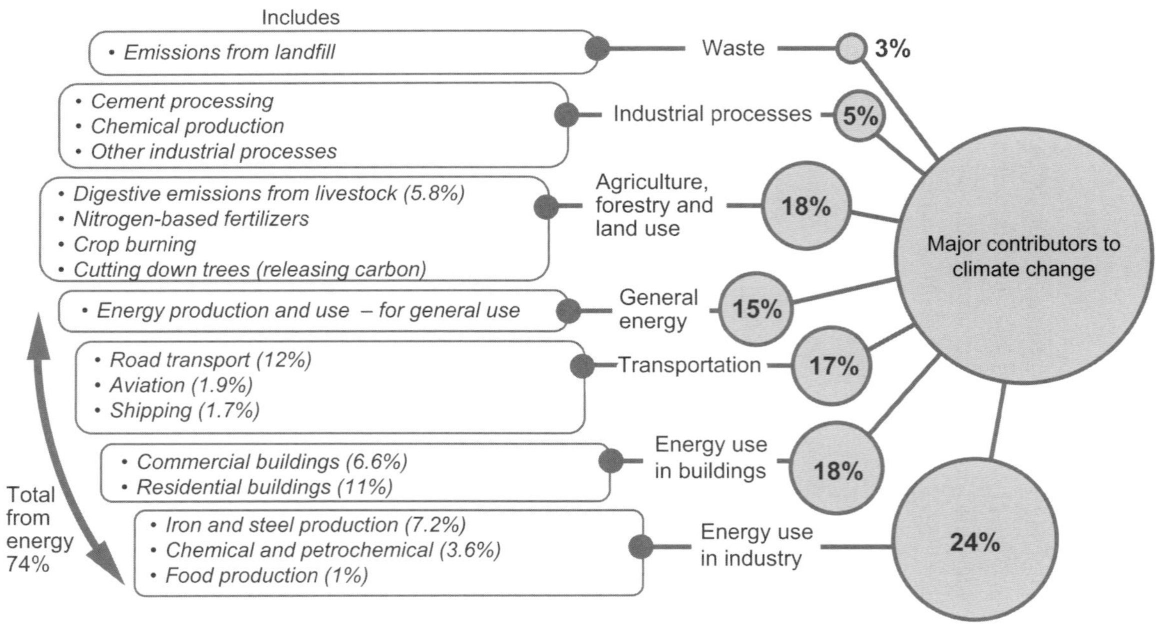

SOURCE Adapted from Ritchie et al (2020)

ambition. More on that shortly too. The hard reality is that if no policies for emission reduction are realized, greenhouse emissions will triple and cause an increase between 4.1°C and 4.8°C by the end of the century (Ritchie et al, 2020). Gates (2021) suggested this figure could be as high as 8°C and IPCC put the worst-case scenario at an 8.5°C raise.

While we see the signs of renewable energy sources emerging around us in the form of wind turbines, solar, biofuels and so on, worldwide the sources of fuel used for energy production have changed only marginally in the past 50 years with fossil fuel still accounting for a round 80 per cent of all energy produced. Of all the fossil fuels coal is the most polluting and the biggest contributor to greenhouse gas emissions, along with many other nasty chemicals that find their way into the water and food system and impact air quality. Around 37 per cent of energy worldwide comes from burning coal (IEA, 2021). Despite pledges in recent years by world nations to reduce coal, coal is alive and well and by the end of 2022 China had 1,118 coal-fired power plants, India had 281 and the US 252. In contrast China is also the biggest producer and user of renewable energy.

Of the 38 billion tonnes of CO_2 emitted each year, China is the biggest emitter accounting for just under one-third of this. China, the US, India, the 27 EU countries together with the UK, Russia and Japan represent the largest CO_2 emitters (Figure 1.5). Together these territories account for 51 per cent of world population, 62.5 per cent of gross domestic product and produce 67 per cent of all fossil fuel CO_2. Emissions continue to rise globally; however, both the EU27+UK and US saw reductions from 2019 (Crippa et al, 2020).

Emissions are also a major cause of air pollution with 91 per cent of the world living in places where air quality exceeds World Health Organization limits (World Health Organization, 2016). Burning fossil fuels releases gases, chemicals and particles into the air, exacerbating global warming and in turn increasing temperature, which in turn further worsens air pollution. Add to this, as we learnt earlier, increasing and more severe dust storms – a product of soil degradation turning soil to dust, which then gets swept up into the air. Poor air quality accounts for an estimated 4.2 million deaths each year due to due to stroke, heart disease, lung cancer and chronic respiratory diseases (World Health Organization, 2016).

Figure 1.5 Top 10 emitters by percentage of total global emissions

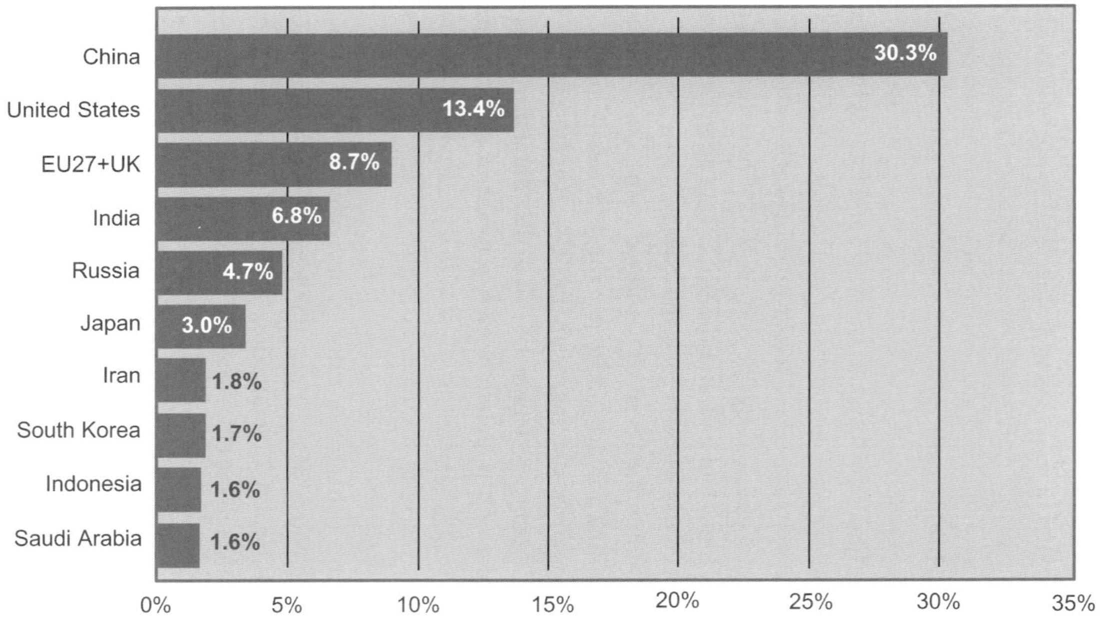

Country	Percentage
China	30.3%
United States	13.4%
EU27+UK	8.7%
India	6.8%
Russia	4.7%
Japan	3.0%
Iran	1.8%
South Korea	1.7%
Indonesia	1.6%
Saudi Arabia	1.6%

SOURCE Adapted from Crippa et al (2020)

The inconvenient truth of climate change

Exactly what the increase will be depends upon what the countries of the world manage to do in the very near term to reduce emissions and so far, global action has fallen too short of various pledges and targets nations have made. Worse, until very recently the nations of the world and their leaders have found ways to ignore, reject or delay the inconvenient science-based truth of climate change. The situation today is one where, on a global scale, we have so far failed to take the necessary action needed to avoid the dire consequences that climate change is bringing and also failed to prepare for the changes that are already certain, irrespective of whether we halt further increases.

In 2021, when the representatives from 200 countries, 120 of them world leaders, came together for the COP26 summit in Glasgow, they made a new deal. This was considered by many to be the last chance to find a way to address the spectre of climate change. As the entire world watched it was evident that getting 200 countries to agree to something meaningful for our children's future would be nothing short of a miracle. Indeed, many of these nations would need to pledge extensive and sustained actions that would bring huge economic and social change and impact and demand eye-watering funding. Following many long and protracted negotiations a deal of sorts was made and in the closing press conferences world leaders talked of how they were keeping the ambition of 1.5 °C alive at this historic moment. Others were less ready to claim victory. Greta Thunberg described the deal as 'very, very vague' with 'still no guarantee that we will reach the Paris Agreement' and news stories focused on where the deal had been watered down, especially regarding phasing out coal.

While it might be possible to limit the rise to 1.5°C, it doesn't follow that the nations of the world will honour their pledges, or they may lack the ability to realize their commitments. Indeed, one year later, and as leaders stated at COP27, countries are falling short on meeting stated commitments. We know from history that there is a world of difference between what world leaders agree to at summits and what actually happens. In the science of game theory, we could regard this as a global game of prisoner's dilemma. It is easy to stand on the sidelines and criticize the politicians but take a moment to reflect on the incredible situation we face. The science is clear that any rise in temperature above 1.5°C would be catastrophic, yet achieving this requires *all* nations of the world to reduce their emissions of CO_2 each year to net zero before 2030. If this feels impossible, that is because it probably is. Indeed, Bill Gates suggests that solving climate change would be 'the most amazing thing humanity has ever done' (Rowlatt, 2021) because the scale of what needs to happen here is like nothing the human race has ever faced before. Key reasons that make this a near-impossible ambition are:

- It is almost entirely dependent upon China (the biggest emitter) decarbonizing.
- Sovereignty of nations means countries can ultimately choose to do what they want.
- Pledges require new legislation that may not be supported, e.g. the US Senate needs to continue to back climate legislation and a change in administration could see previously agreed pledges or legislation overturned.
- Developing nations, including many that contributed little to the crises, face the biggest impacts and lack the resources to make the required changes.

It would be easy at this point to assume we are all doomed. However, in terms of what COP26 and subsequently COP27 achieved there were some key turning points in the rhetoric that give hope and will shape what we do here. These are:

- It created a coalition of countries to decarbonize.
- Countries agreed, for the first time, to report on progress.
- A programme was agreed for funding for developing nations to help tackle the consequences of climate change they face (a principle that later became a key sticking point in countries making a deal).
- 130 countries signed up to halt deforestation by 2030.
- One-third of the world's car market agreed to go to electric vehicles by 2035.
- New funding models to enable commercial sector funding to support climate change initiatives.
- It was the first deal to plan explicitly to tackle coal.
- 90 per cent of countries committed to achieving net zero.
- Loss and damage funding to be provided for vulnerable countries hit hard by floods, droughts and other climate disasters.

The outlook for our climate

It is clear that what happens next depends upon the degree to which all nations of the world manage to work in concert to avert climate change. The predicted small rises in the earth's temperature might seem inconsequential; however, this could not be further from the truth.

As the earth warms up the biggest impact will be to the earth's water cycle.

By 2050 1 billion more people will live in severely water-scarce areas representing about a third of the earth's even larger predicted population (projected to be between 2.7 and 3.2 billion). We will see an increase in fatalities as a result of poor water quality, and water shortages will be greater, more widespread, last longer in these regions and given that developing nations typically use 90 per cent of their water for agriculture, food supply will be severely threatened. Today 90 per cent of natural disasters are water related and the most severe are drought and flood. In the future we can expect more, and of greater magnitude (World Meteorological Organization, 2022), along with more extreme heatwaves, wildfires and the resultant increased pollution levels.

Some regions in the world have already become too hot to sustain human life. Today this is about 1 per cent of the earth. By 2070 it could be 19 per cent (Lustgarten, 2020) and we will see more such regions in coming years. Sea levels will continue to rise and will change the world map for good with some entire regions being lost, and with them the homes and livelihoods of the people in those areas today along with extensive animal habitats. Arctic sea-ice melt and the rising of sea levels is now happening at a faster rate than previously predicted as these regions continue to warm at more than twice the global rate. As the thawing continues, permafrost will melt and will release more carbon into the atmosphere. Permafrost is the frozen ground under the ice in arctic regions made up of decomposed plants, animals and other organic matter that has previously been metabolized. It is, in essence, frozen carbon and methane. The world's permafrost contains approximately 1,700 gigatonnes of carbon, which is nearly twice as much carbon than currently in the atmosphere (Goncalves, 2019). As permafrost melts, it releases carbon and the surface stops reflecting sunlight and starts absorbing it, thus further melting the permafrost and releasing more CO_2 into the atmosphere and creating a spiralling increase of the earth's temperature.

All this means we can expect to see more than one billion climate change migrants by 2050 (Baker, 2020). Whoa! Stop right there and take in that fact once more:

ONE BILLION CLIMATE CHANGE MIGRANTS BY 2050!

Think about what that means. Millions displaced. Millions trying to cross borders, seeking relief in big cities, spurring rapid and overwhelming urbanization. Those who can't migrate 'get stuck' near borders where population and poverty surge, hunger deepens while it gets hotter with less available water. Countries on the 'right' side of the borders then get a new problem to deal with, of course assuming compassion is still some factor in the decisions that nations will make. What is clear when we consider the outlook for our climate is that the poor have the most to lose. Richer countries will adapt or migrate to other parts of the world; poorer countries will lack the ability to do this and the rest of the world will need to figure out how it responds to a humanitarian crisis of proportions never contemplated.

As I mentioned earlier, the relationship between climate change and biodiversity loss is a worrying one, so much so that scientists have given it the term the 'escalator to extinction'. It is worrying because climate change amplifies all other impacts of biodiversity loss, and in doing so biodiversity loss accelerates climate change as the ecosystems get degraded and lose their ability to absorb and store CO_2. Therefore, in order to progress towards sustainability, we must address both biodiversity loss and climate change and the interactions between them concurrently.

Resource depletion and waste mismanagement

Our ancestors could not have imagined the incredible advancements the human race has made and all the things we have conquered, understood and created to give us the world and lifestyles we have today. Yet human activity leaves a footprint and today that footprint is damaging the natural world, impacting people and communities and creating detrimental consequences for future generations to deal with.

As we have seen, the threats we now face with loss of biodiversity, ocean degradation and climate change are as a result of human activity, in particular how we use the earth's resources and dispose of that we don't need. For centuries now the earth has been an unlimited source of all the resources we need and also a convenient sink or dump for our waste. We mine, extract, farm, fish or harvest that we need, and a good amount we don't need too, for our consumption or to process it to create our modern world and all the things we utilize. All of this happens in plain sight. Own a piece of land or water, and with the right government permits companies are largely free to take vast resources, many of which will not be replenished. Then, when we are done, we dispose of what we decide we don't need or want any more, much of it going straight back to the earth or our oceans. Where this is no longer possible in our country, we ship it somewhere else, again all in plain sight and the majority of this happening legally.

Evidence of fishing and farming at scale dates back tens of thousands of years, extracting materials for construction further still and early mining for stones most appropriate to making tools predates *Homo sapiens*. Early examples of waste-water management involving a system of human waste being transported away from urban areas can be found as early as 6500 BC in Mesopotamia and archaeological evidence of landfill sites dating back to 3000 BC have been found in Crete (Encyclopedia.com, 2021). Once the idea that the earth could both provide us with everything and take away that we didn't need was entirely reasonable. This is because nature acts like a giant recycling system and continually evolves to decompose and produce new. The problem, however, is that human activity has pushed many parts of nature's ecosystem so its natural recycling system can no longer function. In addition, human brilliance means we have managed to defeat nature and create materials and substances that endure, bringing with them a new consequence that impacts our natural world (more on that shortly). In essence, human activity has already rendered many aspects of the world's ecosystem unsustainable and if unchecked will render more and more. How did we get here? Future generations may well be aghast at how our generation let this happen and how we viewed the planet as an unlimited resource and disposal route. Yet, it is important to remember that there is no one single point of failure here, but rather a slow dawning realization that what we thought was progress, and what nations permitted, brought with it consequences. We are only beginning to face up to these. There are many drivers here, and various reasons behind each of these (Figure 1.6). At the heart of all of these is our mindset of how we view human activity on our planet and the degree to which we value needing to be sustainable. We will explore the key themes here in turn.

A rapidly growing population

We are in the midst of a period of two centuries of rapid population expansion. There will be 2 billion more people on the planet within 30 years as the world's population is set to increase to reach 9.7 billion by 2050 and peaking at 10.9 billion by the end of the century (Roser et al, 2019). Population growth is higher in underdeveloped countries and 8 out of 10 of these new inhabitants will live in Asia or Africa. While the rate of growth is slowing, it will be the next century before this has any meaningful impact (Figure 1.7). In the meantime, our planet somehow has to sustain this unprecedented population expansion.

Figure 1.6 Key drivers of unsustainable resource use and waste management

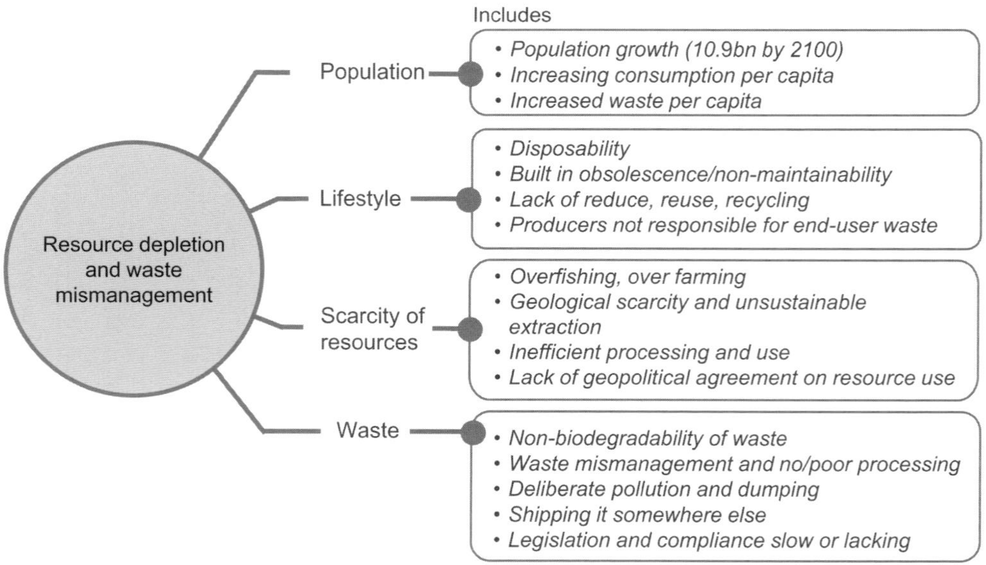

Includes

Population
- Population growth (10.9bn by 2100)
- Increasing consumption per capita
- Increased waste per capita

Lifestyle
- Disposability
- Built in obsolescence/non-maintainability
- Lack of reduce, reuse, recycling
- Producers not responsible for end-user waste

Scarcity of resources
- Overfishing, over farming
- Geological scarcity and unsustainable extraction
- Inefficient processing and use
- Lack of geopolitical agreement on resource use

Waste
- Non-biodegradability of waste
- Waste mismanagement and no/poor processing
- Deliberate pollution and dumping
- Shipping it somewhere else
- Legislation and compliance slow or lacking

Resource depletion and waste mismanagement

Figure 1.7 Projected world population growth and rate of growth

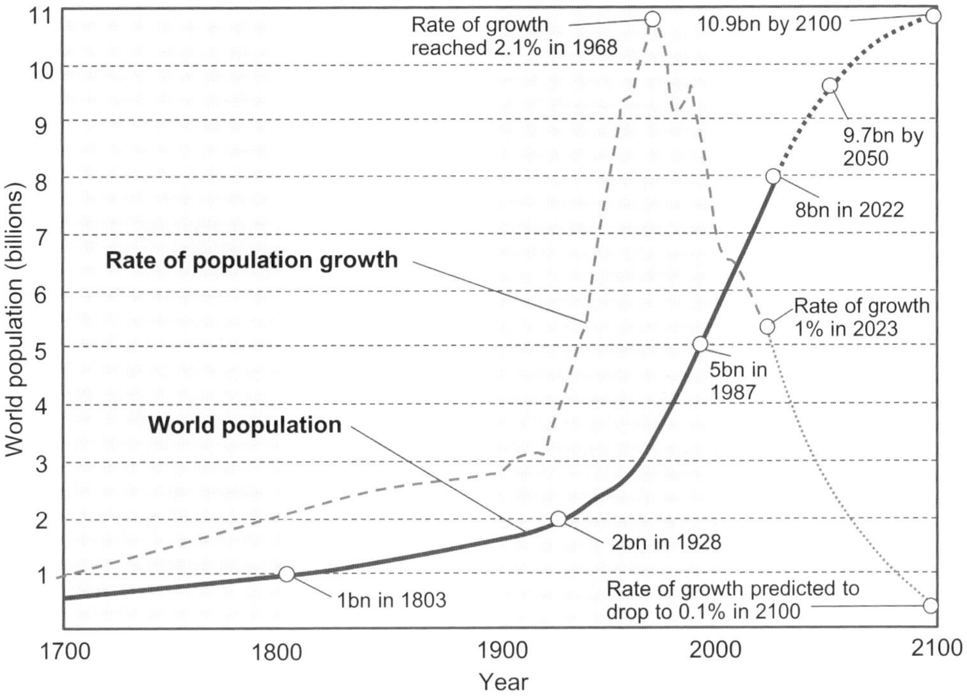

[Chart showing world population and rate of population growth from 1700 to 2100. Key data points: 1bn in 1803; 2bn in 1928; 5bn in 1987; 8bn in 2022; 9.7bn by 2050; 10.9bn by 2100. Rate of growth reached 2.1% in 1968; Rate of growth 1% in 2023; Rate of growth predicted to drop to 0.1% in 2100.]

SOURCE Roser et al (2019)

Unsustainable levels of consumption

The underlying driver behind all the threats I have outlined this far is the unsustainable consumption and depletion of resources to support human activity. Add to that an increasing population, an increasing rate of consumption for some resources and the limits to what this world can provide or sustain. Based upon current levels we will need 1.8 planet Earths to provide sufficient resources and absorb our waste into the future (The World Counts, 2021a).

Overconsumption and unsustainable consumption is not a global problem but one that resides in wealthier nations along with all consequences it brings. For example, globally the extraction of minerals is increasing rapidly. There is a relationship between a nation's GDP and metal consumption. The wealthier a country, the higher its metal use per capita (Graedel and Cao, 2010). This is set to continue to rise globally until 2050 and then stabilize (Henckens et al, 2016). Also, today, around half the world's habitable land is used for agriculture and this still is not enough to meet our increasing consumption of resources. The average person in the UK consumes four times the resources of a person in India. In the US this figure is seven times (Attenborough, 2020a). If the world's entire population adopted the average diet of the US we would need to convert all our habitable land to agriculture and would be 38 per cent short. For a New Zealand diet we would be nearly 100 per cent short (Ritchie, 2017).

EVs – can the world supply enough to meet the new demand?

Sales of new electric vehicles (EVs) are predicted to reach 70 million by 2040, which will represent approximately 65 per cent of the share of technology in the market. EV batteries are resource intensive and depending upon the exact battery technology being used, current lithium-ion EV batteries need to contain about 8 kg of lithium (about as much as a bowling ball), 20 kg of manganese and 14 kg of cobalt (Castelvecchi, 2021). None of these is considered scarce today. There is an estimated 21 million tonnes of lithium remaining in the earth, 1.3 billon tonnes of manganese and 7.1 million tonnes of cobalt (US Geological Survey, nd), which is sufficient to meet EV battery production through to mid-century at least by which time half the current lithium reserves will remain. However, there are other impacts from increased consumption. Cobalt extraction brings a high risk of mistreatment of people in the supply chain (more on that shortly). Then there are the resources needed to upgrade the electricity supply infrastructure for charging, especially home charging, requiring new higher-capacity copper (which is already moderately scarce) and steel cables. Add to this the copious amounts of energy, water and other impacts from the mining process and EV battery production is set to drive incredible levels of consumption in coming decades. Finally, EV battery recycling is in its infancy, meaning the levels overall of available resources are diminishing. This will not be an issue for current generations as there will be sufficient resources through this century; however, we may be creating an issue for future generations. The reasons for this are manyfold. Currently it is cheaper to mine new lithium rather than recycle old batteries and legislation compelling EV manufacturers to be responsible for recycling is slow. This is changing, with new battery requirements in the EU from 2023, and in the US the existing legislation, which requires batteries to be treated as hazardous waste and therefore safely disposed of, naturally favours recycling options (Castelvecchi, 2021).

Depletion of resources

Unsustainable consumption drives resource depletion. Many of the natural resources we need or demand to support the world's growing population, and in particular the lifestyles of developed nations, are getting scarce.

All resources on this planet are finite. If you put all of the gold extracted to date from all over the world in one block it would form a cube 28 metres on each side. It is estimated only 20 per cent of the world's gold as yet unextracted is left on or below the earth's surface (US Geological Survey, nd). That is only a 16.4 metre cube, equivalent to the size of a house.

The notion of the earth's resources becoming scarce would have been unthinkable 50 years ago and yet now we face some significant threats around certain resources we will need in coming years. What resources should we be worried about? It is difficult to know for certain. While we can quantify scarcity for some resources and even predict when they will become a cause for concern or even run out, for others it is less certain, and this is due to the fact that we might not know exactly how much is available to us, for example how much of a specific mineral lies below the earth's surface. There does not seem to be a single reliable list available so Table 1.1 provides a list I have compiled of what I believe are the most-scarce resources today. This comes with a health warning as I keep stumbling across something new to add to this list, so further research is recommended if you need a truly definitive list.

Table 1.1   The earth's most scarce resources

Resource	Why scarce?	Future impacts and risk
Fresh water	Drinking water is set to become the most scarce resource in future years as the world's population expands and the impacts of climate change take hold. Despite the fact the most of our planet is water, fresh water only makes up 2.5% of the total volume of water in the world and 70% of this is locked in ice and permanent snow cover (Ruz, 2011).	Severe impacts, especially for developing countries: • More severe and frequent droughts • More deaths from poor water quality • Food security threatened

Table 1.1 *continued*

Resource	Why scarce?	Future impacts and risk
Sand	The most consumed raw material after water and the primary material for all global construction, glass and modern electronics. Key is the type of sand – sharp 'water-eroded' particles that bind well with cement are required rather than the round 'wind-eroded' grains found in the desert. Global consumption of the right sand is about 50 billion tonnes per year and rising. This exceeds the natural rate at which sand is replenished (Meredith, 2021).	• Sand mafias controlling illegal harvesting and sale from developing nations • Coastal resilience threatened
Topsoil	At current rates usable topsoil could be gone in less than 60 years. 95% of world food production requires topsoil. It is one of the most important components in our food system. Quality topsoil is becoming scarce because of soil degradation at a rate of 30 soccer fields every minute – modern intensive agricultural methods and chemical treatments strip vital nutrients, minerals and microbes, literally turning it to dust. The usable depth is also reducing due to wind or water whisking away or thinning the amount of usable topsoil. About one-third of the world's topsoil is already degraded. It takes 1,000 years for 3cm of topsoil to regenerate (Arsenault, 2014).	• Food security threatened • Dust storms • Flooding
Fossil fuels	It is hard to be certain and the position seems to keep changing. Currently it seems there is less than 50 years of oil and natural gas left based upon current consumption and about 178 years of coal (Ruz, 2011).	If nothing changes to stop using fossil fuels future energy supply will be impacted

Table 1.1 *continued*

Resource	Why scarce?	Future impacts and risk
Phosphorus	Phosphorus is finite and non-renewable. It is an essential nutrient in fertilizers and without it we cannot produce food at the levels needed to feed the world. Reserves are in decline and demand will exceed supply this century (Cordell, nd).	Significant threat to world food supply
Antimony	The world's rarest metal. Used to make alloys to improve properties and in the electronics industry to make some semiconductors such as infrared detectors and diodes. Also essential for bullets, fireworks, flame-retardant materials, paints, enamels, glass and pottery. 22% of the world's resources were extracted between 2003 and 2014. Extractable resources predicted to be exhausted by 2050 (Henckens et al, 2016). Less than 10% recycled. Found in, or controlled by, China, Bolivia, Russia and Tajikistan.	Threat to multiple industry sectors
Gold	Extractable global resources predicted to be exhausted by before 2150.[1] 30–55% recycled. Produced or reserves held by China, Australia, USA, South Africa and Russia.	Threat to multiple industry sectors
Helium	Helium is the only element on the planet that is completely non-renewable. Once released into the atmosphere it escapes the earth into space. Formed over many millions of years, helium is generated deep underground from radioactive decay of elements such as uranium and thorium. There is about 110 years' worth of helium left on earth. Helium is only found in the US, Algeria and Qatar	Threat to multiple industry sectors

Table 1.1 *continued*

Resource	Why scarce?	Future impacts and risk
Rare earth metals	There are 17 rare earth metals: scandium, yttrium, lanthanum, cerium, praseodymium, neodymium, promethium, samarium, europium, gadolinium, terbium, dysprosium, holmium, erbium, thulium, ytterbium and lutetium. Rare because they are either in short supply or difficult to mine. Used in, and critical for in some cases, production of high-tech electronics including smartphones, computer hard drives, monitors and EVs. Key to multiple defence electronics. Also used in vehicle exhaust systems, as chemical catalysts and to make metal alloys more durable. More than a third come from China (who are now limiting exports), a further third from the US.	Threats to electronics and defence industry
Molybdenum	Used to make metal alloys in aircraft and defence, nuclear, heating elements and to strengthen drill bit and saw blades. Resources will be exhausted within 100 years. Only about 30% gets recycled.[1]	Impacts to some industries without substitution
Tantalum	Key for electronic capacitor production. Less than 10% gets recycled. Resources could be exhausted by 2060.	Threats to electronics and defence industries
Zinc	Used to galvanize steel, in batteries and in construction. Could become scarce within 30 years.	Threat to multiple industry sectors
Indium	Abundant in the earth but a by-product of zinc mining. With decline of zinc use (e.g. with moving to aluminium car bodies) it becomes economically scarce and predicted to be unavailable by 2035 (Desjardins, 2014).	LCD panels, smartphones and other displays

Table 1.1 *continued*

Resource	Why scarce?	Future impacts and risk
Copper	Essential in all electronics. Potentially scarce by 2040.	Threat to multiple industry sectors
Silver	Used in electronics and medical industries. Predicted to be scarce within 15 years (Desjardins, 2014).	Threat to multiple industry sectors
Platinum	Used in a wide range of technologies including catalytic converters, turbine blades, dental fillings, spark plugs and within electronics. The amount of platinum left would occupy a cube 2.26 metres on each side (Anderson, 2019).	Impacts to some industries without substitution
Gallium	Used in displays and solar panels and some semiconductors. Reserves could be exhausted in 15 years. Less than 10% gets recycled.[1]	Threat to multiple industry sectors

NOTE [1] Royal Society of Chemistry (various pages from rsc.org)

There are different reasons for scarcity:

- **Geological scarcity** – where metals, minerals and other resources available from our planet are being used up and set to be exhausted by 2150 or sooner.
- **Species scarcity** – where species are in decline or facing extinction.
- **Economic scarcity** – where the market price is such that it is uneconomic to mine, extract, farm, fish or obtain a particular resource. Generally, extraction of resources from our world tends to be viable where concentrations of a given resource exist. As geological and species scarcity increase for a resource, market prices rise and what was previously uneconomic becomes viable, further driving geological and species scarcity.
- **Geopolitical control** – where the majority of reserves of a resource are found only in certain countries and those countries exert control over the supply or extraction of resource, or stop or limit export (e.g. by imposing high export tariffs) in order to protect domestic supply, or to establish power over other nations.

Responding to scarcity

For some of the resources we use, scarcity can be overcome in a number of ways and we can expect these to swing much more into focus in coming years. They are:

- **Substitution** of the materials or species we use, e.g. switching to insect-based products instead of meat to provide protein for future generations, or alternative chemicals or metals.
- **Replenish** – e.g. taking steps to allow fish stocks to re-establish, programmes to plant new trees or reintroduction of species previously driven from their habitats.
- **Recycle** – worldwide levels of recycling are still low for many resources yet scarcity is making recycling increasingly necessary and economically attractive.
- **Recreate** – where human ingenuity can develop ways to recreate or synthesize materials that previously occurred only naturally, e.g. 'growing meat' in a laboratory.

This can leave us feeling upbeat about scarcity, especially if human brilliance can find ways to overcome or adapt. For some of the resources we will need in the future this is precisely what will happen. However, many of the earth's finite resources are non-renewable. Not all can be substituted. Indeed, of the 62 main metals used in construction, automotive or electronics, 12 of these have no substitute at all for their major use (Graedel and Cao, 2010). Furthermore, while some non-renewables get recycled there can only be so much in circulation at any time. Population growth and increases in consumption at current levels will mean there is simply not enough of certain resources to go around. Worse, certain non-renewable elements cannot be recycled presently. When these are gone, they are gone for good. These include some elements formed at the dawn of time by the extreme heat and pressure when the universe was formed, where remnants of old stars fell to earth and formed part of the earth's crust as we know it today. There is one final threat, and possibly the greatest future threat we face for availability of resources, and this is the risk of geopolitical scarcity. Today this is far from our politicians' thoughts, yet there is the very real potential for some countries to gain control and effectively hold the rest of the world to ransom to gain access to the resources needed.

CASE STUDY Should we be worried about phosphorus?

Phosphorus is becoming scarce. Phosphorus is an essential nutrient in fertilizers and without it we cannot produce food at the levels needed to feed the world. As the world's population grows so does demand for phosphorus, especially because of increases in meat and dairy consumption (which are more phosphorus intensive). The world's phosphorus is finite and non-renewable (unless you are prepared to wait 10–15 million years). Many recent studies predict phosphorus reserves are in significant decline and that demand will exceed supply this century (Cordell, 2021). While alternatives can be substituted for other scarce natural resources, there is no substitute for phosphorus in food production. This threat is exacerbated by inefficient use of phosphorus in the world's food systems, with an incredible 80 per cent lost in the supply chain and poor agricultural practice causing pollution to rivers and oceans. In addition, phosphorus mining, processing and transportation is energy intensive and therefore currently a major CO_2 emitter (30 per cent of energy use in agriculture in the US is from fertilizer production and use). Today the average diet results in the depletion of around 22.5 kilograms of phosphate rock per person per year. This is 50 times greater than the 1.2 grams per person daily recommended intake. All farmers worldwide need phosphorus and yet five countries control 88 per cent of it, with the majority found in Morocco and some in China, Algeria, Syria and South Africa. The US has some reserves, which are set to be depleted within 20 years and China has already imposed a 135 per cent export tariff to secure its domestic fertilizer supply (Cordell, 2021). Despite being one of the world's most critical resources there is no international organized effort to take responsibility for phosphorus security in the long term. Without action to improve efficiency of production and use worldwide the world's phosphorus will be depleted sometime in the next century. Without geopolitical intervention, we face the potential for these countries to control the world's food production.

Waste and 'disposability'

The levels and mismanagement of waste in its various forms arising from human activity present a significant and increasing impact on our world. Waste production is directly proportional to population growth and consumption so if nothing changes the impacts caused from waste are set to escalate.

Worldwide we dump over 2 billion tonnes of municipal solid waste each year (Sensoneo, 2022) with predictions of this rising by 70 per cent by 2050 at current rates (World Bank, 2018). Today, that equates to every human on this planet producing a third of a tonne each year, and that is just individual municipal waste. Except it isn't every human because when it comes to waste production there is a wide disparity across the planet. As you might imagine it is the developed nations that produce the most waste. The US is the biggest waste producer with nearly one tonne produced per person each year. This is nearly three times that of those in Poland. Denmark and New Zealand are also big waste producers (Sensoneo, 2019) and across the UK and EU each person produces on average about half a tonne of waste each year.

Approximately 1.3 billion tonnes of edible food, one-third of the total produced for human consumption worldwide, is lost or wasted annually (UNEP, 2015). This waste happens throughout the supply chain, from how the product is harvested or sorted at the point of origin, transported to, handled and stored for the consumer. In developing countries 80 per cent of losses occur on the farm or point of origin or during transportation. In developed countries 80 per cent of losses occur in retail, catering and in the home. In particular, significant waste here is attributed to the modern phenomena of stringent cosmetic standards imposed by retailers seeking to ensure the product we see in the shops are perfect specimens, beautifully presented (UNEP 2015).

Plastic has had a bad press in recent times, largely because, as we have already seen, plastic waste is highly visible. However, it is important to keep in mind that plastic is a unique and highly versatile material that has enabled us to transform our world and lives for good. Plastic, in itself, is not the enemy, rather it is the misuse of plastic in single-use disposable applications and the mismanagement of plastic waste that has caused harm. We produce 350 million tonnes of plastic each year, which gives rise to about 275 million tonnes of plastic waste and this is increasing year on year. Only about 20 per cent of this waste gets recycled, 25 per cent is incinerated and the remainder is discarded (Ritchie and Roser, 2018). About half of this waste is from packaging. China and the US are the biggest plastic waste producing countries. Germany, the Netherlands, Ireland and the US are among the biggest producers of plastic waste per person, however, in every country except China plastic waste is managed well. Plastic waste mismanagement is highest in India, African countries, China and the majority of the rest of Asia. (Jambeck et al, 2015).

These are only some of the waste streams we create and these volumes of waste pale into insignificance when compared with the total waste humans on this planet produce and especially those associated with industry. Numbers are sketchy but it seems this could be in the range of 650 billons tonnes per annum across all waste. Within this are some big volumes of waste, however it doesn't follow that the higher the number the bigger the impact. Instead each of these needs to be understood more fully to make sense of the numbers so as to determine the degree to which these wastes get recycled or managed effectively. The waste streams and total global annual volumes of waste produced are:

- Animal waste – 5 bn tonnes, most of which releases high amounts of the greenhouse gas methane (Cox, 2019)
- Agricultural waste – 5.5 bn tonnes (Wight, 2019)
- Sewage – 359 bn cubic metres (~359 tonnes) of which about half is released untreated (Utrecht University, 2021)
- Healthcare waste – total volume not known but it is a $15 billion market worldwide. 85 per cent is non-hazardous and 15 per cent is hazardous including 16 bn needles and syringes consumed annually (WHO, 2018)
- Construction and demolition waste – 2.2 bn tonnes (Fabris, 2018)
- Extraction and mining waste – ~200 bn tonnes (Fortune Business Insights, 2021)
- Oil and gas production waste – estimated 15 bn tonnes globally of ~6 bn tonnes of waste fluid pa in the US alone (EPA, 2021)
- Waste produced by combustion of fossil fuels – 38 bn tonnes CO_2 (EPA, 2021)
- Radioactive waste – estimated 0.3 m tonnes of highly radioactive waste in storage worldwide (NIRS, nd)
- Hazardous waste – 400m tonnes (The World Counts, 2021b)
- Industrial non-hazardous waste – 7 bn tonnes (Vignesh et al, 2021)

Non-biodegradability

The final, and possibly the biggest, contributor to the modern waste problem is non-biodegradability. As we have seen, we have, for now at least, successfully defeated nature in creating modern materials and substances that endure. This gives us the synthetic materials, plastics, fibres, chemicals and metal alloys that create our permanent buildings, lasting products, electronic devices, package our food or clothe us. The problem comes when these materials are disposed of. Unlike everything else in the natural world this waste endures in the environment. The toxic chemicals that are now found in marine animals, the construction waste that goes to landfill, the synthetic fibres that get sent to somewhere else in the world and of course the plastic waste in our oceans. Once again, we should not berate human ingenuity for creating enduring materials as these are not the enemy, rather it is the mismanagement of the waste.

Clearly the high volumes of waste produced have an impact in terms of managing disposal, but also because waste generation, especially the resources, energy and emissions involved throughout the life of a product tends to represent inefficient use of materials. Of greater importance, however, is what we do with our waste.

The disposability culture

The incredible volumes of waste produced by developed nations is a product of our modern lifestyles as well as what has come to be most profitable for the companies we buy from, in particular the disposability of goods and built-in obsolescence. We are wealthier than our forefathers and mothers could ever have imagined, and we can afford the value of convenience. Single-use, disposable, discard, replace, throw away and buy new are all ways of living we have come to accept or have only just begun to question. As a child I can remember finding plastic food packaging that had washed up on the beach and my father telling me that these items would not rot down like other things did and would stay as plastic, at least for many hundreds of years. I remember thinking there was something wrong with this and surely our oceans would soon become full of plastic. However, once again, no one else at the time seemed to be concerned so I assumed the clever people that run the world had it covered, and I didn't need to worry.

In the developed world, we have become part of a disposability culture. These days, we are regularly reminded of how bad we are to have created the waste problem we now face, yet disposability is not something the majority of us set out to do, but rather we have ended up there. Whether by ignorance, ambivalence or assuming the companies we buy from and those that govern our countries were doing what was needed to act in our best interest all along, we have ended up with disposability fully ingrained in our developed societies. The shoots of change are there however, and behaviours are beginning to shift, but disposability is a big ship to turn around and it will take new legislation and real consumer demand and public will to turn it. The problem is moving away from disposability requires a sea change. One of the reasons for this is that disposability is big business. Creating a product that gets thrown away and the customer buys new secures repeat revenues. Why do we throw it away? Because there is some reason we need new or because we are convinced by the marketing and social proof of what others are doing to upgrade or change, because we can afford to and because we like it. Shopping has long since stopped being just a necessity and big brands are all too aware of the thrill of the shop, especially if they can make something unique, scarce or a newer version of something. Fast fashion and consumerism are founded on the principle of disposability. It is easy at this point to demonize the big global brands here, however, the brands we buy have simply responded to customer demand and seized the opportunity. Put simply, with the exception of only a few, disposability has not figured as a concern in the minds of consumers until recently.

We are all familiar with the easy changes – switching to a reusable coffee cup, not upgrading to this year's model or buying an old-fashioned slightly imperfect whole carrot instead of the plastic bag full of pre-chopped pieces! These are the things we control. Harder are the more complex things and the fact that today, disposability is in most cases unavoidable and deliberately planned by the companies we buy from. As an electronics engineer, I used to regularly mend electronic things that had gone wrong. I could sort most things and, equipped with a test meter and sometimes an oscilloscope, I could open up a TV or other appliance, locate the fault and replace the faulty part. Today things have changed – it is rarely possible to repair things these days. This is partly due to miniaturization but also a deliberate design strategy, with products designed to be unserviceable, non-modular and in some cases designed to prevent people trying, and even if someone were to try, the replacement parts are unobtainable. This strategy means users can only throw away old electronic items and get new.

A similar driver of modern waste is built-in obsolescence, where manufacturers design their products to have an artificially limited lifespan and be unusable after that. Like disposability, built-in obsolescence is big business. There is nothing worse for a manufacturer than to be so good at what they do that their products never wear out or need replacing. Therefore, companies build in frailties in their design. Once again, back to my electronics engineering days and one of the jobs I had was to approve electronic components for high-spec telecommunications products. I learnt that it was possible to design some components to last for a set period of time and then fail under certain conditions. Some manufacturers got so good at this they could even design a component to almost always fail after, say, seven years. This is the basis for how many electronics goods were designed. Today built-in obsolescence is more precise and is accomplished via software updates. Perhaps you have experienced doing a software update on your phone that then seems to slow the whole thing down or limit battery life, compelling you to consider a replacement, and that brings me to e-waste.

There's gold in them old laptops

We produce about 50 million tonnes of e-waste (or WEEE – waste electrical and electronic equipment) each year – the fastest-growing waste stream in the world with Europe and the US leading the pack in amount of e-waste per capita. This is predicted to reach 74 million tonnes by 2030 (Feng, 2021). This is all our old computers, televisions, toys, medical devices, tools, lamps, washing machines, mobile phones, printers and electrical appliances. We recycle very little of this, only about 17 per cent in fact (Feng, 2021). For the rest, some ends up in landfill or being incinerated but in the main we ship it to poorer countries, mostly in Asia and Africa because the cheap labour and inadequate environmental legislation in these territories create attractive waste disposal routes for developed nations and a thriving e-waste business for developing nations. And then there are all the devices not yet recycled. In the US an estimated 70 per cent of all computers sold in the US are idle but have not yet been disposed of (Feng, 2021) and only 34 per cent of old smartphones get recycled with as many as 55 million redundant phones estimated to be lying around or sat in drawers in households in the UK alone, due to data security fears or users not knowing how to dispose of old tech (Metro, 2020). Yet smartphones contain up to 64 elements including rare earth metals, the majority of which are only found in China.

Exporting waste (especially toxic waste) to underdeveloped countries is generally illegal. Despite this the global waste trade, or 'toxic colonialism' as it has come to be known, is alive and well with richer countries shipping toxic waste to underdeveloped nations. This includes e-waste. The 1992 Basel Convention international treaty agreed a complete ban on exporting e-waste, however there are exceptions when the export is for 'repair and reuse' which provides a sufficient loophole for developed countries to exploit. Add to this a healthy trade in e-waste disguised as second-hand equipment, the fact the US has not signed up to the Basel treaty and a thriving trade in illegal exports (Feng, 2021) and there is a massive global flow of our old e-stuff from developed to underdeveloped nations to end up in huge graveyards of our old electronic devices.

The first problem with e-waste is it is difficult and costly to recycle. It is also highly toxic and contains heavy and poisonous metals and chemicals including arsenic, mercury, lead, cadmium, chromium, antimony and PCBs, flame retardants and toner. It contains large amounts of plastic (PVC, PE, ABS, polystyrene and polypropylene). Yet e-waste also contains the gold, silver, antimony and other rare earth metals many of which are getting scarce. Remember only 20 per cent of the earth's gold remains in the ground and the good news is gold is recyclable, however levels of gold recycling run somewhere between 30 and 55 per cent, which brings us to the second problem. These precious metals occur in very small amounts within the various components and circuit boards so extraction is difficult but as resources become scarce, the attractiveness of reprocessing old e-waste increases. The third problem is how recycling takes place at the world's e-waste graveyards.

E-waste dumps around the world are generally open dumps in impoverished areas. Recycling efforts are primitive and unorganized – typically e-waste gets left for residents to scavenge and dismantle items. Child labour is common. Water run-offs pollute water courses with highly toxic leachate, open burning (especially to release parts) creates GHG emissions along with a host of noxious gases that local workers and those living nearby breathe, leading to high rates of lead poisoning and miscarriages among communities in close proximity to e-waste dumps.

One such dump is the Agbogbloshie Waste Dump located in Accra, Ghana by the Old Fadama slum district on the Korle Lagoon of the Odaw River. Agbogbloshie has been called the most polluted site in the world (Biello, 2014) and receives 192,000 tonnes of e-waste annually. This site is reputed to be at the centre of an illegal exportation network and the destination for automobile and e-waste mostly from the Western world. However, various studies have failed to confirm this and in fact one study by UNEP and the Basel Convention revealed that this was not the case, in fact despite the informal nature of the waste processing about half of the material was being recovered (Wikipedia, nda). Another e-dump is Bekasi in Indonesia, which receives 230,000 tonnes each year and there are many more. The biggest dump in the world is the Guiyu dump, located in the Guangdong province of southern China. Guiyu processes around 1.2 million tonnes of e-waste each year (Boardman et al, 2020). In 2017 the Chinese government made it illegal to import e-waste; however, despite this, significant volumes of 'second-hand equipment' from the West end up there, presumably helped by the $75 million revenues Guiyu generates. Guiyu started life as an open dump, however today it has become more of an industrial park focused on recycling. While recycling is still primitive with only basic provision to protect workers, the community and the environment, it is evolving. Scavengers have been replaced by 150,000 workers working 16-hour days in 5,000 workshops reprocessing e-waste.

E-waste, it seems, is one of the biggest growing waste problems yet consumers remain unaware of exactly what happens to our old electronics. The irony here is some of the world's poorest and most vulnerable communities are exposed to high levels of toxic substances through having to dismantle devices they do not have access to.

The recycling imperative

The degree to which there is effective waste management varies around the world. Recycling is the best method for managing waste and, as we have seen, recycling is key to addressing future scarcity risk for some resources. It also tends to be the most difficult and expensive. While the US and Denmark are top waste producers, they each recycle about a third of their waste (Sensoneo, 2019) and in the EU about half of waste is now recycled (Eurostat, 2019). In contrast New Zealand is lagging somewhat behind in terms of any meaningful recycling program (Sensoneo, 2019).

The next most effective method of solid waste management is incineration and while overall this is a positive technique for waste management it is significantly less effective than recycling due to the energy involved, potential emissions and the fact that this technique does not recover resources for future use. Then there is landfill where, if sites are properly constructed, they are much more than big holes in the ground and are well-designed facilities that protect human health, and provide a safe repository for waste to decompose in that protect ground water and the surrounding environment. Globally, landfill sites produce around 3 per cent of global emissions. In the US, landfill sites are the third-largest source of methane, accounting for approximately 16 per cent of greenhouse gases. Landfill gets a bad press, however they are not all that bad. Modern sites contain emissions and extract the gas to be used as energy and by design contain waste. Today we view landfill as the final destination for waste, however future generations that face scarcity we can't yet conceive may view them as sites to be mined for resources. The final means of waste disposal found around the world is open dumping. Open dumps exist both legally and illegally and are land disposal where waste is dumped in a way that does not protect the environment, giving rise to toxic water run-off that pollutes ground water and water courses, open burning, emissions and scavengers. Open dumping tends to be found in developing countries that are not equipped to manage waste or where the enforcement of legislation is limited. Open dumping is also alive and well and the means by which almost all waste is handled in Turkey, Mexico and Chile (Sensoneo, 2019).

The problem with linear

I have outlined many of the drivers behind resource depletion and waste mismanagement. The underpinning root cause behind all the impacts I have described and others besides is that developed nations have evolved a one-directional linear society. Our lifestyles today have been founded almost entirely on the concept of consumption of largely virgin resources that are consumed and the resulting waste, containing non-biodegradable components, is simply dumped and we buy new. This linear, one-directional system is unsustainable and threatens future resource security. It also demands much more energy to produce more and more, and then to process the waste, all creating more emissions. We can only begin to become sustainable with a complete shift towards a global society built upon a circular system where resource use and the waste cycle is circular, either through the natural cycle of decomposition and renewal or by managed recycling means – this is known as the circular economy. Doing this will have far-reaching implications for our lives, organizations and, of course, procurement and supply chain functions. We will return to this later.

Animal welfare

The final section is concerned with impacts to animals. This is an area that sits distinct from all other areas, which is why I have left it until now, as it doesn't fit neatly under any one of our six impact area headings. Animals are part of biodiversity and the global ecosystem of which we are all a part and depend upon, so it would seem logical that this was part of *biodiversity loss*. Arguably however, animal welfare does not cause loss of biodiversity unless the mistreatment of animals affects reproduction. For this reason, animal welfare or animal ethics are often omitted in published information about sustainability although this is changing. It is a strand of sustainability because there is a relationship between animal welfare and global ecosystem services (the ability of our ecosystem to provide everything we need) and human welfare. The mistreatment of animals impacts the global food supply. It is also a matter of responsibility (McShane, 2018). Animal welfare is compromised by various impact areas, in particular climate change and loss of habitat causing fear and distress in animals, and drives migration and adaption strategies or reduction in numbers of loss of species. For these reasons animal welfare (or the lack of it) should be considered part of and a contributor to loss of biodiversity.

Animal welfare is becoming a critical issue in the world (Abubakar et al, 2018) and attitudes towards animals, welfare standards and legislation vary around the world. Furthermore, there is no universal definition of what animal welfare means nor any agreed means to measure it, but the five freedoms as explained by Backus et al (2014) seem to be the most widely accepted definition – animal welfare is:

- Freedom from thirst, hunger and malnutrition, e.g. access to freshwater and a suitable diet
- Freedom from discomfort including a suitable environment, shelter and facility to rest
- Freedom from pain, injury and disease including prevention and timely treatment
- Freedom to express normal behaviour, e.g. sufficient space and being with other same species animals
- Freedom from fear and distress and avoiding mental suffering

Chapter checkpoint

So far in this first chapter we have explored four (of the six) critical threats, impacts and drivers that describe our current situation in terms of our environment. These are:

1 *Biodiversity loss* (including poor animal welfare) where extinction of one eighth of the world's species threatens our global eco-system of which we are a part and on which we depend.

2 *Our ailing oceans* where biodiversity loss, pollution, over-extraction of resources and acidification due to climate change are threatening the ability of our oceans to absorb CO_2 and service our needs.

3 *Climate change* where the warming of the earth's temperature and potential acceleration beyond safe limits will bring catastrophic consequences for human life on this planet.

4 *Resource depletion and waste mismanagement* where increasing resource scarcity and regarding use and disposal as linear rather than circular threatens future resource security.

Individually each impact area presents a critical threat to our planet. Collectively these impacts are intertwined and further accelerate each other.

The last two critical threats we face are distinct from, but related to, the environment and are a key component in developing a sustainability approach. They are the mistreatment of people and detrimental impact on communities, and the threat and impacts associated with data privacy and protection, cybercrime and internet freedom, which are the subject of the next chapter.

Situation planet Earth, part 2   02

People and communities

> This chapter continues our exploration of our current 'situation planet Earth' and some of the biggest threats and challenges we now face. We consider our situation in terms of detrimental impacts on people and communities, and we explore why we need to be concerned and what this means for us and future generations. The implications for organizations continue to be examined.
>
> *Pathway questions addressed in this chapter*
>
> 1 What is sustainability?
> 2 Why is sustainability important?

Impacts on people

The next significant threat is concerned with detrimental impacts on people and communities. Much of the published information about sustainability focuses on the environment and omits this dimension, yet it is an integral part of the overall ecosystem that we rely upon – the human race could not survive without social cooperation. People and the communities they live in are the main part of the story behind that which creates the world we live in, the products we use and the services we consume. When we consider sustainability in terms of people and communities 'the ability to exist constantly' takes on a different meaning and encompasses a range of factors and considerations that ensure our collective future. I will return to that but first I will lay out the different impact areas we need to be concerned about if we are driving sustainable procurement in our organization (Figure 2.1).

Figure 2.1 Detrimental impact areas for people and communities

Human rights — Includes:
- Modern slavery
- Child labour
- Discrimination, diversity and inclusion

Working conditions
- Exposure to physical risk
- Workers' rights
- Poor working environment
- Living wage
- Job quality, security and prospects

Illegal trades
- Blood diamonds
- Conflict minerals
- Sand mafia

Communities
- Corporate community impact
- Mistreatment of First Nations people

Impacts to people and communities

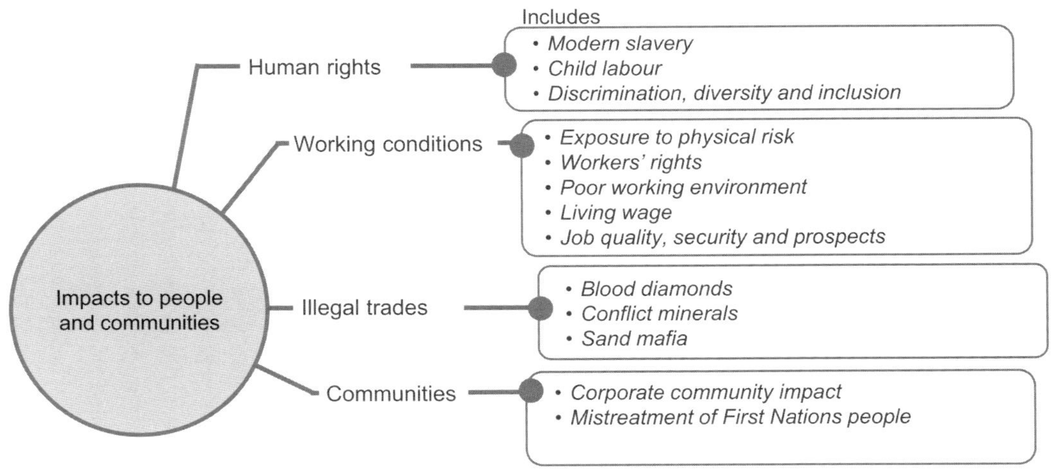

Human rights

Human rights are the starting point to understanding impacts on people. Human rights are inherent to all human beings, regardless of race, sex, nationality, ethnicity, language, religion or any other status. Human rights include the right to life and liberty, freedom from slavery and torture, freedom of opinion and expression, the right to work and education, and many more. Everyone is entitled to these rights, without discrimination (UN, nd).

In 1949 Eleanor Roosevelt posed for photographers, holding up a large poster version of the Universal Declaration of Human Rights (UDHR), widely regarded as a milestone document in human history that set out, for the first time, fundamental human rights to be universally protected. The UDHR was adopted by resolution 217A (III) at The United Nations General Assembly in Paris on 10 December 1948. In 1976, the UDHR, together with two core human rights treaties covering civil, political, economic, social and cultural rights that later came into force, collectively formed the International Bill of Human Rights. Since then, further treaties have been adopted, including treaties to protect and promote rights for children and people with disabilities, and also to eliminate all forms of racial discrimination and discrimination against women. The UDHR was further strengthened some 50 years later by the Vienna World Conference and declared to be universal, indivisible, interdependent and interrelated. The Vienna Declaration and Programme of Action was adopted by 171 UN member states. Today there are nine core international human rights instruments that have been established to implement the UDHR.

Human rights are established through international law that lays down the obligations of the governments that are parties to international law. Governments adopt these obligations that then form part of national constitutions and domestic legislation, typically together with other laws that formally protect human rights. In Europe this takes the form of the European Convention on Human Rights (ECHR) with all 47 member states including the UK having signed the convention. The UK made these rights part of its domestic law through the Human Rights Act 1998. In the US the Organization of American States adopted the American Convention on Human Rights in 1969, which has been ratified by 24 states. Other territories have similar legislation. Measures exist for abuses to be referred to international courts in the event domestic mechanisms and procedures fail.

With such a universal and long-standing commitment to human rights we might expect that the social impacts that give rise to the need for sustainability imperative to be minimal. This is not the case and before

I outline why we will explore some of the areas where human rights are compromised around the world.

Modern slavery

Modern slavery is alive and well. Today there are an estimated 40 million people trapped in modern slavery worldwide. This is more than three times the number in slavery during the years of the slave trade. One in four of those in modern slavery worldwide are children. About three quarters are women and girls (Anti-Slavery International, nd). It is easy to think such things are far removed from our lives, however the reality is modern slavery is all around us. Modern slavery takes many forms (Anti-Slavery International, nd):

- **Human trafficking** – people are recruited, transported and held using violence, coercion or threats in order to exploit them for prostitution, forced labour, marriage, organ removal or criminality.
- **Forced labour** – people are made to work against their will under the threat of punishment or because they cannot leave.
- **Child slavery** – exploitation of children for trafficking, child soldiers, child marriage and domestic slavery.
- **Forced marriage** – someone is married against their will and is unable to leave.
- **Born into slavery** – where traditions dictate that people inherit slave status at birth.
- **Debt or bonded labour** – this the most common form of slavery, where people trapped in poverty borrow money they cannot repay and are forced into work to pay the debt and in doing lose control over their employment conditions and the debt.

To the uninitiated, modern slavery can conjure up the idea of people physically shackled, held captive and forced to work by ruthless taskmasters ready to give out a beating at any opportunity. This does happen, however this impression can prevent us understanding the true problem here because modern slavery can be more subtle and is often right there hiding in plain sight, perhaps even in our own neighbourhood. Modern slavery is possible where an individual can be exploited by one or more people who have a hold or some form of control over them. Control gets exerted through fear, violence, debt or obligation, or inability to escape a given situation. To an outsider, in many cases, modern slavery can go unnoticed. Workers who appear to be coming and going and engaging in their employment freely may in fact be being exploited and controlled in some way to such an extent that they are afraid to speak out. The perpetrators here are adept at creating and maintaining the conditions needed to enslave people without detection. Without intervention by us to prevent such things, many of these can end up as workers in some of the companies that supply us and we, and even those who manage the companies, may be oblivious to it.

We have all heard the stories of people being trafficked, perhaps we have even wondered how such things could actually happen, but the lure of the dream job opportunity, promoted by an accomplished confidence trickster to a desperate poor family in an impoverished remote location may be enough to convince a family member to travel to take up the promise, start a new life and send money back to the family. Then, of course, the promise does not get fulfilled, the individual ends up captive, with no passport or money, forced into prostitution or other work with the threat of violence against the family back home should the individual not comply, try to escape or tell someone. Therefore, modern slavery can be hard to detect. Signs of modern slavery include (ILO, nda):

- Deception
- Restriction of movement
- Isolation
- Physical and sexual violence
- Intimidation and threats
- Retention of identity documents
- Withholding of wages
- Debt bondage
- Abusive working and living conditions
- Excessive overtime

Why the US banned rubber glove imports from a Malaysian firm

Top Glove in Malaysia is the world's largest manufacturer of rubber gloves. Its products are used extensively across the US, UK and EU. In March 2021 the US Customs and Border Protection banned imports of Top Glove products from Malaysia to the US and made a finding that its products are made using forced and indentured labour (CBP, 2021).

The Guardian reported that the majority of Top Glove workers were migrants from Nepal and Bangladesh desperate to gain employment. Many were required to pay high fees to recruitment agents to gain their jobs, and as such created big debts that needed to be repaid from their wages. Workers alleged they were put to work for 12-hour shifts, six days a week with some earning as little as £7 per day and had to live in squalid dormitories shared by more than 20 workers. Top Glove denied all the allegations (Pattisson, 2021). Later in September 2021 the US Customs and Border Protection lifted the ban on import to the US stating that Top Glove had addressed all indicators of forced labour at its Malaysian facilities (CBP, 2021).

By the end of 2021 the Top Glove website had published a commitment to continuous improvement, which identified and provided detailed commitments to five key areas of improvement (Top Glove, nd).

Conflict minerals, blood diamonds and the sand mafia

As resources get scarce, and wherever there is potential to make good money by extracting resources from the earth, there is potential for illegal trade. Most developed nations prevent such things; however, in parts of the world where criminal gangs are able to gain control or access to a resource, the foundation for a lucrative illegal trade operation is born. Add to that bribery and corruption of authorities that would otherwise stop or prevent it and the conditions are set for all manner of human rights abuses. As resources continue to get scarce the stage is set for the rise in mafia- or militia-operated illegal gangs for many other resources in countries that are unable or unwilling to prevent it and the environmental and human rights abuses that they bring. Three examples illustrate this; there are many others besides.

Conflict minerals

Conflict minerals are primarily tantalum, tin, tungsten and gold that originate from the Democratic Republic of Congo (DRC) and adjoining countries (Angola, Burundi, Central African Republic, Republic of Congo, South Sudan, Tanzania, Uganda and Zambia). Here the mines are operated by criminal gangs and warlords who use the proceeds to buy weapons and fund their atrocities and conflict in this region. Intermediaries and those in the immediate supply chains turn a blind eye so long as they make a big profit and smelters mix minerals that originate from both legal and illegal sources, effectively washing away any trace of illegality. As such, conflict minerals can easily end up in the electronic devices we all use and the manufacturer may be unaware. In the US in 2010 there was legislation (widely known as the Dodd-Frank Act) for big Wall Street traded companies to report about the use of conflict minerals.

Blood diamonds

Similarly, blood diamonds are those mined in areas controlled by militia, most typically in the same Central African countries, where proceeds are used to fund arms for rebel groups. Blood diamonds are either sold directly to merchants on the black market or are smuggled into neighbouring countries to be merged with stocks of legitimately mined diamonds and sold on the open market.

Sand mafia

As we saw in Chapter 1, sand is becoming scarce. Not all sand, but the particular sharp sand used for construction that comes from beaches and river beds, needed to meet the ever-increasing demand for fracking, industrial processes such as glass and silicone manufacture, and in construction in the expanding economies of Asia, Africa and the Middle East. As such, in recent years there has been an explosion in illegal coastal sand mining and dredging sand from river banks to sell on the black market in dozens of countries, including Jamaica, Nigeria, India, China and Israel.

Sand trading is big business and as such attracts criminal gangs or 'sand mafia' that set up well-organized illegal operations to extract, transport and sell sand. Gangs exploit those communities and use violence, intimidation and torture to gain control over extraction. Those who try to stop it get killed and battles between rival sand mafias kill hundreds of people including government officials and police officers each year. Officials are bribed so the activity continues unchecked with some countries, including Singapore and Morocco, content to permit the import in the interest of national security, leaving communities to get broken apart because people can no longer earn a living (Stronberg, 2017).

In addition to the social impact, sand gouging leads to severe environmental damage. Currently, on a global scale, sand is being extracted at a rate faster than it is produced naturally. The practice of gouging from river beds causes dried-up river beds or flooding, and dredging causes pollution, compromising water supplies and the food chain, and threatening the lives of hundreds of thousands of people who depend upon the river for food and water.

Child labour

Child labour deprives children of their potential, their childhood and their dignity. It deprives children of an education either completely or in part, for example they are required to leave school prematurely or have to work long hours on top of a school day. It typically involves work that is mentally, physically, socially or morally dangerous and harmful to children. Child labour is often exploitative, with long hours. It is also often dangerous with about half of child labour exposed to hazardous work that risks injury and death. This typically involves working underground, underwater, at dangerous heights or in confined spaces, working with dangerous machinery or tools, carrying heavy loads or being exposed to hazardous chemicals, processes, temperatures, noise levels, vibrations or other risks to health (ILO, ndb). The worst forms include child slavery, trafficking and sexual exploitation and any other form of work that exposes the child to physical, psychological or sexual abuse.

The ILO Minimum Age Convention 1973 (No 138) sets the general minimum age in developed countries at not less than the age of completion of compulsory schooling and in any case not less than 15, or 14 in a developing country, with some exceptions.

Worldwide, it is estimated 160 million children are victims of child labour, that is about one in every ten children on the planet. Of these, 63 million are girls and 97 million are boys. Nearly half of these are in hazardous work. The majority of child labour exists in sub-Saharan Africa and Asia and Pacific countries (ILO, ndb).

Generally, across the regions of the world where child labour is most prevalent it is also illegal. The problems with child labour and the difficulties in addressing it have long been recognized by both developed and developing nations, yet it was only in the 1990s that child labour emerged as an important global issue requiring attention. In 1999, ILO Convention 182 on the worst forms of child labour was drafted and became the fastest convention in history to be ratified by 113 countries within two years. Today 184 countries have ratified this convention and incorporated it into national legislation. Despite this, it continues and is tolerated as part of how things are across many industries and regions.

Child labour is inextricably linked to poverty. Children either work because they are enslaved and forced to or, as is the case for the majority of children in work, because their survival and that of their families depends upon it. Child labour is often ingrained in cultural and social attitudes and traditions in these countries where state and education systems are either not prepared or ill-equipped to deal with it. This is reinforced by commonly cited justifications from employers, such as certain activities require 'nimble fingers' or 'smaller-sized people', and despite the fact that these claims have been disproved repeatedly child labour continues invisibly and is silently tolerated in the nations that have banned it.

The invisibility of child labour makes it a unique social impact and can be the hardest to detect, which is why it continues in such numbers around the world. Where there is a will and the means to address a child labour situation, the tendency is to address the most obvious – that which is visible in a concentrated situation – or to focus on specific trades such as those working in garment factories or picking crops in agriculture. This is a good starting point, yet the majority and indeed the worst type of child labour is found where the children do not work in a single location but are moved around, and situations where the children are less visible or what they do happens 'behind closed doors'. Figure 2.2 gives some examples of different types of child labour situations. Add to this those situations where there is the opportunity and incentive to exploit children without detection and that is precisely what will happen. I have been involved with several companies that have worked tirelessly to eradicate child labour and other detrimental people impacts from the factories they were sourcing from, only to be exposed when (unbeknown to them) it was discovered that children were making the products. Typically, when this happens it is not because a 'big bad greedy top-brand company' is trying to exploit children, but rather because a single corrupt individual in the supply chain is making money through some 'back door' illegal practice.

Efforts to eradicate child labour tend to focus at either extreme of the problem. Most countries have legislation to address the worst types (typically those that are dispersed and invisible) and both nations and organizations target that which is the most obvious, i.e. is concentrated and visible. This means that the most widespread forms of child labour today and those that fail to get addressed are those that are either dispersed but visible or concentrated and invisible. Identifying and addressing these groups, especially in a supply chain, requires new approaches to determine where they exist and being able to address them.

Figure 2.2 Examples of child labour situations

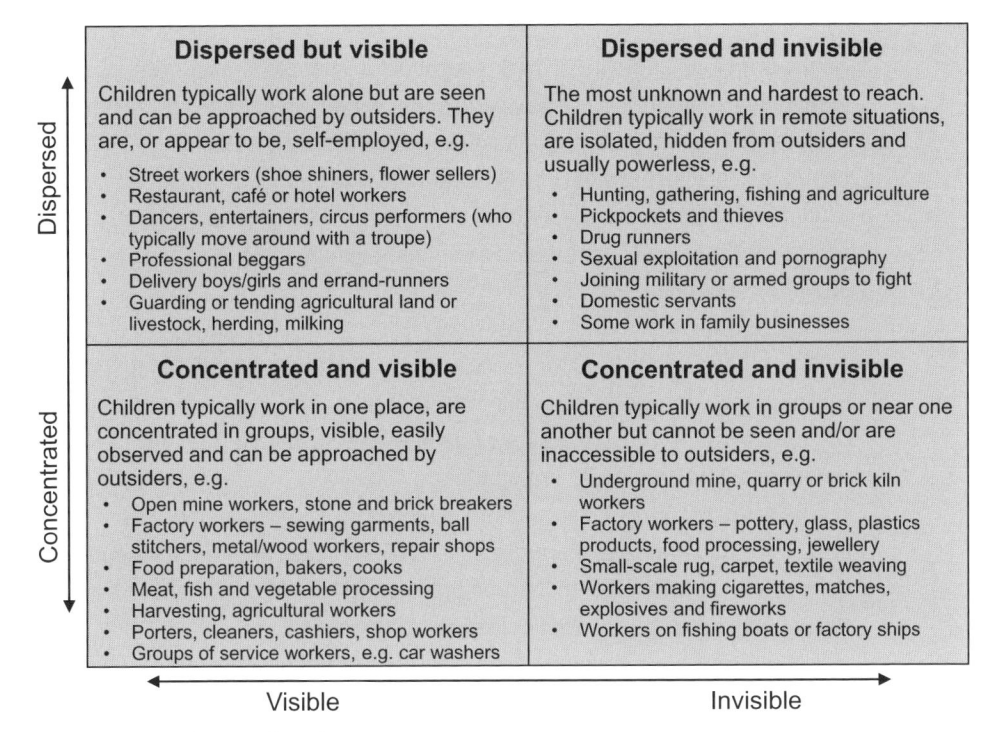

	Visible	Invisible
Dispersed	**Dispersed but visible** Children typically work alone but are seen and can be approached by outsiders. They are, or appear to be, self-employed, e.g. • Street workers (shoe shiners, flower sellers) • Restaurant, café or hotel workers • Dancers, entertainers, circus performers (who typically move around with a troupe) • Professional beggars • Delivery boys/girls and errand-runners • Guarding or tending agricultural land or livestock, herding, milking	**Dispersed and invisible** The most unknown and hardest to reach. Children typically work in remote situations, are isolated, hidden from outsiders and usually powerless, e.g. • Hunting, gathering, fishing and agriculture • Pickpockets and thieves • Drug runners • Sexual exploitation and pornography • Joining military or armed groups to fight • Domestic servants • Some work in family businesses
Concentrated	**Concentrated and visible** Children typically work in one place, are concentrated in groups, visible, easily observed and can be approached by outsiders, e.g. • Open mine workers, stone and brick breakers • Factory workers – sewing garments, ball stitchers, metal/wood workers, repair shops • Food preparation, bakers, cooks • Meat, fish and vegetable processing • Harvesting, agricultural workers • Porters, cleaners, cashiers, shop workers • Groups of service workers, e.g. car washers	**Concentrated and invisible** Children typically work in groups or near one another but cannot be seen and/or are inaccessible to outsiders, e.g. • Underground mine, quarry or brick kiln workers • Factory workers – pottery, glass, plastics products, food processing, jewellery • Small-scale rug, carpet, textile weaving • Workers making cigarettes, matches, explosives and fireworks • Workers on fishing boats or factory ships

SOURCE Adapted from ILO (2002)

Most people would agree that child labour is wrong; however, not all work done by children is wrong. Work that does not affect the health, well-being and development of a child, and does not interfere with schooling, can be beneficial to a child who is old enough to engage in work, for example, through learning new skills, earning money or helping in a family-run business (ILO, ndb). Furthermore, when it comes to children in work, we should be careful not to view child labour through Western eyes or jump to the course of action that would be normal in our societies. Consider the example of a 13-year-old child who has left their education early to work and is the only income provider for their entire family. This would seem to fit the definition of child labour, yet stopping this practice would have more damaging and far-reaching consequences as her entire family would get plunged into poverty and be on the streets. Understanding child labour, and more importantly how to respond, is therefore not straightforward.

The cobalt children who power our EVs

Cobalt is a unique hard metal that is particularly suitable for modern battery technology. Therefore, it is a key component within the batteries for electric vehicles (EVs), with an average long-range Tesla battery containing 20 kg of cobalt. It is also used widely in all our electronics and other consumer products. EV producers are actively trying to find alternatives to cobalt or at least solve some of the problems with obtaining it; however, this is not straightforward because the problem with cobalt is what happens at the original source.

More than two-thirds of the world's cobalt is produced in the Democratic Republic of Congo (DRC), the remainder in Russia, Canada and Australia. Of the 19 mines in DRC, 15 are now Chinese owned, bought from the Americans who previously owned them.

The growth in EVs has brought an explosion in cobalt demand. The majority of reserves, and therefore all the cobalt mines, are near the capital Kolwezi and also IN the remote area of Kisanfu – one of the poorest communities with no access to clean drinking water.

Cobalt extraction is commercially operated by the big companies where the sustainability arrangements required by the automotive companies and other customers can be introduced, measured and monitored. However, much of the extraction occurs away from the big operations at artisanal mines where most of the cobalt is mined by hand. Here teams of workers chip away at rock in dire and dangerous working conditions. There are many accidents and tunnel collapses, and back injuries are common. There have been several examples of human rights abuses including child labour, as well as environmental damage (NS Energy, 2021). Artisanal mining happens because the mines are open mines and so people from the surrounding community simply 'rock up' and start chipping away. Some artisanal mines are situated on their own, and some are part of sites owned by the commercial mine companies where companies struggle to prevent artisanal miners, desperate to make a living, illegally accessing their sites. Artisanal mining is the only source of income for much of the community who are unable to get other work, and there is no shortage of middlemen to sell their hand-mined cobalt to those who it seems have ways to get their product into legitimate supply chains.

The automotive giants are quick to point out that their cobalt is sourced responsibly. The problem, however, is how difficult it is in practice to realize this promise or even know for certain if this has ever been achieved. As long as cobalt continues to be sourced from DRC and artisanal mining remains possible, with middlemen ready to buy cobalt and mix it into legitimate supply chains, it is impossible for an automotive company to claim they source responsibly. The introduction of blockchain to track and provide confidence in all sourcing may hold the solution to the cobalt problem.

Discrimination, diversity and inclusion

Discrimination harms someone's rights because of who they are or what they believe and perpetuates inequality. Discrimination can be on the basis of race, ethnicity, nationality, class, caste, religion, belief, sex, sexual orientation, gender identity, sex characteristics, language, age, health, or other differences, distinguishing factors or status. Discrimination occurs when a person is unable to enjoy their human rights on an equal basis, typically because an unjustified distinction is made in law, policy, or how groups, societies or individuals are treated, and takes one of three forms (Amnesty International, nd):

- **Direct discrimination** – for example when a government permits and promotes unequal treatment towards specific peoples, usually with horrific consequences. History is full of such examples including the Holocaust, apartheid, genocide in Rwanda in 1994, the ethnic cleansing of the Rohingya people in Myanmar in 2017 and other real or alleged genocide since then.

- **Indirect discrimination** – when a law, policy, treatment or practice appears to be non-discriminatory but it disadvantages specific individuals or groups. For example, a supplier in a developing country recruiting workers from a local community might specify a minimum qualification or level of education. However, if that society denies or restricts the education of girls then the minimum requirement would be a form of indirect discrimination.

- **Intersectional discrimination** – when two or more forms of discrimination converge to create even greater disadvantage. For example, a company that allows pay disparity between women and men for the same job and also does not promote individuals of certain ethnicity to senior positions would double disadvantage a woman of this certain ethnicity.

Understanding the nature of and degrees of discrimination is an important factor in driving sustainability in supply chains. Gender inequality is relatively easy to determine. Globally, the gender gap across 156 countries stands at 68 per cent. This means, on average, across a range of areas women are 32 per cent short of gender parity (World Economic Forum, 2021). At current rates it will take 136 years to close the gap. Iceland, Finland and Norway have the lowest gap. The UK ranks 23rd and the US ranks 30th. As might be expected Afghanistan ranks the lowest closely followed by many Middle Eastern and African countries. When it comes to work, globally women are at 58 per cent of parity with men in terms of opportunities, participation, taking up positions and pay. Worldwide, when it comes to gender parity, the US ranks 30th and the UK is down at 55th position. Women in leadership positions are significantly lacking with women representing just 27 per cent of all manager positions. When it comes to education the gap is much less. Globally, attainment by women is 95 per cent that of men with 64 countries having achieved educational gender parity. Among them are 28 advanced nations and 36 developing countries. It is a similar situation with health and survival (World Economic Forum, 2021).

When we consider racism, it is less easy to measure or establish degrees of racism around the world. This is largely because a surprisingly high number of countries do not track race or ethnicity of citizens, making it difficult to track racist activities against them. Furthermore, racism takes many forms and its very nature is such that it is not always apparent how racist an individual or society is and can only be established by examining actions. Published research in this area therefore tends to be questionnaire-based findings and it can be difficult to establish if a person is racist or not from a questionnaire (World Population Review, 2022c). According to US News & World Report, the worst countries for racial inequality are Bulgaria, Slovakia, Qatar, South Korea, Israel, Russia and Belarus. The US ranks in 65th place out of 85 countries assessed (US News & World Report, 2022), its ranking having dropped significantly in the wake of the police-involved deaths of African Americans George Floyd and Breonna Taylor. The picture is different when we consider racism based upon the degree to which individuals in a region have experienced it, witnessed it or how comfortable individuals would feel living near neighbours of different race. Here India emerges as the most racist country with just under half of the population claiming to prefer no foreign neighbours and three-quarters report having witnessed racism. India is followed closely by Lebanon, Bahrain, Libya, Egypt, Philippines, Kuwait, Palestine, South Africa and South Korea (World Population Review, 2022c). Racism in all its forms increased worldwide during the Covid-19 pandemic, and through and beyond 2020. The crisis fed fear, which manifested itself in xenophobia and discrimination including a backlash against Asians in particular. US law enforcement warned about a growing threat from the rise of white supremacist groups, calling it the biggest domestic terrorism challenge. Yet 2020 also saw a 'racial reckoning' originating in the US in the wake of George Floyd's killing by a police officer and sparking solidarity around much of the developed world. Prior to this Americans were indifferent to racism and police brutality but this event shook the nation out of this. The Black Lives Matter (BLM) movement created a catalyst that compelled individuals, companies, institutions and entire nations to reflect on racism and take a stand against those areas where it remained, whether intentionally or by ignorant default. Statues of former heroes, whose involvement in the slave trade or other racial atrocities were omitted from the narrative on the plaque, were torn down. Athletes and others besides 'took the knee' and corporates considered their actions and adjusted trajectories in line with the movement. BLM marked a turning point for attitudes to racism in the US and Western Europe. Elsewhere it briefly touched the entire world. BLM dealt a blow to racism; however, the hard reality is it continues to be a worldwide problem and is growing in some regions where we are witnessing the dawn of some nations using modern technology to perpetuate racial discrimination. While BLM had a positive impact, the scale of and nature of racism globally means it only scratched the surface. To truly grasp the problem we need to consider racism in all its forms that exist for different reasons across the societies of the world and all the races that suffer discrimination: Jews, the Rohingyas (Myanmar's Muslim minority), the Uyghurs in North-West China, the Hazara ethnic minority in Syria, Australian Aborigines and other First Nations people, the Shia in Saudi Arabia and the Gulf, the Romani people that originated from northern India and are now dispersed across Europe. The list goes on.

Poor working conditions and job quality

We might object to working past our set hours or finding the coffee machine still hasn't been fixed and some of us might even have experienced a work-related issue that needed to be dealt with via an internal process operated by law by our employer. For the majority of us, ensuring a safe and good working environment is our employer's primary concern. Yet few of us will be familiar with having a job that we know endangers our health, life, or violates our dignity and human rights every day. Yet this is the reality for many workers across the world.

Figure 2.3 Hierarchy of working conditions

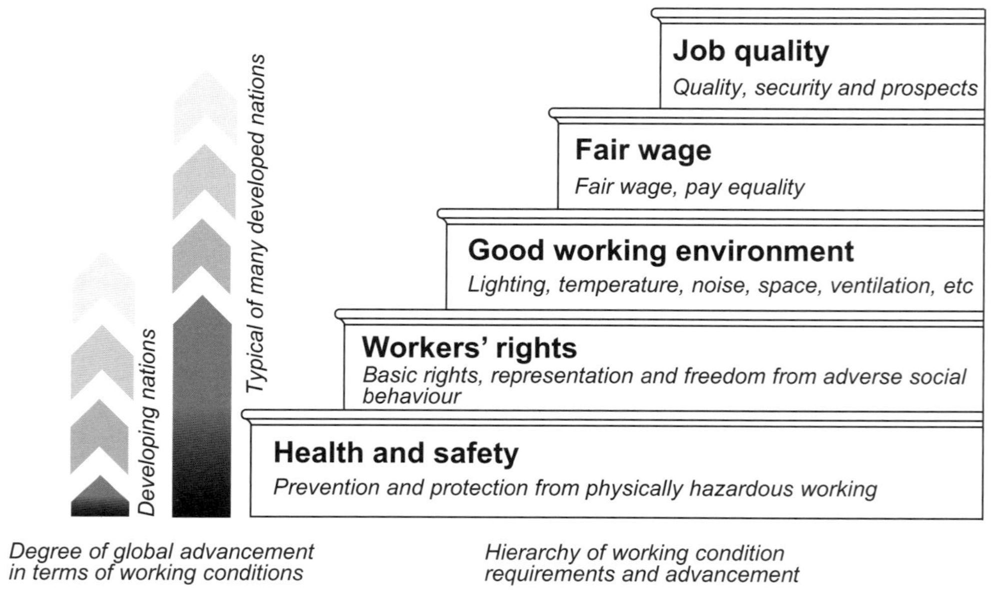

The global workforce is about 3.4 billion and, despite shrinking during the Covid-19 pandemic, overall the workforce is steadily increasing. When it comes to working conditions, this is both a broad topic and one where there are vast differences around the world, both in terms of what is required by law or considered acceptable and the actual conditions workers experience. Crucially there are vast differences between wealthy, developed nations and the developing countries. Working conditions fall under five headings and these form a natural hierarchy (Figure 2.3), ranging from the basic health and safety requirements or expectations, to the more aspirational aspects associated with job quality, security and prospects that currently would typically be found only in some developed nations. I have shown these as a hierarchy because working conditions are inextricably linked to the degree of freedom and advancement of a nation. In general, the more developed a nation is and how free the people are, i.e. not subjected to an autocratic or oppressive regime, the more advanced the nation has progressed up this hierarchy. There are, of course, exceptions.

As we will see in later chapters, determining how far we might expect our suppliers to have progressed within this hierarchy is not straightforward. Under each of these headings there are many considerations and potential detrimental impact areas. These are expanded in Table 2.1, which we will return to later as a basis to assess our suppliers, along with the current global situation where information is available.

Table 2.1 The detrimental impact areas associated with poor working conditions

Impact	What this includes	Current situation globally
Physically hazardous		
Posture-related	Uncomfortable working, non-ergonomic, sustained tiring or painful working positions resulting in musculoskeletal complaints and potentially serious diseases	Limited data available
Unsafe working	Not maintaining safe equipment, inadequate cleanliness, no/lacking fall prevention or other physically dangerous environments, inadequate health and safety arrangements	Workplace accidents account for 360,000 deaths worldwide (WHO, 2021)

Table 2.1 *continued*

Impact	What this includes	Current situation globally
Air pollution/ biological or chemical risk – by inhalation	Breathing in smoke (including tobacco smoke from other people), fumes (e.g. welding or exhaust), powder, dust (e.g. mineral, cement, wood), vapours (e.g. solvents and thinners)	Accounts for 450,000 deaths worldwide (WHO, 2021)
Biological or chemical risk – by contact	Handling or being in contact with chemicals, infectious materials, waste, bodily fluids, biohazardous materials, laboratory materials	Limited data available
Manual handling	Lifting or moving heavy loads, repetitive lifting, lifting or moving people	Limited data available
Repetitive	Repetitive hand and arm movements resulting in permanent injury	The most reported physical risk: >50% of workers affected across many regions and countries worldwide
Vibration	Vibrations from machinery, using hand tools, etc	Limited data available
Working hours	Hours per day, days per week worked, working unsociable hours, limits on working hours set and enforced by company, commuting time, work demands requiring work during free time	In the UK + UE27 15% work more than 48 hours. In China and Korea it is 40%. Chile >50% and Turkey nearly 60%. In most countries >10% work during their free time. Men work longer hours than women overall for paid work. For unpaid work the reverse is true Long working hours linked to 750,000 deaths worldwide (WHO, 2021)

Table 2.1 *continued*

Impact	What this includes	Current situation globally
Intensity of work	Working at high speed, to tight deadlines, insufficient time to complete the work, interruptions/disruptions with negative consequences, having to meet unreasonable performance targets or keep up with pace setting/automatic speed of machine or movement of produce/goods	30% in the EU and 50% in the US, Turkey, El Salvador and Uruguay experience intensive work. (Eurofound and ILO, 2019)
Workers' rights		
Basic rights	Right to civil liberties, free speech and right to assembly, right to justice	41% of the world's countries restricted free speech and assembly (ITUC 2022)
Representation of workforce	Right to establish a trade union, works council or similar committee, representation of employees, fair resolution of workplace conflicts, health and safety representation of employees, protection under labour laws, collective bargaining, right to strike	77% of the world's countries exclude workers from the right to representation (ITUC 2022)
Adverse social behaviour	Verbal abuse, unwanted sexual attention, threats, humiliating behaviours, physical violence, repression of workers, sexual harassment, bullying, other harassment	Workers experience violence in 34% of countries (ITUC 2022), extent of other abuse not known but estimated to be much higher
Working environment		
Bad lighting	Inadequate, poor or inconsistent lighting where the work is carried out, flickering or wrong colour temperature (causing eye strain, headache, etc)	Limited data available

Table 2.1 *continued*

Impact	What this includes	Current situation globally
Temperature	Sustained and ongoing high temperatures (that make workers perspire even when not working) and/or low temperatures either indoors or outdoors	>20% of workers worldwide are exposed to high temperatures, slightly lower figure for low temperatures
Noise	Excessive, sustained, unprotected, typically so loud you would have to raise your voice to be heard or talk to others, sustained exposure resulting in permanent hearing damage	20–33% of workers worldwide are exposed to loud noise
Inadequate space	Inadequate space to work safely	Limited data available
Inadequate ventilation	Inadequate ventilation/access to good air quality	Limited data available
Fair wage		
Living wage	Living wage, getting paid on time, unfair deductions, paying a fee to get a job (and creating a debt)	700 million people live in extreme poverty despite having employment and as such have jobs that do not provide a way out of poverty for them and their families (Eurofound and ILO, 2019)
Pay equality	Pay differences on the basis of gender, race	Average gender pay gap is 68% globally (World Economic Forum, 2021)
Job quality		
Flexibility	Availability of flexible working hours, degree of choice regarding working, ability to take time off for personal or family matters	Limited data available

Table 2.1 *continued*

Impact	What this includes	Current situation globally
Social environment	Quality of management, direct control of supervisor/boss, handling angry clients, customers, patients, pupils, social support, having to work in situations that are emotionally disturbing, support, respect and praise from peers and managers, fair distribution of work	25–40% of workers have jobs with emotional demands (Eurofound and ILO, 2019)
Skills and discretion	Adequate skills for the work, decision latitude, availability of training (paid by employer), consultation and participation in the organization (e.g. ability to influence decisions that affect the employee), support for personal development, cognitive development	Limited data available
Job security and prospects	Employment contracts, career prospects for advancement, job security	Limited data available
Leave	Paid holidays, paid maternity and paternity leave, paid sick leave, ability to take other time off unpaid	Limited data available

SOURCES Eurofound and ILO (2019); ITUC (2022); WHO (2021); World Economic Forum (2021)

Exposure to physical risk and poor working environment

In the Western world we are used to and expect effective arrangements for health and safety in the workplace. Typically, workers have the ability to voice concerns and expect resolution, and companies face tough penalties for failing to ensure safe working. It is hard to imagine a workplace that does not have this; however, workplaces where employees are exposed to physically hazardous conditions can be commonplace in some supply chains.

Approximately 1.2 billion workers in 41 countries around the globe have poor working conditions. Women face the worst conditions. Exposure to physical risk exists in nearly all countries, especially those associated with repetitive hand and arm movements. Data is lacking in this area, especially in developing nations, so the scale of the problem is almost certainly very underestimated.

Around 1.9 million people die from work-related causes each year with a disproportionately large number of work-related deaths in South-East Asia and the Western Pacific, and also in males and people over 54 years. Overall, this figure has declined in the first part of this century, yet deaths from work-related heart disease and stroke associated with long working hours (more on that shortly) rose by up to 41 per cent. Of the 1.9 million, occupational injuries and accidents account for 360,000 deaths (WHO, 2021).

Each year, globally, around 1 billion workers worldwide are exposed to hazardous substances. These include pollutants, dust, vapours and fumes, with the biggest exposures being to asbestos, silica, heavy metals, solvents, dyes, toxic chemicals, EDCs (endocrine-disrupting chemicals), pesticides and MNMs (manufactured nano materials – tiny particles with exceptional characteristics and as such are easily inhaled with potential health consequences). The majority of this exposure happens in developing countries. Many of the hazardous chemicals that cause health problems have long since been phased out in developed nations, yet these are still commonly found in the workplace in poorer regions. In addition, workers being exposed to poor air quality or pollution in the workplace is most acute in developing nations and is estimated to be responsible for 450,000 deaths each year mainly from cancer (ILO, 2021). Globally asbestos accounts for more than 233,000 deaths annually and exposure to pesticides account for more than 300,000 deaths. Cancer is the main cause of work-related death, with over 200 carcinogens regularly found in workplaces around the world. Other health concerns include toxic effects on the body including reproductive, cardiovascular, respiratory and immune systems as well as specific organs such as the liver and brain (ILO, 2021).

Each year, 750,000 deaths worldwide are attributed to long working hours (WHO, 2021). Long working hours is the new psychosocial occupational risk factor globally, across both developed and developing nations. When it comes to the most affluent nations, Denmark, Norway, Germany, Netherlands and Iceland work the least hours, averaging between 30 and 35 hours per week. Some of the countries with the highest working hours near or exceeding 50 hours per week include Mauritania, Egypt, Qatar, Cambodia, Myanmar and Bangladesh (World Population Review, 2022a). These might not seem high; however, these are the average hours across all forms of employment. If we look further, in the EU 15 per cent of workers work more than 48 hours per week, yet in China, Republic of Korea, Chile and Turkey as many as 60 per cent of workers pull more than 48 hours each week (Eurofound and ILO, 2019). Workers in richer countries earn more and work fewer hours, and crucially have more choice regarding their hours than workers in poorer countries (Giattino and Ortiz-Ospina, 2020).

Workers' rights

When it comes to workers' rights the worst regions in the world are the Middle East and North Africa. In 2021, the ten worst countries were Bangladesh, Belarus, Brazil, Colombia, Egypt, Honduras, Myanmar, the Philippines, Turkey and Zimbabwe. Worldwide representation of workers is declining along with an increase in countries suppressing the right to join or form a trade union, strike or collective bargaining. In 2021 there was a 19 per cent increase in countries that impeded or repressed independent union activities. These include Hong Kong, Kyrgyzstan, Iraq, Belarus and Egypt among others. In 2021 trade unionists were killed in six countries, three of which were in the Americas and freedom of speech and assembly of workers that was constrained increased by 13 per cent to 64 countries (ITUC, 2021).

Living wage

Working poverty is a reality for many worldwide. Approximately 700 million people are living in extreme or moderate poverty despite having employment and as such have jobs that do not provide a way out of poverty for them and their families. There is no universally agreed definition of what constitutes a living wage (otherwise referred to as a fair wage or decent wage). It is interesting to note the differences; for example, Luxembourg, Australia, France, New Zealand and Germany have the highest hourly minimum wage at $11–$14 per hour while contract workers in Mexico only have to be paid $1.05. Yet there is no universally accepted monetary amount that would constitute a living wage and notwithstanding the obvious stark differences quoted here, comparisons are not straightforward. There is, however, a broad consensus among countries of the world regarding what a living wage is and that is one that enables workers and their families to meet their basic needs (UN Global Compact, 2022a). Hungry and desperate individuals with little choice will end up working for a pittance and there are plenty of companies ready to capitalize on this. Here is it easy to demonize these as 'the big greedy corporates' for taking advantage of their workers and while this label could rightly be applied to some organizations, the reality is it is a product of the capitalist economic model that drives global trade that we are all part of. Within procurement, this means the predominant driving force that shapes everything we do has almost always been founded on realizing first and foremost some form of a cost-based objective. This, together with opportunism, greed of those involved and lack of regulation in developing nations means 'low cost' flows right back up some supply chains to the vulnerable and unprotected workers. Those sourcing from these supply chains are either oblivious to this or the complexity of supply chains can conveniently hide this. Whether the employees of a company in a supply chain are receiving a living wage is one of the most difficult areas to determine. We can work to understand a supply chain, audit factories and check safety and how workers are treated, yet it can be hard to know whether or not employees are receiving a living wage relative to their circumstances and the local economy. It can be harder still to create mechanisms that then enable workers to receive a living wage and even if we try, preventing corruption and abuse can be harder still. We will return to this theme later as here we are touching on one of the fundamental challenges in driving sustainability.

Covid-19 worsened working conditions for many employees and was used as an excuse to single out trade union members, force unpaid leave and suspend or terminate employment without compensation. In some cases workers were dismissed for raising concerns or requesting additional safety measures for Covid-19 (ITUC, 2021). Covid-19 also exposed the reality of the economic fragility of our world and the impact on human capital development.

Job quality

The final aspect of working conditions is concerned with job quality and might be regarded as the more aspirational dimensions of work, more akin to wealthier developed nations. Indeed, it is these nations, and especially the EU, that have legislation in place to protect workers in these areas, whereas many aspects of job quality do not figure in developing countries. Job quality covers many aspects and includes job security, career advancement prospects, scope for skills development, availability of training paid by the employer, decision latitude and the degree to which a role provides cognitive development. It includes how much flexibility is afforded to us, the ability to take time off or enjoy paid leave for holidays, being sick, maternity, paternity and other needs. For many, such things would be either expected or might be differentiators that are evaluated in determining whether or not to take a job. Many others, however, do not have such choice when finding work and can only rely upon what they are entitled to under prevailing regulations of their country. Job quality extends to the social environment, such as the quality of management, support, respect, praise and fair distribution of work. It includes the emotional demands placed upon the employee within their job, such as having to handle angry clients, patients, pupils or work in situations that are emotionally disturbing. Twenty-five to forty per cent of workers claim to have jobs with emotional demands (Eurofound and ILO, 2019).

Bribery and corruption

Bribery and corruption has many dimensions. Core to this is the idea that a corrupt act involves the abuse of entrusted power for private gain. Corruption has been a persistent feature of human societies since time immemorial.

By its very nature, corruption is hidden, so difficult to identify and measurement is only possible based upon assessing experience and perception. The most widely recognized indicator of country-level corruption around the world is Transparency International's Global Corruption Barometer and Corruption Perception Index (transparency.org). Other measures exist too. However, the limitations of assessing perception mean there are wide differences across the various published indicators out there. The most corrupt countries are to be found in the African continent and the Middle East. They include Somalia, South Sudan, Syria, Venezuela, Yemen, Equatorial Guinea, Libya, Democratic Republic of Congo, Haiti and North Korea (Transparency International, 2020). Other perception-based studies find that the most corrupt countries include Iraq, Colombia, Mexico, Brazil and Russia (World Population Review, 2022b). The least corrupt countries are to be found in North America, northern Europe and Australasia with Denmark, New Zealand, Finland, Singapore and Sweden emerging as the highest in terms of least corruption (Transparency International, 2020). Corruption is judged as most prevalent within police, elected representatives, government officials (national and local) and business executives.

Corruption at a country level means ordinary people in are forced to pay a bribe for such things as access to a doctor or finding a school place. Worldwide, about one in four citizens have to pay bribes in order to access public services. In those situations, it is those who are less able to pay the bribe that suffer the most. This is especially high in countries where the public sector is highly corrupt (e.g. Moldova, Yemen, Lebanon, Liberia and

Venezuela) but also highly prevalent in India, Mexico and Vietnam (Transparency International, 2017).

Attitudes towards corruption tend to be shaped by the prevailing culture and context. If our experience is that of a low corruption environment, chances are we will view corruption as a negative force. Yet others, especially in parts of the world where corruption is commonplace, frequently argue that corruption is necessary, that it has a value and is a positive economic force because it generates parallel economic flows that 'grease the wheels' of an economy and cut through red tape. As such, it is often argued that corruption actually helps economic growth by creating a parallel catalyst for productivity and entrepreneurship, especially in countries that lack an effective governmental framework (Houston, 2007; Méon and Weill, 2008). While many studies have shown that corruption may initially help reduce costs incurred by cumbersome administrative processes in certain environments, it has a long-term detrimental effect on individuals, companies and nations, undermines government by eroding the efficiency and legitimacy of state institutions, and ultimately undermines sustainable development (Chêne, 2014). Consequently, attempts to counter corrupt practice where it is rife come up against deep cultural and well-established ways of working. For this reason, corruption is one of the main obstacles that prevents or inhibits driving sustainability, especially in supply chains.

A key measure of sustainability is the growth in genuine wealth per capita along with sustainable improvements in human welfare. Empirical analysis across multiple nations consistently indicates that corruption reduces this and inhibits this growth, and rampant corruption can put an economy on an unsustainable footing and seriously erode its capital base (Aidt, 2010). Corruption also affects the equitable distribution of resources, which widens inequalities and undermines social welfare programmes.

Sustainable economic development is not possible in countries suffering from corruption. Corruption has a significant social impact by preventing or inhibiting communities from becoming or remaining sustainable.

Mauro (1997) and Myint (2000) suggest this happens for a number of reasons:

- It retards economic development – corruption lowers investment as the funds are diverted elsewhere and tax income is reduced, impacting a nation's ability to reach its short- and long-term goals. Any foreign aid directed to a help a developing nation is misdirected for the gain of corrupt players, further hindering economic growth.

- It impairs the fair distribution of resources, which weakens the economy. Health, education and public services suffer as the state's resources get misdirected. The gap between rich and poor increases and the disadvantaged and vulnerable groups in society suffer disproportionately. The overall happiness index of the people declines.
- It reduces capability of the available legitimate labour pool, as those with talent are lured away to engage in parallel corrupt economic activity, and it deprives people of the right to hold positions of power.
- It leads to lower quality of infrastructure (as bribes are paid for substandard specifications) and public services that are further hindered by corrupt government players mismanaging public expenditure to benefit themselves rather than the best interests of the people of that nation.
- The government's role in implementing state policy and plans is undermined, weakening democratic reform, creating political instability and ultimately the collapse of social structure due to the spread of hatred among the nation's people, resulting from injustice and inequality.
- It negatively impacts the enjoyment of all human rights.
- Unchecked environmental damage and associated impacts as a result of bribes to turn a blind eye to unsustainable extraction, e.g. sand mafia, soil erosion, illegal mining causing irreparable damage and impacting societies, e.g. through flooding, depriving communities of the ability to fish, farm, etc.
- The safety and well-being of people is compromised, especially the poorer, as safety measures are weakened, e.g. bribes paid for buildings not to meet fire regulations.

However, it doesn't follow that all corruption leads to such things and a nation's GDP is not an indicator of whether or not corruption exists. Many developed nations including China, India, Mexico, Indonesia and Turkey have moderate or high levels of corruption but continue to be highly sustainable in terms of GDP (Aidt, 2010). It is the degree of development of the nation and specifically the context of the country's legal and institutional framework and effectiveness of the political regime that determines how sustainable a nation is in terms of defeating or at least minimizing the detrimental impacts of corruption.

So far, I've talked about corruption at a country level, which is a good starting point to gauge whether a supply chain might involve corruption in a region we are sourcing from. However, corruption takes many forms and is not confined to 'high-risk' countries. In order to truly understand and begin to assess corruption and the specific impacts it causes, we need to be able to spot it within organizations, public bodies, societies and so on. Being offered a bribe is obvious, however, other forms of corruption are less obvious, many of which we may not think of as corruption. Table 2.2 lists these and all the different types of corruption.

Table 2.2 Forms of corruption

Form of corruption	What this involves
Bribe or inducement	A payment or other advantage in return for something, such as being awarded a contract.
Kickback	A form of bribe where an individual or company receives benefit as a result of their action, e.g. a decision maker in a firm receives a kickback for granting the contract.
Secret commissions	An individual, company or agent that is supposed to be acting impartially requests or accepts a payment in return for securing or placing a contract with a particular company, gaining favourable terms or even disadvantaging a competitor to the benefit of the payer.
Future promise	Promise made or implied to an individual or company, asking them to provide some benefit now that would not otherwise be provided, in return for the promise of receiving some benefit later – e.g. 'do this now and I'll ensure you get the future contract'.
Pay to play	Being required to pay a fee to access services, get a job, participate in a process or receive privilege to engage in certain activities. Here an individual or company must pay to 'get in the game.'
Cronyism	Favouring or granting partiality to friends or colleagues in connection with awarding jobs, recruitment, procurement or other decision making. Legitimate networking can easily become cronyism and it can be hard to delineate between where one stops and the other starts. Phrases such as 'the old boy's network', 'the inner sanctum' or 'the golden circle' often get used under the guise of networking but can easily be cronyism.

Table 2.2 *continued*

Form of corruption	What this involves
Nepotism	Favouring or granting partiality to family members in connection with awarding jobs, recruitment, procurement or other decision making.
A 'bit on the side'	A provider of goods or services fulfilling a government or commercial contract provides something additional to one or more individuals that remains invisible or is absorbed and unreferenced in what gets billed. For example, a construction company working on a large project undertakes some construction work at the house of a senior individual from the company that awarded the contract but this does not appear on any project paperwork.
Dual role	Individuals operating in a duel capacity influence a process or decision to the advantage of a player, e.g. an individual in public office is also a board member for a company bidding for work. The individual is deliberately not involved in the selection and award process but is able to influence the specification and award criteria.
Distorting competition	Discriminating, imposing restrictions or setting unreasonable qualification criteria on providers that limit competition in order to favour one or more certain providers.
The 'revolving door'	Movement of individuals between positions of public office and the private sector where they use their past experience or connections to create advantage and even reward in their new position.
Lobbying	When an individual, business, trade union or other body tries to persuade a government to change its policies, often involving financial contributions in support of this. Lobbying can be a force for good that drives change in a society; however, the difference between lobbying and bribery can be hard to detect. Lobbying, as a good legal activity, is an effort to influence power, e.g. by like-minded individuals, companies or industries organizing themselves to influence those in power to realize a change in legislation that will benefit society, whereas bribery is an effort to buy power in order to gain advantage, typically happening outside normal practices.

Table 2.2 *continued*

Form of corruption	What this involves
Extortion	Securing advantage, money, services or other benefits from an individual through actual, or the threat of, violence, sextortion, intimidation to the individual, their family and friends or to the individual's property.
Parochialism	Favouring local or known individuals or entities.
Patronage	Support, encouragement, privilege or financial support from an individual or organization to another – becomes corruption when the patronage then better enables the other to win business or gain advantage.
Influence peddling	Use of position or ability to influence (e.g. as a politician) in return for money or favours.
Graft	A form of political corruption where public funds get misdirected by a government official for the benefit of private interests. Graft most commonly takes the form of the preferential award of contracts in return for financial kickbacks.
Embezzlement	A form of financial fraud; the misappropriation of money, resources or assets entrusted to an individual who dishonestly appropriates these for their own personal gain.

Impacts on communities

The 2019 film *Dark Waters* dramatizes corporate defence attorney Robert Bilott's case against a chemical firm, DuPont, after it contaminates a town with unregulated chemicals (Rich, 2016). According to Wikipedia (ndb), Bilott begins by investigating a series of unexplained animal deaths from unusual medical conditions and discovers that DuPont has dumped thousands of tons of a toxic sludge containing a chemical used to make Teflon into a landfill site adjacent to a farm. The chemical is not regulated by the US Environmental Protection Agency and therefore not reported. Bilott discovers DuPont had been running tests on the chemical for decades, finding it caused cancer and birth defects. A long and protracted battle eventually led to DuPont settling more than 3,500 cases for more than $671 million. The film portrays the battle of the big company that was all powerful in the community, the struggles of those that spoke out against something that was not right and the backlash from the community for doing this to their main employer.

It is a familiar story and this, and others like it, have been told many times in the movies, most with a story based upon real events. The coal or copper mining company dumping toxic waste into rivers, the hydroelectric dam projects displacing entire communities and so on. There are plenty of cases where the misdeeds of companies have impacted communities. Some have a Hollywood hero to call it out, battle against the company, the system, face the backlash from the community but get justice in the end. Many others don't have such happy endings. Sometimes there is a clear and obvious impact a company can have on a community and it might involve illegal action, corruption or corporate incompetence in some way. However, companies can impact communities in many other ways that are not corrupt, operating entirely legally and with the support of authorities. Furthermore, there are many other situations where a company might try to work proactively with the community yet still causes impacts.

The relationship between companies and the communities they inhabit or affect can be complex. Whether it is a new pipeline, renewable energy farm, oil field, fracking, mining and extraction, agriculture and farming, a factory or just an office building, any company creates a footprint in the communities it exists in, operates in, travels through, transports its product through, extracts from, sells to, employs and so on. Any company has neighbours and cannot exist without becoming a part of a society somewhere. This might be the simple occupation of a building and employing some local staff. However, for some companies, this footprint can be much more than that with the potential for significant detrimental impact to a community or entire society. Imagine a poor remote town in an underdeveloped nation with little legislation (or little enforcement of) to protect workers or the environment, where the major employer, and the only choice of employment available to the majority of the community, is a large wealthy corporation. The corporation becomes all-powerful and often without reproach. On the one hand the company provides jobs and almost single-handedly keeps the local economy going. On the other it has almost ultimate control over the community and few would try to stand in the way of progress at risk of being marginalized by the rest of the community. If the company elects to act responsibly, it can be a force for good in the community, addressing problems that the authorities have not been able to. Yet, put pursuit of profit above responsibility to a community, add in some corruption and you get a mini authoritarian state that can drive all sorts of detrimental impacts to a community that will go unchecked. The thing of Hollywood movies? No, a very real reality in parts of the world where the conditions are ripe for this to happen. Ways in which a company can impact a community include:

- Mining and extraction of resources – especially where the extraction brings impacts to the community by changing the landscape and water courses, depletion of resources a community needs and impacts of processing.
- Major employer with significant power – hampering economic development, paying less than living wage or establishing mini mafia-type structures to exert control.
- Dumping waste – environmental damage, spoiling the landscape, pollution.
- Occupying or clearing land, e.g. for palm oil plantations, impacting biodiversity in the region.
- Carrying goods through, over or under land – visible impacts, e.g. pipeline, impacts of increased road, river, sea, rail or air freight.
- Displacing inhabitants – forced relocation for development, e.g. to build a hydroelectric dam.

While potential for community impact by companies is clear, many corporates have long since recognized their obligation to act responsibly but more so there are a growing number of companies that recognize investment in communities, especially fragile ones, brings huge benefit for both company and community. It is a quid pro quo. If a company extracting resources in Africa keeps losing significant numbers of its workforce to HIV/AIDS, investment in programmes to promote protected sex and make condoms freely available is an easy win. If workers cannot access basic services because they have no identity papers (common in parts of Africa), then a company providing ID for its workers enables them to take a step into a more sustainable place within a community. Another easy win. There are a huge number of examples of companies supporting communities and making a positive impact. Key here is the recognition that any company by default has a relationship with the community or communities it touches and outside of legislation there is a choice about how it elects to approach that relationship.

Protecting First Nations people

First Nations people are the indigenous, aboriginal or native population of a country that existed and developed their territories pre-colonization. There are an estimated 220–350 million First Nations people worldwide (Bodley, 2015). In Australia the indigenous peoples account for around 3.3 per cent of the population, most of which are Aboriginal Australians. In North America there are more than 80 million with Native Americans or Alaska Natives accounting for 2 per cent of the US population and in Canada there are 634 First Nations communities, including the Inuit peoples south of the Arctic Circle and the Métis, that account for 5 per cent of the total population (Assembly of First Nations, 2022). First Nations people can be found the world over.

History is littered with accounts of battles where explorers and colonists threatened the sovereignty of First Nations people and drove them from their land to gain access to the resources upon which their cultures depended. These accounts are further troubled by a history of persecution or treating First Nations people as lesser citizens, something that continues to this day in some places. Many of the countries that we now look to to uphold human rights and good moral practice harbour these histories, yet common across these same countries is modern legislation and practice that seeks to protect these people and actively re-balance their place in society. This includes, for example, the United Nations Declaration on the Rights of Indigenous Peoples, which sets out the policies and rights member states must establish, and includes provision for diversity in employment, appointment of suppliers, protection of culture, preservation of language, access to health, education and natural resources.

First Nations people have their own culture and to this day strive to preserve this within the wider country cultures in which they exist. In doing so, they create competing systems between Western-imposed norms and traditional group norms. The various legislation here generally seeks to address this to prevent actions from impacting First Nations people and also seeks to ensure that the rights of these people are accommodated.

Today, in the US, Canada and Australia, First Nations people occupy and enjoy the rights to designated territories. There are many scenarios where there are impacts to the land of the indigenous people, such as for construction of dams, pipelines or for mining. Within the protection of these people, companies seeking to embark on such projects must engage in consultation to assess the impact, preserve and accommodate the rights of the First Nations people.

Figure 2.4 Drivers for detrimental impacts around data and digital

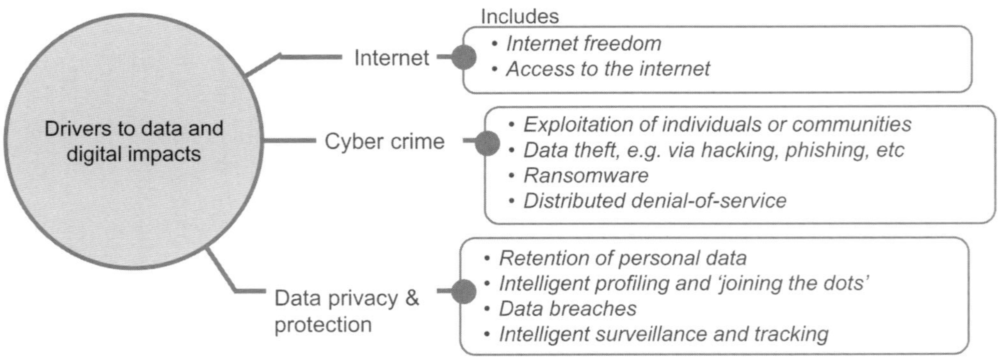

Drivers to data and digital impacts

- Internet
  - Includes
    - *Internet freedom*
    - *Access to the internet*

- Cyber crime
  - *Exploitation of individuals or communities*
  - *Data theft, e.g. via hacking, phishing, etc*
  - *Ransomware*
  - *Distributed denial-of-service*

- Data privacy & protection
  - *Retention of personal data*
  - *Intelligent profiling and 'joining the dots'*
  - *Data breaches*
  - *Intelligent surveillance and tracking*

Digital world impacts on people

The final significant threat continues to consider impact on people and communities but specifically in terms of the digital world that drives much of the physical world we inhabit today. This is not an area that is traditionally considered part of sustainability, largely because the recognition of the risk posed to people and communities is only just beginning to be grasped. Digital is an area that represents a key threat to our societies and the 'ability to exist constantly'.

It's all about data – ours!

Today we are witnessing a new gold rush to get and control data. Data about us! The importance of data protection and privacy has rapidly come into focus in recent years. Yet, there is a lag between the rapid emergence of our digital world and governmental regulation. The tech companies and many others that have long since realized the value in data and have built the digital world we now inhabit with a keen eye on collecting data about us on the way through. Many of the systems and apps, and much of the hardware that we use today, all have secondary data-collection purposes, if we allow it, in this modern age. Governments came late to the party and are only now figuring out how to respond or regulate the digital world and finding it is not that easy. It would be an understatement to suggest we are 'locking the door after the horse has bolted' because the horse has long since left and has been running rings around us all for many years. Add to this the fact that data is global so unless you physically stop it flowing across borders (as China has worked hard to do) then regulation and control is not easy. The world of data and information is somewhat of a wild and free untameable beast. It is this freedom that autocratic regimes fear more than anything as it holds the potential to undermine their existence. It is the untameability that threatens us all.

Today, despite the legislation that is in place, our personal data remains the biggest target, with all manner of companies and even nations finding ever more creative ways to get, retain, control, and use for current and future advantage as much data about us as possible. About 69 per cent of countries have introduced legislation for data protection and privacy, typically with big fines for breaches. Yet, the gold rush to get our data has abated little and arguably much of the legislation has failed to have the intended potency with the exception of a handful of high-profile cases. Put simply, the value of our data, and the revenues companies can generate by getting it, is attractive enough to find ways to circumvent or simply ignore the legislation. We've seen the news stories where large corporates get fined for a major data breach. Understandably regulators target these to demonstrate legislative enforcement. However, it is the immense scale of lots of small breaches that happen every day to each and every one of us, perpetrated by a vast number of organizations, that regulators around the world are unable or unwilling to tackle in a meaningful way. This means the very legislation that companies have set up to attempt to protect us just might not be enough. Should we be worried? Yes, and that is why data protection and privacy, internet freedom and cybercrime are a key component in considering sustainability. There are several areas we need to consider.

Freedom on the internet

Who controls the past controls the future. Who controls the present controls the past.

(GEORGE ORWELL, *1984*)

Governments have clashed with technology companies on users' rights in at least 48 countries, attempting to pursue new rules for tech companies on content, data or competition. Freedom of expression online has come under strain like never before with some governments arresting users for non-violent political, social or religious expression. Access to social media platforms was blocked in 21 states in 2021. The worst environments for internet freedom can impose prison terms for online dissent, independent reporting and mundane daily communications. It is possible, and also a reality today in some parts of the world, to have a nationwide-imposed firewall with comprehensive and sophisticated control of data flow in and out of a country that imposes government-operated censorship. Levels of internet freedom declined in the US leading up to 2021 as a result of the increase in false, misleading and manipulated information, even affecting public acceptance of the 2020 presidential election results (Freedom House, 2021a).

The internet is possibly the greatest and most powerful evolution humankind has ever made. Its emancipatory power depends upon its egalitarian nature, i.e. everyone is equal and has a voice. It is therefore understandable why an authoritative nation would seek to curb this to perpetuate its own being. Digital authoritarianism is a growing force that works against democracy and the future good of humankind. It can only be countered with regulations to enable users to express themselves freely and share information across borders, holding the powerful to account (Freedom House, 2021a). Stifling freedom on the internet has grave consequences for all of us. It leads to the denial of the basic human right of freedom of expression and perpetuates fake news, with potential for deliberate, mass-scale fake news targeting a nation, which in turn undermines democracy. It also creates the conditions for the manipulation of market practices as well as online harassment, victimization, hatred and discrimination.

The increasing threat of cybercrime

Cybercrime is the deliberate targeting of individuals or communities, or the exploitation of security vulnerabilities in order to steal passwords, data or money, or to gain control over something, for example for ransom or extortion. Cybercrime most commonly involves hacking (e.g. to access social media or email), phishing, malicious software such as ransomware or distributed denial of service (DDoS) attacks against websites or systems. Cybercrime costs many trillions of dollars worldwide each year and reached a new high during the Covid-19 pandemic as perpetrators sought to exploit the situation. Cyberattacks are on the increase and we have all seen more and more examples in recent times.

Cybercrime can severely hurt corporates and much of it goes unreported. Contrary to what is declared publicly, big companies often elect to pay the ransom for DDoS attacks rather than risk the loss of consumer confidence and brand damage. However, cybercrime impacts people and communities, and especially the vulnerable, the most severely.

Cybercrime needs to be considered in driving sustainability because of the risk of people becoming victims of cybercrime through no fault of their own. Clearly there is personal responsibility here to take all the necessary steps to protect ourselves in the digital world; however, even if we do this and notwithstanding the fact that cybercrime originates from criminals, it can become possible because of vulnerabilities and poor practice within the companies we rely upon. If a company we trust with our information has a major data breach, that can impact us. Modern data protection legislation is designed to compel companies to ensure robust arrangements but despite this major data breaches continue to happen. Yet it is the people in less-developed countries where companies are not so compelled who face greater risk of impact as a result of cybercrime. Key impacts include identity theft, financial crimes and loss of money, discrimination, victimization, persecution, extortion and sextortion from accessing sensitive information. Preventing cybercrime in the supply chain is a key consideration within sustainable procurement.

Data privacy and protection

Our surprisingly big digital footprints

How big is your digital footprint – all the data about you that resides somewhere in cyberspace? Chances are you would be surprised by how much is out there. Around 1994, the big tech companies started collecting data and since then we have each progressively created more and more data, and more and more of this has been retained, somewhere, by some company, for some reason or other. On average each human on the planet creates 1.7MB of information every second. Wow! Worldwide, we can only estimate how much data exists today, but the consensus seems to be that there is around 175 zettabytes (or 175 billion terabytes or 21 zeros) of data today and that is growing fast. Google is thought to hold about 8 per cent of this, a good proportion of which is data about us. This data resides in one of an ever-increasing number of supersized data centres, with data co-located across two or more data centres to give continuity. For example, the Switch SUPERNAP data centre complex in Las Vegas, Nevada (one of many around the world owned and operated by Switch) serves some of the biggest-name companies on the planet. It occupies more than 2.3 million square feet and consumes more than 180 megawatts of electricity (now all generated from renewable sources), which is equivalent to the power consumed by six small towns. Each year the size and number of data centres increases. Today China is home to some of the biggest data centres on the planet.

The game in play is to legally collect and store as much data as possible about us and use this to profile us and create intelligence about us that can be used for advantage. Legislation means it has become more difficult for companies to do this without our permission yet companies including Google, Facebook, Microsoft, Amazon and others besides comply with data legislation while managing to retain pretty much everything since their inception and all with the permission that was granted by us at some point, and most of us would not have truly realized what we were signing up for. This happens because the useful new technology that helps and enriches our lives, some of which is given for free, comes with the price tag of sharing data about us. Generally, however, we are reasonably aware what is happening but still elect to make the trade. More on that shortly.

In essence, each of the big tech giants have a diary of everything we have done since about 1994. This can include every website we have ever visited, every email we have ever sent, every file uploaded to a cloud (including those we have long since deleted), every location we have ever visited with our phones somewhere near us, every event we have ever attended, all our contacts in our phone, photos we have taken on a device and uploaded including the metadata of when and where each was taken (Curran, 2018). Many other companies have since joined in further growing our digital footprint out there in cyberspace and it includes such things as: if we use an internet-linked fitness monitor, when and how we exercise, how fit we are, how much sleep we get, some of what we have said near to a smart speaker, phone, TV or voice-activated remote, everyone who has ever rung our internet-linked doorbell video camera, everywhere we have driven in our car and so on.

Modern data laws require companies to declare how long they keep our data and to then delete it; however, this is typically a default position and we all unwittingly give permission for our data to be kept and used in many other ways when we agree to use a particular platform. Key here, however, is while we can do this with the big-name platforms, there are many other companies out there that also store our data but either do this in a less visible way or we simply have no idea who they are or that we ever agreed to them having our data.

An advert for the very thing you happened to be looking for at that precise moment

Ever wondered how it is that you visit a website and right there is an advert for something you have been thinking of buying? Sometimes it is the thing you talked about with a friend or family member earlier that day. This is not a coincidence but happens because these days many of the websites or companies we visit will employ 'programmatic advertising' – the modern secret revenue generator for big-name brands and a whole industry of companies you won't have heard of. Every time we click on a web link to load a page that uses programmatic advertising we set off a lengthy chain reaction. As our page loads up, the website we are visiting also asks our computer to send details of the browser we are using, its ID and IP address, which gives a rough location, and as much other information as it can get from the cookies stored on our machine.

The website we are visiting then effectively auctions off our information to the highest bidder willing to pay to get our attention. To do this it sends the information it has collected about us to hundreds or even thousands of bidders, spread all over the world in regions with varying privacy laws, if any. The advertiser (or demand-side platform) that wins the auction, based upon the best fit with what they are selling, and what they know about us and what this is worth to them, then gets to serve us a targeted advert that appears on the website as it loads up. And all of this happens in a fraction of a second. It doesn't stop there because once the ad has been served to us the provider askes our computer to send it another small packet of information on our browsing data back (Ball, 2018).

Key to enabling this is the world of internet cookies – small bits of information that websites we visit send back that are then retained on our computer, every time we go online. They can be helpful because they retain local details about our preferences for a particular site so next time we visit the site the experience is much smoother (e.g. 'keep me logged in' or 'remember me' options). So far, so good. However big companies, and especially the tech giants, were quick to realize the potential cookies hold to harvest data and so entered the 'tracking cookie' where, without intervention or computer settings set to limit these, information about all our online browsing as well as much other information about us is sent back to the company that placed it there, like an invisible spy watching our every move and collecting data about us. The ideal scenario for data collection is therefore where a company can put a tracking cookie on our device and create a situation where we choose to keep their application permanently on, such as a social media platform we access daily. Add to this the potential for data collection from what we say anywhere near our smartphone, voice-activated remote control, TV or smart speaker and it begins to get a bit sinister. While conspiracy theories abound here, it is worth noting that while all voice-activated devices are listening constantly, this is only to detect the activation command and only then do they spring into life and start recording and sending this information to the cloud. It seems they stop doing this quickly after they have finished their task. The tech companies provide some privacy settings that can be used here and, once again, many users do not set these up. Despite this, it is worth remembering we are surrounded by the means to be listened to and we rely upon the prevailing determination by the tech giants as to the extent to which our data gets used. It also seems more than a coincidence that I, and most people I know, seem to get ads served to them for something they

> only talked about earlier that day. Programmatic advertising online is an ongoing data breach happening on a vast global scale that most are oblivious to.

Joining the dots – why is this a problem?
Big Brother is watching you

(GEORGE ORWELL, *1984*)

I read George Orwell's book *1984* in 1982 while at school. Two years away, I thought, thankfully such a societal-changing philosophical prediction is never going to be realized but what an interesting work of fiction. Turns out he was about 40 years too early; perhaps not in its entirety, or even globally, many aspects of what George Orwell predicted have and are now being realized in parts of the world, and that should be a grave concern for each and every one of us.

Why should we worry about all of this if we have nothing to hide? This holds true if that data is safely retained by the giant tech companies we trust (which one would presume might include Google and Facebook) within the bounds of legislation to protect us. The problem comes when a company has or can get our data and starts joining the dots.

Joining different bits of data about us and what we do builds profiles about us with such things as our general state of health, how we drive, where we like to go, our preferences, what events we like to attend, who we spend time with, how much money we spend and on what, and so on. This can be a good thing. Just before the time I am due to leave work to go home, my phone now routinely flashes up with a notification to tell me that the traffic on the route to my home address is looking good. It also gives me an estimated journey time. I've never asked it to do this, but I like it.

These profiles and insights can also be used legitimately for profit or reduce the risk for companies we engage with. However, imagine such things as our car insurance quote being based upon how we have been driving and where we go, or a healthcare company contacting us about private treatment for a medical condition they have determined we might have from various sources of data about us, but we don't realize it yet. So far, less good but perhaps OK and inevitable.

Adding artificial intelligence to profiling allows companies to join more dots and start predicting what will happen to us, such as if we are about to get ill, we have a medical condition we don't yet know about or if our psychological well-being is deteriorating, which might impair our ability to do something, or if we need help. It can even identify certain citizens most likely to present a risk to others, or predict when a citizen is about to commit a crime. So far, OK in part if it helps but getting a bit scary now.

Finally, consider this intelligent profiling or the insights it brings falling into the wrong hands or being used against us, and the potential for blackmail, extortion, harassment, victimization, cybercrime and discrimination. Consider also governments deliberately using this as a means of discriminatory control over its citizens. Imagine compulsory facial recognition that can detect what race you are, with location monitoring and automatic access to every bit of data about you, and artificial intelligence to determine your emotional state and whether you are likely to commit a crime against the state. Imagine if that state then locked up those citizens judged to be future criminals, or even made them disappear, just in case. So far, not OK and surely this is the stuff of Hollywood movies? No, it is becoming real today with live facial recognition systems already being used in some countries (Healy, 2021; Rollet, 2021; Wakefield, 2021) and trialled by police in many other parts of the world including the UK, US and India (Yang and Murgia, 2019).

Data and digital now needs to be regarded as one of the detrimental impact areas and is a key consideration in driving in sustainability, especially in terms of the supply base as this area holds the potential to significantly impact people and communities.

Figure 2.5 The six impact areas for situation planet Earth fully expanded

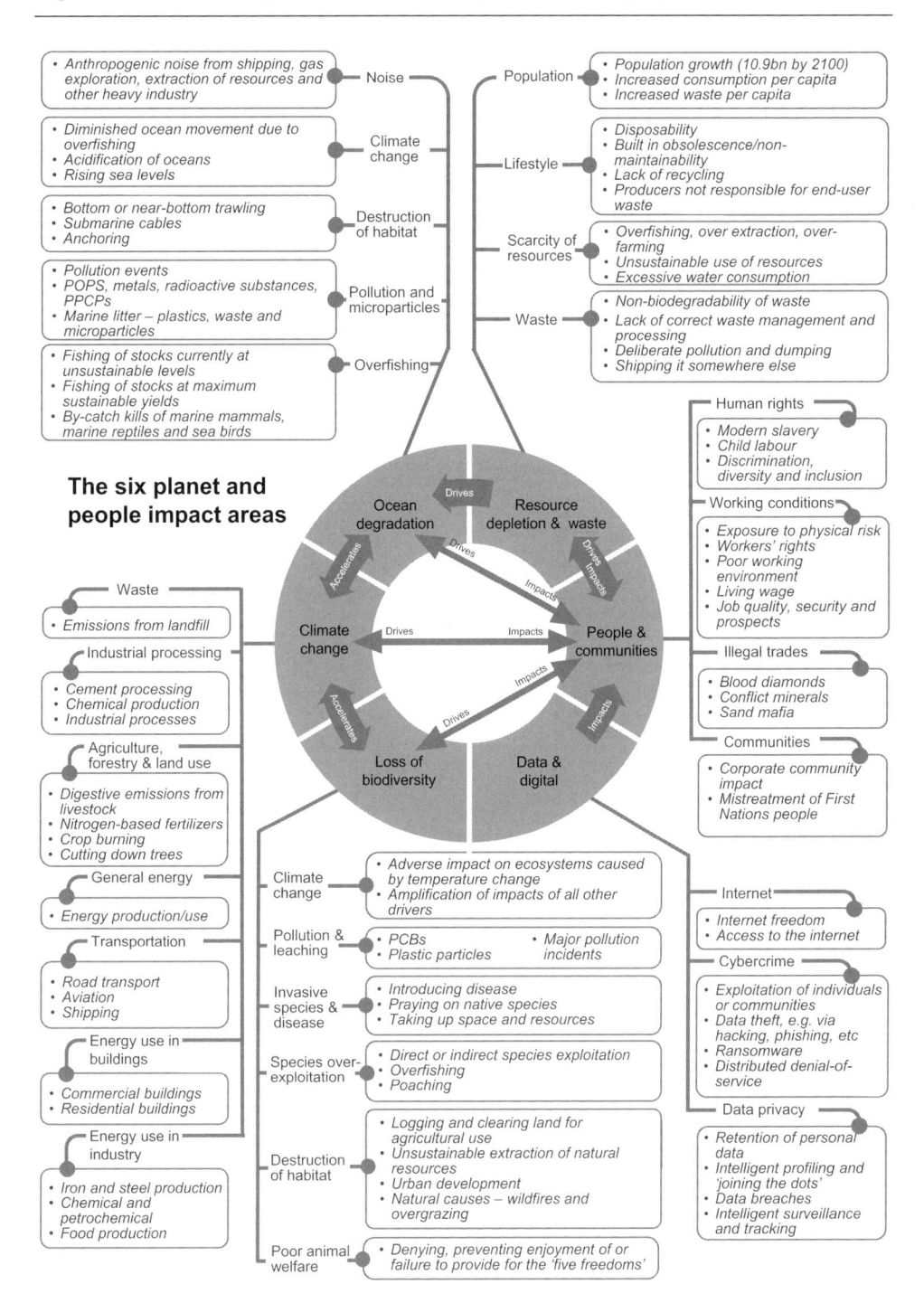

- Anthropogenic noise from shipping, gas exploration, extraction of resources and other heavy industry — **Noise**
- Diminished ocean movement due to overfishing
- Acidification of oceans
- Rising sea levels
  — **Climate change**
- Bottom or near-bottom trawling
- Submarine cables
- Anchoring
  — **Destruction of habitat**
- Pollution events
- POPS, metals, radioactive substances, PPCPs
- Marine litter – plastics, waste and microparticles
  — **Pollution and microparticles**
- Fishing of stocks currently at unsustainable levels
- Fishing of stocks at maximum sustainable yields
- By-catch kills of marine mammals, marine reptiles and sea birds
  — **Overfishing**

Population
- Population growth (10.9bn by 2100)
- Increased consumption per capita
- Increased waste per capita

Lifestyle
- Disposability
- Built in obsolescence/non-maintainability
- Lack of recycling
- Producers not responsible for end-user waste

Scarcity of resources
- Overfishing, over extraction, over-farming
- Unsustainable use of resources
- Excessive water consumption

Waste
- Non-biodegradability of waste
- Lack of correct waste management and processing
- Deliberate pollution and dumping
- Shipping it somewhere else

The six planet and people impact areas

Central diagram: a circular wheel with six segments — Ocean degradation, Resource depletion & waste, Climate change, People & communities, Data & digital, Loss of biodiversity — with arrows labelled Drives, Accelerates, Impacts between them.

Waste
- Emissions from landfill

Industrial processing
- Cement processing
- Chemical production
- Industrial processes

Agriculture, forestry & land use
- Digestive emissions from livestock
- Nitrogen-based fertilizers
- Crop burning
- Cutting down trees

General energy
- Energy production/use

Transportation
- Road transport
- Aviation
- Shipping

Energy use in buildings
- Commercial buildings
- Residential buildings

Energy use in industry
- Iron and steel production
- Chemical and petrochemical
- Food production

Climate change
- Adverse impact on ecosystems caused by temperature change
- Amplification of impacts of all other drivers

Pollution & leaching
- PCBs
- Plastic particles
- Major pollution incidents

Invasive species & disease
- Introducing disease
- Praying on native species
- Taking up space and resources

Species over-exploitation
- Direct or indirect species exploitation
- Overfishing
- Poaching

Destruction of habitat
- Logging and clearing land for agricultural use
- Unsustainable extraction of natural resources
- Urban development
- Natural causes – wildfires and overgrazing

Poor animal welfare
- Denying, preventing enjoyment of or failure to provide for the 'five freedoms'

Human rights
- Modern slavery
- Child labour
- Discrimination, diversity and inclusion

Working conditions
- Exposure to physical risk
- Workers' rights
- Poor working environment
- Living wage
- Job quality, security and prospects

Illegal trades
- Blood diamonds
- Conflict minerals
- Sand mafia

Communities
- Corporate community impact
- Mistreatment of First Nations people

Internet
- Internet freedom
- Access to the internet

Cybercrime
- Exploitation of individuals or communities
- Data theft, e.g. via hacking, phishing, etc
- Ransomware
- Distributed denial-of-service

Data privacy
- Retention of personal data
- Intelligent profiling and 'joining the dots'
- Data breaches
- Intelligent surveillance and tracking

SOURCE © Positive Purchasing Ltd 2022

Chapter checkpoint

In this chapter we explored the remaining two (of the six) critical threats, impacts and drivers that describe our current situation in terms of people. Sustainability has traditionally focused on environmental impacts; however, these two are equally relevant and necessary to drive sustainable procurement. They are:

1 *People and communities* where there are multiple impacts around the mistreatment of people, including worsening failure to uphold human rights around the world and the detrimental impact on communities.
2 *Data and data privacy* where inadequate provision means the resultant threat and impacts of data privacy and protection, cybercrime and internet freedom has potential to severely impact people.

Our journey to understanding the individual impact areas that are situation planet Earth is complete and it would be easy at this point to give up and go home. However, what we do not have is a basis to understand, and a framework for where to look, in terms of the areas we need to address for sustainability in an organization and, in particular, sustainable procurement. I shall now continue to explore what this all means and how we can move forward to a better planet and our role in making this happen. The complete picture of situation planet Earth across the six impact areas is given in Figure 2.5.

Homo sapiens: extinct in 100 years?

03

> This chapter concludes and summarizes our exploration of our current 'situation planet Earth' and what this means for all of us. We consider how unsustainable we are overall and examine a model to help make sense of this as a basis for driving sustainability. Finally, we explore the degree of choice that exists in terms of the action we take.
>
> *Pathway questions addressed in this chapter*
>
> 1 What is sustainability?
> 2 Why is sustainability important?

Future planet – with or without people?

Time for a surprise

Today, across the entire planet, including the deepest ocean, no natural or pristine systems are found in nature that have not been affected in some way by the impact of human activities (UN, 2016). We are interdependent on nature. Ecosystems can exist without humans in them, but humans cannot survive without ecosystems.

Depending upon whose analysis you consider we, the human race, are staring into the very real possibility of our own extinction in the near term unless we change things. Ord (2021) suggests that humanity faces unprecedented risks over the next few centuries and even puts the likelihood of human extinction within the next century at one in six. An overly apocalyptic suggestion? Maybe. Others suggest that we are an intelligent, interconnected species, capable of adapting to survive. Longrich (2020) suggests that *Homo sapiens* has survived over 250,000 years of ice ages, eruptions, pandemics and world wars; we could easily survive for another 250,000 years or longer. Perhaps we've been lucky until now, yet what is clear is we are vulnerable and the evidence to date suggests that large, warm-blooded animals like us don't handle ecological disruptions well.

The problem here is, as we began to see in the previous chapters, everything is interconnected, and many impacts accelerate other impacts. The jeopardy we now face results from all six of the impact areas placing a combined squeeze on our planet. Rockström and Klum (2015) suggest there is an additional factor, which is the element of surprise. Surprise is the big wild card when it comes to sustainability and is possibly the most worrying dimension as it means things may not follow the scientific projections we have today, and things could, and even have in some areas already, worsen at a far higher rate. At the heart of this lies the fact that the earth has become less resilient. For example, today it is possible to measure individual impact areas such as GHG levels in the atmosphere, model the future of global warming and quantify the degree of correction needed and seek to translate this to action. However, this assumes the planet's ecosystem continues to behave as expected. The surprise dimension comes when we consider that climate change accelerates loss of biodiversity and also ocean acidification. Loss of biodiversity and the effects of ocean change accelerate climate change and so on. All our systems are interconnected, and all regulate and buffer the planet's ecosystem. The surprise is also when our scientific modelling at an individual system level is invalidated because the combined system does not behave as the sum of the parts. It is a surprise because we simply do not know how resilient the planet will be in future years and we could be facing scenarios ranging from needing to make a course correction to plunging over a precipice and possible extinction of the human race.

The worrying trend against human rights

In terms of the people on this planet, we are witnessing a worrying anti-democratic trend and challenge to the universality of human rights, with the potential for misuse of our data and artificial intelligence systems to further compound this.

While the science shows us that we all need to be concerned about the planet because if we don't we will all suffer, when it comes to people and communities here we come up against more of a choice depending upon the degree to which all people and communities of the world matter to us and whether or not we need to or seek to care beyond our immediate family and society. As history has shown us, in the absence of environmental threats to our planet it is entirely possible for the people and communities of the world who have wealth, resources and ultimately some control to exist constantly. Less so for those without or with less. This is a key point to understanding sustainability in terms of people and communities and I will return to that shortly.

We began the last chapter by exploring our universally agreed human rights as ratified and made law by nearly all the countries of the world and how they have become what they are today. Despite this, all the people impacts we have explored, and many more besides, still happen. Child labour exists in some of these countries, including India, Uzbekistan and Tanzania (Posner, 2014). In much of the Islamic world, equality among women is seriously lacking, religious dissenters are persecuted and political freedoms are curtailed. Women's rights remain subordinate by law in Middle Eastern countries and autocratic nations still commit genocide. Furthermore, civilized countries engage in torture, sometimes as a matter of policy and sometimes deliberately kept out of sight, indeed the US set up a centre for torture at Guantanamo Bay following the World Trade Center towers attacks in 2001. The list goes on.

International human rights law is supposed to give rights to all people regardless of nationality and prevent governments engaging in abuse. The problem with human rights is that in order for them to be effective everyone needs to play by the same rules with meaningful consequences for those who do not. The sovereignty of nations means governments can make their own decisions around the degree to which they will ensure their citizens enjoy their human rights. When we look back at the 70-year history of the evolution of human rights legislation, it is easy to assume that the notion that human rights are universal is robust. This is not the case and increasingly nations are electing to rationalize and justify departures from human rights legislation in part or in its entirely. Critics assert that human rights are expressive of Western values and there is a worrying trend in the universality of human rights being increasingly challenged (Shaheed and Richter, 2018).

Posner (2014) argues that human rights law has failed to accomplish its objectives and that human rights were never as universal as people hoped, and the belief that they could be forced upon countries through international law was misguided. He argues the UDHR did not create legally binding obligations, was not ratified by the nations but rather approved by the

UN General Assembly and was vague, aspirational and open to interpretation by governments. Furthermore, authoritarian states including Saudi Arabia and the then Soviet Union and Yugoslavia abstained. At the core of this were fundamental differences in the belief of what human rights should be. At the time, the West argued human rights were about political freedom – the right to vote, free speech, freedom of religion and so on, while the Soviet Union argued human rights were about social and economic rights – the right to work, access to healthcare and to education. Distil this down further and world nations either supported political rights (democracy) or economic rights (socialism). The result was two of the later treaties that separately addressed political and economic rights (Posner, 2014).

What were a few cracks back in 1948 have become growing and worrying fissures across the geopolitical landscape today. The commitment to human rights has declined since the 1990s and despite the fact that each of the six major human rights treaties have been ratified by more than 150 countries, many of these still remain hostile to it (Posner, 2014). Russia showed its true colours when it invaded Ukraine in 2022 and China has risen to become a formidable global power and has steadily weakened international human rights. It rejects international criticism of its repression of its citizens or political assertions, citing the 'right to development' as its rationale.

Furthermore, democracy is in decline worldwide with an unparalleled deterioration in democracy in the past decade. The number of countries that can be considered a democracy reached its lowest point in 2021 (Freedom House, 2021b). Democracy provides freedom and the structure that gives the greatest chance of human rights being the foundation for how a society operates. The world's wealthiest societies are democracies; these are the least corrupt and seek to preserve liberty of citizens. Yet this is not the case across much of the world and we are witnessing a rise in autocratic regimes. The notion that countries can simply make their own choices within their borders as far as democracy is concerned is misguided. Globalization means the fates of all countries are interlinked.

We should be worried about the fact that in order for an autocratic regime to maintain its power at home, it must find ways to deny honest elections and isolate itself and its people against ideas such as free speech, accountable government, and effective regulation and control over police, military and other institutions (Freedom House, 2021b). Increasingly we see this at play around the world with more and more stories of apparent election rigging and control of information. These same countries control what internet content its citizens can see.

It gets worse. Crucially, democracies are under threat because in order to maintain and grow power an autocratic regime must actively seek to undermine democracy and suppress debate *outside* its borders. This is happening all around us with social media offering the perfect platform here and we may not even be aware and worse still, our governments may still be playing catch-up. It might seem an absurd idea that an autocratic regime outside our border could wield sufficient power to undermine Western democracy but that is exactly what is happening. Moscow and Beijing are single minded in their identification of democracy as a threat to their oppressive regimes, and as such pour vast resources into deliberately working, with increasing sophistication, to undermine its institutions and cripple its advocates (Freedom House, 2021b).

Autocratic regimes outside our borders can't and don't need to rig our elections, they only need to sow distrust in Western democracy by undermining candidates and spreading disinformation. The 2016 US presidential elections were influenced by Russian interference. Prior to the election, Russia hacked the personal emails of hundreds of government employees and also hacked voter registration databases, created fake online groups, and selectively shared specific bits of information to undermine the Democratic Party's campaign. Whether or not this action influenced the outcome is not clear, but the fact that it happened is very clear (Abrams, 2019). Similar Russian misinformation and interference in the run up to Brexit has been widely alleged, however, the UK government claimed there was no evidence of such but crucially chose not to investigate it anyway (Lis, 2020). Democracy and human rights are further eroded when autocratic regimes form unexpected alliances with, and provide economic and diplomatic support to, the countries that violate human rights that Western countries condemn, isolate and impose sanctions on.

Sustainability in the digital world

The final summary of situation planet Earth is the misuse of data, or failure to protect data that can significantly impact people and communities, deny their human rights, fuel bribery and provide the means for autocratic nations to control its citizens, or worse. Our reliance upon the internet, modern connectivity or computer-controlled systems means our entire world depends upon the digital infrastructure that surrounds and supports us. These days few systems have an 'old world' back up as things have progressed so far it is no longer considered necessary or cost effective to provide for such things. For example, utility companies that utilize the cell phone network for the essential data communication and telemetry between sites, which would once have used a secure internal network or radio system, or the computer-controlled infrastructure for a supply pipeline that uses a secure network over the internet to connect to remote parts of the infrastructure, which would once have required a human presence and perhaps a telephone. Create a major interruption and the economic and social impact can be immense.

Data and digital is therefore the key to modern power and this power is increasingly being recognized by criminals and nations that are becoming ever more ingenious and sophisticated, seeking to undermine democracies in order to obtain, control, use and profit from data or the control of infrastructure. Few take data risk seriously enough, many remain unaware of how much data could hurt us – creating the perfect conditions for data to be exploited. Yet, even with the most advanced measures to protect ourselves, ultimately, we rely upon the companies we deal with to do the same. As we have seen, many lack the systems or ability to do this adequately and when it comes to data their vulnerabilities become our problem.

Data and digital is such that we cannot fully protect ourselves. We might look to effective legislation in the hope that it will protect us and it will to a degree, but not completely. People in the regions of the world where legislation is lacking are wide open to detrimental impacts from misuse or lack of protection of data. However, arguably these are generally developing nations and as such the data risk is less, as fewer people are online and societies are not yet as data driven as we are, therefore citizens don't yet have much, if any, digital footprint, but it will come. It is easy to assume that in a civilized nation with good data privacy and protection regulations we would not need to be concerned, yet the global nature of data is such that criminal activity will not respect our borders and so the legislation in our country will help us little. Therefore, the biggest digital threats we face are from overseas where the potential to obtain, retain and exploit our data is greatest.

Data and digital is such that it has the potential to impact us all where criminals are able to exploit weaknesses or where certain nations are able to use it to strengthen their autocratic regimes. The risk of detrimental impacts from data is particularly prevalent for those that have the biggest digital footprints or rely upon it the most and are therefore the most at risk. Data risk to people and communities is therefore unique and vulnerabilities don't follow the same rich/poor divides as many other aspects of sustainability.

Except, however, when the state is collecting and using the data about people, and so those who live in regions where a nation elects to utilize data and digital as a means of control over its citizens are unwittingly impacted by the power of data being misused.

Add to all of this how attractive the exploitation of data is to criminals, along with how easy it to do this, how unprotected or unaware most individuals and corporations are, how behind the curve governments are and the ease with which criminals can exploit and remain undetected or untraceable, and the stage is set for people and communities to be impacted by data and digital and be left powerless to do anything about it.

How unsustainable are we?

We are already in trouble. The stability we all depend on is breaking. This story is one of inequality, as well as instability. Today, those who've done the least to cause this problem, are being the hardest hit. Ultimately, all of us will feel the impact, some of which are now unavoidable.
Sir David Attenborough, COP26 Climate Summit Glasgow opening address, November 2021 (Attenborough, 2021a)

An uncertain future

How unsustainable is our planet? It is an important question if we are to begin to prioritize where we are to direct our efforts and have a baseline to work from. Yet measuring how unsustainable we are at a planetary level is not straightforward. As we will see later, measuring it at a supply chain level is equally challenging. Across these first three chapters I have laid out the various impacts and as much science-based fact as I could muster to provide a comprehensive assessment of situation planet Earth. We know in detail what is happening to our planet and the people and communities that live here and as the science shows we are already unsustainable in many different areas. Yet, despite this, it is hard to see a clear picture of the overall combined level of unsustainability or indeed which areas most need to be addressed. Add to this the uncertainty of the surprise factor and a good pinch of scientific debate about how at risk we might be, versus the earth's or humankind's ability to adapt, innovate, compensate, correct or adjust our trajectories, and there is no certain measure. However, what we can say with certainty is we have now reached the point where the future is uncertain and in a few specific areas we can also be certain we are at high risk.

If we are unsustainable now, the big question is are we past the tipping point, i.e. the point beyond which we cannot recover? Here there is much debate and the general consensus within the scientific community suggests that we are at or at best perilously close to a tipping point. In addressing the G7 summit in Falmouth, UK in 2021, the environmentalist and broadcaster Sir David Attenborough told leaders from the world's seven most advanced economies that the question science forces us to address is 'are we on the verge of destabilizing the entire planet? If that is so, then the decisions we make this decade – in particular the decisions made by the most economically advanced nations – are the most important in human history' (Heffer, 2021). The good news is the general consensus also suggests we have the skills to recover from this.

How unsustainable are people and communities? It is difficult to say. Furthermore should we consider all people or some people, and what is the minimum that needs to be in place for a citizen of planet Earth to enjoy sustainable life for them, their families and future generations? The imperative to act for environmental impacts is clear and science based. Whether to act to protect people and communities is more of a choice and one where human nature is such that without good, universally agreed and enforced legislation the choice made may not necessarily be for the good of all.

The replacement of democracy with authoritarian practices is the ultimate unsustainable global practice that will slowly grind down its people and communities and with it their human rights. This means the outcome of elections is a forgone conclusion, any challenge or opposition gets marginalized and tyrannical leaders presenting themselves as the single, best-suited and most powerful individual devoted to the interests of the nation. This is reinforced, and the autocracy is maintained, through state-controlled internet, press and social media, censorship, propaganda and active misrepresentation of information. The people and communities that exist under these regimes will only ever know lies and disinformation and will be more subject to injustice, persecution, discrimination and all manner of other mistreatment that compromises human rights.

Past the tipping point

In an attempt to determine how unsustainable we have become, a team of scientists led by Johan Rockström and Will Steffen considered the resilience of the earth's ecosystems and their ability to function reliably. They found nine critical thresholds – the nine *planetary boundaries* where if we keep our impacts under these thresholds we remain safe. (Persson et al, 2022; Rockström and Klum, 2015; Steffen et al, 2015). If any one threshold is exceeded, we risk destabilizing our planet's ecosystem and at best our future becomes uncertain. A significant excess beyond a threshold places us at high risk and makes us unsustainable. The planetary boundaries model is worth further examination and can be found on the Stockholm Resilience Centre website at stockholmresilience.org. Today we are in the unsustainable high-risk zones for four of the nine and our future is uncertain for another two. The highest risk areas are identified as:

- loss of biodiversity;
- over-use of chemical fertilizers (causing severe soil degradation);
- weakening of the earth's natural nitrogen flows (caused by GHG emissions and over-use of chemical fertilizer further causing soil degradation); and
- chemical pollution and plastics (the most recent to be considered high risk (Persson et al, 2022).

In addition the following areas are identified as at risk and uncertain:

- land use (clearing of land for agricultural use and over farming); and
- climate change.

The planetary boundaries model is quite scientific and requires a degree of interpretation to relate it to the six planet and people impact areas we have explored so far. Crucially, the model specifically relates to environmental impacts and does not include impacts on people and communities. Figure 3.1 provides a summary of how unsustainable we are. It incorporates, is based upon and adapted from the data given in the planetary boundaries model with some interpretation in order to relate it back to four of the six threat and impact areas identified in Chapter 1 that relate to environmental threats. There is no data or measure of sustainability for the remaining two – people and communities or impacts from misuse of data or lack of data protection. Therefore, for these I have provided an estimate of the current level of sustainability based upon what we know and have explored so far in this book. Figure 3.1 therefore provides a combined summary and interpretation of how unsustainable we are against all the major threats and impacts we face.

Figure 3.1 Current levels of sustainability

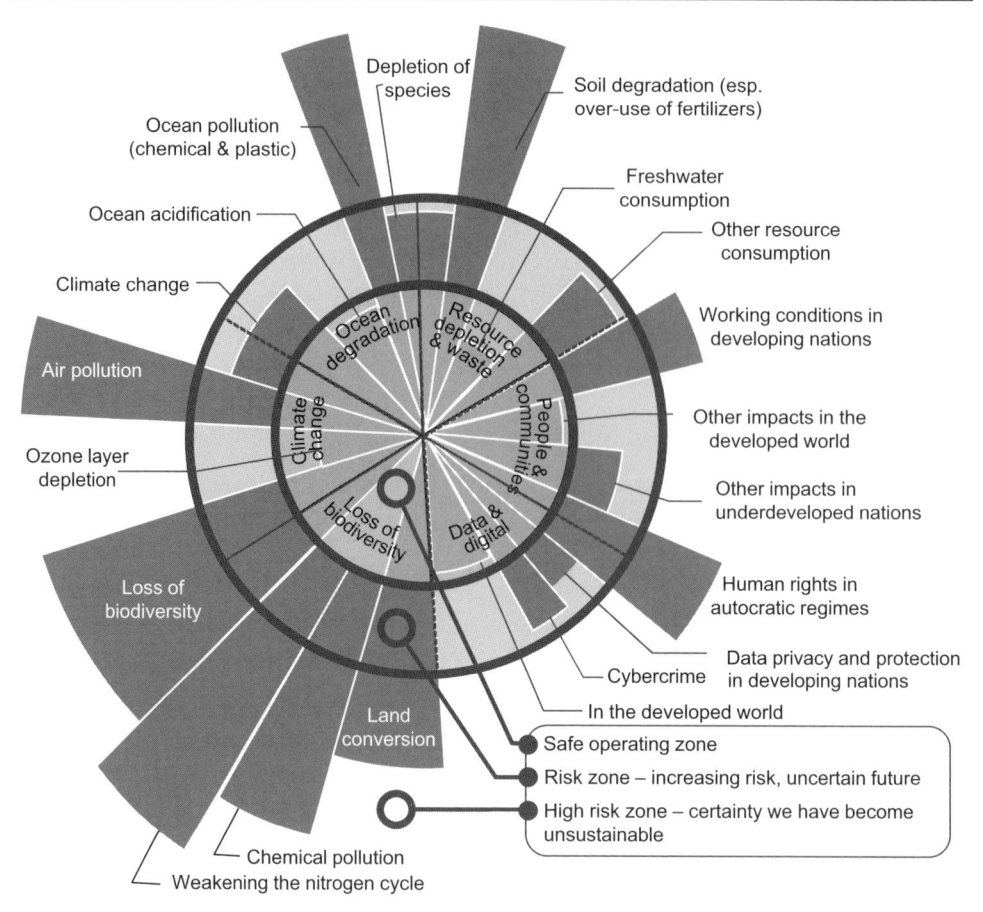

Labels around the diagram:
- Depletion of species
- Soil degradation (esp. over-use of fertilizers)
- Ocean pollution (chemical & plastic)
- Freshwater consumption
- Ocean acidification
- Other resource consumption
- Climate change
- Working conditions in developing nations
- Air pollution
- Other impacts in the developed world
- Ozone layer depletion
- Other impacts in underdeveloped nations
- Loss of biodiversity
- Human rights in autocratic regimes
- Data privacy and protection in developing nations
- Cybercrime
- In the developed world
- Land conversion
- Safe operating zone
- Risk zone – increasing risk, uncertain future
- High risk zone – certainty we have become unsustainable
- Chemical pollution
- Weakening the nitrogen cycle

Inner ring sectors: Ocean degradation; Resource depletion & waste; People & communities; Data & digital; Loss of biodiversity; Climate change

SOURCES Incorporating content from, based upon and adapted from Attenborough (2020b); Persson et al (2022); Rockström and Klum (2015); Stockholm Resilience Centre (2021), Steffen et al (2015)

Everybody wants to change the world

So you might think, but in fact not everybody wants to change the world or necessarily change the world for good. Laying out the basis for sustainability will resonate with those who get it, yet many reject it and cite all sorts of reasons for this – 'the science is flawed', 'it is the natural rhythm of the planet', 'there is little point until the rest of the world does their bit,' 'it's a dog-eat-dog world so we should only look after ourselves' and so on.

I know a good number of people who argue these points viscerally and refuse to adopt any sort of sustainability agenda. While the science of our current environmental peril and unsustainability is absolutely irrefutable, it doesn't follow that everyone will buy it. Furthermore, for those who do get it there are different schools of thought regarding the degree to which we must act. Some follow the idea of 'strong sustainability' – based upon the idea that current generations should not deprive future generations from having an effective global ecosystem and the same resources we have available to us today. Others, however, reject this in favour of 'weak sustainability' – the idea that continuing as we are and exhausting resources today is not necessarily bad for future generations and that current generations need these resources today to construct a society and invent human-made equivalents to scarce resources, in order to improve living conditions for current and future generation (Henckens et al, 2016).

We must therefore recognize that individuals, organizations and entire nations may, if free to do so, exercise their choice as to whether or not to work towards a more sustainable future or to choose do it at different rates. It is easy for us to condemn no or slow action as ignorance, selfishness, protectionism and so on. Yet such a polarized stance against solid scientific fact is usually borne out of the inconvenient truth that sustainability carries with it the threat of losing something. Whether this is aspects of lifestyle as an individual, profit as an organization, a government not being able to keep sectors of an economy thriving or the wealthy nations that created much of the current problem asking a developing nation to switch off their coal-powered energy generation just as they are managing to get themselves together.

The point here is one of choice and today much of the action required to move towards a sustainable future is based upon those doing it making that choice to do so. Arguably the environmental crisis we face is such that we don't have any choice but to act if future generations are to have any sort of good future. After all, as we have seen, people cannot survive without the environmental ecosystem; however, the ecosystem will adapt and survive just fine without people. It follows therefore that we need to look after it if we want to be part of it. As long as there is choice, any action towards this today requires buy-in from those who would need to fund, support or make any sort of change or sacrifice. Legislation is emerging that will compel individuals and organizations in some areas; however, this is slow, and legislation will not address the geopolitical challenges. The hard reality here is that the actual degree of change requires all 200 nations of the world to start working together simultaneously to halt the impacts and actively begin a programme of restoring the planet and reinforcing human rights. Without this we risk expending massive effort and getting nowhere, like two people in a rowing boat both claiming they want to get to the other side of the lake, but only the rower in the front is rowing and as such the boat is making little progress and won't reach the other side. Add to this the fact that 50 per cent of humanity's environmental impact on the living world thus far is attributable to 16 per cent of the human population (Dasgupta, 2020) and so the expectations on the wealthier nations to dig deeper to fund this might halt progress somewhat. This is the reality of the global situation we face. Similarly, preserving human rights requires true universal commitment and, as a minimum, a tolerance of democracy. Can we do this? We have yet to see but what is clear is that we have entered the most challenging decade since the earth's creation.

Should we make the planet better for all people, or just the ones who matter?

The imperative to act takes on a different dimension when we consider sustainability in terms of impacts to people and communities. As we have seen, for many of us, the impacts on people and communities are either far removed from us or don't impact our lives. They are more often than not problems that exist elsewhere – in another part of the world, in another community or a distant country, or for any other reason that might cause us to regard someone as different or less deserving. After all, while we have to act to fix the planet's ecosystem because all our futures depend upon it, when it comes to people we are not so co-dependent. So how does that 'ability to exist constantly' apply when we consider people? Should we make the planet better for all people or for just the ones who matter? Should our aim be to further establish the two-tier world we already inhabit; to further polarize those who have and those who may not have and concentrate our efforts on preserving the future and lifestyles of the elite?

As you read that, perhaps a part of you was inwardly shouting 'of course we need to care, why wouldn't we? We are all equal!' or perhaps your response was more 'not unless it impacts what I need; it's unfortunate, but that is life'. Perhaps you were somewhere between the two. The point here, once again, is we have choice where we sit here as individuals, organizations and even entire nations. History has shown that without universally upheld legislation to prevent it, those with power or those in wealthier nations will act in a way that fails to consider impacts on people and may even elect to focus on only the few that matter to us. This might sound somewhat Machiavellian, yet it is the reality today, due in part to deliberate actions by some but more often than not through ignorance, apathy or the belief that someone else is sorting this stuff out. As consumers, without realizing it much of what we buy has been tainted by some sort of detrimental impact on people along the way, whether it is modern slavery, child labour or poor working conditions and the companies that supply us are more often than not equally unaware or at best are struggling to address the issues.

Add to this the fact that we live in a capitalist world and it is a finite planet that runs based upon a system of capitalism. Companies create wealth within that system and politicians maintain the system to ensure economic prosperity. It follows then that without regulations to prevent it, commercial companies will seek to maximize wealth by increasing profit and the most effective way to increase profit is to minimize input costs. Minimizing the costs of people is something we are all familiar with; however, in the Western world regulations prevent this to a degree. Take that regulation away and have companies operating in a global market and, depending upon how far you are prepared to go or how much you actually know about what is happening in the supply chain, there is the ability to access cheaper and cheaper people and make more money. This gets us to one of the fundamental points regarding sustainability and that is that capitalism, as we know it today, would indeed appear to be incompatible with anything even vaguely resembling sustainability (Porritt, 2005).

Yet when it comes to people and communities, while we may have choice as to how far to go, in a global economic system that naturally works against sustainability, addressing social impacts is not optional. Remember, the ability to exist constantly means considering the capacity of the earth's global ecosystem and human civilization to coexist today without compromising the ability of future generations to meet their own needs. Fail to address the impacts on people and we fail to deliver sustainability. As we know, nature provides us with food, shelter, protection and provides the basis to engage in cultural activities. Our social systems that we rely on cannot exist or thrive without all the people and communities that created them, or the support of nature. Perpetuating inequality, poor working conditions and compromising human rights threatens the long-term social and economic development. It hampers the process of eliminating poverty and destroys people's feeling of self-worth. As people get poorer, they become more desperate, need more support, this in turn can breed crime, disease and environmental degradation. Poverty denies nations the resources and incentives to innovate and support a global effort to recover our planet and also drives local protectionism, for example driving choices that harm us all such as choosing coal-powered energy over something more sustainable.

The diversity of influences here are summarized by Granovetter (1985), who suggests that business decisions are influenced by both sociological and economic concerns and that how we approach a business decision exists somewhere on a continuum between these two (Figure 3.2). At one extreme the sociological and altruistic concerns such as fairness, honesty, equality, trust and common interest drive business decisions. Here we would find the utmost care and consideration for people and communities and how they might be impacted, either positively or detrimentally, by the decisions we take as an individual acting alone or on behalf of an organization. At the other extreme are business decisions that are totally influenced by economic concerns. As such, this drives self-interest behaviour that is cut-throat, dishonest, opportunistic or involves wrongdoing. Granovetter (1985) suggests that acting at either extreme is counterproductive and acting at either extreme will not succeed. Extreme sociological concerns thwart progress, stifle economic growth and compromise outcomes from the fear of upsetting, harming or unfairly treating anyone. This has been the traditional positioning of many advocates for sustainability in past decades and as such has failed to gain traction with initiatives that 'lack teeth' by focusing only on good intent without considering what might be commercially viable. Extreme economic concerns drive action to maximize profits and returns but individuals and organizations acting here may struggle to win or retain support. This suggests the extremities of a capitalist economy or 'capitalism that doesn't care'. Here sustainability initiatives beyond the legal minimum get rejected unless there is worthwhile payback. There is also the potential for false claims around sustainability if it will maximize profit. Granovetter (1985) suggests that the optimum approach lies somewhere in the middle. He calls this 'embeddedness' and provides the basis for how organizations need to approach sustainability and the basis to develop the business case for sustainability, i.e. balancing sustainability initiatives against economic considerations. We will explore how we do this soon, but first we need to get to what sustainability actually is and, in particular, what is sustainable procurement, and that is the subject of the next chapter.

Figure 3.2 Granovetter's continuum

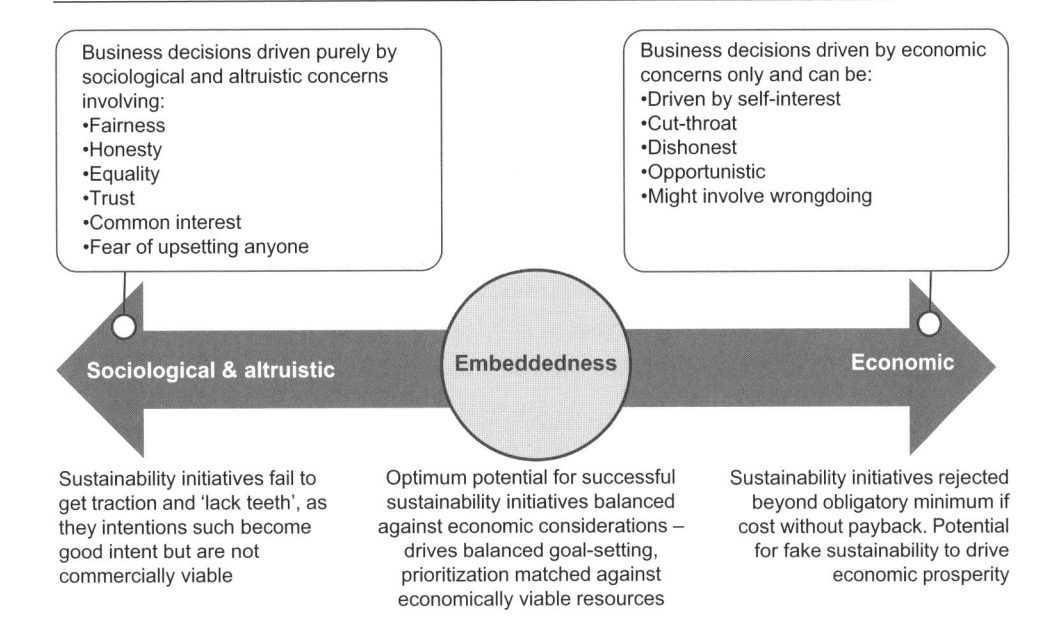

Business decisions driven purely by sociological and altruistic concerns involving:
- Fairness
- Honesty
- Equality
- Trust
- Common interest
- Fear of upsetting anyone

Business decisions driven by economic concerns only and can be:
- Driven by self-interest
- Cut-throat
- Dishonest
- Opportunistic
- Might involve wrongdoing

Sociological & altruistic ← **Embeddedness** → **Economic**

Sustainability initiatives fail to get traction and 'lack teeth', as they intentions such become good intent but are not commercially viable

Optimum potential for successful sustainability initiatives balanced against economic considerations – drives balanced goal-setting, prioritization matched against economically viable resources

Sustainability initiatives rejected beyond obligatory minimum if cost without payback. Potential for fake sustainability to drive economic prosperity

Chapter checkpoint

In this chapter we considered what our current situation in terms of planet and people means and what the future might hold. In particular:

1 *The planet can survive without us* but we need the planet and its ecosystem to work for us in order to survive, with one prediction putting the likelihood of extinction of the human race at one in six within the next hundred years.

2 *We are at, or close to, the tipping point* and while there is much debate regarding how bad things are there is general consensus that, for certain impacts at least, we have reached, and in some cases exceeded, what is sustainable, making our future uncertain.

3 *There is a surprise factor* – while we can model individual impacts, the combination of effects of one impact on another could make the Earth's entire ecosystem behave in an unexpected way and further accelerate the decline in the earth's ability to sustain human life.

4 *Worrying trend against human rights* – human rights and democracy globally have been eroded in recent decades and continue to be

eroded, with an increase in autocracies. Increasing impacts on people and communities are now key considerations for supply-side sustainability.

5 *A choice regarding people* – we have no choice but to make the environment sustainable – our survival depends upon it. However, for people and communities, until there is good, universal legislation and compliance by nations, there remains a choice regarding how people and communities get treated. There are vast differences around the world and no shortage of nations and companies ready to put economic prosperity above how people are treated. This has significant implications for supply-side sustainability.

We have reached the end of Part 1. In Part 2 we will explore what sustainability is and the sustainability imperative, and what needs to be in place to set the direction for sustainability at an organizational level and drive sustainable procurement.

PART 2
The sustainability imperative

Introducing sustainable procurement

04

> In this chapter we will explore what sustainability is and how it came to be what it is today. We then define sustainable procurement and conclude by introducing the process that enables organizations to implement sustainable procurement as part of an overall strategic procurement and supply chain approach.
>
> *Pathway questions addressed in this chapter*
>
> 1 What is sustainability?
> 3 What is sustainable procurement?

It seems we have managed to sleepwalk into where we are at right now and the risk is that we keep going, oblivious of the cliff edge we are walking towards with our eyes closed. Sustainability is the movement that wakes us from our sleep and holds the solution if we can drive in the right thinking and more importantly effect change at a global level. Sustainability needs more than recycling our yoghurt pots or rushing out to buy an electric vehicle (EV). Instead it requires a global effort across all of the areas I have outlined. Such change is beyond that achievable by governments alone but might be possible with economic change driven by the need to survive, the scarcity we are about to face and ultimately by the people demanding change. This means the changes needed will happen in the companies that collectively power the world's economy and because research shows, at a minimum, 50–70 per cent of these changes involve the supply chain in some way (Staal, 2021), it means that procurement has a mission critical role to drive sustainability and global change in coming years. First, however, I will bring our journey through situation planet Earth to a meaningful conclusion that sets the scene for the rest of this book, which provides the route map for how we respond. I will lay out an effective approach for sustainable procurement that, if well implemented, will deliver breakthrough change to any organization.

The ability to exist constantly

Sustainability is the ability to exist constantly. A simple statement yet one that stirs up all manner of reverberations when we try to consider if we are sustainable as people, as communities, as organizations, as the entire human race, as the planet; collectively, the global ecosystem of which we are part. The idea of needing to be sustainable would have been fairly irrelevant to all but a few in the decades towards the end of the last century. The cries of the few who could see we might be barrelling towards catastrophe and tried to warn the rest of us to 'act now' fell largely on deaf ears and we continued to head towards what is now a very real risk of a bleak future, but there is hope.

The big problem today is that we may not have the ability to exist constantly or if we do, we are perilously close to losing it. As such, today sustainability is hard to ignore. Advertising campaigns that once focused on how a brand would enrich something in our lives, now emphasize how they help us be more sustainable because many companies and consumers have started to make sustainability part of the buying decision-making process. While it may feel like the imperative to become more sustainable has suddenly appeared, the reality is that it has been growing steadily in the background for a long time now but been conveniently ignored by nations, politicians, companies and, of course, by us.

The blueprint for the idea of a practice needing to be sustainable has been around for over three centuries and originates from the world of international forestry. In 1713 Hans Carl von Carlowitz coined the phrase *nachhaltiger Ertrag* meaning 'sustainable yield' which related to the need to meet the challenge of a predicted shortage of timber while ensuring that woodlands could remain undiminished. For all practical purposes however, it is largely a post-World War II phenomenon and it wasn't until the 1960s that it began to surge in importance (Carroll and Shabana, 2010). Since that time there has been a succession of legislation, conventions, turning points and new scientific understanding that brings us to where we are today.

Figure 4.1 This history of sustainability

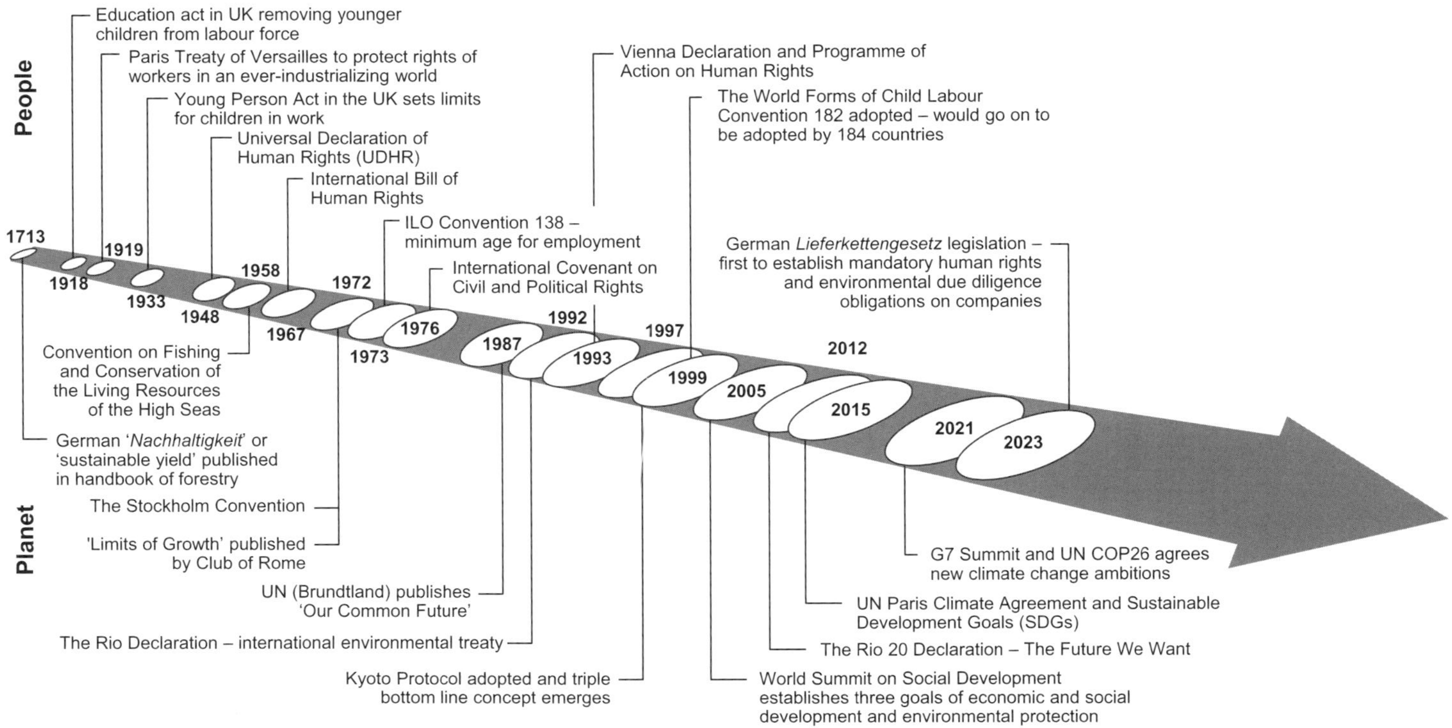

Figure 4.1 gives some key milestones in the evolution of sustainability. There are more than 300 interpretations of what sustainability is out there (Henckens et al, 2016) and many names for this, including:

- Corporate social responsibility (CSR)
- Corporate responsibility (CR)
- Social responsibility (SR)
- Socially responsible investments (SRIs)
- Environmental, social and governance (ESG)
- Ethical business
- Green
- Intergenerational responsibility
- Green capitalism
- The circular economy

Despite the many names and different emphasis each suggests 'sustainability' seems to be the label that is emerging the strongest. As we have seen, this label is a broad topic with many considerations that demand attention and a long list of issues that impinge on our ability to exist constantly. When we hear the word 'sustainability' we may well place our own interpretation on what this means based upon how we see the world and what this means to us or our view of the most critical issues. It is the new buzzword for companies extolling the features and benefits of their brand offering. It is the word consumers are starting to resonate with and it is the word companies are using to redefine values, missions, aims and objectives.

Therefore, sustainability is not one single thing but many things. It is a movement that has become the new zeitgeist. Sustainability is:

> Considering the capacity of the earth's global ecosystem and human civilization to coexist and therefore taking action to ensure we can meet our needs today without compromising the ability of future generations to meet their own needs. It is the ability to exist constantly.

Sustainable procurement

As we will see in coming chapters, organizations pursue sustainability for a variety of reasons, many driven by choice and increasingly driven by obligation. Furthermore, action around sustainability must be linked to the overall global sustainability agenda, including science-based targets.

Sustainable procurement is a component of an organization's overall sustainability approach. It is virtually impossible for a procurement or supply chain function to pursue sustainability in isolation to or at odds with what the rest of the organization is doing.

Moreover, sustainable procurement is unique in that, if it isn't there already, it catapults a procurement and supply chain function to having a strategic role to drive the business forward. Why? Simply because, as I stated earlier, research shows around 50–70 per cent of sustainability issues cannot be solved within an organization but need to be solved with a supply chain perspective (Staal, 2021). Furthermore, more than 90 per cent of the impact on natural resources, including air, soil and land, is due to supply chain activities with more than 80 per cent of GHG emissions for consumer goods occurring in the supply chain (Bové and Swartz, 2016).

Sustainable procurement – the most difficult thing to achieve

Procurement is fundamental to a company's efforts to drive sustainability. Yet it is the hardest area to tackle because:

- What happens outside our organization is not readily visible and is harder to change, especially when many contractual steps removed from us. Understanding what actually happens in our supply base can be the greatest challenge of all.
- Typically, we have no direct contractual relationship beyond our immediate suppliers.
- Just because we require change, it doesn't follow that will happen. Suppliers and those in the supply chain may lack the will to change or they may lack the resources and ability to change, meaning they will need our help to do so.
- Organizations typically lack the capability to do this or do not know where to start.
- It can increase the total cost, typically when viewed in isolation (yet, as we will see later, also holds the potential to reduce total cost along with creating new social and environmental value).

- It requires organization-wide engagement, participation and alignment. Suppliers don't 'belong' to procurement, instead, they are the organization's suppliers. Similarly, what we buy is determined by what the firm does.
- It requires a shift in approach from an 'inward-out' determination of what the business does and how it operates to an 'outward-in' supply-side driven approach.

This last point is particularly important as, unlike anything else a company may embark upon, when we work to understand the supply base and determine how misaligned it may be from our corporate sustainability goals, we establish a new basis to drive change right back up the organization. Until now, whether approached tactically or even strategically, the role of procurement has been largely to respond to what the organization determines it needs to buy. Specification, selection of materials, determination of potential providers, basis for selecting suppliers, etc have had an 'inward-out' focus, i.e. driven internally looking out from the organization. In a strategic procurement and supply chain environment, the procurement and/or supply chain function has had more of a seat at the table in this determination. Therefore, with good cross-functional engagement, strategic procurement and supply chain functions have been able to connect supply-base possibilities with end-user needs and aspirations, capitalizing on innovation and other value possible within the supply base – an 'outward informing inward-out' focus.

However, sustainable procurement is fundamentally different because it can only work with a paradigm shift towards an 'outward-in' focus. This is much more than programmes that check a supplier's sustainability rating, include contractual terms or seek to drive improvements. Instead sustainable procurement can only truly impact an organization when what is happening in the supply base, and what needs to change, drives change back in the organization in terms of materials used, specification, design, where things come from, how it is processed, how it performs, how it is sourced, the people involved and so on. In some cases, an intervention to drive sustainable procurement may require the organization to fundamentally redesign and change what it does and what it offers. Procurement now finds itself as the function leading the rest of the organization to drive change and find a way to engage the wider business to do this effectively. In practice, how we achieve this builds on the same approaches we use to drive any sort of strategic sourcing, whether it is category management, supplier relationship management or key negotiations, and that is simply about close working together with other internal functions. Cross-functional working is therefore a critical success factor for sustainable procurement.

Defining sustainable procurement

Definitions for sustainable procurement, and there are many out there, mostly tend to be a variation on the original Brundtland Commission definition of sustainable development that centre around describing an approach to procurement that is able to meet the needs of the present without compromising the ability of future generations to meet their own needs. Walker and Brammer (2009) define it in terms of procurement that is consistent with the principles of sustainable development, which they suggest incudes ensuring a strong, healthy and just society, living within environmental limits and promoting good governance. Miemczyk et al (2012) review all the established definitions and conclude that it must consider environmental, social, ethical and economic issues in the management of the organization's external resources so that across everything it sources it secures value not only to the organization but also provides value to society and the economy.

The problem with the majority of definitions out there is threefold. First, they tend to focus on the intent around procurement delivering good social and environmental and outcomes yet omit the key qualifier that this can only happen if it is part of a wider organizational initiative contributing to the corporate goals and informed or influenced by some or all of a firm's stakeholders. Second, the definitions out there tend to be quite nebulous, framing sustainable procurement as an aspirational philosophy, yet key to realizing a philosophy is establishing a structured and systematic approach to do so. Third, definitions out there tend to limit the scope to specific elements of a supply base. Some describe it as dyadic interventions with individual suppliers, others extend this to include the entire supply base and what happens right back up our supply chains. Others recognize that a *supply chain* is better regarded as a *value chain* as Michael Porter told us back in 1985. Porter defines value as 'what buyers are willing to pay' and suggest this value exists through the entire supply chain and on to the end customer to become a *value chain* (Porter, 1985). In any supply chain there are many 'flows' including, of course, the flow of goods or services in one direction and cash flowing the other way. Yet calling it the *value chain* recognizes other flows such as the flow of demand and information, and also the flow of value as each step in the chain transforms inputs to create new value, thus progressively building value throughout the chain. Crucially this transformation at each step is based upon creating the outputs that the next customer and ultimately the end customer seek.

When we consider a supply chain or value chain in terms of sustainability, we are interested in how sustainable value is added or areas where it is inhibited due to detrimental impacts as driven by the new requirements of buyers through the chain. Others look further to recognize that what we have come to call a supply or value chain is more than the linear supply-side sequence of steps they are often represented as. Instead they are more like a network of interconnected entities that extend right back to the original factory, raw material, original agricultural source, etc, and extend right forward to the final end customer, consumer, user, client, patient, citizen, etc, with multiple interconnections. This has many names: the supply network, ecosystem, value network, etc. As the terminology here can get a bit cumbersome, the name that best encapsulates what we are referring to without diluting established language is the supply and value chain network, or SVCN. From this point on I will use the term supply chain to refer to only the upstream supply base and SVCN when referring to the entire end-to-end network. If you want to understand this further I expand this concept more fully in my other book, *Supplier Relationship Management*, also published by Kogan Page.

Finally, there is the age-old debate about whether this thing we do is purchasing, procurement or sourcing or something else. *Purchasing* and *procurement* have been used interchangeably for many years. Some say one is tactical and the other is strategic, yet which it is which varies depending upon which part of the world you are in. Others duck this by calling it *sourcing*. Indeed, for sustainability, the term *sustainable sourcing* has gained some popularity, especially by NGOs and charities to attempt to indicate that the focus is on all aspects of what is sourced, how it is sourced and where things come from, and what happens along the way. Increasingly however, the term *procurement* is more universally used to describe the systematic strategic supply-side interventions of a firm, aligned with the wider organization and in support of realizing corporate goals.

Therefore, bringing all this together, the focus for sustainable procurement has to consider what we buy, who we buy from and what happens across the entire supply and value chain network. Figure 4.2 illustrates the different areas of focus for strategic procurement. Sustainable procurement is therefore defined as:

> A structured and systematic approach to assess the supply base relative to the firm's stated direction and objectives for sustainability, as informed by its

stakeholders, and to work in concert with the wider organization to identify, implement and embed new procurement approaches and improvement programmes for what we buy, who we buy from and what happens in the entire supply and value chain network, prioritized against available resource so as to deliver the required social and environmental value alongside economic value as appropriate to make a strategic contribution to realizing the firm's mission overall.

Figure 4.2 Areas of focus for sustainable procurement

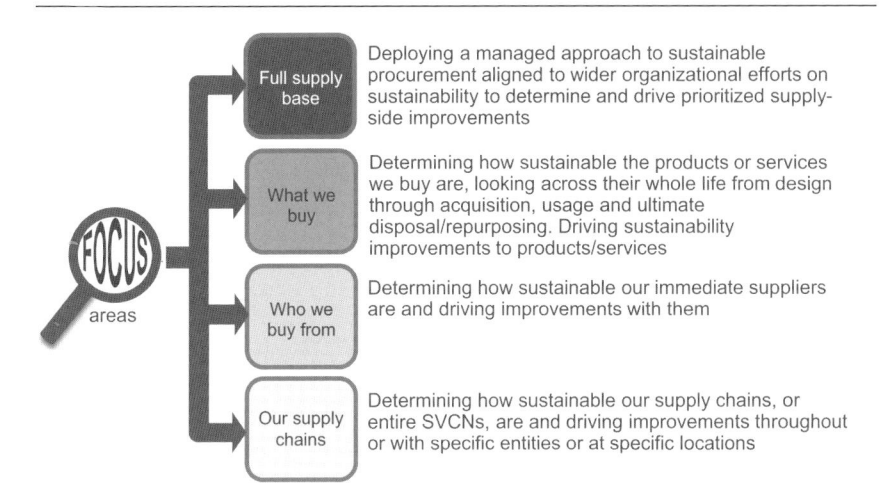

FOCUS areas

- **Full supply base**: Deploying a managed approach to sustainable procurement aligned to wider organizational efforts on sustainability to determine and drive prioritized supply-side improvements
- **What we buy**: Determining how sustainable the products or services we buy are, looking across their whole life from design through acquisition, usage and ultimate disposal/repurposing. Driving sustainability improvements to products/services
- **Who we buy from**: Determining how sustainable our immediate suppliers are and driving improvements with them
- **Our supply chains**: Determining how sustainable our supply chains, or entire SVCNs, are and driving improvements throughout or with specific entities or at specific locations

Introducing the OMEIA® sustainable procurement process

Sustainable procurement requires a structured approach. It is not something that can simply be bolted on but rather in order to be effective, it needs to be embedded and run throughout everything the organization does.

OMEIA® is the methodology for sustainable procurement and the full process is given in Figure 4.3. This forms the basis for the structure of the rest of this book.

OMEIA® is a five-step process based upon the established principles of driving business improvement. The OMEIA® methodology is the route map to implement sustainable procurement as well as to determine, realize and accelerate the value from individual sustainable initiatives and full-scale projects.

As we have seen, sustainable procurement flows from the wider organizational goals for sustainability, as informed by the firm's stakeholders and the global agenda for sustainability. Therefore, the first step has a mostly organization-wide focus to either drive this or respond to it if already well formed. Our response here is the determination of a sustainable procurement strategy and goals, ideally science-based, flowing from the wider organizational science-based goals. These are translated into the three focus areas of 'what we buy,' 'who we buy from' and 'what happens in our supply chains'. These focus areas will ultimately lead to specific initiatives and projects but before that we measure and assess the supply-side detrimental impacts and then determine and prioritize the areas for action relative to our goals. A key consideration for any aspect of sustainability is the recognition that we cannot change everything. Therefore, prioritization is essential, and we do this at three levels to reflect things we must do to avert critical risks, things we want to do in order to meet our sustainability goals and a third level of the things that will unlock new opportunities and growth. This gives us the basis to plan individual initiatives or create full-scale sustainable procurement projects and set up the governance to drive success.

Putting on the sustainability hat with our existing approaches

The individual sustainable procurement initiatives/full strategic projects are the main event. The OMEIA® process is about everything that needs to happen leading up to these to determine what we need to do, to ensure success and then augment the social and environmental value balanced with economic value. This is not about a new process or approach, but rather applying the existing approaches that have enabled effective procurement at all levels but with sustainability in mind. Sustainable procurement is, in effect, continuing to do what we do well but with a 'sustainability hat'. In other words we are applying the same processes, approaches, tools, techniques and systems that any well-equipped procurement professional will know intimately but with sustainability being a key driver. This is key to success and so sustainable procurement is not another initiative, but is something that completes what has already been shown to be successful. We will return to how we don the sustainability hat as we move through this book.

In the same way that this book completes the series of five titles I have written around key procurement practice, in order to put sustainable procurement into practice, it needs to be read in conjunction with the other publications that provide the full detail of each methodology and its process and toolset. The key linkages to each focus area are:

Category management

The process and approach for 'what we buy'. 5i® Category Management is the proven methodology to determine and implement sourcing strategies for individual market-facing categories of spend. Category management is the single most effective way for an organization to drive out significant benefits across its spend. Traditionally the focus has been around realizing dramatic price and cost reduction; however, in recent years there has been a shift towards application to drive in increased security of supply, reduce supply-side risk and unlock new value and innovation from the supply base. Well-executed category management is such that, while the process remains the same, the results change according to what you set out to achieve, hence the shift in recent times. Therefore, by applying 5i® Category Management *with a sustainability hat on*, perhaps alongside other drivers, the methodology provides a highly effective means to deliver sustainability in terms of what we buy.

In Chapter 10 we will explore some of the key tools from 5i® Category Management where the shift in application is significant; otherwise the full process and resources can be found in *Category Management in Purchasing*, also published by Kogan Page.

Supplier relationship management

The process and approach for 'who we buy from'. Supplier relationship management (SRM) holds a variety of different meanings depending upon whom you talk to. It is therefore best considered an umbrella term for the different types of supply-side intervention that we might need to manage supply-side risk, unlock value and innovation, and create new competitive advantage from the supply base. If well implemented, it is an approach to determine which suppliers (and supply and value chain networks) are important, what makes them important and then, based upon this, determine and implement supply-side interventions to realize these benefits – all aligned to the goals of the organization.

The various different components of SRM are critical to success for sustainable procurement except, once again, we are putting on the sustainability hat as we deploy them. This includes supplier performance measurement, how we drive supplier improvements, how we manage individual suppliers, managing new contracts that include sustainability factors, reviewing and managing progress, managing supplier risk and ensuring the relationship works to support this on an ongoing basis. It also includes how we might work jointly and collaborate with the critical few suppliers who hold the potential to change the game for us in sustainability terms, because they present incredible risk to hold the potential to bring dramatic new value.

In Chapter 11 we will explore how we apply key aspects of SRM to support sustainable procurement. We will cover some new tools and explore some of the key tools from the Orchestra of SRM® including the 5S and 5A SRM methodologies where the shift is application is significant; otherwise the full approach and resources can be found in *Supplier Relationship Management*, also published by Kogan Page.

Supply chain management (SCM)/management of the SVCN

This is the process and approach for 'what happens in our supply chains or in the supply and value chain network'. Until recently SCM as it is most commonly termed or management of the SVCN has been distinct from procurement, often with organizations having separate functions. Supply chain functions have traditionally focused on aspects of logistics, agility and efficiency within the SVCN while procurement focus on securing the most effective way to source the goods or services from our immediate suppliers. However, there are a number of factors, with sustainable procurement being the primary one, that are driving a convergence here. This is because sustainable procurement is almost impossible if we only consider our immediate suppliers. Instead, to be effective, we need to understand what is happening right back up the supply chain, and in some cases forward on the customer in the SVCN, to properly assess detrimental impacts and begin to know where to drive changes. As we have seen, organizations have not, until recently, been compelled to understand everything that happens in their supply chains/SVCNs, so they have not done so and bad practice can be conveniently washed away through ignorance. SCM/management of the SVCN is part of SRM and a section within the Orchestra of SRM®.

It is an approach to understand and optimize supply chain/SVCN considering logistics, the various flows (demand, information, money, goods and services, and value) and, if well developed, will be optimized using such things as Lean, Six Sigma and, more recently, predictive modelling using artificial intelligence and machine learning. By understanding and mapping a supply chain/SVCN it is possible to identify risks and opportunities. This is also a key enabler for sustainable procurement to identify where detrimental impacts might or do occur and what would need to change to address them. Supply chain/SVCN tools, good practice and expertise are therefore crucial to enable sustainable procurement.

Figure 4.3 The OMEIA® sustainable procurement process

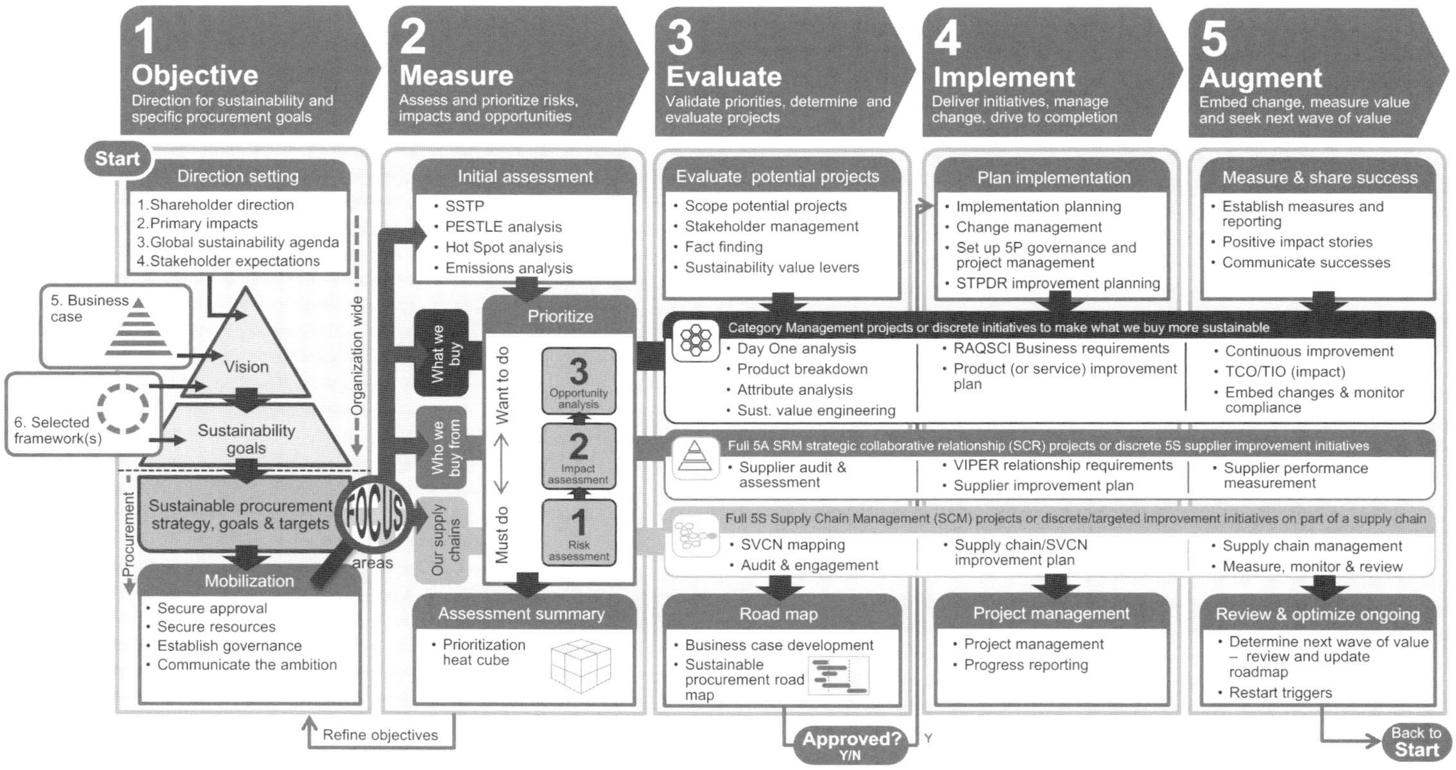

© Positive Purchasing Ltd 2022. All rights reserved. OMEIA® is a registered of Positive Purchasing Ltd

In this book we will explore how we apply key aspects of SCM/management of the SVCN to support sustainable procurement. We will include some of the tools that from the 5S SRM methodology (which, once again can be found in *Supplier Relationship Management*, also published by Kogan Page); however, we will build on some of these quite significantly to provide a means to drive sustainable procurement throughout a supply chain/SVCN.

Chapter checkpoint

Sustainability can take many different forms and is known by many names. In this chapter we explored what sustainability is and provided a definition of sustainable procurement. Key points we explored were:

1 *The ability to exist constantly* – across all the definitions of sustainability, it all its forms, the key underpinning concept is driving action to establish the ability to exist constantly.

2 *Sustainable procurement* is the most difficult aspect of sustainability to achieve largely because most of what happens, and the change required, happens outside the firm, perhaps many contractual steps removed.

3 *50–70 per cent of change* typically required to happen to make an organization sustainable needs to happen in the supply base.

4 *Putting on the sustainability hat* – sustainable procurement is not an entirely new approach, but rather becomes the backbone and driving objective and principles behind existing strategic procurement approaches, including 5i Category Management and SRM.

In the next chapter we will explore the business case for sustainability and the basis to begin to determine goals for sustainable procurement.

The business case for sustainable procurement

05

> This chapter explores the business case for sustainability at an organization-wide level and also in the supply base. It provides a model to determine the basis for action according to wider corporate aims and objectives and explores the nature of investment organizations need to make when pursuing sustainability.
>
> *Pathway questions addressed in this chapter*
>
> 2 Why is sustainability important?
> 4 What is the business case for sustainable procurement?

The business of business is business

The economist and Nobel Prize winner Milton Friedman stated in 1970 that for business, there is one and only one social responsibility, which is to use its resources and engage in activities designed to increase its profits so long as it stays within the rules of the game (Friedman, 1970).

Since that time this quote has been much used to suggest companies should not get diverted into matters of sustainability but focus on what most businesses are there to do – to increase profit for the firm's owners and shareholders. In fact, over the years the arguments against corporate sustainability have not been based upon this but have gone much further than insisting the primary pursuit of business should be profit. They also include:

- It dilutes the businesses' primary purpose
- Businesses are ill-equipped to drive sustainability
- It gives already powerful businesses too much new social power
- It compromises business competitiveness on the global stage

These arguments, however, were introduced decades ago (Carroll and Shabana, 2010) and no longer hold true in our modern context. Furthermore, the idea that a company should focus only on increasing its profit for the owners and shareholders is missing Friedman's point as what he was in fact saying is engaging in social responsibility is the decision of its shareholders. In other words, it is for the owners of the business to determine rather than from the bottom up or as a result of inward initiatives. This point remains fully relevant today and any corporate action towards sustainability must flow from the top-level vision, mission, aims, strategy and objectives, which of course will be determined by the owners of the business. We will explore this some more later in this chapter.

The sandal-wearing, tree-hugging hippies

The difference between 1970 and today is that previously businesses had little need, or were not conscious of any need, to be concerned with anything other than satisfying their shareholders. Indeed, that is the basis upon which the global economy today has been built. Once, anyone trying to convince an organization of the need to consider its social or environmental impacts would have been regarded as a sandal-wearing, tree-hugging hippy; an activist whose motivations were misaligned with that of business. Those who attempted to call things out were not taken seriously and gained little wider support. Sustainability did not make it to the boardroom agenda. Looking back, it seems there was an almost universal acceptance that the business of business was business.

By the turn of the 21st century, little had changed and few corporate boards held any interest in pursuing sustainability, except for the few that were doing so to protect or recover the business from the harm of exposure. Fewer still did things because they believed it was the right or necessary thing to do. Instead most organizations opted to concentrate on the single bottom line of business.

The business case for sustainable procurement

Today however, things are different and sustainability is firmly on the boardroom agenda and for some companies the hippies are now running the board (minus sandals). While Friedman's point is still sound, we are part of a shifting paradigm in terms of who are the shareholders of an organization. In 1970 it was simple – a commercial firm's shareholders were its financial owners and public corporations were owned by the government. Today however, no firm is able to ignore the fact that its shareholders now go beyond those who have a financial stake but extend to include all those who have a stake for other reasons. This is anyone who is impacted by, or who stands to gain or lose by what the company does – in other words a firm's stakeholders – and includes:

- its employees
- its customers, consumers, clients and users of its products or services (either directly or indirectly)
- its suppliers
- those in its supply chains
- the local community and the regions or communities where the company operates or travels through
- business partners, group or associate companies
- trade unions
- investors and environmental rating companies
- industry sector bodies
- for the public sector – citizens, patients, pupils, etc
- those who own, need, rely upon or are impacted as a result of the resources the company needs in order to operate
- and ultimately, the planet and all the people on it

These stakeholders have not traditionally been thought of as having a share in a company, yet we are the first generations to understand, with scientific basis, our current global situation, which ultimately demonstrates we all share the consequences of how a firm impacts our world. As a result, no company in this world can operate or be successful unless it considers its stakeholders, whether compelled by legislation, demands of the financial shareholders, customer expectations or the desire to do good. The business case for sustainability is therefore not about whether or not to do it, it is about which of the different drivers for action to respond to and how far to go. This is the basis for the business case for sustainability.

The business case for sustainable procurement

The business case for sustainable procurement is the reason to act. It supports the overall business case for sustainability within the wider organization and that is our starting point. Driving sustainability at the organizational level to any meaningful degree requires resources, investment and time, and can be a significant diversion from what the business is there to do. It can also become the driving force behind what the business chooses to be there to do and the basis to drive growth and future success. Sustainability is not something that can be bolted on to run alongside the firm's operations but needs to be interwoven with the other corporate aims and underpin the entire firm's strategy and ways of working. As we will see later, when we consider sustainable procurement there are some things we can get on and do now by changing how we apply existing procurement approaches by wearing the 'sustainability hat'. In other words, considering and embedding sustainability within all of our current procurement activities. This is a good start but will only get us so far. True sustainability needs to consider all of the firm's activities and every stakeholder it impacts and this might lead to some fundamental changes to the design of the goods/services it produces, the materials used, the suppliers involved, where we source from, the processes we rely upon, how we get the goods/service to the user, how the user uses or interacts with what we do and so on. True sustainability requires us to consider everything we do, end to end, and drive in actions to address the areas of detrimental impact, and remember that typically 50–70 per cent of this will require action in the supply base (Staal, 2021).

Counting the cost

Sustainability has a cost and that cost can be significant depending upon what the organization does, and the degree of change required. It extends to the cost of change, cost of innovation, additional resources, establishing new organizational capability, changing processes and logistics, switching supply, reporting, compliance, marketing and so on. The natural response in a world where organizations are structured around top-down financial controls is for organizations to view this as a sunk cost. Add to this the fact that sustainability expenditure for a firm is a new, perhaps unknown, thing, appearing to lack tangible payback in the short term or at all, and the 'we have done OK without having to do this so far' factor and the cost of driving sustainability can cause a CFO to break out in welts. The problem here is how organizations understand the business case behind sustainability which, if well considered, establishes sustainability not as a sunk cost but an investment that can offer significant returns across multiple areas. Sustainable procurement is a key enabler here and can even be the driving force across the entire business.

A multidimensional business case

The business case for sustainability is not a single justification but is multi-dimensional. Kurucz et al (2008) suggest it is fourfold and can enable an organization to reduce cost and risk, gain competitive advantage, build its reputation and legitimacy and find win/win outcomes through synergistic value creation. However, this assumes the motivation for sustainability by an organization is largely around how it can benefit from it. Increasingly we see a wide range of motivations including some less inward-focused.

The business case for sustainability is therefore a multilayered hierarchy according to what is driving us to pursue sustainability. As we have seen, when it comes to sustainability organizations still have a surprisingly wide degree of choice regarding how far they want to go. This is tightening and increasingly organizations are being compelled to do more; however, significant choice still remains. Therefore, the business case for sustainability has many degrees according to a firm's objectives in this area and the degree to which it needs to act versus wants to act. This is shown in Figure 5.1 and this hierarchy forms the business case for sustainability for an entire organization and also provides the basis to determine the business case for sustainable procurement. It is a hierarchy because each layer builds upon the one below it. In other words, we progress up the hierarchy depending upon how far our organization determines it needs or wants to go. Each tier is a separate heading for each of the progressive reasons to pursue sustainability, and each brings new levels of value and benefits (see also Figure 5.4 later).

The growing legal imperative

Few organizations would seek to operate outside the law, therefore compliance with legislation forms the ultimate irrefutable, non-optional business case to act. Yet, when it comes to sustainable procurement legislation is some way behind, but it is on the way and procurement functions need to be ready.

There are many turning points in human history where something changes things dramatically for future generations – where there is a dramatic change both in how something is viewed and the legislation that makes the change happen. Once smoking was promoted as good for you,

Figure 5.1 The business case for sustainability

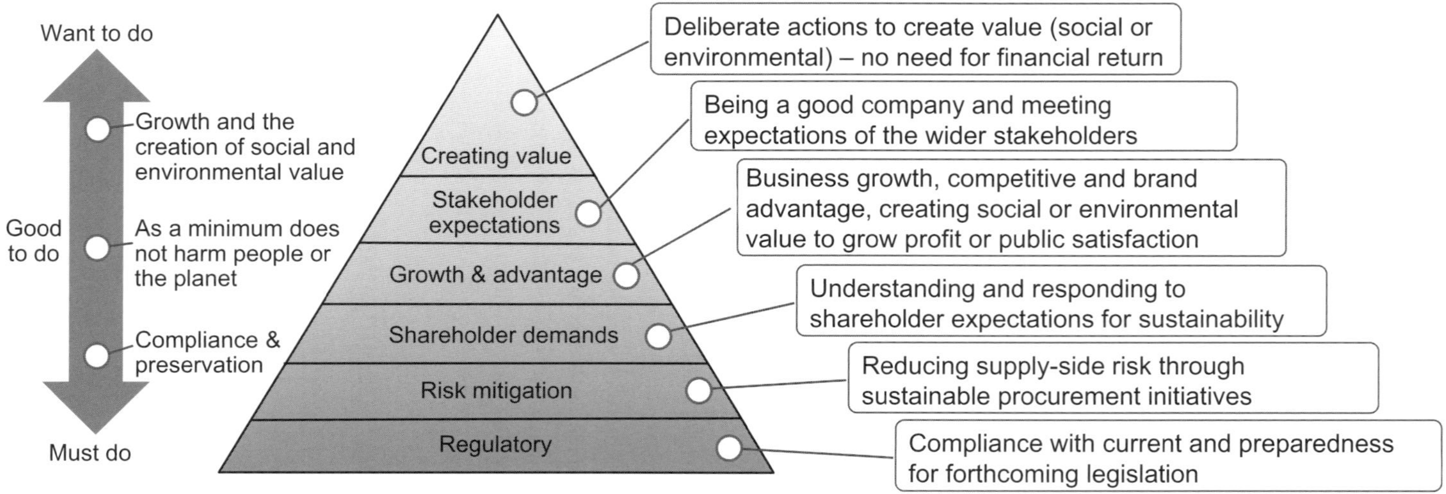

the idea of strapping yourself into your seat in a motor car was absurd and airplane cockpits didn't need to be kept locked. We are witnessing the start of what is set to become a new turning point and that is how we view, and the legislation that drives, the obligations of corporates be to responsible for what happens throughout the entire supply base. This is no small development but may well change the world or at least establish 'capitalism that cares'. It is unlikely to happen at pace, but it is beginning and at the heart of this is the principle that for all our futures a company's responsibilities must extend far beyond its boundaries.

Organization-focused legislation

Legislation for aspects of sustainability at the organization level are generally well advanced in many wealthier or more developed nations. As we have seen, international human rights legislation and others beside it remain reasonably well ratified around the world and form the basis for the various national legislation that ensures good protection of people and working conditions. Similarly, in most of these nations we can expect to find rafts of environmental, social and other legislation that place various obligations on firms across all relevant areas. The vast majority of this legislation is mostly inward focused on the organization. Today, at a global level, there is relatively little legislation that creates obligation on companies for aspects of sustainability outside the firm. While few companies would ignore health and safety legislation or fail to protect themselves against liabilities for their products or services causing harm or loss, when it comes to the supply base it is a different story. The de facto approach has most typically been for firms to not get involved in how the supply base beyond our immediate supplier provides what we need, but to focus only on what we need and use contractual means to compel our suppliers to warrant what they provide is good. This can conveniently, or through ignorance, hide all manner of things in a supply chain. Clearly the way a firm contracts with its immediate suppliers must comply with relevant legislation, but beyond this it gets a bit sketchy.

In essence, firms have not needed to understand what happens in their supply chains beyond the immediate supplier with a few exceptions. Indeed, over the last 30 years or so that I've had the privilege to work with some of the biggest-name companies around the world to help transform procurement, the single common factor, even in the most strategic or advanced teams, is that the perspective of procurement extends only to immediate suppliers. Few procurement practitioners possess the capability required to understand and drive improvements back up a supply chain. Those from supply chain functions are better equipped yet are typically used to working on how things flow rather than sustainability. Again, this is understandable because there has been no real need to look beyond immediate suppliers, except perhaps to force supply chain efficiencies such as optimizing logistics, reducing inventories or ensuring traceability for critical applications. This means that today it is entirely possible for a company to trade with a reputable supplier and be fully compliant with all relevant legislation where it operates, but for some elements of what happens in the supply chain, many contractual steps removed in other parts of the world would fall far short of our legislative standards. These elements may well be fully compliant with local legislation, or may not be, but happen due to lack of enforcement, or perhaps there is no legislation in these regions. This sets the stage for exploitation by companies and those in the supply chain keen to take advantage of the remarkably cost-effective sourcing that is possible and enjoy corporate impunity. It has, in effect, been one of the factors that has enabled wealthy nations to enjoy decades of highly affordable consumerism.

Why have we ended up here? If you read the first two chapters of this book perhaps you asked that very question and the answer is that today there is little legislation in developed nations to oblige companies to take responsibility for what happens in their supply chains. Yet, as I stated earlier, that is now changing.

Supply-side focused legislation

When we consider the specific legislation in place or emerging around the world that specifically obliges companies to be responsible in some way for what happens in their supply base, we find that it is the countries in North America, Europe and also Australia that are leading the charge here. Table 5.1 provides some of the key pieces of legislation. This comes with the health warning to check for latest developments as legislation is a constantly evolving.

Where legislation exists, it is generally quite fragmented and typically has a narrow scope for only specific facets of sustainability overall. For example, legislation specific to anti-corruption and bribery is well established in 46 countries yet this is probably the only example of any form of sustainability legislation established so globally. Other legislation exists to create obligations on companies around modern slavery in the UK, Canada and Australia and also in the US as part of the Tariff Act, which prevents import of anything that has involved forced, indentured or child labour. The Netherlands also has specific legislation around child labour in supply chains. Europe

Table 5.1 Key legislation for sustainable procurement

Region	Legislation	Applies to	What this covers
Various	Anti-corruption and bribery	Public sector and some extend to private sector	Various legislation in 46 jurisdictions – sets legal framework and penalties for corruption in various forms, including with the supply base
UK	Modern Slavery Act 2015	Commercial UK companies with annual sales >£36m	Requires companies to publish annual report setting out steps take to address modern slavery in the supply chain
UK	The Public Services (Social Value) Act 2012 – effective for supply chains 2021	UK public sector	Requires public bodies to include and evaluate social value factors in all major procurements
UK	Streamlined Energy and Carbon Reporting (SECR)	UK companies with ->250 employees or ->£36m turnover	Mandatory reporting of energy usage and emissions as well as efficiencies over the previous year
UK	Mandatory Greenhouse Gas Reporting (MGHGR)	UK listed companies	Mandatory reporting of 'carbon footprint' (scope 1 and 2 emissions). It is aligned to SECR
UK	Energy Savings Opportunity Scheme (ESOS)	UK companies with >250 employees or £50m turnover	Mandatory energy assessment. Requires companies to undertake assessments and progress savings opportunities
US	Tariff Act (1930) – section 307	US imports	Prohibits importing anything that has involved forced, indentured or child labour

Table 5.1 continued

Region	Legislation	Applies to	What this covers
US	Uyghur Forced Labour Prevention Act UFLPA	US imports	Establishes the presumption that anything produced in Xinjiang Uyghur Autonomous Region of China is prohibited under section 307 of the Tariff Act
US	CAATSA – Countering America's Adversaries Through Sanctions Act (2017)	US imports and exports	US Federal law that imposes sanctions on Iran, North Korea and Russia
US	Supplier Diversity	US government contracts above $700k ($1.5m for construction)	Requires companies to set and meet aggressive goals to subcontract spend with minority-owned organizations (including ethnic, woman, LGBT, disadvantaged, veteran, service-disabled veteran and HUBzone owned enterprises)
Canada	Transparency in Supply Chains Act – Not yet enacted	Likely to apply to companies with sales – >CAD 40m or – balance sheet >CAD 20m	Will require companies to report on and take reasonable steps to avoid modern slavery in their supply chains
Switzerland	Swiss Responsible Business initiative	Publicly traded companies with – >500 employees and either sales of – >CHF 40m or – a balance sheet of >CHF 20m	Requires companies to report on environmental and social matters, respect for human rights and anti-corruption in all controlled entities, and conduct due diligence relating to child labour and conflict minerals in supply chains

Norway	Transparency Act – effective 2022	Companies with any two of – >50 employees, – total annual sales of NOK 70m or – balance sheet >35m NOK	Requires companies to conduct human rights due diligence on entire supply chain, take steps to prevent and limit violations, and publish reports
Netherlands	Child Labour Due Diligence Act – effective 2022	All companies that sell to Dutch consumers	Requires companies to conduct due diligence related to child labour in their supply chains and submit a statement
Italy	Legislative Decree No 254 – effective 2017	Italian companies that trade on Italian or EU-regulated markets, banks and insurance companies with – >500 employees, balance sheet – >€20m and – €40m pa sales	Requires companies to publish a statement of information about their impact on environmental, social, human rights, anti-corruption and bribery
India	Business Responsibility and Sustainability Reporting – effective 2021	Top 1,000 listed companies in India	Requires companies to report on certain business responsibility and sustainability indicators
Germany	Lieferkettensorgfaltspflichtengesetz (Supply Chain Due Diligence Act) – Effective 1 January 2023	Companies based in Germany or German-registered branches of foreign companies with >3,000 employees – reducing to >1,000 in 2024	Requires companies to conduct supply chain due diligence to ensure social and environmental standards are observed in the supply chain

Table 5.1 continued

Region	Legislation	Applies to	What this covers
France	Corporate Duty of Vigilance Law – effective 2017	Companies with ->5000 employees or ->10,000 employees in the company and direct and indirect subsidiaries	Requires companies to identify and prevent adverse human rights and environmental impacts resulting from their own activities and those of their suppliers and sub-contractors. Companies must publish an annual public vigilance plan
EU	Conflict Minerals Regulation – effective 2021	EU-based importers of tin, tantalum, tungsten and their ores, and gold	Companies must report on supply chain due diligence including source (mine used)
EU	NFRD – Non-Financial Reporting Directive – Effective 2018	Certain large listed companies, banks, insurance companies and other public-interest entities	Requires companies to publish reports on environmental, social, human rights, anti-corruption and bribery and diversity policies they implement
EU	SFDR – Sustainable Finance Disclosure Regulation – effective 2021	Fund and asset-management companies, institutional investors, financial advisors and certain other regulated firms	Requires companies to disclose whether they consider detrimental impacts on environment and social justice of their investment decision and advice
EU	HREDD – Human Rights Environmental Due Diligence – Draft legislation – anticipated by 2027	Large EU companies and some non-European companies doing business in Europe	Will require companies to assess their human rights and environmental impacts (and potential impacts) in their operations and in the supply chains and to take action to prevent, mitigate and remedy harms. Administrative penalties and civil liabilities for companies that fail to do this. CSDD is a means to implement this.

EU	CSRD – Corporate Sustainability and Reporting Directive – effective October 2022	All companies in the EU or those wanting to access the EU market with – >€40m turnover – €20m balance sheet and/or – >250 employees	Amends and broadens scope of NFRD. From 2024 mandatory requirement for large companies to report on sustainability policy and performance. Designed to be applied in tandem with CSDD
EU	CSDD – Corporate Sustainability Due Diligence – not yet enacted	Companies with – >500 employees and – >€150m turnover or for high-impact sectors – >250 employees and – €40m turnover	Basis to implement HREDD and will establish corporate due diligence duty for companies to identify, prevent, end or mitigate detrimental impacts of their operations (including supply chains) on people and the environment. Designed to be applied in tandem with CSDR
EU	Timber Regulations – EU Regulation 995/2010 – effective 2010 with additional new legislation due to be enacted soon	Companies that sell domestic or imported timber into the EU	Requires companies to exercise due diligence. Proposed new legislation on deforestation-free supply chains on the way
Australia	Modern Slavery Act 2018 – effective 2019	All companies operating in Australia with sales > AU$100m	Requires companies to report annually on risk of modern slavery in their operations and supply chains and take action to address risks

SOURCES Includes some content adapted from Sedex (nd) and Ecoact (2022)

has specific legislation around timber and conflict minerals and Norway has legislation around human rights in the supply chain. Across Europe, legislation has emerged in recent years that creates obligations on certain companies to report on and disclose information related to social and environmental impacts in the supply chain.

At first examination, Table 5.1 would suggest the degree of legislation is well evolved; however, looking further it is clear that where legislation exists much of this only goes so far as creating obligations for reporting and perhaps some due diligence. In 2017 France's Corporate Duty of Vigilance Law went further and set a clear obligation for companies to not only report on but prevent adverse human rights and environmental impacts resulting from their own activities and of their suppliers and subcontractors. New legislation in Germany came into force on 1st January 2023 with the highly memorable title for non-German speakers of Lieferkettensorgfaltspflichtengesetz, otherwise known as the Supply Chain Due Diligence Act. Lieferkettensorgfaltspflichtengesetz obliges large German companies or German-registered branches of foreign companies to conduct supply chain due diligence and ensure social and environmental standards are observed in the full supply chain. The EU has continued the tightening here with its Corporate Due Diligence and Corporate Accountability Directive, which makes it mandatory for all companies in the EU or wanting to access the EU market to identify, prevent, mitigate and remedy human rights abuses and environmental damage, including in supply chains.

The new legislation that is emerging across some of the developed world takes a big step forward and compels corporates to do more than due diligence and reporting, creates obligation to take clear action and crucially now has teeth to bite companies that do not in the form of some eye-wateringly high fines. This would seem to offer the perfect solution to fix the world. However, it is not quite yet the magic bullet we need and there are a number of reasons behind this:

- Currently, most legislation only applies to the biggest of companies. For the new EU legislation, this will only apply to companies with more than 250 employees and sales turnover exceeding €40million – that means the legislation will apply to less than 0.2 per cent of EU companies.
- Globally, supply-side legislation remains fragmented. That which is emerging is only in some parts of the developed world. North American countries have not yet gone quite as far as Europe has and there is little emerging from across Asia Pacific and the Middle East.

- In less wealthy and developing nations, legislation, and crucially compliance to that which is in place around sustainability for what happens in the company, is less well developed, which means that legislation for what happens in the supply base is some way off.

Despite the fact that legislation driving supply-side sustainability may still be somewhat fragmented and not necessarily universally applicable to all companies, what we can see here is a clear trajectory. Legislation in this area is emerging around the world fast and countries are recognizing the crises we now face and responding with legislation that addresses companies' obligations for the supply chain. We can expect to see legislation progressively tighten and we can expect it to be applied progressively to more and more companies, big and small. It is likely that the urgency of some areas such as decarbonization, as recognized by global leaders at the COP26 summit in 2021, will drive a general acceleration in legislation in this area. If we are not already compelled to drive sustainability in the supply base, we will be in the short term. Legislation therefore represents the most fundamental business case driver for action to drive all aspects of sustainability in the supply chain.

The risk of corporate social irresponsibility

Mitigating supply-side risk is a compelling reason for sustainable procurement. Forward-thinking companies are well versed with considering the traditional procurement supply-side risk in terms of risks associated with a supplier failing, geopolitical uncertainty or other volatility in the supply base. However, here we are considering new and growing risks around the six main impact areas. The second component of the business case for sustainable procurement is therefore the imperative to understand, mitigate or develop contingencies for the supply-side risks associated with these impact areas that hold the potential to cause serious damage to an organization.

In recent years security of supply has swung into the spotlight of virtually all procurement functions and is now centre stage for many. Covid-19 showed us the volatility and vulnerabilities of our supply chains. The Russian invasion of Ukraine shook global supply routes some more. Yet what we soon learnt was that things would never return to where they were. Not only had the world changed but we could now see clearly the fragility of our global supply chains. This was the cue, to enter stage left, the idea that we need to think about whether we can rely upon our supply chains. What we didn't see before was suddenly obvious and that was the rapidly emerging risk to security of supply as a result of more permanent disruptions. This includes risks arising from resource depletion, scarcity and volatility, the risk of quality impact as a result of scarcity or environmental degradation driving the need to switch to lesser alternative raw materials, the risk of loss of competitive advantage due to price hikes as supply capacity fails to meet demand and the increasing cost of compliance with new and emerging legislation. One of the biggest future risks companies face is not being able to obtain the reliable, cheap materials and labour they have been used to as the consequences of the six planet and people impact areas take hold. Companies ignore this at their peril as these risks, if not addressed, hold the potential to bring a company to its knees or drive loss of competitive advantage to the competitors that are already planning ahead here.

Risking our brand and reputation

The second significant risk area is that increasingly companies face a growing risk of brand or reputational damage as a result of exposure for poor practice in supply chains. This risk area has been steadily growing yet companies have only begun to take it seriously in recent years. The risk of brand damage can be immense. Today, the Nike brand still has echoes of its association with sweatshop labour, yet it was more than 30 years ago that this news story broke worldwide, following a report published by the activist Jeff Ballinger exposing low wages and poor working conditions in the factories making Nike products (Nisen, 2013). Following that exposure Nike worked to become an exemplar for sustainable supply chains and maintained this for many years, slightly slipping back in recent years according to the sustainable brand rating website, Good On You (Robertson, 2022). However, it is not Nike's efforts to make itself a sustainable brand that it gets remembered for but rather its history with how the workers in its factories were treated may years ago. Brand and reputational damage can be catastrophic and can happen in an instance but last a lifetime.

Corporate social irresponsibility

There are many examples over the years where companies have suffered financial and reputational damage resulting from an event or something the company did or did not do – the BP Deepwater Horizon oil spill in the Gulf of Mexico in 2010, benzene in Perrier water in 1990 and the

Volkswagen CO_2 emissions scandal in 2015, to name but a few. Yet brand and reputational damage doesn't need a catastrophe to wound a big corporate. It only takes one exposure, of one detrimental impact, one photo of a child sewing a football that goes viral, one news report showing orangutans being displaced from their habitat and a brand once trusted becomes permanently tainted in the minds of its consumers. There is even a name for it now: corporate social irresponsibility (CSI) is one of the factors that can halt mergers, acquisitions and corporate expansions. Research suggests that the media coverage that surrounds announcements of potential takeovers or acquisitions plays a role in determining if it will go the distance with 12 per cent of announced acquisitions failing where examples of CSI surface as part of media coverage (Hawn, 2021).

The risks of supply failure and brand and reputational damage are so potent and therefore why risk mitigation is one of the fundamental reasons for driving sustainability. These are not the only risks, in fact there are seven types of supply-side risk (Figure 5.2). Overall, it seems companies have been slow to respond to the growing risks here and this may be because when it comes to the specific social and environmental impacts that give rise to these risks we find that the risks are unique because:

- They manifest themselves over a longer term
- The potential scale of future risk exposure is hard to determine
- They are largely outside the organization's control
- They hold the potential to impact an organization on many dimensions
- Organizations do not currently possess the capability or are not set up to fully understand and respond to these risks or plan long term

This means that tacking supply-side sustainability risk requires us to create agile and adaptive strategies for keeping the operation going and consider a much longer planning horizon than has been typical. Figure 5.2 gives the seven supply-side risk areas, of which sustainability is one, and examples of how these relate specifically to some of the detrimental impact areas. We will return to risk assessment and how we do it in Chapter 8.

Figure 5.2 The seven supply-side risk areas and how they relate to sustainability impact areas

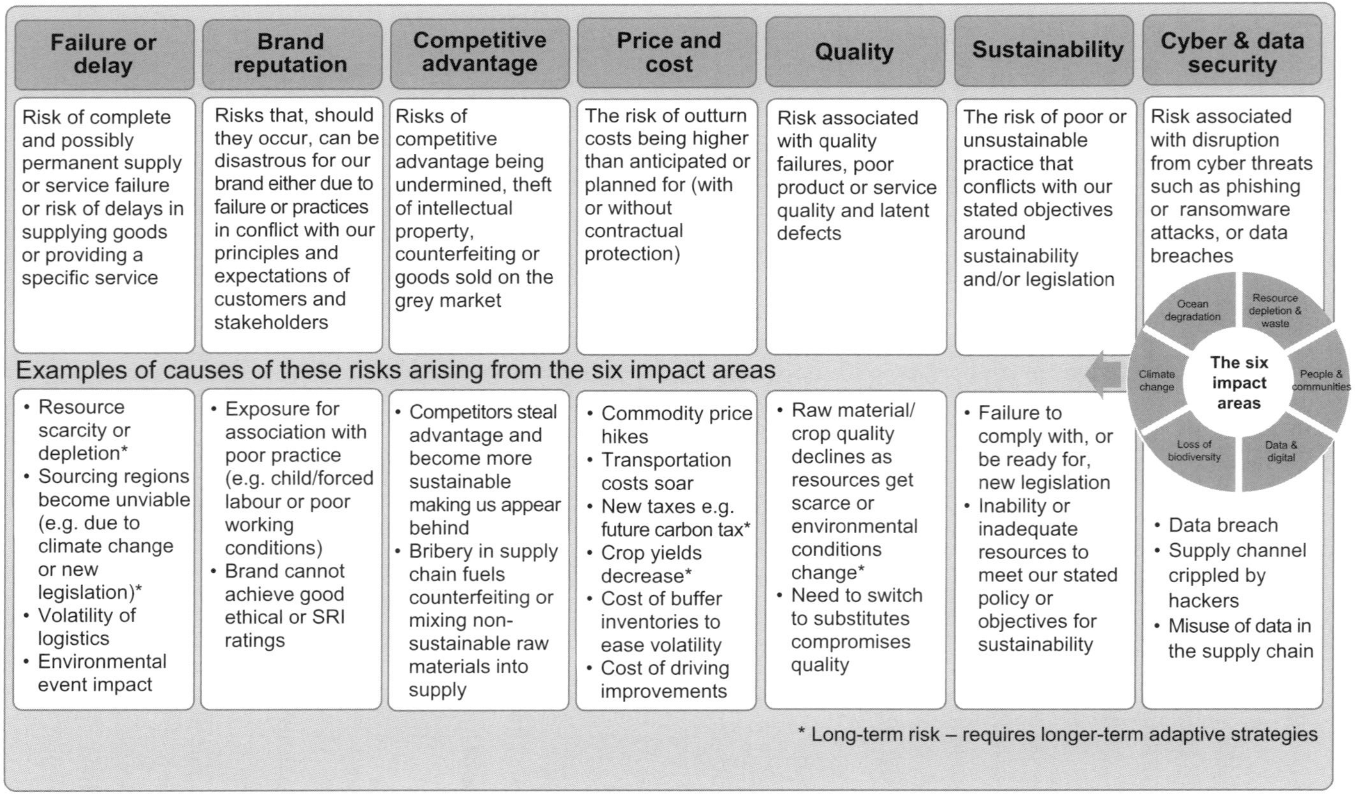

Failure or delay	Brand reputation	Competitive advantage	Price and cost	Quality	Sustainability	Cyber & data security
Risk of complete and possibly permanent supply or service failure or risk of delays in supplying goods or providing a specific service	Risks that, should they occur, can be disastrous for our brand either due to failure or practices in conflict with our principles and expectations of customers and stakeholders	Risks of competitive advantage being undermined, theft of intellectual property, counterfeiting or goods sold on the grey market	The risk of outturn costs being higher than anticipated or planned for (with or without contractual protection)	Risk associated with quality failures, poor product or service quality and latent defects	The risk of poor or unsustainable practice that conflicts with our stated objectives around sustainability and/or legislation	Risk associated with disruption from cyber threats such as phishing or ransomware attacks, or data breaches

The six impact areas: People & communities, Data & digital, Loss of biodiversity, Climate change, Ocean degradation, Resource depletion & waste

Examples of causes of these risks arising from the six impact areas

• Resource scarcity or depletion* • Sourcing regions become unviable (e.g. due to climate change or new legislation)* • Volatility of logistics • Environmental event impact	• Exposure for association with poor practice (e.g. child/forced labour or poor working conditions) • Brand cannot achieve good ethical or SRI ratings	• Competitors steal advantage and become more sustainable making us appear behind • Bribery in supply chain fuels counterfeiting or mixing non-sustainable raw materials into supply	• Commodity price hikes • Transportation costs soar • New taxes e.g. future carbon tax* • Crop yields decrease* • Cost of buffer inventories to ease volatility • Cost of driving improvements	• Raw material/ crop quality declines as resources get scarce or environmental conditions change* • Need to switch to substitutes compromises quality	• Failure to comply with, or be ready for, new legislation • Inability or inadequate resources to meet our stated policy or objectives for sustainability	• Data breach • Supply channel crippled by hackers • Misuse of data in the supply chain

* Long-term risk – requires longer-term adaptive strategies

What the shareholders want

What the shareholders want is the third component of the business case for sustainability. Increasingly, sustainable investments are outperforming traditional investments and shareholders are demanding or at least expecting the firms they invest in to be actively advancing sustainability.

From time to time I have worked with large global companies that are still majority-owned by a family or a handful of individuals. There is a notable difference between these companies and other large corporates in that these companies tend to have an obvious 'way' about them – manifested through the tangible signs of culture, philosophy, ingrained values, reporting structures and lines of control that flow from the owners. Sometimes the owner's reluctance to let go runs like deep veins to every corner of the organization. Sometimes it stands in the way of progress. Yet sometimes it establishes what the owners believe in and hold as true and important across every aspect of the organization in a way other corporates never manage to achieve. Sometimes the entire company becomes the embodiment of the owner. If the owners believe some or all of the aspects of sustainability are important you can be sure this drives how the entire company works.

For such family-owned companies, the business case for sustainability is simply what the owners want or believe must happen. However, such companies are the minority. The majority of large companies out there are owned by multiple shareholders. A large corporate can have hundreds of thousands of owners of its share capital, with perhaps a few thousand owners of a significant stake (which may still be a fraction of a percent overall) that typically are made up of the banks, pension and investment companies. This means that apart from any large majority shareholders, power is typically diluted and values held by those who own shares have little influence on the company. A lone minority shareholder standing up at an annual general meeting advocating action contrary to the company's direction of travel will have little impact. Yet a major pension fund with a significant holding voicing a concern will get listened to and taken seriously.

Shareholders drive action and change in a company yet they may not be directly involved in it day to day. The power that all shareholders have is the power to decide whether or not to invest or to continue to invest in the organization. Companies therefore place keeping their shareholders happy above everything else. Early in my career I recall a senior executive in a utility business telling me that satisfying the shareholders came first and foremost above the needs of customers, employees and even the regulator although this was not something that was ever said outside closed doors.

Keeping the shareholders happy has, until recently, been entirely about delivering good financial returns. The large financial institutions that power our banks and pension funds typically select and hold sizeable shareholdings in global corporations with the sole aim of securing good financial returns. That has, until recently, been almost entirely the basis for how the developed world works. However, we are seeing a shift in where individual investors are seeking to direct their money, which is making financial institutions sit up and consider their position.

Earlier I suggested that environmental, social and governance (ESG) is an alternative name for sustainability. It is here, within the world of sustainable investment that we most see ESG referenced. ESG is the most commonly applied term to describe all the arrangements a company puts in place to drive sustainability within a governance framework. Socially responsible investments or SRIs (also known as value-based investments, sustainable investments and ethical investments) offer both financial returns and environmental and social returns for an investor. SRIs are investments that are considered socially responsible due the nature of the business the company conducts. This includes companies that offer a positive sustainable impact and exclude companies making a negative impact (e.g. tobacco, gambling and alcohol companies).

Three decades ago SRIs were on the fringe – left to the minority who were determined to invest ethically. They had higher fees and delivered lesser financial returns. As such, banks and pension funds didn't go anywhere near them and individuals seeking financial advice would rarely be urged to look towards SRIs. Since then, investment in SRIs has grown exponentially with a 25-fold increase including a doubling from 2019 to 2020. 2021 was a record year for SRI investment with around $120 billion being poured into ESG funds; this was more than double the $51 billion in 2020 (Figure 5.3).

Worldwide around $100 trillion is invested in publicly traded securities. Today an estimated one-third of this contain sustainable investments. The Covid-19 pandemic and climate change imperatives have helped boost the momentum; furthermore, SRIs didn't suffer so much in the initial economic downturn, signalling their stability with 77 per cent of those from 10 years ago having survived versus 46 per cent of non-SRI funds (Visram, 2021). Investments in ESG companies now outperform counterparts and show lower volatility than peers while simultaneously having a positive effect on equity return (Milinchuk, 2021). SRIs therefore have become more than investments for those who seek to combine investment with making an impact but have also become wise investments for those not driven by any sort of moral principle or desire to consider social and environmental issues. SRIs now form an important component within the portfolios of banks and pension funds. That said, with this growth also comes more scrutiny and challenge of SRIs to sift out those that are little more than 'greenwash' but rather are founded upon more robust, evidenced-based verification of the activities of the companies that make up the funds against ever more stricter criteria. This is good and is an indicator of the wider movement towards sustainability in all aspects of business with transparency, accountability and demonstrating compliance more and more part of how business operates.

Figure 5.3   Growth and projected growth in investment in SRIs since the 1990s

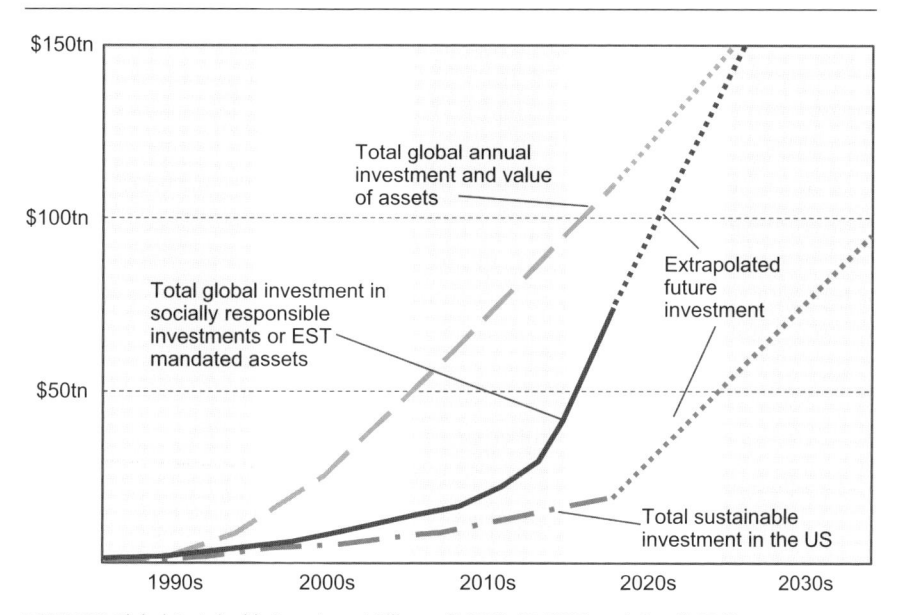

SOURCES Global Sustainable Investment Alliance (2020); US SIF Foundation (2020)

The proportion of investors seeking to make a positive impact with their money select SRIs on the basis that a company's activities and sources of revenue align with their individual values beyond financial return. Therefore, investors will select different SRIs according to what they hold important. Those demanding decarbonization may invest in renewable energy providers while others who care about the advancement of women may seek women-run companies. For those who choose SRIs, 67 per cent value social and environmental factors as more important than financial returns, with only 17 per cent of investors choosing financial returns as the top priority.

More than half of those investing in SRIs claim to have more than 20 per cent in SRIs, and human rights is the most important value for investors, closely followed by environmental impacts. Interestingly, the baby boomer generation tends to care most about human rights while millennials focus on environmental impacts (BusinessWire, 2018).

Why baby boomers and Generation X love SRIs

The exponential growth in SRIs is likely to continue, partly due to their resilience and proven financial return, but increasingly because of shareholder pressure from the next generations of investors. The demand for responsible investment exists across generations. Yet the majority of investment today comes from the baby boomer generation and Generation X. Millennials and Generation Z may not yet have the money to invest in their values, so instead are acting as cultural catalysts to urge large banks and institutional investors to engage more (Visram, 2021), and when they do have the money they will further fuel the growth.

SRIs are promoted and compete with each other on the basis of the ESG standing within the SRI portfolio. Companies therefore pursue a good ESG rating as a basis to attract and retain investment. A company's ESG standing is typically represented as a rating against one of the many unique, investor-specific, frameworks or requirements for ESG which include:

- The Global Reporting Initiative (GRI)
- The Climate Reporting and Performance (CRP)
- UN Principles for Responsible Investment (PRI)
- World Economic Forum Stakeholder Capitalism Metrics (WEF)
- The Sustainability Accounting Standards Board (SASB)
- The Climate Disclosure Standards Board (CDSB)

There are many others and I will return to frameworks for sustainability in the next chapter. Crucially, however, much of the world of ESG is based upon disclosure and reporting to specific standards. As we will see later, this approach has limitations and scope for 'chasing the ratings' rather than necessarily addressing difficult issues in supply chains.

ESG-based funds are now big business for any asset management company with, on average, two new ESG funds being launched every day. However, with this comes a fair degree of 'greenwashing' where the fund is packaged to appear green but is home to funds that would disappoint many investors should they know how to look closer. *The Economist* found that across the 20 biggest ESG funds, on average each of them holds investments in 17 fossil fuel producers. Some invested in coal mining, gambling, alcohol and tobacco (The Economist, 2022). When it comes to shareholder behaviour, appearing to be green can be more lucrative than actually doing it. Whether this is by choice or ignorance, we can conclude it is still early days for SRIs yet the trajectory is clear and steep and growth in sustainable investment will continue to grow. We can expect more regulation in these areas to prevent greenwashing, which only seeks to strengthen this component of the business case for sustainability.

Listening to the shareholders in a public company

In a public company we, as citizens, are the shareholders. However, we don't choose whether or not to invest in a public company but rather expect government-owned companies to be acting in our interests. Public opinion drives legislation, which in turn drives change. The drivers here therefore work slightly differently, and instead come from legislation – specific public sector legislation. In recent decades there has been a steady growth in new measures across public sector organizations in the developed world to consider and implement arrangements that drive social value in public sector procurement. As we have already seen, this includes legislation such as supplier diversity in the US, protection of First Nations people in Canada, and the Social Value Act in the UK to name but a few.

A basis for growth and advantage

As we move up the business case for sustainability the emphasis changes from 'need to do' to more 'want to do.' Until now the basis for investing in sustainability and the benefits we can secure have been around compliance and preservation. Now benefits and the basis for sustainability shift to everything that is possible if we choose to create social and environmental value. This begins with sustainability as a means to drive growth and advantage. Traditionally, such benefits have not been associated with sustainability, which historically was considered a cost drain rather than something that brings new value. Yet a shift in mindset allows us to consider the vast potential sustainability can bring to an organization.

Figure 5.4 The benefits from sustainability

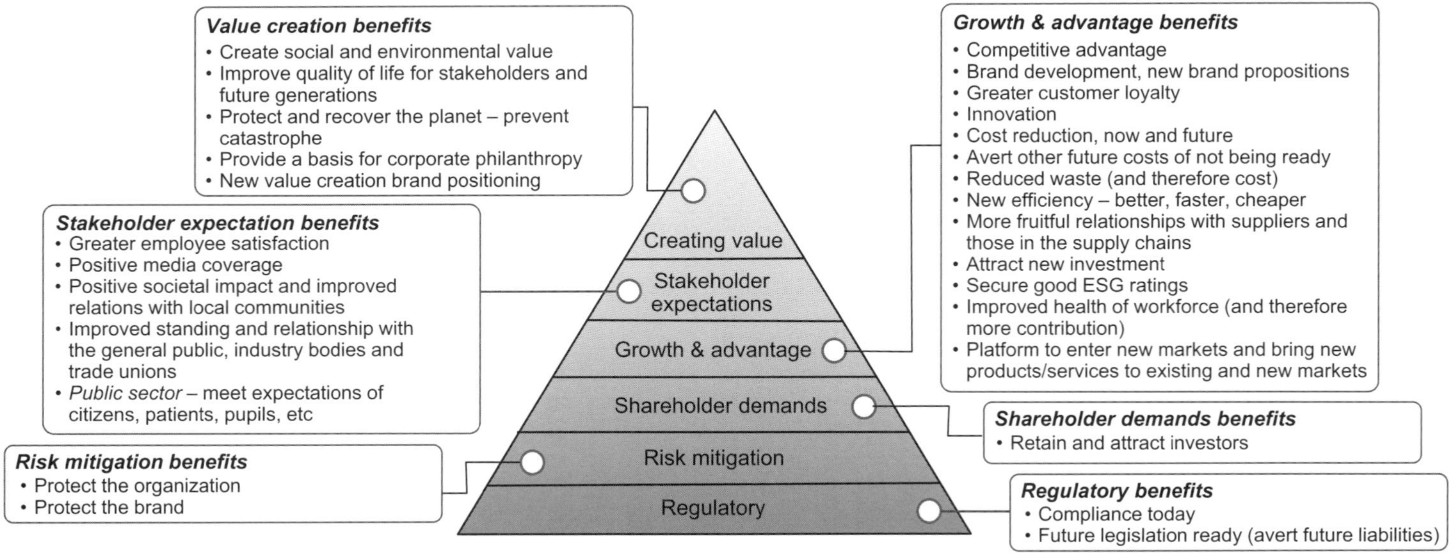

Value creation benefits
• Create social and environmental value
• Improve quality of life for stakeholders and future generations
• Protect and recover the planet – prevent catastrophe
• Provide a basis for corporate philanthropy
• New value creation brand positioning
Stakeholder expectation benefits
• Greater employee satisfaction
• Positive media coverage
• Positive societal impact and improved relations with local communities
• Improved standing and relationship with the general public, industry bodies and trade unions
• Public sector – meet expectations of citizens, patients, pupils, etc
Risk mitigation benefits
• Protect the organization
• Protect the brand
Creating value
Stakeholder expectations
Growth & advantage
Shareholder demands
Risk mitigation
Regulatory
Growth & advantage benefits
• Competitive advantage
• Brand development, new brand propositions
• Greater customer loyalty
• Innovation
• Cost reduction, now and future
• Avert other future costs of not being ready
• Reduced waste (and therefore cost)
• New efficiency – better, faster, cheaper
• More fruitful relationships with suppliers and those in the supply chains
• Attract new investment
• Secure good ESG ratings
• Improved health of workforce (and therefore more contribution)
• Platform to enter new markets and bring new products/services to existing and new markets
Shareholder demands benefits
• Retain and attract investors
Regulatory benefits
• Compliance today
• Future legislation ready (avert future liabilities)

A means to grow sales and build brand value

Sustainability has become a key selling point and even a differentiator or the unique selling proposition (USP) for what some firms now offer. The battle is on to secure the customer who this resonates with. Companies now go to great lengths to include some sort of reference to sustainability when they promote what they do. Cleaning products that once focused on how soft our hands would be if we chose that brand now show us a pristine garden on a sunny day. Car adverts that once showed safety features or driving performance now show the bumblebees and birds that the car is helping. The message is clear. Buy something that is sustainable, and you are doing your bit to help save the planet and the people on it. This selling proposition now drives big business.

At the turn of the century while about a third of consumers, when surveyed, said they would choose a sustainable brand over a non-sustainable brand, in practice only about 3 per cent actually followed through on this in their shopping baskets. Today, more than a third of shoppers are selecting and buying a product or service based upon stated ethical or environmental practices and values, even when this requires them to pay more for it. Similarly, just under a third (and perhaps not the same third) made conscious buying decisions not to purchase certain brands or products due to ethical or sustainability concerns (Statista, 2022). This is doubled in the fashion sector, and accelerated heavily during Covid, with nearly 60 per cent of consumers stating they had changed their behaviour to buy fashion based upon some sort of sustainability principle (Granskog et al, 2020). Once companies could fool the consumer by simply adding some sort of green credential; today consumers are savvier and many now scrutinize the claims being made with a rise in consumers checking how brands stack up in terms of sustainability via one of a growing number of brand sustainability check apps and websites.

Offering sustainable products and services creates the opportunity for companies to create new products and align with the now significant customer base that are ready to buy these. It also provides opportunity to enter new markets, especially the growing number of market places made up of companies with a 'sustainable only' positioning. Sustainability builds market share and creates new brand value and competitive advantage over others not quite there yet. What's more, sustainability now builds customer loyalty.

Advantage from sustainability is not limited to retail or B2C market places. In public companies the competitive advantage from growth can be translated to the effectiveness of delivery of public services. Increasingly in the B2B world, sustainability, or at least some aspects of it, now forms a key component and criteria for award within tendering activity. Once this was a cursory tick against some sort of compliance to supplier diversity or modern anti-slavery. Now an increasing number of large organizations are making sustainability a key basis for selection and award with verification and even audit.

Fostering innovation

As we will see later in this book sustainability can require a complete redesign of what the organization does as well as its supply base and what happens in the supply chains. Redesign can involve finding new materials, new processes, new ways to do things and new ways to move things around. It brings into question old principles of globalization in favour of more localization. It means we need new approaches to energy and water use and all of this is not only within the confines of our organization but is required through the entire supply chain and indeed the end-to-end value chain. Innovation drives productivity in both commercial and not-for-profit areas and all of this offers huge new opportunities and is set to power an entire new global economy in coming years. We are talking some big changes here, the scale of which most will not have seen. This change is not a case of flicking a switch but demands deep and sustained innovation, and as many of the challenges outlined in Chapters 1 and 2 begin to take hold it is innovation that will provide the hope to manage out of the crisis. This drives the need for better relationships and more collaboration with those suppliers that can help as well as the need to have intimate knowledge and full control over everything that happens in a supply chain. With this comes a raft of benefits including efficiency, reduced waste, optimized cost, reduced risk and crucially achievement of sustainability goals and so on. In fact, I've just summarized sustainable procurement in one paragraph so we could end the book here, but there is much more we can explore to help us make this a reality.

What is expected of us

The fifth component of the business case for sustainability is doing what is expected of us by all our stakeholders. Traditional business approaches seek to create value for shareholders, often at the expense of stakeholders. In contrast, sustainable businesses seek to create value for all stakeholders including shareholders. Here action is a choice not an obligation, so we are firmly into the territory of companies deliberately seeking to respond positively to what their stakeholders expect and pursue sustainability to create social and environmental value. We are part of a growing global movement here that is driving a fundamental shift in our economic system. I will return to this at the end of this book, but for now we will focus on the specific drivers behind how expectation are shifting.

Earlier in this chapter I listed all the different stakeholders of an organization and this is our starting point because our each of our stakeholders holds expectations to different degrees regarding the way our company operates. Whelan and Fink (2016) suggest that the strategic potential of sustainability comes from the need to continually talk with and learn from key stakeholders and that it is through this ongoing dialogue and interaction with stakeholders that a company with a sustainability agenda is better placed to anticipate and react to economic, social, environmental and other changes as they arise. Therefore, one of the first activities for an organization serious about sustainability is to determine its direction of travel and the goals it will pursue. Integral to this is the identification of the firm's stakeholders and stakeholder groups and taking the time to understand their expectations as well as establishing an ongoing dialogue with them. While the specific expectations of each and all of our stakeholders will be unique to the organization, and need to be determined, there are some general trends we can consider.

In her book *No One is Too Small to Make a Difference*, Greta Thunberg talks of what she will do on her 75th birthday in the year 2078. She contemplates that if she has children, then maybe they will spend that day with her and suggests they might ask about the older generations and those who ran things and perhaps they might ask why they didn't do anything while there still was time to act (Thunberg, 2019). She has a point. Whatever you may think about Greta Thunberg, what is notable here is how Greta became the voice of a large swathe of the people, and especially of her generation. It seems that Greta went from that 15-year-old girl sitting outside the Swedish Parliament in Stockholm with the now iconic '*Skolstrejk för Klimatet*' placard to figurehead for a global movement demanding that governments and those who make decisions take action to avert a climate catastrophe. Greta voiced the expectations of the people, the people we now need to regard as stakeholders.

Consumer expectations

As consumers we are loyal to the brands that we believe in. This is typically more than preference or based on how something performs, but we come to form a connection with a brand and view it as 'good' otherwise we wouldn't be buying it. It therefore comes as a shock when a brand we have come to trust gets exposed for some sort of bad practice. It can feel like betrayal. Perhaps as consumers we have been naive to trust that the companies we buy from are good. This has changed and consumers are now much more aware of what could be hidden behind what they buy. Consumer sentiment reflects what people and the public at large now expect with clear trends around the world and increasing expectations on companies. Today's consumers expect more transparency, honesty and a tangible global impact from companies and crucially now have a good choice of providers here (Whelan and Fink, 2016). Furthermore, stakeholder expectations are reflected by the abundance of news stories in recent years and the rise in investigative journalism specifically targeting corporate action to find stories of human rights abuse or environmental impact. Journalists exist because they target stories that are in the public interest. What they target serves as a barometer for the expectations of society as a whole.

Employee expectations

The expectations of our employees don't change because they work for our company but rather employees are part of the general public and hold the same expectations as the public at large. Post pandemic we witnessed what came to be termed as 'the great resignation' where those who had re-evaluated what was important in their lives during the Covid-19 pandemic then took decisive action to rebalance their work/home life, with many resigning to do this creating a shortage of key talent. Ensuring employee satisfaction for key individuals suddenly became key to retaining talent. Increasingly, a firm's approach to sustainability has a bearing on employee satisfaction overall. Working for a progressive company in sustainability terms instils pride and loyalty and can even be a basis for talented individuals to select or deselect an employer. Tension arises when advocates for sustainability end up working for a company that is contributing towards, rather than helping fix, the global issues we all face. Such tensions end up needing to be resolved, which usually means leaving and going to work somewhere else. Someone close to me worked for a large privately owned company that trades on cost leadership. The founder/owner's only objective, which he is honest about publicly, is to maximize his profit and rejects anything else he doesn't need to do in pursuit of this. As such, the individual loved the job but hated the company and everything it stands for, so could only view the job as transitional until the right opportunity came up elsewhere. The company has a very high churn rate for employees.

Expectation of communities

One final point here is the expectations of the communities that companies exist within or impact. As we have seen, there are many examples where the big bad company has blighted a community in the pursuit of its own profit. There are also many examples of where a company has made it part of its mission to support its workers and have a positive impact on the community in which it operates. While the latter may be the exception, it is reasonable to assume any company should be a good neighbour to those around it. In the same way that in our domestic neighbourhoods we expect to do our bit and hold an expectation that others will do so as well, to keep the neighbourhood clean, tidy and safe with consideration and respect for each other. A similar expectation for consideration and respect exists within the communities that companies exist in or travel through.

Understanding and responding to all our stakeholders' expectations for sustainability is a choice based upon how we might want to drive new social and environmental value but it is also one that further enhances benefits from the previous tiers of our business case, including reducing risk, increasing shareholder value and building competitive advantage and growth.

Creating social and environmental value

The ultimate basis for pursuing sustainability, and the top of our business case pyramid is the altruistic creation of social or environmental value above profit. Here, companies make a clear choice rather than respond to any sort of obligation or compelling force. This was what used to be referred to as corporate philanthropy, however, I'm cautious about using this term here as corporate philanthropy may not necessarily be centred around the true altruistic creation of social and environmental value above profit but rather motivated by profit, directly or indirectly. There will be more on that shortly.

It is hard to imagine the idea that a commercial business could function with the primary aim of delivering social and/or environmental value, yet this is exactly how public sector and not-for-profit organizations operate so here, at the top of our business case hierarchy, is where we find the main business case for the public sector.

All organizations need to be financially viable in the sense that they need enough cash to operate effectively ongoing, whether provided or generated as revenue, meet their aims, objectives and reason for being, and ideally end up with something left over. The only difference is that in the commercial sector the something left over is called profit and benefits the owners and shareholders, and in the public and not-for-profit area this is called the surplus for reinvestment in what the organization is there to do. How we view this is all about mindset around the fundamental purpose of an organization – does the company exist to create profit or value, or both? Milton Friedman might turn in his grave at the very suggestion of a value-driven business, arguing that diverting funds to a good cause prevents individual shareholders from deciding how they should use their profit. Friedman argued that if charitable contributions are to be made, they should be made by individual shareholders or, by extension, individual employees and not by the corporation (Friedman, 1962). Yet, as we have already seen, while shareholder expectations have shifted since then, shareholder choice still drives investment. Therefore, and in a commercial sector company, when it comes to an overarching business strategy of social and environmental value over profit this is only possible if driven by the owners or collectively by all the shareholders. Consequently, businesses owned by a small number of like-minded individuals rather than tens of thousands of shareholders are much more likely to operate at this top tier of the business case. This might help Milton rest more easy, so too the fact that today things are different and 'value-first' strategies no longer mean the company will not be profitable, in fact quite the contrary.

I've worked with many public sector organizations and some not-for-profit companies over the years and for some, but not all, it can be like stepping into an impoverished dark age. One publicly owned company I worked for was so cash strapped it couldn't afford to replace the defective light fittings in the basement meeting room, and I ran an entire workshop in semi darkness with people huddled around the projector (that I had to bring) for light. It reflected how the entire organization was run. It doesn't follow, however, that value over profit means badly run. Indeed, it is therefore entirely possible to create a company and even a brand that exists for the greater good, where those involved are paid well and the company operates with everything you would expect in any other company, but that the value goes to people and planet not to shareholders.

CASE STUDY The Patagonia principle

Patagonia states on its website 'We're in business to save our planet' (Patagonia, 2022). Alongside the online store for outdoor clothing and adventure wear are links to find out more about Patagonia activism and some of the stories of how, since 1985, the $161 million dollars given in Patagonia grants have helped fund grassroots environmental projects to defend air, land and water globally – all funded by what the company calls its 1 per cent self-imposed Earth tax (Patagonia 2021). It has established a global community to spread knowledge and information. Its core values are to 'build the best product, cause no unnecessary harm, use business to protect nature and not be bound by convention' (Patagonia, 2022).

Patagonia has driven sustainability throughout its customer proposition deliberately setting out to not create limited-time fashion clothing but long-lasting products. There is even a repair and reuse programme. It has scrutinized every corner of its operation and the make-up of its products – minimum use of only sustainable virgin fabrics, using recycled fabrics in 94 per cent of its line, use of organic cotton and regenerative farming, and big leaps in eliminating chemical use, minimizing water consumption and CO_2 emissions in its production. It looks after those in its supply chains and is a founding member of the Fair Labor Association (FLA) with 85 per cent of Patagonia's products Fair Trade Certified Sewn. As of 2020, 39 per cent of Patagonia's clothing factories paid workers a living wage. It is aiming for 100 per cent as well as working towards circularity in the garment industry (Langridge, 2022). The consumer sustainable clothing rating website Good On You rated Patagonia as 'good' and praised its extensive work to drive environmental impacts, labour conditions and animal welfare throughout its supply chains (Wolfe, 2022).

Patagonia's CEO, Ryan Gellert, avoids using labels such as sustainability and responsible to describe the company, stating instead that it still has some way to go. Yet you only have to read the stories it publishes on its website, or watch its YouTube channel, or read some of the buzz on social media (not paid for by Patagonia as it stopped all Facebook and Instagram ads as part of its Stop Hate for Profit campaign in June 2020) to realize they are possibly one of the most responsible brands on the planet (Langridge, 2022). Alongside its annual accounts, it publishes an impact report – it is compelling reading with impressive statistics of the social and environmental improvements it has enabled.

Patagonia is a highly profitable $1 billion annual sales company that keeps going from strength to strength. It is a global success story that has built itself upon sustainability, placing determined action and a degree of altruism to make a positive impact on our planet first and foremost, and profit as a natural consequence rather than the driving aim. It seems to have made it work quite well and shows us that a 'be sustainable and profit will come' business model can overturn traditional thinking.

The creation of social and environmental value with no need for financial return sounds like another term for corporate philanthropy yet, and in order to understand the business case for sustainability, it is important to consider the firm's motivation as philanthropy takes different forms. In fact, there are three ways companies place value over profit. All are good but only one is truly altruistic and only one belongs at the top of the business case. They are:

- Corporate philanthropy as a means to improve its competitive context so it can be more effective.
- Corporate philanthropy practised strategically as a means to create profit.
- Truly altruistic creation of social and environmental value as the primary objective over profit. There is a likelihood profit may also be diverted into value.

Corporate philanthropy is not a new concept; it has been around for centuries, from the Quakers in the 17th century, Andrew Carnegie in the 19th century who directed wealth to improve access to facilities for the community, to the emergence of major corporate foundations in the 1940s and 50s by Ford, AT&T, Philip Morris and so on. Despite the Covid-19 pandemic, corporate philanthropy is on the increase with an increase in schemes such as employee contribution matching or donating to support a range of local or general causes, universities and charities. In general, corporate philanthropy tends to be diffuse and is often unfocused. However, increasingly there are examples of companies considering it more strategically.

The virtuous circle of philanthropy

Porter and Kramer (2002) suggest that targeted philanthropic activities and competitive advantage can become a virtuous circle. Philanthropy can influence the firm's competitive context – the quality of the business environment in the location or locations where they operate – and in doing so improve a firm's long-term prospects. When philanthropy is targeted at where the firm operates it brings social and environmental value and profit into alignment thus contradicting Friedman's assertion. For example, a firm investing in education in the local community – in so doing ensures it has the capable workforce it needs in the future, by investing in local infrastructure and telecommunications it can be more efficient and improve quality of life for its workers and so on. This enables the company to improve its competitiveness while fulfilling the needs of some of its stakeholders. Here philanthropy is used to drive growth and advantage (i.e. profit from value) by taking a long-term view and therefore is part of this tier, not the top tier of the business case.

Similarly, a further dimension to corporate philanthropy is the growing trend in recent decades for corporate giving to be used as a form of public relationship or advertising to promote a company's image or brand through cause-related marketing or other high-profile sponsorship (Porter and Kramer, 2002). In practice this might manifest itself as a corporation giving, say, $100 million as a charitable contribution and then spending $200 million on an advertising campaign to publicize it. This is also part of '*growth and advantage*' and not the top tier of the business case.

True altruistic creation of social and environmental value is distinct from the above and drives different behaviours through the business. Once the need to secure financial return over and above running the firm is removed, everything changes and the purpose of the organization becomes twofold – the organization equips itself to maintain an effective commercial operation whilst simultaneously determining where to direct its resources to create value. Managing the right balance and ensuring the creation of the right amount of value becomes as much the business as what the business does, it is not simply a by-product. Get it right and value over profit can be highly profitable and 'highly profitable' takes on a new dimension because it represents a greater fund to create social and environmental value rather than shareholder wealth alone. This doesn't mean the owners live an impoverished life; quite the contrary, as in a successful operation as it is possible to create sufficient profit and good social and environmental value alongside. It can be hard to identify the truly altruistic companies as all organizations make profit – the key way to tell is what companies do with their profit.

As we have seen there are two distinct corporate motivations here: first, profit as a happy consequence to the primary objective of social and environmental value creation, and second, profit as the primary objective but using the creation of social and environmental value as a means to build green brand credentials and increase market share. This second motivation is entirely acceptable; however, it should be noted that in terms of our business case this sits better under the 'growth and advantage' tier with true altruistic value creation the pursuit at the top tier.

Selling the business case

The business case for sustainability provides organizations with the basis to set corporate aims and objectives for sustainability overall. With the direction of travel determined, the next question is likely to be 'how much will it cost?' No matter how altruistic a firm wants to be, cost justification is inescapable. There is a reason why the predominant system of corporate governance has evolved to be based upon financial performance and that is simply about preservation of the firm and the fabric of the economic system it exists within (more on that later). Therefore, balancing the pursuit of sustainability with financial viability and performance is essential. Without it sustainability doesn't make it to base camp.

Do I need a 'green budget'?

The mindset of sustainability as an added cost alone is limiting. Equally so is the stance of 'only if it doesn't increase cost'. Sustainability undoubtedly requires investment, and it may well mean creating some sort of fund or 'green budget' as it has come to be known in certain organizations. In some of the organizations I have worked for this is the point where the CFO wobbles and reaches for the brake lever. Rightly so because it would be folly to suddenly burden the business with costs that might plunge it into a state of no longer being competitive or at worst failing. That is why the business case for sustainability is so key to balancing investment with returns in all their forms at all tiers, some of which may not be realized immediately or in monetary terms depending upon the direction of the firm.

Yet, no matter how you look at it, investment will be required if an organization is serious about pursuing sustainability and so it will need to plan and budget for it in terms of both direct and indirect costs. For example, a retailer seeking to ensure its entire range meets its declared sustainability standards may have no choice but to accept, initially at least, an increased unit cost to source the right products from the right suppliers and regions. It may also need to start getting to know its supply chains and even getting close to the original producers as well as supporting their development. An initial uplift in cost is almost inevitable, but by doing so it enables the retailer to meet its stated policies, satisfy shareholder and stakeholder expectations, and hopefully increase market share. It may also be a basis to increase margin with some higher price points in some areas. The new relationships it creates with its providers might also, in time, create the platform for a new type of cost reduction.

Action towards sustainability might increase cost short term, yet it doesn't follow that sustainability needs to cost more overall. Indeed, the scene is set for procurement and supply chain functions to work with, perhaps new, producers, processors, materials, providers to find new ways and build the next generation of supply base where cost is not the only/primary driver. Furthermore, as we know from applying category management and SRM, this sort of focus on an area of supply is a very powerful way to optimize and reduce costs.

In essence we must move to thinking about sustainable procurement in terms of a convergence of social and environmental value alongside commercial excellence. We will return to this in the next chapter. This is how the business case for sustainable procurement is brought to life in real terms and while we should not consider it a cost burden, organizations do need to budget for how they will invest in driving sustainability. This might include providing for:

Direct costs

- Potential increased costs of goods and services that meet sustainability requirements
- Cost of audit and assessment or visiting and working with producers, providers, etc
- Cost of implementing change
- Cost of increased reporting and monitoring

Indirect costs

- Setting up a sustainability function
- Evaluating new innovation and R&D
- New technology to enable sustainability, e.g. supply chain traceability and transparency
- Conversion of assets, processes, e.g. moving to EVs
- Costs of certifications or being reported on by third parties

Selling the business case for sustainable projects

The final consideration for the business case is how we communicate and sell it, and the means by which we justify and secure the budget for individual sustainable initiatives, full-scale projects or a complete organizational change. Figure 5.5 gives the range of benefit types and how the approach to secure support and investment shifts.

Investment based upon a direct financial return in a set period of time is straightforward. Similarly, it is often possible to quantify other non-financial benefits in financial terms where a direct correlation can be established, for example, reducing water consumption in a process by 7 per cent will save $200k per annum. However, it gets harder when non-financial benefits cannot easily be translated into financial returns or the direct correlation is less clear. It is here where organizations struggle the most to invest, especially when shackled to traditional forms of top-down financial management and governance.

'How do I sell the non-financial benefits?' is a question I have been asked regularly by companies practising category management or SRM with a good degree of maturity. It is something most companies struggle to do. Yet there are established precedents here. Investing in innovation, R&D, sales initiatives to find new markets and others like this are all investments where the correlation to a known financial return at the outset is, at best, indistinct. Yet organizations still do these things and it is often these things that make an organization great above others. Taking a considered leap into the

Figure 5.5 Selling the business case for sustainability initiatives

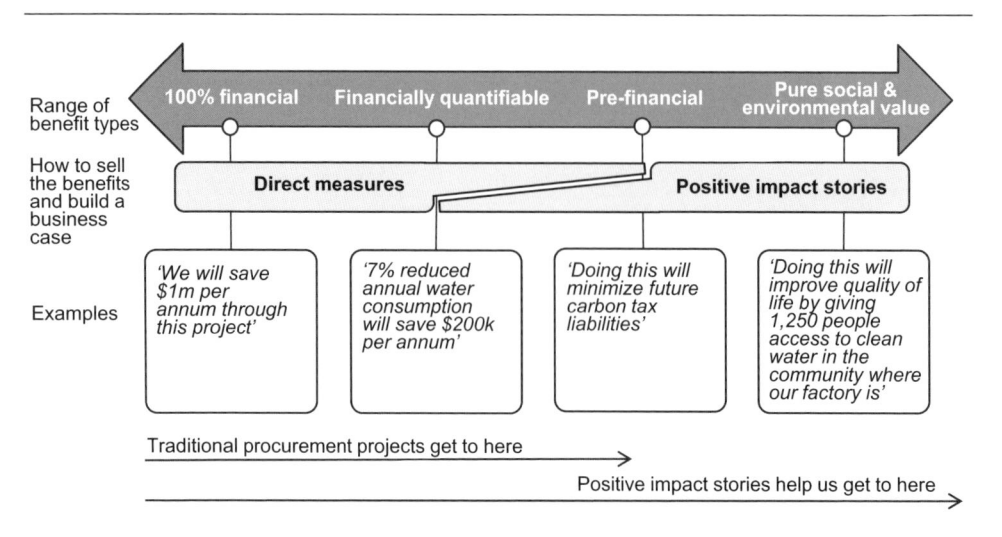

Range of benefit types	100% financial	Financially quantifiable	Pre-financial	Pure social & environmental value
How to sell the benefits and build a business case	Direct measures		Positive impact stories	
Examples	'We will save $1m per annum through this project'	'7% reduced annual water consumption will save $200k per annum'	'Doing this will minimize future carbon tax liabilities'	'Doing this will improve quality of life by giving 1,250 people access to clean water in the community where our factory is'

Traditional procurement projects get to here →

Positive impact stories help us get to here →

unknown and being prepared to try something new is a key characteristic of those that succeed over competitors. While such things might involve some sort of financial modelling, usually the primary basis to move forward happens because someone tells a compelling story of what is possible and others take a risk on it.

When it comes to sustainability and sustainable procurement the same principles apply to the non-financial benefits. These fall into two categories. First, those where there are no quantifiable benefits today, but by taking this course of action now it will avert future cost impacts. These are called *pre-financial* benefits and represent the often-quantifiable financial benefits yet to be realized by action now. Some of these can be predicted, some assumed. Examples of pre-financial benefits include:

- Averting future additional taxes, e.g. tax on carbon use, waste disposal, etc
- Averting future cost increases, e.g. where materials are getting scarce or in higher demand
- Securing availability of future resources
- Preventing fines for non-compliance

Second are the non-financial benefits that are difficult to quantify because they centre around the realization of environmental and social value.

In both cases the approach required to sell the benefits is around creating a positive impact story.

Positive impact stories

A positive impact story is the means by which the business case for a project or initiative that will deliver partially or entirely non-financial value, which cannot readily be correlated with quantifiable financial returns in the near term at least, can be defined and communicated. It works by effectively describing the proposed investment or course of action and then telling the story of the positive impacts the investment will bring. A positive impact story is a key means to secure support for sustainable procurement projects and initiatives. For it to be compelling it must:

- Resonate with and support the realization of the wider sustainability objectives of the organization.
- Describe the initiative, change, action, project as fully as possible with supporting outline costings and resource needs.

- Describe the full range of positive impacts that will be realized and quantify as many variables as possible, e.g. how many people will benefit, for how long, what will it mean day to day.
- Tell the story of how it will create environmental and/or social value and how it will change lives now and into the future.

We will return to positive impact stories in Chapter 14.

Chapter checkpoint

While some economic thinking from decades gone by might suggest the business of business is business and any consideration of responsibilities beyond this is folly, things have shifted and the business case for sustainability has never been stronger. Key points we explored in this chapter are:

1 *Sustainability is on the boardroom agenda* – with a multilevel, multidimensional business case for action according to that the company wants to be and sustainable procurement the key enabler.

2 *The business case for sustainable procurement* supports the overall business case for the organization and with 50–70 per cent of all sustainability initiatives involving the supply base procurement is critical to the organization realizing its goals.

3 *The growing legal imperative* – irrespective of whether or not a company wants to pursue sustainability, no company can ignore the increasing legislation that is driving sustainable procurement.

4 *Risk of corporate irresponsibility* – action towards sustainability in the supply base reduces risk to the organization.

5 *Shareholder expectations* – increasingly, those who own corporates expect and are demanding their firms become more sustainable with differing priorities according to the type of shareholder.

6 *A basis for growth and advantage* – sustainability, enabled by supply base possibilities, can be a rich source of opportunity.

7 *Stakeholder expectations* – typically across all the various internal and external stakeholders for a company there are firm expectations for the company to act sustainably.

8 *Creation of social and environmental value* – without the need for payback. The ultimate and somewhat altruistic dimension of the business case that can also be very profitable.

9 *Selling the business case* – sustainability in the supply base can increase cost, yet it can also unlock new revenues and so we need new approaches to sell the business case not based solely upon short-term financial payback.

In the next chapter we will explore the business case for sustainability and the basis to begin to determine goals for sustainable procurement.

Setting the direction for sustainability

06

> This chapter explores how we set the direction for sustainability in an organization and in particular sustainable procurement. Key frameworks for sustainability are explored and these are linked to the six impact areas. We cover stage 1 'Objectives' of the OMEIA® methodology to determine the strategy and goals for, and therefore the basis to implement, sustainable procurement within an organization.
>
> *Pathway questions addressed in this chapter*
>
> 5   How do we determine sustainability goals for the organization?
> 6   How do we determine goals for sustainable procurement?

Sustainability is now on the boardroom agenda and no organization can ignore the imperative to respond in some way. Forward-thinking corporations recognize the strategic importance of sustainability no matter where on the business case they are starting from. As such, we have seen the rise in new sustainability functions, some with C-level representation. The starting point for a firm that recognizes it needs to do something but is not quite sure where to start is to appoint someone to figure it out and recruit a team to help do so. Typically, new corporate sustainability functions are home to a new breed of individual, usually recruited externally and perhaps with deep knowledge of sustainability, perhaps scientists in a relevant field, perhaps recruiting graduates with one of the many new degrees in sustainability or related areas, or perhaps individuals who know how to drive change and market it hard. So important, new and unproven are the new sustainability functions that they typically have the ear and attention of the CEO with close reporting lines. In recent years I've worked with several new teams, typically brilliant individuals desperate to make a difference. There is, however, one thing in common and that is sustainability functions don't typically have strategic procurement skills or know-how to drive supply-side change, so it is not long before they knock on the procurement door to start working together to do this stuff in the supply base. This is a key point because driving sustainability in the supply base requires the marriage of leading expertise in sustainability with procurement and supply chain expertise. If the organization has established a sustainability function, then a true symbiotic relationship between functions is essential. Otherwise, the only way sustainable procurement can be possible is if the team can add new sustainability capability.

Defining the vision for sustainability

Sustainability in any organization begins by defining the vision for what the organization is setting out to achieve and by when. From this, all efforts for sustainability including sustainable procurement must flow. As we have seen, it is virtually impossible for a procurement or supply chain function to progress very far in terms of supply-side sustainability if it sets its own vision independent from the rest of the organization. Imagine the scenario where a procurement function is organizing sourcing based around a long-term sustainability strategy and a cost uplift to achieve this but within an organization that is built around the owner's 'lowest cost, bare minimum for compliance' edict. Clearly incompatible.

Sustainable procurement therefore begins with the organization's vision and direction for sustainability. If this is clear and well articulated you could skip to the next section where we define the specific goals for procurement and supply chain. However, in most organizations the overall vision is rarely clear, or it is still forming. Key here also is the fact that a meaningful vision needs procurement and supply chain input to consider how what happens and could happen in the supply base must shape the direction. Procurement and supply chain are therefore key collaborators here. Through this section and the next we will explore the steps for an organization to define its vision for sustainability and the role procurement and supply chain functions play in collaborating to accomplish this. This is represented in section 1 of the OMEIA® process as given in Figure 6.1, which gives the six steps to define vision. I will explore each in turn.

Figure 6.1 Setting the direction for sustainability

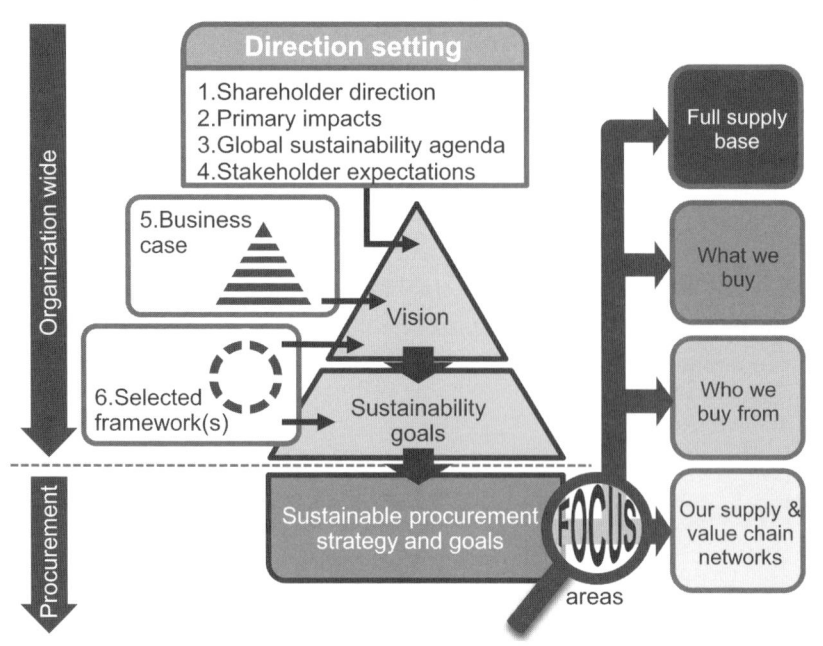

What do the shareholders want?

The first step to defining the organizational vision for sustainability is what the owners of the firm want or the direction they set.

Remember that for a public sector organization, the shareholders are the citizens, patients, pupils, etc, with the role of government to set the direction for sustainability within an organization and legislate accordingly. Therefore, in a public sector company 'shareholder direction' is straightforward, it is a case of complying with the relevant legislation. For commercial organizations this can be less straightforward. As we saw in the last chapter, a firm owned by a small number of individuals, say a family-owned business, may have a clear vision and be able to articulate it to provide the fundamental driving vision for the firm. I worked with one large organization that remained in family ownership. The family were no longer part of the day-to-day running of the organization, however, once a year the family would issue a simple, concise unformatted and plain document running only to a few pages of type that would set out the direction the owners wanted the business to take. It was then down to the executive team to interpret and realize it. In recent years the owners' growing thoughts and concerns regarding sustainability manifested itself in a shift in focus away from profit and cost management to a new sustainability agenda. The business pivoted accordingly. In such a scenario the direction is clear. However, as we also saw in the last chapter, where ownership is highly dispersed, perhaps across tens of thousands of shareholders this is not so straightforward and requires intervention to understand what the shareholders want. Furthermore, in these situations shareholders typically don't know what they want and need to be shown the possibilities and why it makes good sense in the hope they will invest or continue to invest. Shareholder consultation is therefore a key step in defining the direction for sustainability and there are two approaches here that can help to accomplish this.

1 **Shareholder round tables** – meetings with small group of key shareholders (majority owners, owners of large numbers of shares, those with influence, etc). The aim is to establish what is important to shareholders, what they value and would support in terms of future direction. Round tables need careful facilitation as there can be a world of difference between an aspiration that feels good voiced in a session versus the reality. Therefore, while round tables need to solicit direct feedback regarding what they believe the future direction should be, they should also triangulate this by offering a range of scenarios, rating different scenarios according to importance and questions that pressure-test ideas such as 'do you agree we need to invest X to realize Y?' etc.

2 **Shareholder consultation** – relevant where there are many shareholders and typically accomplished via some form of survey. Key here is ensuring the communication messaging that supports the survey demonstrates the participative approach. Questionnaire structuring is critical, with a mix of quantitative and qualitative questions, ranking by importance, pressure-test questions, etc. As such, good questionnaires require professional design and deployment, ideally using an external provider with a proven track record.

Determining the primary impacts

The direction for sustainability with an organization needs to be relevant and respond to what the firm does. It is impossible to fix everything, so focus is essential. Determining the right focus is a critical early step to establishing a meaningful sustainability programme and requires the firm to focus on how it will begin to tackle the biggest impact areas as a result of what the firm does, both directly and indirectly, within the organization, externally across all stakeholders including the end-to-end SVCN and the world at large. These are called the primary impacts of the firm.

A sustainability programme cannot be meaningful unless it is based around the primary impacts. For example, consider a mining company operating in developing countries that takes resources from the ground, and where the prosperity and welfare of the local communities are highly dependent upon the company. If this company set out a sustainability vision based upon ensuring all staff restaurants would only serve sustainable line-caught fish and fair-trade products, then it is missing the point. Instead a sustainability programme can be relevant only if it starts to directly tackle the primary impacts such as use of resources, waste processing, support to the community and so on. Yet, it is important also to consider the limit of what can be achieved and still enable a business to exist and have a future. Mining companies still need to extract resources, oil and gas companies still need to supply fossil fuels, and airlines still need to burn them if they want to continue to be an airline. That is for now at least, because as sustainability gets driven much harder from all camps, future legislation and demand patterns will drive change. Oil and gas companies are already driving massive research programmes to figure out how they can develop new technologies that will keep them in the game. Airplane manufacturers together with the airlines are working on the next generation of electric propulsion systems and battery systems capable of powering a passenger aircraft over distance. None of this eliminates the primary climate change impact, although it may in time, but it means the companies understand their impacts, are measuring them, have publicly committed to doing something about it and have set out on programmes to address these impacts. While electric airlines are quite some way away, what airlines are doing today is replacing old aircraft with more modern fuel-efficient aircraft, switching to sustainable jet fuel, optimizing fuel use, reducing engine running time on the ground, minimizing holding pattern times and so on. It could be argued that the motivation is self-preservation or token gestures to be 'seen to be green'. Yet it is much more than that. All of these are steps towards sustainability and begin to reduce CO_2 impact, yet also help airlines be ready for new legislation and reduce their operating costs – therefore acting at multiple levels of the sustainability business case we explored in the last chapter. What is also clear in the boardroom and to the shareholders of the major airline corporates around the world is the days of air travel that freely burns fossil fuel are numbered and long-term survival depends upon future innovation. Therefore, when a company is publicly transparent about its primary impact areas and outlines its response and a timeline of action, this is open to scrutiny by all, including the firm's stakeholders, and demonstrates long-term strategic thinking. Increasingly, as we have seen, this makes a difference.

Figure 6.2 provides a simple primary impact assessment tool based upon the six impact areas (a template is also provided in the Appendix). It is applied by considering what the organization does and the impacts it has in each area. The initial assessment should be a high-level determination, ideally worked in a small team of those who know what the business does and are familiar with its operations. It is possible a company does not fully understand its primary impacts or needs to set about measuring them to understand them. For example, few companies could state how much CO_2 they are responsible for, either directly or indirectly, as, until recently, there has been no imperative to measure such things. Therefore, at this stage we are not quantifying the impacts, just determining a judgement of a relative level of severity. This provides the starting point to baseline, measure, fur-

Figure 6.2 Primary impact assessment

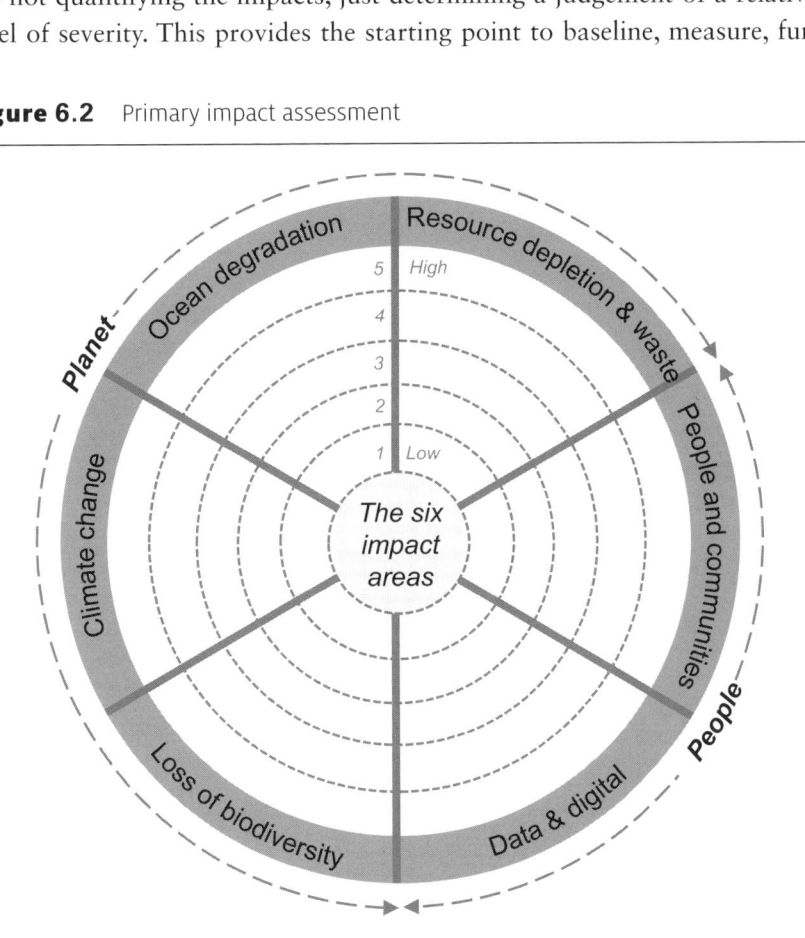

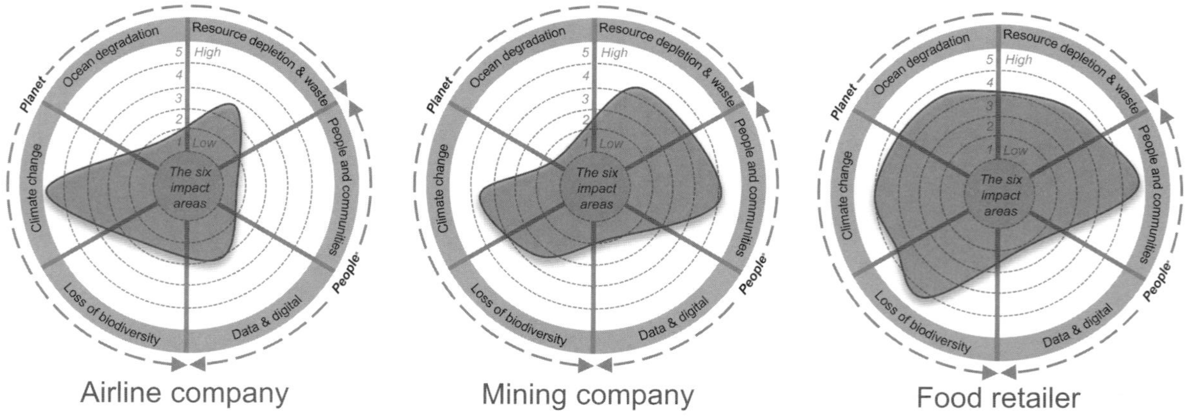

Figure 6.3 Examples of an initial primary impact assessment

ther assess and refine our early thoughts as we move through our sustainability approach. This is part of stages 2 and 3 of the OMEIA®.

The steps to determine primary impacts are as follows:

1 Best worked in a small team of those familiar with the organization and all its operations.
2 Consider the six impact areas and for each determine the severity of impact caused by the organization based upon what it does and everything that happens externally end-to-end across the entire SVCN.
3 Determine a relative level of impact severity between 1 and 5 for each impact area (5 being a significant impact).
4 Note the rationale of the determination.
5 Determine where baselining or further measurement or assessment is required to verify or quantify the impacts. Determine actions to do this.

Linking sustainable procurement to the global sustainability agenda

An organization's direction for sustainability must also resonate with the global sustainability agenda. This is all the insight and thinking supported by science-based facts and data, and general opinion by those who are informed that shapes the consensus throughout the world in terms of where we need to be taking action. This is not a single, defined thing but emerges through the frameworks for sustainability (especially the United Nations Sustainable Development Goals – we will explore that shortly), legislation targeting specific areas (that responds to public opinion) and what is said in the various papers, research pieces, books, programmes and contributions of people who have credibility or experience in this space. This is distinct from the expectations of our stakeholders (we will cover that separately next).

Understanding the global sustainability agenda is necessary to ensure the direction for our sustainability programme and to set both quantitative and qualitative objectives in response to our primary impacts, which are aligned with the facts-and-data-based consensus regarding the global priorities for action. It might also appear a good means to publicly demonstrate we are responding to what matters in the minds of our customers, consumers, users, citizens, patients, pupils, etc. However, there can be a disconnect between these two, and public opinion (and therefore what our stakeholders expect of us) may be based around the topic of the moment or what impact gets the most airtime. The big issues of the moment today, i.e. the ones that are driving the general public most to make changes to aspects of their lives, would most likely be climate change and single-use plastics. This is largely due to the fact that both of these topics have had significant exposure in recent years. The impact of single-use plastics is also one that we all see. Both these impacts are highly important in sustainability terms and, as we have seen, climate change is arguably the biggest threat we face, which therefore demands urgent attention. Yet, if we look at the facts-and-data-based consensus regarding where we need to act, then addressing loss of biodiversity and ocean degradation are also critically important because they present other serious threats to our existence and are also major factors that accelerate climate change. Neither of these gets the same airtime as climate change but arguably are equally important. From the facts-and-data-based perspective, single-use plastics is an issue but is quite some way down the list when compared with the other threats we face. Therefore, the global sustainability agenda is primarily about determining the facts-and-data based priorities. Separately we will consider the expectations of our stakeholders and balance both of these to shape our direction of travel for sustainability.

A key challenge here is it can be difficult to discern global targets for key impacts. For climate change the target is clear as first established in 2015 during COP21, where parties to the UN Framework Convention on Climate Change made the Paris Agreement, which included a commitment to limit global warming, which was further tightened at COP26 in Cornwall in 2021 with a commitment to work to keep global warming below 1.5°C. This goal was then translated into programmes of pledged action by participating nations including new global reporting commitments. From here organizations were able to begin to determine their response, with various different motivations, and a whole industry of measuring CO_2 emissions and 'net zero by 2030' initiatives was born. The phrase 'science-based targets' has come to be specifically associated with climate change action, indeed the Science Based Targets initiative (SBTi) is based around this (we will explore this shortly). However, it is important to remember that we need to consider all the impact areas in terms of their 'science-based' urgency or, to avoid terminology confusion, their 'facts-and-data based' urgency. Where there is no universally agreed target it is down to us to figure out some sort of quantifiable goal that adequately responds to the impacts we are responsible for relative to the global problem.

An organization cannot determine a meaningful direction or objectives for sustainability unless it has understood and considered the global facts-and-data-based agenda for sustainability. In practice this starts with the firm establishing expertise here, perhaps by recruiting suitably experienced individuals or the services of specialist consultants. Furthermore, it helps if those in the firm responsible for driving sustainability, and especially those in procurement and supply chain functions, have a good base knowledge here, typically established through a training programme and ongoing managed development.

The six impact areas provide a good starting point to determine what current targets exist. We do this, and work towards determining the global agenda for sustainability by:

- Recruiting expertise and training those involved
- Ongoing research into current scientific thinking (papers, published research and the wealth of online resources available)
- Talking to experts, engaging specialized consultants
- Tracking current and emerging legislation and governmental direction of travel
- Checking with industry bodies
- Press, media, business publications, etc

Determining stakeholder expectations

Determining stakeholder expectations is the fourth step to determine the direction for sustainability for the organization overall and also in terms of procurement and the supply chain. Stakeholder expectations are established by stakeholder mapping – the process of determining all the stakeholders and stakeholder groups and then determining their respective expectations, interests, how strongly they hold these interests and the degree of influence they could have. A stakeholder map is relevant at the organization level but key to this is the recognition that there are a number of key supply-side stakeholder groups and so it is essential that procurement and supply chain functions are part of the stakeholder mapping process. Figure 6.4 gives an example stakeholder expectations map and a template is provided in the Appendix. Note that the format of this is different to that we use for stakeholder mapping within an organization where we might classify stakeholders or groups according to their role (perhaps using a *RACI – Responsible, Accountable, Consult or Inform* classification model) and also according to the degree to which they might support or oppose an initiative.

These approaches are unsuitable here, instead here we use a more simplified approach to determine what a wide variety of both internal and external groups value or expect and therefore the nature of our engagement with them is primarily, in RACI terms, those we need to *consult* with. In addition, stakeholder engagement should also seek to *inform* as this can be highly beneficial. This is because participation is key to driving effective change and those who might need to embrace a change, for example to our product/service, how we operate, increased cost, etc, are more likely to do so if they feel they have participated in determining the change. The process of asking the opinion of stakeholders values them and creates this sense of participation, even in the largest of surveys. Therefore, stakeholder engagement should not be viewed only as a means of solicitation but a key communications vehicle to inform stakeholders of our intentions regarding sustainability, even if they are not fully formed. Finally, there are some aspects of stakeholder expectations where our role is purely about listening. We cannot necessarily engage all our stakeholders, in fact when we consider the public at large as a stakeholder we can only tune into the general mood, areas of dissatisfaction and frustration, beliefs and trends, and how people are acting towards sustainability. This is about research, evaluating published data and survey results, watching press and media, watching what competitors are doing, listening to what people talk about and picking out the aspects of sustainability that people or specific stakeholder groups care about.

Stakeholder expectation mapping for sustainability is therefore about how we *consult* with, *inform* and *listen* to each stakeholder or stakeholder group. There are different approaches here and Table 6.1 provides some of the approaches that can be used, with some guidance on application. Effective stakeholder management requires a single point of ownership and accountability in the company ongoing with support and input from procurement and supply chain functions. Build a stakeholder expectation map as follows (template provided in the Appendix):

1 Determine all the relevant internal and external individual stakeholders and stakeholder groups – the list of stakeholders already provided in Chapter 5 provides a good starting point here.

2 Determine key central messages to communicate as part of stakeholder engagement.

3 For each group, determine the means of engagement as appropriate (see Table 6.1), incorporate communication messages and conduct the stakeholder consultation for each group.

Figure 6.4 An example stakeholder expectation map to determine expectations

Stakeholder group	Means of engagement	Interest areas, what they value and expectations	Influence	Consult	Inform	Listen	How we will manage this group ongoing
1 Shareholder community	Annual meetings Forums	Responsible investment performance, good returns & compliance	High – share price	✓	✓	✓	Managed communications and engagement
2 Customers	Focus groups, voice of the customer	The product they buy is sustainable in all ways at no or marginal additional cost	High – direct revenue impact	✓	✓	✓	Marketing communications and brand positioning
3 Employees	Annual employee survey	To work for a responsible employer and know what it does is making a contribution	Med – attracting and retaining talent	✓	✓	✓	Internal communications
4 Suppliers	Supplier reviews, RFIs	To understand and align to our requirements and future direction of travel	High – ability to deliver on sustainability	✓	✓	✓	Code of conduct, reviews, direct engagement
5 Local community	Local meetings	That our operations don't adversely impact on those nearby	Low – noise and disruption			✓	Annual meetings with representatives
6 Wider global community	Website	We are a responsible business	Med – future brand value		✓		Marketing communications, brand positioning & PR

4 Establish their interests, what they value and any expectations they hold. Depending upon the means of stakeholder consultation used this may be quantitative results, for example where stakeholders are asked to rank a list in order of importance, or qualitative statements.

5 Determine their degree and nature of influence. Influence factors include all the things a company uses to measure its performance (revenue, share price, reputation, brand value, future viability, etc).

6 Determine if we need to consult with, inform or listen to each group and how we will manage them ongoing.

7 Deploy.

Table 6.1 Approaches to determine stakeholder expectations

Stakeholder engagement method	Suitable for	Key success factors
Round tables	• Shareholders • Key investors • Customer groups • Trade unions • Other small groups	The aim is to establish what is important to shareholders, what they value and would support in terms of future direction. Good facilitation can help. Watch out for the difference between an aspiration that feels good voiced in a session vs the reality. Questions to use: Use simple questions such as 'what do you feel about human rights, the environment, etc?', 'what do you want to know about what we are doing?' and 'what do you think must change?' Determine a range of scenarios and use ranking to determine the most important. Pressure-test those that emerge – use questions such as 'do you agree we need to invest X to realize Y', etc.

Table 6.1 *continued*

Stakeholder engagement method	Suitable for	Key success factors
Surveys	• Employees • Customers • Consumers/users • Larger shareholder groups	Shareholder consultation – relevant where there are many shareholders and typically accomplished via some form of survey. Key here is ensuring the communication messaging that supports the survey demonstrates the participative approach. Questionnaire structuring is critical, with a mix of quantitative and qualitative questions, ranking by importance, pressure-testing questions, etc. As such, good questionnaires require professional design and deployment, ideally using an external provider with a proven track record.
Voice of the customer (VOC)	• Customers • Clients • Consumers/users • Citizens, patients, pupils	Engagement forums, focus groups, customer round tables, surveys, feedback, online data harvesting, etc – VOC is a specialized area often with specialized functions and providers to do this well. This is a key approach to understanding expectations. Use professional support to ensure representative sample size across relevant demographics and the right approaches to understanding expectations. Incentives are often key to obtaining feedback.
Request for Information (RFI)	• Suppliers • Supply chain/SVCN players	Conducted via an e-sourcing platform or can simply be done via an email request. Create an RFI template that solicits both quantitative and qualitative responses, keep it simple (<5 mins to complete) and communicate why you are doing this, how you will use the responses and timescales for responses.

Table 6.1 *continued*

Stakeholder engagement method	Suitable for	Key success factors
Audit/visit them, meet with them (face-to-face or online)	• Suppliers • Supply chain/SVCN players	Use to both inform and consult, and potentially combine with an audit to assess current position and gauge capability for improvement programmes.
Townhall or gatherings	• Communities • Employees	Multi-individual transmit-only sessions, so good for informing. Can be difficult to solicit representative feedback in such forums. Large group 'in the moment' voting rarely yields meaningful results so if consultation is required consider including something people go away and do after the event.
Research, press and trends, published data and surveys	• Understanding the general public sentiment	Watch the press, structure online research and look for related trends on social media. Sometimes asking those you come into contact with can give good insight. Generally, the more research you do the better the outcome.

Frameworks for sustainability

We could simply determine our direction for sustainability based upon our assessment of the impacts and improvement areas we determine we want to focus on, indeed many organizations do just that. However, there are many frameworks for sustainability at a company level and also specifically for sustainable procurement that provide a predetermined structure for assessment (potentially including detailed measurement) and action, in some cases including a schedule of impact areas against which this happens. There are scenarios where a company might need to adopt and demonstrate compliance with multiple frameworks, for example to satisfy different regulatory, shareholder or industry requirements. While this might bring an administrative burden, generally once a company can demonstrate progress for sustainability it will be able to satisfy multiple frameworks, perhaps with a data engine supplying the same data in different forms to show compliance across all the frameworks.

The six impact areas in this book establish a suitable framework that can be used and these have been translated to provide a framework for sustainable procurement specifically, which is given at the end of this chapter in Figure 6.9. Alternatively one of the many frameworks out there could be used instead. Part of setting the direction for sustainability is for the company, and procurement and supply chain functions, to determine what framework(s) it will adopt. Reasons to adopt a framework include:

- Structured means to build a sustainability programme
- Achieve regulatory compliance
- Give confidence and make us more attractive to investors
- Universally recognized measure of progress
- Establishes a common language to describe progress
- A basis to achieve a recognized badge, accreditation or certification
- Brings confidence that all relevant areas are being covered
- Clear demonstration to stakeholders of turning intent into action

Frameworks tend to fall into a number of categories depending upon the purpose they serve, which seem to include:

- Legislative (we covered some of these in Chapter 5)
- Investor
- Emissions and carbon (in particular reporting)
- Standards and guidance notes
- Industry sector specific (e.g. textiles, food, etc)
- Frameworks for general sustainability action

Table 6.2 lists some of the key frameworks along with any industry context where they are typically used. We will explore some of most relevant frameworks together, as well as some concepts that can be applied to any framework. We will examine seven approaches here. These are the circular economy, the triple bottom line, the United Nations Global Compact, the United Nations Guiding Principles, the United Nations Sustainable Development Goals (SDGs), ISO 26000 and ISO 20400, and the GHG Protocol.

Table 6.2 Frameworks for sustainability

Framework	Areas of focus	Description
Emissions and carbon reduction		
ACT – Assessing low-Carbon Transition	Carbon reduction	Provides benchmarking against science-based metrics to help companies to develop low-carbon operations
GHG Protocol	Emissions	Voluntary, international framework that provides accounting methods and reporting for GHG emissions. One of the more established frameworks that helps companies quantify emissions, set reduction targets and measure emissions
SBTi – Science Based Targets Initiative	Climate	Approach and resources for science-based target setting with assessment
Sustainability and reporting		
GRESB	Real estate	Sustainability performance in the global commercial real-estate sector (including asset- and entity-level disclosures)
EcoVadis	Sustainability ratings	Voluntary universal sustainability ratings provider – mainly questionnaire-based with performance tracking against 21-point framework
Global destination sustainability index	Destinations	Sustainability benchmarking and improvement framework and approach for destinations
GRI – Global Reporting Initiative	Climate change, human rights and corruption, many others	International independent and vast range of standards for organizations and governments to help them understand and report their impacts. Includes recommendations on key topics

Setting the direction for sustainability

Table 6.2 *continued*

Framework	Areas of focus	Description
ILO Declaration on Fundamental Principles and Rights at Work	Human values and rights at work	Framework and expression of five key commitments by governments and organizations to uphold basic human values that are vital to our social and economic lives
OECD Guidelines for Multinational Enterprises	Standards for responsible business	Standard for responsible business across a range of areas including human rights, labour rights and the environment, including in the supply chain. Includes a government-backed international grievance mechanism
UN Global Compact	International framework for sustainability	UN pact that sets the minimum requirements for sustainability in organizations according to 10 principles around human rights, labour, the environment and preventing corruption
UN Guiding Principles	International principles for human rights	Framework of 31 principles that sets out the minimum expected responsibilities of companies to respect human rights
UN Sustainable Development Goals (SDGs)	International goals for sustainability	Seventeen interlinked global goals designed to be a shared blueprint for peace and prosperity for people and the planet, now and into the future
The United Nations Declaration on the Rights of Indigenous Peoples	First Nations people	Universal framework of minimum standards for the survival, dignity and well-being of the indigenous peoples of the world
World Economic Forum (WEF) Stakeholder Capitalism Metrics	Stakeholder capitalism reporting	Framework to measure stakeholder capitalism with metrics and reporting for sustainable value creation

The sustainability imperative

Table 6.2 *continued*

Framework	Areas of focus	Description
\multicolumn{3}{l}{**Investor and finance reporting**}
AA1000	Investor-led sustainability reporting	Assurance standard for assessing and strengthening credibility of an organization's sustainability reporting by AccountAbility
CDP	Investor-led sustainability reporting	Sustainability reporting framework and disclosure system. Largest repository of GHG emission data and energy use. Now includes forestry and water impacts
CDSB – Climate Disclosure Standards Board	Investor-led environmental reporting	Two frameworks focused on reporting environmental information when reporting to investors
European Green Taxonomy	Investor led environmental reporting	A classification framework for companies to define which of their economic activities are environmentally sustainable
FTSE4Good	UK investor-led sustainability reporting	Index of top 100 socially responsible companies
DJSI – Dow Jones Sustainability Index	US investor-led sustainability reporting	Index of top 10% of socially responsible companies with economic, environmental and social focus
IR – Integrated Reporting	Reporting, accounting and ESG	Framework for connecting financial statements with sustainable value creation from a global coalition of regulators, investors, companies and those who determine standards. Part of IFRS Foundation
MSCI – Morgan Stanley Capital International Global Standard Index	Investor-led ESG reporting	Significant player in ESG investment indexes to help institutional investors. Rates international companies based on performance in environmental, social and governance (ESG) aspects

Setting the direction for sustainability

Table 6.2 *continued*

Framework	Areas of focus	Description
SASB – Sustainability Accounting Standards Board	Sustainability accounting	Sustainability accounting framework with industry-specific reporting standards focused on financially material issues
TCFD – Task Force on Climate-related Financial Disclosures	Investor-led sustainability reporting	Framework and recommendations for accounting for climate-related risks and opportunities within financial disclosures
UN Principles for Responsible Investment (PRI)	Investor-led ESG reporting	A framework of six principles and ESG indicators for UN network of investors
Standards and guidance		
ISO 26000:2010	International guidance standard for social responsibility	Intended to help organizations develop and implement an approach to sustainable development
ISO 20400:2017	International guidance standard for sustainable procurement	Provides guidance on sustainable procurement specifically that is designed to help organizations of any size integrate sustainability
ISO 14064	International standard for GHG emissions	ISO14064-1:2018 is the international standard and specification with guidance for an organization to quantify and report its GHG emissions and develop plans for removal. Similar to the GHG Protocol, it distinguishes between direct and indirect emissions
ISO 14001	Environmental management system	Framework and criteria for an organization to set up and maintain an effective environmental management system. Companies can be certified to ISO14001

Table 6.2 *continued*

Framework	Areas of focus	Description
ISO 50001	Energy management systems	Voluntary international standard for organizations of any size. It provides requirements for establishing, managing and improving energy consumption and efficiency
PAS 2050	International standard on carbon footprinting	Provides a process life cycle approach to evaluating GHG emissions with goods and services
PAS 2060	International standard for carbon neutrality	Provides requirements to quantify, reduce and offset carbon emissions and means to demonstrate net zero claims are robust

SOURCE Includes content adapted from Ecoact (2022)

The circular economy

The circular economy is less of a framework and more of a philosophy from which we can extract a set of operating principles to establish a sustainable organization. It is not mutually exclusive to other frameworks or concepts but rather a principle of system design to be embedded within whatever direction, goals and action towards sustainability a company might set or take.

As we saw in Chapter 1, the underlying root cause to all the planet impacts is the fact that we have evolved to be a one-directional linear society. Organizations and our lifestyles have typically been founded on consumption of often virgin resources and the resultant waste, much of which is non-biodegradable, that is then dumped and we buy new. As we have seen, this linear, one-directional model is no longer sustainable. It threatens future resource security, it is energy-intensive to create and dispose of more and more, which also creates significant emissions.

In contrast, the circular economy is a concept that seeks to changes this by stopping the waste being produced in the first place and redesigning how we operate as individuals, companies and entire economies in order to move from the linear model to a circular one (Figure 6.5). The concept first appeared as early as the 1960s but the term 'circular economy' was first coined by Allen Kneese in the 1980s (Kneese, 1988). However, the idea has only really gained traction this century, initially by China as a national policy and subsequently in the UK, Europe and the Americas. The Ellen MacArthur Foundation has been instrumental in promoting the concept with the EU launching a New Circular Economy Action Plan in 2020.

The well-known 3R approach (Reduce, Reuse, Recycle) is, in part, what the circular economy is about; however, this only focuses on the use of raw materials whereas circular economy thinking also requires new systems thinking and a redesign of all aspects of how a company operates. There are three guiding principles for doing this (Ellen MacArthur Foundation, 2022):

1 **Eliminate waste and pollution**. We have come to accept waste and pollution as inevitable by-products of what we make. Instead, in the circular economy there is no such thing as waste or pollution – this requires a shift in our thinking to view these as design flaws and design them out. In practice this means changing the materials we use, our processes, using new technology and finding innovative ways to achieve zero waste and zero emissions. For example, we might recover heat from industrial processes or move away from plastic packaging to something fully recyclable or a container that stays in circulation and gets reused, or how about edible packaging made from seaweed?

2 **Circulate products and materials**. Redesign products so they can be reused, recycled, repaired, repurposed or remanufactured in their entirety or in part. While this places an obligation for companies to move away from deliberate built-in obsolescence, it does not mean designing things to last forever, but rather designing both products and the infrastructure to keep things in circulation as long as possible and ultimately avoid anything going to landfill. Circularity offers huge benefits, for example if packaging is owned by the producer and disposal becomes the responsibility of the producer this could reduce emissions globally by 10–15 per cent (UNEP 2015). In practice this means careful selection of input materials so they are non-toxic and don't deplete natural resources. It also means that once something is used or needs to be changed there is a route to do this rather than simply throwing it away. It means how things are recycled is as much a part of the design process as the products themselves – it is essential that materials are recycled properly and that components and raw materials remain of high quality in these cycles

Figure 6.5 The circular economy

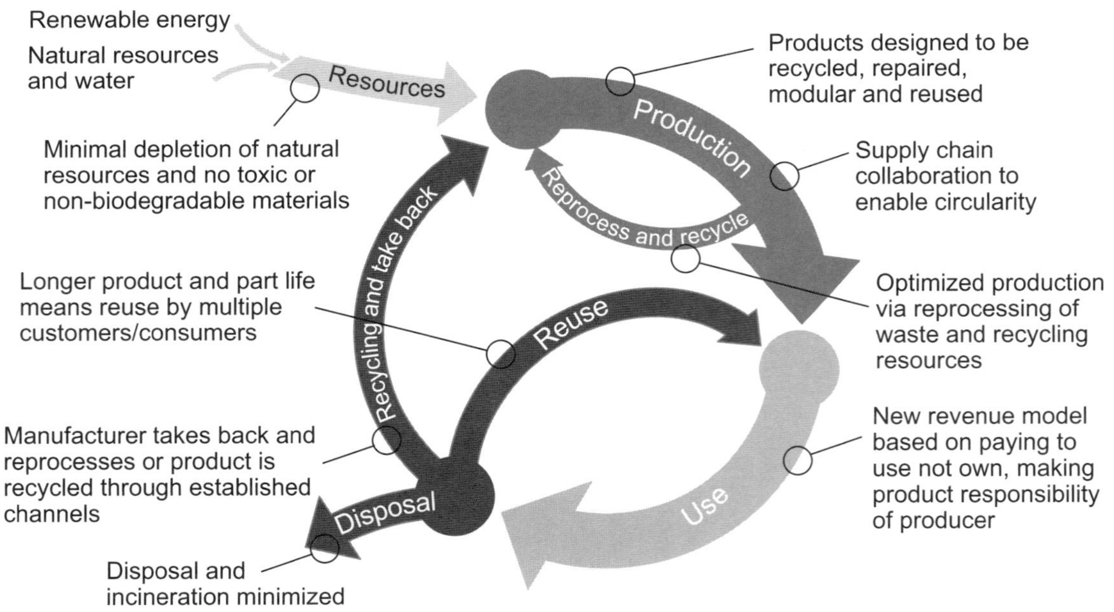

- Renewable energy
- Natural resources and water

- Minimal depletion of natural resources and no toxic or non-biodegradable materials

- Products designed to be recycled, repaired, modular and reused

- Supply chain collaboration to enable circularity

- Optimized production via reprocessing of waste and recycling resources

- New revenue model based on paying to use not own, making product responsibility of producer

- Longer product and part life means reuse by multiple customers/consumers

- Manufacturer takes back and reprocesses or product is recycled through established channels

- Disposal and incineration minimized

(Korhonen et al, 2018). Current municipal recycling routes won't cut it but rather manufacturers need to create return routes, industry needs to change processes and society needs new thinking on disposal streams. Examples of circularity include:

- Cars at end of life go back to the manufacturer to be stripped down and parts recycled/reconditioned.
- Electrical items go back to the manufacturer to get reprocessed and key raw materials and precious metals extracted.
- Furniture gets returned to processing companies that strip it down and reprocess or recycle component materials.
- Demolition or road resurfacing waste in construction gets sorted, reprocessed and reused in new construction – often *in situ* to minimize transportation.
- Discarded clothing first gets resold as 'vintage or pre-loved' and then when next discarded is reused in developing countries prior to finally being recycled into cloths or new raw materials. Key to this is fashion designers designing out microfibres to make garments more recyclable.
- Agriculture waste streams become organic fertilizers or animal fodder.

3 **Seek to regenerate nature**. The ultimate circular economy is one that strives to replicate the perfection of nature in the sense that nature has no waste – everything one part of nature produces gets used by another to create a perfect circular ecosystem. Therefore, the final component of the circular economy is how we can return things to nature in a way that will regenerate it. In practice this means returning nutrients to soil, returning water to its source and so on.

In the same way that use of materials becomes circular, the circular economy is underpinned by a transition to renewable energy. Energy is not circular, and it is not possible to recycle energy, but it is possible to ensure all input energy is from renewable sources and convert energy produced (e.g. heat produced to power). Therefore, the principles of a circular economy can only be upheld if all energy used comes from renewable sources and no fossil fuels or other resources are depleted.

Achieving circularity requires a new form of closer and more collaborative relationships with key suppliers, and indeed back up the SVCN. Therefore, procurement and supply chain functions are key enablers in order to establish new joint working relationships with key providers and establishing new, more circular, logistics.

The circular economy is a principle of system design rather than responding to specific impact areas. Key to establishing this principle is the decoupling of the economic activity of a firm from the consumption of finite resources and redesigning the system accordingly. Critics of the idea suggest true circularity is impossible, that there will always be waste and that it is impossible to stop primary production. While this may hold some truth, what is clear about sustainability is that we cannot attain perfection, but we can take big steps forward. Furthermore, others suggest that in a free-market economy where there is choice not everyone will opt for circular products – if given the choice of new or refurbished in some way, many people will reject the latter. This choice may not be available to us for much longer and there is much companies can do to reposition products and re-educate consumers and customers.

Triple bottom line

Triple bottom line (or TPL/3BL/3P) is an accounting framework based upon the idea that an organization can measure and report its performance and progress not just based upon *profit* but also *people* and *planet* (Figure 6.6). The idea of a triple bottom line seems to have been first articulated by Freer Spreckley (1981) and established by John Elkington in 1994 (The Economist, 2009).

Organizations have, in the main, been structured around top-down financial-based management with profit in all its various stated forms including EBITDA being the single most important measure of business performance. Arguably, this is how much of the capitalist world runs. Antagonists would be quick to cite greed and pursuit of profit by the big corporates as the root of all our problems; however, it is not that clear cut.

I have worked for many profit-only driven companies that I would consider good firms that worked to do the right thing in all they did, long before sustainability was a thing, yet the only measure of performance that drove everything the firm did was profit and ultimately shareholder value. Milton would be pleased. As such, the organizations were built upon a framework of financial budgetary controls of performance against financial projections. Decisions would require a business case with financial justification core to any approval. Investing in something without this would be a bold move and securing approval would be unlikely. This is how most companies are structured and function and the reality here is companies have not so much chosen pursuit of profit over other value, but rather managing an organiza-

Figure 6.6 The triple bottom line

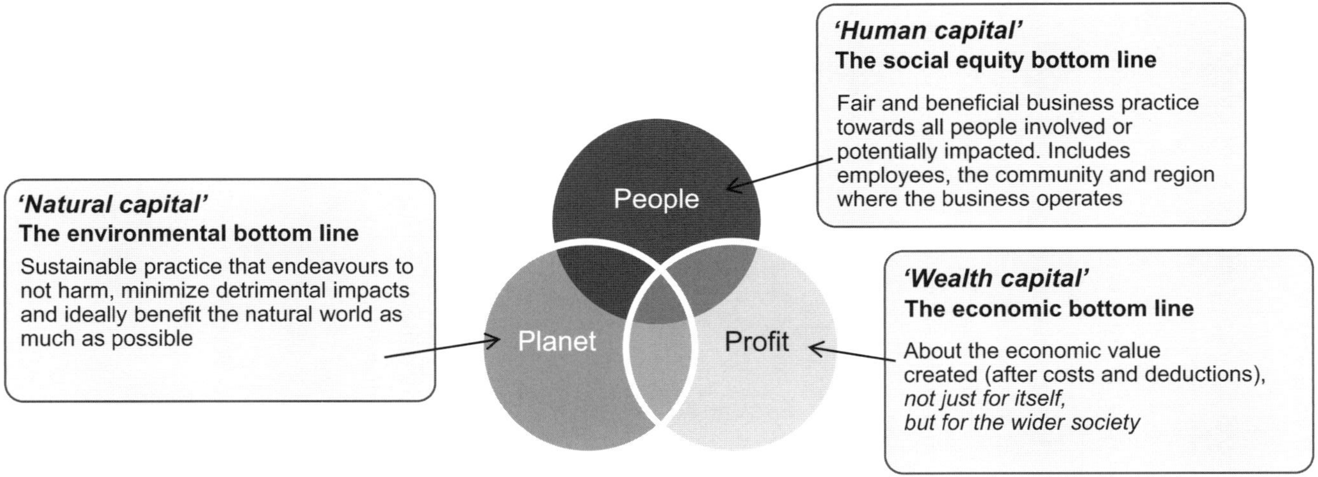

'Natural capital'
The environmental bottom line

Sustainable practice that endeavours to not harm, minimize detrimental impacts and ideally benefit the natural world as much as possible

'Human capital'
The social equity bottom line

Fair and beneficial business practice towards all people involved or potentially impacted. Includes employees, the community and region where the business operates

'Wealth capital'
The economic bottom line

About the economic value created (after costs and deductions), *not just for itself, but for the wider society*

tion based upon financial performance and profit is the only established system for how an enterprise can function, survive and grow and manage its risks. There is no other system that works to any degree. Even in a not-for-profit or public sector company financial performance is critical to the firm's existence and future, except the goal is something other than profit or to ensure funds for reinvestment. If a company fails to perform in financial terms or runs out of cash it is doomed unless a lifeboat turns up to save it. In contrast, today, companies don't fail if they miss social or environmental goals; however, as we have seen, that is changing and new/emerging legislation now holds the potential to cripple a company that fails here also.

Few companies have dared to stray away from the safety of profit-driven performance and decision making and those that have tend to be more towards the entrepreneurial side of the spectrum. Virgin Atlantic was the first airline to introduce a bar on board its planes where passengers in Upper Class could socialize during a flight. Famously, Richard Branson was advised against doing this by his finance team because the number of seats that would be sacrificed to create the space needed for a bar would have a significant impact on revenues. Yet the Virgin Atlantic in-flight bar went ahead and remains part of the brand attribute of the airline. Here was a decision not made on the basis of immediate financial returns but based upon how it would heighten the customer experience, create a unique selling proposition and build brand value. It could be argued that the future financial return from increased passenger demand in the Upper Class cabin would make the business case. Yet even with this there remains a degree of uncertainty along the lines of 'something really good will happen that will make us great if we spend money doing this and the finances will take care of themselves'. These sorts of 'non-finance-based' decisions are classic traits of entrepreneurs who just have a feel for how greater new value can be created beyond immediate financial returns and where, and where not, to take such a punt. It is, in essence, about taking a risk.

Learning from entrepreneurs – taking a balanced approach

When it comes to sustainability, we can learn from how entrepreneurs make decisions and take risk. Here we are doing the same thing – we are making what are often non-financial or pre-financial based decisions on a course of action that will create greater value. If we do this without care, there is a risk we rush off to save the world and bankrupt the firm. Therefore, sustainability needs a balanced approach that combines financial performance with sustainability performance. This concept of balance is not new. Kaplan and

Norton (1996) introduced us to the Balanced Scorecard – a means of measuring the performance of a firm so that it is guided not only by the financial indicators of performance but also by other value drivers that enable the organization to be successful and achieve outcomes. It was *balanced* because the approach dealt with the challenge that no single type of measure can provide a clear focus for attention and so sought to strike a balance between disparate strategic measures. The approach combined measures of financial performance, customer satisfaction, effectiveness of internal business processes and innovation, learning and growth. Back then sustainability did not make it as a balanced measure, although since then many have adapted the model to leverage it in and a quick internet search will reveal the many takes on this original model.

The problem with traditional financial measures

Financial and profit-based performance management systems are inherently risk adverse. They are also the most quantitative – a table of figures tells the absolute truth. You can't measure people and planet in the same way as you measure profit. Financial performance considers direct and immediate indirect costs whereas people and planet consider other costs, i.e. the six impact areas from Chapters 1 and 2. If sourcing from Brazil means indiscriminate deforestation in order to supply food ingredients or textile sourcing means child labour has been denied both education and a childhood there is an environmental and social cost. As we have seen, historically these costs have laid conveniently hidden from Western consumers, however, and also as we have seen, and whether by choice or compulsion, companies are now having to consider these costs. Furthermore, measuring people and planet value (or the avoidance of social or environmental cost impact) has historically been quite subjective, requiring qualitative measures. Despite the fact that qualitative measures don't fit with traditional financial measurement systems they are a necessary part of driving sustainability. They are also exactly what entrepreneurs use – if we put a bar on an airplane it will drive growth and brand value! We shouldn't shy away from qualitative measures but rather learn to embrace them and recognize that to drive sustainability effectively we need to be prepared to take some level of risk with some decisions based on little other than a positive impact story of what social and environmental value is possible from a course of action. The triple bottom line is a key enabler here. That said, increasingly people and planet factors can be measured quantitively and as legislation becomes established together with new reporting obligations a new world of quantitative measures are emerging. This includes such things as compliance to legislation, amount of CO_2e produced, diversity ratios at suppliers and so on. More on that later.

A new approach to drive organizational success

The triple bottom line is therefore not so much a framework for sustainability but the new underpinning means to manage the organization and measure progress and success that needs to form part of any initiative to pursue sustainability, whatever framework is adopted. The old adage 'what you measure is what you get' is highly relevant here and so the triple bottom line is about preparing three different and quite separate bottom lines – the traditional *profit* line and then a *people* line that measures how socially responsible a company has been throughout all its operations, and the *planet* line as a measure of how environmentally responsible it has been. The 3Ps have no hierarchy and the performance across them cannot be summed or combined to give a single measure. They are separate and as such require a shift in how the firm organizes itself to serve all three individually and collectively. TBL therefore aims to measure financial, social and environmental performance over a period of time and in so doing takes account of the full cost involved in doing business (The Economist, 2009).

The United Nations Global Compact

The UN Global Compact is a non-binding set of principles set out to provide organizations with a framework to adopt sustainability. They are widely regarded as the 'ticket to the ballpark' and 'must dos' of sustainability. Indeed, the route several companies have adopted to navigate towards sustainability has been to use the principles set out within the UN Global Compact as the minimum that must be met, adding additional layers of perhaps more aspirational or medium-term goals that it wants to achieve, perhaps using a second framework such as the UN SDGs (up next) here.

The UN Global Compact is therefore a framework for companies to meet their minimum or fundamental responsibilities in areas of human rights, labour, the environment and preventing corruption. The 10 principles have been derived from the Universal Declaration of Human Rights (UDHR), the International Labour Organization's Declaration on Fundamental Principles and Rights at Work, the Rio Declaration on Environment and Development, and the United Nations Convention Against Corruption. The 10 principles (UN Global Compact, 2022b) are

Human rights

1. Support and respect the protection of internationally proclaimed human rights; and
2. make sure that they are not complicit in human rights abuses.

Labour

3. Uphold the freedom of association and the effective recognition of the right to collective bargaining;
4. the elimination of all forms of forced and compulsory labour;
5. the effective abolition of child labour; and
6. the elimination of discrimination in respect of employment and occupation.

The environment

7. Support a precautionary approach to environmental challenges;
8. undertake initiatives to promote greater environmental responsibility; and
9. encourage the development and diffusion of environmentally friendly technologies.

Anti-corruption

10. Work against corruption in all its forms, including extortion and bribery.

The United Nations Guiding Principles

The UN Guiding Principles (UNGP), or to give it its full name the Guiding Principles on Business and Human Rights, is a framework that defines 31 principles to implement the UN 'Protect, Respect and Remedy' framework (UN, 2011). These principles are set out in three sections or pillars, which are:

1. The state duty to protect human rights
2. The corporate responsibility to respect human rights
3. Access to remedy for victims of business-related abuses

The UNGP was the first global corporate human rights responsibility initiative endorsed by the UN – endorsed in 2011 by the UN Human Rights Council. It sets out the expected responsibilities of companies rather than their mandatory obligations. That said, the UNGP is referenced and underpinned by new and emerging legislation including the CSRD and CSDD (expanded in Figure 5.1).

The UNGPs are widely regarded as the 'ticket to the ballpark' and 'must dos' of human rights to mitigate risk. Indeed, there has been a strong take up of global companies confirming their commitment to it. The route many of these companies have adopted to navigate towards sustainability has been to use the principles set out within the UNGPs as the minimum that must be met, perhaps also with some of the other principles set out in the UN Global Compact, adding additional layers of perhaps more aspirational or medium-term goals that it wants to achieve, perhaps using a second framework such as the UN SDGs (up next).

The UNGPs set out the global standard for preventing and addressing the risk of adverse human rights impacts linked to business activity. Established 12 years after the UN Global Compact, the UNGPs provide further clarity and reinforcement for the two human rights principles championed by the Global Compact. The key difference between these two is that the Global Compact provides a broader set of principles for sustainability, but also for the two human rights principles the Global Compact requires organizations to go further than respecting human rights and commit to the promotion of human rights and how they can make a positive contribution to do this through core business activities, investment and philanthropy.

Once a company commits to the UNGPs the principle of 'know and show' becomes important, and therefore the need to report on it progress. There are different approaches out there including a UNGP reporting framework developed through a joint initiative between the non-profit company Shift and the international accountancy firm Mazars backed by a coalition of investors.

The United Nations Sustainable Development Goals

Possibly the most useful, most global, most widely adopted and elegant framework is the United Nations Sustainable Development Goals (SDGs). Naturally building upon the prerequisites of the UN Global Compact, the SDGs form part of the 2030 Agenda for Sustainable Development that was adopted by all United Nations Member States in 2015. They provide the blueprint for peace and prosperity for people and the planet, now and into the future. There are 17 SDGs (Figure 6.7) crafted by a global partnership, which form an urgent call for action by all countries. They recognize that ending poverty and other deprivations must go hand-in-hand with strategies that improve health and education, reduce inequality and spur economic growth – all while tackling climate change and working to preserve our oceans and forests (UN, 2022a).

The 17 SDGs include environmental, social and economic development goals and are interlinked, global and designed to be achieved by 2030. Each goal has specific targets with indicators to be used to monitor progress towards each. Some targets have end dates, some are open ended. Monitoring and reporting progress towards goals is the remit of the UN, which publishes annual reports of progress. As we have seen with the six impact areas, impacts are interlinked, and therefore action to address these is synergetic. Similarly, synergies exist across the SDGs where progress towards one goal supports another. For example, SDG 13 (take urgent action to combat climate change and its impacts) drives and is driven by SDG 3 (ensure healthy lives and promote well-being for all at all ages), SDG 7 (ensure access to affordable, reliable, sustainable and modern energy for all), SDG 11 (make cities and human settlements inclusive, safe, resilient and sustainable), SDG 12 (ensure sustainable consumption and production patterns) and SDG 14

Figure 6.7   The 17 UN Sustainable Development Goals

SOURCE Courtesy of United Nations

(conserve and sustainably use the oceans, seas and marine resources for sustainable development).

The UN SDGs provide a framework for global action and are translated into action at a country level through legislation, funding and governmental initiatives. The framework also provides the starting point for organizations to determine their direction of travel for sustainability. However, the 17 goals and the 169 individual targets contained within them represent an incredible aspiration and beyond what can realistically or practically be pursued by a firm or indeed many governments. As we have already seen it is impossible to fix everything and it would be folly for a company to try, but we can take positive steps. The SDGs therefore enable a company to determine which of the 17 goals are most relevant for the firm given the primary impacts of what the firm does, and pick one, two or possibly more to aim towards. Of the companies I work with, it would seem picking about three SDGs is a good place to start, and then perhaps planning to adopt further goals along the way as momentum builds. Selecting which SDGs to pursue provides the direction for a sustainability programme. From here the organization can translate the goals, and associated measures, into specific areas of focus in terms of what we buy, who we buy from and what happens in our supply chains. More on the UN SDGs and extensive resources can be found at un.org/sustainabledevelopment.

Note the content of this publication has not been approved by the United Nations and does not reflect the views of the United Nations or its officials or Member States.

ISO 26000:2010

ISO 26000:2010 is the international guidance standard for social responsibility. As a guidance document it is intended to help organizations develop and implement an approach to sustainable development. It is not a management system standard and does not contain requirements, and therefore it is not a basis for certification. It is built around seven core areas of organization impact or areas of responsibility, which are human rights, labour practices, the environment, fair operating practices, consumer issues, community involvement and development, and the central organizational governance. For each, the document provides a full listing of the various impacts for each core area and a schedule of the various initiatives that can be put in place in response to each. ISO 26000:2010 is specifically aimed at creating a framework and approach for sustainability across an entire organization.

ISO 20400:2017

IS0 20400:2017 is also a guidance standard and is designed as a subset of 26000:2010. It provides guidance on sustainable procurement specifically that is designed to help organizations of any size integrate sustainability, as described within ISO 26000, within procurement. As a guidance document, it does not lay out requirements and so it is not possible to obtain any sort of certification to ISO 20400. It is helpful insomuch as it lays out what sustainable procurement is, the key drivers for it and it sets out the principles and considerations for a firm attempting to implement sustainable procurement. As such, it provides a useful checklist of what to plan for and put in place for procurement at a strategic level and throughout the procurement cycle against the framework for sustainability as defined in ISO 26000. There is an online not-for-profit global community where practice and experience of ISO 20400 can be shared at iso20400.org.

GHG Protocol

The Greenhouse Gas Protocol is an organization that was formed in 1998 between the World Resources Institute and the World Business Council for Sustainable Development and is now a multi-stakeholder partnership of governments, NGOs and businesses. Its mission is to provide frameworks to measure, manage, report and reduce GHG emissions. As such, the GHG Protocol standard was published in 2001 and updated in 2011 to include emissions across the entire SVCN and is the most established (and probably the most widely used) approach for GHG emissions assessment, accounting and reporting. The standard identifies three areas where an organization needs to consider its emissions (Figure 6.8):

- Scope 1 – the direct emissions of the organization.
- Scope 2 – the indirect emissions of the organization arising from purchased electricity, steam, heating and cooling for its own use.
- Scope 3 – all the indirect emissions of the organization across the entire SVCN, upstream from the original raw material, agricultural source or factory to the end customer or consumer, its use during its life and on to end-of-life processing. Scope 3 emissions also consider other indirect sources such as business travel, employee commuting, leased assets, franchises and investment.

An alternative framework to the GHG Protocol standard is ISO 14064. We will return to emissions assessment in the next chapter.

Figure 6.8 The GHG Protocol – areas of emission assessment and reporting

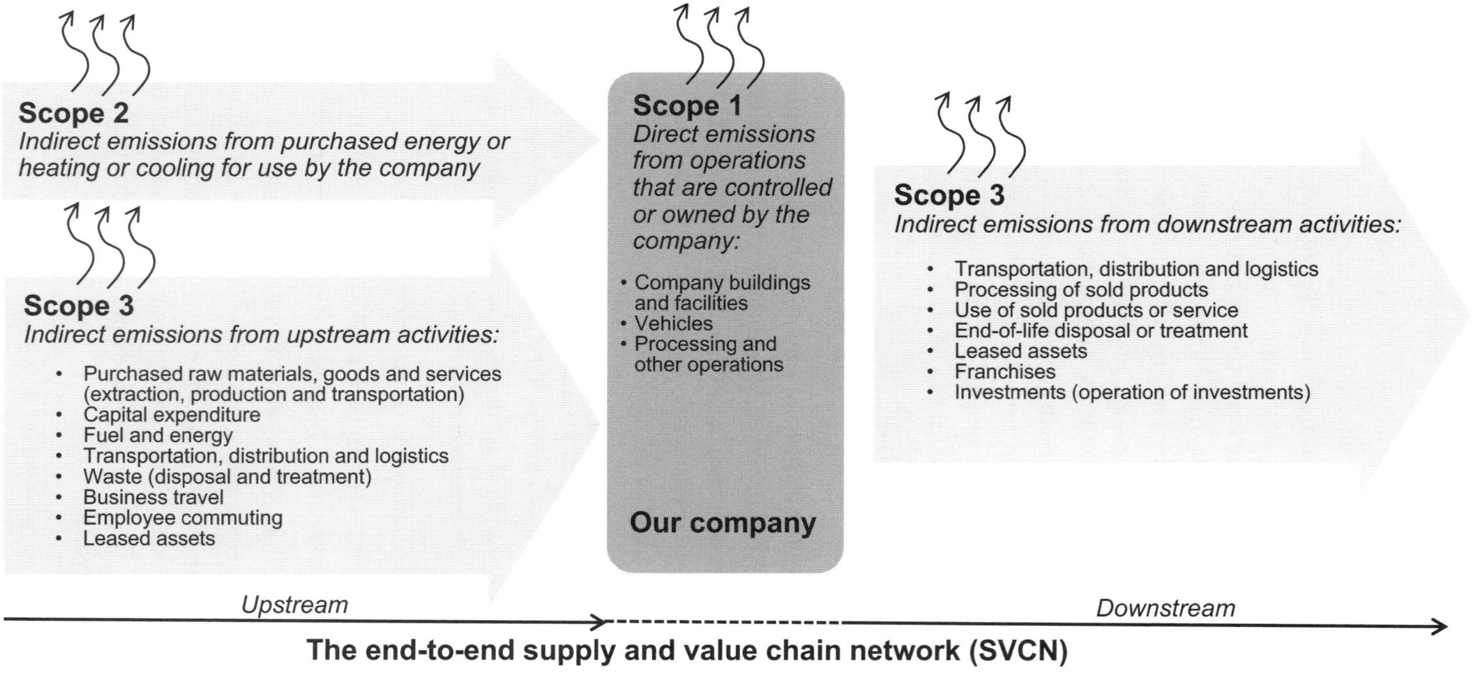

Scope 2
Indirect emissions from purchased energy or heating or cooling for use by the company

Scope 3
Indirect emissions from upstream activities:
- Purchased raw materials, goods and services (extraction, production and transportation)
- Capital expenditure
- Fuel and energy
- Transportation, distribution and logistics
- Waste (disposal and treatment)
- Business travel
- Employee commuting
- Leased assets

Scope 1
Direct emissions from operations that are controlled or owned by the company:
- Company buildings and facilities
- Vehicles
- Processing and other operations

Our company

Scope 3
Indirect emissions from downstream activities:
- Transportation, distribution and logistics
- Processing of sold products
- Use of sold products or service
- End-of-life disposal or treatment
- Leased assets
- Franchises
- Investments (operation of investments)

Upstream → Downstream

The end-to-end supply and value chain network (SVCN)

SOURCE adapted from GHG Protocol (2022)

A framework for sustainable procurement

Almost all of the frameworks out there (except ISO 20400) are for an entire organization. This is logical because, as we know, the goals for procurement are part of and flow from the wider organizational vision and goals. However, there can sometimes be a disconnect between a general aim of a firm and how this translates to the specific actions needed within the supply base.

Therefore, I have included a sustainable procurement framework (Figure 6.9), which has been constructed to respond to the six impact areas we have explored (and therefore would align with some or all of other frameworks out there) but with specific interpretation for procurement and supply chain functions. The six impact areas are translated into 30 individual goals that represent all the potential areas that could be focused on as part of a sustainable procurement programme. These are expanded in Table 6.3. The sustainable procurement framework therefore provides ambitions and objectives for an organization in terms of its supply base and sourcing arrangements. It can be used as stand-alone or complementary to and could encompass many established frameworks and approaches. It is particularly applicable where the overall corporate aim for sustainability is a general ambition (rather than aligned to specific outcomes such as the UN SDGs) as it provides the necessary goal precision to guide what needs to happen in the supply base. Furthermore, and despite what I have said earlier here, if the organization has not set any goals it can be possible to establish a 'procurement-up' sustainability programme but only with top-down support and agreement.

We use the sustainable procurement framework by determining which goals we will pursue and within what time frame, and then determining specific time-bound targets in support of this.

198 The sustainability imperative

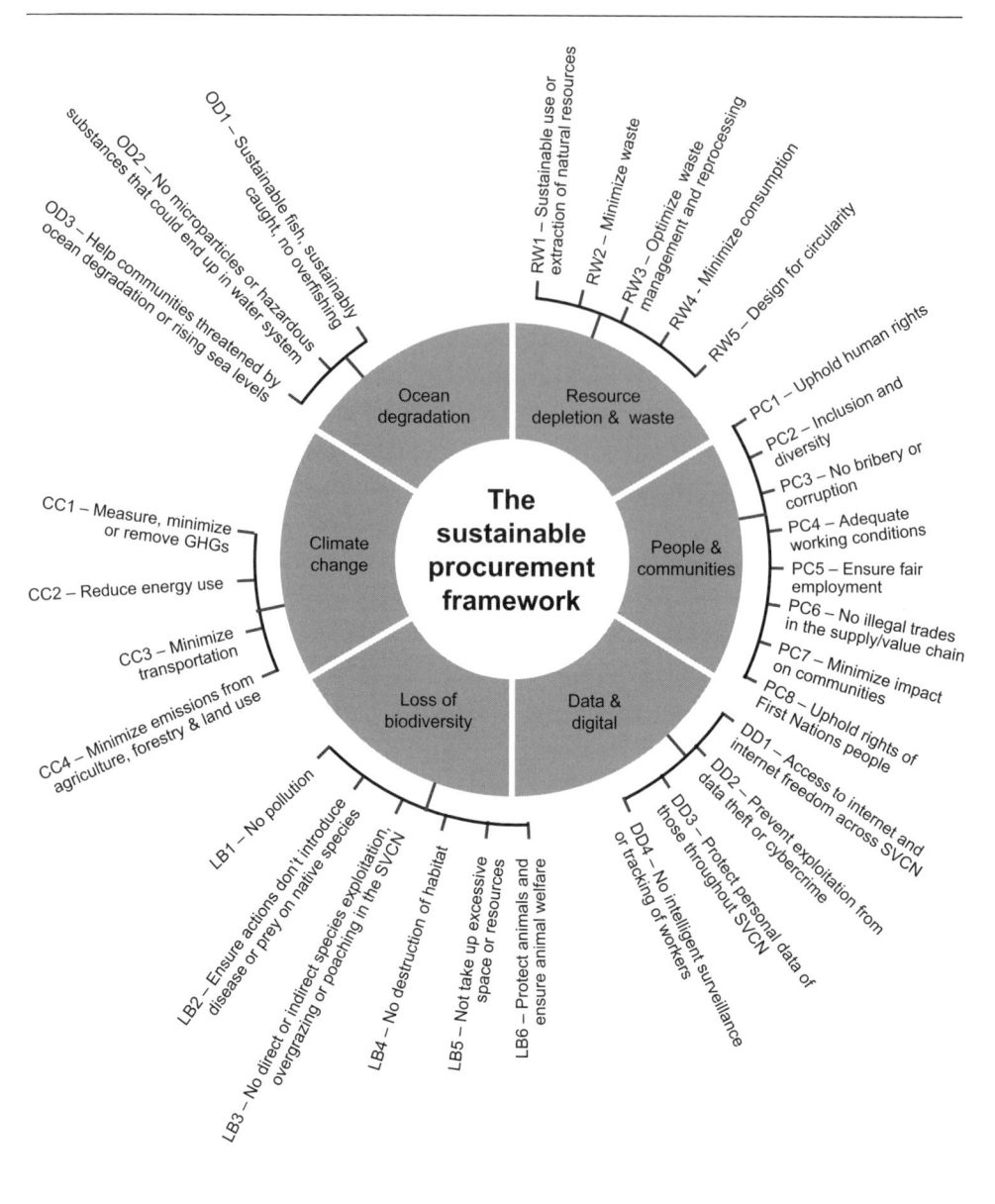

Figure 6.9 The sustainable procurement framework – goals for the six impact areas

Ocean degradation
- OD1 – Sustainable fish, sustainably caught, no overfishing
- OD2 – No microparticles or hazardous substances that could end up in water system
- OD3 – Help communities threatened by ocean degradation or rising sea levels

Resource depletion & waste
- RW1 – Sustainable use or extraction of natural resources
- RW2 – Minimize waste
- RW3 – Optimize waste management and reprocessing
- RW4 – Minimize consumption
- RW5 – Design for circularity

People & communities
- PC1 – Uphold human rights
- PC2 – Inclusion and diversity
- PC3 – No bribery or corruption
- PC4 – Adequate working conditions
- PC5 – Ensure fair employment
- PC6 – No illegal trades in the supply/value chain
- PC7 – Minimize impact on communities
- PC8 – Uphold rights of First Nations people

Climate change
- CC1 – Measure, minimize or remove GHGs
- CC2 – Reduce energy use
- CC3 – Minimize transportation
- CC4 – Minimize emissions from agriculture, forestry & land use

Loss of biodiversity
- LB1 – No pollution
- LB2 – Ensure actions don't introduce disease or prey on native species
- LB3 – No direct or indirect species exploitation; overgrazing or poaching in the SVCN
- LB4 – No destruction of habitat
- LB5 – Not take up excessive space or resources
- LB6 – Protect animals and ensure animal welfare

Data & digital
- DD1 – Access to internet and internet freedom across SVCN
- DD2 – Prevent exploitation from data theft or cybercrime
- DD3 – Protect personal data of those throughout SVCN
- DD4 – No intelligent surveillance or tracking of workers

The sustainable procurement framework

Table 6.3 The sustainable procurement framework goals expanded

Goal	Ambition	Requirements for this goal to realize sustainable procurement
Resource depletion and waste		
RW1	Sustainable use or extraction of natural resources	Assess and quantify proportion that is sustainable: • for all purchased goods and services • within suppliers • across those in the supply chain/SVCN Set prioritized targets and improvement actions to reduce or eliminate what is not sustainable
RW2	Minimize waste	Eliminate or minimize waste: • in our operation resulting from what we buy • at suppliers • throughout the supply chain/SVCN • with customers/consumers and beyond
RW3	Optimize waste management and reprocessing	For suppliers/those throughout the supply chain/SVCN: • optimize waste management and reprocessing to maximize recycling • no or minimal waste to landfill • take responsibility for end-user waste, return or recycling (create circular economy) • 100% responsibility for all waste streams end-to-end – no 'shipping it somewhere else'
RW4	Minimize consumption	For suppliers/those throughout the supply chain/SVCN: • Minimize consumption of raw materials • Minimize water consumption

Table 6.3 *continued*

Goal	Ambition	Requirements for this goal to realize sustainable procurement
RW5	Design for circularity	• Design to preserve resources and eliminate harmful waste • Minimize disposability of products • Eliminate built in obsolescence – create maintainability • Optimize product recyclability • Eliminate or reprocess non-biodegradable waste • Minimize single-use plastics
People and communities		
PC1	Uphold human rights	• Eliminate and prevent modern slavery • Eliminate and prevent child labour
PC2	Inclusion and diversity	• Eliminate and prevent discrimination • Ensure diversity and inclusion
PC3	No bribery or corruption	• Eliminate and prevent bribery and corruption
PC4	Adequate working conditions	• Health and safety for all • Uphold workers' rights • Ensure good working environment • Ensure air quality • Prevent exposure to harmful substances • No excessive working hours
PC5	Ensure fair employment	• Those throughout supply chains earn living wage • Employers seek to create job quality, security and prospects
PC6	No illegal trades in the SVCN	No products or use of suppliers that are involved in, or source products or materials that have any connection with, illegal trades including: • Conflict minerals • Sand mafia • Blood diamonds

Setting the direction for sustainability

Table 6.3 *continued*

Goal	Ambition	Requirements for this goal to realize sustainable procurement
PC7	Minimize impact on communities	Assess and actively minimize impact of our operations, our suppliers' operations and those throughout the supply chain/SVCN in the communities they operate so as to: • Minimize impacts from extraction of resources • Prevent operators becoming all-powerful • Minimize impacts from transportation of goods through communities • Minimize changing the landscape • Ensure no displacement of inhabitants
PC8	Uphold rights of First Nations people	• Uphold rights of First Nations people • Protect and respect cultural elements
Data and digital		
DD1	Access to internet and internet freedom across SVCN	Those in our suppliers and the SVCN enjoy: • access to the internet • internet freedom
DD2	Prevent exploitation from data theft or cybercrime	Actively prevent exploitation by our suppliers or those in the SVCN of individuals or communities via data theft or cybercrime
DD3	Protect personal data of those throughout SVCN	Controls for personal data retention for all those in the SVCN
DD4	No intelligent surveillance or tracking of workers	No utilization of intelligent surveillance and tracking of workers: • No use of facial recognition specifically combined with worker tracking (except for essential security in a closed system) • No use of race recognition software • No use of artificial intelligence to predict individual behaviour

Table 6.3 *continued*

Goal	Ambition	Requirements for this goal to realize sustainable procurement
\multicolumn{3}{c}{**Loss of biodiversity**}
LB1	No pollution	No pollution to land, air or water
LB2	Ensure actions don't introduce disease or prey on native species	All operations and activities by suppliers and throughout the supply chain/SVCN must not: • introduce disease • introduce non-native species • prey on native species
LB3	No direct or indirect species exploitation, overgrazing or poaching in the SVCN	No over farming, over harvesting, over extraction: • Where species are at or close to unsustainable levels • Where a consequence of the main operation exploits or threatens other species • Where farming methods are unsustainable • Where illegal
LB4	No destruction of habitat	Suppliers' processing, production or transportation must not cause destruction of habitat: • No logging and clearing land for agricultural use
LB5	Not take up excessive space or resources	Procurement related: suppliers and those in supply chain/SVCN operations and processing must not occupy a disproportionate space or use an unnecessary amount of resources
LB6	Protect animals and ensure animal welfare	No mistreatment of animals Animals must enjoy the 'five freedoms' (see Chapter 1)

Table 6.3 *continued*

Goal	Ambition	Requirements for this goal to realize sustainable procurement
\multicolumn{3}{c}{**Climate change**}
CC1	Measure, minimize or remove GHGs	Measure GHG emissions, identify time-bound reduction or elimination targets and actively pursue these for: • Scope 3 emissions – at our suppliers • Scope 3 emissions – throughout the SVCN • Scope 2 – for the energy we purchase
CC2	Reduce energy use	Measure energy use, nature of energy used, proportion of overall energy that is sustainable and identify time-bound improvement targets and actively pursue these: • To reduce energy use overall • To reduce or eliminate energy from fossil fuels • To increase use of renewables • To capture and convert and reuse energy produced from processes and production
CC3	Minimize transportation	• Minimize transportation of goods throughout the SVCN • Minimize storage and the use of resources required for storage • Reduce and eliminate GHG emissions from transportation
CC4	Minimize emissions from agriculture, forestry & land use	Minimize or eliminate: • Digestive emissions from livestock • Nitrogen-based fertilizers • Crop burning • Cutting down trees

Goal	Ambition	Requirements for this goal to realize sustainable procurement
Ocean degradation		
OD1	Sustainable fish, sustainably caught, no overfishing	No fish directly or indirectly obtained by suppliers: • Where stocks currently at or close to unsustainable levels • Fishing methods must not include bottom- or near-bottom trawling • Fishing methods must minimize by-catch kills of marine mammals, marine reptiles and sea birds • Minimize anthropogenic noise from industry
OD2	No microparticles or hazardous substances that could end up in water system	• No purchase, use of or discharge of hazardous substances (including POPs, metals, radioactive substances, PPCPs) • Product design or return/recycling arrangements to prevent microparticles that could end up in water system
OD3	Help communities threatened by ocean degradation or rising sea levels	Actively support and help communities where we operate or that support our operation that are threatened by the impacts of ocean degradation or rising sea levels

Setting the sustainable procurement strategy, goals and targets

Once there is clarity of direction for both the organization and the procurement and supply chain function in terms of sustainability, the next step is to crystallize this within a strategy, define the specific aims and timebound targets that the function will work towards (Figure 6.1) and communicate it internally and externally to establish the ambition and align efforts towards it. A template to do this is provided in the Appendix.

Defining the sustainable procurement strategy

A strategy is the articulation of the high-level approach or plan of action to accomplish a (usually long-term) goal or ambition. It is 'how' we will make sustainable procurement happen. In its simplest form the sustainable procurement strategy could be something along the lines of *'we will establish and manage delivery of a programme to realize the company sustainability goals in the supply base'*. However, a more detailed strategy will help secure greater understanding and alignment with those who will be part of implementing it.

The process of strategy determination requires the procurement or supply chain function to think about the various things that will need to be put in place to enable the strategy to be realized. This might include the people and resources needed, organizational structure, required capability, systems, ways of working, governance and the sort of culture that will get results. Therefore, it can be useful to define the 'how' with a more fully formed series of statements. Ultimately the strategy should be something that makes it easy to understand how the function will move forward while comprehensive enough to reference the various essential elements that form part of it. Sustainability is not a strategy in itself, but achieving sustainability or moving closer towards it drives our overall procurement strategy. An example is given in Figure 6.10. The sustainable procurement strategy should define in the simplest terms possible:

- How it will meet legislative obligations, now and future
- How the procurement or supply chain function will organize itself to work towards achieving the wider organizational objectives for sustainability within the supply base
- How it will determine and prioritize what it will focus on
- How it will enable the firm to be accountable and transparent in what it does with respect to the supply base
- The role of innovation to support this
- The capability and systems it will deploy to support this
- The relationship between cost and sustainability value
- How sustainability will be integrated and embedded in every aspect of procurement and the supply chain
- How it will measure, monitor and report on progress

Defining the sustainable procurement goals

The sustainable procurement goals are a subset of the strategy and define the specific aims for the function. They are high-level statements that define the ambition, direction of travel and therefore priorities that the procurement or supply chain function will work on. Goals here should respond to the primary impacts of the firm. They must also flow directly from, and support the realization of, the wider organizational goals. For example, if the firm has set a goal to reduce GHG emissions, then our goal might become to reduce GHG emissions across the supply base.

They are typically imprecise and qualitative, and articulate the long-term direction rather than short-term target outcomes; and may or may not have a time dimension. While this might seem somewhat vague, being clear about the aims is a necessary step before determining specific targets. It is also necessary because a target may not be achieved or may need to be revised along the way but the overall goal, and direction of travel, remains robust. It is like shining a light on the way we want to go so we can take steps towards it. Develop the goals as follows:

1 Determine if the wider organization has set or can articulate goals for sustainability.
2 If so, interpret these in the context of the supply base and determine the specific goals that flow from and will support realization of corporate goals.
3 Or where corporate aims are less well-defined, consult with shareholders and stakeholders to determine the ambition. Interpret this for the supply base and use the sustainable procurement framework as a basis to define goals.

Setting the targets

Targets for sustainable procurement are the individual measurable and time-based outcomes required to achieve or work towards the goals and realize the strategy. Targets are typically linked to the required outcomes of specific projects and initiatives and are often quantitative although certain aspects of sustainability also require qualitative targets in some cases. Where the wider organization has set specific targets for sustainability the sustainable procurement targets must directly relate to these. For example, if the organization has set a quantitative target to reduce GHG emissions by 50 per cent within three years, then we must have a 'flow through' target along the lines of 'reduce GHG emissions from the supply base by 50 per cent within three years'. Targets should be:

- Designed to realize the ambition of the sustainable procurement goals
- Linked to and work towards wider organizational targets and, where appropriate, linked to the global sustainability agenda
- SMART (specific, measurable, achievable, realistic and timebound) – so you know when you have achieved them
- Science based, where possible
- Regularly reviewed and revised and perhaps re-established annually or at another suitable frequency

Figure 6.10   Example of sustainable procurement strategy, goals and targets

Sustainable procurement strategy

To enable and support the timely realization of organizational goals for sustainability by

1. Ensuring compliance with current and future legislation that involves the supply base
2. Prioritized and targeted supply-side interventions and managed improvements
3. Balancing cost and sustainability value across all sourcing
4. Determining short-, medium- and long-term sustainable procurement goals and targets
5. Establishing a dedicated, highly capable, cross-functional sustainable procurement team
6. Utilizing current and future data and digital technology
7. Actively seeking supply-side innovation and opportunity

Sustainable procurement goals

1. Understand, measure and report our supply-side sustainability impacts
2. Only source from suppliers that meet our minimum sustainability requirements
3. No human rights violations and fair treatment of all in our supply chains
4. Net zero supply base by 2035
5. Enable corporate positive contribution through supply side innovation

Sustainable procurement targets

1. Code of conduct mandatory for all suppliers by end yr1
2. Scope 3 emissions reduction of 35% by end yr3
3. Reduce non-renewable energy use in top 25 suppliers by 50% by end yr3
4. Circularity 'take back' supplier reprocessing in place by end yr2
5. Reduce supply-side waste by 50% by end yr3
6. Tier 1 supplier audit and monitoring regime by end yr1
7. 70% water reduction in tier 1 processing suppliers by end yr2
8. Vertically integrate source and primary processing for top two spend area by end yr2
9. 50% use of recycled raw material by end yr3
10. Five major supply-side positive impact projects each year

The supply base areas of focus

One of the main reasons why sustainable programmes fail to adequately address the supply base is the inability to relate a specific goal to exactly what needs to happen on the supply side. This is typically because procurement operates in three dimensions:

- **Products and services** – the products or services we are buying and therefore the optimum way to source these to fulfil the needs of the organization. Here the strategic approach of category management provides the means by which firms organize themselves to do this effectively.
- **Our supply base** – the suppliers we are buying from and how we need to work with our most important suppliers to maximize the value they can provide to us, using the established strategic approach of supplier relationship management (SRM).
- **Our supply chains** – how we understand and can optimize effectiveness of our entire SVCNs using supply chain management.

A crucial step to establishing a sustainable procurement programme is to translate the ambition set by the strategy, goals and individual targets into actions we will take to assess and drive change across each of these and also all of these. As we have already seen, we do not need new strategic approaches but rather to continue to apply category management, supplier relationship management and supply chain management but with a sustainability hat on. Therefore, to enable us to do this we need to consider how our ambition for sustainability will be realized specifically in terms of:

- what we buy;
- who we buy from;
- within our supply chains (and in some cases the full SVCN);

but also considering:

- all of these together as the full supply base.

These form the individual areas of focus for sustainable procurement and success comes by considering each of these separately with our sustainability ambition in mind and determining where we are today and how we will drive change to realize this ambition. They also provide the basis to quantify the gap against our strategy, goals and targets for sustainable procurement and how we will prioritize efforts. Once we have completed the assessment it is possible we may need to refine our goals and targets. The OMEIA®

process and indeed the rest of this book is structured to help do this and we will cover assessment in the next chapter.

Programme mobilization

The final step to establishing a sustainable procurement programme is to mobilize it. A strategy, goals and targets should be carefully considered so they can realistically be achieved. Targets soon become worthless if a function regularly sets targets but fails to achieve them. Therefore, implicit within setting the direction for sustainable procurement is ensuring the right top-down alignment, resources, structure, leadership and governance are in place to create the right conditions for the sustainable procurement ambition to be achieved. There are four key steps within mobilization:

1 **Secure approval** – a sustainable procurement strategy needs top-down approval in order to have credibility and the basis to secure resources. It should also then be incorporated into wider organizational strategies and a fundamental part of what the organization is attempting to achieve.

2 **Secure resources** – as a minimum the function will need to organize itself to deliver the strategy and agree roles and responsibilities, and perhaps a change of structure. It is likely the additional resources will also be required, both in terms of people and the investment to develop capability and systems. It is also likely the organization will need to recruit new capability for sustainability.

3 **Establish governance** – governance is all the interconnected arrangements the organization establishes to enable sustainable procurement and ensure it delivers its objectives. This is given by the 5P governance framework and includes:

   a *People* and how the company organizes and structures itself for sustainable procurement.

   b *Plan* – the sustainable procurement road map and a solid project management approach to deliver it.

   c *Payoff* – how the organization will define and measure sustainable procurement improvements.

   d *Proficiency* – ensuring the right capability, systems and tools for success ongoing.

   e *Promote* – managed communications to drive success.

We will return to the 5P governance framework and how we use it to make sustainable procurement a success in Chapter 14.

4 **Communicate the ambition** – the last 'P' is something we need to get going on right away and so our fourth point for project mobilization is to communicate the ambition. This vital and often neglected step can be the key to success, as it is the activity that secures alignment and support to a common cause. Communication should be both internal (within and outwith the procurement or supply chain function) and externally to suppliers and potentially wider stakeholders, customers, consumers, etc. Each audience may require different messages and communication approaches. Communication is effective by identifying the different stakeholder groups (as we covered earlier) and developing and implementing a communication plan to engage with them. We will also return to this in Chapter 14.

> ## Chapter checkpoint
>
> In this chapter we have explored how we set the direction for sustainability for an organization and in particular for sustainable procurement. Key points we explored are:
>
> 1 *The vision for sustainability* – sustainability in an organization begins by defining the vision for what the organization is setting out to achieve and by when. Procurement must inform this and the vision and direction for sustainable procurement then flows from this.
>
> 2 *The vision and direction of travel* for sustainability is informed from what the shareholders and owners of the company want, by considering the primary impacts of the organization, the current global sustainability agenda and stakeholder expectations.
>
> 3 *Frameworks for sustainability* – there are many frameworks for sustainability available. These vary according to the purpose they serve, which might be legislative, investor, emissions reporting, general standards and industry-specific frameworks.
>
> 4 *Frameworks or philosophies that are relevant for sustainable procurement* include the circular economy, triple bottom line, the UN

Global Compact, the United Nations Guiding Principles, the UN Sustainable Development Goals (SDGs), international standards ISO 26000 and ISO 20400 and the GHG Protocol.

5 *A framework specifically for sustainable procurement* with 30 individual goals was included in this chapter.

6 *The sustainable procurement strategy, goals and targets* can be defined once there is clarity regarding the organizational aims and objectives. Specific goals and targets are set for procurement overall and also for the focus areas of what we buy, who we buy from and our supply chains.

7 *Mobilizing the programme* – The final step to establishing a sustainable procurement programme is to secure approval for the direction of travel, secure resource, establish governance and communicate the ambition.

This concludes Part 2 and our exploration of the sustainability imperative. In the next chapter, and as we move into Part 3, we will begin to explore sustainable procurement and how to realize it within an organization, starting with how we assess the supply base.

PART 3
Sustainable procurement

Assessing the supply base   07

> In this chapter we explore how we assess our organization's position with respect to sustainability in the supply base relative to the strategy, aims and goals we have set. We explore how to assess the gaps from our supply-side sustainability ambition in terms of what we buy, who we buy from and our supply chains by considering the areas of greatest impact or 'hot spots' that we can use to determine and prioritize sustainability projects to realize our goals. We also explore how to assess supply-side GHG emissions.
>
> *Pathway questions addressed in this chapter*
>
> 7 How can we assess sustainability within our procurement?
> 8 What improvement areas should we focus on first?

Where to start with assessment

The sustainability assessment is the process of determining, and where possible measuring, how sustainable procurement is with respect to the ambition and direction of travel we have set for sustainability. It is, in essence, about determining the gap from where we are today against the goals we have set. From here we can begin to shape the potential improvement initiatives needed to move towards our goals and prioritize which ones we will work on, and when, and how, and direct our precious resource accordingly. In many ways, setting the goals for sustainable procurement is the easy bit, the hard bit is understanding how we stack up against them. This is for all the reasons we have explored so far that make the supply base the most difficult area to understand and effect sustainability as large parts of it are not within our direct sight or control.

Furthermore, assessment is no small task and could easily require an entire army if we set out to examine every supplier, every supply chain and every product or service we sourced. This is clearly impractical so we need a more targeted approach to measure and assess how sustainable our supply base and what we source is relative to our goals. Get this right and measurement and assessment will provide the muscle for effective sustainable procurement. Get this wrong, or without it, our efforts would be nothing more than aimless good intention based upon our inward-facing understanding.

Measurement: the muscle for sustainable procurement

We are assessing sustainability in our supply base relative to our goals, but we also need to measure how sustainable we are if we are to have some sort of baseline to work from. Ideally the goals we have set are SMART so we can know when we have reached them or how far away we might be from them. That is why measurement is a key component within assessment, yet it is not possible to measure all aspects of sustainability. Once, there were precious little aspects of supply-side sustainability that could be measured; however, that has now changed and across the world companies have been figuring out how to measure things that weren't previously measured. This in turn in is driving new methods of corporate reporting and governance. Indeed, in recent years there has been an explosion of companies that can help measure aspects of supply-side sustainability. A decade ago, no one had any idea where to start to measure GHG emissions – now it is fast becoming a core skill for some of those in procurement.

While measuring sustainability is more possible there remain many aspects that are more challenging. We can figure out ways to quantify emissions, pollution levels, resources consumed, volumes recycled and so on, but it becomes much harder when we consider aspects of sustainability that are less quantifiable. The degree to which human rights are upheld, working conditions are acceptable or if workers are fairly treated becomes harder to quantify. However, we can assess such things and determine if they meet minimum requirements set by us or by an international standard or legislation. The problem here becomes how any assessment can be truly credible. Today many of the sustainability claims made by companies are based upon some form of supply-side assessment conducted remotely. Indeed, there are many companies out there, some industry specific and others more generalist, who specialize in providing supplier sustainability ratings determined based upon collection of information about the supplier provided via a remote questionnaire approach. While this is somewhat good, any remote assessment has limitations in terms of fully understanding what is happening with suppliers, especially those in distant geographies where responses cannot easily be verified and where those suppliers are hungry to ensure the right boxes get ticked. That said, this assessment approach is a good first step, but it is by no means definitive. The hard reality is that to truly understand what is happening on the ground within a supply chain we need eyes on it, and not just one time but ongoing. This will be covered in more detail later.

We measure and assess supply-side sustainability across four focus areas; an initial assessment that considers a high-level view across our entire supply base and also more detailed assessments for what we buy, who we buy from and our supply chains. There are a number of steps and tools to help us do this well and these form stage 2 of the OMEIA® sustainable procurement process (Figure 7.1). We will explore each in turn in this and the next chapter.

Start with an SSTP

Begin the initial assessment with the SSTP – Sustainability Situation, Target, Proposal. If you know my other books you will know that I am a big advocate of the STP tool; well, here it is again used specifically to consider our position with respect to sustainability hence the extra 'S.'

The SSTP helps us clarify our initial current situation and starting position, our direction of travel and our next steps for sustainable procurement (or indeed any business scenario, problem or project). It is a hugely powerful means to secure alignment and common purpose within a team. If we have a cross-functional team this tool provides the perfect starting point to pool thinking and get everyone pointing in the same direction. It is incredibly simple to use and best worked collaboratively as a team. Remember to use the tool to consider our starting point, as we will not have many answers yet, but this will help us figure out our initial steps. A template is provided in the Appendix. Build the SSTP as follows:

1 Start with the *Problem statement* – this is the simple definition of the issue or problem we are setting out to address and therefore frames the discussion to complete the SSTP. This might be along the lines of 'we do not know how our supply base compares to our ambition for sustainability or where and how to start driving improvements'.

Figure 7.1 Stage 2 of the OMEIA® process – measure, assess and quantify risks and opportunities

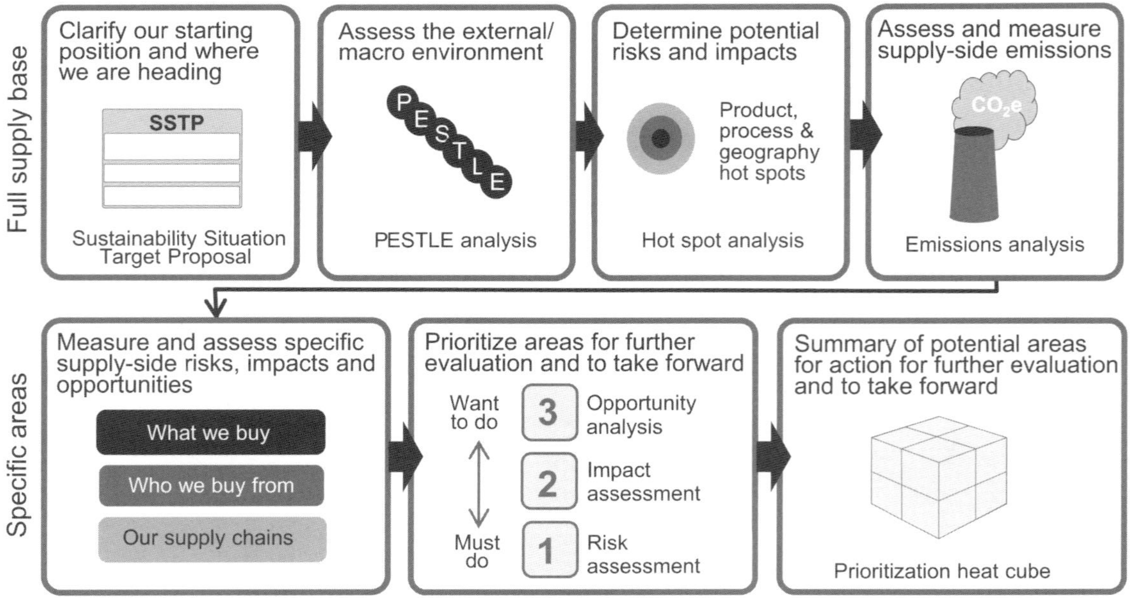

2 Define the *Situation* – consider all the different things we know, facts and data we have, insights, unfounded suspicions, knowledge gained from work done so far and so on. This is a free-flow list and the chance for all involved to pool their knowledge.

3 Determine the *Target(s)* – here we are considering the overall target(s) for our sustainable procurement programme. Remember, by now, we should already have clarity regarding our corporate goals and the specific goals for sustainable procurement, and these are the targets overall, so they do not need to be restated. Instead here we need to state the specific SMART targets for our sustainable procurement programme in order to progress through the OMEIA® process and therefore realize our overall ambition and goals. This might include such things as key deliverables and their associated timings for aspects of the supply-side assessment, having the programme plan finalized, setting up governance and so on.

4 Determine the *Proposal* – the proposal is where we define our next steps or the specific course(s) of action we will go and take. Once again, this is specifically about how we progress our sustainable procurement programme, not the improvement projects we might go and do within our supply base as we have yet to determine these. Therefore, the proposal must directly respond to the targets we have set with statements that define what we will do to meet our targets.

Figure 7.2 gives an example of a completed SSTP.

Using PESTLE to understand the macro environment

Arguably the PESTLE tool is one of the most important tools to support a sustainable procurement programme (Figure 7.3). PESTLE (or one of the many variants using a slightly different acronym) is the tool we use to assess the external or macro environment within which we exist and operate and the specific drivers, forces, trends, changes or potential impacts we need to consider or respond to in terms of our sourcing. If you know my other books you will know it is a key tool to help determine a category strategy, it helps determine how we might need to manage key supplier relationships and is part of how we approach negotiation planning. The PESTLE tool became invaluable for procurement practitioners following Covid-19 and subsequently the invasion of Ukraine by Russia, as global supply chains and

Figure 7.2 An example SSTP for a sustainable procurement programme

SSTP (Sustainability Situation, Target, Proposal)

Date: 4th November

Problem statement

We do not know how our supply base compares to our ambition for sustainability or where and how to start driving improvements.

Situation

- For sustainable procurement goals, we suspect only a small number of suppliers could meet these currently, but we don't know
- We have circa 10,000 suppliers but we only have some knowledge of around 150 suppliers and good knowledge of around 30 key suppliers
- We are not equipped or ready to measure GHG emissions yet - legislation requires us to do this within 2 years
- Supplier onboarding asks only basic compliance questions around bribery and corruption. We do no other form of supplier qualification for sustainability
- We suspect human rights issues, especially forced labour for some ingredients within our choc-me-up range where we cannot be certain of country of origin
- We do not understand the vast majority of our supply chains but rely upon immediate suppliers to ensure supply chains are managed

Target

- Initial assessment of our supply base relative to the sustainable procurement goals complete by end May
- Prioritized wave-based programme of improvement projects agreed by end June
- Sustainable procurement improvement projects underway within by end July

Proposal

- Recruit the team and secure the resources needed to progress the programme
- Undertake training in sustainable procurement
- Process sustainable procurement and work through the OMEIA process
- Conduct the focused supply base assessment
- Establish project management, governance and reporting for sustainable procurement

SOURCE © Jonathan O'Brien, 2015

everything we had come to rely upon changed in an instant. Here PESTLE analysis helped to consider the changing macro environment and how to best respond and adapt sourcing.

PESTLE stands for Political, Environmental, Sociological, Technological, Legal and Environmental and is an important tool within sustainable procurement to help us identify areas where we may need to drive sustainability improvements. When we apply PESTLE in this context, we consider both the general trends, changes, drivers, etc but also those specifically within the supply base. This gives a slightly different interpretation of the headings and in this context we consider the people or social dimensions under the sociological heading and the planet or environmental dimensions under environmental. Table 7.1 provides a list of areas to consider when using PESTLE to support sustainable procurement and Figure 7.3 gives an example for EV battery sourcing. A template is also provided in the Appendix. PESTLE analysis is best done in a team as follows:

1 Determine the theme or scope for the PESTLE analysis – PESTLE can be applied at multiple levels to serve different purposes. This could be a product, category, area of supply, supplier, supply chain, company, industry sector or the world at large. Each of these can be useful and provide different insights so the PESTLE tool should be applied throughout a sustainable procurement programme.

2 For each of the headings, *Political, Environmental, Sociological (including people), Technological, Legal* and *Environmental (including planet)*, explore and consider the various drivers, trends, changes, forces or potential impacts for the theme or scope being considered with specific emphasis on the supply base.

3 Ask 'so what does this tell us?' and determine the key insights as well as the areas where further fact finding might be necessary.

4 Determine the potential risks and opportunities and use these, together with all the other insights we will gain, to determine potential sustainability projects.

Sustainable procurement

Table 7.1 PESTLE analysis – areas to consider for sustainable procurement

PESTLE heading	Areas to consider
Political	• Political stability of territories we source from/goods pass through • Socio/environmental regulations and degree of enforcement for the territories/suppliers/supply chain we source from • Government grants or subsidies for sustainable initiatives/progress • Tariff or trade barriers, import or export rules based upon socio/environmental factors • International trade policies • Renewable energy and climate policies • Environmental permits • Sustainable industry job creation
Economic	• Growth of market (esp growth in demand for sustainability) • Economic outlook for us and for those in the supply base and what this means • Uplift in cost of raw materials that are becoming scarce • Cost of sustainability • Cost of labour if human rights are upheld • Cost of logistics • Regional tax regimes and tax incentives for sustainability • Interest rates and how this impacts those in the supply base • Inflation and its effects • Exchange rate fluctuation and how this impacts those in the supply base • Cost savings from waste reduction

Table 7.1 *continued*

PESTLE heading	Areas to consider
Sociological	• Respect for human rights through the supply base • Attitudes towards First Nations people • Future demand from population growth and lifestyle consumption • Diversity and inclusion • Distribution of wealth (and in particular living wage and to poor households) in the supply base • Education of consumer/customer re supply-side sustainability factors • Changes in expectations (of customers, stakeholders and those in the supply chain) • Demand for sustainability • Working conditions • Health impacts from poor sustainability
Technological	• New technologies especially those to help sustainability, e.g. carbon capture, new recycling technologies, etc • Energy demands and means of production • Speed of obsolescence • Access to, and freedom on, the internet through the supply base • Protection of personal data for those in the supply base • Infrastructure changes or emerging infrastructure that drives sustainability, e.g. EV charging capacity, renewable energy, etc • Use of technology to monitor compliance at remote factories • Logistics technology changes • Packaging technologies and reduction of waste
Legal	• Supply-side sustainability legislation – now and on the way • Socio/environmental regulations for the territories/suppliers/supply chain we source from and levels of enforcement • Legislation that makes us responsible for the entire supply chain

Table 7.1 *continued*

PESTLE heading	Areas to consider
Environmental	• Impact of natural changes, catastrophes and threats • Impact of climate change • Waste, recycling and disposal trends • Pollution • Impacts to habitats and biodiversity • Emissions produced • Resource scarcity and consumption and volatility of raw materials

Hot spot analysis

Using hot spot analysis to determine priorities

Hot spot analysis is a pragmatic approach to identify those supply-side areas that are most misaligned with our sustainability ambition. As we have already seen it is virtually impossible to assess our entire supply base and consider everything we source, all our suppliers or supply chains, yet we need to start somewhere. Hot spot analysis helps here and works by reviewing what the organization does, the key areas of spend and identifying those areas that are known to have potential sustainability issues in one or more of the six impact areas. These are the 'hot spots'. It is similar to conducting a risk assessment except here we would be checking against a list of known possible risks.

If you tune in to all the discussion and information being exchanged around sustainability, there are a number of areas that regularly get flagged up as problematic. Ask someone what the most concerning products are, and you might hear cocoa beans, textiles, palm oil, etc. Clearly these are hot spots yet there are many more besides. In fact, hot spots fall into three categories:

- **Product hot spots** – raw materials or products where there are known or potential social or environmental impacts.
- **Process hot spots** – known industry sectors or processes that potentially give rise to detrimental social or environmental impacts.

Figure 7.3 An example PESTLE analysis for EV battery sourcing

Heading	Drivers, changes, trends, impacts, risks & opportunities
Political	- New legislation prohibiting sale of hydrocarbon-powered vehicles in near term - China dominates and controls global extraction and processing of most raw materials – almost impossible to set up alternative supply chains of any capacity - Chinese industrial policy to gain control provides a risk of single point of failure – China already own most cobalt mines in DRC, they continue to acquire rights to other raw material reserves and are taking stakes in key players including EV start-ups enabling them to integrate supply chains - Risk of impact of new geopolitical tensions could completely disrupt supply chains - Incentives by South American countries to support lithium mining crowds out the agricultural sector
Economic	- Exponential growth in market for EV batteries - Risk China applies export tariffs - Cost of lithium extraction becoming less cost prohibitive closer to home. Old closed lithium mines now reopening (e.g. in Cornwall) - Impact and risk from future increased likelihood of greater exchange rate volatility
Sociological	- Consumer expectations of action to halt climate change – perception of EVs being clean solution - Massive shift to EVs and exponential demand (circa +500 million new vehicles over the next 20 years) - Growing concerns and consumer awareness regarding impact in battery production - Significant human rights abuses and poor working at most raw material sources. - Lithium reserves and mineral rights being taken from indigenous peoples by government in Bolivia - Child labour involved in some cobalt mining in DRC – difficulties detecting and policing
Technological	- Likely shift in battery technology in the short term could pivot this industry in an instant - Higher-capacity battery technology holds potential to reduce cost and detrimental impacts - New processing technologies to reduce water use for lithium processing in development - Potential for silicon to replace use of graphite for anode source (lithium-ion only) to open up new supply chain option
Legal	- New legislation making companies responsible for everything that happens in the supply chain difficult to meet due to lack of ability to gain control over original parts of the supply chains
Environmental	- High transportation miles – raw materials shipped to China for processing and then to the West - Energy-intensive production – China increasing use of renewables - Current recycling of old batteries inadequate and a significant amount of materials are not currently being recycled - Mass impacts to agricultural land from pollution and waste from lithium mining in Chile, Argentina and Bolivia - Lithium mining highly water intensive

SOURCES Baxter (2020); Picarsic (2020)

- **Geography hot spots** – specific territories or regions where there may be concerning practices and any sourcing from these regions may be tainted by detrimental social or environmental impacts.

Just because we source a particular hot spot product, or it comes from a hot spot geography, doesn't mean we are sourcing unsustainably, but rather it means there is a likelihood there may be some impacts and so these become the areas we need to give the most attention to initially and investigate more fully what happens before the goods (or service) get to us.

Over the next three sections I will expand each of the three hot spot areas and provide a list of potential hot spots for each. These are by no means definitive and new hot spots are emerging all the time. Therefore, it is a good idea to develop and maintain your own supply-side hot spot register, perhaps using what I have included here as the starting point. Building a hot spot register is simply a case of getting a group of people with knowledge in this area to think about and document potential hot spots and augment that with research, then maintaining it ongoing. Typically, within an organization, there is already a built-up knowledge of what the hot spots might be, but this is rarely rounded up. In the same way that an organization might maintain a risk register, we should maintain a hot spot register and use this on an ongoing basis. There are a number of good sources of information that can help to build and maintain a hot spot list and these help with sustainable procurement in many other ways too. These are given in Table 7.2.

Table 7.2 Sources of information to build a hot spot list (and to help support a sustainable procurement programme)

Source	How this helps	URL
General useful information		
United Nations Environment Programme	Wide range of publications and data including some real-time data tools for global environmental information	unep.org
FedCenter	Range of US environmental data	www.fedcenter.gov
The World Bank	Entire section dedicated to data sets about world issues, sustainability and economic factors	datacatalog.worldbank.org

Table 7.2 *continued*

Source	How this helps	URL
Eurostat	EU data and statistics including sustainability and environmental	ec.europa.eu
Global Corruption Barometer	Interactive map and extensive resources on corruption around the world	transparency.org
Sedex – Sustainability legislation	Membership organization providing online platform and tools, including list of sustainability legislation by country	sedex.com
IPBES	IPBES – intergovernmental science-based platform on biodiversity and ecosystems services	ipbes.net
Worldometers	Website that provides counters and real-time statistics for various subjects	worldometers.info
Fraser Institute	Publishes the Human Freedom Index	fraserinstitute.org
Global Atlas of Environmental Justice	Incredibly useful website that lists all the instances of where industry or other human activity is significantly in conflict with the planet	ejatlas.org
World Business Council for Sustainable Development	CEO-led community of 200+ sustainable businesses with a range of papers and downloads	wbcsd.org
World Resources Institute	Global research organization for sustainability with a range of data and publications	wri.org
SRI BES index	Comprehensive set of global data on biodiversity loss, including the SRI BES index	swissre.com

Sustainable procurement

Table 7.2 *continued*

Source	How this helps	URL
Sources about resources and waste		
Royal Society of Chemistry	Periodic table based information on elements including scarcity, sources, global risk, etc	rsc.org
US Geological Survey	Wide range of publications and information about world resources and earth conditions	usgs.gov
Sources about emissions		
GHG Protocol	Sets the standards to measure and manage emissions with a range of very useful resources	ghgprotocol.org
The Carbon Trust	Company that specializes in helping organizations achieve net zero emissions	carbontrust.com
CO_2 Everything	Website that provides kg CO_2 data for household products	co2everything.com
Sources about people		
International Labour Organization	US focused – sets labour standards, develops policies and programmes promoting decent work for all women and men	ilo.org
World Economic Forum	Global Gender Gap Report – benchmarks gender-based gaps globally and tracks progress towards closing these over time	weforum.org
Freedom House	Country-by-country reports and data on degree of freedom, internet freedom, democracy and human rights	freedomhouse.org
International Labour Organization	Extensive website of child labour survey reports by country (part of ILO)	ilo.org

Table 7.2 *continued*

Source	How this helps	URL
Global Rights Index	Rates countries depending on their compliance with collective labour rights and violations by governments and employers	globalrightsindex.org
US Department of Labor	Vast range of resources including full listings of child and forced labour and human trafficking by country or product	dol.gov
UNCTAD data protection and privacy	Interactive map and resources about degree of data protection and privacy worldwide	unctad.org
Ethical brands		
Good On You	Website that rates thousands of apparel brands	directory.goodonyou.eco

Product hot spots

Product hot spots are products or services where there is a high likelihood that there are detrimental impacts associated with the raw materials, production, processing, provision, transportation, use or disposal of a given product or service. By considering whether we are sourcing any hot spot products we can quickly identify if there are any areas worthy of further investigation. Product hot spots are possibly the most obvious as they tend to be the starting point for targeting sustainability actions and what most companies will naturally start with. Published articles or those providing instruction on sustainability will be quick to illustrate impacts by citing problematic products; if you buy chocolate perhaps the cocoa beans might have been picked or processed by forced labour, depending upon where they originate from, or if you buy cotton then the washing process has consumed huge amounts of water, and so on.

Product hot spots is a great place to start. Indeed, this is exactly how retailers have typically approached sustainability – by considering what products on the shelves might have the highest likelihood of detrimental impacts in their supply chains. The UK retailer B&Q, owned by the Kingfisher Group (that also includes Brico Dépôt and Castorama in Europe) was one of the first retailers to take sustainability seriously at the start of this century. It set out to create a store where the products on its shelves were sustainable. The challenge, however, was where to start with the circa 44,000 items it stocked. The answer it came up with was to consider the product hot spots and identify those products that were known could involve potentially problematic impacts in their supply chains or indeed within the specification of the product. In effect it developed a product hot spot list and then used this as a basis to prioritize efforts to drive sustainability. Starting with a handful of products including rugs, timber (lumber) and paint, B&Q took the first steps on a sustainability program that would overhaul its standing in this area one range at a time.

Table 7.3 lists the potential product hot spots and the nature of the potential impacts where further investigation might we warranted. This can be used as a starting point to further build a company-specific hot spot list.

Table 7.3 Potential product hot spots

Product area	Potential impact
Beef	Drives deforestation and livestock farming produces significant GHGs (varies according to feed used). Risk of child labour to manage livestock in some regions
Bricks	Significant risk of forced labour and child labour[2]
Cereals (excl rice)	Drives tropical deforestation (accounts for 9.6% of deforestation)[1]
Cocoa	Drives deforestation, risk of forced labour and child labour for harvesting and processing[2] in some regions
Coconuts	Risk of monkey labour (chained monkeys trained to scale trees to retrieve coconuts) – especially in Thailand and Sri Lanka
Coffee	Risk of forced labour, child labour in some regions[2]
Cotton	High water consumption for washing process, risk of child labour harvesting and processing in some regions

Table 7.3 *continued*

Product area	Potential impact
Diamonds	Risk of child labour, forced labour, poor working conditions and other human rights violations. Very high environmental impact from mining process (up to 400 times amount of earth removal for each diamond). Very high risk of supporting war and terrorism if 'conflict' or 'blood diamonds' from areas including Democratic Republic of Congo, Angola and Sierra Leone. Applies to all diamonds except those sourced under the Kimberley Process (a certification scheme that tracks each diamond from mine to store)
Electronics	Use of scarce resources (especially precious metals) and inadequate disposal routes
Fish	Risk of overfishing (species dependent) or unsustainable fishing methods with high by-catch or damage to seabed. Risk of child labour for fishing and processing in some regions
Garments	Risks vary depending upon location and by supplier. High water consumption industry and risk of pollution discharge. Risk of potential worker exposure to hazardous substances (e.g. silica). Standards for workers in big manufacturers at key garment locations generally much improved but less so in lower-tier suppliers – watch for long working hours, poor working conditions, forced labour and child labour[2]
Gold	Potential conflict mineral depending upon source, risk of child labour for extraction in some regions
Soya	Drives deforestation
Oilseeds (incl soya and palm oil)	Drives tropical deforestation (nearly 20% of deforestation comes from expansion for oilseed production, mostly soybean and palm oil)[1]
Palm oil	Drives deforestation
Paper and wood	Drives tropical deforestation (accounts for 13% of deforestation)[1]
Pornography	Risk of forced labour and child labour[2]

Table 7.3 *continued*

Product area	Potential impact
Rare earth metals	Seventeen rare earth metals (scandium, yttrium, lanthanum, cerium, praseodymium, neodymium, promethium, samarium, europium, gadolinium, terbium, dysprosium, holmium, erbium, thulium, ytterbium, lutetium). Some are becoming scarce due to increasing demand for electronics applications, some are less scarce but only found in small, highly dispersed quantities making extraction high impact in terms of mining. More than 80% come from China with regulation of exports being introduced
Rice	Risk of child labour for harvesting and processing in some regions,[2] drives tropical deforestation (accounts for 5.6% of deforestation)[1]
Rubber gloves	Risk of poor working conditions in some parts of the world (esp Malaysia)
Rugs	Risk of forced labour[2] and poor working conditions
Sand (for building)	Risk of illegal trades for extraction (sand mafia), risk of over-extraction especially in developing countries with impacts to communities if river beds and ocean shoreline are impacted
Sugar cane	Risk of child labour harvesting and processing in some regions[2]
Tantalum	Potential conflict mineral depending upon source
Tin	Potential conflict mineral depending upon source
Tobacco	Risk of child labour harvesting and processing in some regions[2]
Tungsten	Potential conflict mineral depending upon source
Vegetables, fruit and nuts	Risk of child labour in some regions. Drives tropical deforestation (accounts for 7.3% of deforestation)[1]

SOURCES Adapted from [1]Pendrill et al (2019); [2]USDOL (2022)

Process hot spots

Process hot spots are processes or entire industries where there is a high likelihood there are detrimental impacts associated with what suppliers in this space do (i.e. their primary impacts), the processes they use, the resources consumed, the likely working conditions, etc. By considering if we are sourcing from suppliers with hot spot processes or in hot spot industry sectors, we can identify suppliers we might want to get closer to and understand more fully. It also enables us to understand what processes or practice we might want to target for change if we are driving sustainability improvements. There is, of course, a close correlation between product and process hot spots in some areas. For example, the product hot spot of 'fish' means if we buy fish there might be impacts in the supply chain whereas the process hot spot of 'fishing' means the process of extraction might be unsustainable (e.g. by-catch, bottom trawling, etc). It is important to consider both dimensions. Table 7.4 lists the potential process and industry hot spots

Table 7.4 Potential process or industry hot spots

Process or industry	Potential impact
Agriculture	Depending upon set up – risk of loss of biodiversity for crops and livestock
Cement	Produces large-scale GHGs
Chemical industry	Massively energy intensive and produces large-scale GHGs
Electronic waste processing	Poor working conditions, exposure to hazardous substances, exposure to poor air quality. More than 60 chemical elements are typically found in electronics
Fishing	Depending upon the methods used, risk of loss of biodiversity from by-catch or bottom trawling. Also risk of illegal fishing
Food and tobacco	Energy intensive
Logging	One of the biggest causes of loss of biodiversity, and supports clearing forests and grassland for livestock and crops as well as for wood, biofuel, paper and pulp
Paper and pulp	Energy intensive and potentially driving deforestation

Table 7.4 *continued*

Process or industry	Potential impact
Petrochemical	Massively energy intensive, driving over-extraction of resources and perpetuating use of fossil fuels
Mining	One of the biggest causes of loss of biodiversity. Risk of overextraction of resources, poor working conditions, exposure of workers to hazardous substances (especially silica), risk of child labour and forced labour in some territories
Machinery	Energy intensive
Smelting process	Risk of raw materials from unsustainable sources being blended with sustainable raw material, e.g. corrupt workers mix a proportion of ore mined by child labour with the good ore. Risk of poor working conditions and exposure to hazardous substances
Textiles/garments	Potential issues with forced labour, poor working conditions, exposure of workers to hazardous substances (especially silica), gender inequality and child labour. Resource intensive (especially water consumption for washing)
Tourism	Intensive and nature based – risk of loss of biodiversity
Waste processing	Produces significant GHGs

A key factor that determines process and industry hot spots is poor working conditions and the specific risks, scenarios or exposure to certain chemicals or substances. We can therefore consider process hot spots by looking at what is involved or what is happening within the process rather than the industry. This approach might bring to light other hot spots not readily apparent by the industry. Table 7.5 lists potential process hot spots due to exposure to poor working conditions. Both Tables 7.4 and 7.5 provide a starting point to build a company-specific process hot spot list.

Table 7.5 Potential process hot spots based upon exposure of workers to hazardous working conditions

Process or chemical	Typical industry sectors	Potential impacts
Exposure to asbestos	Mining, construction, agriculture, automotive and some protective textiles	Poor working conditions and exposure of workers to hazardous substances – accounts for >233 million deaths worldwide annually[1]
Sandblasting/exposure to silica	Mining, construction, agriculture, oil and gas, manufacturing, sandblasting and textiles	Poor working conditions and exposure of workers to hazardous substances – accounts for >65,000 deaths worldwide annually (lung cancer and silicosis)[1]
Exposure to heavy metals (lead, mercury, arsenic, cadmium, chromium)	Mining, construction, agriculture, manufacturing, metal production, shipping, utilities, textiles and engineering	Poor working conditions and exposure of workers to hazardous substances (e.g. handling lead, lead poisoning from paint, batteries, etc), poor air quality (e.g. from use of gasoline with lead) – exposure to lead potentially accounts for >900,000 DALYs[2] worldwide annually and exposure to mercury accounts for >2 million DALYs[2] worldwide annually[1]
Solvent-based processes	Printing, construction, plastics, rubber, textiles, leather, manufacturing, dry cleaning, food and drink, tobacco and chemical	Poor working conditions and exposure of workers to hazardous substances, exposure to poor air quality (causes cancer, neurotoxic effects and reproductive toxicity)[1]

Table 7.5 *continued*

Process or chemical	Typical industry sectors	Potential impacts
Dye-based processes	Textiles, food and drink, cosmetics and pharmaceuticals	Poor working conditions and exposure of workers to hazardous substances (causes bladder cancer)[1]
Processes involving nanomaterials	Chemical, food, drink, tobacco, healthcare, engineering and textiles	Risk of poor working conditions by exposure (potential cause of cancer but limited data)
Endocrine disrupting chemicals (EDCs)	Chemical, food, drink, tobacco, healthcare, engineering, textiles, oil and gas, agriculture and construction	Poor working conditions and exposure of workers to hazardous substances
Exposure to pesticides	Agriculture, plantations and chemical	Poor working conditions and exposure of workers to hazardous substances – potentially accounts for 358 million acute poisoning events which affect 44% of farmers annually and >300,000 deaths worldwide annually[1]
Exposure to perfluorinated chemicals (PFAS), including >4,730 man-made chemicals	Chemical, food, drink, tobacco, textiles, construction, electronics, aerospace and automotive	Poor working conditions and exposure of workers to hazardous substances

SOURCES Adapted from [1]ILO (2021); [2]DALYs – Days Adjusted Life Years – a time-based measure that combines years of life lost due to premature mortality

Geography hot spots

Geography hot spots are countries or regions of the world where there is a high likelihood that there are detrimental impacts if we are sourcing from suppliers in these territories, or if the goods or services we are sourcing pass through or are processed in some way in these territories. By considering if we source from geographies where there are known potential problems, we can identify those suppliers and supply chains we might want to examine more fully. It doesn't follow that just because a supplier or supply chain is present in a geography hot spot their operations are causing detrimental impacts or we should not use them, but rather that we need to examine what they do more closely as there is potential risk.

Establishing a reliable set of geography hot spots is the most difficult of all. This is because there is little data for some areas and for others there are multiple sets of data that consider various impacts. Furthermore, there is no single or established measure by country but rather we can establish geography hot spots only by considering a range of available information; some at country level, some at a regional level and, as is the case for biodiversity impact, some based upon the geological features of the world rather than its political boundaries. There are many data sources out there that help build and maintain a register of geography hot spots (given in Table 7.2) and these provide a starting point. However, for a geography register to be useful it needs to consider as many of the potential impact areas as possible and this presents a further challenge as available data tends to focus on one specific area.

Table 7.6 provides a list of the potential geography hot spots. This was compiled from several sets of impact data and were combined with interpretation to provide a single visual measure. There is a health warning with this as it is only intended to provide a starting point; further, more rigorous research is recommended to establish a geography hot spot register for an organization or indeed as the basis to determine a given course of action to drive sustainability. The indicators in Table 7.6 are determined from a number of factors:

- Degree of child labour and forced labour by country based upon the extent of different industries and ranges of products produced by that nation that have been found to have a strong likelihood of involving these practices. This gives an indication of a key aspect of human rights violations by country.
- Level of CO_2 emissions by country as in indicator of overall GHG risks.
- The level of corruption by country.
- The perceptions of freedom of citizens by country (including perceptions of rule of law, legal system, security and safety, freedom of movement, religion, expression and information, etc).
- An indicator of biodiversity loss risk based upon how biologically rich or unique in terms of biodiversity a region is, together with how much this region is threatened or already impacted and also the lack of regulation or enforced protection to safeguard nature.

Table 7.6 Potential geography hot spots

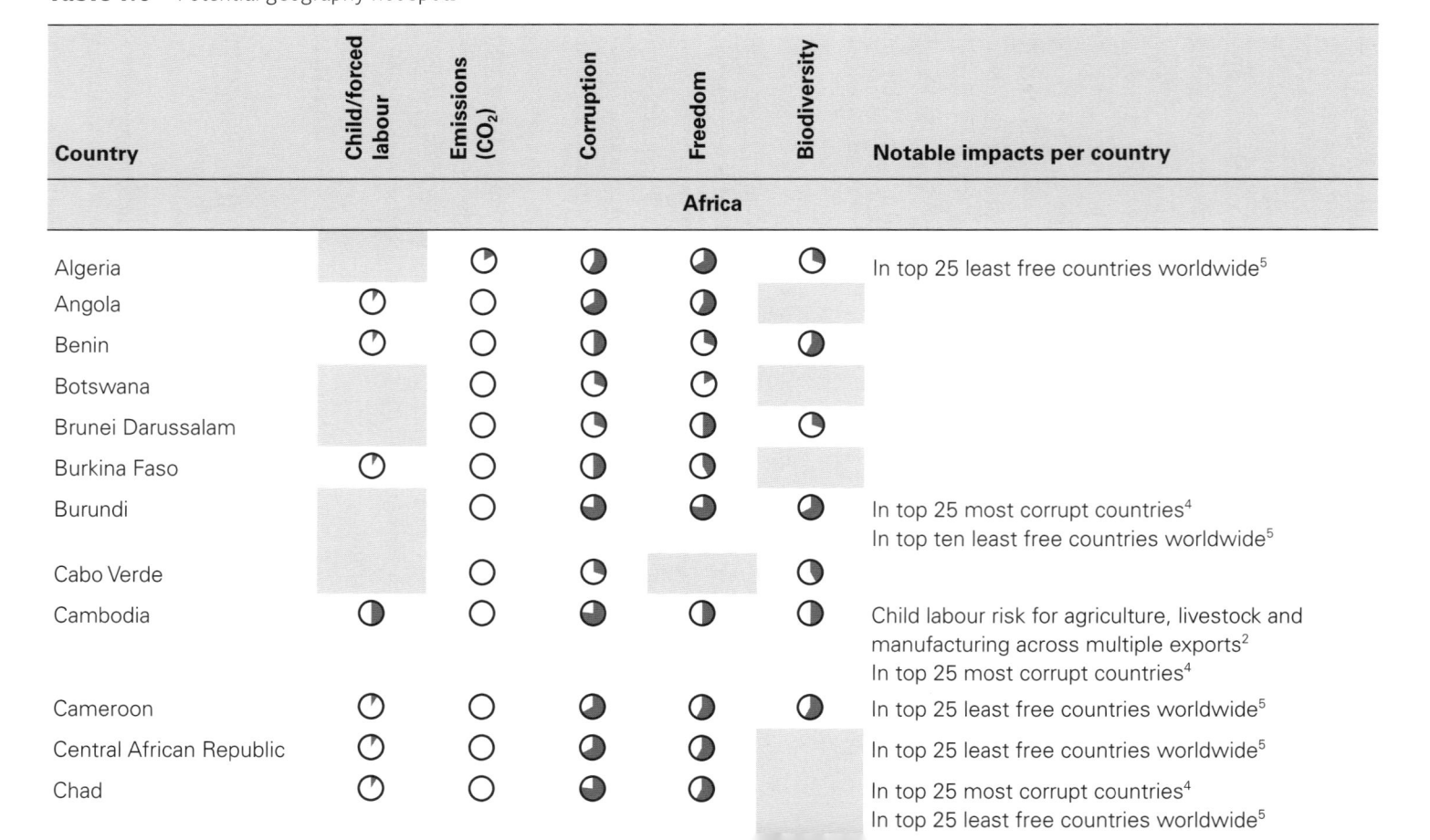

Country	Child/forced labour	Emissions (CO$_2$)	Corruption	Freedom	Biodiversity	Notable impacts per country
			Africa			
Algeria		○	●	●	◐	In top 25 least free countries worldwide[5]
Angola	◐	○	●	◐		
Benin	◐	○	◐	◐	◐	
Botswana		○	○	◐	◐	
Brunei Darussalam		○	◐	◐		
Burkina Faso	◐	○	◐	◐	◐	
Burundi		○	●	●	◐	In top 25 most corrupt countries[4] In top ten least free countries worldwide[5]
Cabo Verde		○	◐			
Cambodia	●	○	●	◐	◐	Child labour risk for agriculture, livestock and manufacturing across multiple exports[2] In top 25 most corrupt countries[4]
Cameroon	◐	○		●		In top 25 least free countries worldwide[5]
Central African Republic	◐	○	●	●		In top 25 most corrupt countries[4] In top 25 least free countries worldwide[5]
Chad	◐	○	●	◐		In top 25 most corrupt countries[4] In top 25 least free countries worldwide[5]

Country						Notes
Comoros						
Congo						In top 25 most corrupt countries[4]
						In top 25 least free countries worldwide[5]
Côte d'Ivoire						Child and forced labour risk for coffee and cocoa exports[2]
Democratic Republic of the Congo						Child and forced labour risk for mining cobalt, copper, diamonds, gold, tantalum, tin and tungsten[2]
						In top 25 most corrupt countries[4]
						In top 25 least free countries worldwide[5]
Djibouti						
Egypt						Fifth least free country worldwide[5]
Equatorial Guinea						One of the ten most corrupt countries[4]
Eritrea						In top 25 most corrupt countries[4]
Eswatini						
Ethiopia						
Gabon						
Gambia						
Ghana						
Guinea						Child labour risk for cashews, coffee, cocoa, diamonds and gold[2]

Table 7.6 continued

Country	Child/forced labour	Emissions (CO_2)	Corruption	Freedom	Biodiversity	Notable impacts per country
Guinea Bissau		○	◐		◐	In top 25 most corrupt countries[4]
Kenya	◐	○	◐	◐		Child labour risk for exports that are harvested and some gold mining[2]
Lesotho	◐	○	◐	◐		
Liberia	◐	○	◐	◐	◐	
Libya		◐	◐	◐	◐	One of the ten most corrupt countries[4] In top ten least free countries worldwide[5]
Madagascar	◐	○	◐	◐	◐	
Malawi	◐	○	◐	◐		
Mali	◐	○	◐	◐		In top 25 most corrupt countries[4]
Mauritania		○	◐	◐		
Mauritius		○	◐	◐	◐	
Morocco	◐	○	◐	◐	◐	
Mozambique		○	◐	◐	◐	
Namibia		○	◐	◐	◐	In top 25 least free countries worldwide[5]

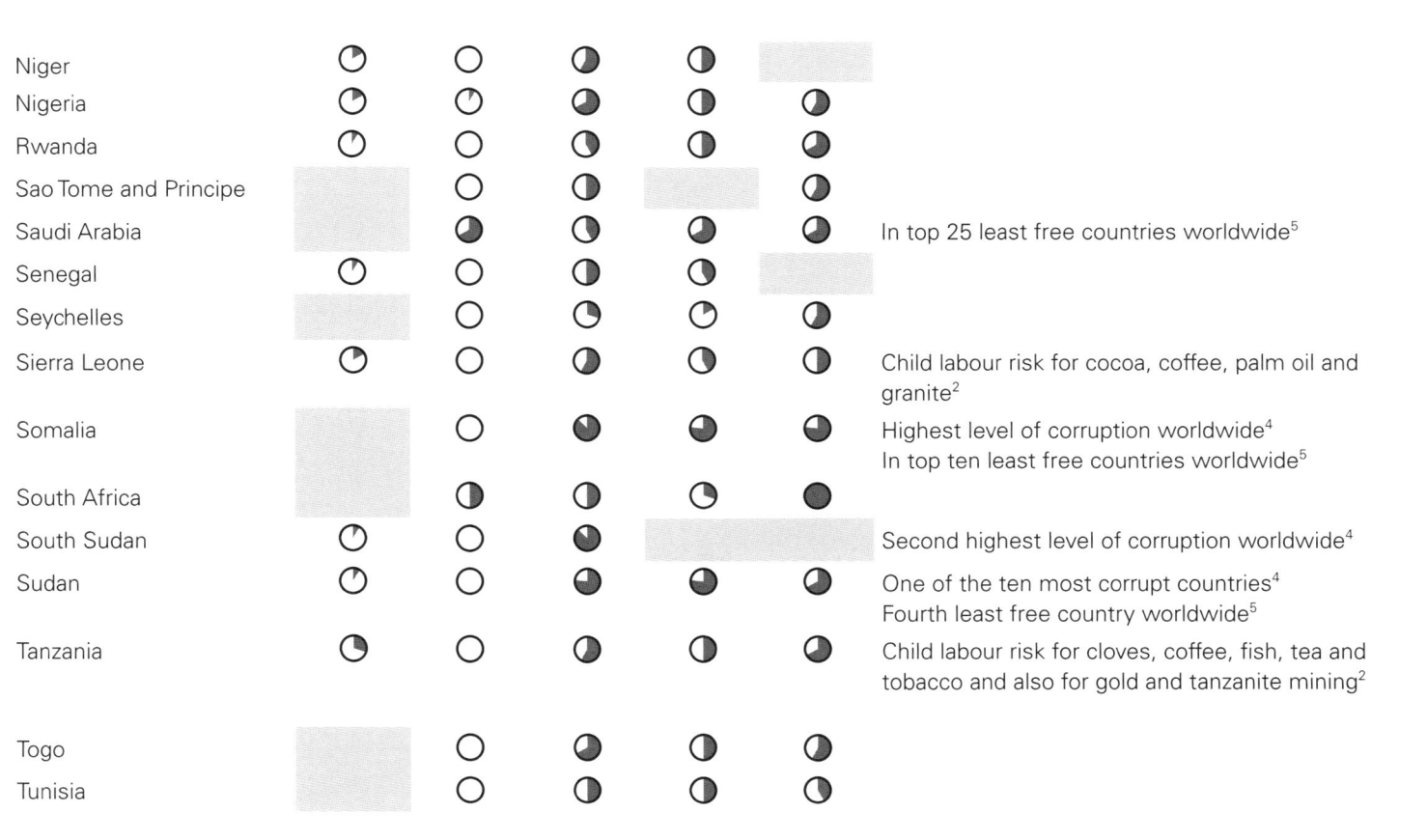

Country					Notes
Niger	◐	○	◐	◐	
Nigeria	◐	○	◐	◐	
Rwanda	◐	○	◐	◐	
Sao Tome and Principe		◐	◐	◐	
Saudi Arabia	◐	●	◐	◐	In top 25 least free countries worldwide[5]
Senegal		○	◐	◐	
Seychelles	◐	○	◑	◐	
Sierra Leone		○	◐	◐	Child labour risk for cocoa, coffee, palm oil and granite[2]
Somalia		○	◐	◐	Highest level of corruption worldwide[4] In top ten least free countries worldwide[5]
South Africa	◐	◐	◐	●	
South Sudan	◐	○	◐	◐	Second highest level of corruption worldwide[4]
Sudan	◐	○	◐	◐	One of the ten most corrupt countries[4] Fourth least free country worldwide[5]
Tanzania	◐	○	◐	◐	Child labour risk for cloves, coffee, fish, tea and tobacco and also for gold and tanzanite mining[2]
Togo		○	◐	◐	
Tunisia		○	◐	◐	

Table 7.6 continued

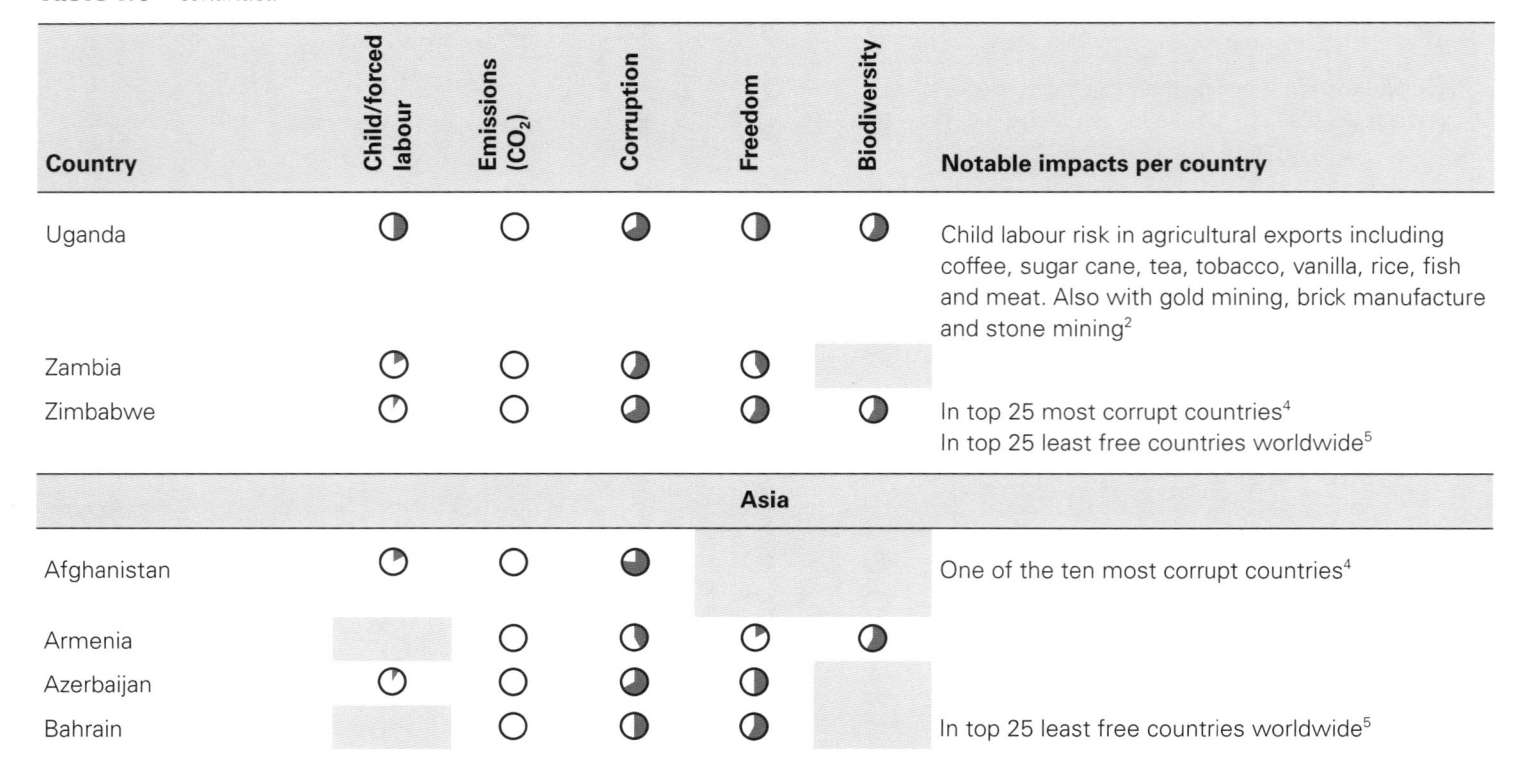

Country	Child/forced labour	Emissions (CO$_2$)	Corruption	Freedom	Biodiversity	Notable impacts per country
Uganda	◐	○	◐	◐	◐	Child labour risk in agricultural exports including coffee, sugar cane, tea, tobacco, vanilla, rice, fish and meat. Also with gold mining, brick manufacture and stone mining[2]
Zambia	◑	○	◕	◕		
Zimbabwe	◑	○	◕	◕	◐	In top 25 most corrupt countries[4] In top 25 least free countries worldwide[5]
Asia						
Afghanistan	◑	○	◐	◐	◐	One of the ten most corrupt countries[4]
Armenia		○	◕	◕		
Azerbaijan	◑	○	◕	◕		
Bahrain		○	◕	◕		In top 25 least free countries worldwide[5]

Bangladesh	◐	◐	◔	◐	◐	◐	Child labour risk across multiple industries including footwear, furniture, garments and other textiles, leather, glass, brick manufacture, poultry, salt, shrimp and soap. Forced labour risk in fishing industry[2].
In top 25 least free countries worldwide[5]
Bhutan		◐	◐	○	◐	◐	
Burma			●	○			Child and forced labour risk across multiple industries including brick manufacture, rice, rubber, beans, sugar cane, teak, precious stones, sesame, shrimp, sunflowers and garments[2]
China	◐	◐	●	◐	◐	◐	Child labour risk in fishing industry, footwear, garments and textiles, hair products, tomato products, artificial flowers, Christmas decorations and coal. Forced labour risk in brick manufacture, cotton and yarn, electronics industry, fireworks, textiles and toys[2]
Biggest CO_2 emitter >10bn tonnes pa[3]
In top 25 least free countries worldwide[5]
Hong Kong		◑	◐	◐	◐		

Table 7.6 continued

Country	Child/forced labour	Emissions (CO$_2$)	Corruption	Freedom	Biodiversity	Notable impacts per country
India	●	◐	◔	◐	◐	Child labour risk across multiple industries especially where items are manufactured including footwear, leather goods, silk, cotton and yarn, soccer balls, sugar cane, precious stones, fireworks, incense, locks, matches, brasswear and fireworks. Child and forced labour risk for brick manufacture, carpets, rice, garments, sandstone, stones, cottonseed[2] Accounts for 1.41% of tropical deforestation[1] Third biggest CO$_2$ emitter (2.5bn tonnes pa)[3]
Indonesia	◔	◐	◐	◐	◐	Child and forced labour risk for footwear, gold, tin, rubber, tobacco, fish and palm oil[2] Accounts for 13.9% of tropical deforestation and supplies 57% of world's palm oil[1]
Iran	◔	◐	◐	◐	◐	In top ten least free countries worldwide[5]
Iraq		◔	◐	◐	◐	In top 25 most corrupt countries[4]
Israel		◔	◔	◔	◐	In top ten least free countries worldwide[5]

Japan				●	Fifth biggest CO_2 emitter (1.2bn tonnes pa)[3]
Jordan	◐			○	
Kazakhstan				◐	
Kuwait	◐			○	
Kyrgyz Republic (Kyrgyzstan)				○	
Laos	◐			○	
Lebanon	◐			○	
Malaysia				◐	Forced labour risk in electronics, garments rubber gloves and palm oil. Some child labour risk for palm oil also[2]. Supplies 27% of world's palm oil[1]
Maldives	◐			○	
Mongolia	◐			○	In top 25 least free countries worldwide[5]
Myanmar				○	Child and forced labour risk for brick manufacture, carpets, stones and some textiles[2]
Nepal	◐			○	
North Korea	◐			◐	Forced labour risk for brick manufacture, cement, coal, gold, iron, textiles and timber[2]. One of the ten most corrupt countries[4]
Oman				◐	

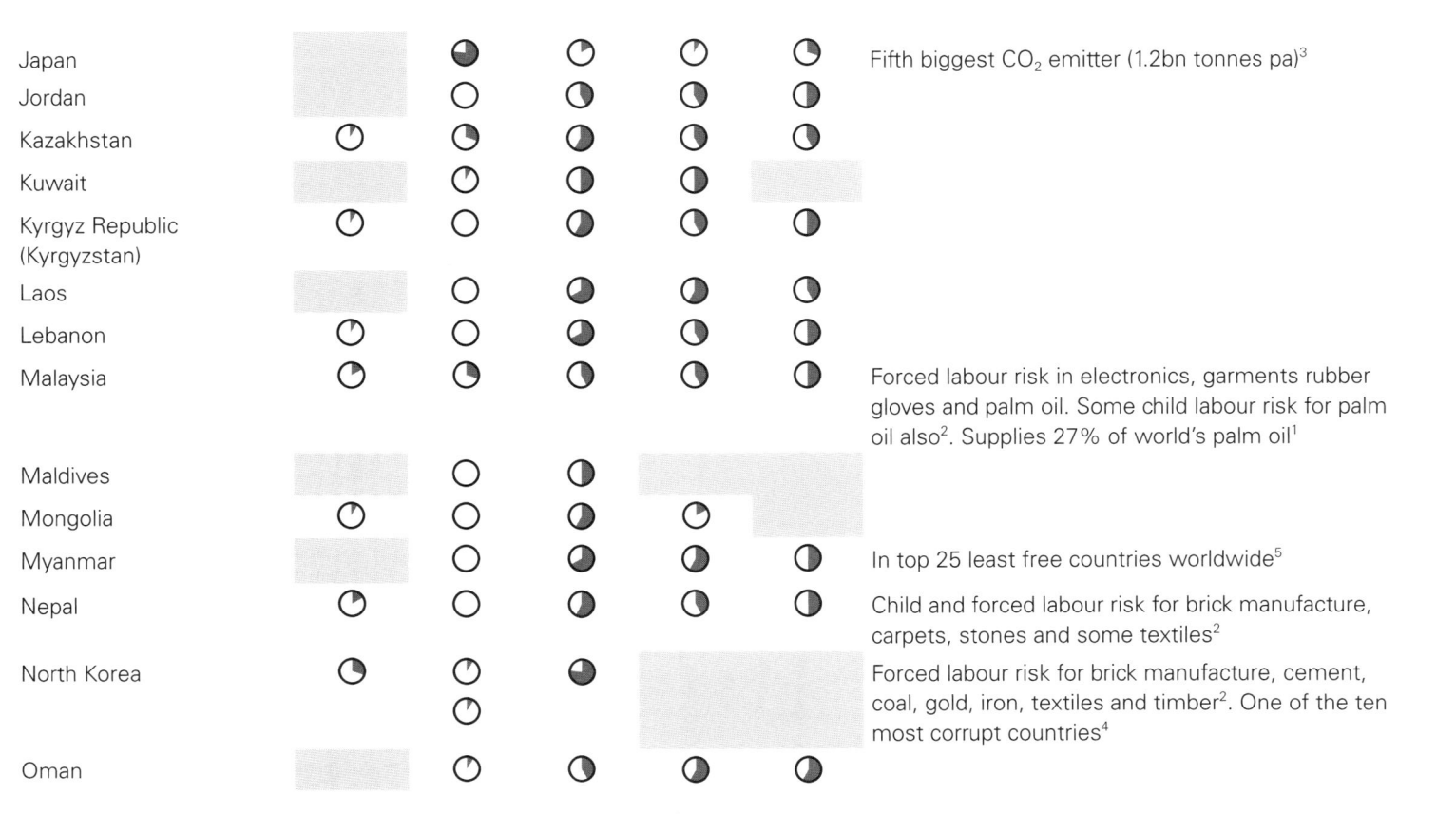

Table 7.6 continued

Country	Child/forced labour	Emissions (CO$_2$)	Corruption	Freedom	Biodiversity	Notable impacts per country
Pakistan	◐	◐	◐	◐	◐	Child and forced labour risk across leather, cotton, sugar cane, wheat, bricks, carpets, coal and surgical instruments[2]. In top 25 least free countries worldwide[5]
Philippines	◐	◐	◐	◐	◐	Child labour risk in agriculture including bananas, coconuts, corn, fish, rice, sugar cane and tobacco. Also in fashion accessories, rubber and pyrotechnics. Risk of child exploitation for pornography[2]
Qatar		◐	◐	◐	◐	
Singapore		◐	○	◐		
South Korea		●	◐	◐		
Sri Lanka		○	◐	◐	◐	
Syria		○	●	●		Third most corrupt country worldwide[4]. The least free country worldwide[5]
Taiwan	◐	◐	◐	◐		

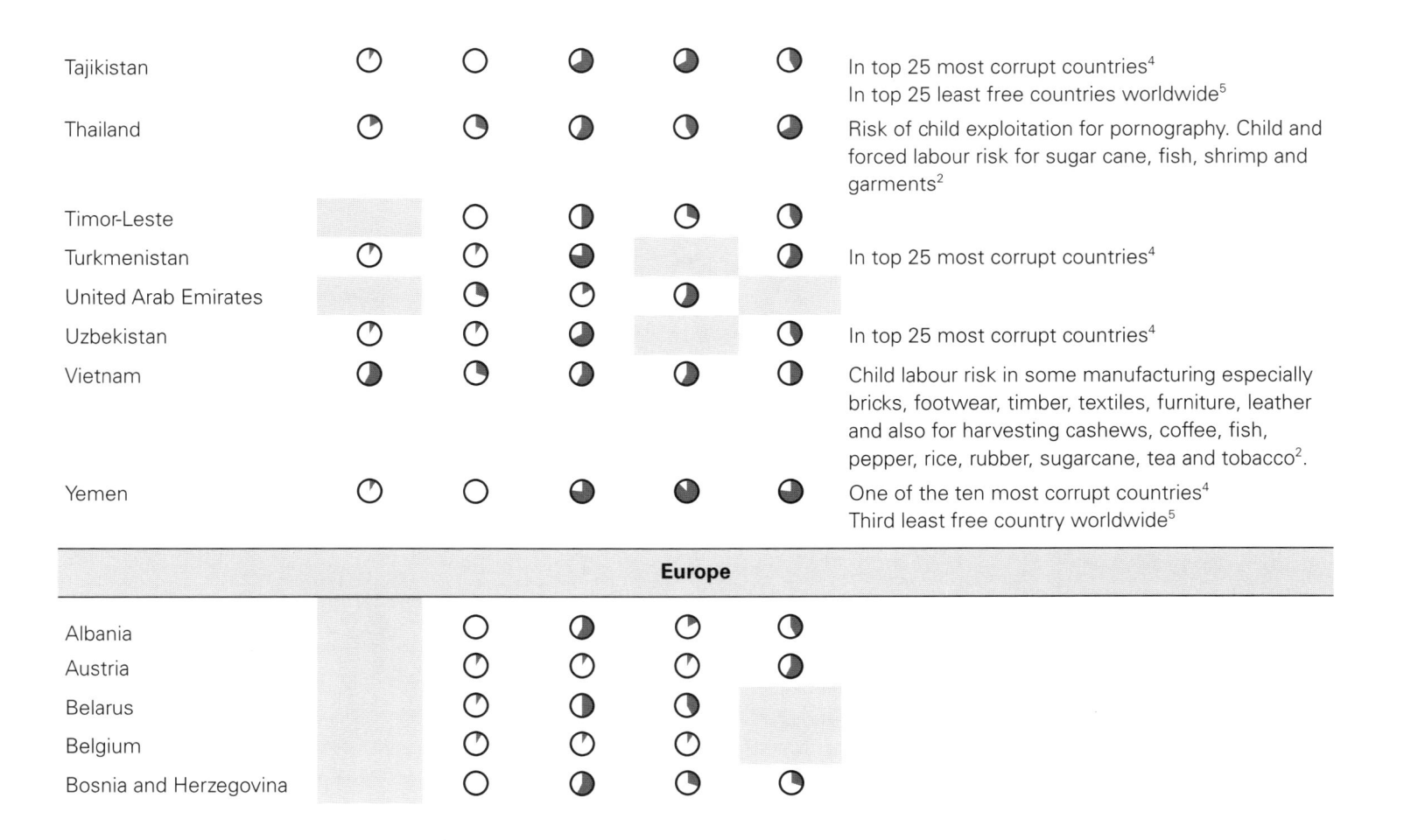

Tajikistan	◐	○	◐	◐	In top 25 most corrupt countries[4] In top 25 least free countries worldwide[5]
Thailand	◐	◐	◐	◐	Risk of child exploitation for pornography. Child and forced labour risk for sugar cane, fish, shrimp and garments[2]
Timor-Leste		○	◐	◐	
Turkmenistan	◐	◐	◐	◐	In top 25 most corrupt countries[4]
United Arab Emirates	◐	◐			
Uzbekistan	◐	◐	◐	◐	In top 25 most corrupt countries[4]
Vietnam	◐	◐	◐	◐	Child labour risk in some manufacturing especially bricks, footwear, timber, textiles, furniture, leather and also for harvesting cashews, coffee, fish, pepper, rice, rubber, sugarcane, tea and tobacco[2].
Yemen	◐	○	◐	◐	One of the ten most corrupt countries[4] Third least free country worldwide[5]

Europe

Albania	○	◐	◐	◐
Austria	◐	◐	◐	◐
Belarus	◐	◐	◐	
Belgium	○	◐	◐	
Bosnia and Herzegovina	○	◐	◐	◐

Table 7.6 continued

Country	Child/forced labour	Emissions (CO$_2$)	Corruption	Freedom	Biodiversity	Notable impacts per country
Bulgaria		◐	◐	◐		
Croatia		◯	◐	◐	◔	
Cyprus		◯	◐			
Czechia/Czech republic		◯	◐	◯		
Denmark		◯	◯	◯		
Estonia		◯	◯	◯	◐	
Finland		◐	◐	◐	◐	
France		◯	◐	◐		
Georgia		◐	◐	◐	◐	
Germany		◉	◐	◐		Sixth biggest CO$_2$ emitter (775m tonnes pa)[3]
Greece		◐	◐	◐		
Hungary		◐	◐	◐	◐	
Iceland		◯	◐	◯		
Ireland		◐	◐	◯	◐	

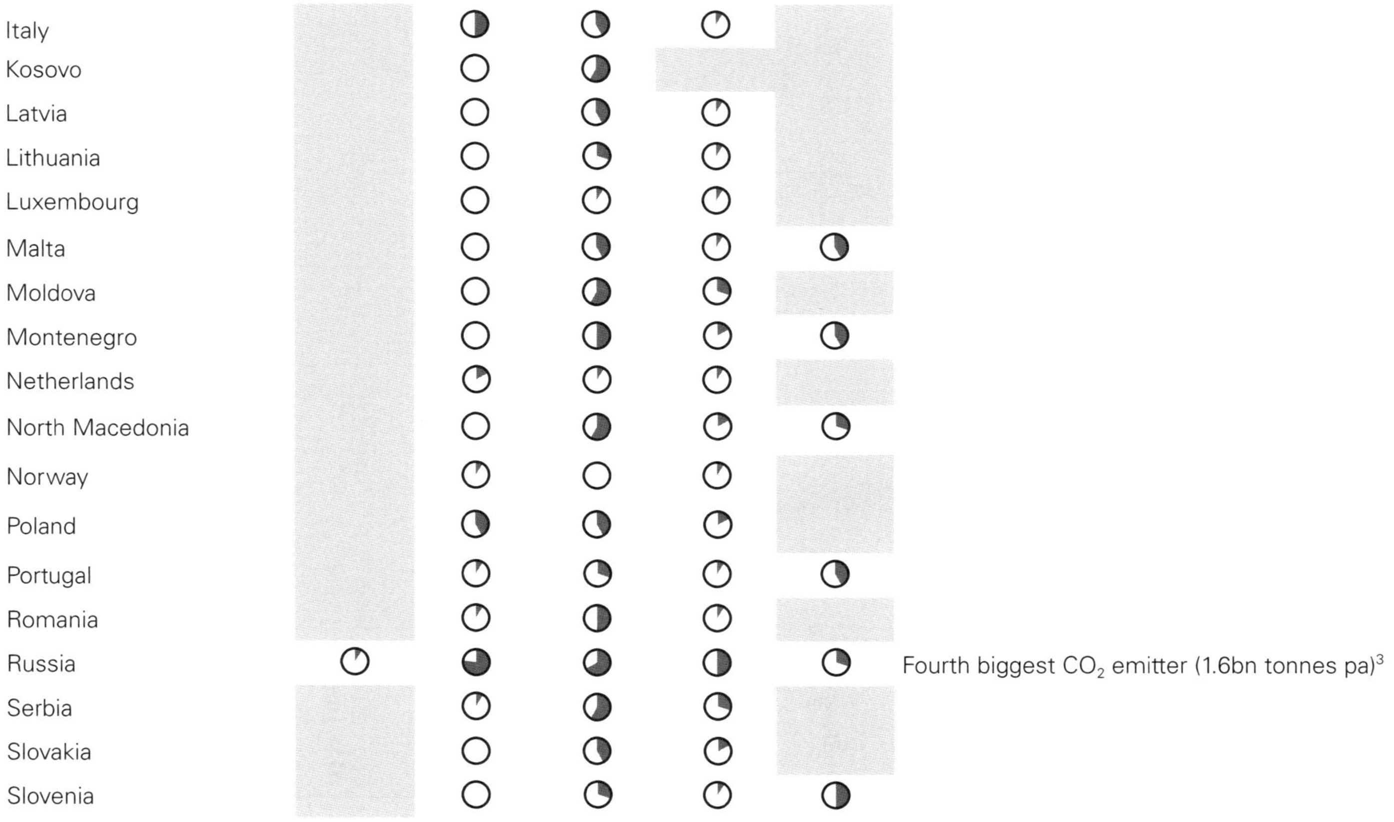

Fourth biggest CO_2 emitter (1.6bn tonnes pa)[3]

- Italy
- Kosovo
- Latvia
- Lithuania
- Luxembourg
- Malta
- Moldova
- Montenegro
- Netherlands
- North Macedonia
- Norway
- Poland
- Portugal
- Romania
- Russia
- Serbia
- Slovakia
- Slovenia

Table 7.6 continued

Country	Child/forced labour	Emissions (CO$_2$)	Corruption	Freedom	Biodiversity	Notable impacts per country
Spain		◑	◐	◑	◑	
Sweden		◑	○	◑		
Switzerland		◑	○	○		
Turkey	◐	◐	◐	◐	◐	
Ukraine	◑	◑	◐	◐		
United Kingdom		◐	◑	◑		

North America

Country	Child/forced labour	Emissions (CO$_2$)	Corruption	Freedom	Biodiversity	Notable impacts per country
Bahamas		○	◑	◑	◑	
Barbados		○	○	◑	◑	
Belize	◑	○	●	◑	◑	
Canada		●	◑	○		Seventh biggest CO$_2$ emitter (0.67bn tonnes pa)[3]
Cuba		○	◑	○	◑	
Dominica		○	◑		◑	

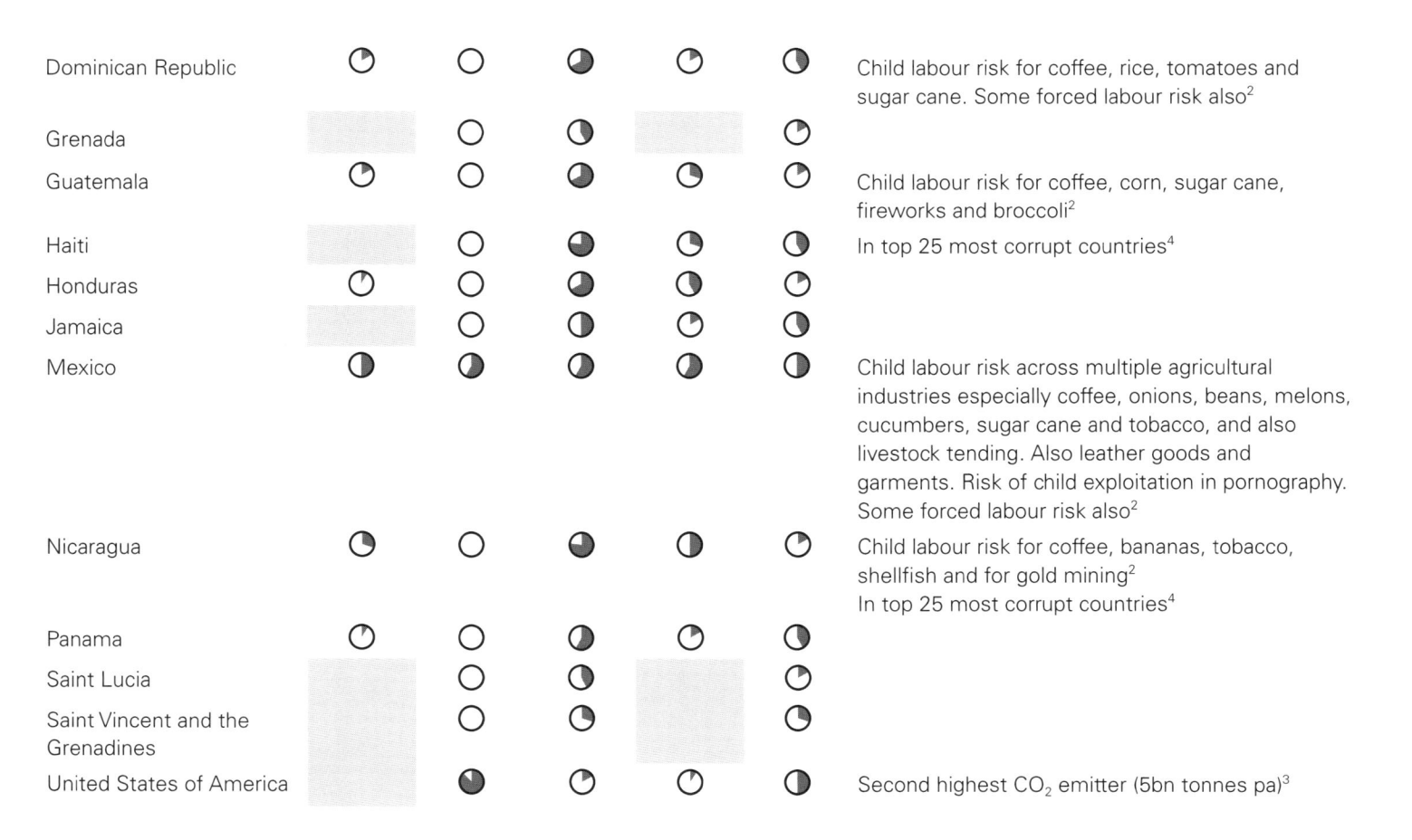

Dominican Republic	◐		◕	○	◕	◔	Child labour risk for coffee, rice, tomatoes and sugar cane. Some forced labour risk also[2]
Grenada	◔			◕	○	◔	
Guatemala	◔		◔	◕	○	◔	Child labour risk for coffee, corn, sugar cane, fireworks and broccoli[2]
Haiti	◔		◕	◕	○	◕	In top 25 most corrupt countries[4]
Honduras			◕	◕	○	◕	
Jamaica	◔		◕	◕	○	◕	
Mexico	◐		◕	◕	◕	◕	Child labour risk across multiple agricultural industries especially coffee, onions, beans, melons, cucumbers, sugar cane and tobacco, and also livestock tending. Also leather goods and garments. Risk of child exploitation in pornography. Some forced labour risk also[2]
Nicaragua	◔		◕	○	◔		
Panama	◔		◔	◕	○	◕	Child labour risk for coffee, bananas, tobacco, shellfish and for gold mining[2]
Saint Lucia			◕	○	◕	◔	In top 25 most corrupt countries[4]
Saint Vincent and the Grenadines			◕	○	◔	◕	
United States of America			◕	●	◕	◐	Second highest CO_2 emitter (5bn tonnes pa)[3]

Table 7.6 continued

Country	Child/forced labour	Emissions (CO$_2$)	Corruption	Freedom	Biodiversity	Notable impacts per country
Oceania						
Australia		●	◐	○	◐	
Fiji		○	○	◐	◐	
New Zealand		○	○	○	◐	
Papua New Guinea		○	◐	◐		
Solomon Islands		○	◐	○	◐	
Vanuatu		○	◐		◐	
South America						
Argentina	◐	◐	◐	◐	◐	Child labour risk across multiple industries, mostly agriculture, including cotton, grapes, strawberries, olives, tomatoes, blueberries, tobacco and bricks. Some forced labour also[2]
Bolivia	◐	○	◐	◐	◐	Child labour risk in mining (gold, silver, tin and zinc), nuts, corn, sugar cane. Forced labour risk also in some areas[2]

Country					Description
Brazil	◐	◐	◐	◐	Significant child labour risk and forced labour risk across multiple industries including agriculture, textiles, meat, ceramics and timber. Risk areas include cocoa, bananas, pineapples, cotton, coffee, fish, footwear, sugar cane and many others[2]. Accounts for 33% of tropical deforestation[1]
Chile		◐	◐	◐	
Colombia	◐	◐ ◐	◐ ◐	◐ ◐	Child labour risk for bricks, coal, mining, precious stones, fruit and sugar cane. Risk of child exploitation for pornography[2].
Costa Rica	◐ ◐ ◐	◐ ◐ ◐	○ ◐ ◐	◐ ◐ ◐	
Ecuador					
El Salvador		◐ ◐	◐ ◐	○ ○	Child labour risk for grains, shellfish, sugar cane, meat, coffee, fireworks and baked goods[2]
Guyana					Significant child labour risk for land-based agriculture (various crops, meat, nuts, beans), fish and brick manufacture. Some forced labour. Risk of child exploitation for pornography[2]
Paraguay	●				
Peru	◐	◐	◐	◐	Risk of child and forced labour for brick manufacture, nuts, timber, fish, mining (gold) and fireworks[2]
Suriname	◐	○	◐	◐	

Table 7.6 *continued*

Country	Child/forced labour	Emissions (CO$_2$)	Corruption	Freedom	Biodiversity	Notable impacts per country
Trinidad and Tobago		○	◐	◐		
Uruguay		○	◐	◔		
Venezuela	◔	◑	◕	●	◔	One of the ten most corrupt countries[4] Second least free country worldwide[5]

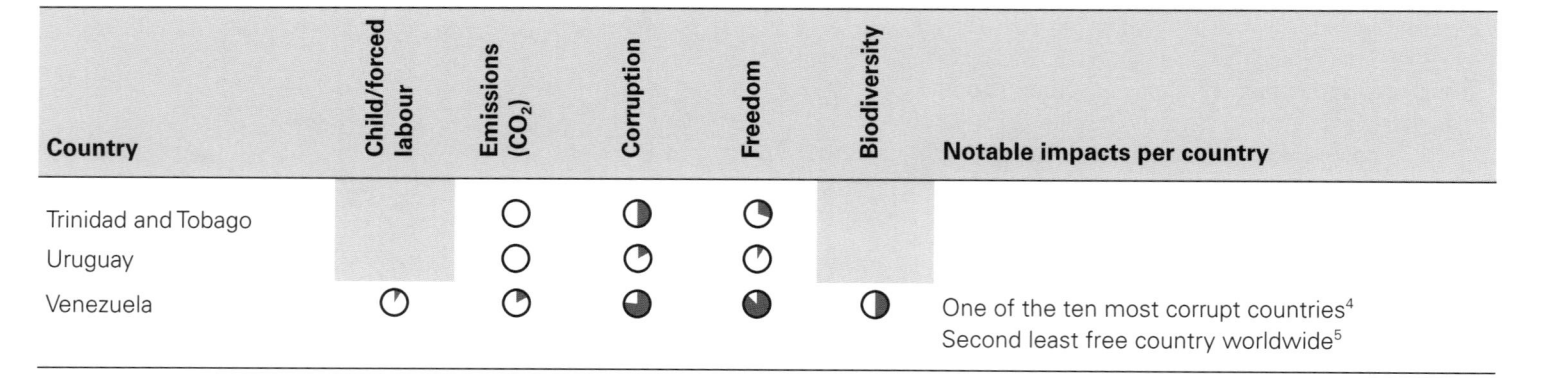

Notes re indicators: Indicators adapted with interpretation and built upon various sources:

1. Biodiversity indicator based upon combining data about territories rich in biodiversity or significantly threatened (Conservation International, 2022; Mittermeier et al, 2002; Myers, 1988, 1990; Pendrill et al, 2019), degree to which territories are already compromised (Swiss Re Institute, 2020) and the lack of regulation or enforced protection in the region (IPBES, 2019)
2. Child and forced labour indicators – based upon the count of industries and products per territory where child and/or forced labour risk has been identified (USDOL, 2022)
3. Emission indicator based upon total volumes of CO$_2$ per year per country relative to overall CO$_2$ global emissions, with rankings adjusted for highest emitters to create indicators (Worldometer, 2022)
4. Corruption indicator based upon Global Corruption Barometer ranking (Transparency International, 2020a)
5. Freedom indicator based upon Human Rights Index (Fraser Institute, 2021; WorldPopulationReview, 2022d)

The importance of biodiversity hot spots

This last factor is worth more exploration to help understand geography hot spots. Biodiversity is not the same the world over but rather there are parts of our planet that are critically important in terms of biodiversity as they are home to extraordinarily diverse ranges of species, or are unique in terms of the species they are home to. If such areas get destroyed, for example to make way for agriculture or development, then the impact is many times greater than for other less-diverse regions.

In 1988 Norman Myers published what was to become a seminal paper that discussed the principles of irreplaceability and vulnerability to guide global conservation (Myers, 1988). Myers identified ten tropical forest hotpots on the basis of extraordinary plant endemism and high levels of habitat loss. His early work has subsequently been further built upon by him and others and was adopted in 1989 by Conservation International, which has been systematically updating the global list of hot spots since that time to become a comprehensive indicator of geographical biodiversity loss. Today Conservation International identify 36 hot spots and these are shown in Figure 7.4 based upon two criteria (Conservation International, 2022):

- It must have **at least 1,500 vascular plants as endemics** – which is to say, it must have a high percentage of plant life found nowhere else on the planet. A hot spot, in other words, is **irreplaceable**.
- It must have **30 per cent or less of its original natural vegetation**. In other words, it must be threatened.

Collectively these regions hold more than 50 per cent of vascular plants and more than 42 per cent of terrestrial vertebrates (amphibians, mammals, birds and reptiles) as endemics (Mittermeier et al, 2004). As a result of extreme habitat loss across these hot spot regions the wealth of biodiversity is concentrated in remaining habitat, which totals around 3.4 million km^2 (2.3 per cent of the world's land area), which is just one-sixth of what it was originally.

Conducting a hot spot analysis

Conduct a hot-spot analysis as follows:

1. Best worked collaboratively – assemble a small team of key individuals who are familiar and knowledgeable with the operations of the organization, the make-up of the products/services it provides and what it sources.

Figure 7.4 The Conservation International Global map of biodiversity hotspots

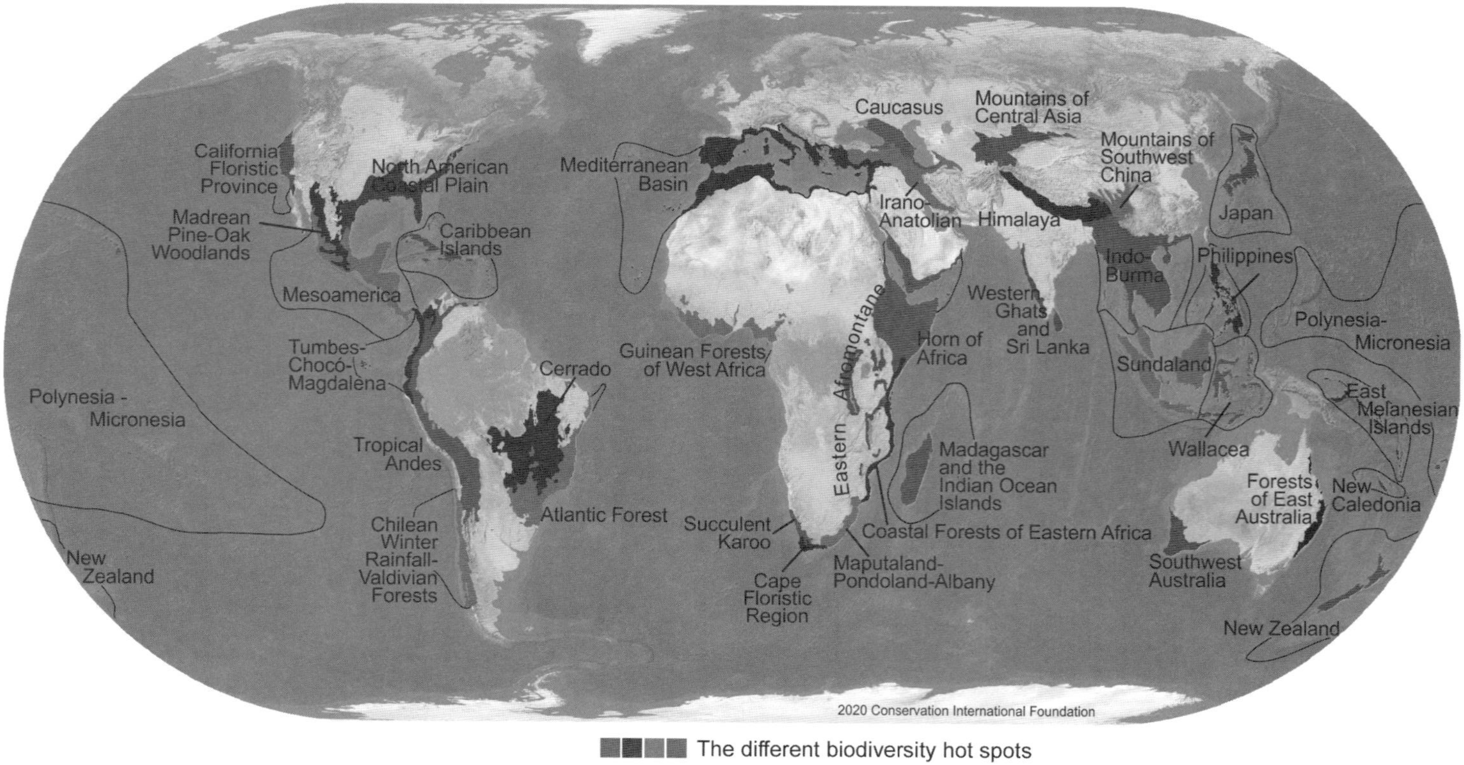

SOURCE Reproduced with permission, available at cepf.net

2 Consider what the organization sources in terms of product, process/industry and geographies – consider and note possible hot spot impacts for each. Use the hot spot lists and/or knowledge from the group of known risk areas to inform the activity.

3 Make a longlist. Identify areas where further information is needed and determine actions to fill the gaps or validate assumptions.

GHG emissions analysis

The challenge of assessing supply-side GHG emissions

Measuring GHG emissions is an important component of assessing supply-side sustainability and provides the basis to determine priorities for improvement in terms of what we buy, who we buy from and our supply chains. If it is not already mandated by legislation for a given country or company, it almost certainly will be and so must become part of what we all need to do. Measuring and driving improvements in terms of emissions can make a significant positive impact and therefore is a key part of our overall sustainability assessment to understand our overall emissions. This begins at the company level, however; to achieve sustainable procurement we need to determine the scope 3 and potentially scope 2 emissions (see the GHG Protocol section in the last chapter) in terms of the specific goods, services, suppliers and supply chains that are part of what we do.

The challenge here is it is impossible to address supply-side GHG emissions unless we address GHG emissions of the company overall (i.e. scope 1, 2 and 3 emissions). It is difficult for procurement to reduce GHG emissions just by buying better. For example; if we are sourcing high-CO_2 raw materials, due to composition, miles travelled, energy required, etc, then changing these may not be a procurement decision but become a business decision. Therefore, whilst we talk about considering the scope 3 and potentially scope 2 emissions as part of sustainable procurement, in fact any work to drive supply-side improvement can only happen in concert with the entire business. Once again, we come back to the critical importance of cross-functional working to drive sustainable procurement. That said, the supply-side GHG emissions assessment informs the debate and shapes the priorities for wider business improvement.

Right now, companies all over the world are scrambling to measure their GHG emissions, either because they are now required to or expected to, yet typically struggling to know how to do this. This has led to a flood of companies ready to help and follow up with a programme to drive emission reduction. Professional help can be very useful here, especially if the organization lacks resources to do it itself. Measuring GHG emissions is not rocket science, yet to do it well it can be resource intensive and require some specialist in-house skills or know-how. The skills and know-how can be learnt easily so it is entirely possible for an organization to put together a team and direct them to investigate and establish supply-side GHGs. The next section provides some simple guidance here.

The principles of GHG emission measurement

There are many different greenhouse gases that cause warming of the earth when in the atmosphere, produced as a result of different activities of our societies or across the planet. Of these, seven are identified as the gases we need to measure and reduce, as originally identified by the Kyoto Protocol in 1996 and regular updates by the IPCC (IPCC, 2021). These are given in Table 7.7. Each of these gases contribute to heating the planet when released into the atmosphere. Some do this much more than others according to how much they absorb infrared radiation and how long they stay around – for ease of calculation globally it is assumed greenhouse gases remain in the atmosphere for 100 years. For example, methane (CH_4) from non-fossil sources can heat the planet 29.8 times more than CO_2 and sulfur hexafluoride (SF_6) can heat the planet up to 25,200 times more than CO_2 (Gillenwater, 2022). This different capacity to heat the atmosphere is called the Global Warming Potential (GWP). CO_2 has been assigned a GWP of 1 and all other GHGs have a GWP factor. GWP factors are regularly updated by the IPCC and the 2021 figures are given in Table 7.7.

All GHG emissions are represented as CO_2. This is because it is the gas that is produced in such vast quantities when compared with all others. Therefore, other non-CO_2 GHG emissions are represented as their CO_2 equivalent – denoted as CO_2e, CO_2eq or CO_2-e. When we measure GHG emissions, we are measuring the mass of the GHG in metric tonnes and converting it to the CO_2 equivalent. For example, if a waste landfill site releases one metric tonne of non-fossil methane per hour, then the GHG emissions are 29.8 tonnes CO_2e per hour. Straightforward enough, but how do we begin to establish that a tonne of methane was released in the first place? Or how might we know how much CO_2e an industrial process or power station is emitting?

Table 7.7 The seven GHGs we need to measure and reduce and their GWP factors.

Greenhouse gas	Global Warming Potential (GWP), over 100 years[1]
Carbon dioxide (CO_2)	1
Methane (CH_4)	Non-fossil sources = 27.2 Fossil sources = 29.8
Nitrous oxide (N_2O_4)	273
Hydrofluorocarbons (HFCs)	HFC-23 = 14,600 HFC-134a = 1,530
Perfluorocarbons (PFCs)	7,380
Sulfur hexafluoride (SF_6)	25,200
Nitrogen trifluoride (NF_3)	17,400

SOURCES Gillenwater (2022); IPCC (2021)[1]

One way would be to capture the gas being given off and weigh it (just as we might have done as part of a school physics experiment), analyse its composition to see how much air is mixed in and adjust our measure of gas accordingly. Imagine if we had to do this to assess all our supply-side emissions? It would make emissions assessment almost impossible for the vast majority of us. There are scenarios where a method like this might be employed but fortunately, there is a much easier way.

When we measure CO_2 we are measuring the mass of the gas. Mass and weight are not the same thing, although both are measured in grams, kilograms, tonnes, pounds, etc. The weight of something changes according to gravity and so the volume of CO_2 that weighs a tonne on earth would only weigh about 160 kg on the Moon. The distinction is irrelevant for greenhouse gas emissions as we are concerned with those in our atmosphere, where gravity is pretty constant. So, if we were to attempt to establish emissions by weighing actual amounts of gas we would not be off the mark. That said, there are scenarios where we might want to consider CO_2 in the ocean, which would change things. Therefore, emission measurement considers the mass of the gas. The mass of an object or gas is a product of how dense it is (things that are very dense have smaller, more massive atoms that are closer together) and its volume, or:

$$\text{Mass} = \text{Density} \times \text{Volume}$$

We have long since known the density of CO_2 because we know how its atomic structure and although density will vary according to temperature and pressure, at 15°C and atmospheric pressure the density of CO_2 is 1.87 kg/m^3. In contrast the density of dry air under the same conditions is 1.22 kg/m^3 making CO_2 heavier than air. This means we can establish that the volume of CO_2 with a mass of one metric tonne would occupy a cube 8.3 metres on each side (27 feet). Therefore, all we need to determine is the volume of CO_2 an industrial process or activity produces. There is good news here too because the relationship between the mass of carbon and mass of CO_2 that is produced when it is burnt was established many years ago. We know that every atom of carbon burnt will produce one CO_2 molecule and we also know the relationship of the mass of a carbon atom and a molecule of CO_2. We know that the mass of an oxygen atom is 1.33 times that of a carbon atom, so a CO_2 molecule would have a mass of 1 carbon molecule + 2 oxygen molecules, or (1 + (2 × 1.33) = 3.67.

3.67 is therefore the multiplier we can use to determine CO_2 emissions from the carbon that gets burnt or released from an industrial process. This means if we can establish the carbon content of what goes into an industrial process, we can calculate the CO_2 emissions it produces. For example; we know that coal is about 70 per cent carbon, so if a power station burns 1 million tonnes of coal then that equates to 700,000 tonnes of carbon and therefore, using the multiplier of 3.67, will produce 2.56 million tonnes of CO_2 (NIWA, nd). This is the basis for how we begin to establish supply-side emissions and the basis to determine an emissions factor that results from a specific activity, for example kg CO_2e emitted per kg coal burnt, kg CO_2e emitted per litre of fuel consumed or kg CO_2e emitted per kg of material produced. Therefore, in order to determine supply-side emissions for what we source, we need to collect data for all scope 3 and potentially some scope 2 emissions in terms of:

1 **Activity or volume data** – what and how much is consumed or purchased for each step within the SVCN.
2 **Emissions factors** – for each instance of consumption or use.

Increasingly firms are being required to determine and report the emissions factor for their products or service. Book a flight and the airline will be obliged to inform you of the total kg CO_2e for your flight, equipping you to make comparisons with other airlines or evaluate the need for the flight in the first place. Comparison with other airlines operating the same city pair routes can reveal vast differences in the total kg CO_2e quoted revealing the impact airplane type, age and airline operating procedures can have – data that was once hidden from all of us. If everything we purchased came with information about its kg CO_2e then supply-side emission calculation would be very simple. However, the reality is that until such data is widely available it is down to us to do the detective work to determine emissions but a lot is, in fact, available already.

Measuring GHG emissions through the entire SVCN

To fully understand supply-side emissions, we would, in theory, need to examine every product or service we source and examine its entire SVCN, everything that gets consumed at each step, the resultant emissions factors at each step and the collective total of all of these for the given product or service. Combining all of these across all our spend would give us the total supply-side emissions and a basis to determine where we might prioritize action to reduce emissions. Imagine being able to access a dashboard of emissions by what we buy, who we buy from and our supply chains – this would be the ultimate in management information to drive sustainability within a company. One day, all companies will have such a dashboard, but until then we need to find a different way and clearly examining every SVCN in its entirely is impractical. Instead we need to be selective where we direct our resources.

Mapping the supply chain or entire SVCN is not a new concept, it is part of good SRM and a topic I have expanded at large in my book *Supplier Relationship Management*. For detailed emissions measurement we use the same approach – we determine each and all of the upstream steps right back to the original factory, raw material acquisition, agricultural source and also potentially downstream on to the end of life and disposal, and determine risks to address and/or opportunities to drive improvements at each step. Therefore, for supply-side emissions there are two approaches for assessment:

1 Assess all the supply chain upstream emissions – everything produced at all steps up until the point of sale or delivery by the supplier (also called *cradle to gate* or *cradle to shelf*). This is typically how we determine supply-side emissions.

Sustainable procurement

2 Assess all emissions through the entire SVCN including upstream *and* downstream to the end customer and on to end-of-life disposal. These are called *life cycle emissions*.

Increasingly, it is possible to obtain good information about cradle to gate or life cycle emissions for specific raw materials or products purchased. If it is not available, we can ask our suppliers and if they don't know we can push them to find out. The age of everything that is for sale having both a price tag and a kg CO_2e tag attached is with us, whether driven by legislation, consumer pressure or the will to do the right thing. Search 'what is the average CO_2e per kg of x?' and most of what you put in will return a value. Alternatively utilize the many websites that serve up this data, with many databases and listings providing life cycle emissions factors, most for free (Table 7.2). For example, a quick search reveals it takes over 15.3 kg CO_2 to produce 1 kg of coffee beans, the emissions factor for cotton is 8.3 kg CO_2, for an iPhone it is 72 kg CO_2 and manufacturing a single-use plastic bag produces 1.58 kg CO_2 whereas it takes 5.52 kg CO_2 to produce a single-use paper bag – that was a surprise (CO2 Everything, nd). The abundance of good data also allows us to compare emissions for the same material or product from different geographies. For example, a 1 kg ingot of aluminium produced in Europe generates 6.7 kg CO_2e whereas the same ingot produced in China will generate 20 kg CO_2e, due to the high energy required that is largely produced by burning coal. The global average is 18 kg CO_2e (European Aluminium, 2020). Using data like this to calculate emissions based upon taking the mass of the materials that we source or are consumed along the way and multiplying this by the life cycle emissions factor is called the activity-based method and is an effective approach used to build up a detailed picture of an area of the supply base.

Another, less accurate and less precise method is the spend-based method where we take spend data and multiply it by a spend-based emissions factor to determine an estimate of emissions. Again, there is a wealth of data out there providing lists of spend-based emissions factors. Developed nations publish information about their carbon footprint and the total emissions per sector. This, combined with the total revenues the industry generates, means we can establish the CO_2e per £1 or $1 or €1, etc for a given industry. Once again, a quick internet search revealed that in the UK £1 of meat creates 0.63 kg CO_2e, pharmaceutical products would create 1.31 kg CO_2e and a £1 ticket on public transport would create 16.7 kg CO_2e (gov.uk, 2022).

Even with readily accessible data, mapping a single supply chain/SVCN remains a huge undertaking, let alone mapping all of them, and so success comes by being laser-focused in determining where to invest time in doing it. It also means that, just as we have considered the hot spots in terms of impacts, we need to identify the overall hot spots in terms of emissions so we can decide where to establish specific projects to look deeper. Supply-side GHG emissions assessment therefore has two stages:

A   Helicopter hot spot view – The main supply-side areas where we believe there may be high supply-side emissions or potential hot spots as a basis to direct our efforts.

B   Down on the ground detailed assessment – The specific areas in terms of what we buy, who we buy from and our supply chains, where we identify there is value in measuring emissions more precisely and driving improvements.

I will explore each in turn.

A 'Helicopter hot spot view' GHG emissions assessment

The helicopter hot spot view is what we would get if we could fly above the entire organization and see all its end-to-end supply and value chain networks and just as you might use a thermal imaging camera to detect heat hot spots, we would use a special emissions camera to reveal the high emissions hot spots. From here we could look more deeply at these areas.

In reality, and without access to a helicopter or special emissions camera, we establish this high-level view in a more practical way as follows:

1   Best worked collaboratively in a small team.
2   Review the primary impacts previously identified and determine the areas of sourcing that most contribute to the highest primary impacts.
3   Review the product, process or geography hot spot analysis and identify those that relate to emissions.
4   Considering the entire supply base, identify any other areas where there could be potential high emissions, e.g. where there is high energy use, high temperature or lengthy processing, burning (especially fossil fuels), heat generation, significant transportation or movement of goods, or emission of gases as part of processing.
5   Create a shortlist from steps 2–4 and refine and validate to identify the main hot spots – use spend-based assessment and spend-based emission factors where available to help roughly quantify emissions here.

B 'Down on the ground' detailed GHG emissions assessment

For the specific areas of the supply base where a more detailed assessment of emissions is worthwhile, we can determine the actual emissions (or as close as we can get to this), for what we buy, who we buy from and our supply chains. This might be in response to our 'helicopter hot spot view' or might be part of how we are assessing and determining improvement areas for specific products or services, suppliers or entire supply chains or SVCNs. We will return to this through successive chapters; however, I will outline the process for establishing these emissions here as it is the same process for all aspects of our supply base.

Key to a detailed and focused supply-side GHG assessment is a breakdown of the area we are concerned with and securing the data needed to determine emissions for each element. There are a number of ways we can secure this data:

- Primary data we collect – data we have, can measure or can get, e.g. volumes or amounts purchased from corporate systems, records of purchasing transaction, metered processes, goods inwards monitoring, product specifications, direct measuring mass produced, etc.
- Primary data from suppliers – getting our suppliers to do as much of the data gathering as possible can help, specifically emissions data relating to:
  - The products or services they provide – life cycle or cradle-to-gate GHG emissions.
  - Processing – if not factored into product or service information, then GHG emissions generated from a specific process, activity, production lines, etc. Emissions are calculated by assessing all the inputs required by the process such as energy, water, processing and environmental inputs.
  - Their facility – again, if not factored into product or service information, then GHG emissions generated from the facility/facilities where goods are made or processed. This could be a specific site, entire business unit or the company overall.
- Secondary data – published information we can access regarding emissions factors by industry or product type or other useful information, e.g. cradle-to-gate or life cycle emission factors per mass of a material, or spend-based emission factors.

Assessing the supply base 265

The process for conducting a detailed assessment is broadly the same across what we buy, who we buy from and our supply chains for any given scenario, by building an emissions model as follows:

1 Break it down – start by breaking down the area of interest, e.g. the components and processes that make up a product, how a supplier is organized, the steps in the supply chain, etc.
2 Determine the units – are we looking at the total emissions per year, per consignment, per service delivered or something else?
3 Gather any primary data about each component, step, etc.
4 Where there is no primary data use secondary data and calculate the estimated emissions.
5 Where neither primary nor secondary data exist, attempt to fill the gap either through research, sample measurement or estimation using the closest spend-based emissions factor data. Accept that it may not be possible to fully determine all emissions but rather an emissions model should be refined and updated as new information becomes available.
6 Build the emissions model – create a full list of all the individual elements that contribute emissions and their actual or calculated emissions value and calculate the sum of all the elements.

Establishing supply-side scope 3 and potentially scope 2 emissions provides the basis to determine improvement activities, perhaps by changing the make-up of what our firm does, sourcing different materials or buying from a different geography. It provides the basis to either select or switch suppliers or work with those suppliers that are important to us to better develop their emissions assessment or drive improvements. It also enables us to change our supply chains or target areas for improvement. Finally, by determining the scope 2 and 3 emissions for our firm, this together with the scope 1 emissions enables the organization to know and publish its emissions.

Assessing supply-side GHG emissions might seem daunting; however, it is in fact quite simple but can be an extensive and time-consuming undertaking. Yet in procurement, as I said earlier, we already map and optimize specific SVCNs. We also do product breakdowns as part of a purchase price cost analysis (PPCA) to determine what something should cost. For emissions we are using the same approach, except we are not only looking at price, cost, risk, opportunity, etc but also at CO_2. As we become familiar with approaches to determine emissions this will become part of what we do. Once again, we are applying the procurement approaches and tools

Figure 7.5 Example supply-side emissions for a coffee cart vendor

Annual supply-side CO₂e based upon annual sales of 71,760 12 oz/354 ml cups of coffee

Areas	Calculation notes	Mass + units	Emissions factor	Total CO₂e
Annual coffee sales				
Coffee beans	71,760 cups at 18 g per cup = 1,587 kg	1,291 kg	15.3	19,763 kg
Paper cups	71,760 × 12 oz/354 ml cups per annum. Manufacturer supplied data provides CO₂e at 0.11 kg per cup = 7,893 kg			7,893 kg
Plastic lids	71,760 pa polypropylene lids 100 = 340 g so 71,760 = 244 kg	244 kg	1.58	386 kg
Stirrers	30,000 pa birch wood 100 = 140 g so 30,000 = 42 kg. 1 m³ kiln-dried birch wood = 710 kg and creates 51.3 CO₂e so 42 kg = 3 kg CO₂e	42 kg	N/A	3 kg
Milk	7,620 litres pa 1 l = 1.032 kg = 7,863 kg	7,863 kg	3.2	25,161 kg
Sugar	229 kg pa	229 kg	0.43	98 kg
Utilities & other				
Water	17,783 litres pa 1 l = 1 kg	17,783 kg	0.59	10,491 kg
Electricity	Barista rated at 1.5 kW with 45 seconds per cup = 1,345 kWh + lighting, tills, etc = 300 W for 2,496 hrs pa – 748 kWh = 2093 kWh pa using electricity produced in the UK at 0.193 kg per kWh = 404 kg equivalent	260 kg	2.6	1,050 kg
	Total annual supply-side CO₂e for coffee cart			64,845 kg

we know but with our sustainability hat on. A template is provided in the Appendix and Figure 7.5 provides a simple example of a supply side-emissions assessment for a small coffee cart vendor.

The net zero imperative

The global science-based target, as set by the United Nations and ratified by 193 countries is that we must reach net zero emissions by 2050 and to have halved emissions by 2030 if we are to avert a climate change catastrophe (UN, 2022b). Currently we fall short of meeting these targets and despite commitments made at the COP26 and COP27 the vast majority of countries have failed to make progress or indeed submit any sort of updated climate plan (UN, 2022b).

Pledges to achieve net zero abound. Companies, our favourite brands, municipal bodies, cities, films, bands are publishing their commitment to reach net zero by some point in time in the next decade or two. It is trendy and expected to be on the road to net zero. For some it is an important commitment to tackle climate change with robust systems and action behind it. For others it is an intent, maybe genuine or maybe with a bit of greenwash to look good. After all, unless the company is bound by or has committed to some form of reporting here, there is no law against having an intent and telling the rest of the world about it.

Net zero is the balance between the amount of GHG a company produces and the amount removed from the atmosphere. When these balance a company has reached net zero. Net zero is subtly different from carbon neutral in that net zero is concerned with all GHGs rather than only CO_2.

There are various ways an organization can pursue net zero:

- **Reduce emissions** – getting to 'real zero' is unattainable; however, reducing emissions can get some way towards this.
- **Remove GHGs** from the atmosphere and offset this against our emissions. This involves establishing ways to capture carbon. This is more than simply planting some trees but needs a more measured approach. There are many ways to do this and entire new industries have sprung up here to help companies do this:
  - *Trees* – tree planting is good; however, the more you look at carbon capture the more complicated it gets. Across the full life of a tree it will both emit and absorb carbon. Planting trees creates GHGs and at the end of life when a tree rots or is burnt it emits carbon. That said, over the life of the tree, and if the right variety is planted (typically non-

invasive species with the biggest leaves that grow fast tend to work best) then trees are great carbon absorbers.

- *Planting other types of vegetation* – grassland is particularly effective.
- *Carbon capture* – emerging technology that literally sucks the carbon out of the atmosphere. The technology is there, but in its infancy and currently can only capture carbon in small amounts but as this develops and becomes scalable we can expect an entire new carbon capture industry to be born.

- **Preserving carbon sinks** – the world's vegetation, oceans, soil, peatlands, mangroves, salt marshes and seagrasses are critical and exceptionally good absorbers. Companies cannot create new oceans or find new soil, but they can ensure their actions and what happens in the supply chains don't compromise what we have. While this cannot be directly measurable in terms of a net zero calculation, it is an important factor in a company's overall commitment to addressing climate change.

Net zero is critically important because it is the only way we can tackle climate change and what happens in the supply chain is part of this story. There are big watch-outs here and if our organization is pursuing net zero then measurement and reporting become essential to give it credibility. Similarly, when we consider our supply base we need to look beyond suppliers' claims and ambitious net zero pledges and evaluate the robustness of the arrangements they have put in place to achieve this, how they will measure and report on it, and how real and achievable the ambition is. After all, there is little point kidding ourselves that all our key supply chains will be net zero or at least halfway towards it by 2030 only to face a wave of suppliers repositioning their ambitions in 2029.

Chapter checkpoint

In this chapter we have explored how we assess our organization's position with respect to sustainability in the supply base relative to the strategy, aims and goals we have set. Key points we covered were:

1 *The sustainability assessment* – the process of determining, and where possible measuring, how sustainable procurement is with respect to the ambition and direction of travel we have set for sustainability.

2. *The measurement muscle* – measurement is the muscle for sustainability and provides the basis to determine and manage improvements.
3. *The SSTP tool*, which provides the basis to start considering our sustainability situation and determine how we will move forward.
4. *The PESTLE tool*, which is key to understanding our macroenvironment and how that might shape our direction of travel for sustainability.
5. *Hot spot analysis* – it would be impractical to assess everything, so hot spot analysis helps us determine where there might be risks, impacts and opportunities to focus on. There are three types of hot spot – product, process (or industry) and geography.
6. *GHG emissions analysis* – the process of measuring GHGs in terms of their equivalent CO_2 (or CO_2e) for what we buy, in our suppliers and throughout the supply chain. This measurement gives us the basis to determine priorities for reduction and what would need to change to achieve this.
7. *Net zero* is when our GHG emissions balance that we remove from the atmosphere. Working towards net zero in our supply base is a key contributor here. Net zero pledges can lack substance and so we need to understand and verify the arrangements within our suppliers, and monitor and measure improvements.

In the next chapter we will explore how we make sense of our supply-side sustainability assessments and how we begin to prioritize and determine the risks, impacts and opportunities that we will work on.

Prioritizing risks, impacts and opportunities

08

> This chapter continues to explore stage 2 of the OMEIA® process and how to make sense of the various assessments and hot spot analyses in order to determine and prioritize the areas to work on. We examine how to conduct a risk assessment to determine the priority areas and how to conduct an impact assessment to determine and prioritize which other impacts we wish to address to meet our sustainability goals. Finally we will consider how to conduct an opportunity analysis to determine other areas that can unlock new benefits that we might want to pursue. The chapter concludes with the prioritization heat cube as a means to bring all the outputs of assessment together to give a single visualization of the sustainable procurement areas we will progress in one way or another.
>
> *Pathway question addressed in this chapter:*
>
> 8 What improvement areas should we focus on first?

Determining what to work on is about making sense of the outputs of our initial assessment and, with our sustainable goals in mind, prioritizing which areas we might want to work on and then deciding how these translate into specific projects. It is important to recognize that there are two distinct steps here, as defined by stages 2 and 3 of the OMEIA® process, which are the principles we establish using the SSTP – we must first measure and assess the situation, i.e. the priority impacts we will address or areas where we will initiate some improvement, before we evaluate and determine the specific projects to do this. It is easy to slip from a risk, impact or opportunity straight to a solution – often something we need to fix becomes the thing we will do to fix it, typically without conscious thought. To some degree this is unavoidable; however, as we progress through this chapter the principles of Situation – Target – Proposal should be kept in mind. Figure 8.1 shows the elements within the OMEIA® methodology we will cover in this chapter.

Figure 8.1 The key steps within stages 2 and 3 of the OMEIA® process that relate to how we prioritize and determine projects

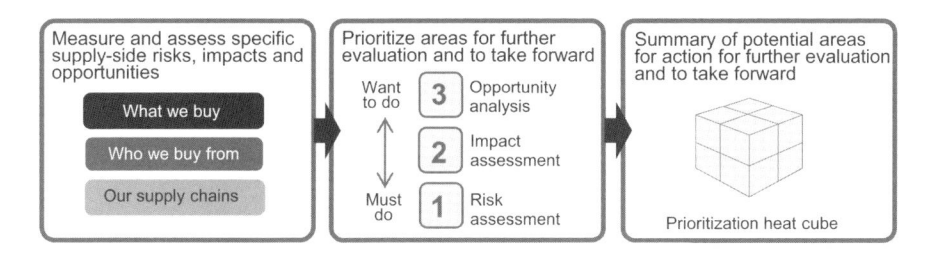

Don't boil the ocean, don't even let it warm up a bit

Earlier in this book I suggested that we cannot fix everything and that we need to be focused in directing our resources. This is true, however, it is also important to have an eye on the bigger picture, no matter how impossible it might be. I frequently hear those who are working on sustainability espousing the principle that we should not try to 'boil the ocean' – a metaphor with uncertain attribution and depending upon which source you trust comes from either Will Rogers, Mark Twain or Lewis Carroll. While a somewhat paradoxical metaphor for sustainability and ocean temperatures rising, nonetheless it is a phrase we all know – designed to suggest that when it comes to problem solving, we should avoid focus on the whole where we try to do everything but rather keep our focus of problem solving deliberately narrow. Yet, for sustainable procurement this is, in fact, not such good advice. If we only focus on improvements to individual problems, we will fall short. The thing about addressing sustainability is that the impacts, and therefore the problems we are setting out to address, are interconnected, constantly changing, dynamic and often non-deterministic (i.e. we don't necessarily know the answer to, or how to address, the problem we need to solve). Therefore, in determining our road map of sustainable procurement projects, establishing a programme with a series of stand-alone, potentially unrelated, improvement projects is a good start. Yet, establishing a programme that sets out to have a much bigger ultimate goal in mind, no matter how unachievable it might be today, establishes the basis for individual projects to be related and intertwined in pursuit of a common ambition. This common ambition should, of course, be our overall sustainability goals. Therefore, the sustainable procurement road map we are working towards should be designed to have multiple time horizons – near term for urgent priorities, medium term for the impacts or bigger projects we determine we want to progress, and the less well defined longer-term sustainable procurement initiatives, which may be an ambition rather than a specific course of action. These would typically take many years to realize, if at all realizable, in terms of available resources, supply base readiness, appetite for change or just the scale of change. In this and the subsequent four chapters we will explore how we progress to build the sustainable procurement road map that will deliver on our goals and that begins with prioritization of the areas to work on.

Prioritization

We have arrived at the point where we have the outputs of the various assessments done so far and potentially one or more longlists. By now it is likely we are immersed in a mass of assumptions, possibilities, ideas and firm assertions that represent possible risks, impact areas we might need or want to address and also some opportunities to drive new value. Collectively, these will typically have come from:

- Primary impact assessment
- Any initial risk assessment carried out as part of business case determination and goal setting
- SSTP
- PESTLE analysis
- Product/service hot spot analysis
- Process/industry hot spot analysis
- Geography hot spot analysis
- Emissions analysis

To move forward we need to determine which of these are the priorities, and why. This will then enable us to establish the necessary projects and establish our sustainable procurement programme. To make sense of this we conduct three separate steps or levels of prioritization, each a separate pass through our longlists and each focusing on a different response. The three steps and levels are:

1 **Risk assessment** – to identify the top priority areas we must address
2 **Impact assessment** – with our sustainability goals in mind, to identify the impacts we need and want to address to meet our goals
3 **Opportunity analysis** – to identify areas where we can unlock new value and benefit

These three steps represent a progression from those areas where we 'must do' something, for example to avert dire consequences, to areas where we 'want to do' something because of the potential benefit that can be secured. As we have seen, this same motivational hierarchy forms part of our business case determination and so there is a degree of correlation between at what level our organization sits within the business case model and how far we go in terms of determining priorities. For example, a firm only interested in sustainability in terms of basic compliance and averting negative PR might want to stop at the risk assessment. However, the correlation diminishes slightly further up the business case as it doesn't follow that only philanthropically motivated organizations can benefit from an opportunity analysis. The process of prioritization can therefore challenge our sustainable procurement objectives. Figure 8.2 illustrates the prioritization process and the loose correlation to the business case determination. We will explore each step in turn:

Risk assessment

Purpose – to identify the most significant supply-side sustainability risk areas where we must take action to protect the organization.

Alignment to sustainability goals required? No – risk assessment should consider all areas, not only those where we have set a goal.

Focus – can be applied enterprise wide, entire supply base, what we buy, who we buy from, our supply chains or other specific scenarios.

Typical time frame for action – typically short–medium term, possibly some urgent projects.

Risk assessment is the first step within prioritization. It is the process of identifying and assessing potential supply-side risks and, for those we ascertain to be significant, determining actions to either eliminate or mitigate the

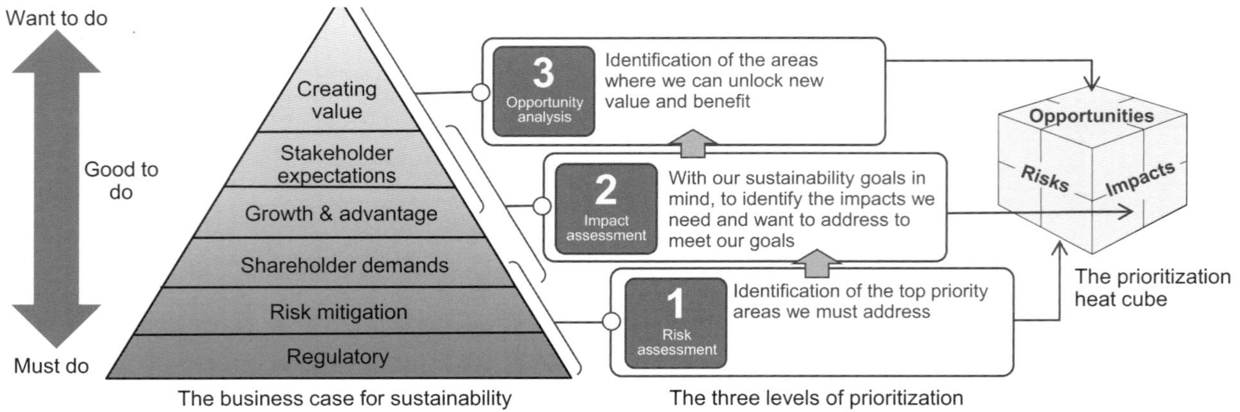

Figure 8.2 The process of prioritizing what we should work on

risk, or where this is not possible or practical, determine contingency actions. The process of risk assessment is the same whether applied at an enterprise level, full supply base, or specific areas or projects. We explored risk and minimizing or preventing risk in Chapter 5, as one of the foundations for establishing a business case for sustainability. Here we will develop the specific plans to address the risks we identify.

Potential risks will have surfaced from the various assessment work we have done so far. Furthermore, we may also be aware of other risk areas we need to tackle. Figure 5.2 can help here to identify potential risks against the seven supply-side risk headings. The first step is therefore to establish a single list of all the potential supply-side sustainability risks. This might include risks within all three focus areas (what we buy, who we buy from and our supply chains). From here we determine the priority risks to address. We do this by considering each risk in turn and deciding the likelihood of the risk occurring and then the severity of impact should it occur. For each a simple H/M/L (high/medium/low) assessment is enough. More sophisticated assessment approaches are out there using weightings and scoring, etc; however, generally a simple and easy to use approach will do just fine. Figure 8.3 gives an example of a simple supply-side risk assessment (the template for this is given in the Appendix). The risk prioritization matrix (Figure 8.4) provides the basis to then determine our response to the risks and the priorities for action.

Finally, we convert the risks we have identified we must address into specific projects or actions. For example, the risk 'possible negative press stories and reputational damage due to current sourcing from Malaysia factories' might become 'pre-prepare positive PR responses', or longer-term 'move sourcing away from Malaysia factories within one year'. Therefore, this is where our sustainable procurement programme begins to form – with the individual projects and courses of action we identify we need to progress. This will continue to build as we work through our impact assessment and also opportunity analysis.

Conduct a supply side-risk assessment as follows:

1 Best worked collaboratively as a team.
2 Determine the scope of the risk assessment (e.g. a supplier, area of spend or entire supply base).
3 Identify all the possible supply-side risk areas using the outputs of the assessments and the seven supply-side risk headings as a prompt.

Figure 8.3 Example of a supply-side risk assessment

Supply side sustainability risk assessment – for *Moving to an outsourced customer call centre in India*							
Supply-side risk	Likelihood of occurrence	Severity of impact	Priority for action	Mitigation or contingency action in response to risk	Owner	By when
Poor working conditions	M	H	3	Establish minimum requirements, regular audit and remote monitoring	JT	31 Mar
Workers don't get paid the living wage	H	H	1	Establish minimum requirements, regular audit and interviews with staff	NO'C	31 Mar
Customer data is compromised en masse	M	H	2	Put ISO27001 in place. Upgrade data security on site. Retain EU data hosting	MD	30 Nov
Workers access individual data and sell it	L	H	6	Staff training and incorporate user-tracked record access with regular audits	MD	Ongoing
We get exposed for poor treatment of staff	L	H	7	Prepare contingency communications PR statement in advance	MH	31 Mar
High non-green energy usage at facility	H	M	4	Regular energy audit and agree a programme of installing solar panels	JH	Ongoing
High carbon footprint at facility	H	L	5	Measure and agree a programme of improvement	JH	30 Apr
Redundant IT equipment doesn't get adequately recycled	L	L	Low	Define requirements within agreement	MD	31 Mar

Prioritizing risks, impacts and opportunities

4 Begin to compile a risk assessment matrix using the template or format given in Figure 8.3.
5 Assess each risk – for each risk discuss, debate and determine the potential likelihood and severity. Apply a simple H/M/L score to each.
6 Using the risk prioritization matrix (Figure 8.4), classify each risk onto the matrix to determine its priority.
7 For each risk, determine the potential actions to either ignore, live with, mitigate the risk or develop contingencies as appropriate.
8 Where actions are identified, take these forward and establish individual projects as part of the overall sustainable procurement programme (covered in the next chapter).

Figure 8.4 The risk prioritization matrix

Mitigation or accept the risk	Priorities for action
Depending upon the degree of severity and the practicalities of any action, either accept the risk or determine and implement mitigation action to reduce or eliminate the risk	*These are the top priorities for action. Determine mitigation and/or contingency actions and prioritize in terms of timing and securing resources to address*
Limited work or ignore	**Develop contingency plans**
Do nothing or, if easy, practical and agreed worthwhile, basic work to mitigate or prepare contingency action	*Accept that there is a low chance of these risks being realized and prepare and maintain contingency plans, e.g. prepare a plan to handle negative PR, etc*

Likelihood (y-axis) → Severity (x-axis)

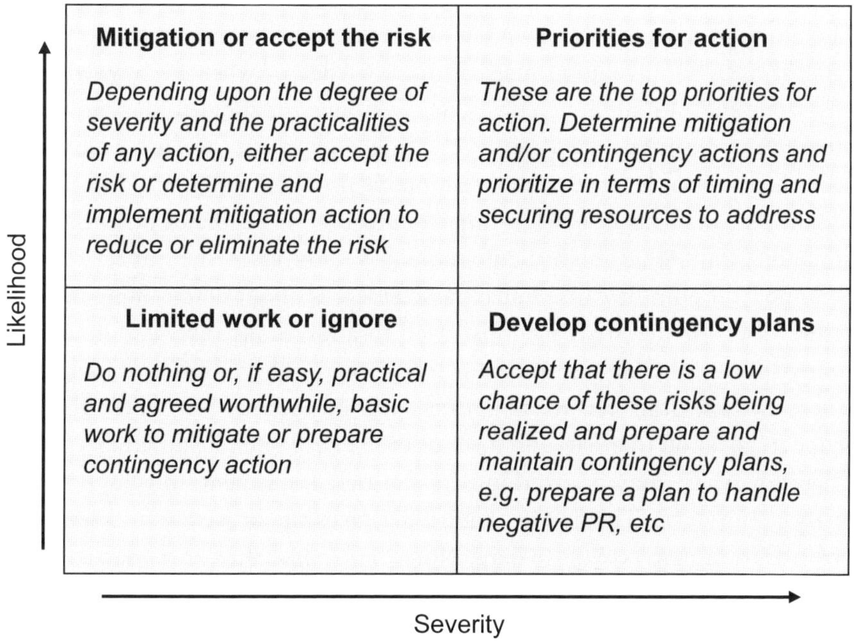

Impact assessment

Purpose – to realize our sustainability goals.
Alignment to sustainability goals required? Yes, essential.

Focus – apply to consider what we buy, who we buy from and our supply chains.

Typical time frame for action – typically medium term, possibly some longer-term projects or at least ambitions.

Impact assessment is the second step within prioritization. Impact assessment is where we respond to the sustainability goals we have set and determine the specific impact areas where what we buy, who we buy from and our supply chains are misaligned to or fall short of the goals we have set. This is the means by which we develop a sustainable procurement improvement programme that is laser-focused only on the projects that will contribute directly to realizing our goals.

In a similar fashion to how we approached risk assessment, we begin by determining a longlist of the potential impact areas by making a second pass through the various assessment work done so far and adding any new areas we can identify from our knowledge of the business and its supply base. Therefore, once again, this step is best accomplished collaboratively with a small team who have good first-hand knowledge of what we buy, who we buy from and our supply chains. Once we have the longlist, we can determine the potential priorities by evaluating each impact we have identified according to its relevance to our sustainable procurement goals, and also its significance in terms of level of impact currently or degree of potential sustainability value that might be possible if we addressed the impact. This is an important point because impact assessment is about determining the priorities both for the areas we most need to address because we fall significantly short of the targets and goals set, i.e. we must fix a problem, and also where current practices are not necessarily of concern but where there is scope to go 'good to great' and meet or even exceed our sustainability goals. Therefore, there may be overlap between risk assessment and opportunity analysis (up next). This is OK. Figure 8.5 gives the impact assessment and prioritization matrix we use here. Note that unlike the other matrices, the horizontal axis works right to left for this tool to enable us to integrate it into the prioritization cube later.

Finally, and only for the impact areas we identify as priorities or where we will progress some form of action, we determine the specific projects that will address the impact. This is where we might group together similar impacts we have identified into a single course of action. For example, if we have set a goal to reduce CO_2 emissions in our supply chain by 50 per cent by 2030 and we have identified a number of potential high-emissions impact area hot spots across several key suppliers and supply chains, and also associated with some key raw materials, then combined we might determine a single 'supply-side CO_2 reductions project'. As part of this project we would then target the individual impact areas we identified to do more fact finding and establish improvement plans. The individual projects we identify will form part of our sustainable procurement improvement programme.

Conduct an impact assessment as follows:

1. Best worked collaboratively as a team.
2. Begin with a reminder of the sustainable procurement goals we have set.
3. Identify all the possible supply-side impact areas using the outputs of the assessment work thus far as a prompt.
4. For each impact, discuss, debate and determine where it sits in the impact assessment and prioritization matrix (Figure 8.5) – classify it according to its relevance to our goals and significance in terms of potential impact (either degree of misalignment from goals or potential to meet goals if addressed).
5. Group together similar impacts that might be addressed collectively, e.g. via a single project.
6. Where the matrix suggests priorities or potential action determine the potential projects that would address the individual impacts.
7. Take these forward and establish individual projects as part of the overall sustainable procurement programme (covered in the next chapter).

Opportunity analysis

Purpose – to secure advantage or create new value from sustainable procurement.

Alignment to sustainability goals required? Yes, but potential to consider other areas if a significant benefit potential is identified.

Focus – can be applied to what we buy, who we buy from, our supply chains.

Typical time frame for projects – typically medium term.

Opportunity analysis is the third step within prioritization. It is an approach to identify areas where sustainable procurement intervention or action would unlock new value or benefits beyond addressing existing risks or impact areas. Opportunities can take two forms:

Figure 8.5 The impact assessment and prioritization matrix

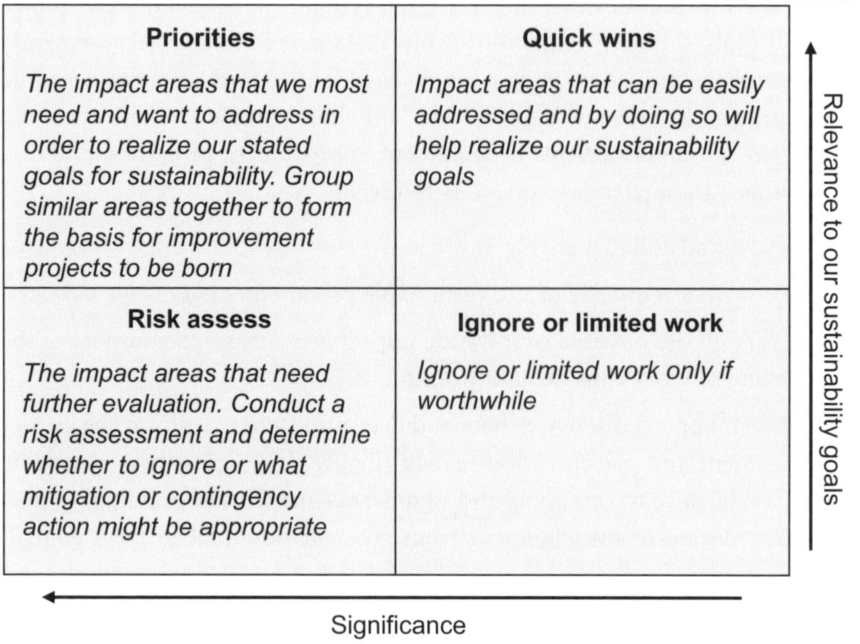

Priorities	Quick wins
The impact areas that we most need and want to address in order to realize our stated goals for sustainability. Group similar areas together to form the basis for improvement projects to be born	Impact areas that can be easily addressed and by doing so will help realize our sustainability goals
Risk assess	**Ignore or limited work**
The impact areas that need further evaluation. Conduct a risk assessment and determine whether to ignore or what mitigation or contingency action might be appropriate	Ignore or limited work only if worthwhile

← Significance →

↑ Relevance to our sustainability goals

1 New supply-side value to the organization such as competitive advantage, brand growth, revenue growth or increased effectiveness and efficiency for the organization.

2 For companies operating towards the top of the sustainability business case it could also be altruistic action to unlock new supply-side social or environmental value that is not directly related to addressing supply-side impacts. These might include such things as electing to improve quality of life for a community or establishing a wildlife protection programme – typical of companies that set out to fund specific projects out of their profits, or could also be part of strategic collaborative relationships with key suppliers.

Opportunities are distinct from action to address risk or impacts as they represent the 'want to' rather than 'need to' interventions. However, the lines between these will inevitably be blurred.

The process of opportunity analysis is similar to risk and impact assessment, where we begin by establishing a longlist of the possible opportunities that emerged from the various assessment work done so far, along with any new ideas. Once again, this step is best accomplished collaboratively with a small team of those with good first-hand knowledge in this area. Opportunities ideas are evaluated and prioritized using the opportunity analysis matrix (Figure 8.6) by evaluating each according to the scale of benefits that would be realized, either to us or in terms of altruistic social or environmental benefits, and the ease of realization.

Conduct an opportunity analysis as follows:

1 Best worked collaboratively as a team.

2 Identify all the possible supply-side opportunities that would create new value or benefits using the outputs of the assessment work thus far as a prompt.

3 For each impact, discuss, debate and determine where it sits in the opportunity analysis matrix (Figure 8.6) – classify it according to its potential scale of benefits and ease of realization.

4 Where the matrix suggests priorities or potential action, group similar opportunities together and determine the individual projects that would realize the opportunity.

5 Take these forward and establish individual projects as part of the overall sustainable procurement programme.

Figure 8.6 The opportunity assessment matrix

	Worth the effort	**Priority projects**
	Opportunities that hold great potential but not easily realizable - further evaluate and determine if worth the effort. Consider deferring until later or securing additional resources to deliver	*Opportunities we want to realize that can bring new supply-side value, such as competitive advantage, brand growth, effectiveness, etc or more altruistic value such as social or environmental value*
	Ignore	**Maybe**
	Limited work or ignore	*Opportunities that are easy to realize but low or moderate benefits. Further evaluate if worthwhile, potentially pursue as a quick win*

Benefits ↑

Ease of realization →

Figure 8.7 The prioritization heat cube

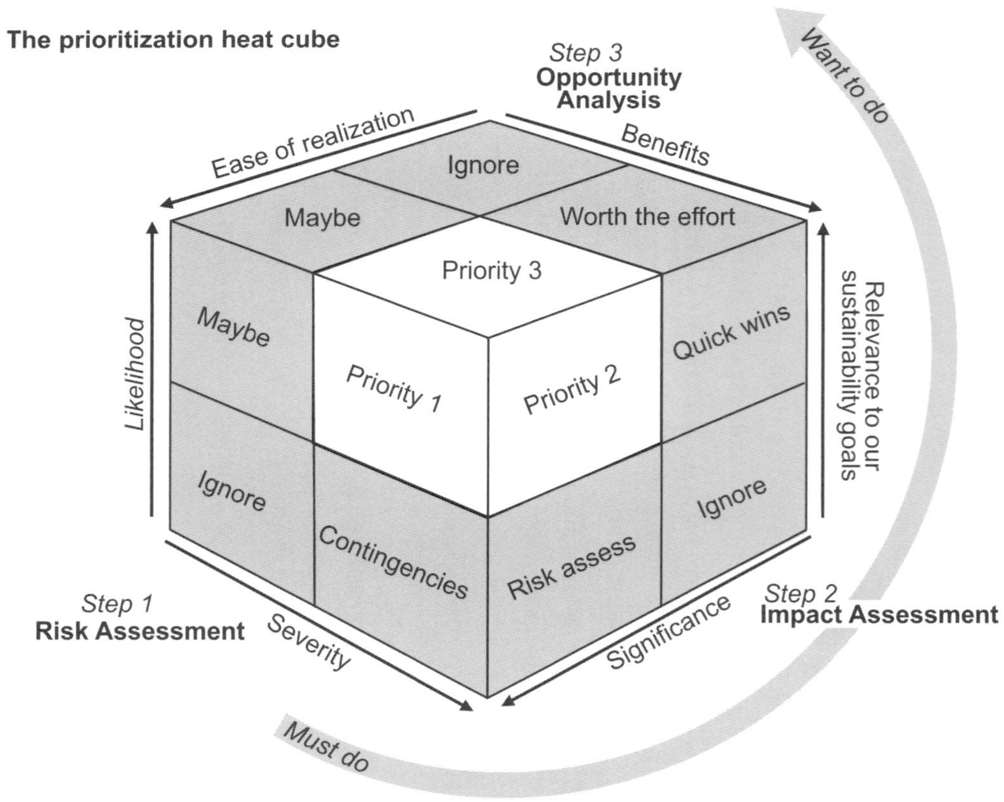

Building a prioritization heat cube

The prioritization heat cube brings together the risk and impact assessment and opportunity analysis to give a single representation of all the supply-side sustainability areas we need or want to address. So far, we have considered and evaluated the sustainable procurement risks, impacts and opportunities separately as our focus and resulting actions are different in each case. This yields three separate groups of priority actions, some being more critical than others. However, a sustainable procurement programme requires a single plan and the final step in prioritization is to bring the three assessments together using the prioritization heat cube.

The prioritization heat cube (Figure 8.7) combines the three assessment matrices to create a single view at all levels and a combined 'heat map' of our supply base that enables us to consider the relative priorities overall. From here we can then begin to scope the individual projects that will form part of our sustainable procurement road map.

Refining our targets

The final step within prioritization is to check back to our original goals and targets. It is possible that the priority areas we have identified might suggest a refinement to our original targets in light of what we have now established. If so, adjust as necessary.

> ### Chapter checkpoint
>
> In this chapter we explored why prioritization is a critical step in building a sustainable procurement road map in order to determine the areas we will work on. Key points we covered are:
>
> 1 *Prioritization has three levels* – these align to our business case for sustainability and are a hierarchy ranging from the areas where we must take action to those where we want to take action.
> 2 The first level is *risk assessment*, where we identify the top priority areas we must address.
> 3 Second is the *impact assessment* where, with our sustainability goals in mind, we identify the impacts we need and want to address to meet our goals.

Sustainable procurement

4 Third is *opportunity analysis*, where we identify areas where we can unlock new value and benefit.

5 The outputs of prioritization at each level are summarized using the *prioritization heat cube*, which forms the basis to determine the actions, initiatives and projects we will potentially move forward with, subject to further evaluation and determining which will ultimately form part of our sustainable procurement road map.

Evaluating potential sustainable procurement projects

09

> This chapter expands the first part of stage 3 of the OMEIA® process and explores how to convert the summary of our assessment as defined in our priorization heat cube into potential actions, initiatives or projects. Key tools are provided to further evaluate these potential ways forward as the first step towards building a sustainable procurement road map.
>
> *Pathway questions addressed in this chapter*
>
> 8   What improvement areas should we focus on first?
> 9   How do we build a strategy and road map for sustainable procurement?

We concluded stage 2 of the OMEIA® sustainable procurement process with a comprehensive assessment of the supply-side areas where we want or need to take action in terms of sustainability. The priority risks, impact areas or opportunities we have identified tell us where we might take action. However, many of these we will be informed ideas, based upon high-level knowledge or data only. This is our starting point for progressing sustainable procurement, and to do this we will need to scope out the potential projects that will address the risks and impact areas and respond to the opportunities we have identified. From here, we conduct further evaluation and more detailed fact-finding to validate our priorities and further scope individual projects centred around what we buy, who we buy from and our supply chains that will come together to form our sustainable procurement road map. Stage 3, evaluation (Figure 9.1), is where we do this. The assessment work we completed in stage 2 helps us know where we need to take action, subject to further investigation to validate our assumptions; stage 3 is about determining what this action will be. Stage 3 includes a range of tools and approaches to help, culminating in a fully formed sustainable procurement road map. We begin by scoping out our potential projects.

Figure 9.1 Stage 3 – Evaluation

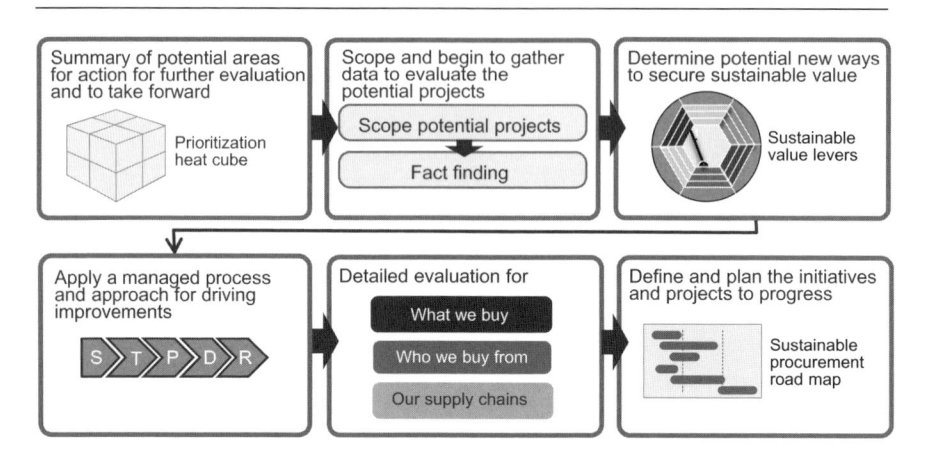

Scoping potential projects

Scoping potential projects is the process of converting the priorities we have identified into possible specific projects or actions that we might move forward with subject to further evaluation.

We do this by taking the outputs from our assessment work as summarized in our prioritization heat cube and then determining how we might respond in each case. This means we will translate risks into mitigation or contingency actions, progress quick wins, translate impact areas into improvement projects and convert opportunities into new initiatives and so on. Figure 9.2 shows the typical responses within the prioritization heat cube. And for each we determine a timeline according to overall business goals, our prioritization and available resources. We might also group together similar risks, impacts or opportunities to establish a single project that addresses multiple individual areas. This is where our sustainable procurement programme is born – as an initial collection of possible actions, initiatives and projects, which collectively begin to form our sustainable procurement road map. More on that later.

Before we get to that, however, further and more detailed evaluation may be needed to determine if the project or initiative we think we need is viable and also to determine exactly what that project or initiative might be. For example, if we identify a supply chain where we believe there are significant detrimental impacts, then we can determine we need a project to change what happens in that supply chain. However, at this stage we may not understand the precise nature of the supply chain and what happens in it or what exactly we would need to do in order to change it. Furthermore, there may be other related supply chains we also need to consider. We therefore would need to map the supply chain/SVCN, and potentially others also, in order to determine what needs to change and only then can we establish the right initiative to do this.

Scope potential projects as follows:

1 Best worked collaboratively in a small team of well-informed individuals.
2 Review the outputs of stage 2 as defined in the prioritization heat cube.
3 For that which we have placed in each quadrant against risk, impacts, opportunities, quick wins, etc (see Figure 9.2), determine how each entry would translate into a specific action, potential initiative or full project.
4 Determine potential timelines for each – this might change as we progress through stage 3.
5 Create a summary tentative 'the story so far' list or a draft project plan of the possible actions, initiatives or projects we believe might adequately respond to our assessment findings.
6 Determine next steps to validate and further evaluate these starting with a fact-find plan (up next).

Taking stakeholder management to new levels

As we will see in coming chapters, how we engage and collaborate with the wider organization has to go up a few notches for sustainability procurement when compared to what went before. Traditional approaches based upon functions trying to engage with each other are unlikely to cut it. In the main, it is unlikely that most organizations will be agile enough to restructure their entire operation to drive sustainability. Therefore, success from sustainable procurement means working within existing constraints, typically

Figure 9.2 Converting priorities into projects

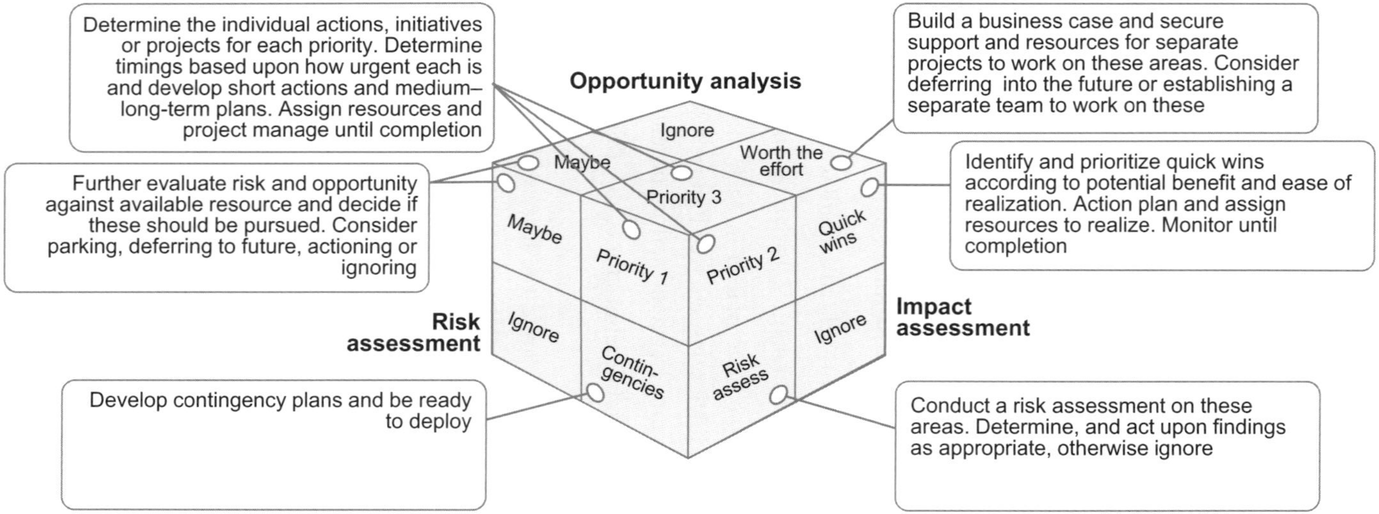

Build a business case and secure support and resources for separate projects to work on these areas. Consider deferring into the future or establishing a separate team to work on these

Identify and prioritize quick wins according to potential benefit and ease of realization. Action plan and assign resources to realize. Monitor until completion

Impact assessment

Conduct a risk assessment on these areas. Determine, and act upon findings as appropriate, otherwise ignore

Opportunity analysis

		Quick wins	Ignore
Ignore	Worth the effort	Priority 2	Risk assess
Maybe	Priority 3	Priority 1	Contingencies
	Maybe	Maybe	Ignore

Risk assessment

Determine the individual actions, initiatives or projects for each priority. Determine timings based upon how urgent each is and develop short actions and medium–long-term plans. Assign resources and project manage until completion

Further evaluate risk and opportunity against available resource and decide if these should be pursued. Consider parking, deferring to future, actioning or ignoring

Develop contingency plans and be ready to deploy

those of a silo, top-down driven company. Within such an environment good stakeholder management and cross-functional working become critical enablers. These are both topics I have covered extensively, and provided various tools for, within all my other books so if you are not fully familiar with approaches here additional reading is recommended.

As a minimum, stakeholder management begins by mapping who our stakeholders are. These could be both individuals and groups and may be different or might include others from those we would have previously identified as part of a commercially focused procurement project. The approach is different to that we covered in chapter 6 to determine stakeholder expectations. Here we apply the established method of stakeholder mapping and management which means once identified we classify stakeholders both in terms of role (using RACI analysis – whether they are *responsible*, *accountable*, need to be *consulted* or kept *informed*) and propensity to support us (are they *against it happening*, will they *let it happen*, can they *help it happen* or will they *make it happen?*). You can find this model explained at length in my other books.

Fact finding

Fact-find planning

Fact-find planning is about structuring the work we will do to progress through stage 3. It is the means by which we further evaluate areas of what we buy, who we buy from and our supply chains, following the risks, impacts and potential opportunities we have identified. This then equips us to validate and finalize the precise nature of the specific initiatives, projects or actions we will move forward with as part of our sustainable procurement programme. Core to this is how we plan our fact finding.

As for any strategic procurement initiative, fact finding is integral to sustainable procurement. It is almost impossible to determine and implement a programme to drive sustainable procurement without extensive data gathering and much of this will be in new areas to those procurement practitioners will be familiar with as part of category management, SRM or negotiation planning. As far as these methodologies are concerned, I have expanded the fact-find and data-gathering activities that underpin these across my other books, so here we will explore the specific and additional areas that support sustainable procurement.

Good fact-finding can make all the difference in determining where to direct resources or drive improvements. It is all too easy to assume we know enough to make a good decision, however, sticking with 'I know what I know' can be result limiting. 'I know what I don't know' is a good step forward and means we can establish a fact-find plan to go and plug the gaps in our knowledge. However, it is in the 'I don't know what I don't know' where the biggest opportunities and breakthroughs for sustainable procurement and supply chains can lie. This means the principle of conducting an extensive fact-find and pushing beyond the limitations of our current understanding and mindset is of paramount importance. This can strike the difference between attempting to source a traditional area of spend differently in an attempt to make it sustainable, versus reengineering what we are buying or what it is incorporated into, to remove what makes it unsustainable in the first place. This requires a new way of thinking beyond procurement as solely about acquisition.

In practice, the quest for 'I don't know what I don't know' is about keeping looking and finding out more and more, beyond the point where one might assume we know enough. That said, we must also strike a balance between pushing beyond what we know and avoiding getting lost in perpetual data gathering. This is something that becomes clear with practice (and if in doubt it can help to ask someone who has done lots of research). Notwithstanding the slightly 'free-flow' approach I've outlined here, a good fact-find also needs structure in order to direct our resource in the best way. A fact-find plan helps to respond to 'I know what I don't know' and some of 'I don't know what I don't know'. Fact-find planning is about listing all the different bits of data and information we know we need to go and get, as informed from our work so far, and then establishing a plan to do this. This provides the ability to plan efficient data collection and optimize the use of available resource as well as to combine different data needs within one fact-find activity. An example is given in Figure 9.3 and a fact-find plan template is provided in the Appendix.

Fact-find planning can be conducted for a specific project we are evaluating or across multiple projects and initiatives. For example, we might use a single request for information (RFI) or survey to collect information that supports multiple sustainable procurement initiatives.

Fact finding can be more productive with a small team. The process of fact finding need to be closely managed through to completion to ensure those tasked with gathering data and information follow through. As we progress, review the new information and understanding that emerges to further validate, shape and provide the starting point for the sustainable procurement projects and initiatives we have determined. Fact-find planning is not a once-only activity, but an ongoing approach. Develop a fact-find plan as follows:

1 Best worked collaboratively within a team of informed individuals.
2 Determine the scope for our planning – single initiative or project, or multiple?
3 Review the outputs of our assessment, especially the situation we determined as part of our SSTP and the scope of the project or initiative we have identified.
4 Determine the information and data we have already and where it is – round it up so it is available to all the team.
5 Identify the additional information and data we need but don't currently have against the different focus areas (product, service, supplier, market, supply chain) as appropriate. Use the fact-find planning template (see Figure 9.3 and the Appendix).
6 For each, determine how we will get this data – this might be discrete areas of information gathering or more substantial activities such as conducting sustainable value engineering on a product or auditing a supplier.
7 Where possible and practical identify where information or data gathering needs can be combined and satisfied with a single activity, e.g. one RFI to key suppliers to collect information across multiple data gaps.
8 Identify any other areas where we believe we might want to go and look further (to inform the 'I don't know what I don't know').
9 Assign actions, owners and agree timing.
10 Go do it. Manage and review regularly until completion.

Equipped with a good fact-find plan, we conduct fact finding in up to four areas as informed by our assessment and the potential actions, initiatives and projects we have identified. These are facts and data about what we buy, who we buy from, our supply chains and also the fourth area of the market.

Product/service or category fact-finding

Where we have identified potential projects or initiatives that focus on what we buy, our fact finding is concerned with everything we might need to find out about the products, service or categories we are sourcing. Table 9.1

Figure 9.3 An example fact-find plan

Sustainable procurement fact-find plan

Focus areas: product, service, supplier, market, supply chain or multiple

For: Cotton-based textiles
By: Sustainable Proc Team

	Focus area	Data to collect	How data will be collected	By whom	By when
1	Supplier	Countries of origin used and how much supplier understands its supply chains	RFI to immediate supplier + follow up discussions, talk to expert consultant, desktop research	Gina Bryant	End Jan
2	Supply chain	Map each of the supply chains by country of origin	Internal workshop with sustainability team and supplier collaboration	Gina Bryant	End Jan
3	Multiple	For Uzbekistan and Turkey supply chains determine all cotton producers and who the traders and ginning owners are	RFI with immediate supplier. Talk to in-country experts. Desktop research. RFI to SC players	Gina Bryant	End Mar
4	Product	Understand ginning process and how to reduce water consumption in ginning process	Desktop research, talk to expert consultant, visit and assess key players	Paolo Carlos	End Feb
5	Multiple	Water consumption for irrigation and at ginning mills	RFI to immediate suppliers, visit and assess key players	Gina Bryant	End Apr
6	Multiple	Total scope 3 CO_2e	Start with immediate suppliers. RFI to key supply chain players, audit and assessment.	McKenna Shute	End Apr
7	Multiple	Analyse cultivation providers in Turkey (circa 57 k), how big, spread, methods used, GMO vs organic	RFI to immediate suppliers, visit some, consult country industry experts	Erik Bergmann	End Jan
8	Multiple	Analyse thread manufacturing companies and market globally, including where supplemented with imports	RFI to immediate suppliers, visit some, consult country industry experts	Erik Bergmann	End Jan
9	Multiple	Supply chain movements – volumes of imports and exports by country or supply chain and where things travel most	RFI to immediate suppliers, visit some, consult country industry experts	Gina Bryant	End Jan
10	Product	Volumes of cotton-based textiles sourced globally and spec/requirements	Internal ERP system	Paolo Carlos	End Apr
11	Product	Determine impacts around soil erosion, fertilizer use, crop protection and future thinking in this area	Talk to specialist	McKenna Shute	End Feb
12	Supply chain	General data about cotton pickers by region – typical demographic, pay, likelihood of child or forced labour, etc	Published data, desktop research, consult country industry experts	Gina Bryant	End Mar

provides the potential data to collect here. There are various sources and approaches we can use, with different degrees of rigour – the more rigorous also being more demanding.

Breakthroughs for what we buy are only likely to emerge if we challenge some of the fundamentals around what we are buying in the first place, how we are using this and the need we are satisfying. Reactive procurement directed by the business leaves no room to find supply-side breakthroughs in sustainability, but rather these come when the organization together with procurement is able to reconsider what it does and how it does it, informed by understanding supply-side impacts and possibilities in this area. There are three key tools here that can help. These are sustainable value engineering, attribute analysis, and understanding the total cost and sustainable impacts of ownership. These are core to evaluating and determining projects centred around what we buy and are expanded in the next chapter.

Table 9.1 Potential data to collect and possible sources for what we buy

Potential data to collect/fact find for sustainable procurement	Possible sources of data
About the product/service<ul><li>What are we buying?</li><li>How is the product/service used (by us, by our customers)?</li><li>Specification</li><li>Certifications</li><li>Disposal/ability to recycle, reduce, repurpose</li><li>Product life cycle</li><li>Built-in obsolescence</li><li>Single use or ability to maintain</li><li>Related categories (potential synergies)</li><li>Future needs and wants for product/service</li></ul>**About how it is made**<ul><li>CO_2e generated</li><li>Processes involved</li><li>Methods of construction/fabrication</li></ul>	**Level 1 – basic and easy**<ul><li>Desktop research</li><li>Review specifications</li><li>Conduct an internal RFI</li><li>Internal R&D or NPD experts</li><li>Stakeholder interviews</li><li>Internal survey</li><li>Published information, indices, research and also that provided by governmental bodies</li></ul>**Level 2 – rigorous but hard**<ul><li>Take it apart</li><li>Break it down</li><li>Involve those who know about it</li><li>Focus groups</li><li>Ask the supplier</li><li>Map the supply chain</li><li>Take a view</li></ul>

Table 9.1 *continued*

Potential data to collect/fact find for sustainable procurement	Possible sources of data
About what goes into it • For categories and products • Materials used • Where is it made? • Inbound and outbound packaging • Where do the raw materials come from? • What happens in the supply chain and how do logistics work • Miles/kilometres travelled *For services and people involved in products* • Who does what? • Where do they do this? • How far do they travel? • Human rights upheld for workers? • Working conditions • Fair terms of employment? *Any 'hot spot' materials or products?*	**Key approaches to use here** • Sustainable value engineering • Attribute analysis • TCO/TIO (total cost of ownership/ total impacts of ownership)

Supplier fact-finding

For potential projects or initiatives required with specific immediate suppliers we will need to conduct a fact find to understand these companies more deeply. Table 9.2 provides the potential data to collect here with potential sources we can use. A supplier audit and assessment are the key tools we use to determine how sustainable a specific supplier is and there are many approaches we can use here. I will cover these in Chapter 11.

Market fact-finding

An experienced procurement practitioner will be quick to point out the importance of a thorough and deep understanding of any given sourcing market. It is by doing this that we can find commercial and traditional value breakthroughs from widening the potential supply market, creating new

Table 9.2 Potential data to collect and possible sources for who we buy from

Potential data to collect/fact find for sustainable procurement	Possible sources of data
About our suppliers • What do they do? • Location(s) and geographies they operate in • Certifications (e.g. ISO 9001, ISO 14001, ISO27001) • Any sustainability reporting? • Their plans or commitments for sustainability • Contingency planning • Reputation • Bad press • History of accidents or incidents **About how they operate** • CO_2e generated • Processes involved • Waste management • What are their supply chains? • How do they manage what happens in their suppliers? • Their logistics **About their workforce** • Who are their workforce? Where are they based? • Upholding human rights? • Working conditions • Diversity • Equality *Any 'hot spot' suppliers?*	**Level 1 – basic and easy** • Supplier's information • Online research • News stories • Talk to those who know • Published information including that provided by governmental bodies **Level 2 – rigorous but hard** • Request for information (RFI) • Remote assessment • Visit them, interview them • Industry publications • Third-party expert **Key approaches to use here** • Full supplier audit and assessment

markets or finding other ways to increase competitive tension. These are core principles that underpin category management, SRM and negotiation. The same is true for sustainable procurement, except here we look at a supply market through a different lens – that of seeking a supply market or players that either comply with legislation and our sustainability

Sustainable procurement

Table 9.3 Potential data to collect and possible sources for the supply market

Potential data to collect/fact find for sustainable procurement	Possible sources of data
About the marketplace • What 'sustainable' supply options are out there? • What are the market trends for 'sustainable practice'? • What factors might hinder sustainable practices? • Suppliers in this market today • Potential future suppliers in this market • Competitiveness within the market (and comparisons to less-sustainable market options) • Technology trends/emerging technology for sustainability in this market • Market conditions and factors driving these trends • Market segmentation (geographical, by product/service, etc) • Possible future opportunities • Possible future threats to this market • Our relative power within this market	**Level 1 – basic and easy** • Published information • Consult experts • News stories • Specialist market reports • Published information and research including that provided by governmental bodies **Level 2 – rigorous but hard** • Commission focused market insight and analysis • Request for information (RFI) • Interviews/discussions with suppliers • Interviews/discussions with experts • Business newspaper articles • Specialist consultants • Trade shows

requirements or offer the potential to progress with us to do so. Table 9.3 provides the potential data to collect here with potential sources we can use.

What we are seeking here is different to that we seek when cost is our main focus. This doesn't mean we should abandon how we optimize our approach to the supply market to secure sustainability in lieu of best cost, but rather we need to do both side by side. Looking at a marketplace through the lens of sustainability can limit the potential market available to us, and increase cost. Not all players may want to or be able to meet our requirement, others are quick to convey the increased cost of sustainability, whether founded on fact or attempting to give plausibility to higher pricing. The key here is understanding how sourcing sustainably impacts our competitive position and the specific factors that hamper leverage and competition. This equips us to make an informed decision but crucially it shows us what needs to change so that sustainable procurement can also mean best cost, if not now then later, which might also come from what we do across the products/services we source and the suppliers and supply chains we are sourcing from. It is for this reason that understanding the marketplace in terms of sustainability is important and why it should be part of our fact finding.

Supply chain fact-finding

The final area of fact finding centres around our supply chains/SVCNs. Table 9.4 provides the potential data to collect here with possible sources we can use. Arguably this is the most onerous part of a fact find as gathering meaningful information for just one supply chain is a considerable undertaking, let alone multiple supply chains. Deciding where to conduct a fact find must therefore be precisely focused and this comes from the outputs of the assessment process we have conducted, which point towards the specific supply chains where we have identified potential risk, impacts or opportunities and where we have identified potential supply chain projects or initiatives.

Supply chain (or SVCN) mapping is a key approach here and one I will expand on in Chapter 12.

Table 9.4 Potential data to collect and possible sources for what happens in our supply chains

Potential data to collect/fact find for sustainable procurement	Possible sources of data
About the supply chain • What is the structure? • Who are the players? • Where are they located? • Certifications held by individual players (e.g. ISO 9001, ISO 14001, ISO27001) • What geographies does it span? • How do things move from one place to another? • CO_2e generated at each stage *Any 'hot spot' elements?*	**Level 1 – basic and easy** • High-level desktop research • Map it with experts **Level 2 – rigorous but hard** • Detailed mapping and analysis • Consult/visit players • Specialist consultants **Key approaches to use here** • Supply chain/SVCN mapping • Audit and assessment of key players

Driving new sustainable value

Sustainability value levers

Value levers are a core tool within category management and SRM and a tool I have covered extensively within *Category Management in Purchasing* (also published by Kogan Page).

Just as a small force on a lever can create a big shift, value levers are the different interventions or actions we can take that will secure a big shift in value in all its forms from the supply base. It is a tool we use early on and throughout a category management or SRM project and practitioners will be well versed in the application of this tool and using it as a key means to shape the sourcing strategy. Value levers are traditionally used to find ways to unlock value in the form of cost or price reduction but also serve to determine ways to leverage value such as risk reduction, innovation, improved effectiveness and so on.

The value levers tool, given in Figure 9.4, is equally core to sustainable procurement to consider the different actions or interventions we can take that will yield a big shift in sustainable value. We use the same tool as we use for category management and SRM except here we consider the specific actions to drive sustainable value. In sustainable procurement, while the levers are the same, the application is different. Our focus shifts to the interventions we can take to release sustainable value, therefore we apply these levers in a different way to secure different benefits. For example, in category management we might have applied the value lever *change specification* to source a more generic product and therefore open up competition and leverage price reduction. With our sustainability hat on, *change specification* becomes interventions to specify and source a more sustainable product. Typically, this might include limiting our sourcing options, for example only to suppliers that can comply with a new, harder to achieve, specification or excluding sourcing from certain territories. Clearly limiting our supply options is at odds with the traditional application of this particular lever, which seeks to open up supply options. Here we see the potential for conflict between lowest cost and realizing sustainability being played out. While this scenario might only emerge in a handful of situations, nevertheless such conflicts will arise as sustainable value levers are applied. However, a practitioner familiar with applying both sets of value levers will be able to respond to any juxtaposition and use this to inform the decision as to what to pursue or how to counter any compromise in our commercial strength of position. If pursuing sustainable procurement means we narrow our supply options, then it may follow we need a different sourcing strategy to that we might have arrived at previously. For example, we might need to err more towards building closer relationships with fewer suppliers as an alternative means to retain leverage whereas previously a lowest-cost-only focus might have resulted in arm's-length competitive market tenders with no or low relationships. *Change relationship* is also a value lever so here we might then seek to apply this lever also whereas previously we would not have done. It is therefore essential to watch for where sustainable value compromises commercial value and determine an appropriate sourcing strategy in response to this.

The sustainable value levers tool becomes a key means by which we can determine areas where we will drive change and also to determine our sourcing strategy for a given area as well as the precise action we will take to realize it. For this reason it is essential to work towards sustainable procurement as part of, rather than in parallel with, company initiatives around category management or SRM.

There are 18 sustainable value levers under six headings that represent all the potential ways we can unlock sustainable value either for what we buy, who we buy from or within our supply chains. These are expanded in full in Table 9.5. For any given area of focus, we review the sustainable value levers and determine which ones might be relevant and effective. It would be highly unlikely to use all sustainable value levers at the same time, instead it is about picking out those that can work for the given area of focus and revisiting this ongoing. Apply as follows:

Clarify the specific area of focus (i.e. the category, product, supplier, supply chain, etc) identified from the assessment work so far as an area we will work on.

1 Review the sustainable value levers and determine which ones would be relevant and would yield the sort of sustainable value improvement we are seeking.

2 Check any conflict with how the traditional value lever might be applied or any areas where commercial value might be sacrificed for sustainable value and identify other value levers that might need to be applied in response to this.

Figure 9.4 The sustainable value levers

Sustainable value levers — Potential ways we might be able to drive supply-side sustainability

- **What we buy (category and product)**: Change specification; Change design; Aggregate spend
- **Supply chain**: Analyse, restructure & optimize; Improve process efficiency & capability; Improve logistics
- **Supply market**: Restructure supply base; Change market; Use market competition
- **Who we buy from (supplier relationship)**: Seek innovation; Improve relationship; Performance development
- **Supplier incentivization**: Offer commitment; Improve payment terms; Support route to market
- **Demand management**: Buy less or eliminate; Policy and compliance; Optimize (resource/asset utilization)

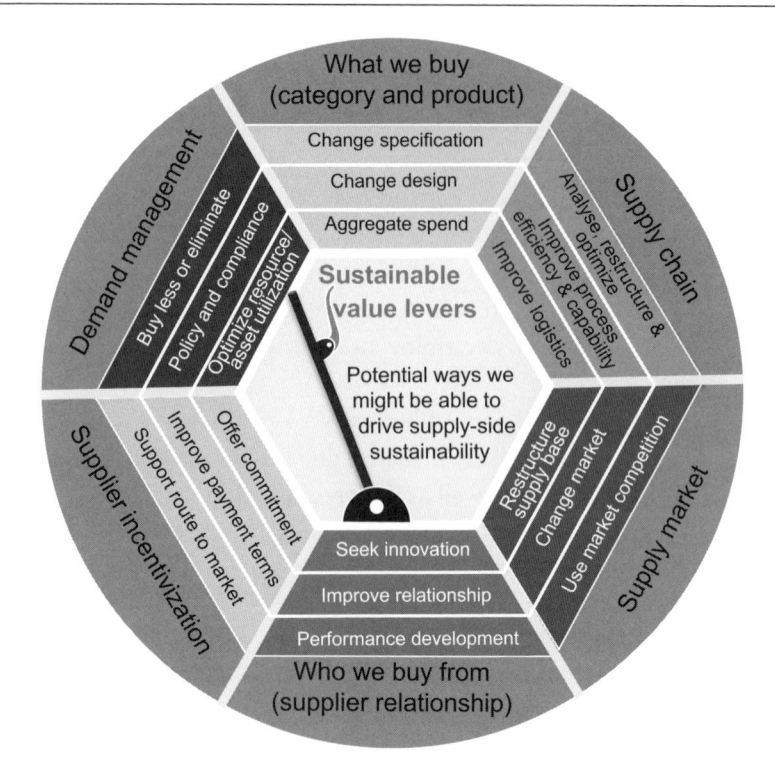

3 Determine the overall sourcing strategy the combined value levers we have selected point towards.
4 For each chosen lever, determine the precise course of action we will take.
5 Action-plan or scope sourcing project or improvement project and incorporate within sustainable procurement road map.

Table 9.5 The sustainable value levers explained

Sustainable value lever		Intervention to drive sustainable value
What we buy – category and products	*Change specification*	• Change specification to be sustainable (e.g. less-impactful alternative materials) • Limit specifications (e.g. permitted sources) • Introduce requirement for transparency or traceability • Add some sustainable feature or function to drive growth *Watch for interventions here compromising competitive position – balance sustainability with commercial good practice around making generic, consolidation or standardization*
	Change design	• Change materials or how processed • Substitute materials or components • Review 'fitness for purpose' and sustainable value-engineer • Make it circular – reuse/use recycled materials/components and design for recycling, reuse, return or managed disposal • Adapt how it can be used • Incorporate sustainable innovation to drive growth
	Aggregate spend or demand	• Aggregate spend or demand across the business – increase buying power to give leverage that can drive sustainability • Consortia buying with partners • Consolidate volumes to optimize logistics/minimize transportation/ reduce CO_2e

Table 9.5 *continued*

Sustainable value lever		Intervention to drive sustainable value
Supply chain	**Analyse, restructure and optimize**	• Map the end-to-end supply and value chain (including our internal process) and identify sustainability risks/impacts/opportunities – drive in changes • Restructure the supply chain, e.g. vertically integrate or integrate steps • Eliminate unnecessary steps • Understand the total cost of ownership and current/future cost impacts of unsustainable sourcing (e.g. future carbon tax) and optimize
	Improve process efficiency & capability	• Improve capability (process, knowledge and skills of people around sustainability) • Improve flow of information • Improve/change flow of cash • Reduce or eliminate waste/improve what gets recycled • Introduce tracking or traceability back to source • Introduce monitoring at key risk points • Make it more efficient and improve flow
	Improve logistics	• Optimize flow of material • Optimize packaging (size, spec, number of components, quantities, pallet load, reusable, recyclable, etc) • Reduce miles/kilometres travelled • Ullage reduction for packaging and transport • Optimize logistics (least-impactful means, trailer/container fill, combine loads, back hauling, etc) • Make warehouses more efficient (fit solar panels, reduce heat/cold loss through open loading doors • Change form of logistics or extend delivery times to use less impactful routing • Reduce CO_2e – EVs, eTrucks, hydrogen fuel-cell trucks, minimize air freight, etc • Use alternative transport

Table 9.5 *continued*

Sustainable value lever		Intervention to drive sustainable value
Market	**Use market competition**	• Switch to more sustainable suppliers • Run a tender or competitive market exercise built upon sustainable requirements for both product/service and supplier – select supplier and contract based upon best fit
	Change markets	• Look beyond current market – what other markets can be less impactful? • Move away from 'hot spot' geographies • Right shoring, onshoring or localization • Exclude markets where there is risk/impact we can't influence • Look at new/other markets where similar capabilities exist *Watch for loss of competitive advantage by limiting market options to pursue sustainability. Counter with longer-term development and relationship building with fewer, more important suppliers while retaining competitive tension*
	Restructure the supply base	• Make vs buy/insource vs outsource decision • Rationalize supply base – work more closely with fewer, more-important suppliers to drive sustainability • Create new suppliers • Backwards integration (start doing what your suppliers do) • Vertically integrate (acquire your suppliers)

Table 9.5 *continued*

Sustainable value lever		Intervention to drive sustainable value
Who we buy from – supplier relationship *(Immediate suppliers and those upstream in the supply chain)*	*Performance development*	• Supplier performance measurement • Set sustainability improvement objectives and targets • Contract for sustainability improvements • Drive in supplier improvement plans • Have suppliers measure and report CO_2 and agree a pathway to net zero • Provide support to develop supplier capability in this area • Introduce performance incentives or penalties • Ensure measures for data and privacy protection
	Improve relationship	• Change or develop the relationship • Get to know our suppliers better (and those upstream in the supply chain) • Agree a structure for how the relationship works for sustainability improvements • Build a 'sustainable focused relationship' • Manage supplier interfaces better • Joint working and collaboration to drive joint sustainability improvements • Drive in shared objectives and values around sustainability with common aim and purpose
	Seek innovation	• Check for and pursue potential innovation to drive sustainability with suppliers • Collaborate, align innovation initiatives and agree focus areas with key suppliers • Offer incentives, seek new value – possibly exclusivity in some cases • Look for new opportunities for growth from supply-side innovation

Table 9.5 continued

Sustainable value lever		Intervention to drive sustainable value
Supplier incentivization (Immediate suppliers and those upstream in the supply chain)	*Offer commitment*	• Offer potential or firm contractual commitment in terms of volumes, spend or length of contract to immediate supplier • Offer commitment, financial help or support direct to upstream players • Promise of future volumes of spend • Agree new pricing based upon cost breakdown (potentially with increased cost of sustainability) • Invest in supplier development • Invest in supporting local communities
	Improve payment terms	• Offer improved payment terms • Offer stage payment • Prompt settlement discount
	Support route to market	• Help the supplier improve their route to market through our organization • Help the supplier find new markets through joint innovation with us
Demand management	*Buy less or eliminate*	• Reduce need or buy less • Eliminate need • Reduce consumption • Reduce processing • Educate customer to accept less
	Policy and compliance	• Change existing/introduce new policy to manage demand or drive sustainable behaviour • Track and manage compliance to policy
	Optimize resource/asset utilization	• Reduce/minimize/eliminate use of resources • Improve/optimize asset utilization – make it more efficient/less impactful • Switch to renewable energy • Measure, monitor and reduce CO_2 • Optimize asset disposal for sustainability

Chapter checkpoint

In this chapter we have continued working through OMEIA® stage 3 and explored how we begin to determine what potential areas to work on and what further evaluation is necessary as we move towards establishing a sustainable procurement road map. In practice this means:

1 *Translating outputs of assessment into possible ways forward* – responding to our prioritization heat cube we determine how supply-side risks translate into actions and we determine the quick wins, initiatives or full projects that respond to the priority impacts or opportunities we have identified. Here we *scope the potential projects* to further evaluate.

2 *Fact-find planning* to determine how we will evaluate each potential project, the information and data we need to collect and analysis we will conduct.

3 *Fact find and detailed analysis* for what we buy, who we buy from and supply chains as well as the market place

4 *Sustainable value levers* help us to determine the different approaches we can use to secure supply-side sustainable value.

Across the next three chapters we will continue to explore stage 3 and how we make what we buy, who we buy from and our supply chains more sustainable. We will cover different analysis tools and approaches that enable us to continue our evaluation leading up to defining our way forward within our sustainable procurement road map.

Making what we buy sustainable 10

> This chapter continues our evaluation of potential sustainable procurement initiatives and projects. In this chapter we shall explore different analysis tools to evaluate what we buy for the priority areas we have identified and what would be required to make these more sustainable.
>
> *Pathway questions addressed in this chapter*
>
> **10** How can we make 'what we buy' sustainable?

We are continuing to evaluate where we need to direct our resources and now we turn our attention to what we buy. To do this we are continuing our journey through OMEIA® stage 3 and also moving into stage 4 to consider how we begin to implement changes.

Making what we buy sustainable is about driving change and improvements to the goods or services we source and how we use them. In most organizations, it would be nearly impossible to consider everything that gets purchased, so once again focus and prioritization are essential. The assessment work we have completed during stage 2 of the OMEIA® process will have identified the priority areas of spend to consider and now we need to further evaluate these and, where viable and worthwhile, determine actions to address these specific areas. This can be realized at two levels:

- Discrete mini-projects to drive an improvement for an area of spend.
- Full 5i Category Management projects with sustainability as a primary objective to determine and implement a new sourcing strategy for a category-based area of spend, working together with the wider business.

At each level, the traditional approaches for good strategic procurement remain the most effective means to drive change; however, our goals and focus change – we are doing what we know wearing our 'sustainability hat'. What is different is that we need to look at things in a slightly different way, and so we need some new tools to help do this. We will explore them in this chapter and they are summarized in Figure 10.1. We also need to work with the wider business in a different way. In fact, we need a completely new approach.

Figure 10.1 The key tools and steps in making what we buy sustainable

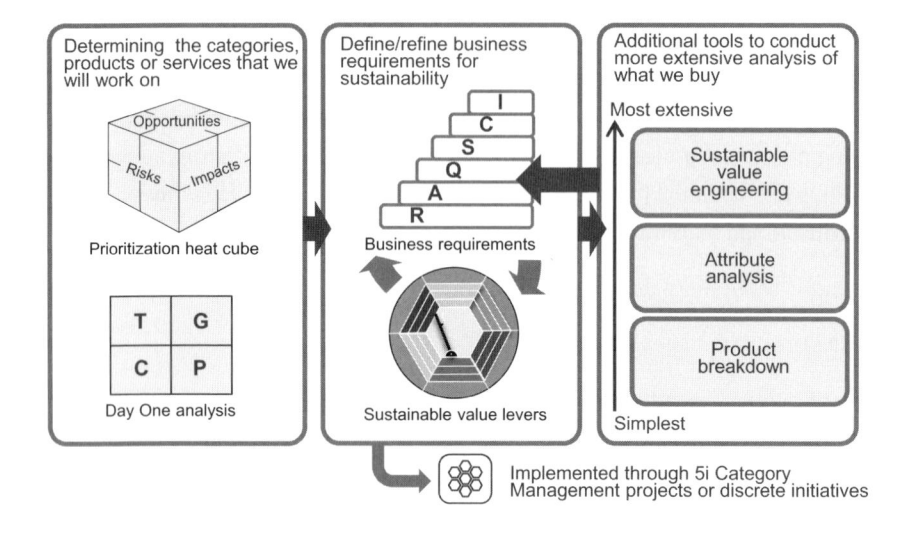

A completely new approach

Procurement practitioners will be familiar with the idea of optimizing what we buy, challenging what the business is specifying and questioning 'need' versus 'want' within the buying decision. Indeed, the notion of procurement being more than a reactive function and one that drives the right interventions to shape what gets sourced based upon what the firm is trying to achieve, coupled with supply-side possibilities, underpins modern strategic procurement. This notion also forms the basis for good category management and one I've previously described in my other books as the *3S (sourcing, satisfying and strategy)* model, which describes the necessary linkages between how we source, how our firm satisfies its customers and how procurement influences and responds to corporate strategy.

As we saw earlier, sustainable procurement takes this to another level where we not only challenge what we are buying, based upon our understanding of what is and is not sustainable on the supply side, but we can end up challenging aspects of the way our organization works, the design of our organization's product and/or service, and the overall strategy of the firm. Making what we buy sustainable will, in many cases, require more than buying something different or from a different source to that previously. It may require a complete rethink of our organization's proposition. In fact, when it comes to sustainable procurement, our interest in and influence on what happens in the supply base mushrooms beyond traditional acquisition to include:

- Determining and specifying what we buy (business requirements)
- Reviewing how we obtain the goods/service
- Reconsidering how our firm uses the goods/service
- Being prepared to change the design of what our firm offers to the market
- Taking account of how our customers use and dispose of our goods/service

Experienced procurement practitioners in organizations with mature procurement functions will be used to working closely with internal functions to deploy the optimum sourcing strategies. Once again cross-functional working, joint teams, stakeholder engagement and management are essential. However, to achieve sustainable procurement, we need more again because even with a cross-functional approach, this may not be enough to challenge some of the fundamental aspects of what the firm does. Arguably, when it comes to sustainable procurement, the idea of procurement as a separate function fails to create the right conditions for true sustainable procurement. Instead sustainable procurement needs to become a driving philosophy that runs through the entire organization coupled with the ability of the organization to work in a flatter, more collaborative cross-functional structure. This may not be something most firms can simply transition to immediately. For a procurement function to be effective and actively contribute to realizing the future strategy of the firm, it will need to become even more embedded within the wider organization and become a key protagonist for sustainability in everything the firm does. The good news is we already have a well-proven approach here that can help and it is category management.

Using 5i Category Management to drive sustainability

For some areas of spend a simple desktop review and improvement project may be sufficient, perhaps with cross-functional engagement. However, given everything we have explored previously, driving change to a significant area of spend will typically require much more. As I touched on earlier in this book, 5i Category Management is the most proven and effective means by which an organization can realize its strategic goals in terms of what gets sourced. Practitioners will be familiar with its application to drive reduced price, mitigate price increases, reduce cost, reduce risk, drive supply-side innovation or improve efficiency for third-party spend. Practitioners who have been part of a well-implemented category management approach will understand the strategic contribution it can make to an organization as well as the unrivalled scale of benefits made possible by good application. With our sustainability hat on, category management also provides the perfect, well-established, approach to drive sustainability for categories of spend and the individual products and services these categories might include. It also enables us to determine and implement sourcing strategies that balance meeting commercial objectives along with supply-side sustainability goals. Furthermore, it is the means by which an organization that has established good governance for category management projects can utilize this same governance approach to realize sustainability objectives.

Once again, refer to *Category Management in Purchasing*, also published by Kogan Page, to access the 5i methodology in detail. Within the application of this approach there are a number of steps or tools where a shift in their application while *wearing the sustainability hat* becomes particularly relevant to sustainable procurement. These are specifically included within the OMEIA® process and covered within this book. However, beyond these, nearly the entire 5i methodology and the majority of steps that make it up are relevant to some degree when sustainable procurement is part of or our entire ambition. Therefore, 5i Category Management should be regarded as the go-to process and approach for driving sustainable procurement for what we buy beyond simple improvement projects.

That said, there is one important shift and consideration in doing this. 5i Category Management is based upon the principle of gaining leverage for an area of spend by working at the category, not product or service, level and ensuring our categories are market facing. This means that we maximize our leverage by developing sourcing strategies for the entirety of what we spend in any given marketplace. Therefore, good commercial-based category management is market focused rather than internally focused. However, when we consider sustainable procurement, we can encounter a disconnect with this principle for three reasons, which I will expand:

1 The category perspective might be too broad.
2 We might cause a dilution of competitive position.
3 Sustainability might drive alternative more relationship-based sourcing strategies.

Category versus product or service perspective

Some aspects of sustainability for what we buy can be driven at a category level (e.g. compliance with legislation, meeting a sustainability policy, etc). However, some aspects of sustainability improvement might be needed at the level of individual products or services. In practical terms this means that while we might be applying 5i Category Management at the category level we will drive individual improvements at a product or service level. I will return to this later when we look at business requirements.

Preventing a dilution of competitive position

If a marketplace is moving towards offering more sustainable products or services that fit with our internal requirements, then the market-facing approach fits as we can simply define new sustainable business requirements and select a supplier based upon their ability to meet these. However, the disconnect comes where the changes we need to make to what we are sourcing in order to drive sustainability mean we create unique or differentiated products or services not generically available within the market. This can dilute the commercial leverage we might have otherwise enjoyed if not pursuing sustainability. Here we reach one of the challenges with sustainable procurement and the hard reality that sometimes we need to trade commercial advantage to meet our sustainability goals. It might also mean that to counter this we need to look to alternative sourcing strategies.

Driving sustainable procurement for what we buy means we not only need to consider how we change what we buy or how we use it, etc, but we also need to consider the marketplace we are sourcing from and the impact our decisions to source more sustainable products or services will have on our competitive position in the market place. Key tools within 5i Category Management can help. Portfolio analysis and supplier preferencing are key tools to determine the optimum sourcing strategy in commercial terms (Figure 10.2). For example, a category in the Leverage quadrant within portfolio analysis, which is viewed as Development to the suppliers we engage with (supplier preferencing), might point to a sourcing strategy built upon running a competitive tender and selecting a small number of preferred suppliers with whom we will agree short–medium-term contracts. However, add in the need to meet new sustainable goals and a tightening of our business requirements to do this and what was previously generic with multiple suppliers in the market might become more unique and therefore limit our market options. This might then push us into the Strategic quadrant (portfolio analysis) and as such we might seek a different sourcing strategy to select and work with a single supplier, in a long-term contract (Core in supplier preferencing). This therefore prevents the dilution of our competitive position through creating a more strategic, mutually dependent relationship.

Alternative relationship-based sourcing strategies

As we will explore more in the next chapter, the shift from traditional pure leverage-based approaches with key suppliers towards more collaborative relationship-based procurement is an inevitable consequence of working towards sustainable procurement. This is not a bad thing – quite the contrary, as it provides a platform from which we can create new value. It is also the natural trajectory of travel of procurement globally as a response to how global marketplaces and supply chains have changed in recent years and become more volatile, less predictable and less reliable, driving closer relationships. When we feel safe, we are happy to swim alone. When we are in deep water, we want to be close to others.

What this means is the relationship between related categories becomes more important with the opportunity to pursue advantage by closer relationships with a smaller number of suppliers that we are working longer-term with to meet new sustainability across multiple categories.

5i Category Management therefore remains perfect whether we are seeking commercial advantage and/or sustainability advantage, and as our goal changes so too do the different strategic sourcing strategies that emerge to balance commercial and sustainability objectives.

Another important tool used in 5i Category Management and across all areas of strategic sourcing is Day One analysis, which is particularly useful to help evaluate what we will work on and the type of sourcing strategy we might move forward with.

Figure 10.2 Using portfolio analysis and supplier preferencing to shape alternative sourcing strategies that drive sustainable procurement for what we buy

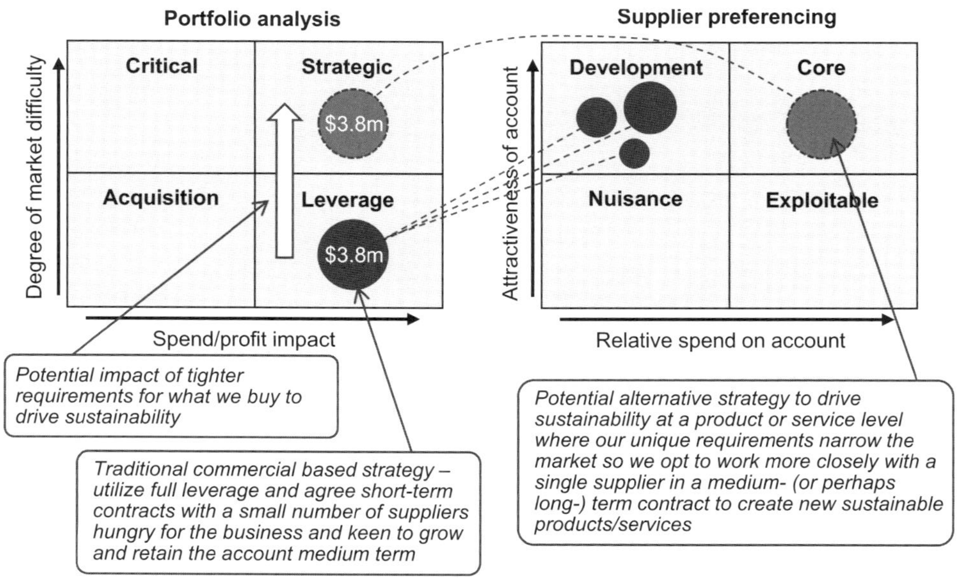

Using Day One analysis to evaluate what to work on and select the right approach

Day One analysis is a key tool in strategic procurement, and one used early on to gain an insight into our current situation for an area of spend. It enables us to determine our relative power position and what we might need to change to gain commercial leverage. It is particularly useful within sustainable procurement, and especially when we consider goods and services, to provide an early indication of the potential sourcing strategy and the primary areas to focus on. Day One analysis (Figure 10.3) works by considering what we are buying and the number of suppliers as well as the number of buyers (of which we are one). A template is provided in the Appendix. The axes are binary, rather than graduated, so we consider if there is one, or more than one, in each case. When we consider the number of suppliers, we can encounter a different classification based upon the potential number of suppliers available in the market versus how this might be limited as a result of internal decisions we have taken. This might include the impact of tighter business requirements for sustainability, which, as we have seen, will drive us towards alternative sourcing strategies.

Once again, this tool and its use is expanded in full in *Category Management in Purchasing*, also published by Kogan Page. However, Figure 10.3 includes a summary of our position for what we buy for each quadrant along with our potential responses. Day One analysis should form part of any sustainable procurement project and should be used early on to establish how we might proceed in driving sustainability for an area of spend. Use as follows:

1 Best worked collaboratively within a team.
2 Apply at a category, product or service level.
3 For each of the areas of spend we have identified as potential priorities, classify them onto the Day One matrix strictly by the axis (a template is provided in the Appendix).
4 Where there is debate, e.g. where an internal policy changes the classification, plot both outcomes and discuss the basis for the difference. This will give a key insight.
5 Review the completed Day One matrix and discuss – 'so what does this tell us?'
6 Agree next steps and plan as appropriate for each of the areas of spend being evaluated.

Figure 10.3 Using Day One analysis to determine our approach for sustainable procurement

	One	More than one
More than one (Number of suppliers)	**Tailored** We have commercial power because we have choice - there are many suppliers that can do this, and strong ability to drive sustainability because we are buying to our specification *Focus on:* Selecting and working with right suppliers to deliver to our specification, including sustainability requirements	**Generic** We have commercial power because we have choice and can switch suppliers but limited influence on how sustainable what we buy is – we are buying a generic specification that the market offers *Focus on:* • If spec is OK – supplier selection • If spec not OK – change spec to be sustainable and move to tailored. Watch for loss of competitive tension if spec changes limit supply choices
One	**Custom** Usually a shared commercial power relationship to mutual benefit. Strong basis to drive sustainability because we are working together with a single supplier (possibly co-development) to meet or create a unique specification *Focus on:* Working closely with the supplier, developing the relationship and pursuing innovation to drive sustainability (for mutual advantage)	**Proprietary** We have no or very little commercial power and no or very little influence on how sustainable what we buy is. We are buying to the supplier's specification. They hold the power *Focus on:* Changing specification to get out of proprietary and open up choice, or lobbying supplier to change what is unsustainable

Number of buyers (including us)

Analysing what we buy

For the areas of priority spend we have determined there are a series of tools and approaches that enable us to analyse what we buy and provide the basis to determine what needs to change to make the goods and services more sustainable. These are, in order of difficulty and complexity:

- Redefine **business requirements** to include sustainability
- Conduct a **product breakdown** with a sustainability focus
- **Attribute analysis** and redefining business requirements/specification
- Full **sustainable value engineering** – the most extensive, resource-intensive and all-encompassing approach

Each of these serves a different purpose and so we would not necessarily seek to conduct all of these, but rather the one or ones that are relevant and possible based upon available resources. I will cover each in turn.

Redefining business requirements

Business requirements is both the starting point and end point for driving sustainability for what we buy. It is the starting point because it is the simplest and most easily achievable means to review and redefine what we are buying. It is the end point because it is the means by which we will redefine what we are buying following a more extensive review and redesign of what we buy.

Business requirements is one of the most fundamental tools within 5i Category Management, and also within supplier relationship management and is an essential part of negotiation planning. Business requirements (covered at length in my other books) are specific to what we buy but by implication can also need to include requirements for the suppliers that will provide the goods or services. The RAQSCI model (Figure 10.4) provides the framework to define business requirements. It is a hierarchy and hence represented as a staircase (or a pyramid) to illustrate the concept that, in the same way you need to step on the first stair to get to the second, the bottom-most requirements must be achievable and satisfied in order to then consider the next level. When contemplating supply options, unless the requirements for the lower tiers can be satisfied, options that meet upper tier requirements such as best cost or great innovation potential become irrelevant.

Business requirements are the needs and wants, now and into the future, as determined by the business and ratified by procurement to form a single, overarching definition of requirements for what we will buy. We often need multiple levels of business requirements definition to define the overarching requirements of the category and then perhaps for individual (or groups of) products or services. Whatever the application, business requirements can be the hardest step to complete as achieving a good set of business requirements demands extensive fact-finding and stakeholder engagement. It also requires us to make sense of the multiple, varied and often conflicting wants, aspirations, preferences and desires, often expressed as essential needs, into a single definition of business requirements. Intrinsic to established good strategic procurement is how we challenge what the business is setting out to buy and refine the multiple inputs to arrive at a set of business requirements that will maximize our commercial leverage. Here we are seeking to get behind stakeholder preferences to arrive at a single definition of what the business need is. This can often result in shifts in what those in an organization thought they were setting out to buy and can result in alternative goods and services from alternative markets that satisfy the need while optimizing leverage within a marketplace. These shifts are typically informed by considering the various value levers that might be used. Business requirements is therefore a key source of breakthrough within procurement and the most important and difficult step in terms of wider business engagement.

Using RAQSCI to define sustainability requirements

The RAQSCI tool and the process of defining business requirements is particularly important for sustainable procurement. It is the means by which we can engage with multiple stakeholders to define current and future needs and wants for sustainability for an area of spend. Crucially, the same process of engagement with, and challenge to, internal stakeholders is a key means by which we can drive sustainability for what we buy, guided by the sustainability value levers. There are four dimensions within this:

- Challenging the business based upon our understanding of the supply base and the risks, impacts and opportunities for sustainability.
- Optimizing the balance between maximizing our commercial leverage and making what we buy sustainable – once again we see that the redefining of requirements for sustainability could dilute our commercial position and so we can quantify this and adjust our sourcing strategy accordingly.
- Challenging what we buy and how we use it.
- Determining the specific, additional requirements for sustainability.

Building upon this last point, sustainable business requirements should not be separate from traditional business requirements, but rather integral. After all, everything we already know and need regarding what we buy and the best way to define this remains entirely relevant, but we need to put on the 'sustainability hat' and extend, modify or adapt our business requirements to include the specific sustainability needs and wants. This is unlikely to be a case of simply bolting on additional sustainability requirements, instead it is entirely possible that new sustainability requirements might drive a fundamental shift in existing or commercially focused requirements – providing the opportunity to balance both objectives into a single set of business requirements.

The sustainability business requirements, and the process of creating them, is the point of convergence for everything we are setting out to achieve in terms of sustainability for what we buy. It is where the sustainability goals for the organization and those of procurement get translated into that which will steer what we buy. It is the means by which modern thinking for driving sustainability can be realized. This might include defining requirements that move closer to circularity (see Chapter 7) or respond to scarcity of resources (e.g. through requirements that substitute, replenish, recycle, recreate). For commercial business requirements it is the means by which we translate market possibilities into our requirements. For sustainability this becomes the means by which we respond to the supply-side risks, impacts and opportunities we have identified. The sustainable value levers are a key driver in defining business requirements and both these tools work together and inform each other to determine a definition of what the business needs and wants while maximizing sustainability value. Finally, as I've already outlined above, it is where the needs and wants of the business, following challenge, synthesis and ratification by the business get defined. Figure 10.4 summarizes the inputs along with potential additional sustainability requirements to consider under each heading.

Once again, stakeholder engagement is key to determining sustainable business requirements and this should be planned and managed as part of the fact-find activity. Approaches such as remote internal surveys can help, especially for large groups of stakeholders, but to be effective defining requirements for sustainability requires engagement with key individual stakeholders in order to be able to have the right conversations and open discussions that might challenge specific aspects. We then have the task of fusing all the outputs of these individual discussions to weave together a single definition of business needs and wants. Only once this is agreed by the business, which in practice requires us to go back and negotiate agreement with the various individual stakeholders, do we have a basis to move forward and make what we buy more sustainable. Achieving this is nothing short of an art form that can require the same tact, tenacity and resilience of an international diplomat brokering peace between warring nations. Procurement practitioners of 5i Category Management will be well used to this; however, when it comes to sustainability this can be even more difficult as we can end up challenging what we buy much more deeply than before. The good news, however, is that whereas before the goal of improving commercial outcomes rarely resonated with the alternative goals of the wider business functions, when it comes to sustainability this goal is universal and therefore cooperation should be more forthcoming. Therefore, in developing business requirements and engaging with the business it helps to sell why we are doing this – support early on can make all the difference to the process of challenging and changing what we buy to make it more sustainable.

Figure 10.4 Business requirements – inputs and potential additional sustainability requirements to consider

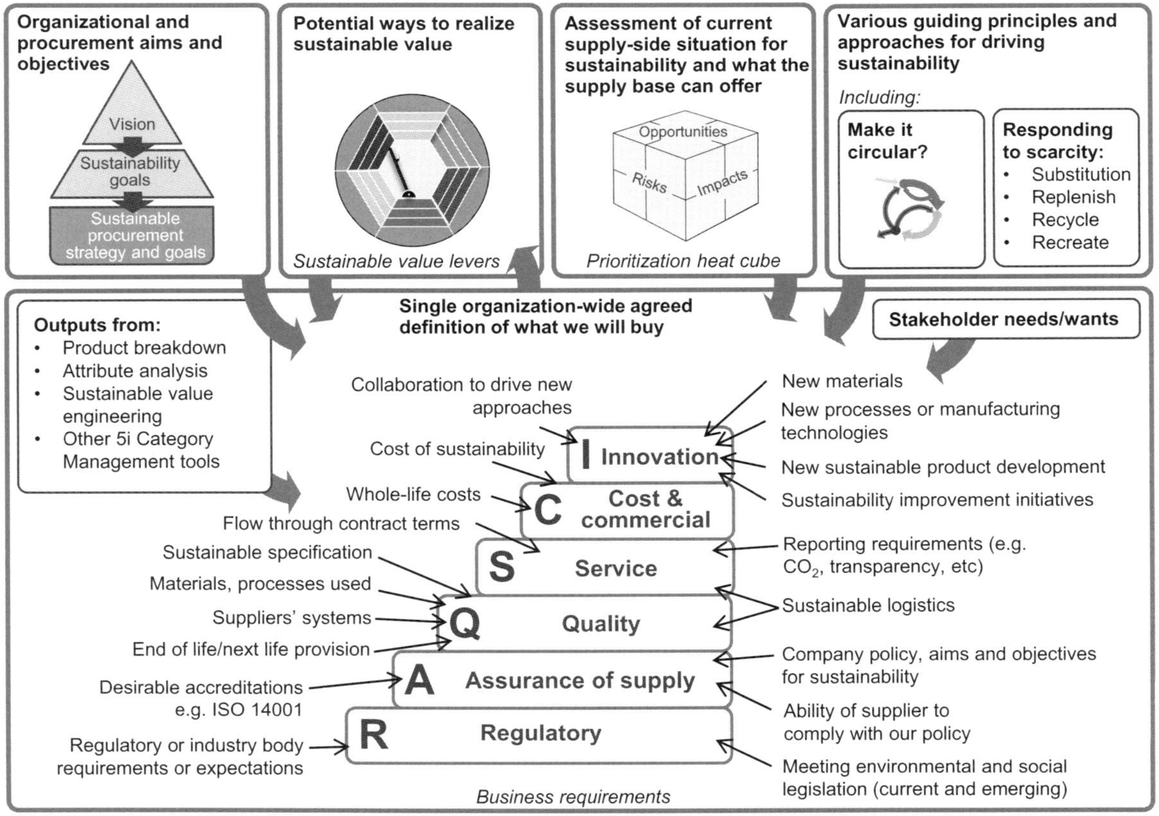

Sustainable procurement

Table 10.1 provides some supplementary questions we can use internally to determine sustainability business requirements. These should be used together with the established questions and as a means of data gathering for business requirements.

Define sustainability business requirements as follows:

1 Best worked collaboratively in a small cross-functional team.
2 Begin by determining the scope of the requirements – entire category, product or service? Or multiple levels?
3 Where existing commercially focused business requirements are already in place, use these as a starting point (but be ready to change them), otherwise develop a single set to define combined commercial with sustainability business needs.
4 Interpret the organizational and procurement goals for sustainability and determine specific requirements that flow from these.
5 Translate the sustainable value levers we have identified into specific requirements.
6 Determine the potential requirements that have emerged from our assessment as captured in the prioritization heat cube.
7 Determine any opportunity to bring in sustainability concepts (e.g. circular economy, dealing with resource scarcity) and translate into requirements.
8 Translate the outputs from any product breakdown, attribute analysis or sustainable value engineering activity into requirements.
9 Build a 'first draft' set of business requirements under each of the RAQSCI headings, distinguishing needs from wants and whether needed now or in the future. Avoid stating vague requirements or defining aims and work to make each a precise definition of the outcome to be achieved. Make requirements as SMART as possible.
10 Identify key stakeholders, not already engaged, to involve and determine a fact-find plan for stakeholder engagement.
11 Engage with the stakeholders, share the first draft and establish sustainability needs and wants. Use the questions in Table 10.1 to guide discussions.
12 Challenge, debate, discuss, combine and refine together with stakeholders to arrive at a single, agreed, definition.

Making what we buy sustainable 321

13 Use as the basis for sourcing to determine the sourcing strategy, engage with the market and negotiate and select suppliers, and for contract planning, supplier management and performance measurement.

14 Review regularly, update as needed and act upon any significant changes.

Table 10.1 Supplementary stakeholder questions to shape sustainability business requirements

Requirement	Sample stakeholder questions
Regulatory	• What current and future legislation at organization, product, service, supplier or supply chain level must we comply with?
Assurance of supply	• What organizational policies must be complied with? • What standards do we want suppliers to hold (e.g. ISO 14001, ISO27001)? • What needs to be in place within our suppliers here in order for them to comply with legislation and our policies? • Should we exclude certain potential suppliers and if so on what basis (e.g. hot spot location, historical factors, size, knowledge of them, etc)? • Are there any internal qualification requirements suppliers here must meet (e.g. successful internal audit)? • What data privacy and protection requirements apply here?
Quality	• Are there any specifications to be met? • What could change within the specification to make it more sustainable (attribute analysis)? • How sustainable is the use of resources, what proportion is recycled, how can we improve this? • How sustainable is the processing that goes into this? What could we change to improve this? • What, if any, management systems do we require the supplier to have in place here (e.g. ISO 9001)? • What needs to happen at end of life of what we buy? How can we make this circular, sustainable or provide for next life? • How much waste is produced in the supply chain or by us? Can we change this? • How can we get more transparency regarding what happens in the supply chains?

Table 10.1 *continued*

Requirement	Sample stakeholder questions
Service	• How do we want to manage sustainability improvement initiatives with suppliers? • What do we want the supplier to report on in terms of sustainability? • What performance measures do we need here? • Do the suppliers have the capability to drive sustainability?
Cost/commerical	• What is the cost of making it more sustainable? How can we verify this? What would need to change to optimize this cost? • What terms around sustainability might we include within contracts? • How might we make sustainability improvement targets contractual? • What commitment would we need to give the supplier to incentivize them to drive sustainability?
Innovation	• What innovation would help here? • How do we want to work with the supplier to collaborate on new sustainability initiatives?
	General questions
General questions that will help 'unlock' key sustainability business requirements	• How can we make this more circular? • How can we reduce waste and optimize waste management? • How can we minimize the use of resources? • How can we change the specification of what we buy?

Product breakdown

Product (or service) breakdowns are nothing new for the experienced procurement or supply chain practitioner. Conducting a purchase price cost analysis (PPCA), or should-cost analysis, is a key tool used within category management and one I've covered at length in *Category Management in Purchasing*, also published by Kogan Page. PPCA traditionally helps us determine what a product or service should cost by conducting a full breakdown of every cost component it contains and determining, via research and investigation, what each 'should cost' to calculate the total should-cost of the product or service. This allows comparison with suppliers' pricing and provides the basis for negotiation and driving improvements. As such, PPCA is only suitable for non-complex, non-proprietary areas of spend and not usually helpful where the market is competitive and therefore market forces drive price. In Day One analysis we would mostly consider using PPCA if what we are buying is in tailored or custom quadrants.

Our traditional application of PPCA has been based around seeking out areas for cost improvement. However, when we consider sustainability in terms of what we buy, a product or service breakdown becomes highly useful to start considering the materials, processing, logistics, methods of provision and who gets involved for a given product or service. This provides the basis for driving sustainability for what we buy and when coupled with a PPCA also provides the basis to quantify what any changes should cost and therefore assess the cost of sustainability at a product or service level. Table 10.2 shows the difference (and similarities) in component elements we are identifying between a cost based PPCA and sustainability-focused product breakdown. This table also highlights the conflicts between cost and sustainability objectives. This is good as it informs the debate about how we balance these two objectives. The process for conducting a breakdown versus a PPCA is identical, it is just our perspective and objectives that change. When we put our sustainability hat on we are able to determine where elements of a product or service must change while also determining where we want to accept an increased cost or alternatively what the new goals are for driving cost reduction with sustainability.

This last point is important because it doesn't follow that making what we buy sustainable must increase cost. Time to put our commercial hat back on and challenge the basis for this increased cost. If it is because historically a product has been made with low-cost labour in an underdeveloped country, then the cost increase here is necessary. However, if switching the source of a raw material comes with a cost increase we should question why and how this could be improved. Remember, for many suppliers sustainability is a new concept demanding new ways of working and management time to do things differently, which increases indirect costs. The aim here should be that sustainability is business as usual. Therefore, understanding what is driving the cost of sustainability in our suppliers is essential to determining what is justified and for how long, and what are the longer-term plans to reduce supplementary costs and not pay more for something to be sustainable.

Sustainable procurement

Table 10.2 The differences, similarities and conflicts between a cost-based PPCA and sustainability-focused product breakdown

Cost and sustainability driver	Includes	Cost-based PPCA	Sustainability focused product breakdown
Materials	All the components used, raw materials, ingredients and packaging	What each component should cost and potential to impact costs	How sustainable is each component and what could be changed to improve it?
People	Labour that goes into making/providing it, who does it, where are they?	Time and cost of labour involved	Can we be confident re upholding human rights, working conditions, living wage and general fair treatment of those involved?
Processing	How and where it is processed?	Equipment used, cost of processing	CO_2 produced, environmental impact, likelihood of pollution
Logistics, transportation and inventory management	Logistics, transportation and inventory management	What logistics, cost of each element and potential to impact costs	Miles/km travelled, CO_2 produced, impact on communities
Overheads	Direct and indirect overheads	Direct costs – people and equipment that makes the goods/delivers the service + indirect overheads (cost of sales, general admin, marketing, R&D, etc)	Adequate ability for suppliers to reinvest to ensure sustainable operations
Profit	Supplier margin	How much margin is the supplier making? Is it reasonable?	Are suppliers or supply chain entities making sufficient margin?

Those familiar with PPCA in cost terms will know that conducting a breakdown is no small task and therefore it is essential to target resources where worthwhile. For driving sustainability in terms of what we buy, a breakdown should be contemplated only where a product (or service) breakdown will work. This would be for a specific, non-complex product or service (not a category) where worthwhile (check Day One analysis). It should also be relevant, i.e. there are risk and impact areas and opportunities that emerged as priorities from our assessment. A template for product breakdown is provided in the Appendix.

Conduct a product breakdown for sustainability as follows:

1 Best accomplished collaboratively in a small team of those with knowledge of the product or area in question.
2 Determine the scope of the breakdown (what product, what service, what is and is not included, focus on sustainability or cost also).
3 For the item in question break it down; if possible and a physical thing – take it apart. Identify all the elements, and if physical components, what they are made from, where they might come from, how much there is of each, etc.
4 Under each of the headings in Table 10.2 or using the template in the Appendix, start making a list of all the components and cost drivers.
5 Using the six impact areas as a prompt, consider how sustainable/unsustainable each cost driver is and identify areas we may want to change. Inform this via research online, asking suppliers, asking experts, etc.
6 Repeat for people, processing, logistics, overheads and profit.
7 Review the total assessment, combine with any PPCA conducted, and determine 'so what does this tell us?'.
8 Determine the potential changes required and further evaluate as needed, then define the new product using RAQSCI business requirements.

Attribute analysis

Attribute analysis is a creative thinking technique based around reviewing a specific material, product, assembly or service and identifying all the different characteristics that make it what it is and, in particular, what can make it distinct from other products. Attributes are therefore the features, functions, benefits and the experience of using a particular product (or service), and the collective analysis of these attributes provides a basis for comparison to drive new value. For example, consider an apple – it has shape, size, weight, colour, variety, texture and taste. That is about as far as most of us get initially, but think harder and it also has smell, perhaps a stalk, pips, freedom from disease, insects or other parasites, grown using pesticides, a label, inner carton packaging, outer packaging, shelf life, country of origin and possibly other things besides that I haven't thought of. Some of these are tangible attributes (i.e. things we can see, measure, compare, etc) and some of these are intangible (things based upon how it makes us feel, e.g. the unpacking experience, how it tastes, our judgement regarding quality and so on). The list of tangible and intangible attributes is almost endless.

Typical applications of attribute analysis

Attribute analysis is typically utilized as an optimization tool looking either customer facing or supplier facing, and both work very differently:

- **Optimizing the customer-facing product (or service).** This is the most common application for attribute analysis and typically a marketing technique to optimize a product and influence the customer buying decision thereby maximizing profit or market share. By considering the attributes of a given product and determining which attributes customers expect or value, along with those that are invisible or those that the customer doesn't care about, it is possible to optimize the product both in terms of cost or efficiency as well as attractiveness to the customer.

- **Optimizing what we source.** Here we consider the attributes of products or materials we are sourcing as a basis to review and optimize the specification of what we buy, or to compare attributes across multiple items we are sourcing as a basis to refine or harmonize specifications and determine opportunities for cost improvement or efficiency.

Attributes help establish the end-to-end value flow

The second application is, of course, the most relevant to procurement and supply chain functions. However, key here is that the use of attribute analysis on the supply side is very different to the marketing-led approach, demanding a very different mindset and approach to using it. That said, the two are inextricably linked.

When customer facing, we are concerned with the attributes that might influence a customer decision. In procurement, it is less about how attributes might influence our decision, indeed it is unlikely we would be quite so market led, but rather we would be interested in the attributes where there might be opportunity to find new value by driving an improvement to the specification. This typically results in us focusing on a different set of attributes on the supply side. For example, imagine if our business produces ready meals. We might work on optimizing such customer-facing attributes as taste, smell, texture, size, labelling, packaging, quality marks, shelf life and so on. Perhaps there might also be a sustainability mark or claim. On the supply side, we are considering how we can optimize sourcing the ingredients that will create the product and so attributes for a specific ingredient might include materials, processing involved, type of logistics, origin, and if we add in sustainability, energy used, CO_2e consumed, certifications and so on. Attributes such as taste, texture, etc would still be relevant but these would typically be part of the specification for what we are sourcing, perhaps verified by testing on incoming goods, rather than areas we might focus on for driving supply-side improvements.

Crucially, the customer-facing attributes that are important drive the specification of the product, which determines the business requirements for what we source. Customer-facing and supply-side-facing attributes are therefore not separate but rather codependent, and establishing the linkage between the two is a key enabler of true end-to-end category management and the basis to drive end-customer value enabled by supply-side possibilities.

The importance of comparability

When we consider the attributes for an area of spend (materials used, outcomes achieved, size, volume, specification, how processed, shelf life, origin, logistics involved, etc) we quickly find we are making a similar list to that we compile when we conduct a product breakdown. While a product breakdown can provide a good starting point, attribute analysis takes our understanding of a product or service to a new level. Key here is how we compare attributes, either to a target, a benchmark or other products or services. Therefore, attribute analysis is distinct from a product breakdown because we quantify the attribute in terms of how much value it provides to make it comparative and therefore inform our decision making. Comparative attributes are something we all use every day to guide our personal buying decisions – price per kg on supermarket shelf labels, time per session, pixels per inch, quantity per carton, etc.

In procurement comparative attributes form the basis to leverage benefit from the supply base through optimizing the specification. As such, attribute analysis acts as an enabler to utilize specific value levers and so we might use comparative attributes such as volume per unit, thickness of carton, length of cable, per cent dilution, hours attended and so on. Such attributes would typically form part of a specification and the broader business requirements for an area of spend. Therefore attribute analysis can be a key means to challenge a specification and challenge business requirements as a means to drive new value.

For example, consider a global business buying cans to package its canned food products where there is legacy buying from different suppliers by various business units around the world. The firm has ended up buying to a variety of in-country specifications with various thicknesses of can, different plating thicknesses and different openers being specified for what is a common part used by all business units. By considering the attributes of can thickness, can material, number of ridges, plating type, plating thickness, type of opener, etc, this provides the basis for comparison. The firm can establish a single new more efficient global specification to provide the basis to drive down material cost and aggregate spend with fewer suppliers. This is how attribute analysis can drive significant value for procurement, and building upon a product breakdown and PPCA provides the basis to develop a new, challenged, set of business requirements.

Using attribute analysis to drive sustainable procurement

Attribute analysis is a key tool for driving sustainable procurement. By identifying the comparative attributes of a product or service in terms of sustainability, we can use this as a basis for comparison and driving improvements to make what we buy more sustainable. If done well, it can provide the most comprehensive basis to assess how sustainable a given product is, perhaps together with, or distinct from, a product breakdown. Furthermore, as we have already seen, sustainable procurement means we also may end up driving a more fundamental change in what our organization does and the goods or services it provides. Therefore, we may also end up being part of a more end-to-end project using attribute analysis to optimize the customer-facing proposition of our organization along with the supply-side sourcing. The resultant improvements also provide the basis to for the organization to publish benefit reports that demonstrate improvements made in sustainability.

With our 'sustainability hat' on, the typical comparative attributes we need to consider are different to those we might use for cost or efficiency comparisons, but rather we focus on identifying how we can begin to quantify how sustainable what we buy is (or specific elements of it). This might include considering attributes such as CO_2e per unit, litres of water consumed per unit, miles/kilometres travelled, percentage of recycled materials used and so on (Table 10.3 gives some of these). This same principle can also be applied to consider the comparative attributes for a supplier or supply chain.

The challenge of good attribute analysis

Attribute analysis is difficult to do, initially at least, as it can be hard to identify the attributes. As for a product breakdown, attribute analysis is no small task and should only be contemplated for a product (or service) where worthwhile and relevant. This means the risk and impact areas and opportunities that emerged as priorities from our assessment. It could also be where comparison across products or services is needed or we anticipate the need for a more end-to-end redesign of what our firm does and how the product or service area in question supports this. Furthermore, the product or service would ideally be in Tailored or Custom within Day One analysis. Figure 10.5 gives an excerpt from an attribute analysis being used for product comparison to identify areas for sustainability improvement. A template is provided in the Appendix.

Conduct an attribute analysis for sustainability as follows:

1 Best worked collaboratively in a small team of individuals with good product or service knowledge.
2 Determine the product (or service) to review.
3 Determine all the attributes for the item in question and make a longlist.
4 Decide which attributes are important and hold potential for sustainability improvements, i.e. where there might be risks, impacts or opportunities. Make a shortlist of them (template available in the Appendix).
5 Add a quantifier to make it comparative. Typically, this means adding the 'per x' to the attribute (e.g. CO_2e per consignment, life expectancy per unit, per cent sustainable packaging per carton, etc).
6 If evaluating multiple products, create a table to drive comparisons.
7 Working collaboratively with the wider business as appropriate, challenge where needed and determine opportunities for change.
8 Define new specification and business requirements using the RAQSCI model and build a change plan/initiate a project to transition.

Table 10.3 Some possible attributes to consider

Attribute area	Some of the many product attributes used (customer and supply side)	Examples of comparative attributes for sustainable product analysis
Physical properties	Size, shape, weight, length, height, quantity, thickness, feel, colour, appearance, shiny/matt, holes, cracks, hard/soft, elasticity, volume, etc	• Thickness per part • Volume per unit
Type	Manufacturer, brand, sub-brand, variety, country of origin, product classification, type (e.g. diet vs regular), design, processed, etc	• Sustainable source Y/N? • Sustainable certifications • Constituent parts from non-approved countries/sources
Materials	Materials, ingredients, content, recyclability, reusability, what characterizes the product, etc	• % sustainable materials • % organic • % recycled materials used • % recyclable at end of life • % reusable
Packaging	Labelling, inner packaging, outer packaging, pack size, visuals	• % sustainable • % recycled materials used • % recyclable at end of life • Ratio product volume to packaging volume • Units per carton/pallet/load
Product life	Shelf life, life expectancy, warranties, etc	• # weeks shelf life • Life expectancy
How it gets to us	Type of logistics, where it travels, where/how it is stored, etc	• Miles/km travelled per unit • CO_2e per unit • CO_2e per consignment

Table 10.3 *continued*

Attribute area	Some of the many product attributes used (customer and supply side)	Examples of comparative attributes for sustainable product analysis
Processing	Type of processing, people involved, where processed, materials consumed, etc	• Litres of water per unit • Miles/km travelled per unit to process it • CO_2 per unit • Kw energy consumed per unit • % renewable energy per unit • % workers receiving living wage
Declarations and instructions	Descriptions, instructions, declarations, certifications, safety statements, health statements, allergen statements, claims, nutritional claims, etc	• Fair trade certified • Sustainability certifications
Quality, performance and sensory	Top-rated, high-quality, reliability long-lasting, taste, aftertaste, flavour, odour, smell, feel, texture, sweet, bitter, sour, salty, savoury, creaminess, resistance to bite, moist/dry, solubility, easy to clean, made with x, one of a kind, artisan, regional, original, real, etc	• Build in obsolescence Y/N? • % modular/replaceable/repairable

Sustainable value engineering

Sustainable value engineering takes a product breakdown and attribute analysis to another level and is the all-encompassing approach to assess the design and end-to-end life cycle of a category, product or service, to determine how sustainable all aspects of it are and what would need to change to

Figure 10.5 An excerpt from an attribute analysis used to compare sustainability attributes for a product.

Attribute	Target	Product 1	Product 2	Product 3	Product 4
1 CO_2e per pack	320 gm	340 gm	420 gm	330 gm	550 gm
2 Total miles/km travelled	300 km	300 km	2335 km	1500 km	8000 km
3 % recyclable packaging	100%	80%	70%	90%	65%
4 Weight (delivered) per pack	1 kg	1 kg	1 kg	1 kg	1 kg
5 Origin	EU	EU	Albania	EU	China
6 Energy used per 1 kg pack	1.2 kWh	1.2 kWh	1.35 kWh	1.3 kWh	1.4 kWh
7 Packs per carton	96	96	24	192	48
8 % air per carton	5%	10%	13%	5%	7%
9 Shelf life	3 months	3 months	3 months	2 months	3 months
10 % dilution	17%	20%	22%	17%	19%
11 Main method of logistics	EV truck	Diesel truck	Diesel truck	Hybrid truck	Shipping
12 Traceable to source?	Yes	Yes	No	Yes	?

drive new sustainable value. The approach is distinct from that we have covered so far as we take our assessment one step further to consider the context of how what we buy gets used. For example, how changing the design of what we buy, or of that into which it is incorporated, could drive sustainable benefit or how a change to specification could make use by the end customer more sustainable.

Those familiar with product or specification optimization will be familiar with the concept of value engineering – an approach to:

- review the design, materials and fabrication methods (or how the service is provided) for a product;
- redesign a product and remove unnecessary elements and cost;
- change aspects of the design, often that are invisible or unimportant to the customer; and
- make it fully fit for purpose without overengineering it.

Value engineering is used extensively across automotive companies to optimize cost versus performance for key components. Traditionally, key assemblies would be bolted onto the car to provide rigidity, certainty of fastening, etc. However, take a deeper look at a modern car and it is not uncommon to find headlight clusters fixed with tape strips or key components fixed together with nothing more than a sealant adhesive. These are not compromises, but innovations utilizing specialist modern adhesive technology well proven to perform its job for the life of the vehicle. In value engineering the focus and overall aim is traditionally concerned with realizing the value of reducing cost, reducing complexity, increasing automation and driving production efficiency, and sometimes improving the performance of the component over traditional methods.

Sustainable value engineering is based upon the same principle of examining something we buy in detail but instead with a view to determine how to bring new sustainable value to the item in question. We don't ignore cost and efficiency – these remain key considerations – however, our overall driving focus becomes making the category, product or service more or entirely sustainable. This is more than considering what we buy. In the same way that value engineering looks beyond the product being acquired to aspects of how it is used, total cost of ownership and disposal considerations, sustainable value engineering is typically more than sourcing the same thing but from a different source or changing its specification (although such changes may well figure). Instead it is about considering every aspect of what we buy, from its design, how it is made, where it comes from, how we buy it, how we use it, how we incorporate it into what we do and ultimately how our next and end-customers use it. It is a means by which we consider the total impact of ownership (TIO). Elements of what we might consider as part of a product breakdown or attribute analysis figure here, but crucially we are looking end to end, which is the only way we can make what we buy truly sustainable. Figure 10.6 gives the eight end-to-end areas we consider. Only by considering what we buy in the wider context, the product (or service) and what it gets incorporated into, and the design of this through to end of life, can we begin to make what we buy sustainable. Remember changing the specification or source of what we buy gets us so far; however, driving change to the overall proposition of our company based upon supply-side possibilities for sustainability has much greater potential. Sustainable value engineering will therefore only succeed if done together with the wider business and with its full support.

There are many approaches to considering TIO out there. Essentially this is about compiling a full-life view of all the impact areas for a given product or service. Sustainable value engineering does this by considering the main aspects of sustainability that emerge from, and are common across many of, the six impact areas. Essentially, this means that for any given product or service, we consider how sustainable it is for each phase of its full life in terms of:

- use of resources;
- emissions/CO_2e produced;

Figure 10.6 The end-to-end areas where we consider the sustainability of a product or service we source

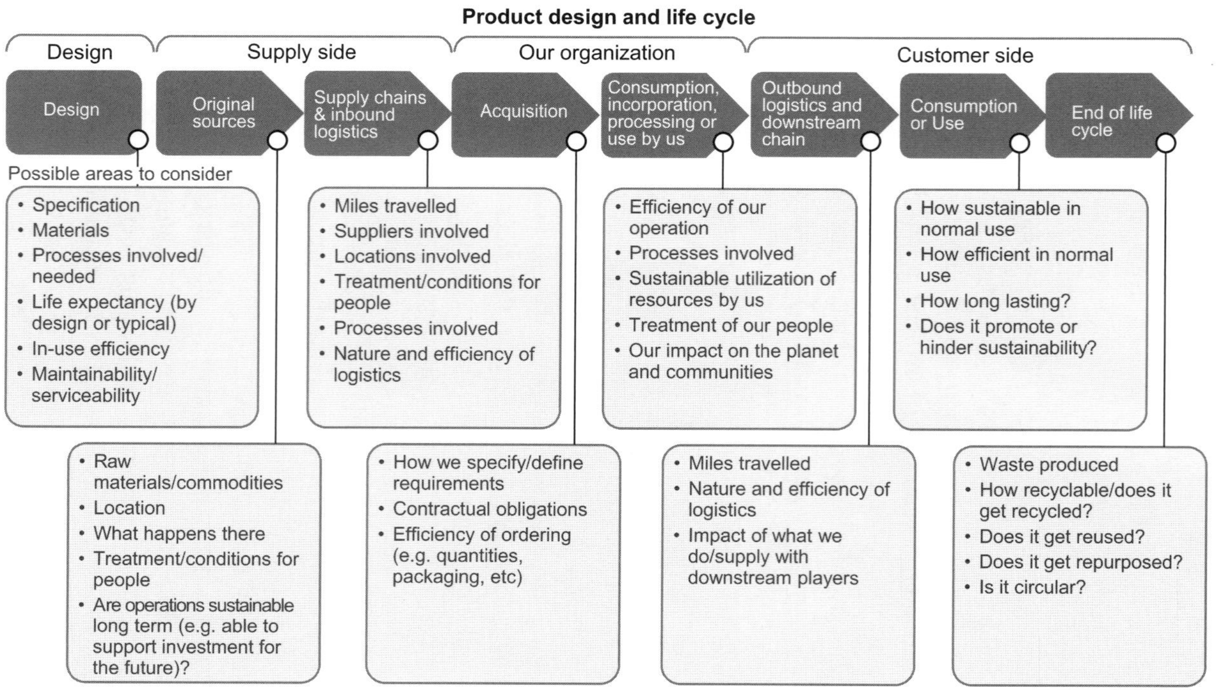

Product design and life cycle

Design	Supply side	Our organization	Customer side

Design

Possible areas to consider
- Specification
- Materials
- Processes involved/needed
- Life expectancy (by design or typical)
- In-use efficiency
- Maintainability/serviceability

Original sources
- Raw materials/commodities
- Location
- What happens there
- Treatment/conditions for people
- Are operations sustainable long term (e.g. able to support investment for the future)?

Supply chains & inbound logistics
- Miles travelled
- Suppliers involved
- Locations involved
- Treatment/conditions for people
- Processes involved
- Nature and efficiency of logistics

Acquisition
- How we specify/define requirements
- Contractual obligations
- Efficiency of ordering (e.g. quantities, packaging, etc)

Consumption, incorporation, processing or use by us
- Efficiency of our operation
- Processes involved
- Sustainable utilization of resources by us
- Treatment of our people
- Our impact on the planet and communities

Outbound logistics and downstream chain
- Miles travelled
- Nature and efficiency of logistics
- Impact of what we do/supply with downstream players

Consumption or Use
- How sustainable in normal use
- How efficient in normal use
- How long lasting?
- Does it promote or hinder sustainability?

End of life cycle
- Waste produced
- How recyclable/does it get recycled?
- Does it get reused?
- Does it get repurposed?
- Is it circular?

- waste and waste management;
- pollution or risk of pollution;
- preserving biodiversity;
- upholding human rights, ensuring fair treatment and good working conditions for people and protecting and supporting communities; and
- ensuring data and digital protection and privacy.

Conducting sustainable value engineering is a significant undertaking, so we need to be clear it is worthwhile. It is also one of the most useful approaches to begin to determine how to drive improvements in terms of what we buy. It is also the most suitable means to galvanize internal collaboration. Figure 10.7 gives an example of sustainable value engineering for the plastic moulding used in an inhaler. A template is provided in the Appendix. Conduct sustainable value engineering as follows:

1 Best worked collaboratively in a small cross-functional team – identify key stakeholders and those who are responsible for the product to be part of it.
2 Determine the category, product or service to evaluate.
3 For each of the eight steps from design through the product or service life cycle, review each of the aspects of sustainability. For each, discuss, debate and rate how sustainable this aspect of the product is for this part of its life. Decide from high (yes, it is sustainable), medium, low or not sustainable. For each, and using the template provided in the Appendix, draw an arrow from left to right to give a visual indicator of how unsustainable each area is. Record any notable assumptions or the basis for determinations.
4 For areas that are difficult to determine due to lack of knowledge, identify, plan and conduct fact finding to bridge gaps.
5 Review each step and, using the sustainable value levers, determine potential changes that could be effected to address key areas where sustainability is most lacking.
6 Summarize the proposed changes.
7 Secure agreement (e.g. from key stakeholders).
8 Develop an updated specification and set of business requirements.
9 Plan project, actions or changes required and manage the transition.

Figure 10.7 An example of sustainable value engineering for the moulded plastic parts used in a medical inhaler

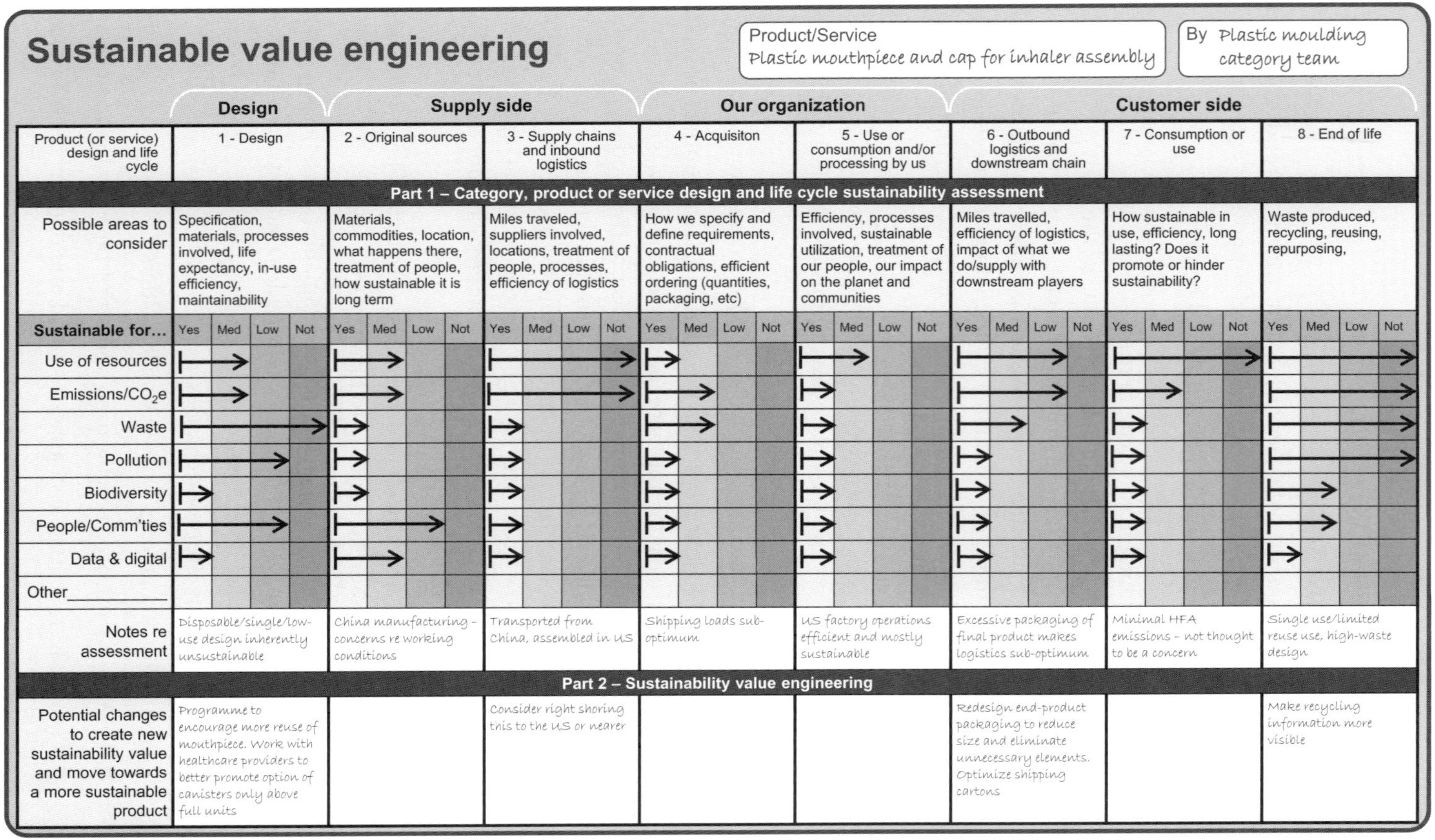

Making what we buy sustainable

Chapter checkpoint

In this chapter we have continued working through OMEIA® stage 3 and explored key analysis tools to evaluate what we buy for the priority areas we have identified and what would be required to make these more sustainable. This includes:

1 *A completely new approach* – making what we buy more sustainable requires us to look beyond what and how we source, and to lead the challenge and drive change to aspects of what the organization does and how our customers use what we produce (or provide).
2 *5i Category Management* provides the proven strategic approach for making what we buy sustainable with a shift in application of key steps and tools.
3 *Business requirements* is a key enabler. Refining business requirements with sustainability in mind is the easiest means to make what we buy more sustainable and the means by which we define the new requirements we will go to market for.
4 *Product (or service) breakdown* builds on established cost-focused procurement breakdown tools such as PPCA as a means to examine the component parts and what goes into a specific product or service, identify where it is unsustainable and therefore what would need to change to make it sustainable.
5 *Attribute analysis* builds on the product breakdown by considering the attributes of a specific product or service we buy – all the features and defining factors that make it what it is. By determining key comparative attributes it is possible to make comparisons across products and set targets for improvement.
6 *Sustainable value levers* – the most comprehensive means to drive sustainability for what we buy. By considering the end-to-end life of a product or service we buy from its design, and also the design of what it gets incorporated into, through to use and end of life by our end customer, we can determine how sustainable it is at each step. This enables us to determine ways to drive sustainability beyond changing how we source, by working with the wider business to challenge and change the design or end-customer proposition.

In the next chapter we will explore how we drive sustainability in our suppliers.

Driving sustainability in our suppliers

11

> This chapter explores how we will drive sustainability in our suppliers, particularly our immediate suppliers. We will consider how we determine which suppliers we will work with and how we determine what we need to do with them. We will explore the role of contracting to drive sustainability and also how to drive sustainability improvements and developments with suppliers.
>
> *Pathway questions addressed in this chapter*
>
> **11** How can we drive sustainability in our suppliers?

We are continuing to evaluate where we need to direct our resources and now we turn our attention to which suppliers we need to better understand or work with to drive sustainability. To do this we are continuing our journey through OMEIA® stage 3 and also moving into stage 4 to consider how we begin to implement changes.

In part, we continue to respond to the priority risks, impacts and opportunities we identified during our assessment. We also need to consider our entire supply base and how we can determine what we need to do, and the specific approaches or programmes of action with some or all suppliers that will enable us to realize our sustainability goals. The key elements we will cover are given in Figure 11.1.

Figure 11.1 The key elements of driving sustainability in our suppliers

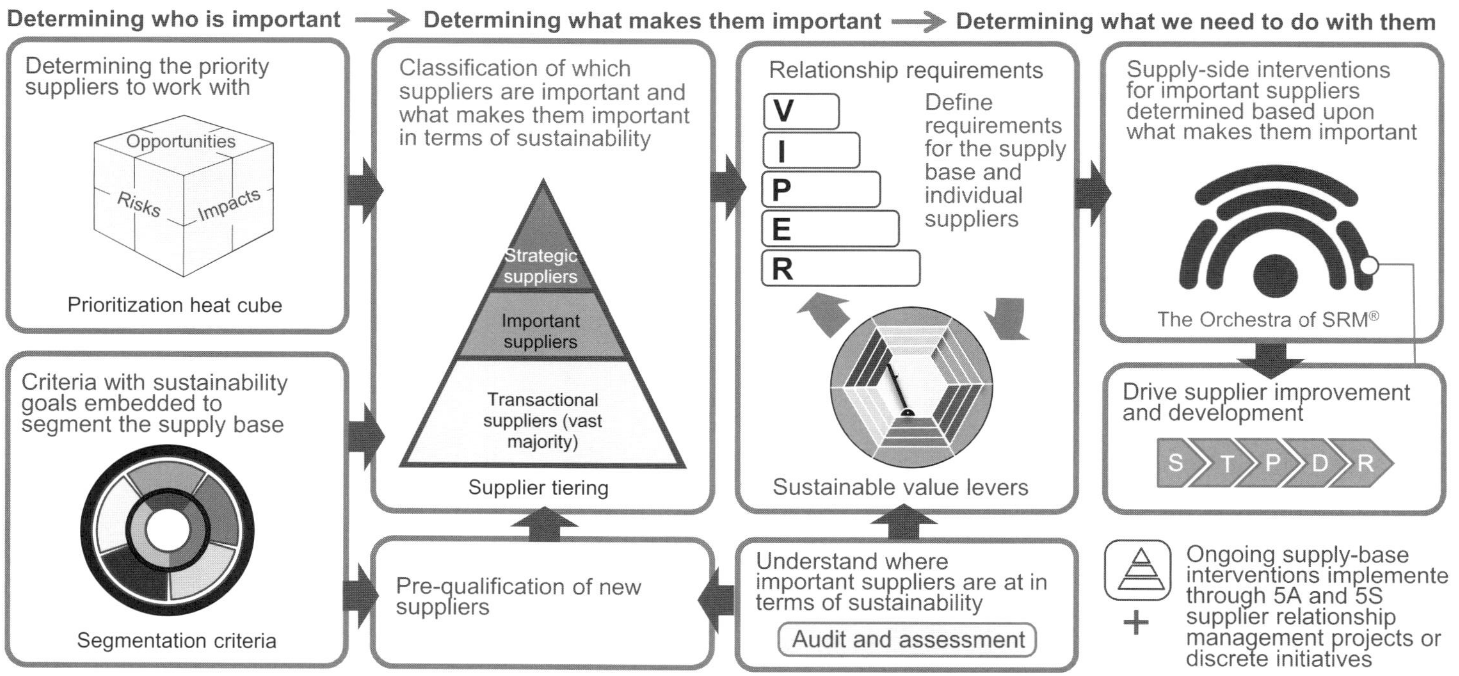

A new dimension to SRM

Experienced procurement practitioners will be familiar with applying supplier relationship management (SRM) approaches to manage and unlock value with key suppliers. It is a methodology and philosophy I have covered extensively in my book *Supplier Relationship Management*, also published by Kogan Page. Many of the approaches outlined within it are key to driving sustainability in suppliers and so further reading is recommended. However, in this chapter I will build on key areas where we utilize new approaches or apply familiar tools in a new way to drive sustainability.

Using SRM to drive sustainability in key suppliers

SRM holds different meanings depending upon whom you talk to and there is no universal definition. It is, in fact, an umbrella term for all the different types of intervention that we can make within the supply base to manage risk and unlock new value from our suppliers and throughout the supply chain. If well applied, that value can be dramatic and can bring great competitive advantage or social value by connecting supply-base possibilities with end-customer needs and aspirations. We use the concept of an orchestra to illustrate the different types of intervention. Just as an orchestra has many different sections and each plays individually or with others and at different times according to the music, each important supplier needs different types of intervention at different times according to what makes them important. All the interventions within the Orchestra of SRM® are necessary for sustainable procurement but once again here we put our sustainability hat on, which drives a shift in our focus and what we are looking to achieve. This means how we manage suppliers day to day encompasses that necessary to drive sustainability. It means supplier performance measurement (SPM) has sustainability embedded and supplier improvement and development (SI&D) is about how we drive supply-side improvements. It means supply chain management (SCM) takes on an entirely new dimension to help us drive sustainability back through the supply chain or SVCN. Finally, it means for the critical few suppliers that are of strategic importance to us in sustainability terms we will need to establish strategic collaborative relationships (SCRs) to drive mutually beneficial new sustainability value. Figure 11.2 shows the Orchestra of SRM and how each section supports sustainable procurement.

Figure 11.2 The Orchestra of SRM® and sustainable procurement

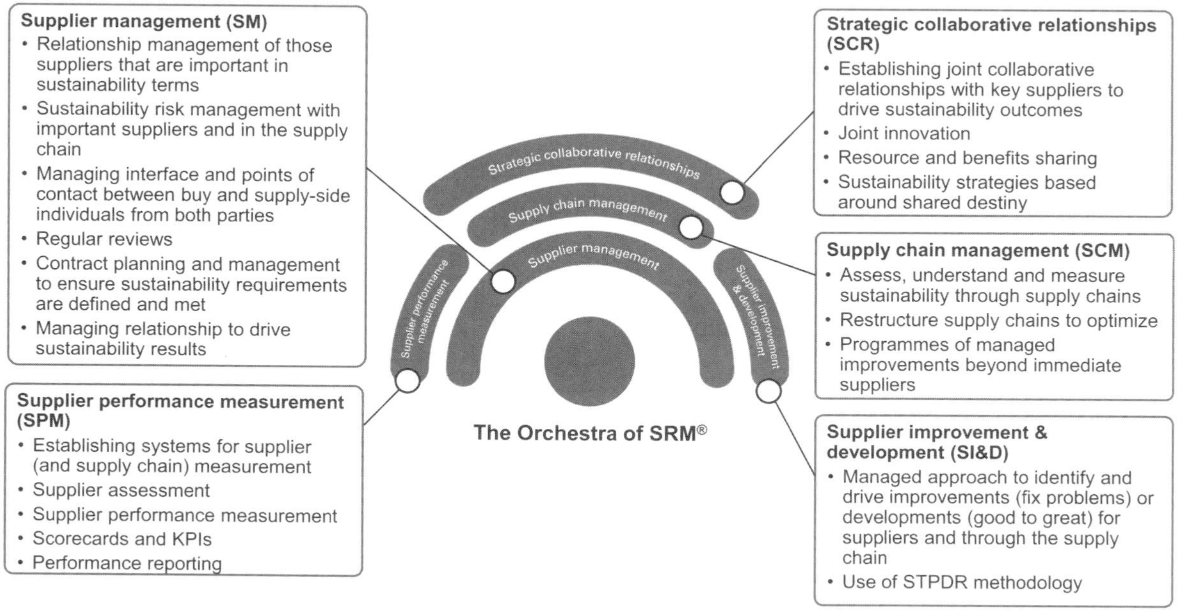

Supplier management (SM)
• Relationship management of those suppliers that are important in sustainability terms
• Sustainability risk management with important suppliers and in the supply chain
• Managing interface and points of contact between buy and supply-side individuals from both parties
• Regular reviews
• Contract planning and management to ensure sustainability requirements are defined and met
• Managing relationship to drive sustainability results
Supplier performance measurement (SPM)
• Establishing systems for supplier (and supply chain) measurement
• Supplier assessment
• Supplier performance measurement
• Scorecards and KPIs
• Performance reporting
Strategic collaborative relationships
Supply chain management
Supplier management
Supplier performance measurement
Supplier improvement & development
The Orchestra of SRM®
Strategic collaborative relationships (SCR)
• Establishing joint collaborative relationships with key suppliers to drive sustainability outcomes
• Joint innovation
• Resource and benefits sharing
• Sustainability strategies based around shared destiny
Supply chain management (SCM)
• Assess, understand and measure sustainability through supply chains
• Restructure supply chains to optimize
• Programmes of managed improvements beyond immediate suppliers
Supplier improvement & development (SI&D)
• Managed approach to identify and drive improvements (fix problems) or developments (good to great) for suppliers and through the supply chain
• Use of STPDR methodology

SOURCE © Positive Purchasing Ltd, 2003–2023

Key to good SRM is how we determine which suppliers are important to us and which are strategic, in other words critical to our future survival and prosperity or hold the greatest potential to change the game for us.

The role of segmentation

In traditional SRM, supplier importance is determined by supply-base segmentation. This is a structured approach to determine which suppliers are important or strategic and why, and use that as a basis to direct what resource we have at working with those suppliers. While many will segment based upon spend, spend alone is not enough as it can exclude lower-spend suppliers that present significant risk or opportunity. Therefore, good segmentation considers supplier importance by applying five segmentation criteria individually, not collectively (i.e. a supplier only needs to score highly in one to potentially require some intervention). These are *risk*, *difficulty* (e.g. market difficulty of what they supply), *current importance* (which would include spend), *future importance* and degree of *alignment*. By applying these criteria, using a non-aggregating method of evaluation scoring, we can determine the suppliers that require intervention and shape that invention according to the specific aspects that made them important. A simpler method is the *help*, *hurt*, *heroes* approach, which is to consider which suppliers could *hurt* us, which could *help* us and which might be the *heroes*. Whichever method is used, segmentation is the means by which we then determine the suppliers that are important or strategic and typically this will be represented by classifying suppliers in tiers (Figure 11.3). This then forms the basis for how we contract with, manage, measure, review and possibly collaborate with some of our key suppliers and, in some cases, back up the supply chain.

A different sort of importance

The same tiering classification approach is relevant for sustainable procurement. However, when we consider sustainability, *importance* takes on a different meaning and with it the criteria we apply to determine tiering. Suppliers become important, and even strategic, in sustainability terms if they present significant risk we need to address, are home to impacts that we want to tackle to achieve our sustainability goals or hold the potential opportunity to help us realize new value through sustainable approaches.

Therefore, this new perspective can drive a shift in the classification of some suppliers, with suppliers that would not have previously been classified as important with a commercial hat on now being so. For example, applying traditional segmentation that didn't consider sustainability to any degree may have resulted in certain suppliers being classified as transactional. However, if there are potential sustainability risks or impacts within these suppliers now that we are wearing our sustainability hat, for example they exist in a hot spot geography or there are questions regarding the sources of origin of key materials, then these suppliers might now be classified as important. On the face of it, this might suggest we then need to get closer to these suppliers or work with them to address the sustainability concerns. Perhaps it is more likely that we have identified a supplier that we should not be working with in the first place. Remember if classification determined a supplier to be transactional without considering sustainability, then it is most likely of little importance beyond the transaction. Trying to make these suppliers sustainable would take effort when that effort would be better placed working with fewer, more important suppliers where our efforts will have the greatest impact. Therefore, in such a situation, the most appropriate way forward would typically be to remove suppliers of low importance that cannot meet our sustainability requirements.

Segmentation that includes robust criteria for sustainability adds another layer of evaluation when selecting and classifying suppliers, and may change the traditional classification outcomes in three ways:

1 Exclude suppliers that cannot meet our sustainability requirements and where it is not worthwhile to try and make them so.

2 Work with some suppliers in a different way. For example, a supplier that might be moderately important in commercial terms might be much more important to help us achieve our sustainability goals if they are working on innovation or new approaches that will provide a unique solution.

3 Make a supplier more important by reducing the available suppliers that can meet our sustainability requirements. As a result our commercial leverage may be diluted necessitating a counter via a closer, more structured relationship with mechanisms to protect and keep our competitive position balanced.

Figure 11.3 gives the traditional pyramid representation of supplier tiering along with the typical different ways we will engage with them and how this might shift when we look at our suppliers through a sustainability lens.

Figure 11.3 Traditional segmentation versus potential priorities for segmentation

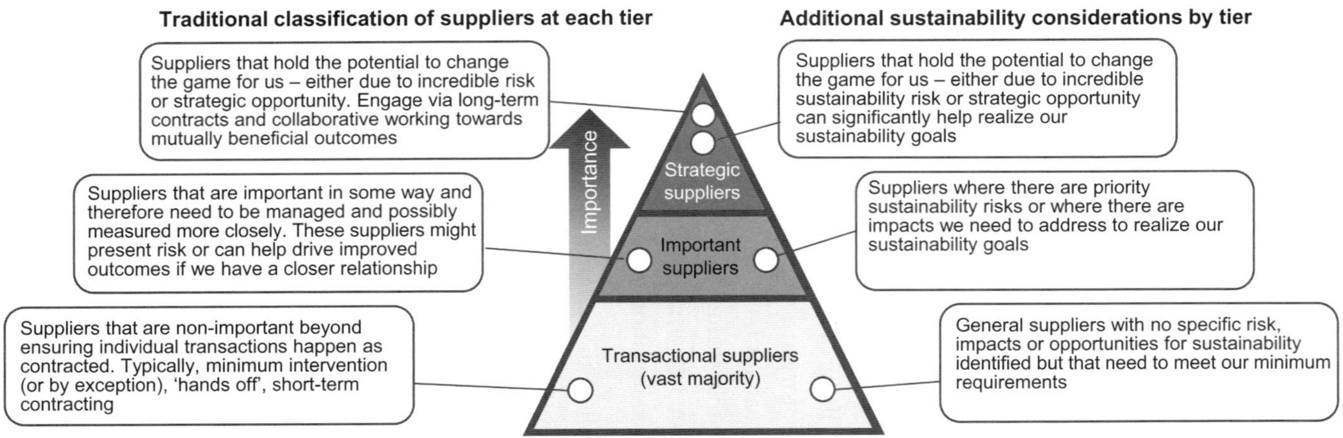

Traditional classification of suppliers at each tier

- Suppliers that hold the potential to change the game for us – either due to incredible risk or strategic opportunity. Engage via long-term contracts and collaborative working towards mutually beneficial outcomes

- Suppliers that are important in some way and therefore need to be managed and possibly measured more closely. These suppliers might present risk or can help drive improved outcomes if we have a closer relationship

- Suppliers that are non-important beyond ensuring individual transactions happen as contracted. Typically, minimum intervention (or by exception), 'hands off', short-term contracting

Additional sustainability considerations by tier

- Suppliers that hold the potential to change the game for us – either due to incredible sustainability risk or strategic opportunity can significantly help realize our sustainability goals

- Suppliers where there are priority sustainability risks or where there are impacts we need to address to realize our sustainability goals

- General suppliers with no specific risk, impacts or opportunities for sustainability identified but that need to meet our minimum requirements

Tiers (top to bottom): Strategic suppliers / Important suppliers / Transactional suppliers (vast majority)

Importance

Embedding sustainability within segmentation criteria

In any organization that has deployed SRM effectively, the approaches used to determine supplier importance and classify them onto the appropriate tier drives everything the organization does in terms of managing its supply base. Similarly, if we are deploying sustainable procurement, then having a means to determine and classify supplier importance in terms of sustainability across our supply base is essential. In practical terms, this means adapting the criteria we apply here to embed our sustainability requirements and establish a single, company-wide system, to classify suppliers according to everything that makes them important and use this as a basis to determine the specific interventions for individual suppliers. When we do this, there are a few things that need to change:

- **Full supply base segmentation** – traditionally, SRM would be implemented by a company conducting a supply-base-wide segmentation exercise using the segmentation criteria to determine which suppliers are important and which are strategic and then reviewing this regularly. Full supply-base segmentation is still valid with our sustainability hat on. However, once we adapt existing segmentation criteria to include sustainability then the entire exercise needs to be rerun and is likely to generate a different list of suppliers at each tier. Adopting dual lists of important suppliers (e.g. one based upon traditional value opportunities and one based upon sustainability) should be avoided. This suggests separate ambitions, which defeats the idea of sustainability being an integral part of what the organization is trying to do. Suppliers can be important for various reasons. If we ensure the segmentation criteria is comprehensive, including all the reasons that make a supplier important, then we will be successful in identifying whom to spend time with.

- **Targeting specific suppliers** – sustainability is unique in that we can identify suppliers we need to work on, and therefore are important, from our sustainability assessment and the prioritization heat cube outputs. Here we are effectively fast-tracking suppliers to a specific tier without going through a full supply-base segmentation

- **Supplier qualification** – supplier segmentation must also consider how we determine importance for a new supplier. How we qualify suppliers also changes to ensure we set out to work only with suppliers that will meet our sustainability requirements in the first place. Ideally this should be an extension of any existing pre-qualification process such as financial, data protection, etc.

Figure 11.4 How sustainability is embedded within supplier segmentation criteria

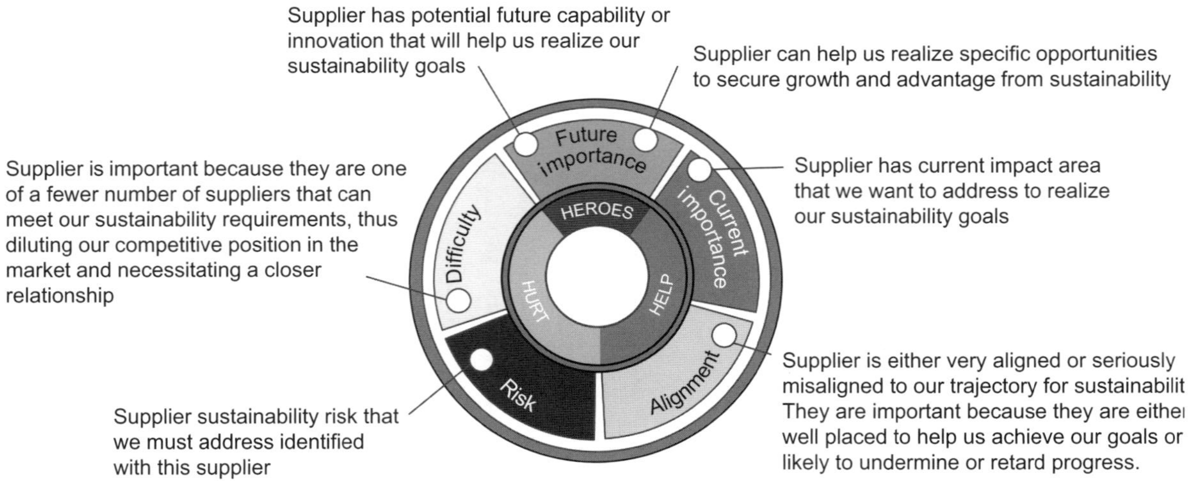

Supplier can help us realize specific opportunities to secure growth and advantage from sustainability

Supplier has current impact area that we want to address to realize our sustainability goals

Supplier is either very aligned or seriously misaligned to our trajectory for sustainability. They are important because they are either well placed to help us achieve our goals or likely to undermine or retard progress.

Supplier has potential future capability or innovation that will help us realize our sustainability goals

Supplier is important because they are one of a fewer number of suppliers that can meet our sustainability requirements, thus diluting our competitive position in the market and necessitating a closer relationship

Supplier sustainability risk that we must address identified with this supplier

- Current importance
- Alignment
- Future importance
- HELP
- HEROES
- HURT
- Risk
- Difficulty

Figure 11.4 gives the traditional segmentation criteria and the specific ways we embed sustainability criteria to determine importance.

Redefining relationship requirements

In the last chapter we explored the RAQSCI business requirements where we define our needs and wants for what we buy. Similarly, relationship requirements are the means by which we define what we need and want from our supply base and specific suppliers using the VIPER model.

The VIPER model

VIPER is how we define the value the organization needs and wants to realize from the supply base (Figure 11.5). VIPER stands for *Value, Innovation, Performance improvements, Effectiveness (of business and operations)* and *Risk*. VIPER is a hierarchical model and the means by which we define our relationship requirements for who we buy from. We can apply it at two levels:

1 **Macro level or entire supply base** – a definition of the high-level requirements of the organization and specific types of value, including sustainability value the organization needs from its entire supply base at large, e.g. 'all suppliers must comply with the UN Global Compact' or perhaps to respond to specific organizational goals, e.g. 'to achieve net zero in the supply base by 2035' or 'to source 100 per cent organic cotton within three years'.

2 **Supplier-specific relationship requirements** – the specific relationship requirements and the nature of intervention needed with individual known current suppliers or the requirements for suppliers we are looking to bring on board.

Defining sustainability requirements for suppliers

VIPER defines our different requirements and the reasons for instigating some sort of relationship or intervention with a supplier. It is used for general relationship requirements but also it is the framework to connect our sustainability goals to supply-side interventions. There are many inputs that inform VIPER but the primary inputs are our goals for sustainable procure-

Figure 11.5 The VIPER model

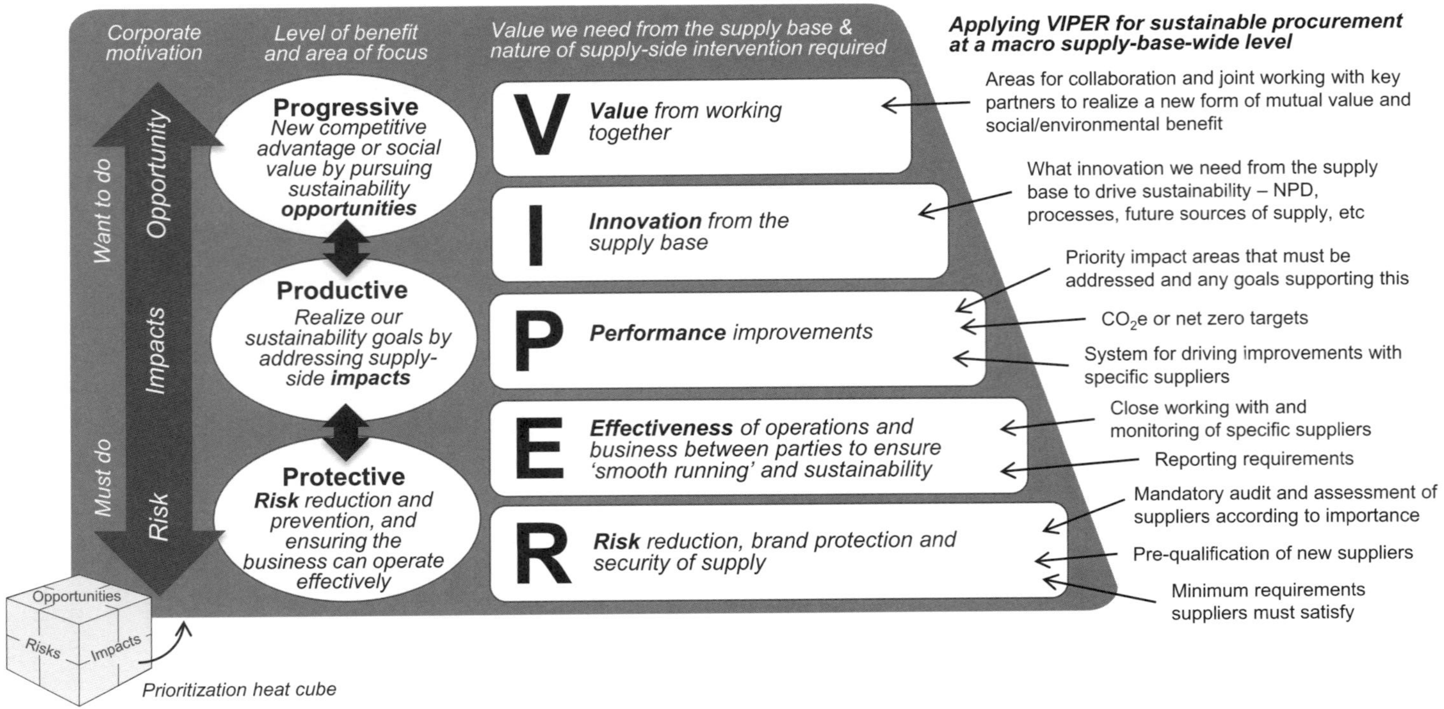

Figure 11.6 VIPER – the convergence of everything that shapes what we need and want from our supply base

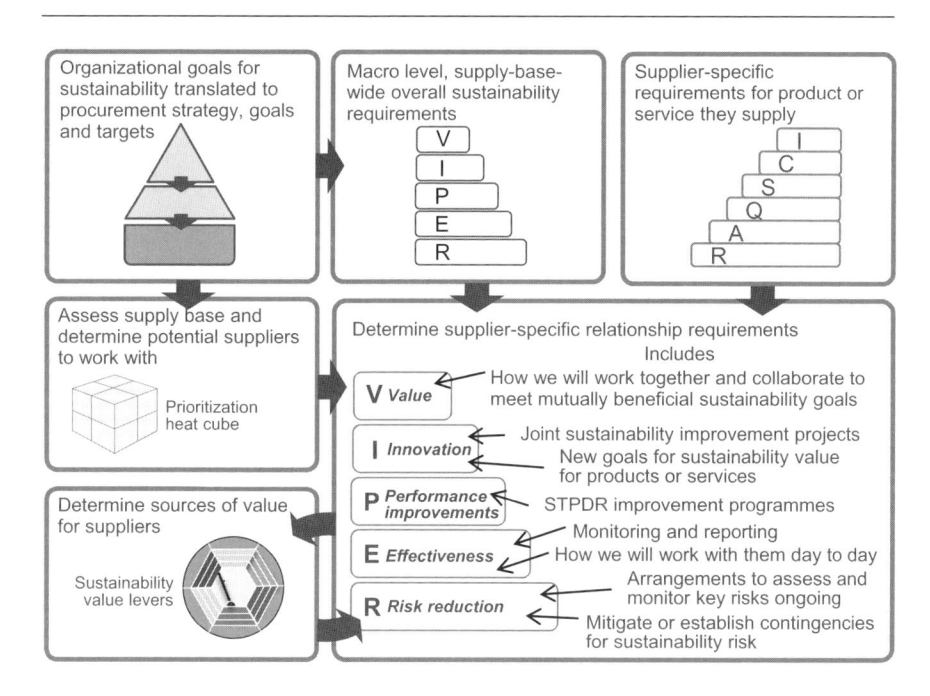

```
┌─────────────────────────┐  ┌─────────────────────────┐  ┌─────────────────────────┐
│ Organizational goals for│  │ Macro level, supply-base-│  │ Supplier-specific       │
│ sustainability translated│  │ wide overall sustainability│ requirements for product or│
│ to procurement strategy, │  │ requirements            │  │ service they supply     │
│ goals and targets       │  │         V               │  │         I               │
│                         │  │         I               │  │         C               │
│                         │  │         P               │  │         S               │
│                         │  │         E               │  │         Q               │
│                         │  │         R               │  │         A               │
│                         │  │                         │  │         R               │
└─────────────────────────┘  └─────────────────────────┘  └─────────────────────────┘
```

Assess supply base and determine potential suppliers to work with
- Prioritization heat cube

Determine supplier-specific relationship requirements
Includes

V *Value* — How we will work together and collaborate to meet mutually beneficial sustainability goals

I *Innovation* — Joint sustainability improvement projects / New goals for sustainability value for products or services

P *Performance improvements* — STPDR improvement programmes / Monitoring and reporting

E *Effectiveness* — How we will work with them day to day / Arrangements to assess and monitor key risks ongoing

R *Risk reduction* — Mitigate or establish contingencies for sustainability risk

Determine sources of value for suppliers
- Sustainability value levers

---

ment. VIPER is a hierarchy ranging from that we must do at the bottom (the 'R') to what we want to do at the top (the 'V').

VIPER is a key tool that helps us clarify and communicate our sustainability requirements to a specific supplier and there are many inputs that converge to enable us to develop a good set of relationship requirements. These are given in Figure 11.6. I will explore each heading in turn, starting at the bottom of the hierarchy with Risk.

'R' – managing Risk

The most critical reason for supply-base intervention is the effective management of supplier and supply chain risk. Taking steps to prevent potential crises or catastrophes – perhaps in response to the priority risks we have identified – or at least being prepared for them, is the most important source of sustainability value an organization can secure from the supply base. 'Risk' therefore forms the foundation of the VIPER hierarchy.

The response to this risk, and therefore the specific requirements for our suppliers under R might include targeted interventions or driving improvements with some suppliers, and upstream in some supply chains. This might be to either prevent or minimize risk, or accept and be prepared for certain risks being realized. It might also include setting a requirement for supply-base-wide arrangements to manage our suppliers, including pre-qualification, setting minimum requirements, how we assess our suppliers and so on. More on these later.

'E' – Effectiveness of operations

The second reason for intervention with specific suppliers and therefore a source of supply-side value is that of ensuring the effectiveness ongoing of what the supplier does. It applies where realizing our sustainability objectives within their operations requires a degree of close working day to day and necessitates ongoing communication with, involvement in or monitoring of certain suppliers.

There are certain situations where close working with suppliers is necessary. For example, a construction company working together with its subcontractor onsite as if it was part of the business, with day-to-day communication and interaction to deliver the project. For sustainability with suppliers this can be a key requirement and applies in different ways but in essence it is about the measures we need in place to ensure a supplier's operation is sustainable day to day and where we need to work with them on this. This might mean we need to set up monitoring or new processes and procedures that provide assurance sustainability requirements are met. For example, consider an outsourced customer service provider. Once again, this company will need to work as if part of the business. They will need to have access to customer data and process it and perhaps we might want them to access our corporate systems. Here we would need to establish the arrangements to do this, perhaps vetting who has access, training the supplier, having safeguards in place or establishing the right contractual terms and conditions. Overall, we would need to be ensuring the effectiveness of the operation to safeguard customer data.

'P' – Performance

The third reason for intervention with suppliers and source of value in the VIPER hierarchy is that of ensuring supplier performance where it is lacking, or driving performance improvement where we want to go 'good to great'. The sustainable value comes by pursuing improvements with specific suppliers where the effort required will deliver worthwhile results. For example, directing and perhaps working with a supplier to address supplier impacts or working more collaboratively to realize opportunities.

Performance in VIPER enables us to define the broad areas where performance improvements might be required. This could include supply-base-wide performance targets, for example net zero by 2030 or bringing working conditions at all factories in India in line with our minimum sustainability requirements. It may be where we identify supplier-specific improvement requirements in response to priorities identified during our assessment.

'I' – Innovation to drive sustainability

As we know, innovation can deliver game-changing value to an organization. When it does happen, it can establish and build a brand, create differentiators, create and grow market share and drive business growth. Innovation alone has the potential to transform a business and unlocking it requires some unique approaches. Innovation can drive sustainability and is therefore the fourth source of value and reason for a closer relationship with some suppliers.

'V' – together we are better; together we create sustainable Value

The ultimate reason for a supplier relationship within the VIPER hierarchy is the additional, perhaps immense, sustainable value that is possible from certain suppliers that possess the capability to help us not only achieve our sustainability goals but realize even greater value if we collaborate and work together with them. This might include jointly developing new products that are more sustainable, perfecting new processes or logistics to remove detrimental impacts or establishing joint programmes that provide social or environmental value and so on. This might typically be how we respond to the priority opportunities we identified as part of our assessment.

Developing relationship requirements

Develop relationship requirements for a specific supplier as follows (a template is provided in the Appendix):

1 Best worked collaboratively in a team and ideally as part of determining all the relationship requirements including sustainability.

2 Determine the supplier (either current, known or requirements for a new supplier).

3 Review the overarching supply-side sustainability requirements (as defined in the sustainability goals and any macro VIPER requirements).

4 Review all the inputs and drivers that establish specific needs or wants from a supplier, including the outputs from the prioritization heat cube, value levers, RAQSCI business requirements for products or categories supplied.

5 Under each of the VIPER headings determine statements of requirements. Make these SMART.

6 Use as the basis to agree improvement plans with the supplier, to establish new relationships, for contract planning and to manage the supplier ongoing.

Contracting for sustainability

Nothing focuses a supplier like a contract! Good contracts not only mitigate risk and provide remedies when things go wrong, they can also add value within the relationship with our key suppliers, but only if they are well put together. If the process of contracting is distinct from what procurement is doing to drive value, say created by a separate legal function and a separate step in the overall process, then its value will only ever extend to putting in place the necessary legal provision. However, if contract development is integral to and joined up with good strategic procurement then our contracts with suppliers can add value. As we have already seen, the RAQSCI business requirements is the means by which we define what we will buy, bringing together all the drivers, needs, wants and aspirations into a single, combined definition. Similarly, the VIPER relationship requirements define what we need and want from our suppliers. Our contracts with suppliers must therefore flow from both the business and relationship requirements, augmenting them with the required legal framework to establish the right obligations between parties. Good contracts will also go further to establish principles for how a relationship might work, or the intent of parties to work in a particular way or harbour a certain ambition – often without being binding and certainly not enforceable with any remedy.

When it comes to sustainable procurement our contracts with suppliers, and any standard terms, must be approached in a similar way. They should be developed collaboratively and working cross functionally with any legal function, to include the provision we need for sustainability. Once again, if we have got our business and relationship requirements right so they include what we need and want for sustainability for what we buy and who we buy from, the contracts we put in place should flow from these and incorporate them within an appropriate wider legal framework.

Ensuring contracts are workable

Contracts must include those minimum sustainability requirements where compliance is required (e.g. meeting specific legislation). We may also include some provision for where we are seeking a degree of commitment in response to setting out an expectation. We could do this by simply including an obligation for suppliers to comply with our code of conduct. Indeed, for standard terms and conditions that may be enough. However, beyond this we will almost certainly need more extensive provision to leave no room for ambiguity. In practice this means we must, working closely with any legal support here, translate our requirements into good legal wording with careful thought to get this right – there is a world of difference in a supplier agreeing to a code of conduct that includes some commitments based upon loose intent and a supplier agreeing to a legally binding contract. For example, consider these two contractual clauses:

> Clause 1 – The supplier shall comply with the Modern Slavery Act and all applicable laws, regulations, codes and guidance made under it or relating to it and ensure that all relevant personnel have received appropriate training on the same.

Such a clause is sufficiently all-encompassing and states a clear legal obligation for compliance. It would be straightforward for most reputable companies to agree to this. However, consider this clause:

> Clause 2 – The supplier shall ensure no use of child or forced labour anywhere within its organization, facilities or in support of the manufacturing of its products or provision of services and shall make best endeavours to ensure there is no child or forced labour in any of its suppliers or supply chains.

We would all agree this is a necessary requirement, so it might seem reasonable to make it contractual with the expectation that a supplier will take all those steps in its power that are capable of producing the desired results. However, consider how many suppliers could actually meet it. Some of the biggest brand names on the planet, that are taking big steps to ensure they are sustainable, would fall foul here simply because they could not be 100 per cent certain of meeting it throughout all its supply chains, irrespective of how much effort they may be putting into prevention here. The reality is that it is almost impossible for any company to be 100 per cent certain. Equally, we should not shy away from establishing bold contractual requirements that set and enforce the required standards for our suppliers in line with our goals and direction of travel. When it comes to sustainability, contractual wording needs careful consideration and in some cases collaborative negotiation with key suppliers to get it right while not diluting what we are attempting to achieve and compelling suppliers to act.

Establishing obligation, intent and incentivization

In addition to embedding minimum requirements within contracts, they should also provide for how the relationship will work and set the scene for specific suppliers to work with us on key areas of sustainability development. This is rarely about creating penalty-based contracts that impose certain obligations but more about incentivizing the supplier and establishing a mutually agreed objective or at least an intent. Once again, this must flow from our business and relationship requirements. Key features of good contract planning in support of this are:

- **Length of contract** – if we need a supplier to make changes or invest in sustainability, we may need to consider a suitable contract duration that provides both the time, commitment by us and therefore incentive for the supplier to act. This means that where we might have once sought advantage by regular market testing and agreeing only short-term contracts for leverage categories, sustainability objectives might now lead us to agreeing longer tenures.
- **Competitiveness clauses** – sustainability should not mean losing competitiveness with our suppliers and contracts should provide for this. If we are replacing advantage by short-term contracting with a long-term agreement, that agreement should include new arrangements to prevent the supplier using sustainability to gain advantage for them. In practice this might include agreed price review mechanisms, perhaps linked to indices and transparency in cost breakdowns including cost of sustainable initiatives.
- **Performance and improvement objectives** – the mutually agreed levels of performance required, agreed KPIs that will be used, improvement objectives and timescales during the contract term. Depending upon what we need to achieve here, some or all of this could be integral to the contract and binding, with remedies if the supplier fails to meet these.

However, for many aspects of sustainability improvement in suppliers, it can be very difficult to give a firm commitment, especially where improvement action is needed back up the supply chain. Therefore, in these areas, good contracts should seek to establish supplier or mutual commitment towards performance and improvement objectives and verify this ongoing. This would typically be defined within an addendum or perhaps an SLA (service-level agreement) separate to the legal framework, where parties signal intent to work together in a particular way, as opposed to clauses that are material to the contract. Failure to achieve objectives would not necessarily be a breach of contract but rather a reason not to renew or extend the contract. For this reason, including contract breaks, where extensions are granted based upon performance, can be a very powerful way of incentivizing suppliers to drive sustainability.

- **How the relationship will work** – good contracts should also go some way to defining how the relationship will work, especially for a supplier we want to work with closely. Once again this might not be binding but more agreed intent defined in an addendum. Typically, here we might seek to establish obligation on parties to name key individuals and define points of interface. We might also define regular joint reviews or obligations around reporting.

Driving supplier improvements

A key dimension to sustainability is how we drive and manage improvements. This could be improvements to what we buy, who we buy from and throughout our supply chains. This section is not unique to supplier improvements but is relevant for any form of improvement. I've included it here as it is most commonly applied in the context of driving supplier improvement.

Using STPDR to drive sustainability improvements

The STPDR supplier improvement process (Figure 11.7) is a simple and straightforward approach for driving all types of supplier improvement. STPDR is a five-stage improvement process that can be applied to a variety of situations. The five stages are *Study, Target, Plan, Do* and *Review*.

Driving supplier improvement and development is part of SRM typically applied across a range of areas. Sustainability becomes an extension of these accomplished by using the STPDR supplier improvement process, linked to our goals for sustainable procurement, VIPER and the needs and wants of key stakeholders.

As we have seen, one of the simplest and most elegant tools to help determine 'where to go from here' in terms of sustainability is the SSTP (*Sustainability, Situation, Target, Proposal*). It is no accident that our supplier improvement tool incorporates an STP, except in a slightly different form. Here we *Study the situation* and our proposal becomes our *Plan* for reasons I will expand on shortly, and, as the other proven business improvement methodologies out there would suggest, we need to add some further steps if our improvements are to be realized and embedded.

The STPDR tool provides structure to drive sustainability improvements and developments and the means to verify these are successful. Crucially the tool can be applied at two levels:

1 **To fix a problem,** correct an issue or address a risk and drive in the right level of improvement.
2 **To go 'good to great'** and further develop something that is already acceptable but could be even better if we drive in some sort of development.

Step 1 – Study the situation

STPDR Step 1 is about determining where we are now and is concerned with studying the precise nature of the issue we are attempting to address, the problem to fix or the area where we need improvement.

If we are to fix a problem then the diagnostic journey starts with analysing the symptoms, just as a doctor would start by asking 'where does it hurt?' If we are solving a sustainability problem with a supplier then our symptoms might be expressed as possible deforestation concerns, a key supplier may have just been exposed for human rights violations or production might be overly water intensive and so on. Here we need to start being precise. When you tell the doctor it hurts, he will ask 'Where exactly? For how long? Does it hurt more if I squeeze here?' Similarly, we need to look further. For example, for overly water intensive production, consider the following:

- What does 'overly' mean?
- What would be good, for all products they make or just ours?
- How much water is used exactly?

Figure 11.7 The five-stage STPDR supplier improvement process

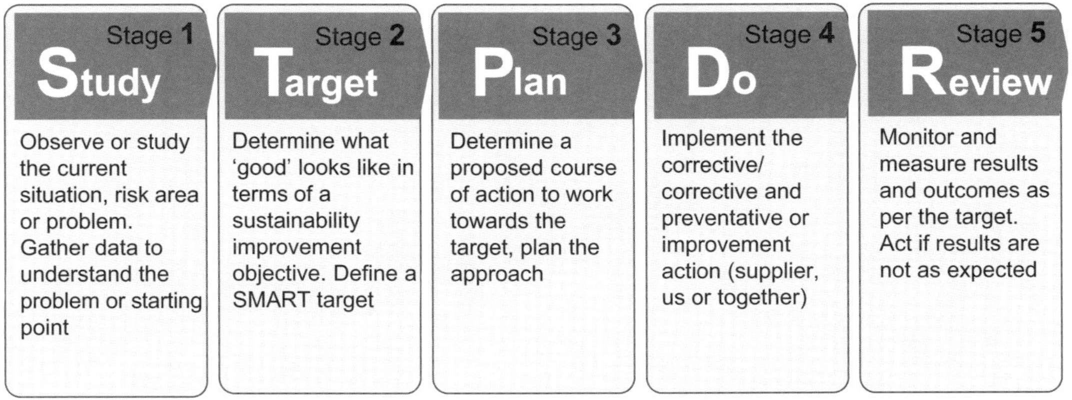

Stage 1 **Study**	Stage 2 **Target**	Stage 3 **Plan**	Stage 4 **Do**	Stage 5 **Review**
Observe or study the current situation, risk area or problem. Gather data to understand the problem or starting point	Determine what 'good' looks like in terms of a sustainability improvement objective. Define a SMART target	Determine a proposed course of action to work towards the target, plan the approach	Implement the corrective/ corrective and preventative or improvement action (supplier, us or together)	Monitor and measure results and outcomes as per the target. Act if results are not as expected

Fact finding and data gathering might be necessary to do this.

Some problems are readily apparent; however, not all supplier-related sustainability problems are that simple and it may not be until later that an issue surfaces. If a small percentage of ore mined from open mines by children gets mixed in with the legitimate ore during the smelting process by a corrupt back-door practice the company could be obliviously promoting themselves as having no child labour until pictures showing the other practice appear around the world. The *Study* step therefore requires us to first define the problem and then, if the cause is not obvious, to study the situation or problem in order to determine its root cause, as if carrying out some sort of autopsy. The word autopsy is derived from the Greek *autoptēs*, which means 'self seen' or 'eyewitness' and this is why this step is called *Study*, because it is vitally important to take the time to properly comprehend and understand the problem before attempting to fix it; to see precisely what the issue is, using hard facts and data to support it. We can waste a lot of time, effort and energy acting upon what someone has told us, what the problem might be expected to be or on a single theory alone. Yet if we decide the rumours of children working in the supply chain are false because we have good systems we could be fooling fooling ourselves.

Supplier improvement to fix a problem therefore begins with good data and taking the time to really see the problem and understand it fully. We need to establish the root cause of any problem and, once we know this, figuring out what to do becomes much easier. Here established techniques including 'fishbone' or 'Ishikawa' diagrams as well as the 'five whys' can help.

For supplier development to go 'good to great', study the situation becomes about understanding all the things that hinder being even more sustainable. Once again we need to immerse ourselves, and ideally others who can help or have an interest, in the situation; to observe and to see with our own eyes what could make things better. Here we are not looking for the root cause of a problem, but rather for potential sources of improvement.

Step 2 – Target for improvement

Step 2 is about determining where we want to be. Here we are looking to set a target that defines the objective for our improvement activity and the specific outcome we wish to achieve. There are three big assumptions here:

1 We know where we want to be.
2 We know exactly how to get there.
3 We are going to take the time to think about both of these.

It is easy to miss this step or for a target to simply be assumed due to our natural human tendency to cut straight to a solution: 'Only 5 per cent of incoming material is recycled' so 'increase the percentage of recycled materials used'. An obvious response and we will automatically make similar responses every day without a second thought, but this is not a target, this is actually a proposal or plan of what we intend to do. Our brains have already processed the problem and decided on the course of action. Worse, we have assumed we know the right solution. Maybe increasing the percentage of recycled material is the right solution, but maybe there are other ways to achieve a better outcome, such as changing the material used in the first place, reducing consumption and so on. If we jump straight to solutions we are losing sight of what we set out to achieve. Defining a target can be the hardest step.

Target is the second step because we need the previous *Study* step to help us identify where we need to be, by revealing the root cause or where our improvements will have the most impact and therefore shape the goal, but it doesn't stop there.

Remember we have already defined certain goals within our business requirements and relationship requirements that flow from our high-level sustainability goals. These may have been used to determine how we have segmented our supply base and identified specific opportunities for a supplier. We may have conducted an audit or assessment (covered in the next chapter). Therefore, targets for supplier improvement may not need to be created anew but, in fact, we may already have them.

This means that for a supply-side sustainability issue or problem we simply need things to reach, or return to, our stated expectations; restating these targets within our improvement process, for example 'supplier to comply with code of conduct'.

For supplier development, target setting gets harder, especially if our aim is less defined and might involve unknowns such as finding new innovations that we can work on together with a supplier. Even if we can be clear about where we want to be, the journey to get there can be even more challenging. If we are setting out to go 'good to great' then here we may be setting out a new level of ambition within a supplier, perhaps collaborating with the supplier to set the target.

Most literature on target setting will be quick to suggest all targets should be SMART (specific, measurable, achievable, realistic and time-related). This helps but sometimes aiming for SMART targets can work against us as it can force us to be overly analytical in our targets. Not every goal lends itself to such an approach, for example targets for an improved relationship using SMART might leave us wondering how to apply the acronym because it might be hard to set specific and measurable targets but rather less specific aims. An alternative approach here is to consider these questions and if we can answer them then we have set a target:

- What specifically do we want?
- Where are we now relative to this goal?
- How will we know we've achieved it?
- Will there be any evidence to know we've achieved it?

Step 3 – Plan

Step 3 is about planning the specific action to fix the problem or drive in the improvement or development in order to meet the target. This may be a simple one-off action (e.g. use only certified waste management contractors and keep records), which would typically be expected for simple supplier problems, or could be a sequence of steps and activities of varying degrees of complexity. The plan connects targets to actions and provides vital alignment, reduces uncertainty, focuses attention and provides detailed direction for all involved. It guides execution while providing a basis for control of actions to ensure they are delivered.

It is tempting to neglect planning and 'cut to the chase'. If we are working alone on something simple this may be all right, but where others are involved everyone needs to understand and be aligned with what is happening, and who is doing what, when and why. Obvious perhaps, yet the importance of good planning is often missed. Anyone who has ever been part of a team activity that required all to contribute but set off without a plan may well have experienced the chaos, tension and lack of traction first hand. Project planning and project management is a subject all of its own and so for complex supplier-improvement projects further reading is recommended.

If we are addressing a simple single sustainability concern with a supplier problem, then we need only a simple action plan using a what, when and who format. Otherwise, for more complex improvement initiatives, planning needs to be a bit more advanced if it is to be successful. Here the use of Gantt charts to define the programme of activities and interim milestones becomes more appropriate, incorporating provision for effective change management, communication and project management.

Step 4 – Do

The *Do* step is just what it says; it is about putting the supplier improvement or development plan into action. If we have completed the first three steps effectively then this step should be the easiest to get right. Success from *Do* comes through good project management in organizing, motivating and controlling resources and those involved to work towards the target.

Plans fail for many reasons: lack of resources, lack of buy-in, competing initiatives, poor goal-setting, resistance to change and so on. However, we can head off many of these simply by making provision for them within the planning process.

For plans to address a simple issue, *Do* may be simply a case of ensuring agreed actions with a supplier are implemented, perhaps by keeping track of progress through email, meetings and so on. For more complex supplier improvements and development, *Do* means there could be a series of actions that need to be completed within a set time frame, maintaining momentum and interest from those involved along the way. It doesn't follow that once a plan is developed and agreed that those involved will do what is required of them. Actions agreed in a meeting can easily drift if there is no apparent pressure, penalty or consequence for non-delivery. Good, determined project management to drive implementation is essential with regular reviews, encouragement and celebrating success with the supplier once complete.

Step 5 – Review

The fifth step is about two things: checking that the improvements have been made and we have reached our target, and instigating any new arrangements to ensure the improvement sticks, otherwise things may simply revert to the previous state.

Checking we have met the target may involve a repeat of some of the initial activities from step 1. Once again, we need to study the situation – we may need to remeasure and re-evaluate the situation to see if our interventions have been successful; ideally our targets provided a clear and measurable definition of what good looks like. We will need to confirm the change is good with stakeholders. If we are satisfied that our improvement has been successful then the cycle is complete. If it has not, we can either effect further corrective actions or simply go back and restart the process again, studying the new problem and so on.

For more complex improvements we must take steps to embed the change. This might include new arrangements to prevent the problem re-occurring and to ensure the improvement is maintained. In practice this might involve:

- Supplier making changes to policies, procedures, processes or systems.
- Retraining or new training of those involved.
- Communicating the details of the new arrangements, and what is expected of those involved.
- Ongoing measurement and monitoring of the supplier, perhaps involving new KPIs.
- Assigning new roles and responsibilities (e.g. to own a new process, monitor effectiveness, etc).
- Contractual changes or arrangements to ensure any new obligations are incorporated.

Supplier willingness and capability to improve

It doesn't follow that just because we want a supplier to improve that they are willing and able to. For a supplier to be willing they need to have reason to want to invest in driving a change they might otherwise not do or not do yet. Ideally, and with the right suppliers, improvements we want align with what the supplier is setting out to do, but this is not always the case. This potentially changes procurement dynamics and once again the traditional leverage, short-term contracting approach will not create the right conditions for a longer-term supplier development programme. Therefore, where we identify suppliers that are important or strategic to us and where improvements are desired, this needs to be coupled with the right incentives and contracts that give more certainty to the supplier. Furthermore we must also structure the relationship and key terms to maintain competitiveness along with the benefits from the relationship. The supplier preferencing tool can help here, and the supplier's likely willingness according to how attractive our account with them is versus our spend with them relative to their overall turnover. Figure 11.9 gives this and the focus of our responses.

Figure 11.8 Using supplier preferencing to gauge supplier willingness

	Development	**Core**
↑	Supplier will be willing to invest in sustainability development but will seek further commitment to do so	Supplier will expect to invest with us in support of mutually agreed objectives and see this as part of the relationship
Attractiveness of account	*Focus on:* Determining the trajectory and potential for this supplier. If they are important to us longer term consider agreeing joint objectives with increased business and/or longer-term commitment with commercial safeguards	*Focus on:* If this supplier is important ongoing maintain a close, collaborative relationship to work together to achieve key sustainability objectives
	Nuisance	**Exploitable**
	Supplier will not be interested or willing to invest in sustainability or work with us. They may not say as much but their actions will confirm this	Risk the supplier appears to be supportive and committed but fails to 'walk the talk' and deliver on key goals
	Focus on: Exiting this supplier if possible, otherwise managing risk and attempting to make our relationship more attractive to them if we need them	*Focus on:* Understanding why we are not attractive to the supplier and if this supplier is important to us longer term take steps to rebuild the relationship

Relative spend on account →

SOURCE Adapted from Steele and Court (1996)

We must also consider if the supplier has the ability to improve. Many may lack this. Even with the right funding they may lack the know-how, people, organization, access to resources, etc to be able to drive an improvement. If a supplier is important to us, then this is where sustainability improvements require us to work with the supplier to help them drive in an improvement. In practice this can mean sharing knowledge and working together with them, perhaps on the ground at facilities, to help them make the change. In essence, this is about providing process and change consultancy to the supplier. This will have a cost and need to be resourced by us so it is important to quantify the investment that will be required and the payback in financial, social and environmental returns. Therefore, such investment should be coupled with a clear plan and contracting approach as part of an overall improvement programme.

Transitioning to organic cotton

Consider a garment producer that has set the goal of having all its products produced using organic cotton. Organic cotton is much more sustainable than regular cotton because the environment is better protected where it is grown, it uses less water during processing, uses no chemical pesticides or fertilizers and limits soil erosion. It also means a greater likelihood of a fair wage for producers. The problem is there are hundreds of individual farmers in the supply chain. Here an improvement plan requires creating a standardized farmer transition programme to share knowledge and prove each with a route map for transition, and then work with them individually to transition them. Yet the farmer will experience lower initial yields and need to invest in time and new processing methods. There would be little incentive to do this if their cotton continues to be openly traded at market price. However, a more direct relationship provides the basis to establish the right incentive for the farmers to want to do this, with a new commitment and agreed price mechanism. The payback for the company is confidence all its cotton is sustainable, not just because of the farmer-level interventions but the new more direct relationship that provides new transparency in the supply chain.

Chapter checkpoint

In this chapter we have continued working through OMEIA® stage 3 and explored how we drive sustainability in our suppliers. Key points we covered were:

1 *SRM provides the framework* – the principles and practice of good strategic supplier relationship management provides the framework to manage sustainability in our supply base using the same approaches and tools we are used to using in procurement but with our 'sustainability hat' on to shift how we do this.

2 *Supplier segmentation* is the means to determine which suppliers are important or strategic. Sustainability criteria should be embedded into existing segmentation approaches, which then drive different outcomes, with some suppliers that would not have previously been considered important now being so in terms of sustainability.

3. *VIPER relationship requirements* is the means to define the value we need from our entire supply base and also from individual suppliers. It is the starting point to define supply-side sustainability requirements and those we need and want from a specific relationship. It is then the basis to establish supplier contracts and put supplier measurement systems in place.

4. *Contracting for sustainability* – our contracts with suppliers must provide for how we will meet our sustainability goals. This includes ensuring contracts oblige suppliers to meet minimum requirements but, for some suppliers, should also provide for defining shared intent, potentially non-binding, for how we want the relationship to work or certain shared aims and objectives.

5. *Driving improvement and development* – key to sustainability is the ability to drive improvements to fix a problem or address a concern and also to go 'good to great' anddrive developments where the current situation is acceptable. Effective management of the improvement and development process with suppliers (and also for what we buy and in our supply chains) comes by application of the STPDR process. STPDR stand for *Study the situation, Target, Plan, Do, Review.*

In the next chapter we will explore the various approaches to audit and assessment for suppliers.

Audit and assessment of suppliers

12

> This chapter explores approaches for audit and assessment of suppliers. We consider how to establish minimum requirements for sustainability across our supply base. We will also explore the different approaches to understand where a supplier is at in terms of sustainability. Practical guidance for how to develop and put in place a suitable audit or assessment approach is provided.
>
> *Pathway questions addressed in this chapter*
>
> **11** How can we drive sustainability in our suppliers?

First-hand understanding

As we continue through stages 3 and 4 of the OMEIA® sustainable procurement process, audit and assessment are a key means by which we understand sustainability in our supply base.

Audit and assessment of suppliers is not new. In procurement we have been doing this, or working with others doing this, since procurement became a thing. The idea that we should check out a supplier that is important to us in some way is basic due diligence. The audit or assessment of suppliers is the basis for supply-side risk management and can also provide a baseline for supplier improvement and development. This typically happens for a variety of reasons including the company's need or desire to assess individually or collectively a key supplier's arrangement in areas including:

- health and safety
- quality management system and compliance
- IT and data protection
- financial standing
- compliance with relevant legislation
- capability and capacity to meet our requirements
- structure, ownership, alignment of certain beliefs or ethics
- potential for acquisition
- potential for innovation or a closer relationship

Typically, such assessments may be conducted by the relevant functional department, a separate dedicated auditing function, an external provider, or it may fall to the procurement function, or a combination of these. Effort to assess suppliers is typically directed to those that most demand it, perhaps due to greatest perceived risk or opportunity, with different degrees of assessment across some or all suppliers for any given organization. Degrees of assessment vary by industry and company; some such as military, financial, banking, government, aerospace and healthcare are typically founded on extensive supply side assessment, others less so. Whichever approach a company might have, procurement might either lead this or at least be part of it in some way.

Sustainable procurement presents a further need for audit and assessment of some or all suppliers, to one degree or another. As organizations run fast to figure out how to embed sustainability, we can observe the birth of entire new functions to do this and many of these have started to audit and assess suppliers. If this activity is stand-alone from other supplier assessment activities then we risk being ineffective, overburdening and creating conflicting objectives for a supplier, and missing key ways we can drive improvements. For example, a well-implemented quality management system, perhaps accredited to an international standard such as ISO 9001, provides a robust means to ensure what the supplier is setting out to do is achieved reliably and consistently. It is therefore a key enabler for many aspects we require when we consider sustainability, for example capability and development of staff, identifying and responding to non-conformances, reviewing adequacy of arrangements to meet stated objectives, etc. Therefore, a single approach to supplier audit and assessment, covering all the relevant areas including sustainability, is essential.

Procurement must be a central player within this, perhaps even leading here. However, the set-up depends upon how the organization is structured. Furthermore, as we have seen, the world of sustainability demands a new skill set of sustainability practitioners. Typically, these individuals lack the procurement experience and procurement practitioners don't typically know sustainability yet. This is changing on both counts but until then working together is key to good supplier audit and assessment.

Levels of audit and assessment

Audit and assessment can be part of an initial pre-qualification activity or ongoing with important and strategic suppliers, either carried out by us or a third party and usually to some form of set standard. Audit and assessment are broad terms defined as:

- **Supplier assessment** – conducting checks or investigations into a supplier or a more structured evaluation to determine their situation and suitability. Assessments are distinct from audits and the easiest to accomplish.

- **Supplier audit** – the systematic assessment of a supplier's systems and arrangements to a specific standard, either set by us or a recognized national or international standard, conducted either first-hand or by a third party empowered to audit and, in some cases, to award accreditation to that standard. Supplier audits almost always involve visiting the supplier and spending significant time, perhaps one or more days, examining the controls and arrangements in place across all the organization and sampling how things work in practice to verify the organization is actually working in the way it claims to be working.

Audit or assessment, and subsequent improvement action, can be a significant undertaking that needs to be properly resourced. Therefore, once again our efforts must be precisely targeted. We must decide the extent to which we will require suppliers to undertake some form of audit and assessment, whether we make this supply-base wide or only some suppliers. We do this, and also determine the required supply-side interventions for sustainability, according to which suppliers are important and what specifically makes them important. The tiering that is derived from our segmentation and also our prioritization heat cube provides the basis to do this, with different degrees of audit or assessment and typically different types of improvement being called for at each tier (Figure 12.1). I will expand each of these and outline the key approaches in turn.

Figure 12.1 Typical types of supplier audit and assessment and types of improvement interventions for each tier

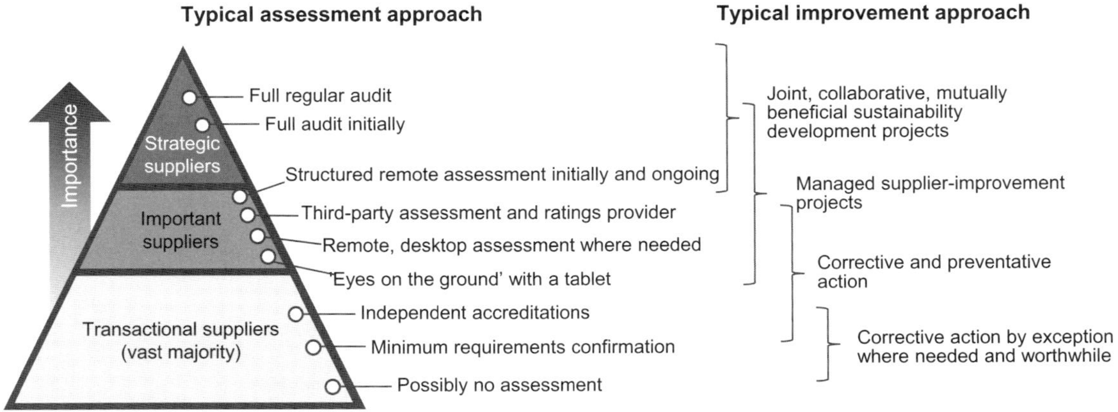

Typical assessment approach

- Full regular audit
- Full audit initially
- Structured remote assessment initially and ongoing
- Third-party assessment and ratings provider
- Remote, desktop assessment where needed
- 'Eyes on the ground' with a tablet
- Independent accreditations
- Minimum requirements confirmation
- Possibly no assessment

Strategic suppliers
Important suppliers
Transactional suppliers (vast majority)

Importance →

Typical improvement approach

- Joint, collaborative, mutually beneficial sustainability development projects
- Managed supplier-improvement projects
- Corrective and preventative action
- Corrective action by exception where needed and worthwhile

Defining the minimum

Sustainability is not something we confine to important or strategic suppliers, but our entire supply base and verifying that all or at least the majority of suppliers meet a minimum standard for sustainability is an essential element of sustainable procurement. This would seem like a no-brainer, yet the vast majority of companies have not managed to do this.

As we have seen, we use the VIPER framework at a macro level, which is derived from our overall corporate and procurement sustainability goals, to define what we need and want in terms of sustainability from our supply base. This then forms the basis to determine the minimum requirements.

Setting a minimum standard

The minimum requirements are those that all, or a good majority we decide, of our suppliers must meet in order to trade with us. It is important because it is the means by which we define all the key legislation our suppliers must meet along with some other areas we determine to be necessary across the supply base. It is the means by which we ensure we establish a base level of sustainable procurement across the supply base. It can be stand-alone but ideally is combined with other minimum requirements for suppliers so we can have a single system.

Setting a minimum standard is harder than you might think. Get it wrong and we either risk excluding suppliers unnecessarily or making compliance burdensome; equally, if we fail to have a minimum or our requirements are weak, we can dilute our efforts to drive sustainability. Setting a minimum can be difficult because:

- The minimum we need could vary according to the nature, size, location and industry sector of the supplier.
- The process of verifying that a supplier can meet a minimum can easily become burdensome on us and them.
- If we ask suppliers to engage with us to confirm they meet our minimum requirements, not all will. For example, we all trade with Microsoft and perhaps other supersized suppliers we have no choice but to use, yet such suppliers will not engage with our request to confirm processes here but will direct us to their published policy statements online. This is fine and we can assume companies such as Microsoft would have at least the

basics in place, but it adds another complexity to how we set minimum standards and verify suppliers meet them.
- Minimum requirements can be hard to implement. To be effective they must be applied as a 'go/no go' gate for suppliers to trade with us. If we have central control of all procurement and vendor approval systems this can be straightforward, but it is harder in an organization with decentralized control, local procurement autonomy, multiple fragmented procurement systems, etc.

Consider carefully what the right minimum should be and how we can establish a company-wide system to verify suppliers meet it. Getting this right will probably demand quite some discussion and debate and key here is determining the absolute minimum and no more, and that which could be easily confirmed by the supplier or verified by us. Our minimum must be that which can easily be met by a small, medium, large or supersized supplier, and the sole-proprietor company that brings the fresh flowers for the reception area each week. Table 12.1 gives some potential things to include when setting minimum requirements.

Minimum requirements should be defined as a series of unambiguous statements that suppliers must meet where something is non-optional (e.g. compliance with legislation). For other areas where there might be different degrees of progress towards, and formalization of, sustainability arrangements within our suppliers, it should state our expectations and seek confirmation. For example, the person who brings the fresh flowers each week may not have a full sustainability management system in place but could agree they are committed to minimizing waste and sourcing sustainably – a small business with a conscientious owner would be doing just this. Setting our expectations is an important part of our minimum requirements. This expectation can tighten as we move forward, and we should signal to suppliers that it will, but we are setting out the direction of travel for our suppliers while leaving it to them to interpret this within their business. This provides both potency and practicality to how we establish a means to ensure suppliers meet our minimum requirements supply-base wide. However, to begin here we need to communicate our expectations to our supply base.

Supplier code of conduct

A supplier code of conduct is a document or information online that sets out the company's expectations of its suppliers for sustainability and defines the minimum requirements they need to meet. It is also a means to secure alignment to values and goals and signal the future trajectory so suppliers can be ready. Sustainability supplier codes of conduct can be set up so compliance is mandatory, desirable or both. Where mandatory, suppliers should be required to formally signal their agreement (e.g. by signing and returning something, online acceptance or via a clause incorporated into a contract).

Setting up a code of conduct is more than defining our expectations to the supplier. It is also a promotional activity to rally suppliers to a common goal with us. To be successful a code of conduct should be:

- simple and easy for any supplier to understand what is expected of them – ideally no more than 10–15 succinct points or statements of requirement;
- given a mini-identity that can be referenced widely;
- in a professionally designed format to show it is important;
- incorporated as a go/no go step within new supplier qualification;
- be incorporated into contracts and standard terms and contracts; and
- something that evolves and is regularly updated.

Table 12.1 Potential things to include when setting minimum requirements

Area	Requirement	Things to consider including
Legislation	Compliance with laws applicable to the supplier's business. Any requirement stated here might vary according to location, sector and size	See Chapter 5 but might include legislation around: • Anti-bribery and corruption • Modern slavery • Data privacy and protection • Carbon reporting • Due diligence and reporting • Supplier diversity • And potentially others
Governance	Corporate leadership and governance of the overall arrangements for sustainability	Confirmation of: • Person with overall responsibility

Table 12.1 *continued*

Area	Requirement	Things to consider including
Health and safety	Compliance with statutory requirements. Consider requiring suppliers to provide supporting evidence	Confirmation of: • Person with overall responsibility • Health and safety policy and arrangements in place • Number of significant or notifiable accidents
Human rights	Adherence to key ethical standards. The degree to which a supplier is required to signal this adherence might vary according to location, industry, etc	Consider requiring confirmation supplier observes a recognized standard such as: • UN Global Compact • UN Guiding Principles • Universal Declaration of Human Rights • ILO Declaration on Fundamental Principles and Rights at Work 1998 (updated 2022)
Environment	Harder to set minimum requirements here as it is very much dependent upon what the supplier does. Emerging legislation will cover big suppliers but for the rest the most we can practically do at a minimum level is seek a degree of commitment from suppliers here. Clearly it is easy for a supplier to simply provider the answers we are looking for, but key is we are setting an expectation and requiring its confirmation with the option to look deeper if we have concerns	Seek confirmation that the supplier is committed to certain principles or ambitions and expectations we set for our suppliers and their supply chains. This might include, for example: • Ensure no pollution • Minimize GHG emissions • Minimize consumption, waste and energy use (where not via renewables) • Minimize unnecessary transportation or movement • Prevent loss of biodiversity • Source sustainably Consider asking supplier to include a statement of what it does and its aims here

Sustainable procurement

Table 12.1 *continued*

Area	Requirement	Things to consider including
People and labour relations	Over and above any legislative obligations, our minimum should be to seek confirmation from the supplier for key areas here	Confirmation of: • No discrimination • Inclusion and diversity is integral to how the supplier recruits and treats people

Supplier assessment

Developing a supplier assessment system

We can adopt a variety of approaches to supplier assessment depending upon what we want to achieve, ranging from verifying a supplier can meet our minimum standards to a more systematic evaluation of the supplier's situation and direction of travel for certain aspects of sustainability. If well implemented, supplier assessments can be highly effective in gaining a better understanding of a supplier's organization and therefore establish a basis to manage risk and drive improvements. Assessments are useful to support sustainable procurement because they are relatively easy to deploy. There are, of course, limitations because there is no substitute for seeing first-hand what happens within our suppliers and supply chains. However, as we will see, for most organizations an assessment approach provides the only feasible means to better understand our suppliers.

A supplier sustainability assessment can take many forms and there are different degrees of assessment we can adopt. It can be a one-time activity (e.g. as part of supplier onboarding) or something that is repeated regularly. Multiple assessment approaches can be effective and across the entire supply base we should know who has been or needs to be assessed, why, when and by what means. Furthermore, we need to then act upon assessment findings with a planned and managed approach to either select, deselect or improve a particular supplier. Once again, organizations typically have such systems to manage other areas of compliance and so sustainability should become an extension of what is already in place.

Supplier sustainability assessments broadly fall into one of two types which I will explore in turn:

- 'Outside-in' remote desktop assessment by us with no or minimum direct engagement with the supplier, using available data and information.
- 'Inside-out' remote structured assessment by us with full engagement with the supplier, perhaps coupled with outside-in data also.

'Outside-in' remote desktop assessment

An 'outside in' remote desktop assessment is the simplest method of conducting checks into a supplier to determine their situation and suitability. This could be done ad hoc as and when needed but ideally is something we approach in a more structured way. It is about taking the time to get to know them and their 'sustainability story' without engaging with them directly. It is therefore how we check the big companies that we need to use but that wouldn't engage with us, or the less-important or transactional suppliers.

A remote desktop assessment is about researching the supplier, and in particular their published information on sustainability, and making a judgement regarding their suitability and acceptability as a supplier. If we have set minimum requirements, we would look for indicators that the supplier would, in all likelihood, meet these.

Clearly a remote desktop assessment has limitations, it depends upon the availability of information about the supplier, what they have published, our interpretation, how the supplier's claims reflect what they actually do and so on. However, it does have its place for low sustainability risk suppliers and can provide a good line of defence against the unexpected, or highlight suppliers we may wish to take more of an interest in. Where we find little information on sustainability about a given supplier, this does not necessarily mean they are not suitable but it might mean we just need to think a bit more about their situation and suitability. For example, presently few SMEs would have good, published information on sustainability, or even sustainability policies, which might mean we may ask such a company we want to use to signal their acceptance of our code of conduct or conduct a more extensive assessment depending upon the circumstances.

It is difficult to have a structured approach to such assessments, but rather this is a data collection exercise and there are certain things we can look for that help determine how serious the supplier is about sustainability and therefore if they are reasonably aligned to our expectations here. These are shown in Figure 12.2.

Figure 12.2 The various means, methods and sources of information to assessing sustainability for a supplier

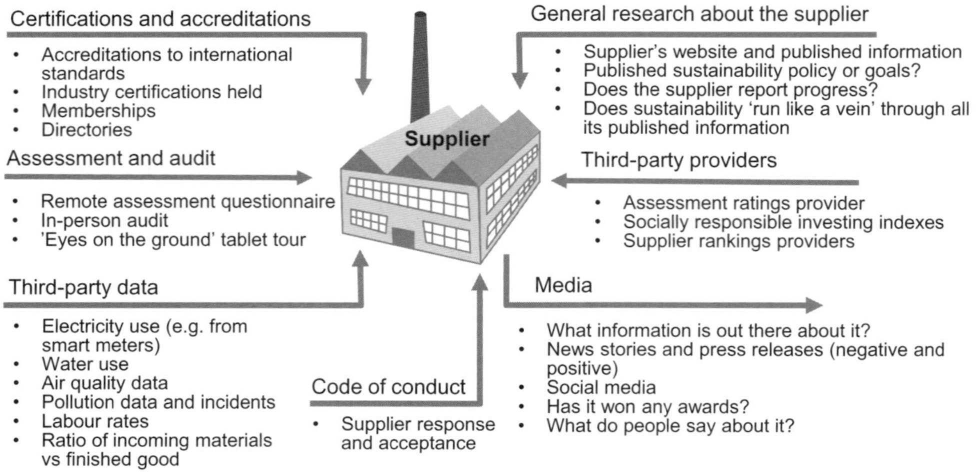

Certifications and accreditations
- Accreditations to international standards
- Industry certifications held
- Memberships
- Directories

Assessment and audit
- Remote assessment questionnaire
- In-person audit
- 'Eyes on the ground' tablet tour

Third-party data
- Electricity use (e.g. from smart meters)
- Water use
- Air quality data
- Pollution data and incidents
- Labour rates
- Ratio of incoming materials vs finished good

Code of conduct
- Supplier response and acceptance

General research about the supplier
- Supplier's website and published information
- Published sustainability policy or goals?
- Does the supplier report progress?
- Does sustainability 'run like a vein' through all its published information

Third-party providers
- Assessment ratings provider
- Socially responsible investing indexes
- Supplier rankings providers

Media
- What information is out there about it?
- News stories and press releases (negative and positive)
- Social media
- Has it won any awards?
- What do people say about it?

Supplier

'Inside-out' structured remote assessment

An 'inside-out' structured remote assessment is a more extensive and focused method of verifying a supplier can meet certain requirements as well as to determine their situation and suitability. This is usually done as part of a planned and managed system of initial or ongoing supplier assessment. Structured remote assessments are either carried out to a set standard (either defined by us or otherwise) or by their very nature establish a standard. It is an approach that is suitable for those suppliers we determine are important in some way in terms of sustainability, and perhaps some that are transactional and where we need to assess these suppliers to qualify them or as the basis to drive improvements.

A structured remote assessment is a form of solicitation of information from suppliers based upon inviting the supplier to answer a series of questions and provide specific bits of information or supporting evidence. Therefore, established approaches here can be used such as e-sourcing platforms with RFI/RFP/RFQ functionality. Alternatively, we can simply provide a document to be completed or use an online survey tool.

Deciding what questions to ask depends upon the nature of the supplier, what they do, what they have in place already and also our expectations. One size does not fit all so it is likely we may require an assessment system that has both core questions and supplementary questions that only apply to suppliers of a certain size, industry, location, etc.

As with any survey-based solicitation method, the design of the questions shapes the value of responses and if this is our only means to gauge a supplier, we need to get it right. Questions requiring quantitative or yes/no responses automate processing and provide easy comparisons across respondents but fail to help us understand the supplier's story. Similarly, qualitative questions requiring suppliers to provide lengthy responses have to be read, understood and interpreted against our requirements. Both approaches have their place. Also, questions need to be carefully constructed to provide no scope for ambiguity or wishy-washy responses. For example, the question 'do all workers have a contract that sets out wages and working hours?' seems reasonable. But does this mean at the supplier's main location or throughout every site and operation around the world? Without tighter definition it can be easy for the supplier to adjust the scope of their responses to make them favourable. Similarly, if we want to get a feel for where a supplier is in terms of developing sustainability then asking 'are you working towards establishing a policy for sustainability?' doesn't really help beyond confirming that we've just made it easy for a supplier to confirm they have good intent. Furthermore, we need to provide for the fact that our suppliers will be at different levels of evolution and the purpose of the assessment is to understand where they are. Some may have well-developed management systems for some or all areas of sustainability and may also have good data they can share. Others may not have started yet. For example, if we asked suppliers to state their CO_2e emissions for a specific site or all operations, only a handful of suppliers could currently provide this. Yet it is a question we will need suppliers to answer, if not now but in the near term. More meaningful is to ask questions along the lines of:

- Do you know the CO_2e emissions per site (and if so please state)?
- How are these measured?
- Are they independently verified (if so please provide evidence)?
- What improvement goals have you set?
- How will you achieve these (please share your plan)?

When designing a supplier sustainability assessment, it is easy to get carried away with creating an extensive assessment that examines all aspects of sustainability. Maybe that is exactly what we need and want. Alternatively, focus the assessment on how the supplier meets the minimum requirements together with where they are against the specific goals we have set. Assessment is not a one-time thing but should be an ongoing process applied when qualifying a new supplier and regularly ongoing for existing suppliers. This also provides the platform for our assessment to change and grow as we move forward and our ambition builds. Therefore, it is important to remember that things we won't assess now we will probably come back to later. This, of course, should be balanced against any key risk areas we need to understand.

The next consideration is what we do with suppliers' responses to our assessment. For it to have meaning and purpose we have to interpret and evaluate responses, apply a judgement and act. There are two areas to consider here:

- **What is an acceptable response?** Decide whether to rate responses and if there is a pass mark, perhaps based upon compliance with our minimum requirements and beyond for some suppliers. Ratings mean we are assigning some sort of measure of sustainable development and ideal value that must be achieved to each aspect we are assessing a supplier against and thereby further establishing a standard for supplier sustainability.

- **What if suppliers fall short?** Assessment must drive action. If a supplier fails to meet a set pass mark, decide if they are de-selected from a qualification process or, if an existing supplier, decide if we will exit them or agree a corrective and improvement action plan with them.

The success factors for establishing a supplier sustainability assessment system can be summarized as follows.

General success factors

- **One size does not fit all** – make it multi-sectional with both core and additional sections for certain suppliers (e.g. based upon size, location, industry, etc).
- **Make it easy** and straightforward for the supplier to complete it, ideally via a simple online portal.
- **Communicate** – what is required, why it is needed, how to complete, how the results will be processed and what happens next.
- **Confidentiality** – commit to confidentiality over the information they disclose to encourage them to share freely.
- **Minimum requirements** – include the minimum requirements with the means for suppliers to signal compliance.
- **Feedback** – include a feedback loop so suppliers get to know the result, or at least if they pass. Ideally, this is automated embedded functionality within an online tool.

Design success factors

- **Focus** – determine questions based upon our macro VIPER, the minimum requirements and the sustainability goals we have set. Update it regularly.
- **Question design** – design questions with how you will analyse and report on responses in mind. Automate processing where possible but don't make this a sole ambition as review and interpretation of qualitative responses is a critical part of the assessment. Use a mix of questions to solicit quantitative and qualitative responses.
- **Clarify scope** – design questions so the supplier must be clear about the scope of their responses (e.g. all sites or just some?)
- **Formal or informal?** Include questions that establish if the supplier has formal arrangements for sustainability, such as a management system and data and reporting that supports it – this is key to establishing if

quality data is available, which might determine the shape of the rest of the assessment.

- **Check policies** – include questions to ask if the supplier has specific policies for key areas of sustainability that cannot be easily assessed remotely (e.g. Do you have a policy for non-discrimination of workers? Do you have an environmental policy?). Decide if you want to receive copies.
- **Evidence based** – where possible, require the supplier to provide evidence of their assessment responses (e.g. supplying policies, data, reporting, etc).
- **Responses by degrees** – where certainty of responses is required, use questions requiring a *yes/no* response, otherwise consider questions that allow the respondent to select what level they have achieved (e.g. *no, working towards it, in place but informal, formal policy and process in place*, etc). This is more powerful if, by selecting the most advanced response, the supplier must provide supporting evidence.

Using an assessment and ratings provider

In recent times there has been somewhat of an explosion of providers of sustainability data on companies. Typically, these providers will review and rate companies using a range of data-gathering methods, typically both inside-out and outside-in with the good ones triangulating data points to verify findings as much as possible. Almost all providers conduct this analysis remotely and in many cases there is engagement with and participation from the company being assessed, especially if that company is keen to secure a tick or certification of some kind. The assessment criteria used and therefore the standard to which these companies are assessing companies tend to be their own assessment framework that they have developed based upon what the markets they serve want to know, with some offering tailored options or the facility for a user to select or set their own criteria and have the assessment process managed by the provider.

The most developed base of review and ratings providers serves the financial and investment community – providing ESG data to support investors and asset managers evaluating companies to include in a sustainable portfolio or to hedge risks. There are many players out there, including providers such as ESG Sustainalytics, Bloomberg, ISS Ratings and Rankings, CDP Climate, MSCI, Refinitiv, RepRisk, FTSE Russell, ESG Book, S&P Global ESG Scores and Moody's ESG Solutions Group.

For supplier review and ratings, ESG investor providers' data is good for evaluating suppliers also, with many of the traditional ESG ratings providers now recognizing the market beyond the investor community and actively establishing themselves as players here. Other providers specializing in supplier review and ratings have now entered the pitch and this space is fast developing as it has huge potential for both supply of supplier sustainability data and also more sophisticated platforms with either a managed or self-service approach for tailored assessment and remote interaction with suppliers in support of this. Notable providers here so far include EcoVadis, CDP, MSCI ESG ratings, Sustainalytics, RobecoSAM and ISS-oekom. Others will follow very soon.

Benefits of using a third-party provider

Developing and maintaining a supplier assessment system requires significant resource and ongoing effort. Alternatively, using a ratings and review provider can, for many organizations, be the most effective method of determining suppliers' sustainability status. Ratings and review providers offer a score of how a company meets certain sustainability criteria based upon a range of assessment and data-gathering activities. Relying upon experts in this field can give greater assurance to all stakeholders and also to shareholders – who may be very familiar with ESG ratings providers and will recognize the value of a similar approach with suppliers. Using review and ratings provides credibility and a great story to tell as a published declaration of sustainability progress, for example '70 per cent of our supply base is rated good or above by an independent sustainability ratings company – our goal is 100 per cent in three years'.

Providers here have amassed significant data and expertise and this will only strengthen. Using a company with expertise that serves both investors and purchasers gives a powerful triangulation. Using providers reduces survey fatigue and we become part of a network with a shared ambition that is growing fast. However, there are limitations and choosing the right provider and the degree to which we will rely upon them now and into the future requires careful consideration.

Limitations of a third-party provider

There is no such thing as a truly reliable third-party metric. There is no single, all-encompassing source of information or tool that does everything. The providers here and the tools they offer have different levels of capability according to the criteria and data-gathering processes used. They serve different markets and tend to be strong in only certain geographic and industry sectors but not across the board. Therefore, the right provider to use depends upon what we are trying to achieve.

Ratings can be subject to a conflict of interest, especially if the providers supply training or consulting services to the company they are assessing. Ratings can lack data verification and it can be hard for us to get behind the degree of verification rigour being applied. Any sort of questionnaire-based or self-determined assessment, even if evidence based, is only as good as that which the supplier submits and without first-hand verification ongoing it can be hard to get the complete picture. Instead, use of multiple data sources can give greater confidence.

It is worth reflecting on where this marketplace is heading. Today supplier assessment is still quite basic but it is perhaps the future of how providers in this space will work that is the most exciting. What is clear is that we will need accurate insight into all our suppliers and supply chains, ideally in real time in the future. Forward-thinking companies in this space are already working on how they do this. Self-assessment will give way to how companies access and utilize a range of real-time data sources from suppliers but also from other indicators and measures of the supplier's operation, their products and how things move through the supply chain. In selecting a provider, it is worth understanding how they intend to develop what they do moving forward.

Selecting the right third-party provider

Considerations in selecting and utilizing a third-party supplier sustainability review and ratings provider are:

- What do they do – rating only, supplier assessment tool we configure or managed assessment uniquely for us?
- Creation and maintenance of rating criteria and rigour with which it is applied.
- Ability to tailor questions to the nature of the supplier.
- Does the platform provide for stakeholder collaboration?
- Process used for data collection – how do they 'meet suppliers where they are at' with the assessment method, question and criteria used, etc.
- Check geographies and industry sectors covered.
- Check their track record.
- Check impartiality and what their agenda is. How independent are they?

- Do they also provide consulting and training services to the companies they assess?
- Sources – is it only questionnaire based or rich triangulation of various data sources? If so what do they use?
- If we are determining or tailoring questions, get stakeholders involved.

Accreditation to known standards

The final consideration and option in how we might assess suppliers is relying upon a supplier's accreditation to a known national or international standard. We can better understand a supplier and gain a measure of risk exposure, or more specifically arrangements that mitigate certain risks, through the accreditations to standards that they hold. Therefore, it is appropriate to be interested in such accreditations, or indeed in supplier's efforts to work towards these, as it tells a story of how serious the supplier is about mastering full and effective control over what they do.

Accreditation to ISO 9001 has long since been a basis to select suppliers or at least gain confidence in them based upon the assurance that they have implemented and maintain an effective quality management system. This might seem somewhat detached from sustainability but the modern iterations of this standard consider what the organization is setting out to be and achieve, with input from the firm's stakeholders, and then how it has organized itself to do this, including the various approaches, processes, procedures, checks and reviews ongoing. Therefore, if a company has made sustainability a key corporate goal then the systems and arrangements that support ISO 9001 accreditation will give confidence in the firm's ability here.

There is no specific, all-encompassing international standard for sustainability to which a company can obtain accreditation. ISO 26000 (international standard for social responsibility) and ISO 20400 (international standard for sustainable procurement), while both highly relevant, are guidance standards and so companies cannot obtain accreditation to these yet. ISO 14001 (environmental management system) is, however, highly relevant and is a standard against which companies can be accredited. So too is ISO 27001 to consider a firms arrangements for data management and information security. What these and other standards in this space have in common is that an effective management system underpins everything a company needs to do for sustainability. Therefore, accreditation to ISO 9001 does not provide an indication of how sustainable a company is but it can provide a good gauge to a company's ability to drive sustainability, providing it has set that as its goal. Accreditation to ISO 14001 takes this one step further to provide an indication that a company has a management system and is organized to determine its environmental impact and meet specific goals it has set. ISO 27001 means we can have confidence in the supplier's ability to process our customer's data or that of those in their supply chains.

Accreditation to international standards is a useful component of assessing suppliers for sustainability but must be combined with other assessments to gain a full insight. Suppliers' accreditations to these standards help us understand them, and potentially negate the need for us to make certain interventions to know them more or assess them as, in theory, this has already been done for their management systems. However, check the scope of the accreditation and to which of the suppliers operations this applies, and verify their certification.

Auditing a supplier

The most effective means to truly understand a supplier is to audit them and audit them regularly. An audit is a first-hand observation and evaluation of a supplier, their management systems, arrangements, ways of working and general set-up. It is also the basis to establish a dialogue about improvements and agree clear plans with a supplier in this respect. A good audit examines every aspect of a supplier to one degree or another and seeks evidence of stated arrangements or control measures in place. Audits are most typically conducted to a set standard that covers all aspects of the operation, either set by an international, national or industry body, or set by us. This defines the framework for the audit and shapes how an audit is conducted. Alternatively, audits, or 'mini-audits' can be conducted without a set standard and become a sort of tourist visit. These are still highly useful as they provide the option to see first-hand a supplier's operation, judge risk and raise questions about what is seen. However, nothing beats a structured audit approach with a supplier to gain true insight into their operation. In my career I've audited a vast number of suppliers and found that with the right approach it is possible to get deep 'under the hood' of a company and discover where there is hidden risk or opportunity.

Auditing for supplier sustainability

Supplier audits can have different areas of focus. Within procurement, audit of a supplier's management system, perhaps conducted by a separate quality or audit function, has been part of how many organizations have typically carried out their due diligence. Other focus areas for an audit might include health and safety, financial or data and IT security. Supplier sustainability audits are no different in terms of how the audit is conducted, except we examine different things and here we encounter greater challenges because we are seeking to verify things that are typically more hidden and difficult to understand, such as how free their workers are, how they are employed, if they cause pollution, where waste goes, etc. The challenges here increase tenfold when the supplier is in a remote developing country, where legislation is less developed or where there is less compliance with legislation, where cultural differences perpetuate certain practices, where corruption abounds, where there are language barriers and where it is difficult to truly understand the socio-economic dynamics in the local region and of the workers, and so on.

A specialist skill

Effective auditing is a special skill; professional auditors train and need to become certified before they can practice on behalf of an awarding body and need to demonstrate ongoing that they are maintaining the currency of their skill. Good auditors know how to stay safe in an unknown and sometimes hostile situation. They know how to understand the expected processes and practices, they know where to look and what to test or examine in order to gauge how effective management controls are. They also know what questions to ask, and how to probe to get behind the veneer of polished answers that the owners or sales representative might be adept at providing. Good auditors are 'worldly wise' and experienced at being able to go into a perhaps unfriendly environment, in another country and in another culture, and remain objective and in control. Such skills are not typically those that reside in procurement but might exist within our organization, say within a quality function where audits have been common practice as part of the company's risk management. Sustainability auditors require further capabilities so as to understand what to look for, what to check and key indicators that help understand a supplier's situation. If existing auditors within an organization can extend their skill set to include sustainability it is possible to expand an existing audit approach to become an all-encompassing first-hand evaluation of a supplier.

Becoming a sustainability auditor

Attempting a sustainability audit without any experience or training is not recommended and doing so may even be dangerous. As a minimum, those auditing suppliers require good auditor training (courses are available), knowledge of how a typical management system operates (part of quality auditing) and deep knowledge of sustainability and what to look for within specific processes, workplaces, etc. The individual(s) who conducts the audit needs to have sufficient gravitas and be assertive enough to lead the situation, often in the face of the supplier attempting to drive their own agenda. Those learning to audit should first be a passenger on an audit and develop from there. Audits work better, and can be safer, when conducted as a small team. This also gives scope to set up a team with a complementary mix of skills. Finally, gender equality is not global yet and attitudes towards women in some cultures are way away from that we view as acceptable, let alone ideal. Consider carefully the situation an auditor is to be placed in, and even if a team of auditors should split up or not. Astonishing as it might seem, a lone female auditor in some cultures may not be taken seriously and could be at risk.

Supplier willingness

Being audited is no small affair for a supplier; it requires them to dedicate resources to accommodating the audit, they may need to protect certain secret or confidential aspects of their business, they will need to ensure the safety of the auditor and that the process of auditing will not impact negatively on their business. They may also go to great lengths to hide things in advance.

A supplier may well need good reason to accommodate a customer audit. If undergoing an assessment is necessary to win or retain a large contract then this will most likely be good reason, but a less significant customer may find the supplier less willing to accommodate being audited or any attempt to impose conditions.

The sustainability audit framework and checklist

Conducting an audit requires a framework of the specific areas to examine. We could use a set standard or framework but more typically organizations design their own framework from which an audit checklist and report format can be compiled. A sustainability audit could be designed to cover all aspects of sustainability to give an overall view of a supplier, or could be specifically aligned to our sustainability goals.

Building an audit checklist

The audit checklist is the means by which an auditor will systematically conduct the audit – an aide-mémoire of what to check (perhaps with a set sequence to do this) and the basis to capture findings and areas of non-conformance or where improvement is required. What gets captured during an audit is of great importance as it provides the basis to select or deselect a supplier, set improvement plans and is a key record that demonstrates how we are managing supply-side risk. It also records the supplier-specific baseline that can be used for subsequent audits or to test improvements have been successful. The record of an audit should be open to scrutiny. It is therefore essential auditors take the time to document findings along the way rather than after the event.

Construct the checklist to cover the relevant areas we are interested in. This could cover all aspects of sustainability or just the specific areas we are concerned with in line with our sustainable procurement goals. The checklist could be merged with other areas also including quality, data, financial, etc to provide a more comprehensive audit approach. Table 12.2 provides some potential check questions and sources of evidence to include.

Supplier audits need to consider more than just the supplier's facilities, but to be effective they need to be contextualized and tailored around the specific products or services the supplier provides and also the end-to-end supply chains or SVCNs it exists within. Hot spot analysis can help here along with outputs from any evaluations we have conducted on what we buy such as sustainable value engineering or for the entire supply chain such as supply chain mapping. Understanding the context is key here to how we conduct the audit. For example, if what the supplier provides involves energy- and water-intensive processing with likely high emissions then our audit must look closely in these areas, whereas another supplier might operate in countries where there are known human rights issues and so we would seek to look closely here. Checklist design should therefore have both core and optional elements that the auditor determines according to the supplier in question.

Determine how to record findings for each check step. Consider whether a check step requires either a 'yes/no' (or N/A) response for areas where you need to test compliance, versus a rating system, in which case define criteria for each level so there is consistency in application. For each step provide for comments to be recorded and non-conformances or areas for improvement to be identified.

Sustainable procurement

Suppliers will be keen to obtain a copy of the audit and will almost certainly ask if the report will be shared. Decide in advance what the approach here will be and whether you will share everything or provide a summary. Sharing everything opens up the risk of suppliers challenging and might make an auditor more careful about recording observations. I favour the approach of stating up front that the auditor's report is confidential but a summary of findings, the audit score (if there is one) and non-conformances or areas for improvement will be shared. This provides greater control over the specific areas we need the supplier to engage with.

Table 12.2 Sustainability audit checklist

Area	Areas to check	Ways to verify
Company and facilities set-up	• Company structure: Who owns it? Group or subsidiary companies? • Facilities: How many and where are they all located? What happens at each location? • What is said about them, what are the rumours, what is on social media or online?	• Research them • Website and annual reports • Talk to those in the area, local bodies, etc • Publicly available company records • Ask them
Context	• What products are made, what services are provided? Where does this happen? What supply chains are involved? • What are the potential risk (or opportunity) areas given the context? Where should we look deeper?	• Hot spot analysis • Ask them • Sustainable value engineering results • Supply chain mapping results
People and governance	• Senior team: Who are they? Experience and qualifications for the role? • Workforce profile at each location and level • Are there individuals with overall responsibility and accountability for sustainability and health and safety?	• Ask them • Organization charts • View HR records • Sample training records • Sustainability reports published • Check intranet, noticeboards and other internal comms

Table 12.2 *continued*

Area	Areas to check	Ways to verify
	• What goals and ambition for sustainability? • Do they audit the company? • What training do people receive? • Communication of policies	• Audit records
Management system	• What management systems are in place – quality, health and safety, environment, sustainability, etc? • Accreditations held: For which facilities and what is the scope? • Do they claim to operate with a code of conduct? • Policies and procedures: What is in place, are they appropriate, are they in use?	• Review policies and procedures • Check accreditations • Check compliance
Suppliers	• Policies for responsible sourcing • Who are the key suppliers? Which impact sustainability the most? Where are they? What do they do? • How do they select and manage suppliers ongoing? Do they visit them? What do they know about them? • What sustainability elements are checked or verified? • Sustainability initiatives with suppliers?	• Check policies • Spend history • Purchase order and invoicing records • Procurement and quality audit records • Interview procurement individuals • Check for hot spots and research key suppliers separately
Transportation	• How are things/people transported? What is the impact and are there initiatives to reduce this?	• Observation • Internal fleet records or supplier records

Table 12.2 *continued*

Area	Areas to check	Ways to verify
Working conditions	• Is there a culture of prevention (of injury, unfair employment or industrial conflict)? • Risk assessment and accident prevention • Check workstations – how long do they stand for? Posture, lifting, repetitive work, vibration? • Environment – noise, temperature • Air quality – fumes, dust, smoke, vapours in the air. Levels of extraction. • Working style – pace required, demands, being placed in difficult or disturbing situations, distribution of tasks, tiring situations. • Protection and prevention, use of right PPE	• Observation • Review health and safety records • Sample worker shift schedules
Child and forced labour	• What is the prevailing political, legislative and socio-economic landscape – is there good, enforced legislation? How likely is child or forced labour? • Do they have a clear position and policy? Is it enforced? What monitoring systems are in place? How do they act on concerns? • Who are the workers – age, sex, location of work? • Is there a culture of prevention? Adequacy of measures to do this • Worker verifications – child labour: birth registration, school attendance records	• Check hot spots • Check policies • Check non-conformance records • Check/sample worker records and check they are validated as original and correct • Observation – look for missing parts of the process or throughputs that don't tally

Table 12.2 *continued*

Area	Areas to check	Ways to verify
Environmental	• What hazardous chemicals are sourced, used, produced? How are they stored, handled, disposed of? • How much energy is used? Plans to reduce or switch to renewables? • How much water consumption? Plans to reduce? • What are the CO_2e emissions of the facility, for what they supply/do, in their supply chains and for the entire company? Do they know? If so, how? Plans to reduce? • Check air emissions management, wastewater management • What waste streams are produced? Where do they go? How is it controlled? • Pollution prevention measures	• Observation • Data from meters • Sample utility bills • Sample waste management contracts and records – check provider's certifications • Internal reporting • Follow waste streams through the process • Local permits • Local authority records – breaches or fines imposed
Employment	• Hours worked, days worked, contracts • Social support and recognition • Pay • Job quality and prospects • Freedom of association and collective bargaining • Freedom from verbal and physical abuse, threats, unwanted sexual attention and humiliating behaviour, bullying, harassment • Non-discrimination	• Sample workers' contracts • Talk to workers • Workforce profile (gender, race, nationality, medical condition, religion, disability, etc at each level) • Observation

Table 12.2 *continued*

Area	Areas to check	Ways to verify
Communities	• Impact on the local community • Activities and initiatives to support the local community	• Local press • Social media groups and forums • Talk to people

Conducting a sustainability audit

With our team ready and a checklist to guide us, all that remains is to conduct the audit and there are a number of considerations here. Key is creating the right audit environment. Ideally, we are there to be collaborative and constructive, to work with the supplier to understand them and help move forward together. Ideally the supplier wants to be open and transparent with us. However not all audits are like this and a supplier, especially one that has something to hide, can become very threatened by the process. Sometimes, audits can become difficult, conflictual and deceitful with the supplier going to great lengths to keep things hidden. Especially if they have a lot to lose. Arguably these may not be the suppliers we ideally want to be using, but we may have no choice. We need to be ready and prepared for all situations and no matter how collaborative it feels it is important to remember to keep at arm's length objectively and not get too close.

We've been expecting you, Mr Bond

When we arrive at the supplier's site it is important to recognize the company will almost certainly have prepared for our arrival. This doesn't mean having coffee and cookies ready but orchestrating things to try to ensure we see only what they want us to see. I have experience of one audit where, prior to the audit, all the things the company didn't want to be seen were loaded into the back of a large truck and the driver instructed to drive around for the day and not to come back until told to do so. Unannounced audits can help here with current suppliers where we have set up the right to do this; however, even unannounced audits are rarely a surprise. Once, as I sat in the bar of the only hotel in town near to the main employer's factory the day before I was due to arrive at the site, the woman behind the bar had clearly been primed to find out who I was, where I had come from, who I worked for and why I was in town. The reality is when we arrive to conduct an audit the supplier has prepared for it. This means our detective work needs us to look for things that don't quite stack up, such as a part of process flow that seems to be missing, there aren't enough people on the premises to be doing the full output and so on. Do this by following the process through and learning to tune in to what doesn't make sense, and ask lots of questions.

Preparing

Pre-preparation matters. If the first time we are learning about the supplier's business is in their boardroom during the audit kick-off meeting, we are already on the back foot. Instead it is essential to engage with the supplier well in advance to set the right expectations and prepare. Conduct pre-research around the company set-up, facilities and context (Table 12.2) well in advance, asking the supplier to provide various bits of information. Determine as far as possible where all the supplier's facilities, factories, premises, agricultural sources and operating locations are based and which ones you will visit. Check transit time, routes, methods between sites. Set expectations with the supplier around how the audit will run and sort out in advance anything that needs to be in place to ensure the audit runs smoothly. This includes:

- **Only setting a loose agenda** – avoid telling them in advance exactly what you want to see but set it up so you may go anywhere. Where relevant, insist the supplier has transport on standby.
- **Understanding any safety requirements in advance** – while a prerequisite, it can also be used as reason to delay you or deny access. Have the supplier share any requirements here and what is needed to access certain areas. Check if inductions will be required, and if so how long these will these take and if any PPE is necessary.
- **Confidentiality** can be a reason for a supplier to deny showing you something, especially workers' records. Ensure the supplier understands you will want to examine but not copy or retain certain records. Get a confidentiality agreement in place ahead of the audit.

Stay safe

Auditor safety must be paramount but don't assume the company you are visiting will put your safety first as you might expect. The supplier's safety arrangements may not be as well evolved or enforced as you expect. They may not have briefed you about certain risks and, in some extreme situations, typically where workers hold some power over their supervisors, workers who perceive the auditor as the enemy can deliberately act dangerously near to the auditor. This is more of a risk than is often realized. I've conducted audits where I had to leap out of the way of forklift trucks, shield my eyes when a welder started arc welding without any screens near to me and dodge a worker who ran through an open doorway pushing a wheelbarrow of molten hot castings towards me. All my guide could say was they have to move them quickly before they go cold. That told me everything I needed to know about the culture. In any and every situation entered, do a mini on-the-spot-risk assessment in your head. Check anything you are unsure about and check if you need any PPE. Maintain awareness of what is happening around you at all times. When two police officers stop and question a suspect, they will stand so they form a triangle with the suspect so they have eyes in all directions and can protect each other from unseen assailants. The same approach, assuming there are two auditors, should be adopted in potentially risky situations. Work so you have each other's back.

Finally ensure the right PPE is available and worn. Don't wait for the supplier to provide this or tell you to wear it. As a minimum, arrive at an audit with your own protective footwear, earplugs, safety glasses, a hard hat and a high-vis jacket. Don't be afraid to be the only one(s) wearing it.

Don't get derailed

Suppliers will use a wide range of practices to derail an audit or prevent or delay an auditor seeing certain things. Most of this can be headed off with good pre-preparation but things to watch for are:

- **The long kick-off** – take control of the kick-off meeting and set out how you want the day to run and timings. The supplier would love to give you a nice welcome and sales presentation that keeps you in the boardroom as long as possible.
- **The long lunch** – a nice lunch at a local restaurant or set out in the boardroom sounds lovely but it also keeps you away from what you are there to do. It is amazing how long a company can make lunch take during an audit. Take control from the outset and set expectations such as setting a 30-minute timeslot, insisting on a light lunch brought into the meeting room. I would often take my own lunch and ask to break off and have a lunch break in a room alone, where I could marshal my thoughts ready for the afternoon session.

- **Avoid the Disney tour** – don't let them give you the standard visitors' tour that guides you through all the bits that they want to show you and nothing else. Instead check the layout, follow the process and checklist and ask to see the relevant areas.
- **We can't show you that** – confidentiality, health and safety, we can't find it, it's not open today, it's Mary's day off, the dog ate it and so on. Be ready for all sorts of reasons why you can't see something. Prepare in advance and set expectations with the supplier as much as possible but during the audit don't take no for an answer, hold your ground and insist on seeing what you are there to see. Remind them they cannot pass the audit unless they fully cooperate.

What really helps

Auditing is about seeing and getting behind the veneer to understand what really happens. The process of auditing is about following a checklist, asking questions, looking at evidence and making a determination about the controls and systems in place. In practice, however, the true picture comes from more subtle signs. With practice it is possible to identify where a supplier is hiding something and what they are uncomfortable with and therefore where to probe further. If we watch and listen closely, those we engage with will tell us everything we want to know without actually saying as much. Key things that help here are:

- **Talk to those who do the job** – with permission, ask those who are doing the job to tell you about it, – what do they do, how long have they worked here, how did they learn to do this, do they enjoy it? Asking about them, rather than what they are expecting or primed to answer can reveal lots.
- **Body language** – watch those who accompany you carefully when you ask them questions and tune in to what is hidden in their responses. Look for differences between when you ask them about general stuff and signs of discomfort when you ask certain audit questions. Where does their gaze fall, what are they trying to guide you towards (and therefore away from…)? What are they not saying in the answers they are giving you?
- **How does it feel?** Think what it would be like if you worked there, how does it feel, how much does the company seem to value its people, how motivated are they? Does it seem a happy place or an oppressive place to work? How do workers look at you – with fear or curiosity?

- **Is the company investing?** Decide if the company is investing in the organization. Growth, new equipment, new people, all show the company is serious about its future, but also might suggest new areas of risk.

Non-conformances and areas for improvement

Sustainability audits are a means to determine compliance to a standard, gauge how sustainable a supplier is or is not, or establish the basis for some sort of improvement. There will almost certainly be areas where a standard is not met or there are things that can be improved. It is important to make a distinction between problems or issues that need to be fixed and opportunities for development. There are four categories we can use here:

- **Major non-conformances** – an audit finding where the supplier fails to meet an aspect of a set standard or there is an area of concern that would present risk and must be addressed urgently. Such findings could potentially prevent us using this supplier until these are corrected.
- **Minor non-conformances** – a minor audit finding or area for improvement that requires addressing, either near or medium term, but the risk is low and we can continue to use this supplier in the meantime. Some audit approaches establish a principle that a certain number of minors constitutes a major.
- **Observation** – an audit finding where we have identified an isolated error or non-compliance with a procedure or something we advise the supplier to address, but will not insist on it.
- **Area for development** – an audit finding that suggests an opportunity to further improve an area that is currently acceptable, to further drive sustainability.

Our audit findings defined across the different categories above form the basis for corrective, and ideally preventative, action by the supplier and also the basis to agree development plans. When we communicate this to the supplier it should not be new to them, but should be areas that were discussed and ideally acknowledged as fair by them during the audit. There are some situations where non-conformances are such that we must impose sanctions on a supplier such as denial of business or penalties until they put corrective action in place. In some extreme situations where we uncover such things as deliberate human rights abuses this is exactly the right response as failing to act could risk brand damage for us. However, in most situations a more collaborative and supportive approach tends to be the most productive – working with the supplier to identify the areas of concern and then agreeing action within suitable timescales with the supplier and project-managing these until completion.

Finally, audits should not be regarded as one-time activities, but we should revisit key suppliers according to risk, opportunity, need (e.g. to follow up corrective and preventative actions) and available resource.

Auditing for child or forced labour

Child and forced labour can be exceptionally difficult to spot during an audit. If child labour exists it won't exist in front of you when you visit. I've heard stories where the moment the auditors entered the front gate, all the children ran out the back gate. In reality, it doesn't happen like this and is harder to detect. Forced labour, however, might be right there in front of you but not detectable as those involved might not risk doing anything that could indicate they are not there freely or are in a situation where all choice has been taken away from them. Therefore, for these areas we need to consider the area and sector and the prevailing political, legislative and socio-economic landscape, and the likelihood of the system working to permit child or forced labour rather than good, well-enforced legislation. The other factor here is if child labour was detected and the children then get removed from work where do they go? Are there social protection measures in place (e.g. children return to and must remain in education, or will they go and work somewhere else, perhaps more dangerous)? In which case we have not solved the issue.

Within a sector it is also important to consider the trends and international standing of the supplier. For example, in the textiles industry, most of the big 'A-list' suppliers in developing nations have long since eradicated such practices as their ability to supply the world depends upon it. However, look at some of the more 'B-list' backstreet companies in the same region, and you will find it.

Auditing for child and forced labour therefore starts by considering the area or sector and where the conditions exist to permit or encourage child or forced labour as well as the likelihood of exposure to violence, bondage, prostitution, etc. Examine carefully and extensively those who do the work – look at the age and sex across the workforce and prioritize verifying the youngest workers, especially young girls. For young people at or above legal minimum ages check how hazardous the work is, the natural environment, working conditions, protection and work performed, taking into account the age and sex of workers and the minimum age for the region. For example, a 14-year-old might be legally employed to pick fruit, but not if this means they have to work at height or have significant exposure to pesticides.

It is also useful to scrutinize the process and all the steps that happen to create a product or deliver a service, and ensure every step of the process can be observed and what you see looks right. For example, if you visit a garment manufacturer and you follow an item through every step of production and at one point the garment is near finished, then the next time you see the garment it is covered in sequins but there is no one sewing sequins, either something magical is happening or there are steps happening elsewhere. Perhaps this step is subcontracted, in which case we can investigate who the supplier is, how they have been approved, how the company ensures the correct practices, etc. Watch also for a similar situation of having token steps, for example if there are two single workers sewing sequins, yet the throughput is 6,000 garments per week and it takes 12 minutes to sew one garment. Even with a 48-hour week, 5,520 garments are being processed elsewhere. Processing elsewhere may be legitimate, but it can also indicate hidden child or forced labour and/or poor working conditions off site.

Talking to or interviewing workers can be useful but with caution and it requires the right approach. First, we need to be certain that it won't put them at risk and respect the fact that they have the right to speak or keep silent. Second, if we can talk to them away from colleagues and superiors listening in it will put them at ease. If an employer is telling us everything is done properly it is hard for them to object to a private conversation. Third, avoid demanding information. Instead talking to workers should be as us asking them a favour to explore a situation. Remember it is not the child or individual who is breaking the law but rather their employer. Work to engage so those we talk to see the benefits of sharing with us. Avoid direct questions but instead ask them to talk about aspects of their experience, both in work and outside. Questions such as 'How do people here treat you?' 'Who here is nice to you?', 'What is the happiest moment you can remember while you have been here?', 'How long do you think you will work here?' and so on can help here (ILO, 2002).

'Eyes on the ground' with a tablet

Having eyes on the ground to see first-hand what is happening at a supplier's facility at any given time, or to tour a remote factory is invaluable. Travelling to visit a factory, agricultural course, producer or processor is often essential. However, clearly, we are only present for a short time. Often it can be necessary to maintain more of a presence. Some companies go as far as employing a local representative as their 'eyes on the ground', which can help; however, it is both expensive and difficult to make work due to risk of the representative 'going native', being marginalized or compromised with some sort of bribe.

However, there is much we can do from our desks with someone from the supplier with a tablet or a smartphone using FaceTime, Zoom, Teams, etc. In effect we can create our own eyes on the ground remotely and have the supplier show us what we want to see. While there can be no substitute for first-hand observation, directing someone remotely to show us the things we want to see can be a highly effective and cheap alternative. Clearly there is scope for the supplier to work this to their advantage or be selective about what we get to see, however the willingness of the supplier here to give us an honest view can also be highly revealing about how serious they are about meeting our requirements. If they find reasons for us not to see certain things then this should ring alarm bells for us. Remote eyes on the ground can enable a remote tour, a degree of audit and can help us manage and maintain a supplier ongoing. However, it needs to be set up for success as follows:

- **Technical considerations** – the locations or areas we are interested in need good access to internet and local 4G-minimum cell-phone coverage or wi-fi. Even in developing nations this is often available. Check the connectivity at the locations we are interested in. It may be worthwhile to help the supplier invest in developing their local connectivity or wi-fi. Also, for locations away from good connection such as agricultural sources, open mines or remote processing there are alternatives using satellite data which, while expensive, can sometimes be worthwhile.

- **Data privacy** – we must ensure we comply with relevant local data protection and privacy requirements. As a minimum, if people are to be observed remotely, they should be informed and know how their video feed will be used, whether any recordings are being made and how these recordings will be used, protected, deleted, etc.

- **Obedient cameraperson** – the person driving the iPad or other device and how they do this makes all the difference. This needs to be someone who has the right skills in filming things. The person operating the iPad must be an 'obedient cameraperson' and must follow our instructions regarding what we want to see, instructing them to pan left, right, go here, go there, show me close up and so on.

- **Access all areas** – set this up with the supplier so they agree we can access all areas. It can help if we have a building plan or site map of all the facilities so we can direct the remote cameraperson. Clarify in advance with the supplier any areas where there is not good connectivity, rather than letting this being brought in as a reason not to go somewhere.

Chapter checkpoint

In this chapter we have continued working through OMEIA® stage 3 to explore approaches to understanding sustainability in suppliers using audit and assessments. Key points covered are:

1 *Sustainability audit or assessment* are means to understand where our suppliers are at in terms of sustainability and there are various approaches.

2 *Minimum requirements* – for sustainability that all or a significant proportion of the supply base must meet. These should check compliance for key legislative requirements and confirm suppliers understand our expectations in other areas.

3 *Supplier assessment* – the easiest method to understand important or strategic suppliers. Conducted remotely by us or a third party. An assessment can be 'outside-in' using published information and data about the supplier, or 'inside-out' requiring the supplier to engage, typically to complete a questionnaire. Use of third-party rating providers is highly effective here.

4 *Supplier audit* – the most effective means to understand a supplier involving an in-person verification of the supplier's facilities, practices and approaches, either to a set standard or a standard we determine, carried out by us or by a third-party or independent assessment body. Audits require great skill and a structured approach and there are many pitfalls and risks to be aware of prior to the engagement.

5 *Eyes on the ground with a tablet* – a great alternative to an in-person visit. With the right set up and relationship with the supplier it is possible to conduct a good level of remote assessment having someone on the ground as a 'remote cameraperson' with an iPad or other device showing us what we want to see.

In the next chapter we will explore how we understand sustainability within our supply chains.

Driving sustainability in the supply chain

13

> This chapter explores how we will drive sustainability through in our supply chains. We will explore how to map and understand a supply chain and full SVCN and consider the complexities and difficulties in driving sustainability. We will explore a series of approaches that can help here.
>
> *Pathway question addressed in this chapter:*
>
> **12** How can we make our supply chains more sustainable?

Understanding supply chains

We are continuing to evaluate where we can best direct our resources and now we turn our attention to which supply chains we need to better understand or work with to drive sustainability. To do this we are continuing our journey through OMEIA® stage 3 and also moving into stage 4 to consider how we begin to implement changes.

Until now we have considered sustainable procurement in the context of what we buy and the immediate suppliers we buy from. With the application of good strategic procurement approaches such as category management and SRM, both applied with our sustainability hat on, we can be effective at driving sustainability in both these areas as we are in control and can define and implement our business and relationship requirements. Figure 13.1 shows the components that we will explore through this chapter that enable us to make our supply chains sustainable.

Figure 13.1 The elements of supply chain sustainability

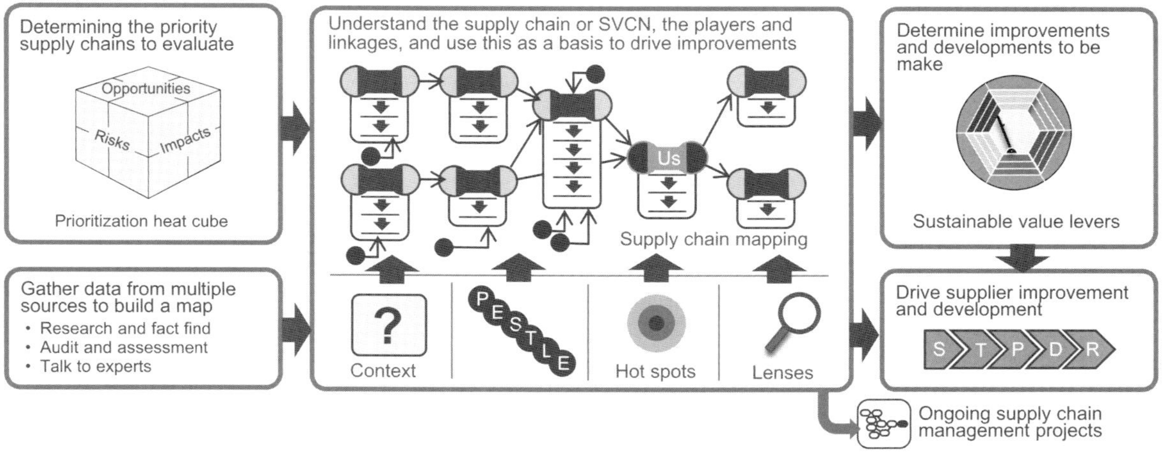

The most difficult challenge

When it comes to the supply chain things are different. Driving sustainability upstream in the supply chain, or even both upstream and downstream in the end-to-end supply and value chain network (SVCN), is much more difficult for four reasons:

- We may not know what happens beyond our immediate suppliers (and also customers) or it may not necessarily be visible or easy to understand.
- Understanding what happens downstream with our immediate and end customers has not traditionally been the concern of procurement and we may encounter resistance internally.
- What happens in our supply chains happens in entities we have no contractual and often no working relationship with, that may not be willing, able or incentivized to accommodate any sort of change of practice. They may not even know who we are.
- Supply chains can be incredibly complex and may run back to remote corners of the world, in developing nations, where sustainability impacts abound, where culture and practice is vastly different or legislation is lacking or not enforced.

Yet the supply chain and also the full SVCN often represents the biggest area of risk and opportunity for sustainability. We cannot make sustainable procurement happen unless we tackle our supply chains, and this is consistently the area companies report as being the most difficult. As we have seen, few companies deliberately set out to act irresponsibly but more typically fall into the 'unaware, unable or have not been required to' categories.

This is due, in part, to the fact that over the last four decades globalization established itself as the blueprint for effective procurement and drove global supply chains and distribution networks, with fewer 'supersized' suppliers. Globalization has worked against sustainability because it means we have become largely disconnected from our supply chains as there has been little reason to do otherwise. Yet the tide is turning here and in recent years we have found ourselves in the situation where we have come to realize the fragility of global supply chains. This has created a whole new trend towards bringing things closer or to a more appropriate location. Sustainability is also a key driver here. Crucially, what is happening here is that in order to drive sustainable procurement in our supply chains we need to undo some of what globalization has established, especially that where transparency has not been needed, where everything comes down to lowest cost and where impacts have gone unnoticed. We are part of a shift from 'unaware, unable or have not been required to', to becoming very aware and being required to. What remains is to establish the capability to effect change.

A new capability and a new perspective on procurement

Procurement functions typically lack the capability to drive sustainability in the supply chain. Getting behind what is happening in a supply chain has not been the primary concern of procurement, but rather we have focused on immediate suppliers. Similarly, supply chain management (SCM) has traditionally been a separate activity and function to procurement, often kept worlds apart. In the same way that procurement was once about buying things, SCM was once about little more than logistics, warehousing, managing demand information through a supply chain, reducing risk and optimizing all the different things that flow to get stuff where it needed to be at the right time. Today, forward-thinking companies regard both procurement and SCM as strategic functions. They recognize the value possible if it can use information and predictive modelling, often powered by new and bigger data sources, to create agile and highly responsive supply chains that better serve its customers. The value of thinking strategically about both procurement and SCM is clear, but crucially with this comes the need for these to operate as one. Furthermore, the need for sustainability is driving a sea change here and now procurement practitioners need to become supply chain experts and vice versa. Both need to be sustainability experts, and we need to work together with others who have knowledge or interests in these areas.

Supply chain management (SCM) and sustainability

If we are to drive sustainable procurement in supply chains we must understand SCM. The science of good SCM is concerned with holistic interventions across the entire supply and value chain network (SVCN) and by doing so significant benefits are possible. SCM has five pillars, which are all the things we need to attend to in order to make an SVCN work effectively. These include sustainability, now widely recognized as an essential component of SCM. They are:

1 **Logistics** – all the activities and arrangements concerned with flow of materials downstream matched with demand.
2 **Demand** – understanding and balancing supply and demand through the entire SVCN including understanding end-customer needs and aspirations

that might trigger future demand. Requires a deep understanding of what drives demand and the nature of any volatility.

3 **Information** – the nature of information, and the way it is transmitted throughout the supply and value chain network

4 **Risk** – understanding and proactively managing supplier and supply chain risk.

5 **Sustainability** – understanding the processes, practices and original sources in the supply chain and specific interventions to ensure a compliance with sustainability requirements and realize sustainability goals.

Supply chain management takes on a new dimension when we apply it to driving sustainability in the supply chain. Here, once again, we put on our sustainability hat. Starting with the priority supply chains we identified during our assessment process as defined in our prioritization heat cube, we need to further evaluate these and determine where specific improvement projects are needed. This begins by better understanding our supply chains and specifically what happens at each step and whether there are any risks, impacts or opportunities. From here we can then determine improvement projects.

It's all about structure and flow

Understanding supply chains is about understanding how they are structured, what flows and how things flow.

The simplest form of supply chain is one where materials flow from the original raw material or agricultural source, are progressively transformed by a series of firms to create goods (or services) that are supplied to an organization. Simple supply chains are often represented literally as a chain, with a number of entities connected linearly. The main concern of those who manage simple supply chains is the flow of materials and therefore how good logistics can optimize it.

In practice few supply chains are simple but have many players. Most definitions of 'supply chain' or 'value chain' conclude that this encompasses the flow of materials or services through a number of suppliers to us and on through to the end customer, each hopefully adding value in some way. A firm is therefore typically part of a chain rather than the end of it, and a more mature focus is on how value is added throughout the entire chain, end-to-end rather than just the flow of materials prior to reaching us. Hence why we encounter the term value chain used instead of supply chain.

Driving sustainability in the supply chain

However, the traditional view of supply or value chains as a linear or near linear series of links actually bears little relationship to how most are actually structured. There are in fact only a handful of scenarios where the linear chain might exist. In practice our suppliers might also be linked to other suppliers, or even directly with our customers and our customers might be linked to suppliers further back upstream and so on. Supply or value chains are typically quite complex affairs and are in fact more like networks (Figure 13.2) and for this reason we use the term supply and value chain network (SVCN) to describe the entire end-to-end network that we are part of. Throughout this book I have been using the term supply chain to refer to the upstream steps and SVCN to refer to the complete end-to-end network, according to our focus.

Figure 13.2 Representation of a supply and value chain network

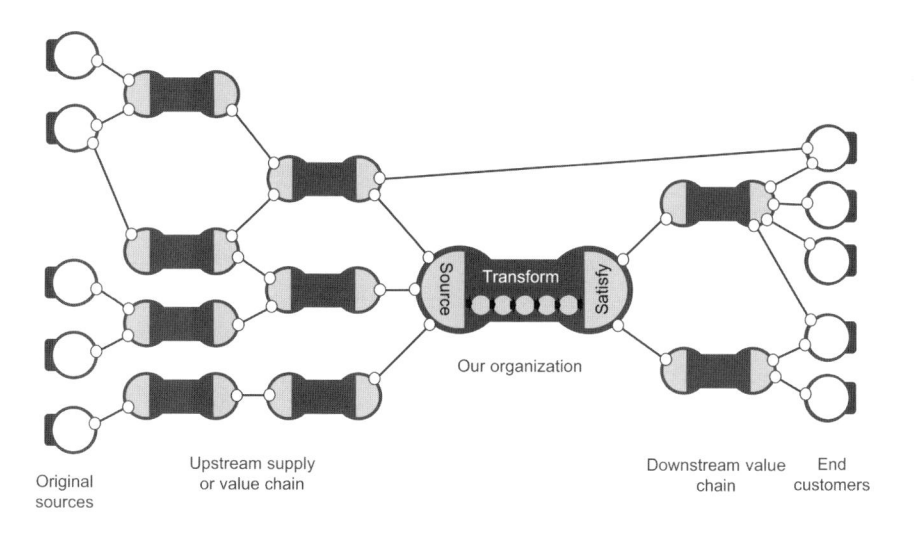

A network is made up of linkages between entities. We can begin to understand a network by understanding the entities, the linkages and considering how things flow within the network. Networks have a number of flows:

- **Materials, goods and services** – flowing from the original sources, being transformed with value added at each stage, towards the end customer.
- **Cash (or other value)** – flowing upstream.
- **Information about demand** – flowing upstream from the end customer. If end-customer demand flows freely and penetrates far back upstream then

the network can work effectively. Otherwise entities have no forward visibility of demand and so are reactive, slow to respond or compensate for this by holding inventories, increasing cost and inefficiency.

- **Other information** – e.g. about factors that might present risk or help others plan better. Traditionally this might include specific local issues holding up logistics, customs delays at a location or shifts in end-customer requirements that will drive future change.

Sustainability flows

In sustainable procurement how things flow is of particular concern. With our sustainability hat on we are particularly concerned with the flow of cash, information and the efficiency in how goods flow.

First, the flow of cash shapes what happens or could happen upstream within a supply chain. We all know the stories of products we pay top dollar for while the original farmers or producers just scrape by: the $4 coffee where the farmer receives 2 cents for the beans but really needs 3 cents to invest in next year's crop, or the fruit that is picked by children because the grower doesn't get enough money from the retailer to employ legitimate workers. Many of these are old stories and today, for example, the big-name coffee chains have done much to address the flow of cash to producers. Yet you don't have to look far to find other examples where those further up the supply chain don't receive enough money or the right amount of money. Paying more to our immediate suppliers rarely addresses this but instead ends up making these suppliers or intermediaries further upstream more wealthy. Instead, if we want to change what producers or farmers and their workers receive we need to examine the flow of cash in the supply chain and identify what might need to change to achieve our outcomes. I will return to this later in this chapter.

Second, the flow of information is the most critical enabler for sustainability, both in terms of how information flows and could flow between firms or players, but also between individuals as part of relationships that get established. Driving sustainability in the supply chain requires us to establish new and deeper understanding of what happens throughout the network and create flows of information to verify ongoing what is happening. This is harder than it might seem for several reasons:

- **Afraid to share** – few players in a network can typically boast good sustainability so would seek to keep hidden that which they fear might fall short for fear of losing business.

Driving sustainability in the supply chain

- **Mistrust** – companies in the network compete with each other to a degree and respond to what is asked for rather than offering more, in case their customer will replicate what they do and they will lose competitive advantage.
- **Distorted information** – in the same way that it is in the buyer's interest to be over-optimistic about demand and future opportunity so as to incentivize suppliers, so too it is in the supplier's interest to be over-optimistic about its sustainability arrangements. However, the consequence here can be distorted information that leads to mistrust.
- **Extracts only** – companies don't share the big picture, just extracts that are just enough to satisfy what they need upstream entities to provide. This can breed mistrust.
- **Differing interests** – players may have different aims and agendas. It is impossible for decisions taken by one individual to fit with the entire network.
- **Lack of clarity regarding who is managing the supply chain** – any one player or individual within a network is only as strong as the contractual relationship with the immediate neighbours. Beyond this any sway or influence can only come through persuasion and getting close to other players. Inevitably other players, many steps removed, may not recognize or respond to attempts here.
- **Lack of willingness** – even with determined attempts to create a network-wide flow of information to drive sustainability it doesn't follow that all players will be willing or able to participate and play their part.

Achieving effective network-wide information flows can transform a supply chain network, create competitive advantage and build the basis to drive sustainability. However, achieving this among mistrust, differing interests and levels of willingness can be incredibly difficult. These obstacles create a compelling argument for vertical integration of supply chains as it removes such obstacles. Where vertical integration is not possible or desirable then these obstacles need to be removed by an evangelical mission to get close to, work with and build relationships with supply chain players. This involves building trust and creating a systematic approach to information sharing that is accepted and supported by all involved without any contractual obligation.

Finally, examining the flow of goods provides the basis to consider how sustainable our logistics are and in particular how much CO_2e is produced, miles/kilometres travelled and optimization of packaging and transport. We will return to these topics later.

Supply chain/SVCN mapping

Supply chain mapping (or SVCN mapping) is the process of creating a representation of the entire network specifically relating to the supply of a certain product or service, as sourced from a specific immediate supplier. It is a means to understand the supply chain and the enabler to identify where intervention is necessary or beneficial. It can take considerable time and resources to do it effectively and the effort required increases with the size and complexity of the supply chain as well as our perspective or the way we choose to study the supply chain. Therefore, directing our resources towards carefully identified priorities is key.

Supply chain mapping is well established in SCM and is not new to procurement but has increasingly become part of SRM within strategic procurement to understand:

- where value is added (or could be added);
- supply chain process flows and how they could be made more efficient or reduce wastage and non-value-adding activities;
- where cost is added to identify specific opportunities to reduce cost; and
- where there is risk and what needs to change to mitigate it.

Typically, considering these areas is about looking at the supply chain through a series of lenses or while wearing different hats helping us to see things in different ways. When we put our sustainability hat on, we can look at the supply chain in terms of the specific risks, impacts and opportunities. This then forms the basis to determine where improvements are required or desirable and provides the basis to establish improvement initiatives. Build a supply chain map as follows; I will explore each of these steps in more detail:

1 Map the physical structure and linkages.
2 Consider the environment and context at each step and determine any relevant risks or considerations using hot spot analysis and PESTLE analysis.
3 Apply the different sustainability lenses in turn.

4 Refine the map, gather further data where needed and summarize findings overall (use the 'so what does this tell us?' format), along with the specific risks, impacts and opportunities for sustainability throughout the supply chain.
5 Determine supply chain improvement projects.

A template for a supply chain mapping is included in the Appendix.

Step 1 – Map the structure and linkages

Supply and value chain mapping is best accomplished by a group of individuals carefully selected for their knowledge and expertise. The process begins by mapping the physical structure of the supply chain and all the linkages. This is, put simply, about creating a big diagram that shows all the players or entities in the network and who is connected to whom, the key steps within each player and what happens. If this can be done in a face-to-face workshop, then a big sheet of paper is essential and unrolling some brown paper onto a large table around which the team can assemble is ideal. If meeting online, a good whiteboard can help.

Do you know how something is made? And where it goes next?

Doesn't that sound like a question we asked back when we looked at sustainable value engineering? When we consider what we buy in terms of sustainability we need to ask questions like 'where is it made?', 'what happens there?', 'how are people treated?', 'is it sustainable?', 'how many miles does it travel?', 'which suppliers are involved?' and so on. We cannot begin to consider sustainability or sustainable value engineer what we buy unless we consider where it comes from and what happens before it gets to us. We must also consider what happens to it next and downstream impacts from the products or services we supply. This is indistinguishable from our fact finding when we consider a supply chain or SVCN rather than a product or service – they are one and the same activity. In practice we cannot begin to truly evaluate a product or service unless we evaluate the supply chain or SVCN at the same time and vice versa.

It's harder than you might think

Start with the product or service and a specific supplier that provides it and determine the key process or transformation steps that the immediate supplier fulfils. Then work back beyond them considering their inputs and where these come from, the second-tier suppliers and the key steps that each of these fulfils and so on. This is where we begin to need some brainpower and data gathering because once we get beyond our immediate supplier things can quickly grind to a halt. We understand our suppliers, but it can be hard enough to understand our suppliers' suppliers, let alone going any further upstream. The problem, as we have seen, is this information may not be readily available and suppliers may be reluctant to share due to fear of loss of competitive advantage or a hidden agenda for backward integration, especially if the supplier is adding little value and fears the consequences of sharing such information. Here we need a bit of detective work, which will be helped if the team doing the mapping has been selected to have as much expertise as possible. Therefore, our first workshop and first pass at mapping a supply chain may become more about making a list of research and data to gather in order to complete it rather than producing a fully formed supply chain map.

We need to be detectives

As a minimum we need to understand all the steps and activities in the supply chain right back to original sources and where these are. Ideally, we understand the individual players that make this up. There are a number of approaches that can help:

- **Desktop research about generic supply chains**. It would be highly unlikely to find a map for the specific supply chain we are evaluating on the internet, but we may be able to find a generic supply chain for the product or service, or some of what goes into it. There are plenty of generic supply chains out there showing all the steps that go into something. These are useful because they help inform us of the key steps and activities. This can then guide our research to figure out where these happen in our supply chain and the specific players that do this. It can give us the 'empty boxes' and how they connect to create our map, and we then need to figure out what is in them.
- **Ask our supplier and start creating obligations**. Our supplier will know their suppliers and may know more beyond that. If suppliers are reluctant to share, the modern imperative sustainability gives us is the arguments to encourage suppliers to be more open. This is especially true where we need to comply with new legislation such as directives to understand

CO_2e in supply chains. Another approach here that can work is to find a way to establish a new obligation for transparency of product (e.g. batch and material traceability is often expected in defence and food industries).

- **Audit and assessment.** Assessment gives us the opportunity to gather information about a player's process and activities and there is no substitute for a face-to-face audit to see what happens. Clearly, this is only feasible for those steps in the supply chain, and those suppliers or players, where we are able and it is worthwhile to do this.

- **Break down the product (or service)** into its constituent parts and attempt to identify where these might be sourced from, e.g. by looking at any identifying markings or evidence of source.

- **Ask an industry, product or logistics expert.** Perhaps these exist within the organization (e.g. in a quality, product technology or R&D function). If not, there are specialist consultants out there who can provide the insight and information needed.

- **Outflank them.** If we can establish that goods flow from a particular region but are struggling to determine the specific original suppliers, then we can research the players in that region and go direct to attempt to establish if they are our original sources.

Figure 13.3 gives an example of a supply chain map for peanut butter. Note the level of detail that has been included but note also many parts of the supply chain have not been expanded – for example there will be further supply chains for salt, sugar, pesticides, labels, pallets, packaging, etc. We could expand the map to include all of these and in some cases that may be appropriate if we identify a particular risk or potential hot spot impact with an ingredient. However, success here is about avoiding trying to create an immense supply chain map but rather focusing on the elements where there is value in understanding them. Even then, supply chain mapping is a considerable undertaking and can take many workshops and background research to get a meaningful representation. A pragmatic approach is essential in deciding when to fully map all the steps and activities right back and when to show something as an input. The same applies for inputs such as energy, water, machinery, labour, finance, insurance and overheads within players. It is important to identify these inputs so we can subsequently measure aspects such as water consumed and energy used to establish a basis to understand and drive sustainability improvements.

Figure 13.3 A supply chain map for peanut butter

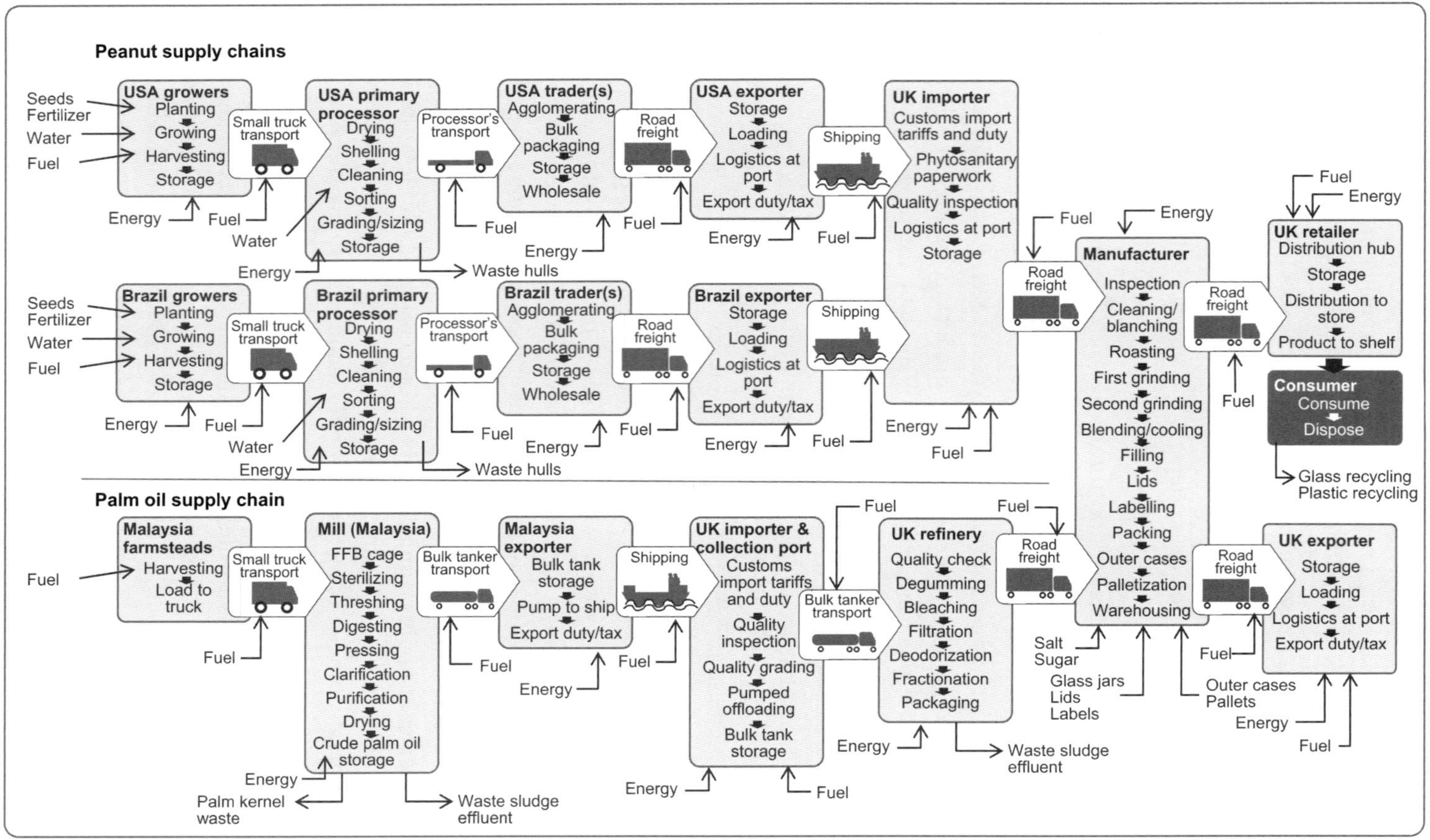

Step 2 – Determine the environment and context

Step 2 is concerned with considering the environment, context and potential hot spots the supply chain exists within, spans or flows through. In order to understand a supply chain, we must look deeper than the sequence of players and steps involved. The nature of the prevailing environment, culture, economic situation, enforced legislation, attitudes towards human rights and so on is highly relevant to understanding a supply chain. Context helps us determine potential risk, impacts and opportunities, and also indicates how certain players might behave or choose to act, especially if we want to drive an improvement. For example, our confidence in upholding good environmental and social standards would vary according to whether a processor is based in the EU or an African country.

Considerations that determine context include:

- Countries and geographies involved.
- Likelihood of corruption, not upholding human rights, failing to protect the environment.
- Cultural differences and therefore how this might drive certain behaviours, or help or hinder development.
- Prevailing political and economic climates.
- Known environmental considerations in the region or industry.
- Complexity – of the network, processes, product or service (which might hide risks).
- Flow of information and how difficult it actually is in practice.

Hot spots and PESTLE

While an understanding of context might naturally emerge throughout the process of building a supply chain map, there are two approaches we can use to help here:

1 **Find the hot spots** – review the supply chain map and further build it to specify locations where things happen and then review the geographies, industries and products/services involved to determine and note any potential hot spots. Here we are looking to identify potential areas of risk or impact that might warrant further investigation.

2 **Apply PESTLE analysis** – the *PESTLE Analysis* tool (political, economic, sociological, technological, legal and environmental) we covered in

Chapter 7 can help us determine the external environment within which the entire supply chain, and specific elements of it, exist. Apply it to help build a supply chain map by considering the forces, drivers, trends or prevailing conditions under each of these headings both upstream in the supply chain and downstream in the SVCN. Apply as a whole, but also identify areas or steps where there are unique or different forces or drivers at play. Determine any potential risks and opportunities relevant to the network under each heading.

Build the supply chain map by noting environment and context factors against each step and overall.

Step 3 – Apply lenses

Step 3 is concerned with successively examining the supply chain for different sustainability risks, impacts (which misalign with our sustainability goals) and opportunities. Here we review the supply chain map several times, each time considering what happens by applying a specific lens to direct our thinking.

Using the lens principle helps us cut through the complexity of a supply chain map and helps us see areas of note. Applying lenses is not a new idea within supply chain mapping where traditionally we would successively examine a supply chain considering process flow (materials, information, demand, etc), where cost is introduced, where value is added and risk. With our sustainability hat on and lens in hand (Sherlock Holmes was definitely on to something) we can use a series of specific sustainability lenses. These lenses derive from the six impact areas and the sustainable procurement framework and are the same seven lenses we use for sustainable value engineering. These are given in Table 13.1.

Apply each lens by reviewing each step and player in the supply chain, evaluate the points where potential risk, impact and opportunity might exist and identify these on the supply chain map. Typically, the most effective approach here is to mark up each point on our map, perhaps using symbols and a key, or with call outs, supported by more detailed notes. Focus on the most relevant or significant risks, impacts and opportunities as we can easily get overwhelmed if we try to highlight everything. We can further build our map later if we needed to.

Driving sustainability in the supply chain 417

Table 13.1 The seven supply chain mapping lenses

Lens	Questions to help identify supply chain risk, impacts or opportunities	Potential value levers to use here (see Chapter 9)
Use of resources	• Where are resources consumed? • What resources are used? • How much is consumed? • Are they scarce? • How much recycling happens within the process? • How much recycled material is used at the input?	• Change specification • Change design • Improve logistics • Restructure the supply base • Performance development • Seek innovation • Optimize resource/asset utilization
Emissions/CO_2e	• Where are the main emissions generated? • Why are the emissions created (e.g. because of energy use or other)? • How much green energy is used? • What is the CO_2e at each step for each player?	• Aggregate spend or demand • Analyse, restructure and optimize • Improve process efficiency and capability • Improve logistics • Change markets • Performance development • Buy less or eliminate • Optimize resource/asset utilization
Waste	• What and how much waste is produced at each step? • Hazardous or chemical waste produced? • Where does it go? • How is it managed? • Proportion recycled/ repurposed/ reused?	• Change specification • Change design • Improve process efficiency and capability • Performance development • Buy less or eliminate • Optimize resource/asset utilization

Sustainable procurement

Table 13.1 *continued*

Lens	Questions to help identify supply chain risk, impacts or opportunities	Potential value levers to use here (see Chapter 9)
Pollution	• Where is there pollution risk to land/sea/air? • Where are controls to prevent pollution lacking?	• Change specification • Change design • Improve process efficiency and capability • Improve logistics • Performance development • Change markets • Improve relationship • Optimize resource/asset utilization
Biodiversity	• What activities contribute to loss of biodiversity directly or indirectly? • What drives loss of habitat or deforestation? • Where might there be animal welfare issues?	• Change specification • Change design • Analyse, restructure and optimize • Use market competition • Change markets • Restructure the supply base • Performance development • Improve relationship • Buy less or eliminate
People and communities	• Where do people work and what do they do? • What is the likelihood of human rights not being upheld? • Where are poor working conditions likely? • Where might there be impacts on communities? • Where do communities need support?	• Analyse, restructure and optimize • Improve logistics • Change markets • Restructure the supply base • Performance development • Improve relationship • Seek innovation • Offer commitment

Table 13.1 *continued*

Lens	Questions to help identify supply chain risk, impacts or opportunities	Potential value levers to use here (see Chapter 9)
Data and digital	• Where is data collected and processed? • Where is privacy not protected? • Is worker intelligent surveillance used at any point? • What activities create the conditions to put people at risk of exploitation from data theft from cybercrime?	• Analyze, restructure and optimize • Use market competition • Change markets • Restructure the supply base • Performance development

Building measurement in the supply chain

A supply chain map provides the starting point for supply chain measurement and the means by which we can establish a baseline of certain parameters and what things we need to measure ongoing. These may include areas such as CO_2e emissions, water consumption, energy consumption, per cent green energy used, miles/kilometres travelled at each step/player or as an input. Such measures are unlikely to exist already supply chain wide so we may need to build a system to gather this ongoing and this starts with our supply chain map by identifying where we will establish measures. From here we can drive in new measurement systems using different data points. More on that in the next chapter.

Step 4 – Refine and summarize

Our early assessment work may have identified this supply chain as a priority for further evaluation; however, it is only once we have fully understood the supply chain, done our research, gathered additional data, filled in the gaps, etc, that we can know if this is a supply chain where we need or want to drive sustainability improvements.

Supply chain mapping requires several iterations and refinement to create something useful. It is possible that early after our initial mapping activity we may decide it is not such a priority after all and stop there (and update our prioritization heat cube accordingly). However, we may also identify all sorts of potential risks, impacts and opportunities as we delve deeper and deeper into our supply chain. Crucially, during our mapping workshops, unless we have all the knowledge and expertise in the room, we may only be able to make assumptions, apply hot spot thinking or identify areas where we need to look further. Fact finding is therefore a key part of supply chain mapping and as we map the supply chain we must also identify the areas where we need to know more and develop a fact-find plan accordingly. Supply chain mapping is an iterative process of mapping and fact finding to arrive at a good, confident understanding of the supply chain and the individual risks, impacts and opportunities at specific points. We can also consider the entire supply chain and summarize our findings by asking 'so what does this tell us?' to complete our understanding. This may well be different from our original assumptions when we developed our prioritization heat cube.

Figure 13.4 shows a supply chain map for vanilla pods, marked up with risks, impacts and opportunities against the individual sustainability lenses and our findings overall. A template to do this is included in the Appendix.

Step 5 – Determine supply chain improvement projects

Once we have a complete supply chain map that we are confident in, where we have verified this supply chain is a priority, we can move forward to determining our actions in response to the risks, impacts or opportunities we have identified. Here we develop and progress individual supply chain improvement projects, which will form part of our sustainable procurement road map. How we do this needs an entire section all of its own.

Driving supply chain improvements

It is a big leap from knowing where we need or want to drive improvements in a supply chain and actually doing it. As we have seen, making change happen throughout a supply chain is the most difficult challenge within sustainable procurement.

Supply chain mapping along with measurement of specific impacts throughout the supply chain will most likely be a difficult and time-consuming step but, if done well, forms the foundation for improvement.

Figure 13.4 A supply chain map for vanilla pods, marked up with our findings

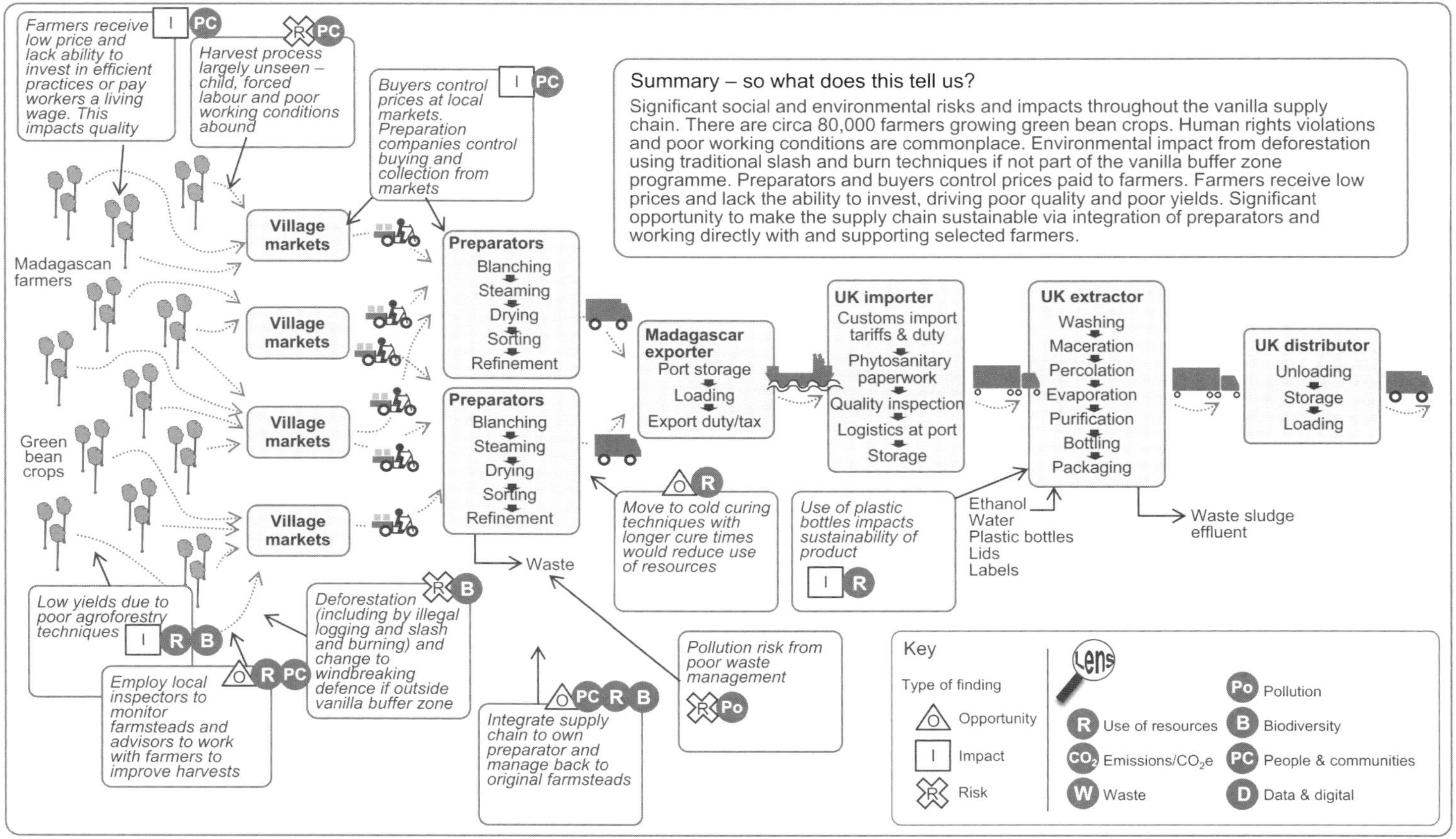

SOURCE Symrise Vanilla (nd)

The STPDR process should be used to manage supply chain improvements with our supply chain map representing much of the study the situation step. From here it is about determining the targets for specific improvements and identifying how this might be achieved in order to make a plan to drive sustainability in the supply chain. This would then become one of our improvement initiatives, incorporated into our sustainable procurement road map.

Types of intervention

In traditional SCM theory there are a number of interventions or 'schools of thinking' that organizations have applied to improve their supply chains (Bechtel and Jayaram, 1997). These have different areas of focus for optimization as follows:

- **Physical material flow** – the origin of the field of logistics as we know it today. This is called the *functional awareness* school of thinking.
- **Linkages** – focuses on the interfaces between entities in the supply chain and how they can be managed simultaneously to work more effectively and smooth the flow of material between partners.
- **Information** – focuses on the information flow between partners both up and down the supply chain so all members have access to all relevant information.
- **Integration and process** – focuses on integrating supply chain areas into a system defined as a set of processes to improve the supply chain overall.

These different schools of thought for interventions remain valid today and underpin good SCM. They are also relevant to drive sustainable procurement. However, with our sustainability hat on interpretation and application shifts somewhat.

Driving improvements to a supply chain demands some unique approaches for all the reasons we explored earlier. We drive sustainability in a supply chain by applying one or more of our value levers (as we explored in Chapter 9), which derive from the schools of thinking above. Three of the value lever groups (Supply chain, Supplier relationship and Supplier incentivization) are particularly relevant and point to five key approaches or interventions we can use to drive sustainability improvements in the supply chain. These are as follows and I will expand each in turn:

- **Restructure the supply chain** (value lever: *Analyse, restructure and optimize* and part of the *integration/process* school of thinking).

- **Collaboration and relationships** among players and sometimes with competitors (*Supplier relationship* group of value levers and part of *linkage* and *process* schools).
- **Improving sustainability flows** – improving the flow of information and cash (value lever: *Improve efficiency and capability*, part of *linkage*, *information* and *process* schools).
- **Make the flow of goods (or services) more sustainable** (value lever: *Improve logistics*, part of *functional awareness* school).
- **Incentivization** (*Incentivize suppliers* group of value levers, part of *linkage* school).

Restructuring the supply chain

Supply chains rarely get designed but rather end up what they are, driven by individual players wanting to succeed and survive thus creating complex dynamics where entities exist and operate independently from each other and also compete with each other. Each handoff adds complexity, hinders flow, hampers supply chain effectiveness and works against sustainability.

We select our suppliers, but we don't design our supply chains and rarely select second-tier onward suppliers. Driving sustainability in the supply chain demands that instead of thinking of supply chains as things we have ended up with, we need to think more strategically about our supply chains. We need to consider and design the supply chains we need to serve our business based upon what we are trying to achieve, i.e. the overall goals of the organization including sustainability and therefore how our supply chains must exist and operate in support of these. This is a concept that companies are only now beginning to grapple with. How organizations can do this remains a mystery for most beyond issuing directives such as 'let's reduce what we source from country X' and so on.

Therefore, when we put our sustainability hat on, a decisive step to restructure the supply chain in response to sustainability risks, impacts and opportunities is the most obvious and effective means to make the required change happen. By reviewing our supply chain map, we can consider areas where we can literally redesign the supply chain and create a new design that will enable us to achieve our goals. This might involve removing handoffs, merging or changing linkages or finding ways to improve flow between players and there are five approaches we can apply here:

1. **Remove entities** – where no value is added and there will be no impact and where adjoining entities can work directly with each other, e.g. remove intermediaries (see later). Useful to drive sustainability by removing entities that hinder sustainability, where transparency gets lost/impacts get washed away, and by reducing complexity overall.

2. **Integration** – merge what is done by two or more players into one (e.g. we push for a player to manage their own transport rather than use contractors). The same integration result can also be achieved where we can establish cooperation and coordination between players working in isolation.

3. **Vertical integration** – possibly the most effective way to drive sustainability, which is to integrate the entire supply chain into our organization, e.g. we acquire the farmer or producer, processors, etc, and take ownership of or use our own logistics, effectively bringing the entire operation under our control.

4. **Add new entities** – create new steps that help drive sustainability, police compliance or ensure transparency.

5. **Add new linkages and establish coordination** – create linkages (e.g. where information flows, for reporting, for inspection or verification, etc) and also ways to oblige parties to work together to drive sustainability.

The problem with intermediaries

Intermediaries are companies that exist within supply chains and connect sellers to buyers in some way or to enable a transaction or supply. Intermediaries exist in a variety of forms the world over serving the need for sellers that lack the ability, size, systems or desire to sell directly to the buyer. Similarly, they serve the need for buyers that lack the ability or are unable to source directly from suppliers. Using an intermediary can be a choice or parties can have no choice if they want to trade. Sometimes intermediaries are government specified or there is some form of licence or permit that only the intermediaries can acquire. Sometimes it is the way things must be done – demanded as established custom and practice in some countries, one where parties would be slow to contemplate working outside an intermediary or there might be consequences. Intermediaries exist in many forms:

- **Market intermediaries** – independent companies that help ensure the smooth flow of goods or services from a supplier or producer to the next customer in the SVCN.

- **Importers** – companies that bring in goods or services from abroad and most typically organize the necessary legal export and import custom clearance formalities. Importers are often representing manufacturers and will sell to distributors.
- **Agents, brokers or financial intermediary** – companies that serve as a link between producers or suppliers and customer, and negotiate and facilitate the transaction between two parties, typically the buyer and seller, either as a one-off or contracted by either the seller or buyer to represent them and take a fixed fee commission on all transactions for doing so.
- **Wholesalers** – create the link between professional buyers and typically small growers, self-employed workers or producers, often with aggregation of output from multiple providers.
- **Distribution companies** – provide the channel or route to market for suppliers, acting as an intermediary between seller and downstream buyers. Distribution companies buy products and then sell on at a profit. Usually involves warehousing and sometimes logistics.
- **Commodity trading houses** – firms or government organizations that buy and sell commodities or commodity futures on behalf of their customers.

A company that establishes itself as an intermediary can enjoy extremely lucrative business, especially if it is able to control the route to market in some way. Therefore, intermediaries will go to great lengths to establish and retain this control, which can often involve corruption and kickbacks. Control is maintained in many ways but primarily by keeping sources of supply and the customers they serve hidden from each other. This works against driving sustainability through a supply chain as intermediaries can effectively hide or wash away any poor practice prior to them and can stand in the way of establishing transparency. Furthermore, until now there has been little need to do anything different, with 'ignorance is bliss' a key feature in how global corporations source. Even when we can broker an agreement where the intermediary is required to maintain transparency and traceability, they may not be organized to do this. For example, in some cases the intermediary may be linking single farmers who get paid cash on delivering a single load of their produce to a central location where it is mixed with that from other farmers and sold on in bulk. The intermediary trades with big companies who provide POs, require electronic invoicing pay by funds transfer 60 days later. The farmers would not be able to contemplate this and get paid immediately in cash, requiring the intermediary to have the financial means to carry the cash flow.

To drive sustainability in our supply chains we need to understand the intermediaries, what role and value they add, and we need to get behind them to see the original sources. We also need to understand how easy it would be to remove them. We cannot drive sustainability in our supply chains unless we can understand the full supply chain. Intermediaries may be reluctant to cooperate here and may even stand in our way or prohibit their suppliers from having direct contact with us. There is no easy way through this and so we need to approach it in one of two ways:

1 To identify alternatives to the intermediary to remove or circumvent them, which might require vertical integration or more direct relationships if we can establish this.

2 To work with the intermediary and drive transformation so they become an enabler for sustainability, with a role to play in establishing transparency, traceability and relationships with producers to develop sustainability.

The power of the pen

Caution is needed in restructuring supply chains as there is a world of difference between redesigning a supply chain in a workshop where, at the stroke of a pen, we can remove entire companies or change how we source something. There may be reasons we cannot remove intermediaries, or they may have a foothold we can't change. Our actions to drive sustainability may displace many workers who may lose their livelihoods. Furthermore, we may lack any power to effect change. Just because it is our supply chain it doesn't follow that we have the sway to direct how entities many steps removed must exist and operate. Therefore, we should consider different options to redesign a supply chain and further evaluate these, including conducting a full risk assessment before moving forward. And when we are confident in how we want to restructure the supply chain the transition needs careful planning. Furthermore, don't underestimate the scale of change that is typically required to restructure a supply chain. Engaging with all involved to establish the required cooperation, coupled with strong and effective change management, is critically important.

Study the situation – don't rush to condemn

Finally, it is easy to rush to condemn practice and restructure based upon assumptions. When we build a supply chain map, we are initially highlighting potential areas of concern or interest and it is our subsequent verification and fact finding that is key to determining if these hold up. Once again, it is essential we study the situation thoroughly before designing wholesale changes to a supply chain. For example, if we had identified palm oil as a key ingredient to a product and we mapped the supply chains that make it up including that of palm oil, we would rightly identify this as a risk area for further evaluation. However, it doesn't follow that there is something we need to change here.

Palm oil is not necessarily bad, yet we are led by the media and other influences to regard it so. Clearly there are some significant issues with sourcing palm oil, with uncontrolled deforestation and loss of biodiversity being the most notable. Yet this is not the case in all sources of supply. Palm oil is an incredibly versatile and useful ingredient. There are few alternatives that perform in quite the same way. Rushing to move away from using palm oil would be sub-optimum. Instead we should look at the supply chain for palm oil and by understanding it we can determine whether it is sustainable or not. Palm oil plantations themselves are not bad things, in fact they can bring new benefits. Rather, it is the uncontrolled clearing of land to grow them that is bad. This doesn't come from a tree but from bad government policy and lack of will or enforcement to do anything different. Many of the plantations were established decades ago, some even exist within other ecosystems where farmers have allowed other plants and habitats to become established around them. These are now good things. If we can have confidence our palm oil comes from a known decades-old source where there are initiatives to rewild around it, and that there is no likelihood our demand will introduce new deforestation, then this can now be regarded as a reasonably sustainable source.

Collaboration and relationships

One of the easiest ways to drive sustainability in the supply chain is to get entities talking to each other and working more closely together. This may be one-to-one but is more effective when relationships can become one-to-many.

Collaboration is an enabler for integration, but it can also achieve the same outcome as integration without actually doing it. Remember an integrated supply chain is one that has evolved beyond a series of entities where there is a flow of materials between the players working in isolation to each other to become one where there is cooperation and coordination between these players.

Within SCM theory there is agreement that the greatest improvement to a supply chain comes through improved connections, relationships, collaboration and sharing between partners. Gradinger (2009) states a lot of leverages can be detected when improving and working on the relationships and interfaces between suppliers and clients within their value chains. Liker and Choi (2004) suggest corporations build *keiretsu* – close-knit networks of vendors that continuously learn, improve and prosper along with their parent companies, and Christopher (2016) states the focus of SCM should be on the management of relationships in order to achieve a more profitable outcome. While traditionally this thinking centred around making supply chains more effective in terms of agility and commercial effectiveness, the same thinking perfectly supports driving sustainability.

Collaboration in the supply and value chain network is not something that just happens. As with any relationship there needs to be a reason to want one and those involved need to get something from it. Traditional supply chains create little need for relationships beyond immediate connections. In fact many of the players beyond these may not even know each other, are unlikely to trust each other and under normal conditions will have little motivation to build relationships beyond their immediate linkages. Obstacles to collaboration and relationships to drive sustainability include:

- **Contractual restrictions** – any contractual obligation that might impede direct discussions upstream or downstream. They may even explicitly prohibit this, e.g. intermediaries protecting their position.
- **Lack of focus for relationship building** – without focus, efforts to build relationships could be seen as little more than a nice to have discussion.
- **Unclear goal or benefits** – collaboration requires effort, commitment and resources and so there needs to be a purpose and business case to justify this.
- **Lack of trust** – players are more likely to be cautious of sharing or relationship building in case it causes loss of competitive advantage.
- **Scale of effort** – getting multiple players in a supply and value chain network relationship to build relationships is no small task.
- **Commitment to information accuracy** – good relationships and the trust within them depends on good information sharing and flow.

Therefore, in order to drive sustainability via relationships, we need to establish a common goal and basis for players to want to cooperate. Sustainability gives us this, yet for it to work we must interpret our goals to make them relevant for players back up the supply chain and with it create the right incentive to want to collaborate. A key incentive here can be business retention or rather the risk of losing business through inaction or not stepping up to meet new requirements. It can also be how working together can unlock new value for all involved. For example, if we want to reduce CO_2e throughout our supply chain or even become net zero, this provides the goal we want players to get behind. There is clear benefit for these players also by cooperating here, as it will help them meet other clients' demands, it may reduce their costs and perhaps it also aligns with their own goals. It also means they are helping fix the planet.

Collaborating with competitors

Collaboration to drive supply chain sustainability should not be limited to getting entities in the supply chain working more closely together. Instead corporations that have been successful here foster collaboration with competitors, and also industry bodies, international organizations and NGOs working in this space. Collaboration with competitors recognizes that no single company can win the fight against poor environmental and labour practices throughout a supply chain. Furthermore, if we were to try we would bear a burden that also benefits our competitors and undermines our competitive position. Our competitors want the same outcomes here and collaboration is the only means by which we can work together to drive change (Villena and Gioia, 2020). Brokering conversations with direct competitors may be a workable approach; however, success here tends to come where this cooperation is driven together with or through an industry body.

Making collaboration happen

Collaboration and relationships need to be brokered; players need to be won over to the cause of increased collaboration and to do this, there needs to be a clear benefit, purpose and goal and a compelling reason to participate. Furthermore, someone needs to take the initiative to broker such relationships and reach out to all involved. In practice, where the potential benefits are worthwhile to us, this means investing in an individual attempting to become supply chain captain and assume a new role to help optimize an entire supply chain, supported by voluntary participation from other players and ideally resources to make the scheme work. Such a scheme is akin to a politician or peace envoy attempting to broker a multi-country peace deal, engaging with and negotiating with a series of country leaders for the benefit of all. Here only someone with sufficient standing will get the attention of country leaders; the same applies for the supply chain so brokering participation needs to be championed by someone senior or with standing. Other key success factors here include:

- Collaborate with major first-tier suppliers, and in particular their procurement functions, to establish and disseminate industry-wide sustainability goals.
- Work to engage directly with lower-tier suppliers and establish cooperation between us and them and also with other players. Create an incentive to get involved, quantifying the benefits where possible and secure commitment from each player to work on realizing specific goals within or outwith their firms.
- Establish collaboration with industry bodies and potentially competitors, international bodies and NGOs to establish common goals and a common programme of improvement supported by all.
- Create a focus for collaboration and improvement initiatives, e.g. a biannual symposium to review progress and a programme of supply-chain-wide improvements, involving all in the design.
- Develop and manage a supply-chain-wide communications plan to improve the flow of information and share progress and successes.
- Manage the activity as if a project, using good project management, reporting and maintaining a current programme of activity.
- Have players sign up to a project charter defining who is involved, the roles each has and how the project team will work together.
- Use a supply chain map and the STPDR approach to guide action.
- Give the scheme an identity and promote it, and the benefits for all, with good marketing communications support.

Contracting to drive improvement

We have already explored the role of contracting with our suppliers and some of the challenges and opportunities within this. When it comes to entities further upstream contracting becomes more challenging. Using contractual terms to drive immediate suppliers to take responsibility, and establish flow through contractual obligations, for what happens upstream in a supply chain is an approach that can have only superficial impact. Typically, when we engage with our first-tier suppliers this engagement rarely penetrates back to their procurement functions. Furthermore, our suppliers are often struggling to get their own sustainability arrangements in place let alone concern themselves with their suppliers' sustainability arrangements. These challenges only get amplified as we work back upstream. There are a number of reasons that prevent a contractual approach from driving sustainable practice throughout a supply chain. These are:

- We don't usually have any direct contractual relationship beyond those we immediately interface with.
- Supply chain complexity or lack of visibility and control of what happens upstream, and enforcement or verification of compliance is difficult if what happens is hidden.
- The difference between legalities and practicalities – even if we agree a watertight contract that obliges our suppliers regarding upstream activities the process of litigation to enforce it could be onerous.
- Supply chains often span jurisdictions.
- Contracts are less recognized or valued in some geographies and cultures.

Having said this, it doesn't mean establishing contractual obligations to run through the supply chain is not worthwhile, quite the contrary in fact, but we should not rely on this alone and we need to be certain that the process of contracting will drive the required action and responses. There are two ways we can approach contracting in the supply chain to drive sustainability:

- **With our immediate suppliers** – focus on working with our immediate suppliers on how they contract with their suppliers. Establish the specific areas our suppliers must contract for with their suppliers and how they will flow these onward.
- **With upstream suppliers** – establish direct commitment and relationships with some specific lower-tier suppliers in the supply chain where the approach can drive benefit. Clearly, if we still require the nearer entities in a supply chain we cannot bypass these with a direct contract with original producers. However, there are situations where a direct side agreement can work. For example, consider a tea farmer where harvested tea gets sold in trading rooms to the highest bidder, effectively washing away the original source of the tea during the commodity buying process. If we want to drive improvements at the specific agricultural source in terms of working conditions, wages and environmental impacts, then the ideal scenario here would be for us to buy the farmer's operation. Yet, if this is not possible and the tea still needs to be sold through the trading process, we could consider establishing a side commitment directly with

the producer for an agreed programme of improvements that we will work with them to accomplish, perhaps supporting financially with a commitment that we will overbid by an agreed amount to buy their produce. Such commitment might be contractual, or might be via a non-contractual joint agreement.

Improving sustainability flows

As we saw earlier, many of the frailties that exist within supply chains that hamper sustainability are around the flow of information, and in particular parties having things to hide or seeking to prevent the right flows of cash. We can drive sustainability in a supply chain by interventions to improve flows, in particular the flow of information in all directions.

Information drives everything, for us and also for those upstream, and there are two considerations:

- How information about our requirements flows upstream to help entities better understand and respond to them outside of the normal contractual cascade.
- How information about what happens in a supply chain flows to us. This includes general information about the supply chain and players' situation ongoing but also information specific to individual goods, services and consignments that the supply chain produces.

We can accomplish improved flows through collaboration and relationships with players and also using our supply chain map to identify where better information could help drive sustainability linkages. However, this only gets us so far. We need to think a little bigger.

Designing the supply chains of the future

Imagine if we could share our goals for improving a supply chain with everyone in it rather than relying on things cascading down, and know how entities were responding. Imagine too if, when goods were delivered, or services were performed, we could know what had happened to get it there down to every original source, company, individual, activity that went into it or truck that moved it. Such insight could give us instant and ongoing confidence in the sustainability of an entire supply chain.

Full supply chain traceability is a form of extensive information flow and is possible today but only in a handful of specialist industries. It is possible to take a critical aircraft casting or surgical implant and see its full history including every raw material source, every individual who worked on it or signed something off. Traceability as part of quality control for critical components is possible because it has been a necessity from the outset. Therefore, the process and supply chain has been designed so every component is uniquely identifiable with systems in place to capture, record and report every step and interaction along the way. Outside of these specialist areas such deep traceability and visibility is mostly out of reach, largely because there has been no driving force to establish it and it would increase costs significantly. Yet, to drive sustainability we need similar levels of transparency and traceability in some areas, especially where we need to have certainty in original sources, or where and how things have been processed or worked on and who did it. The idea of similar levels of information flow to that we have for critical components across all supply chains it not as crazy as it might seem.

If we recognize that strategic procurement including sustainable procurement requires us to design and manage our supply chains rather than accept them then it follows that we need to be thinking about the future here. The driving principle here is to remove that which deliberately or inadvertently stops information flow and create the conditions so players can access more information. Traditional interventions here are difficult and costly; however, it is the adoption of data and digital solutions here that will enable supply chain sustainability through better information flow. Some solutions are there right now waiting to be utilized – social media groups to share information between players, real-time remote video monitoring, RFI tagging and tracking of materials, using a shared cloud-based ERP system to manage supply chain activities and so on. Today it is also possible to start creating real-time supply chain dashboards by combining available data from individual players and at individual steps, and also from other increasingly available data sources. It is also possible to start applying some basic intelligence to flag abnormalities. If a supply chain is super important to us such an approach is worth embarking on and readily accomplished by a good data scientist and creative thinking about data sources. However, there is one other key technology that will change the game and that is blockchain.

Blockchain for supply chain sustainability

Blockchain is the technology that holds the most potential for supply chain sustainability, to provide a single truth about what is happening in a supply chain. It is what lies behind cryptocurrencies. When applied to a supply chain it works by creating an incorruptible record of individual steps, movements of goods/service delivery or transactions in a supply chain. The concept is simple – consider how we manage our money: our bank maintains a single ledger of our money and our transactions (which we access via our banking app). If we withdraw money, they update the ledger and charge us for the privilege. Therefore, there is a single record between us and our bank. If the bank got hacked then someone could change this record as it only exists in one place. Hence banks go to great lengths to make this secure and could roll back if needed. Yet most supply chains work on this principle with each transaction or movement having a single record between parties. Here we are not considering financial transactions but every single activity, handoff or movement of materials/provision of service. The drums of hazardous waste that get handed over to a waste management company but don't all end up where they should, or the fruit picked by children that gets blended with the legitimate stuff before it reaches the processor. All these things mean that where a company thinks it has put sustainability measures in place, it can easily fail where these single company-to-company movements and activities take place because of corrupt practice or where an individual can benefit from skimming a bit here, losing something there, undercounting, overcounting, etc; after all, no one will ever notice!

Blockchain means someone will notice because it uses a different approach called a 'distributed ledger'. Back to our money; if we were using a cryptocurrency then there is no single record but rather the record of our money is kept by many, often hundreds of thousands of people (called miners), as files on computers all over the world. When we go to make a transaction, our computer tells everyone that holds the file. Miners' computers then rush to check our request is possible (i.e. we have the funds) and then the first to reply to everyone to confirm the transaction is possible, together with some proof of workings, gets paid a tiny amount of cryptocurrency for their efforts. Once all the other miners agree, they each update their ledgers. All this is automated and happens in seconds but provides a source of truth that is held by many. As such, it is nearly impossible to corrupt it. Blockchain works in supply chains by recording transactions and movements in the same way and thus removing points where a single point of truth can be corrupted. It makes it impossible for those involved to corrupt the system.

Making the flow of goods more sustainable

How goods (or services) flow in a supply chain is possibly the easiest area to consider in order to drive sustainability improvements, yet one that can bring dramatic benefits. Interventions here would typically consider the areas where we need to improve logistics. This might involve measurement of impacts and targeted activities or interventions around:

- CO_2e reduction
- Right-shoring, onshoring or moving parts or all of the supply chain closer to us or at the right location
- Reducing miles/kilometres travelled
- Making freight travel more sustainably – improving efficiency or changing the means of transportation, e.g. EVs or e-trucks
- Better utilization of freight
- Reducing inventories
- Eliminating wastage due to poor logistics

It is also important to consider where these things happen and the likelihood of being able to drive change. Ideally we would have identified any key factors here during our supply chain mapping when we considered the context, and it is about considering if the changes we want can actually be realized in the places where the supply chain exists.

Incentivization through the supply chain

The final intervention to drive sustainability in the supply chain is how we can incentivize players, especially those back upstream. As we have seen, change to become sustainable can have a cost, initially at least and any sort of change will also demand other resources, time and effort. Where we identify change is needed, those involved must be willing and able. Suppliers will be quick to change if their survival depends upon it; for example, if all customers made meeting a new sustainability requirement a prerequisite, perhaps following introduction of new legislation. However as long as sustainability is a choice by buyers where others are happy to take lowest cost, then supply chain entities may need some encouragement and help here.

As we have seen, sustainable procurement drives a shift away from traditional short-term competitive tendering where we have leverage, to closer and more longer-term engagements with suppliers. Incentivizing immediate suppliers here is straightforward via medium–long-term commitments and contracts or a closer more collaborative relationship with mutual benefits.

However, once again, when it comes to the supply chain, incentivization becomes more difficult beyond our immediate supplier yet it may be here where it is needed the most.

Incentivization does not naturally cascade back up a supply chain. As we saw previously, if we discover poorly paid workers in a supply chain, it doesn't follow that if we decide to pay more to ensure labour gets paid the right wage that those doing the job will see the benefit of this. More often than not we will end up making someone else in the supply chain more wealthy. Instead the only way to drive change to how people are employed way back up the supply chain is to focus on the systems and arrangements on the ground and monitor the effectiveness of any new measures implemented. Therefore, incentivization is typically more than financial, or where it is about changing how cash flows then we need to establish systems and approaches that will deliver the required outcomes.

Incentivization is another area where our investment could end up helping our competitors with whom we share a common objective. Coordination of effort here where possible and practical through some form of coalition can help but is difficult to achieve in practice. Once again, working with industry bodies may be useful.

Incentivization back up the supply chain starts with our supply chain map and the points and linkages we identify where some form of incentivization can drive sustainable value. Then there are several approaches that can help here, each typically requiring some form of direct relationship and engagement with entities back up the supply chain:

- **Help them** – provide consultancy or transfer of know-how to help implement changes.

- **Specify them** – direct how our immediate suppliers buy by specifying a named original source or supplier they must use. Watch, and provide for, potential resultant loss of competitive tension within our supplier's buying. Similarly, a system of mandating approved/not approved sources to our supplier can work here.

- **Invest in them** – direct financial support or investment for improvement projects, with or without a direct commitment by us.

- **Encourage them** – disseminate our future direction of travel and the minimum future requirements upstream in the supply chain and encourage players to work towards where we want them to be.

- **Educate them** – invest in educating players regarding the value possible in changing practices, e.g. savings from energy or water reduction.

Chapter checkpoint

In this chapter we have concluded our journey through OMEIA® stage 3 and part of stage 4 and explored how we drive sustainability in our supply chains. Key points we covered were:

1 *Supply chains present the most difficult challenge to driving sustainability* – it can be hard to know what happens and drive change beyond our immediate supplier, where we have no contractual relationships, especially in a complex supply chain.

2 *Built upon good SCM* – sustainable procurement in the supply chain is built upon the established principles of supply chain management (SCM). With our sustainability hat on we consider how to understand a supply chain in terms of logistics, and flow of information including information about demand, risk and sustainability. Understanding flows in a supply chain provides the basis to drive sustainability.

3 *Supply chain mapping* (or SVCN mapping) is the process of creating a representation of the entire network specifically relating to the supply of a certain product or service, as sourced from a specific immediate supplier. It is the basis to understanding a supply chain and therefore the foundation for driving sustainability improvements.

4 *Applying lenses* helps us make sense of a supply chain. Once we have identified the structure and linkages, and understood the context or environment the chain exists within, we apply a series of lenses to consider different risks, impacts and opportunities for the use of resources, emissions, waste, pollution, biodiversity, people and communities, and data and digital.

5 *Driving change in a supply chain* to make it more sustainable can involve a series of interventions, which can include restructuring the supply chain, establishing collaboration and relationships between entities, improving sustainability flows (especially the flow of information and cash to where it needs to get to), making logistics more effective and incentivizing entities upstream.

In the next chapter we will explore how we make changes happen, how we can measure success and outcomes, and we will conclude with a final section on how to get good at sustainability.

Making it happen, measuring outcomes and driving success

14

> In this final chapter we will bring everything together to establish a sustainable procurement road map. We will explore what is required to drive effective implementation with good change management and also how to establish the governance needed to ensure success. We will consider approaches to measure sustainable procurement outcomes and communicate success. Finally, this book concludes by examining some of the changes we can expect to see and be part of in the future.
>
> *Pathway questions addressed in this chapter*
>
> 13 How can we ensure our sustainable procurement programme is a success?
> 14 How do we measure sustainable procurement outcomes?
> 15 What should we be thinking about for the future?

As we near the end of this book and conclude stage 3, we will cover stages 4 and 5 to complete our journey through the OMEIA® sustainable procurement process. It may seem odd that it has taken this long to only get so far within our process. Yet the split of pages in this book devoted to planning versus doing are representative of how to focus our efforts to drive sustainability in our supply base. To be successful in sustainable procurement we must focus our precious resources with laser precision to where they will have the greatest impact. Hence why putting effort into thorough planning and clarity of forward direction of travel is essential. Only then do we move to action.

I'm going to assume a basic understanding of good project management principles and approaches, so I will avoid explaining these in this chapter. Instead we will explore the key considerations and things we need to provide for in order to effectively implement the individual initiatives and projects we have identified as priorities and also establish sustainable procurement organization wide.

Implementing sustainable procurement

We will begin with the framework for establishing any sort of strategic procurement initiative, which is the 5P governance model. 5P provides the foundation for success by helping establish and provide for the five areas of People, Plan, Payoff, Proficiency and Promotion. 5P brings together all the factors that have been proven to be effective within organizations embarking on any sort of major strategic programme or transformation. It is used extensively by organizations deploying category management or supplier relationship management as the underpinning means to secure results and create traction. In the same way, 5P is how organizations must set themselves up for success in implementing sustainable procurement. The 5P model is given in Figure 14.1 as interpreted for sustainable procurement and throughout this chapter we shall cover how each element needs to be set up and function for success, starting with how we structure the team.

Structuring the team for success

Sustainable procurement requires the right organizational structure and arrangements in order to establish a results-focused, goal-aligned capability. This is the *People P* within the 5P governance model.

The only approach that will deliver sustainable procurement and ensure effective implementation and management of change supported by all is a new approach that not only works across functional boundaries but positively tears them up. Cross-functional working has long since been a mainstay for good strategic procurement. When it comes to sustainability, however, we need cross-functional working on steroids. In practice this

Figure 14.1 The 5P governance model to enable sustainable procurement

People – putting the right structure in place for sustainable procurement
- Clear executive sponsorship
- A steering group responsible and accountable for the programme overall
- Sustainability and procurement functions melded and working as one
- Dedicated programme management and communications resource
- Data scientists and digital experts on the team
- Remit to form cross functional project teams

Plan – managing delivery of the sustainable procurement programme
- Sustainable procurement road map: a dynamic short-, medium- and long-term programme plan combining all initiatives, projects and governance activities
- Dedicated programme manager
- Individual project progress reviews
- Regular programme-level progress reporting

Prioritization heat cube
Sustainable Procurement road map

Payoff – tracking and measuring sustainability value
- Benefits and sustainable values definition
- Benefits tracking and reporting
- Business case development for initiatives and projects
- Measuring improvements to what we buy
- Supplier improvement and development
- Measuring supply chain improvements
- Positive impact stories

Promote – establishing a communications programme for success
- Managed internal and external communications plan
- Dedicated experienced resource
- Internal programme to secure buy-in, create momentum and share success
- External programme to demonstrate sustainable procurement achievements and progress towards goals as part of wider company communications and reporting

Proficiency – ensuring the capability and systems for sustainable procurement
- Competency assessment
- Learning and development programme (advanced procurement, supply chain and sustainability skills)
- Data research and science capability
- Assessment and audit capability
- Processes and toolkits
- Coaching and mentoring
- Educating the wider business

5P Governance: Programme, People, Proficiency, Promote, Payoff

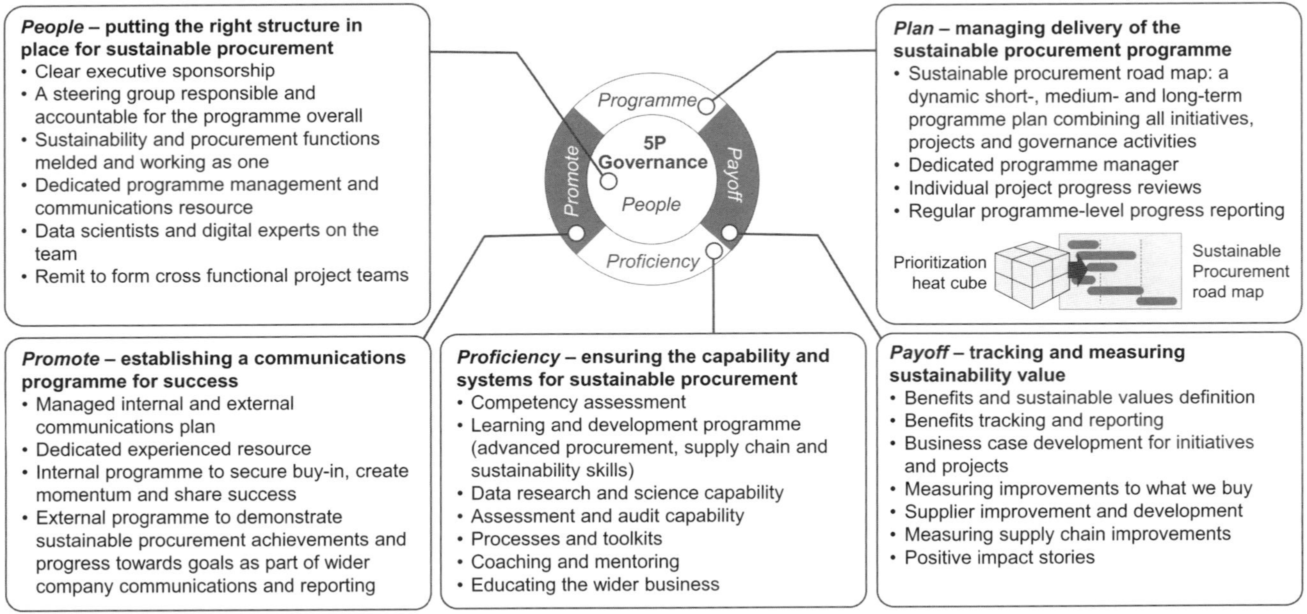

SOURCE © Positive Purchasing Ltd, 2003–2022

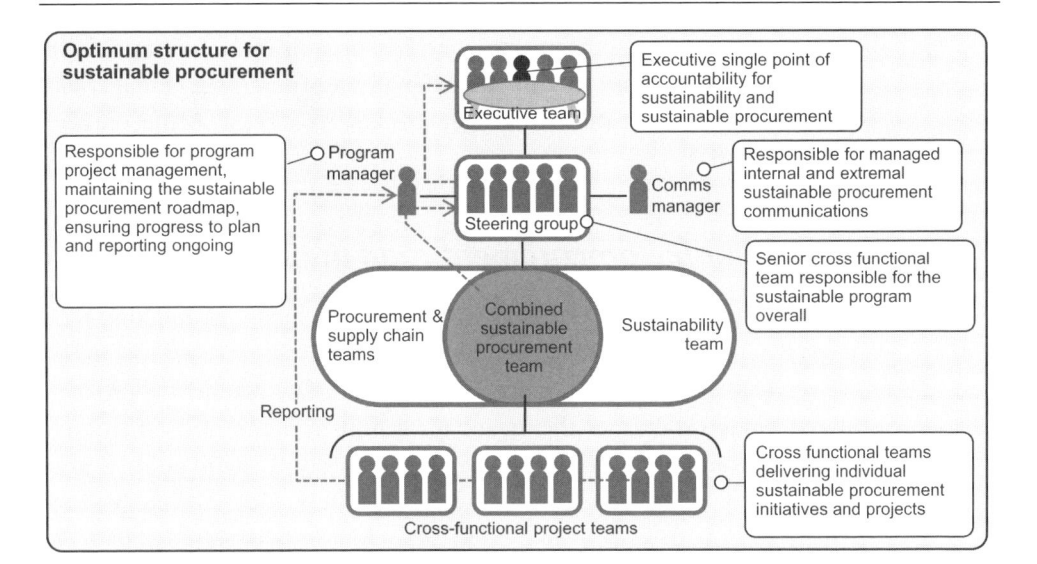

Figure 14.2 A structure for success in sustainable procurement

Optimum structure for sustainable procurement

- Executive team — Executive single point of accountability for sustainability and sustainable procurement
- Program manager — Responsible for program project management, maintaining the sustainable procurement roadmap, ensuring progress to plan and reporting ongoing
- Steering group — Senior cross functional team responsible for the sustainable program overall
- Comms manager — Responsible for managed internal and external sustainable procurement communications
- Combined sustainable procurement team (Procurement & supply chain teams + Sustainability team)
- Cross-functional project teams — Cross functional teams delivering individual sustainable procurement initiatives and projects
- Reporting

becomes more than functions getting together in a workshop, but requires a fundamental restructuring so joint teams with a clear mutually beneficial objective are formed.

The model that is gaining most traction in organizations is setting up a new sustainability function formed of individuals with exceptional knowledge and ideally experience in this area. These are unlikely to have come from within. Where this function is set up so that it works as one team with procurement (and supply chain functions) then we have the optimum marriage of capability and purpose. With this set up, cross-fertilization happens fast where procurement practitioners learn sustainability and vice versa. Even better if these teams are co-located and also report to a single executive individual. Alternatively, where this is not an option, upskilling those in procurement to become sustainable procurement practitioners is the next best option. Add some data scientists and point them at finding data sources, combining them and creating new supply-side insights and we have the perfect team to change the world. Figure 14.2 gives a typical structure for success in sustainable procurement.

Executive remit is essential with a board-level lead for delivering sustainability including sustainable procurement. Establishing a senior steering group is a key success factor. This is a small group of senior individuals tasked with establishing and ensuring the success overall of the programme and realization of the goals set. There could be a steering group for sustainable procurement that reports into one for organizational sustainability overall or it might be one and the same. Finally, a programme manager and potentially a communications manager are key to success. More on both these roles shortly.

The sustainable procurement road map

The sustainable procurement road map is our short, medium- and long-term plan for what we will do, with each of these time horizons expressed in different ways. It is the *Plan P* within 5P governance. The sustainable procurement road map establishes the means for a firm to organize itself to drive supply-side sustainability, put in place the right resources and guide action. It is the centrepiece by which the organization will manage sustainable procurement and ensure effectiveness, and as such it must be a dynamic document – regularly reviewed and updated as things change and progress.

Back in Chapter 6 we explored how we set our sustainable procurement strategy, high-level goals and individual targets. This is the starting point for our road map, with certain goals and some high-level targets now defining the different workstreams of activity into the future and representing our long-term ambitions. Within these we then define all the prioritized initiatives and projects that are required to realize the goals. Our thinking and planning here must be short to medium term. In the short term (12–18 months) the road map should be granular defining the detailed individual activities and milestones. Here the familiar Gantt chart format best serves us. It is difficult to plan beyond the short term with certainty as many things are likely to change. For the medium term (>1year, <3 years), the road map should focus on the high-level projects or programmes that will run, but not necessarily the detailed activities to support them as these will not be fully known at the outset. Figure 14.3 gives an example of a sustainable procurement road map.

All the principles of project planning come into play here to make this successful. Crucially, the road map should be kept as simple as possible and it should be something that key individuals accept, have participated in developing and own. It should be something that can then be easily communicated and understood so as to secure support and buy-in from wider stakeholder and potentially shareholder communities. In order to realize this, it should be developed collaboratively, ideally by a cross-functional

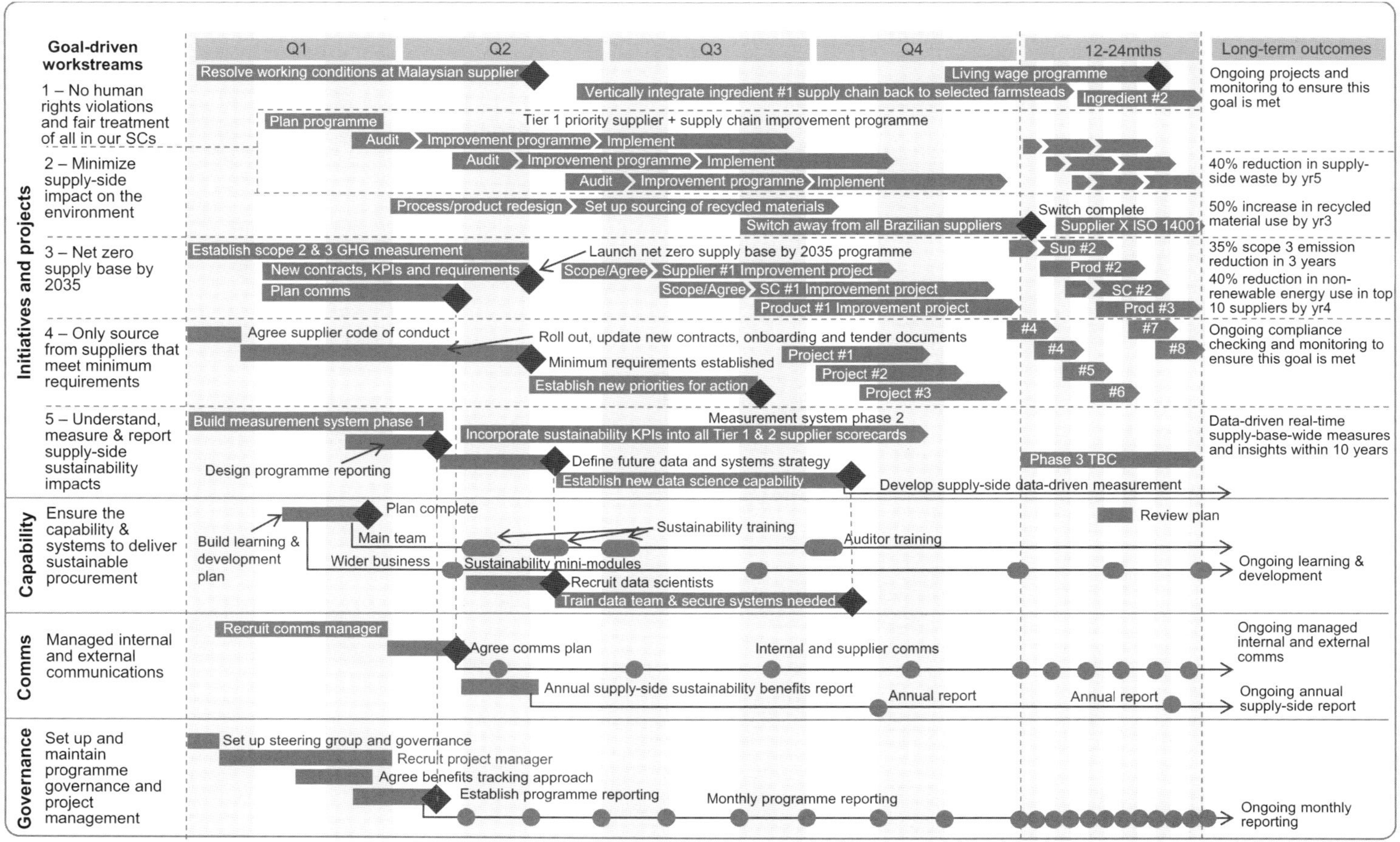

Figure 14.3 An example representation of a sustainable procurement road map

team of key individuals. Workshopping this in a face-to-face meeting using brown paper planning (group draws up a plan on a large sheet of brown paper using Post-it notes, etc) or online via a whiteboard is a great way to build it. Workshop outputs can be drawn up using a variety of professional project management tools or everyday desktop tools such as Excel or PowerPoint.

Building the road map

We compile the sustainable procurement road map by setting out our plans for each of the specific initiatives or projects we have identified we want or need to progress to achieve our strategy, goals and targets. Initiatives are typically short-term activities and projects and are typically more extensive, perhaps with a short- to medium-term time horizon. These come from everything we have done through the first three stages within the OMEIA® process. This includes the initial assessment activities we have carried out in terms of what we buy, who we buy from and our supply chains as summarized in our prioritization heat cube, from which we have further evaluated to validate the initiatives or projects we will progress.

In addition, the road map should include all those activities that are part of how governance for the program will be realized – essentially everything we need to do as part of 5P that has a time dimension or that we need to plan. Each of these should have their own workstream or swim lane within the sustainable procurement road map. They are:

- **Learning and development** (the *Proficiency* P) – the planned activities to develop capability within the team and wider business ongoing or establish new systems in order to deliver the programme.
- **Communications** (the *Promote* P) – the individual planned communications, perhaps covered in detail in a separate communications plan but with key milestones part of the road map.
- **Program management** (part of the *Plan* P) – all the planned activities necessary to deliver the programme, which might include steering group reviews, project stage gates, corporate reporting deadlines.

Build a sustainable procurement road map as follows:

1 Assemble a cross-functional team of key individuals.

2 Set up a blank document to work on – either a large piece of paper if face-to-face, or online whiteboard, PowerPoint slide or Excel document.

Define the timeline – allow 70 per cent of space for the short term with the remainder a compressed representation of the medium term.

3 Determine the swim lanes that define the themes for the various activities. Some or all of these may be determined by reviewing the sustainable procurement strategy, goals and targets and interpreting the long-term ambition into individual workstreams. Set these up on the timeline.

4 Review the specific initiatives and projects we have identified we want or need to progress (those originally identified in our prioritization heat cube that were validated as part of our deeper evaluations).

5 For each initiative and project, brainstorm the individual activities required to deliver it and the key milestones. Agree likely durations for each activity and then determine the sequencing and add to the relevant workstream. The ability to discuss, debate and move things around until the team is happy with it is essential.

6 Continue to build the road map considering the relative priorities of the different initiatives and projects, the relationship between them, the potential resource loading and what is or is not realistically possible. Adjust as needed.

7 Build additional parallel swim lanes for other programme elements including learning and development, communications and programme governance activities.

8 When agreed, crystallize it, perhaps converting team workings into a more manageable format.

The plan forms the basis for how we will manage and deliver sustainable procurement. Therefore, it needs a single point of ownership and it needs to be communicated. Good project management is critical to ensure success and a programme manager is essential; someone with good project management skills is critically important. This individual should manage and maintain the plan, instigate reporting from teams delivering individual initiatives and projects, and form the link between these and the senior team.

Building the business case and securing the mandate

With the sustainable procurement road map defined the final step at the end of OMEIA® stage 3 is to secure approval. What form of approval is needed depends upon the organization and the degree to which the team already have the remit and resources to get on with things.

Despite all the work we may have done to get this far, only now can we quantify the effort and investment required to deliver sustainability in the supply chain aligned to organizational goals. This may well be different to that expected. In my experience, this can often be the point where an engine starts failing in mid-air. Amid the shock, uncertainty and sound of spluttering from outside, we find ourselves no longer flying towards a new more sustainable destination. I have worked with many CPOs who have found themselves being prevented from doing what they were brought in to do because the wider executive team had second thoughts when they understood the scale of change needed. One dynamic here can be resistance to change at a senior level and in some organizations a touch of what C Northcote Parkinson describes as *injelititus* – incompetence and jealousy among senior individuals (Parkinson, 1957). When reality bites and other senior individuals come to understand the scale of change required or get uncomfortable with how sustainable procurement drives a more pivotal role for the function, it can cause a senior team committed thus far to wobble.

Preventing wobble

The other wobble and potential showstopper is cost, especially in enterprises that are heavily built around financial control and performance. One minute everyone is behind the ambition of sustainability in the supply chain, then we hear talk of budget constraints, paring back, shaving off, resetting ambition and so on. The hard reality here is achieving sustainable procurement will require companies to invest in doing so and even the most committed advocates' conviction will wobble when they see what it is going to cost. However, as we have seen throughout this book, good action towards sustainability should not be viewed as only a cost now but a means to avert greater cost later and also to unlock new benefit and competitive advantage. This may not be immediately obvious and so we need to build a business case and justification for individual sustainable procurement initiatives and projects and our programme overall. Clearly the organization has to be able to afford to do sustainable procurement, but this is not a time to let things get pushed back – be aware of the difference between wobble and pushback as if this was an annual internal budget negotiation and genuine difficulty supporting a programme. If we are confident in our sustainability road map it should not be a starting point for what can we avoid or do later, but the basis for investment required. This may demand new thinking regarding how the organization will fund sustainability, perhaps looking to more longer-term funding options where the potential payback stacks up.

Unarguable logic and business cases

The best way to deal with wobble and prevent erosion here is to fight our corner using science-based facts and data and the unarguable logic that is summarized in Figure 14.4. However, there is one final step here that is necessary and that is to ensure that key initiatives or projects have good business cases behind them and ensure the overall business case for the entire programme remains sound (as we explored in Chapter 5).

Remember, a business case is a justification of why we should do something. In its simplest form it is the determination of cost and benefits, most widely used to measure financial payback or return on financial investment. If we invest $X we will get $Y. When it comes to sustainability the same basic approach holds true, except the investment is typically both financial (direct and indirect costs were listed in Chapter 5), as well as non-financial and might include time, know-how sharing, consultancy, commitment and risk sharing. We must also consider a vastly different array of both financial and non-financial benefits. Getting this right is one of the most important enablers for sustainability, not just for creating a business case but for measuring success overall. I will expand this more fully later in this chapter.

Ensuring the right capability

The *Proficiency P* of the 5P governance approach is about ensuring we have the required systems and capability for sustainable procurement. Upskilling of those in procurement around sustainability will almost certainly be needed. However, to be effective we need more than new skills in procurement. Sustainability is an organization-wide concern with sustainable procurement the single most important element of this. This means we need new capability here. It doesn't follow that this resides entirely in a new supersized all-powerful procurement function. Instead it means we need a new organizational capability matched with the right structure to make sustainability happen. Some key skills needed across this include:

- **Strategic procurement capability** – advanced ability in applying modern strategic procurement principles to drive sourcing approaches including category management and supplier relationship management.
- **Sustainability** – advanced knowledge of sustainability and ability to apply it in a range of business scenarios.
- **Data science** – research capability, ability to determine data sources and build algorithms, and present information to give new insight.

Figure 14.4 Summary of the key steps in developing our road map and the logic of arguments to compel others to support it

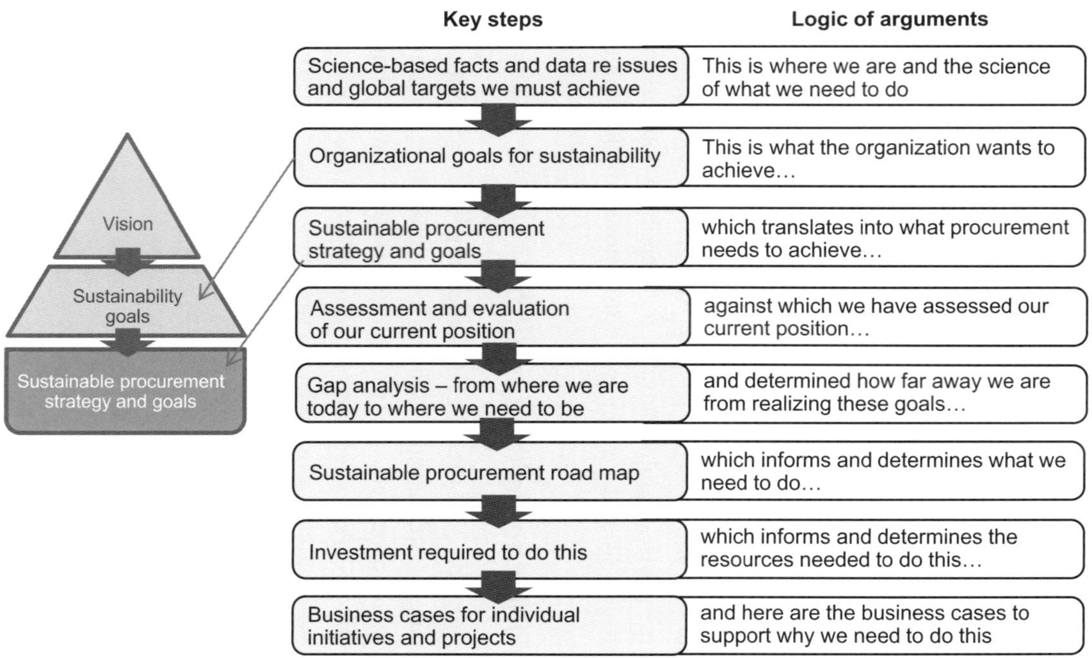

Key steps	Logic of arguments
Science-based facts and data re issues and global targets we must achieve	This is where we are and the science of what we need to do
Organizational goals for sustainability	This is what the organization wants to achieve…
Sustainable procurement strategy and goals	which translates into what procurement needs to achieve…
Assessment and evaluation of our current position	against which we have assessed our current position…
Gap analysis – from where we are today to where we need to be	and determined how far away we are from realizing these goals…
Sustainable procurement road map	which informs and determines what we need to do…
Investment required to do this	which informs and determines the resources needed to do this…
Business cases for individual initiatives and projects	and here are the business cases to support why we need to do this

Vision → Sustainability goals → Sustainable procurement strategy and goals

- **Audit and assessment** – capability to establish assessment programmes or qualified/experienced auditor capability including that required for extreme supply chain situations in unfamiliar circumstances and know-how regarding how to speak to the people in the situations we find.
- **Negotiation** – advanced ability, in particular how to structure and lead negotiation where sustainability is a central requirement.
- **Implementation and project management** – advanced capability and ability to operate at a senior level.
- **Communications** – advanced ability to plan and implement an effective internal and external communications programme using a range of channels.

Managing change

Procurement functions have routinely fallen short when attempting to secure internal buy-in. We can multiply this by a factor of ten for sustainable procurement where any change not only requires cooperation internally but positively challenges internal functions around aspects of design or process. Resistance to change is widely recognized as the biggest cause of project or programme failure and there is even greater potential for resistance to change to scupper what we are trying to do here.

At the heart of resistance to change is fear, often subconscious within the individual but manifested as a complex and varied array of reasons to not do something and, in some cases, positively oppose it. If procurement is advocating significant changes to design, specification, or to switch supplier, or change a manufacturing process, we can expect internal functions that thought they were leading on these things to not to be too ready to support us here. We could even end up being part of an internal power struggle. Clearly this will stop any attempts to drive sustainable procurement in their tracks.

There are four critical success factors to managing change to drive sustainability. They are:

- **Executive leadership** – there must be clear high-level corporate remit with visible and evangelical executive support.
- **Participation** – there must be not only active involvement and participation from across relevant functions but permanent or semi-permanent membership within the team tasked to do this.

- **Communication** – there must be exceptional communication between all involved, in all directions.
- **'Felt-need'** – there must be a felt need or reason to want to do this shared by all those involved.

Fail to provide for any of these and the programme is unlikely to succeed. Therefore, getting the structure right as we explored earlier provides the foundation for managing change. So too does effective communications (I'll cover that later in this chapter) and how people in organizations work together to deliver specific initiatives and projects. These four principles should underpin everything those leading sustainable procurement do.

Measuring outcomes and sharing success

You are what you measure. You get what you measure. What gets measured gets managed. If you measure the wrong things you get the wrong results. Measurement drives action. I could go on. Measurement is the backbone for sustainability and especially the means to ensure effective sustainable procurement. It can also be the hardest thing to establish as it requires new approaches and new ways of thinking about value and benefits that the entire organization will embrace.

Before we rush off to build a big measurement system it is worth reminding ourselves of the role of measurement. Companies frequently get measurement wrong and end up creating systems that take on a life of their own, often requiring a small army to run them, measure the wrong things or focus only on what has happened. All in pursuit of measurement, but for what purpose? This question often goes unanswered as procurement practitioners and suppliers plough through reviewing their longlist of KPIs. Yet this is the question we must start with, for measurement in general and in particular for measuring sustainability. What is the purpose of measuring something, how will it add value and what are we going to do with the results?

Measurement with purpose

Carefully targeted measurement is a key enabler for supply-side sustainability to show progress and quantify benefit. It is the *Payoff P* in the 5P governance model. There are a number of areas where some form of measurement is necessary or can help achieve our goals and there are two levels of measurement.

Strategic, programme level, internal, company-wide and external:

- To demonstrate success overall of the sustainable procurement programme, how it contributes to business goals and thereby reinforce the value contribution of the function driving it.
- As a basis for communication to share success, galvanize support, reduce resistance to change, improve standing with shareholders, build a brand, create social value, secure support from the public at large and so on.

Tactical level, internal and some external:

- To build good business cases for individual initiatives or projects.
- To establish a baseline from which we determine gaps from targets and measure improvement progress.
- To establish how improvements to products or services (or how we buy them) could deliver, or have delivered, new sustainability value.
- To know how a supplier could improve or has improved to become more sustainable.
- To determine how sustainability could be, or has been, improved in the supply chain.

Crucially, any measurement we set up should have a purpose and ultimately that purpose is enabling the organization to move towards the goals for sustainability it has set. Remember, our goals will be shaped by corporate motivation and where on the business case pyramid the company sits. Sustainability measurement systems must be developed to serve our ambition here. If we are only about the legal minimum, we need to do little more than measure compliance. If we want to be known for creating social and environmental value we will need more extensive systems that can measure how effective we are.

Where to start

Resist the temptation to start setting up measurement systems for sustainability based upon what we know or how we have done things before. This is one scenario where 'bottom-up' doesn't work and creating all sorts of systems to measure things can do little more than sap resources. Instead start top-down and determine what measurement we need, where it is needed, why and how we might do this, keeping available resource in mind. We begin with our goals, but then we need to determine what measures we need, both strategic and tactical, in order to know how we are progressing towards these. Obvious enough. However, success here comes from designing new measurement systems that are not constrained by how we have done things before, or today's limitations over what can be measured or ways to measure. For example, today it is very difficult to adequately measure scope 3 or supply-side CO_2e as the required data or information is often unavailable. Yet we know we need to do this and for many companies it is now a legal obligation so we need to be doing this or at least moving rapidly towards it.

A good place to start is to do some visioning around the perfect measurement approach, based upon what we need to know, or would like to know, and work back from there to what is possible today and what might be possible in the future.

Imagine the perfect measurement system

Imagine if everything we bought came with one of those stickers you see on household appliances that tell you how energy-efficient it is, but for sustainability. It would make things a whole lot easier. It is likely such a thing will emerge in coming years perhaps starting with products having to declare 'carbon used'. Imagine if we could access in real time current information about every key aspect relating to sustainability for any given supplier and know it was 100 per cent accurate. Imagine if we had visualizations of the actual full end-to-end supply chains in real time and what is happening in them and could track and trace every single thing we purchased using blockchain technology. Imagine if all these systems were integrated and we could access a real-time dashboard of supply-side sustainability overall with history, progress towards corporate goals and real-time predictive modelling. Imagine too if all these systems were connected to other Big Data sources, and also data about world and environmental events and were intelligent to start predicting where we might need interventions to prevent impacts happening.

It might seem crazy and far-fetched to imagine systems that would be more at home in a sci-fi film. Yet it is not that crazy. In fact, many of the pieces of this vision exist today and will develop, and ultimately this type of intelligent, joined up, highly connected system will exist within a decade. Imagining the perfect system is more than a fun bit of fluffy blue-sky thinking but rather is an essential step to help us step away from that which we know and has gone before towards new ideas and ways to measure supply-side sustainability. It provides the springboard at a strategic level to:

Making it happen, measuring outcomes and driving success

- define the future state and long-term ambition for procurement enablement systems (especially data and digital);
- determine or shape an investment programme, in particular in data or digital systems;
- determine future structure and skills, for example recruiting data scientists to join the team; and

at a tactical level to:

- determine, based upon the ideal future vision, what is possible and practical today and how we can establish the specific systems and arrangements for measurement for what we buy, who we buy from and within our supply chains; and
- determine and plan for what we can do to further develop and enhance these.

This imagining to start designing a measurement system is best done in a small workshop with a group of key individuals as follows:

1. With realizing our goals in mind, start by asking the question 'if we could do anything, what would our sustainable procurement measurement system look like?'
2. Review, sort, discuss, debate and determine the long-term goals and requirements for the sustainability measurement system we want to progress towards (which may not exist or be fully possible today).
3. Determine the strategy for how we will progress towards the long-term goals. Consider systems, capability and what would need to change. Build a long-term plan and incorporate into the sustainable procurement road map.
4. Determine what we can do, or need to do, in the short term and establish individual measurement systems and approaches for what we buy, who we buy from and within our supply chains.

For the last point, I will cover how we do this for each of these in turn shortly, however, it is important to recognize that our aim here isn't necessarily to create separate systems for each. Instead these meld into one and require a joined-up approach. You cannot measure how sustainable something we buy is unless we consider the suppliers we buy from or what happens in the supply chain before them. Figure 14.5 gives the components of sustainable procurement measurement.

There is one final point here in shaping our measurement system and this is the fact that traditional corporate approaches don't fit. Measuring sustainable procurement demands a change in mindset from the top down.

Stories matter

Almost all organizations remain structured and managed based upon quantitative, top-down financial performance. Almost all procurement functions have savings or at least cost management as the fundamental driver and measure of success. This is unlikely to change any time soon as this remains the proven, and seemingly only, viable means to successfully run an organization. However, sustainability requires a paradigm shift in how to measure success and performance beyond financial measures. We cannot let go of cost consciousness or financial management and so success in sustainable procurement is about how we balance supply-side financial performance with sustainability performance (which may or may not be readily financially quantifiable). This shapes what and how we measure in support of this and signals a departure from what we know. The most significant shift required here is not one within procurement but at the heart of the organization, in the boardroom and how the organization at the highest level determines it will judge the success of procurement as a function. A company that states it wants supply-side sustainability but continues to measure procurement success based upon savings only will fail. Instead securing agreement from the executive team to a new way of measuring the contribution from procurement is a prerequisite for success.

Measuring the things we are not used to measuring

Sustainable procurement requires both quantitative and qualitative measures. The use of qualitative measures is commonplace in organizations; however, we typically try to convert that which is qualitative into quantitative because that means we can process results, establish comparators and often quantify the cost – for example 'please rate how you feel about our service, from 1 to 5'. This is typically as far as we go in terms of deviating from the trusted path of quantitative measures that power organizational thinking. I would even go so far as to say that qualitative measurement is frequently dismissed as less valuable, unreliable, merely anecdotal and less important. Yet when it comes to measuring sustainability, embracing the power of qualitative measures is a critical step for an organization.

Figure 14.5 The components of sustainable procurement measurement

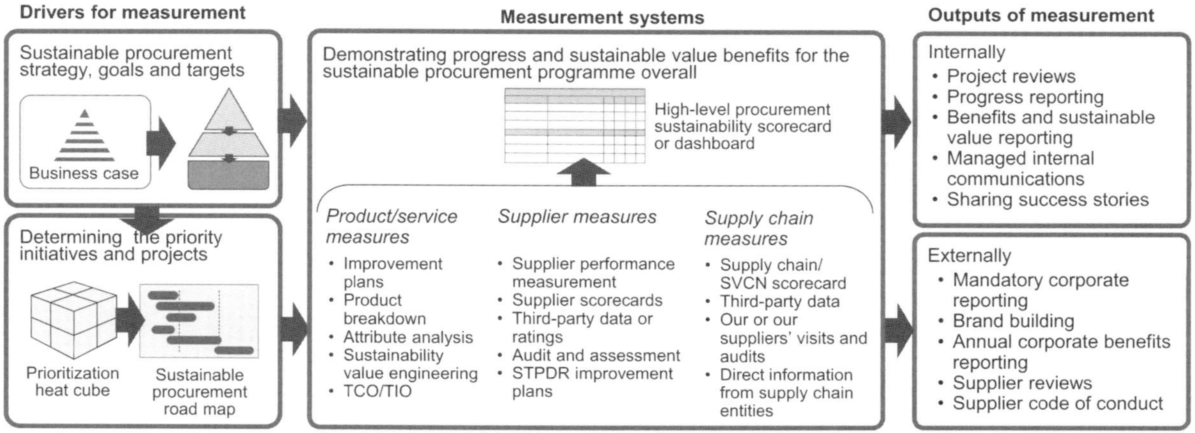

Drivers for measurement

Sustainable procurement strategy, goals and targets

Business case

Determining the priority initiatives and projects

Prioritization heat cube

Sustainable procurement road map

Measurement systems

Demonstrating progress and sustainable value benefits for the sustainable procurement programme overall

High-level procurement sustainability scorecard or dashboard

Product/service measures
- Improvement plans
- Product breakdown
- Attribute analysis
- Sustainability value engineering
- TCO/TIO

Supplier measures
- Supplier performance measurement
- Supplier scorecards
- Third-party data or ratings
- Audit and assessment
- STPDR improvement plans

Supply chain measures
- Supply chain/ SVCN scorecard
- Third-party data
- Our or our suppliers' visits and audits
- Direct information from supply chain entities

Outputs of measurement

Internally
- Project reviews
- Progress reporting
- Benefits and sustainable value reporting
- Managed internal communications
- Sharing success stories

Externally
- Mandatory corporate reporting
- Brand building
- Annual corporate benefits reporting
- Supplier reviews
- Supplier code of conduct

To measure sustainable procurement there are four categories of benefit, as we identified back in Chapter 5. These are *financial, financially quantifiable, pre-financial* and *pure social or environmental value* (see Figure 5.5). These represent a continuum from that which is quantitative and readily quantifiable in financial terms to that which is qualitative and not readily quantifiable in financial terms but brings other value and benefit. These are expanded in Table 14.1, which provides the basis to establish a benefit measurement and tracking approach for sustainable procurement.

The broad range of approaches to measurement that sustainability demands is not an imperfection but an opportunity. There are different approaches to measurement here and these can be applied in a variety of forms for what we buy, who we buy from and our supply chains. They are:

- **Direct measurement** – where there is a comparison to a set value, benchmark or standard.
- **Use of indicators and establishing KPIs** – combination of measures and other information to provide information that is more useful to understand something. Can be lagging (information about what has happened) or leading (information that predicts what is expected to happen). Can be performance indicators (specific indicators about performance) and also key performance indicators (KPIs), which are those designated as the most relevant or important.
- **Quantify potential scale of impact** – converting qualitative data into quantitative measures or indicators.
- **Itemizing and promoting non-financial value** – establishing a list of qualitative value and other benefits that cannot be, or we don't want to be, quantified in financial terms, e.g. reduced risk, increased innovation, improved effectiveness, greater employee satisfaction, improved quality of life, increased collaboration, etc.
- **Positive impact stories** – distinct from the last point and takes this one step further. These are stories of the experiences of people in situations where something changes and how people react to, or are impacted by, a change. They are stories of other circumstances where a change causes a reaction or impact on the environment. Positive impact stories often reveal hidden aspects of the situation and can relate to changes that have happened or are yet to happen.

This last point is more than a type of measurement. It is the new way of thinking that can help change the game and key to this is how we tell the stories.

Table 14.1 Types and examples of benefit for sustainable procurement

Type of benefit	Includes	Ways to measure
Financial	**Direct savings** • Price reduction • Negotiated savings • Below budget • Savings where no baseline exists • Outsourcing, insourcing, right-shoring • Supply chain integration • Market changes	• Direct measurement *Quantitative using primary data*
	Cost avoidance • Eliminating spend (e.g. reduced consumption/waste) • Avoiding inflation • Exchange rates	• Direct measurement • Use indicators *Quantitative and qualitative using primary and secondary data*
Financially quantifiable value	• Efficiency savings • Process improvement • Inventory reduction • Synergy benefits (e.g. sharing resources, facilities, transport) • Benefits from collaboration • Economies of scale	• Direct measurement • Use indicators • Itemize and promote non-financial value *Qualitative converted to quantitative using primary and secondary data*
Pre-financial *Where our actions will, or are very likely to, result in a future positive or negative financial impact*	**Averting future cost** • Risk reduction/avoidance • Future cost avoidance (e.g. carbon tax, projected rise in cost of resources/waste) • Cybersecurity and data protection	• Quantify potential scale of impact • Itemize and promote non-financial value • Positive impact stories *Qualitative with some converted to quantitative using primary and secondary data*
	Creating future revenue • Innovation • New brand value • Competitive advantage • New/increased revenue • Business association • Brand association • Exclusivity • Securing grant or financial support • New financial investment	• Quantify potential scale of impact • Itemize and promote non-financial value • Positive impact stories *Qualitative with some converted to quantitative using primary and secondary data*

Table 14.1 *continued*

Type of benefit	Includes	Ways to measure
Pure social & environmental value	• Protect and recover the planet • Uphold human rights • Inclusion and diversity • Protect vulnerable individuals • Fair treatment of individuals • Improved health • Improved quality of life • Support or help a community • Restore our oceans • Reduce GHG emissions • Restore or protect biodiversity • Protect animals and ensure animal welfare	• Positive impact stories *Mostly qualitative using primary and secondary data*

The power of positive impact stories

As humans we are natural storytellers and we have been doing it since humankind first learnt to talk. Arguably, storytelling, and the ability to share insight and wisdom, played a key role in human evolution.

In Chapter 5 I floated the concept of using positive impact stories to help establish the business case for sustainability. In fact, positive impact stories are a necessary and crucial component to sustainability measurement at both a strategic and tactical level. For them to work we need to consider our approach.

McAleese and Kilty (2019) suggest there is a richness and value in using stories. They suggest they are good for making simple what is complicated and help overcome some of the limitations in using quantitative measures. To use them effectively we need to understand both the value and the impact possible from good storytelling. We must also master the art of using storytelling to our advantage and not giving ground to those who might be quick to dismiss our stories as unfounded to serve their own agendas. We can learn much from those who are skilful in how they use stories – stories are mobilized and simultaneously rejected by those in power according to the agenda needing to be served (McAleese and Kilty, 2019). Often this goes unnoticed. Journalists tell stories to help us understand a news story. Crucially journalists can tell the same story in different ways depending upon the agenda they want to serve. Politicians use stories to expose a dilemma or crisis that requires a governmental response and will narrate the story to serve a political agenda. Stories have huge power to influence change but it depends how good the story is and who takes on or rejects it. If we lack skill in storytelling we end up appearing desperate and ill-informed in front of those who make the decisions, whether internal or external, customers, citizens, shareholders, etc. Therefore, to use positive impact stories we need to perfect the art of creating compelling, unarguable, indisputable stories that leave no option for sitting on the fence. This needs to be a central component within our communications plan and management.

Building systems to measure sustainability

A measurement system is about answering 'what are we going to measure, how will we do this, what sources of information will we use and what will we do with the results?' Figure 14.5 shows the different components of sustainable procurement measurement and how they relate to each other. These all inform the overarching measures of success for sustainable procurement as a whole. In simple terms, this is a high-level scorecard of our overall performance towards the sustainable procurement goals. This gives us the means to demonstrate overall performance and the basis to communicate successes. We create this by determining what measures and indicators we need; however, these will be informed by the results of more detailed measurement for what we buy, who we buy from and our supply chains. I will explore each of these in turn shortly but first we should keep in mind the key considerations in developing a measurement system and what makes it successful. These are:

- **Alignment with goals** – all measurement should support demonstrating how a goal is realized or progress towards it.
- **Simplicity** – carefully craft a shortlist of measures of the right KPIs to give the right insight. Select and craft each measure with scarcity in mind. Determine use of measures or more complex indicators that combine various measures or sources to give more useful information.
- **Business buy-in** – what we measure should be developed with the wider business and aligned to stakeholder expectations to serve the needs of both procurement and the business.
- **Forward-looking where possible** – consider the right measurement approach to help achieve our goals. There are four approaches here:

- *Measure by exception* – where there is a problem or suspected impact requiring corrective action, e.g. we get a report of human rights violations in a supply chain.
- *Measure compliance* – measuring only that which is necessary to verify compliance to legislation or meeting certain standards or criteria.
- *Past performance* – measuring historical performance against set targets and agreeing corrective and preventative action to ensure good future performance.
- *Progress towards joint goals* – collaborative, jointly agreed measures focusing on performance and progress towards mutually agreed goals.

- **One size does not fit all** – make them specific and unique to each scenario – e.g. to what we buy as informed by the RAQSCI business requirements or specific to the supplier as informed via VIPER relationship requirements.
- **Drive required behaviours** – design to foster the right behaviour rather than hit a target. Avoid punitive measures that drive defensive behaviour.
- **Data collection** – design the data collection and measurement system to establish the measure. Consider how the data will be collected initially and ongoing. Should it be closed loop versus open loop, will we use primary or secondary data? Where the data will come from, how will it be collected? Can we use multiple information points to triangulate results?
- **Meaningful outputs** – determine how to output results – visible to the right people, or at the right points in the process, at the right time to enable action and intervention as needed. Decide how these will form part of wider communications or reviews with suppliers.

Measuring sustainability for what we buy

To make products or services we buy sustainable we need a baseline of how sustainable they are now and a means to measure progress towards our goals. Going back to our vision of the perfect measurement system, this is where the ideal would be everything we buy comes with a sustainability rating tag. Until then we need to develop our own approach. Crucially, any measurement activity takes time and effort so this should be aligned to achieving our goals and directed only to those specific priority products we have identified where we need some form of measurement to judge improvements. In Chapter 10 we explored in detail approaches to drive sustainability for products and services, and two tools here that form the basis for measurement of what we buy:

- **Attribute analysis** – a key tool for comparative analysis of products or services and also the basis to identify those attributes that can be used as a baseline for measurement, e.g. CO_2e per product delivered, per cent recyclable, etc.
- **Sustainable value engineering** – enables us to identify the specific areas end-to-end in the life of a product or service where there is risk, impact or opportunity. This helps us target what and where to measure and helps us to identify potential data points or sources to use.

Measuring sustainability for products or services will typically need to be combined with our understanding of the suppliers or supply chains involved to establish a true picture. From here it is possible to determine the measure or indicators for how sustainable a given product or service is and then use this to track improvements.

Using TCO/TIO as a tool for measurement

Total cost of ownership (TCO) is a well-established tool within procurement to determine the full-life, end-to-end cost for something we buy beyond acquisition, including costs to own and use the product or service, deal with end of life and ultimately disposal. TCO has its place for sustainability and in particular aspects of measurement to quantify specific aspects sourcing a product or service. There is a variant on TCO that we can use alongside, which is total impact of ownership (TIO).

TIO works in the same way as TCO where we identify each impact, and its relative magnitude, for each step within the end-to-end life of a product. It is a natural extension of and informed by any sustainable value engineering we have done and useful because it enables us to create a visual measure of sustainability for a given product. We can also use the TIO side by side with a TCO to visualize both sustainability impacts and where cost is added. This can help to establish a means to measure the cost of sustainability improvements. We can use a TIO to show impacts overall or a specific impact area such as emissions. Figure 14.6 gives both the TCO and TIO for a pump over its life.

Figure 14.6 A total cost of ownership (TCO)/total impact of ownership (TIO) for a pump over its life

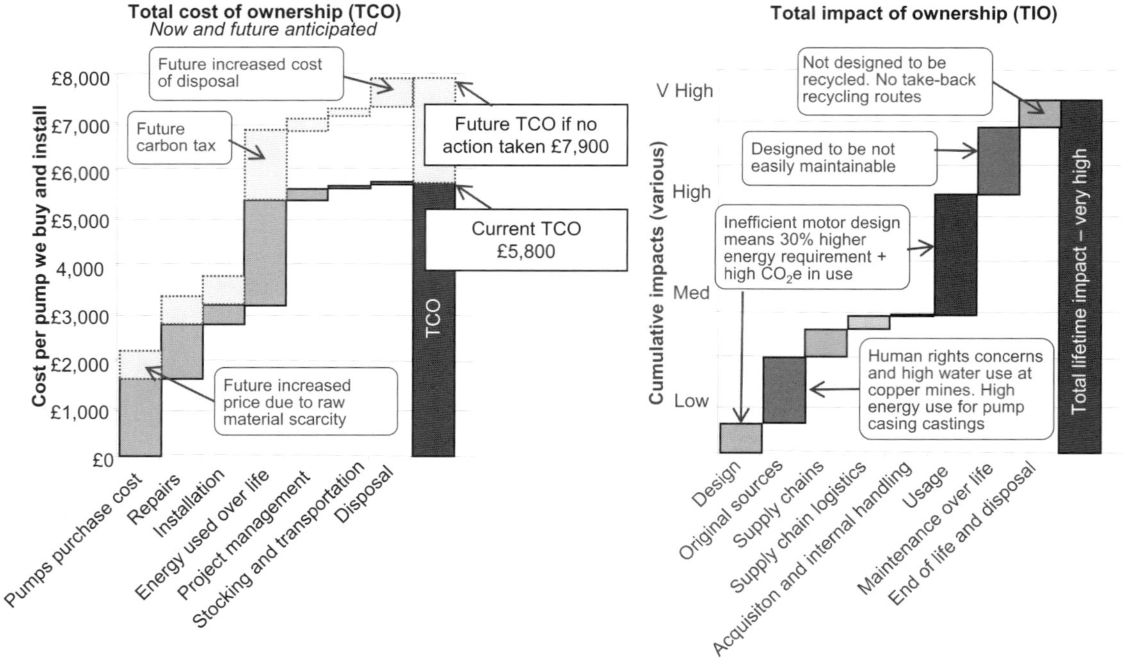

Build a TIO for a product or service as follows:

1 Best worked collaboratively in a small group of individuals with good knowledge of the item in question.
2 Review the outputs from any attribute analysis or sustainable value engineering and any existing TCO that is available for the product/service.
3 Determine each of the steps in the full life of the product or service (use those within the sustainable value engineering tool as a guide).
4 For each step quantify the impact of this step relative to others. We can do this either by assigning each step a score, say using 1–5 with 5 being the most impactful or we can use actual values if we know them, e.g. CO_2e values per step.
5 Create the visual graph and mark up to highlight points of note and potential risks and opportunities for action.

Measuring supplier sustainability

Measuring supplier performance is something we have long since done in procurement. Many practitioners will be familiar with establishing supplier KPIs and agreeing a scorecard, perhaps also incorporating these into a service-level agreement (SLA) within a contract. The same approach is used for measuring sustainability and managing improvements ongoing with suppliers. In Chapter 11 we explored how we drive sustainability in suppliers and the interventions required to do this.

Once again supplier measurement should be precisely targeted so it adds value, and one size does not fit all but rather the measurement approach should be unique to the supplier and what makes them important in terms of sustainability. Using our supplier tiering as a basis, the more important or strategic a supplier is the more likely there will be a good reason to measure them in some way, either to drive improvements or as a basis for supplier development to go 'good to great'.

Building a sustainability scorecard

Measuring supplier sustainability should not be a separate approach to that which might already be in place. If we have already established a system of supplier performance measurement, for example we have agreed scorecards with key suppliers that we regularly review with them, then this should be extended to include sustainability. This is more than adding a bunch of new KPIs to an existing scorecard, but rather rethinking what we need from specific supplier relationships and adapting the system to provide for a simple and effective balanced suite of measures. There are some considerations here and supplier sustainability scorecards, and how we use them, is different because:

- The group of suppliers we need to measure in terms of sustainability may be different from those where we need traditional measures such as delivery, price performance, relationship performance, etc.
- We are more likely to need forward-looking measures of progress towards a target rather than historic review of performance.
- Improvements typically have longer time frames to realize them.
- What we measure and more importantly how we measure it can be vastly different from traditional approaches.

This simply means we need to design and use scorecards differently according to the purpose they need to serve. Even then, it is the determination of the right measures that makes all the difference. Remember a KPI is a 'key' performance indicator – in other words, we have crafted it carefully to select the indicator that will give us the most insight into the supplier performance. If we have a supplier scorecard with 30 KPIs we have missed the point and our measurement system will not be effective.

The final consideration is where the data and information needed will come from, how the scorecard will be compiled and shared, and who is going to do this. We could do this, but it presumes we have the data needed. We can ask the supplier to do this, which is usually the easy way out for procurement practitioners, yet they may not be ready or able to provide this. We must give thought to where the data and information required for each KPI will come from. We might need to work together with the supplier to build it and establish new systems to collect or access the necessary data and information. This could include information from within their operation, but also other data from their supply chain and also the findings of any ongoing assessment or audit we conduct. Figure 14.7 gives an example of a supplier scorecard for sustainability KPIs developed with the principles of good measurement we explored earlier in mind.

Figure 14.7 An example supplier scorecard for sustainability

Supplier sustainability scorecard – *Malaysian Rubber Glove Corporation*

Ongoing performance KPIs	Result area and information source	Target	Q1	Q2	Q3	Q4
Non-compliances – minimum requirements for environment and treatment of workers	On the ground monitoring, audits, workers' council and interviews	Zero non-compliances	1	0	0	0
Water consumption (new, non-returned) per 100,000 units	Facility smart meters and utility bills – volume harvested and recycled	12,000 litre/1,200 m³	11,454 l	11,810 l	9,788 l	13,665 l
Energy consumption – per 100,000 units	Facility smart meters and utility bills	5000 kWh	5,030 kWh	6,100 kWh	4,200 kWh	7,020 kWh
CO₂e per 100,000 units	Emissions calculation based upon inputs	20,000 kg CO₂e	18,500 kg CO₂e	18,500 kg CO₂e	17,700 kg CO₂e	18,200 kg CO₂e
Wastewater – per 100,000 units (effluent and run-offs)	Metering at wastewater processing site + waste contractor invoices	4,000 litres/400 m³	3,650 l	3,400 l	3,550 l	3,400 l
Solid waste – per 100,000 units	Production instrumentation + waste contractor invoices	27.5 kg	26.9 kg	27.1 kg	27.4 kg	28.1 kg

Progress towards med-long-term goals	Result area and information source	Target	Q1	Q2	Q3	Q4
Net zero by 2035 – progress towards target	Emissions measurement + offset calculation + renewable energy	Net zero by 2035		14%		15%
Rubber cultivation improvements – improve yields, methods and reduce CO₂e	Farmstead improvement reports, volumes and emissions calculations	Ave farm efficiency factor of 1.2 in 5 years	0.6	0.6	0.5	0.7

Measuring supply chain sustainability

Establishing measurement for a supply chain can be difficult because it can be hard to know where to direct our efforts, we may need to measure multiple entities and obtaining the data and insight can be onerous. Remember our future imaging? It would be amazing to have a dashboard that showed in real time everything happening across an entire supply chain. However, we should wait for the technology to arrive rather than attempting to create this ourselves, but this thinking does help shape what we are ultimately working towards. Instead success comes by not attempting to measure everything in a supply chain but rather starting with the same questions: what do we need to measure and why, and how can we do this?

The supply chain map for those priority supply chains we identified, and in particular where we have identified risk, impacts and opportunities, provides a good starting point to determine a measurement system. This is typically something we must compile rather than asking an immediate supplier to do it. In practical terms it means using the same scorecard approach we use for suppliers, but for an entire supply chain and it means crafting a small set of KPIs that will help us know everything that is important to us given our goals and targets for specific supply chain improvement initiatives or projects.

We will need to think about how we collect data and information and this may require us to set up a system for data collection from multiple and varied sources in order to bring our scorecard to life. This might be regularly provided by different entities in the supply chain, by accessing third-party data, through remote monitoring, the results of audit, assessment or just visiting entities. For example, if our target is to reduce CO_2e across a supply chain (scope 3 emissions), we will need a KPI for total supply chain CO_2e and we will need to measure this periodically to track progress towards our target. Yet to do this we will need to regularly collect information about emissions at different points through the supply chain and combine these into an overall measure. This is no small undertaking so we must be laser-focused about what supply chain measures we need and the purpose they serve. We must design and manage a system than can cope with the complexities of data collection at the right intervals and process this to compile a supply chain scorecard or measurement system. As such, supply chain measurement may require us brokering direct relationships and channels for entities to provide data and information regularly. They also need to be willing and able to do this so all the factors we explored in Chapter 13 come into play here.

Communication planning

The final P of 5P governance is *Promote*, which is about how we manage communications. Arguably this is the single most important factor to enable success and yet the one that often gets overlooked. Communication cannot be left to chance. Communication, both internally and externally, is essential to make sustainable procurement effective and ensure momentum. Few procurement functions are good at this and the starting point is often one where strategic category- or supplier-related projects have fallen short due to lack of internal buy-in and the resistance to change that arises from this. Procurement functions that get this right recognize the importance of communication and establish a dedicated resource (part or full time) with experience of designing and managing communications.

A managed approach to communication means determining the different stakeholder groups we need to communicate with, both internal and external, and then determining what we need to communicate, crafting compelling central messages to ensure it lands as needed. Then it is about using a range of creative approaches and channels to deliver the communication. Old internal approaches such as intranet pages or email newsletters usually fail to deliver. New approaches such as short fast-paced videos pushed via company social media channels or podcasts work better along with other approaches that better get our attention. The purpose of communication internally for sustainable procurement is to establish the programme in the hearts and minds of the entire business. It is about communicating what the programme is, its executive remit, why it is important, what it is hoped will be achieved and what is needed from all to help do this. If done well internal communications becomes a key means to manage change and minimize resistance. It also galvanizes support and maintains momentum for what will be a long hard slog.

Traditionally there has been only a limited need for external communications from procurement except for those with the supply base. Managed external communications around sustainable procurement are a bit different and much more necessary. The same principles apply for the approach overall, except here our stakeholders are different groups and the purpose of the communication, and therefore our messaging and means, is very different. Blitzing those in the supply base and back up our supply chains with evangelical messaging about our sustainability programme, its goals and our expectations of everyone involved and by when, is vitally important. Remember our supplier code of conduct from Chapter 12? This is a key communications tool.

The corporate sustainability benefits report

Other external communications regarding sustainable procurement should be joined up and integral with wider marketing, brand value positioning and corporate reporting in this area. Organizations increasingly need to communicate what they are doing towards sustainability and are establishing entire new approaches. Whether it is a statement of commitments on a website or an entire new brand proposition, sustainability is now a key thread in a firm's marketing communications. Furthermore, sustainability reporting, whether driven by legislative obligation, shareholder expectations or what the company wants to do to demonstrate its work in this area, is already part of what large corporates do. It will become part of what every company does in coming years. A key challenge here is how to do this. As we have seen, sustainability requires measures way beyond traditional financial measures, so attempting to shoehorn something about sustainability into a corporate financial report doesn't quite work. Instead, as organizations embrace the new economic model of sustainability and organize themselves around the triple bottom line of people, planet and profit, this drives new corporate reporting.

Increasingly companies are electing to publish an annual corporate sustainability benefits report alongside a financial report. Our achievements in sustainable procurement form a core and compelling part of this overall story and so we need to organize ourselves to compile a regular sustainable procurement benefits report as a means to demonstrate the contribution of procurement and supply chain functions to the firm overall. Core to this are the positive impact stories along with other non-financial measures where qualitative results have been quantified in some way. Bringing these together and using infographics, good design and expert copywriting to tell a succinct overall story of how the organization is driving sustainable procurement can be immensely powerful. For example:

- 36% of all our supply chains are now fully sustainable
- 96% of workers in our remote factories now receive a living wage
- 3,200 tonne reduction in CO_2 in the last year increasing progress toward net zero by 2030 to 26%
- 1,016 new nursery places in developing countries created to enable women to work

- $856 of funding for community projects in developing countries
- Free contraception programme for all workers at African facilities to tackle the spread of HIV

The future is (possibly) bright

We started this book by considering situation planet Earth and the immense impacts and threats we face, some of which could ultimately drive the extinction of the human race. We considered how acutely critical our current situation is and the imperative for sustainability globally now, and how this translates at an organizational level and also into the detailed practical steps and actions we in procurement and supply chain functions will need to take.

Sustainability is no fad. There is no loophole and no get out of jail free card. There is no planet B. There are no credible arguments for deprioritizing or delaying sustainability in all its forms, only science-based imperatives to act fast. We have been trading off the planet and people against profit, living for today and putting off tacking critical problems into the future. Today we are still going at full steam while the buffers at the end of the tracks are looming ever larger.

It is easy to despair, to give up, get angry, assume governments will sort this or join the band of angry protestors gluing themselves to government buildings hoping it will achieve something. None of these responses will drive the change needed. Nor will it come from the action of governments alone.

Change is coming whether we like it or not

Greta Thunberg has not held back in telling the world leaders they are failing. Her impassioned speech to the 2019 UN Climate Action Summit made headline news worldwide and still, to this day, is regularly shown in current news stories and documentaries. Key to this speech was one line where she told world leaders that the world was waking up and that change is coming whether they liked it or not (PBS NewsHour, 2019).

Whatever you may think of her, what is clear is that she started a movement. This is key to understanding a deeper change that is happening right now, which is a shift in what we value and how this will drive profound change in coming years.

The established paradigm behind our global political and economic systems is based upon the belief that the world's resources, and our very limited remaining carbon emissions budget between now and 2050, would be exploited without the action of governments to manage them and prevent that which would benefit the few not the many. However, the economist and Nobel Prize winner Elinor Ostrom disproved this with robust field research suggesting that when there is a unifying cause it is not governments that drive change but instead change happens when communities come together and figure out systems to share a common resource. This would suggest that leaving governments to solve issues of sustainability is not the only way. Ostrom stated that community and cooperativity are bigger contributors to global well-being than governments (Ostrom, 2012). They transcend geopolitical tensions and power struggles, war, and can penetrate past autocracy. She has also explained how climate change in particular can be solved by more people stepping up to take charge rather than wait for governments to make policies and enact change (Rangamani, 2012).

Social movements drive action and can drive it globally. Across all the sustainability impacts, it is clear momentum is building. Yet there is more to this than a social movement but right now there is dawning realization that the very fabric of the economic system that makes the world turn is changing right in front of our eyes. This drives how organizations will survive and thrive and in particular the role of sustainable procurement to support them.

The new economics of sustainability

The triple bottom line concept we explored earlier is more than a nice idea but reflects how countries, societies and companies can secure new value and what will become the only viable value into the future. Our capitalist world is founded on the monetary value of assets with our economies and the financial markets built around this. We are already seeing the value of assets impacted making things tangible. This will worsen, but the worst is yet to come. If we continue to think in these terms alone, we are faced with a vast erosion in the monetary value of assets in coming years. With this comes the stark realization that sustainability now drives the future financial value of assets. Climate change predictions alone suggest a fivefold increase in property destruction. Rising sea levels will threaten assets worth 20–25 per cent of global GDP by the end of this century and the cost of climate change is set to equal the equivalent of no economic growth in global GDP growth for a decade (Carney, 2020). Then there is the future pre-financial cost of carbon. Based upon current projections the world has a limited budget of carbon left between now and 2050 in order to avert catastrophe. This is diminishing by the day. Those alive today have a remaining carbon budget equivalent to one-eighth of that of our grandparents (Carney, 2020). At current rates we will spend the entirety of this within a decade. This means a carbon tax is inevitable, which currently would suggest we would pay upwards of €120 per tonne of CO_2 we emit (OECD, 2021). Maintaining the world's living standards with our current economic systems, levels of production and consumption would require 1.7 Earths (Dasgupta, 2020). Suddenly traditional economics based solely upon the monetary value of assets falls short.

Our economic system has become self-limiting because our planet is finite, and it only takes into account that which is priced in the market. We do not value nature as an asset. The loss of species or value to our planet of rainforests, land for grazing or our oceans don't appear on a balance sheet. Yet as we have already seen, loss of nature gives us an asset management problem because our economy is part of, not separate from, nature. Furthermore, we do not place a value on people beyond a market cost to hire figure, nor do we place a value on how social cooperation can make incredible things happen that benefit many. In short, unless an economic system considers the whole ecosystem that it exists within, it cannot function effectively and has no longevity. So how do we change the global economic system away from one that is built around the monetary value of assets? Put simply, we don't need to because it is already happening around us, driven by forces other than governments and these changes are only just beginning.

What society values drives value

The economist and former Governor of the Bank of England Mark Carney argues that we should not fall into the trap of seeing sustainability as a burden. Instead that 'values drive value'. In other words what a society values can drive great new economic value.

Stop for a moment and ask yourself: what do you value and what does society value the most? Perhaps ten years ago we might have said things like prosperity, education, healthcare, etc. Today, however, the answer would be different. Today we are part of a global movement, not one that is organized and not one that is fully aligned in terms of what 'flavour of better' each member wants, and members don't all come together to agree things, but a movement nonetheless and one a with common purpose – to save our planet and ensure a good future for the next generations. This movement means our traditional economic value is being overtaken by a new economic model, one that potentially represents the greatest commercial opportunity of our time and one that is driven by delivering what society values. Net zero by 2050 and the hope it brings would almost certainly be top of the tree here, however, beyond this it is hard to put a hierarchy of importance in terms of what society might value. Take a moment to look back to the sustainable procurement framework towards the end of Chapter 6 and attempt to decide which goal is more important than another. It is almost impossible and that is because everything is interconnected and we are one single global interlinked and interdependent community, so we don't get to pick and choose, although we do have to prioritize. What society values therefore is a sustainable future in all its forms.

This is what will underpin the new economics of sustainability. The more society shares the conviction to drive sustainability for our planet and its people, the more what society values drives new economic growth and opportunity. Greater consumer demand for sustainable products drives investment in creating sustainable products and making supply chains sustainable. The challenges we face spark innovation to create new technology to solve current problems, which drive new industries that generate tax to fund the political investment in implementing green policies. When what society values drives how investors direct their money and what shareholders demand, socially responsible investment outperforms traditional investment ultimately driving what banks and investment funds finance. Suddenly what was once on the fringes gains traction and then gains momentum. Today this momentum is building all around us from the bottom up and along with it our traditional economic model based upon the monetary value of assets is also evolving into one that inherently values people and planet, along with profit.

How we are leading the charge

Organizational thinking must change in order to survive and thrive in a very different future. As those that govern nations grapple with how to make global cooperation happen and follow through on making commitments a reality, every organization will eventually be transformed by the requirements of new legislation. Until then organizations risk being left behind if they wait and fail to grasp the imperative to act right now. It is organizations that will drive Ostrom's community and cooperativity to drive change. Some will do this because they believe they have a responsibility to steward. For the rest, they will respond to the new economics of sustainability and the global movement behind it, or risk failure. It is industry that holds the potential to make the biggest difference and as we have seen throughout this book, sustainable procurement is a critical enabler to do this. Today, there is no question of whether or not to act, the only questions an organization faces today is how fast it should pivot and how far it needs to go.

The greatest and most critical opportunity.

In coming years, the plight towards sustainability will involve every nation, every company, in every sector and every citizen. It will profoundly change all our lives and especially those of future generations who will be impacted much more. The science is clear – 'do nothing' is not an option and so we must find the solutions needed to create a better future. Speed and scale will be critical, which means humankind is staring into the face of what is possibly the greatest and most critical opportunity it has ever had. Industry will drive this change within the shifting economic model I outlined earlier. Procurement and supply chain functions will play a central role and will need to function and contribute to realizing the strategic goals of organizations in entirely new ways to that we do today. Sustainable procurement must become how we do all things. There has never been a more exciting time to be in a procurement or supply chain function, but only for those who are forward thinking and ready for change and a new challenge.

Be ready and equipped for BIG change

Get ready for the ride of our lives followed by gargantuan change beyond anything that has ever gone before. First, as organizations embrace sustainable procurement our role will be figuring out how to tackle all the six impact areas hard and fast with well-enacted action that works to halt, reverse, reduce, repair, recover, replenish, protect, reestablish or do whatever else as needed to become sustainable. This book has been designed to do just that. But there is more. Second, procurement and supply chain will be a key strategic enabler across the many and varied new industries that will spring up before we can blink. The scale and speed of some of these will be eye-watering, with some driven by government directives, but mostly new growth will come from the new economic motivation of sustainability as I outlined above. Innovation and human ingenuity will lead the way with industries and new technologies, many of which have yet to be invented.

Covid-19 revealed new possibilities. During the height of the lockdown we benefited from 11,000 fewer deaths from air pollution in Europe alone, and 2020 saw the biggest ever percentage drop in CO_2 emissions. Commercial air traffic fell by 73.7 per cent compared to 2019 (Cuthbertson, 2020). Despite this reduction in air travel, much of what we do continued in one form or another. While few would want a return to that time, Covid-19 showed us what is possible.

Future energy will drive all our thinking with entire new industries for energy capture or generation and innovation in managing usage on the way. The moment we can move away from hydrocarbon energy to 100 per cent green energy then we take a big step in solving multiple impacts. One hundred per cent renewable of course, using much more solar, wind, tide, etc, but get ready for new ideas to enter the stage such as beaming electricity from space, harvesting energy at altitude or even from our own bodies. The 'electrification of everything' will define the next two decades and breakthroughs in electricity storage will change the game. We will see the biggest upgrade to power distribution systems that could ever be imagined. Get ready too for hydrogen energy storage to help provide short-term electricity storage solutions that bridge the gap between generation and consumption. Then there is energy usage and no longer will we consider energy as a cheap commodity but something precious with boundless innovation around energy efficiency in developed nations and new initiatives to subsidize electricity for developing nations so as to stimulate innovation – all driven by the new economic model of sustainability.

How we travel will change and the industries behind this will see great changes. The automotive industry and those that supply it will see one of the biggest shifts and opportunities as all output becomes EVs, potentially powered by different technologies to that which they are today. Sustainable aviation will become the only viable means of long-distance travel powered initially by sustainable jet fuel (a biofuel with reduced carbon emissions) and then by new propulsion systems and, if these are electric, new means to store the energy needed.

Get ready for huge global industries set up to reverse global warming and other impacts, using technologies that have not been invented yet. One technology that has is carbon capture – a means to literally suck the CO_2 out of the atmosphere. The technology is there but it is early days as currently it can only capture carbon in small amounts, yet it will scale and carbon capture plants may become a familiar sight around the world as an entire new global industry is born. Then there is solar geo-engineering based upon pioneering research from Harvard to put dust into the atmosphere to 'dial down the sun'.

Food and agriculture will be transformed. We will see new ways to overcome the heavy reliance on fertilizers and reduce water consumption. We will see new methods to quadruple yields so we can grow crops to feed the growing global population – hydroponics, growing vertically and genetically modified crops will be essential. Restoring the wild will go hand in hand with farming. We will eat less meat and serve up new sources of protein. Get ready for cultured meat (like meat but grown in a factory, not from an animal) and insect-based protein.

There will be many other new industries born out of the sustainability revolution. In addition, all industries will need new tools, new thinking and new approaches to manufacturing, how we use energy, how we build, heat or cool buildings. As water becomes more valuable, manufacturing processes will change to find new ways that need little or no water with circularity a prerequisite. Ozone or laser washing and other techniques will become key technologies.

The future of organizations to do this

We will be part of organizations that will evolve to work differently with sustainability as an enabling backbone. Sustainability will be a strategic imperative, if it is not already, with new measures of organizational success and a CSO – chief sustainability officer – setting the direction. Functional working will have to give way to a more matrix-based approach as the only way to drive the change and collaboration needed. The new organizational paradigm will be one of transformation, adaptability and persistence. Procurement will be there front and centre and as we transform how organizations buy, we will need new skills and we will be figuring out how to be effective in situations never before encountered. Supply chains will change beyond all recognition. As we move sourcing from one region to another, we will be opening up new as yet unfamiliar territories and changing how supporting supply chains work or integrating them altogether. Get ready too for buying where we never own the thing, just have use of it to serve our needs for a while – an alien concept today but an interesting circular concept and it might become part of how we make sustainability a success. Perhaps some packaging will remain the property of the supplier with a refundable deposit system incorporated into the price we pay so they can be sure they get it back from us.

Anything is possible

I opened this book with a story from my childhood, where I questioned something that didn't seem right. Without knowing it at the time I was calling out something we now know is unsustainable, but not seen as such at the time. I came to accept it based on others not seeing a problem and also the assumption that the people who run the world must know what they were doing. We have all made this assumption to one degree or another or believed the rhetoric that was really hiding the will for profit or economic prosperity. We now see things differently and globally we are starting to do something about all those car exhausts back in 1974 and a good many others besides. Perhaps the real question that a seven-year-old boy should have asked was 'how can we create a world where everyone can have a car, or the things they need, without it hurting the world of the future?' Back then that seven-year-old boy believed anything was possible. He still does.

The future is bright. In coming years we will be part of the largest transformative development since the industrial revolution or indeed ever. The science is clear and unambiguous about the criticality of our current situation yet science also shows us we can achieve a prosperous future if we can move simultaneously and collaborating at a global level to build resilience on a finite planet and uphold human rights. Sir David Attenborough suggests that a new industrial revolution powered by millions of sustainable innovations is under way. One where we will all share in the benefits. One that will deliver affordable clean energy, healthy air and enough food to sustain us all. He points out that no advanced nation is yet sustainable and at a global level we all have a journey ahead of us. He suggests that if we are to be successful that we need to learn together how to do this making sure no one gets left behind. Crucially, he suggests that we have an opportunity to create a world that is more equal and that we should not be motivated by fear but instead by hope (Attenborough, 2021a).

We all have a part to play in this, If you are a procurement or supply chain practitioner, hopefully this book has equipped you to know how you can play your part in the most critical global challenge and opportunity humankind has ever been faced with. Anything is possible if we work together with cooperativity and a common purpose. Anything is possible.

Chapter checkpoint

In this chapter we have concluded our journey through the OMEIA® sustainable procurement methodology and this book. Key points we covered were:

1 *Governance is essential* – sustainable procurement requires effective governance to make it happen. 5P provides the governance framework here and the basis for organizations to consider and plan for *People*, *Plan*, *Payoff*, *Proficiency* and *Promote*.

2 *The sustainable procurement road map (Plan)* is the combined short-, medium- and long-term plan of all the individual initiatives and projects along with the key supporting governance aspects by which we will realize our sustainable procurement goals. Good project management with dedicated resource here is essential.

3 *Measuring sustainable procurement outcomes (Payoff)* demands new approaches to that which has gone before to demonstrate benefits and progress towards our goals overall, for what we buy, with our suppliers and in our supply chains. Key to this is the use of positive impact stories to show the non-financial benefits achieved or possible and therefore supporting a business case for action.

4 *People and Proficiency* – sustainable procurement is an organization-wide concern and requires new thinking in structuring the team so separate functions work as if one, as well as ensuring the required capability for strategic procurement, sustainability, data analysis and others besides.

5 *Effective internal and external communications (Payoff)* for sustainable procurement requires a planned and managed approach with skilled dedicated resource supporting how the organization can demonstrate success and progress overall externally.

6 *The new economics of sustainability* – the traditional economic model based upon the monetary value of assets is giving way to a new model that recognizes financial assets exist within, and depend upon, nature and people, and will be impacted severely in coming years.
Furthermore, the new global movement for sustainability is driving huge new opportunity and creating new triple bottom line economics.

7 *A future of huge opportunity for procurement* – in coming years procurement faces huge opportunity to help make organizations sustainable with the supply chain often representing the greatest contribution. In addition, procurement and supply chain functions will play a central role in the many and varied enormous new industries that will spring up as the world around us changes.

8 *Anything is possible* – governments alone will not drive change but what has been proven to do this more effectively is when communities come together cooperatively. This means industry has the greatest role to play in driving sustainability and the movement behind the new economics of sustainability is already driving this.

APPENDIX

Sustainable procurement toolset

Key tools and templates to begin practising sustainable procurement

This appendix provides a collection of the essential tools and templates for practitioners to apply sustainable procurement. If you have purchased this book then you may copy and reproduce the tools within this appendix for your own personal use as you practise sustainable procurement. They may not be copied and distributed to others or used for commercial gain. They may not be modified and the copyright designation must remain in place.

For more information on corporate licensing of sustainable procurement process and toolsets please contact team@positivepurchasing.com.

Primary impact assessment

Organization	Date

Determine the severity for each of the six impact areas considering what the company does internally and externally, directly and indirectly, across the entire end-to-end supply and value chain network. Rate each between 1 and 5 (5 being significant impact). Plot on the graph and joint the dots to give the 'primary impact area'

Rationale and basis for determination

Areas for further assessment or to baseline

The six impact areas:
- People and communities
- Data & digital
- Loss of biodiversity
- Climate change
- Ocean degradation
- Resource depletion & waste

Axes: People / Planet

Scale: 1 Low — 5 High

© Positive Purchasing Ltd 2022

Stakeholder expectation map

Organization: Date:

#	Stakeholder group	Means of engagement	Interest areas, what they value and expectations	Influence	Consult	Inform	Listen	How we will manage this group ongoing
1								
2								
3								
4								
5								
6								
7								
8								
9								
10								
11								
12								
13								
14								

© Positive Purchasing Ltd 2022

Sustainable procurement strategy, goals and targets

Sustainable procurement strategy, goals and targets should flow from wider organizational vision and goals for sustainability. Determine the strategy and how we will organize ourselves to do this. Then determine the high-level goals (general statements of med–long-term ambition) and the short–medium-term SMART targets

Date

Sustainable procurement strategy

Sustainable procurement targets | By when?

1
2
3
4
5
6
7
8
9
10
11
12
13
14

Sustainable procurement goals

1
2
3
4
5
6

© Positive Purchasing Ltd 2022

SSTP *(Sustainability Situation, Target, Proposal)*

Start with the problem statement or the situation or issue we are considering. Determine everything we know about the current situation. Then determine SMART targets for where we need to be and the proposal for next steps and how we move forward.

Date

Problem statement

Situation

S

Target

T

Proposal

P

© Positive Purchasing Ltd 2022

PESTLE analysis

Determine the trends, changes, drivers, forces, opportunities or risks with the focus of sustainability

Scope or area

Date

PESTLE analysis insights – 'so what does this tell us?'

P *Political*

E *Economic*

S *Sociological*

T *Technological*

L *Legal*

E *Environmental*

© Positive Purchasing Ltd 2022

GHG emissions map

Item being assessed: _____   Date: _____

	Step/area	Calculation notes	Emissions by mass		OR	Emissions by spend		Total CO$_2$e
			Mass+unit	Emissions factor	CO$_2$e	Spend+currency	Spend factor	CO$_2$e	
1									
2									
3									
4									
5									
6									
7									
8									
9									
10									
11									
12									
13									
14									

For a product, service, supply or supply chain, list each of the steps or inputs (raw materials, electricity, transportation, etc). For each, based upon information available, determine whether to calculate emissions by mass or spend. For each, enter either the mass (e.g. of the raw materials consumed) and units or spend and currency. Find the emissions or spend factors (available via internet search) and calculate the CO$_2$e. Capture key notes and then determine to the total CO$_2$e.

© Positive Purchasing Ltd 2022

Risk and contingency planning

Scope or area | Date

Identify all the potential sustainability risks. For each, determine the likelihood of it happening (use a simple high/medium/low system. Then determine the severity should this risk happen. For each assessed risk determine the mitigating or contingency action in response, assign an owner and list by when it must be achieved.

	Risk	Likelihood (H/M/L)	Severity (H/M/L)	Priority	Action	Owner	By When
1							
2							
3							
4							
5							
6							
7							
8							
9							
10							
11							
12							
13							
14							

© Positive Purchasing Ltd 2022

Sustainable procurement fact-find plan

Focus areas: product, service, supplier, market, supply chain or multiple

For (scope of plan): _____ By: _____

#	Focus area	Data to collect	How data will be collected	By whom	By when
1					
2					
3					
4					
5					
6					
7					
8					
9					
10					
11					
12					
13					
14					
15					

© Positive Purchasing Ltd 2022

Prioritization heat cube

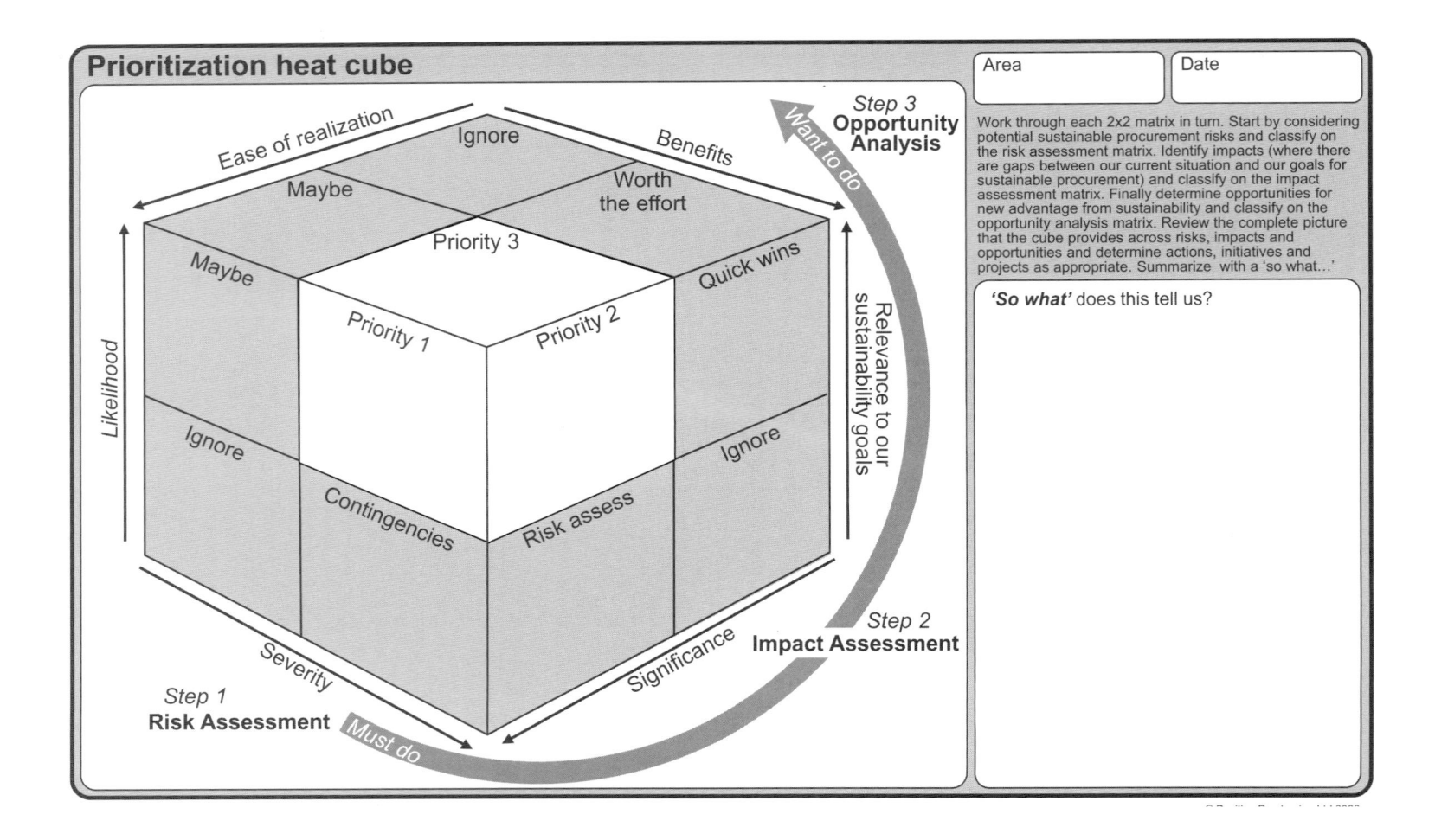

Area	Date

Work through each 2x2 matrix in turn. Start by considering potential sustainable procurement risks and classify on the risk assessment matrix. Identify impacts (where there are gaps between our current situation and our goals for sustainable procurement) and classify on the impact assessment matrix. Finally determine opportunities for new advantage from sustainability and classify on the opportunity analysis matrix. Review the complete picture that the cube provides across risks, impacts and opportunities and determine actions, initiatives and projects as appropriate. Summarize with a 'so what…'.

'So what' does this tell us?

Step 3 Opportunity Analysis — Want to do

- Benefits: Quick wins / Ignore
- Worth the effort / Risk assess
- Ignore / Contingencies
- Ease of realization
- Maybe / Ignore
- Priority 1, Priority 2, Priority 3

Step 2 Impact Assessment — Significance

Step 1 Risk Assessment — Must do

- Severity
- Likelihood

Relevance to our sustainability goals

Day One analysis

| Category/product | Date |

Classify the categories or individual products using the matrix below, then determine the insight (or 'so what does this tell us?'). If in 'Proprietary' determine what circumstances have placed the category or product(s) there and what would be needed to move out of this quadrant.

Insights ('so what does this tell us?')

	Generic	
Tailored		
Custom	**Proprietary**	

Number of suppliers — One ← → More than one

Number of customers — One ← → More than one

Potential actions to improve our position

© Positive Purchasing Ltd 2022

Sustainability business requirements

Under each heading determine the individual requirements for sustainability. Phrase these precisely and as SMART as possible, so we can know when it is satisfied. For each, determine if it is a need or want, and if now or future.

Category/Product/Service:

Date:

	Requirements	Need?	Want?	Now?	Future?
R Regulatory	1 2 3				
A Assurance of supply	1 2 3				
Q Quality	1 2 3				
S Service	1 2 3				
C Cost/ commercial	1 2 3				
I Innovation	1 2 3				

© Positive Purchasing Ltd 2022

Sustainability product breakdown

Supplementary to any PPCA 'should cost' analysis

Product/Service

Materials	Risks, impacts and opportunities	Potential changes required
1		
2		
3		
4		
5		
6		
7		
8		

Other drivers

1 People		
2 Processing		
3 Logistics & transportation		
4 Overheads		
5 Profit		

'So what does this tell us' – what needs to happen next?

© Positive Purchasing Ltd 2022

Attribute analysis

Determine comparative attributes for the product or service. Determine how the product, or multiple products, measures up against each of the attributes. Where relevant, determine a target for each attribute and drive improvements. Ask 'so what?'

Product/Service

	Attribute	Target	Product/Service 1	Product/Service 2	Product/Service 3	Product/Service 4
1						
2						
3						
4						
5						
6						
7						
8						
9						
10						
11						
12						

So what? – findings and summary of improvements to be made

© Positive Purchasing Ltd 2022

Sustainable value engineering

Work through the eight phases and for each of the areas to consider assess how sustainable what we buy is within the context of what it gets incorporated into or used for.

Product/Service (what we buy): _____ Created by: _____

	Design	Supply side		Our organization			Customer side	
Product (or service) design and life cycle	1 - Design	2 - Original sources	3 - Supply chains and inbound logistics	4 - Acquisiton	5 - Use or consumption and/or processing by us	6 - Outbound logistics and downstream chain	7 - Consumption or use	8 - End of life
Possible areas to consider	Specification, materials, processes involved, life expectancy, in-use efficiency, maintainability	Materials, commodities, location, what happens there, treatment of people, how sustainable it is long term	Miles travelled, suppliers involved, locations, treatment of people, processes, efficiency of logistics	How we specify and define requirements, contractual obligations, efficient ordering (quantities, packaging, etc)	Efficiency, processes involved, sustainable utilization, treatment of our people, our impact on the planet and communities	Miles travelled, efficiency of logistics, impact of what we do/supply with downstream players	How sustainable in use, efficiency, long lasting? Does it promote or hinder sustainability?	Waste produced, recycling, reusing, repurposing

Part 1 – Category, product or service design and life cycle sustainability assessment

Sustainable for...	Yes Med Low Not	Yes Med Low Not	Yes Med Low Not	Yes Med Low Not	Yes Med Low Not	Yes Med Low Not	Yes Med Low Not	Yes Med Low Not
Use of resources								
Emissions/CO_2e								
Waste								
Pollution								
Biodiversity								
People/Comm'ties								
Data & digital								
Other _____								
Notes re assessment								

Part 2 – Sustainable value engineering

Potential changes to create new sustainability value and move towards a more sustainable product

© Positive Purchasing Ltd 2022

Sustainability relationship requirements

Under each of the headings determine the requirements for sustainability from this supplier, and the specific value needed from the relationship. Ensure alignment to overall sustainability goals. For each, determine if it is a need or want, and now or future.

Supplier			Date	

	Requirements	Need?	Want?	Now?	Future?
R *Risk*	1				
	2				
	3				
E *Effectiveness of operations*	1				
	2				
	3				
P *Performance improvement*	1				
	2				
	3				
I *Innovation*	1				
	2				
	3				
V *Value by working together*	1				
	2				
	3				

© Positive Purchasing Ltd 2022

Supply chain sustainability map

| Supply chain | Date |

Map the supply chain (or SVCN) – identify the key supply chains and identify each entity. Identify what happens there and how things move or flow between entities. When complete, review and determine risks, impacts and opportunities by considering the chain using each of the lenses in turn. Mark up on the map where these are.

Supply chain map

Additional data gathering required

Data required	How	Who

Summary of findings – 'so what?'

Key

Type of finding
- ◇ Opportunity
- — Impact
- ✖ Risk

Lens
- R Use of resources
- CO₂ Emissions/CO₂e
- W Waste
- Po Pollution
- B Biodiversity
- PC People & communities
- D Data and digital

GLOSSARY

B2B business-to-business relationship, interaction or transaction.

B2C business-to-consumer relationship, interaction or transaction.

EBITDA earnings before interest, taxes, depreciation and amortization. Used as a measure of a firm's overall financial performance.

EV electric vehicle.

GHG greenhouse gas.

KPI key performance indicator. A measure of performance determined as very important, possibly combining a number of measures to create insightful information.

Lean The established practice of considering how to deliver value with fewer resources. It is based upon continuous experimentation to ultimately achieve perfection in terms of value delivery with zero waste.

NGO non-governmental organization. Typically not-for-profit associations, lobby groups, charities or organizations active in environmental or humanitarian support.

RFI/RFP/RPQ request for information/proposal/quotation. Means of soliciting specific responses from suppliers.

Six Sigma A quality management methodology for process improvement, which focuses on reducing variability within manufacturing and therefore improves quality. The process was conceived by American engineer Bill Smith during his time with Motorola in the 1980s.

SMART specific, measurable, achievable, realistic and timebound. Key criteria for goal setting, i.e. create goals that meet all of these criteria and you have a sound basis to know when you have reached your goal.

REFERENCES

Abrams, A (2019) Here's what we know so far about Russia's 2016 meddling, *Time*, 18 April https://time.com/5565991/russia-influence-2016-election/ (archived at https://perma.cc/FPX4-3WEB)

Abubakar, M, Manzoor, S and Iqbal, A (2018) Introductory chapter: Animal welfare – global perspective, in *Animal Welfare*, eds M Abubakar and S Mansoor, IntechOpen, www.intechopen.com/books/6473 (archived at https://perma.cc/TQ5E-P37M)

Aidt, T S (2010) Corruption and sustainable development, in *International Handbook on the Economics of Corruption: Volume 2*, eds S Rose-Ackerman and T Søreide, 3–51, Edward Elgar, Cheltenham

Amnesty International (nd) Discrimination, www.amnesty.org/en/what-we-do/discrimination/ (archived at https://perma.cc/264L-T26P)

Anderson, J (2019) How much platinum is in the world? SD Bullion, 31 August, https://sdbullion.com/blog/how-much-platinum-is-in-the-world (archived at https://perma.cc/87EX-7FZY)

Anti-Slavery International (nd) What is modern slavery? www.antislavery.org/slavery-today/modern-slavery/ (archived at https://perma.cc/L87S-VYC5)

Arsenault, C (2014) Only 60 years of farming left if soil degradation continues, *Scientific American*/Reuters, 5 December, www.scientificamerican.com/article/only-60-years-of-farming-left-if-soil-degradation-continues/ (archived at https://perma.cc/72NC-D3XS)

Assembly of First Nations (2022) http://www.afn.ca (archived at https://perma.cc/9LTM-R5L7)

Attenborough, D (2020a) *Extinction: The facts*, BBC Studios Science Unit

Attenborough, D (2020b) *A Life on Our Planet: My witness statement and a vision for the future*, Witness Books, London

Attenborough, D (2021a) COP26 Climate Summit opening speech, 1 November, www.rev.com/blog/transcripts/david-attenborough-cop26-climate-summit-glasgow-speech-transcript (archived at https://perma.cc/5JU5-EYQR)

Backus, B L, McGlone, J J and Guay, K (2014) Animal welfare: stress, global issues, and perspectives, in *Encyclopedia of Agriculture and Food Systems, Vol 1*, ed N Van Alfen, 387–402, Elsevier, San Diego

Baker, L (2020) More than 1 billion people face displacement by 2050 – report, Reuters, 16 September, www.reuters.com/article/ecology-global-risks-idUSKBN2600K4 (archived at https://perma.cc/GJM7-UNJD)

Ball, J (2018) The anatomy of a click: what happens to your data online, *Huffington Post*, 9 October, www.huffingtonpost.co.uk/entry/what-happens-when-you-click_uk_5bb60455e4b028e1fe3b43a3 (archived at https://perma.cc/8PLB-QBD9)

Baxter, A (2020) Bolivian indigenous people lose out on lithium, Human Rights Pulse, 29 August, www.humanrightspulse.com/mastercontentblog/bolivian-indigenous-people-lose-out-on-lithium (archived at https://perma.cc/X6XE-LNDR)

BBC (2021) Greta Thunberg says 'many loopholes' in COP26 pact, BBC News, 15 November, www.bbc.co.uk/news/uk-scotland-glasgow-west-59296859 (archived at https://perma.cc/SB5K-KCTC)

Bechtel, C and Jayaram, J (1997) Supply chain management: A strategic perspective, *The International Journal of Logistics Management*, 8 (1), 15–34

Biello, D (2014) E-waste dump among top 10 most polluted sites, *Scientific American*, 1 January, www.scientificamerican.com/article/e-waste-dump-among-top-10-most-polluted-sites/ (archived at https://perma.cc/4V39-832A)

Boardman, A, Geng, J and Lam, B (2020) The social cost of informal electronic waste processing in Southern China, *Administrative Sciences*, 10 (1), 7, https://doi.org/10.3390/admsci10010007 (archived at https://perma.cc/K9KA-SWCQ)

Bodley, J H (2015) *Victims of Progress*, 6th edn, Rowman & Littlefield, London

Bové, A and Swartz, S (2016) Starting at the source: sustainability in supply chains, *McKinsey on Sustainability & Resource Productivity*, 4, 36–43

BusinessWire (2018) TD Ameritrade launches socially aware portfolios, expanding access to ESG investing, 6 September, www.businesswire.com/news/home/20180906005134/en/TD-Ameritrade-Launches-Socially-Aware-Portfolios-Expanding-Access-to-ESG-Investing (archived at https://perma.cc/W5WG-Q4D9)

Carney, M (2020) From climate crisis to real prosperity: How we get what we value, The Reith Lectures, Episode 4, BBC

Carroll, A B and Shabana, K M (2010) The business case for corporate social responsibility: A review of concepts, research and practice, *International Journal of Management Reviews*, 12 (1), 85–105, https://doi.org/10.1111/j.1468-2370.2009.00275.x (archived at https://perma.cc/J2AY-3G5U)

Castelvecchi, D (2021) Electric cars and batteries: how will the world produce enough? *Nature*, 17 August, www.nature.com/articles/d41586-021-02222-1 (archived at https://perma.cc/S5SQ-NB6B)

CBP (2021) CBP modifies forced labor finding on Top Glove Corporation Bhd, US Customs and Border Protection, 9 September, www.cbp.gov/newsroom/national-media-release/cbp-modifies-forced-labor-finding-top-glove-corporation-bhd (archived at https://perma.cc/VJ88-WJD7)

Chêne, M (2014) The impact of corruption on growth and inequality, Transparency International, www.transparency.org/files/content/corruptionqas/Impact_of_corruption_on_growth_and_inequality_2014.pdf (archived at https://perma.cc/FYZ4-EWWR)

Christopher, M (2016) *Logistics and Supply Chain Management*, 5th edn, Pearson, Harlow

CO$_2$ Everything (nd) The carbon footprint of everyday products and activities, www.co2everything.com (archived at https://perma.cc/E9MS-88WE)

CoastAdapt (2017) Ocean acidification and its effects, 27 April, https://coastadapt.com.au/ocean-acidification-and-its-effects (archived at https://perma.cc/9FUY-FXJT)

Conservation International (2022) Explore the biodiversity hotspots, CEPF, www.cepf.net/our-work/biodiversity-hotspots (archived at https://perma.cc/DQ2A-6CZK)

Cordell, D (nd) The story of phosphorus: 7 reasons we why we need to transform phosphorus use in the global food system, PhosphorusFutures, http://phosphorusfutures.net/the-phosphorus-challenge/the-story-of-phosphorus-8-reasons-why-we-need-to-rethink-the-management-of-phosphorus-resources-in-the-global-food-system/ (archived at https://perma.cc/7LYV-SUW2)

Cox, D (2019) The planet's prodigious poo problem, *The Guardian*, 25 March, www.theguardian.com/news/2019/mar/25/animal-waste-excrement-four-billion-tonnes-dung-poo-faecebook (archived at https://perma.cc/L3UA-82D3)

Crippa et al (2020) Fossil CO$_2$ emissions of all world countries, JRC Science for Policy Report, European Commission, https://edgar.jrc.ec.europa.eu/report_2020 (archived at https://perma.cc/32XS-V8F5)

Curran, D (2018) Are you ready? Here is all the data Facebook and Google have on you, *The Guardian*, 30 March, www.theguardian.com/commentisfree/2018/mar/28/all-the-data-facebook-google-has-on-you-privacy (archived at https://perma.cc/W46C-DYJA)

Cuthbertson, A (2020) Coronavirus tracked: what the biggest collapse in air pollution levels ever recorded actually looks like, *Independent*, 4 June, www.independent.co.uk/news/coronavirus-pollution-environment-lockdown-carbon-emissions-charts-a9510636.html (archived at https://perma.cc/HCS9-RBRG)

Dasgupta, P (2020) The Dasgupta Review – Independent Review on the Economics of Biodiversity: Interim Report, HM Treasury, UK https://assets.publishing.service.gov.uk/government/uploads/system/uploads/attachment_data/file/882222/The_Economics_of_Biodiversity_The_Dasgupta_Review_Interim_Report.pdf (archived at https://perma.cc/MMN3-XBHG)

Desjardins, J (2014) A forecast of when we'll run out of each metal, Visual Capitalist, 4 September, www.visualcapitalist.com/forecast-when-well-run-out-of-each-metal/ (archived at https://perma.cc/BHF2-EJJW)

Ecoact (2022) *The Big eBook of Sustainability Reporting Frameworks 2022*, Ecoact/Atos, https://eco-act.com (archived at https://perma.cc/M6PA-AA5R)

Ellen MacArthur Foundation (2022) ellenmacarthurfoundation.org (archived at https://perma.cc/7JYC-XVUJ)

Encyclopedia.com (2021) Landfills, www.encyclopedia.com/environment/energy-government-and-defense-magazines/landfills (archived at https://perma.cc/W6ZV-QP9W)

References

EPA (2021) Wastes: What are the trends in wastes and their effects on human health and the environment? United States Environmental Protection Agency, www.epa.gov/report-environment/wastes (archived at https://perma.cc/7SUQ-BY79)

Eurofound and ILO (2019) Working conditions in a global perspective, Publications Office of the European Union, Luxembourg and International Labour Organization, Geneva, www.ilo.org/wcmsp5/groups/public/---dgreports/---dcomm/---publ/documents/publication/wcms_696174.pdf (archived at https://perma.cc/ZSX4-D2PN)

European Aluminium (2020) Vision 2050: European Aluminium's contribution to the EU's mid-century low-carbon roadmap, 15 October, https://european-aluminium.eu/wp-content/uploads/2022/10/sample_vision-2050-low-carbon-strategy_20190401.pdf (archived at https://perma.cc/6GMD-JH9P)

Eurostat (2019) Municipal Waste Statistics, December, https://ec.europa.eu/eurostat/statistics-explained/index.php?title=Municipal_waste_statistics#Municipal_waste_generation (archived at https://perma.cc/PMJ9-4G6H)

Fabris, P (2018) Global construction waste to almost double by 2025, Building Design+Construction, 22 March, www.bdcnetwork.com/global-construction-waste-almost-double-2025 (archived at https://perma.cc/AJX5-LM8K)

Feng, H (2021) Making and unmaking of Guiyu: The global center of e-waste, Duke University Graduate Liberal Studies, March, https://dukespace.lib.duke.edu/dspace/bitstream/handle/10161/23313/Harper%27s%20MP%20revised%201.pdf?sequence=1&isAllowed=y (archived at https://perma.cc/N3PT-XDWT)

Fortune Business Insights (2021) Mining waste management market size, share & COVID-19 impact analysis by source, by waste type, by commodity and regional forecast, 2021–2028, June, www.fortunebusinessinsights.com/industry-reports/mining-waste-management-market-101369 (archived at https://perma.cc/RXV7-FLCE)

Fraser Institute (2021) Economic Freedom of the World: 2021 Annual Report, www.fraserinstitute.org/resource-file?nid=14251&fid=16574 (archived at https://perma.cc/H8SB-VY3M)

Freedom House (2021a) Freedom on the Net 2021: The global drive to control big tech, https://freedomhouse.org/sites/default/files/2021-09/FOTN_2021_Complete_Booklet_09162021_FINAL_UPDATED.pdf (archived at https://perma.cc/KD9T-VDJL)

Freedom House (2021b) Nations in Transit 2021: The antidemocratic turn, https://freedomhouse.org/sites/default/files/2021-04/NIT_2021_final_042321.pdf (archived at https://perma.cc/PRX9-9ZQ9)

Friedman, M (1962) *Capitalism and Freedom*, University of Chicago Press, Chicago

Friedman, M (1970) A Friedman doctrine – the social responsibility of business is to increase its profits, *The New York Times Magazine*, 13 September, www.nytimes.com/1970/09/13/

archives/a-friedman-doctrine-the-social-responsibility-of-business-is-to.html (archived at https://perma.cc/89DG-9RVT)

Gates, B (2021) *How to Avoid a Climate Disaster: The solutions we have and the breakthroughs we need*, Allen Lane & Penguin Random House, UK

GHG Protocol (2022) Corporate Value Chain (Scope 3) Accounting and Reporting Standard, https://ghgprotocol.org/standards/scope-3-standard (archived at https://perma.cc/52RM-U4P3)

Giattino, C and Ortiz-Ospina, E (2020) Do workers in richer countries work longer hours? Our World in Data, 21 December, https://ourworldindata.org/rich-poor-working-hours (archived at https://perma.cc/28GM-9AH8)

Gillenwater, M (2022) What is a global warming potential? And which one do I use?, GHG Management Institute, 28 June, https://ghginstitute.org/2010/06/28/what-is-a-global-warming-potential/ (archived at https://perma.cc/3UMJ-XA7G)

Global Sustainable Investment Alliance (2020) Global Sustainable Investment Review 2020, www.gsi-alliance.org/wp-content/uploads/2021/08/GSIR-20201.pdf (archived at https://perma.cc/PRW2-HMVZ)

Goncalves, A (2019) It was bad and it's getting worse: Melting permafrost is contributing to climate change too, Youmatter, 17 June, https://youmatter.world/en/permafrost-melting-climate-change-28697/ (archived at https://perma.cc/VE7B-GX3R)

gov.uk (2022) UK and England's carbon footprint to 2019, 3 November, www.gov.uk/government/statistics/uks-carbon-footprint (archived at https://perma.cc/336A-NZRE)

Gradinger, G (2009) *Ready for Supplier Relationship Management? A tool for a structured approach*, VDM Verlag Dr Müller Aktiengesellschaft & Co KG

Graedel, T E and Cao, J (2010) Metal spectra as indicators of development, *Proceedings of the National Academy of Sciences*, 107 (49), 20905–10

Granovetter, M (1985) Economic action and social structure: The problem of embeddedness, *American Journal of Sociology*, 91 (3), 481–510

Granskog, A, Lee, L, Magnus, K H and Sawers, C (2020) Survey: Consumer sentiment on sustainability in fashion, McKinsey & Company, www.mckinsey.com/industries/retail/our-insights/survey-consumer-sentiment-on-sustainability-in-fashion (archived at https://perma.cc/26GA-VTL5)

Hawn, O (2021) How media coverage of corporate social responsibility and irresponsibility influences cross-border acquisitions, *Strategic Management Journal*, 42 (1), 58–83

Healy, C (2021) Uyghur Surveillance & Ethnicity Detection Analytics in China: Expert report presented to the Uyghur Tribunal, IVPM, 20 August, https://uyghurtribunal.com/wp-content/uploads/2022/01/UT-211217-Conor-Healy.pdf (archived at https://perma.cc/FTA7-CNCK)

Heffer, G (2021) G7 summit: Sir David Attenborough presses leaders to show the 'global will' to tackle climate change, *Sky News*, 15 June, news.sky.com/story/

References

g7-summit-attenborough-to-tell-g7-leaders-they-face-biggest-climate-change-decisions-in-human-history-12331232 (archived at https://perma.cc/F6GB-G75B)

Henckens, M L C M et al (2016) Mineral resources: Geological scarcity, market price trends, and future generations, *Resources Policy*, 49, 102–11

Hiddink, J G et al (2017) Global analysis of depletion and recovery of seabed biota after bottom trawling disturbance, *Proceedings of the National Academy of Sciences*, 114 (31), 8301–6

Houston, D A (2007) Can corruption ever improve an economy? *Cato Journal*, 27 (3), www.cato.org/sites/cato.org/files/serials/files/cato-journal/2007/11/cj27n3-2.pdf (archived at https://perma.cc/Y7DD-NE7T)

IEA (2021) World energy balances overview: World, International Energy Agency, www.iea.org/reports/world-energy-balances-overview/world (archived at https://perma.cc/U7F9-LPGN)

ILO (2002) *Combating Child Labour: A handbook for labour inspectors*, International Labour Office, 1 December, www.ilo.org/ipec/Informationresources/WCMS_IPEC_PUB_2619/lang--en/index.htm (archived at https://perma.cc/77UZ-ACYX)

ILO (2021) Exposure to hazardous chemicals at work and resulting health impacts: A global review, International Labour Organization, www.ilo.org/wcmsp5/groups/public/---ed_dialogue/---lab_admin/documents/publication/wcms_811455.pdf (archived at https://perma.cc/Q2GL-93L4)

ILO (nda) ILO Indicators of Forced Labour, International Labour Office, www.ilo.org/wcmsp5/groups/public/---ed_norm/---declaration/documents/publication/wcms_203832.pdf (archived at https://perma.cc/XQK4-QWUE)

ILO (ndb) What is child labour, International Labour Organization, www.ilo.org/ipec/facts/lang--en/index.htm (archived at https://perma.cc/RRY7-LXZK)

IPBES (2019) The global assessment report on biodiversity and ecosystem services of the Intergovernmental Science-Policy Platform on Biodiversity and Ecosystem Services, eds S Díaz et al. IPBES Secretariat, Bonn, Germany

IPCC (2021) Climate Change 2021: The physical science basis, Intergovernmental Panel on Climate Change, https://report.ipcc.ch/ar6/wg1/IPCC_AR6_WGI_FullReport.pdf

ITUC (2021) 2021 ITUC Global Rights Index: The world's worst countries for workers, International Trade Union Confederation, https://files.mutualcdn.com/ituc/files/ITUC_GlobalRightsIndex_2021_EN_Final.pdf (archived at https://perma.cc/ATT8-57JZ)

ITUC (2022) 2022 ITUC Global Rights Index, International Trade Union Confederation, www.globalrightsindex.org/en/2022 (archived at https://perma.cc/D4VR-32R7)

Jambeck, J R et al (2015) Plastic waste inputs from land in to the ocean, *Science*, 347 (6223), 768–71

Johnson, T, E, Howard, M & Miemczyk, J (2019) Purchasing and Supply Chain Management, Routledge

Kaplan, R and Norton, D (1996) *The Balanced Scorecard: Translating strategy into action*, Harvard Business School Press, Boston

Kneese, A V (1988) The economics of natural resources, *Population and Development Review*, 14, 281–309

Korhonen, J, Nuur, C, Feldmann, A and Birkie, S E (2018) Circular economy as an essentially contested concept, *Journal of Cleaner Production*, 175, 544–52, https://doi.org/10.1016/j.jclepro.2017.12.111 (archived at https://perma.cc/5AB4-WVVZ)

Kunzmann, K (2021) WHO, China report suggests COVID-19 passed from bats to humans through another animal, ContagionLive, 29 March, www.contagionlive.com/view/who-china-report-covid-19-passed-bats-humans-animal (archived at https://perma.cc/7TMP-MLDE)

Kurucz, E, Colbert, B and Wheeler, D (2008) The business case for corporate social responsibility, in *The Oxford Handbook of Corporate Social Responsibility*, eds A Crane, A McWilliams, D Matten, J Moon and D Siegel, 83–112, Oxford University Press, Oxford

Langridge, H (2022) Patagonia: The environmentally responsible brand, Tiso, www.tiso.com/blog/patagonia-sustainable-brand (archived at https://perma.cc/WHL5-XFV8)

Le Quéré, C et al (2016) Global carbon budget 2016, *Earth System Science Data*, 8, 605–49, https://doi.org/10.5194/essd-8-605-2016 (archived at https://perma.cc/9MTY-LTZZ)

Liker, J K and Choi, T Y (2004) Developing deep supplier relationships, *Harvard Business Review*, December, https://hbr.org/2004/12/building-deep-supplier-relationships (archived at https://perma.cc/W4LN-29Z8)

Lis, J (2020) Was there Russian meddling in the Brexit referendum? The Tories just didn't care, *The Guardian*, 21 July, www.theguardian.com/commentisfree/2020/jul/21/russian-meddling-brexit-referendum-tories-russia-report-government (archived at https://perma.cc/WDX9-E92T)

Longrich, N R (2020) Will Humans go extinct? For all the existential threats, we'll likely be here for a very long time, *The Conversation*, 5 May, https://theconversation.com/will-humans-go-extinct-for-all-the-existential-threats-well-likely-be-here-for-a-very-long-time-135327 (archived at https://perma.cc/G5B5-4MA8)

Lustgarten, A (2020) The great climate migration, *New York Times*, 23 July, www.nytimes.com/interactive/2020/07/23/magazine/climate-migration.html (archived at https://perma.cc/WYA6-QWWA)

Mauro, P (1997) Why worry about corruption? International Monetary Fund, www.imf.org/external/pubs/ft/issues6/ (archived at https://perma.cc/93PC-P6K5)

McAleese, S and Kilty, J M (2019) Stories matter: Reaffirming the value of qualitative research, *The Qualitative Report*, 24 (4), 822–45

McShane, K (2018) Why animal welfare is not biodiversity, ecosystem services, or human welfare: toward a more complete assessment of climate impacts, *Les ateliers de l'éthique/The Ethics Forum*, 13 (1), 43–64

References

Méon, P G and Weill, L (2008) Is corruption an efficient grease? BOFIT Discussion Paper No. 20/2008, https://papers.ssrn.com/sol3/papers.cfm?abstract_id=1304596 (archived at https://perma.cc/22ZN-X5UD)

Meredith, S (2021) A sand shortage? The world is running out of a critical – but under-appreciated – commodity, CNBC, 5 March, www.cnbc.com/2021/03/05/sand-shortage-the-world-is-running-out-of-a-crucial-commodity.html (archived at https://perma.cc/RNN9-AKGU)

Metro (2020) Brits have 55,000,000 unused mobile phones lying around, research finds, 26 November, https://metro.co.uk/2020/11/26/brits-have-55000000-unused-mobile-phones-lying-around-research-says-13657334/ (archived at https://perma.cc/7JRM-MBDS)

Miemczyk, J, Johnsen, T and Macquet, M (2012) Sustainable purchasing and supply management: A structured literature review of definitions and measures at the dyad, chain and network levels, *Supply Chain Management*, 17 (5), 478–96

Milinchuk, A (2021) The growth of sustainable investing, Yahoo! Finance, 5 September, https://finance.yahoo.com/news/growth-sustainable-investing-190000841.html (archived at https://perma.cc/W2AT-6UC9)

Mittermeier, R A et al (2002) *Wilderness: Earth's last wild places*, CEMEX, Mexico City

Mittermeier, R A et al (2003) Wilderness and Biodiversity Conservation, *Proceedings of the National Academy of Sciences*, 100 (18), 10309–13, www.pnas.org/doi/10.1073/pnas.1732458100#fig2 (archived at https://perma.cc/5PBB-U6F4)

Mittermeier, R A et al (2004) *Hotspots Revisited. Earth's biologically richest and most endangered terrestrial ecoregions*, CEMEX, Mexico City

Myers, N (1988) Threatened biotas: 'Hot spots' in tropical forests, *The Environmentalist*, 8 (3), 187–208

Myers, N (1990) The biodiversity challenge: Expanded hot-spots analysis, *The Environmentalist*, 10 (4), 243–56

Myint, U (2000) Corruption: causes, consequences and cures, *Asia-Pacific Development Journal*, 7 (2), 33–58, UN ESCAP, www.unescap.org/sites/default/d8files/apdj-7-2-2-Myint.pdf (archived at https://perma.cc/N4WG-JU75)

NIRS (nd) The global nuclear waste crisis, Nuclear Information and Resource Service, www.nirs.org/the-global-nuclear-waste-crisis/ (archived at https://perma.cc/CH3W-Q2ED)

Nisen, M (2013) How Nike solved its sweatshop problem, Insider, 10 May, www.businessinsider.com/how-nike-solved-its-sweatshop-problem-2013-5?r=US&IR=T (archived at https://perma.cc/A2RX-J2VF)

NIWA (nd) How can carbon emissions can be weighed? https://niwa.co.nz/atmosphere/faq/how-can-carbon-emissions-be-weighed (archived at https://perma.cc/FK6R-5UHX)

NS Energy (2021) Profiling the world's eight largest cobalt-producing countries, 22 February, www.nsenergybusiness.com/features/top-cobalt-producing-countries/ (archived at https://perma.cc/VF2W-5TLH)

References

Nunez, C (2019) Climate 101:Deforestation, *National Geographic*, www.nationalgeographic.com/environment/article/deforestation (archived at https://perma.cc/SJN4-EK74)

OECD (2021) Effective Carbon Rates 2021, https://www.oecd.org/tax/tax-policy/effective-carbon-rates-2021-brochure.pdf (archived at https://perma.cc/SYF3-LLLD)

Ord, T (2021) *The Precipice: Existential risk and the future of humanity*, Bloomsbury Publishing, London

Ostrom, E (2012) *The Future of The Commons: Beyond market failure and government regulation*, The Institute of Economic Affairs, London

Parkinson, C N (1957) *Parkinson's Law and Other Studies in Administration*, Houghton Mifflin, Boston

Patagonia (2021) Patagonia Works – Annual Benefit Corporation Report: Fiscal Year 2021, www.patagonia.com/on/demandware.static/-/Library-Sites-PatagoniaShared/default/dw18ad9c7c/PDF-US/Patagonia-2021-BCorp-Report-Updated-2-15-22.pdf (archived at https://perma.cc/4HXG-AGKS)

Patagonia (2022) https://eu.patagonia.com/gb (archived at https://perma.cc/9BF3-FCKF)

Pattisson, P (2021) US bars rubber gloves from Malaysian firm due to 'evidence of forced labour', *The Guardian*, 30 March, www.theguardian.com/global-development/2021/mar/30/us-bars-rubber-gloves-malaysian-firm-top-glove-evidence-forced-labour (archived at https://perma.cc/5RBH-HL37)

PBS NewsHour (2019) WATCH: Greta Thunberg's full speech to world leaders at UN Climate Action Summit (online video) 23 September, www.youtube.com/watch?v=KAJsdgTPJpU (archived at https://perma.cc/7297-TMS5)

Pendrill, F et al (2019) Deforestation displaced: trade in forest-risk commodities and the prospects for a global forest transition, https://iopscience.iop.org/article/10.1088/1748-9326/ab0d41 (archived at https://perma.cc/L9J3-7GQH)

Persson, L et al (2022) Outside the safe operating space of the planetary boundaries for novel entities, *Environmental Science & Technology*, 56 (3), 1510–21, https://pubs.acs.org/doi/10.1021/acs.est.1c04158 (archived at https://perma.cc/WC57-FW6F)

Picarsic, N (2020) Risky business: the hidden costs of EV battery raw materials, *Automotive World*, 23 November, www.automotiveworld.com/articles/risky-business-the-hidden-costs-of-ev-battery-raw-materials/ (archived at https://perma.cc/5EGT-NL3G)

Porritt, J (2005) *Capitalism as if the World Matters*, Earthscan, London

Porter, M E (1985) *Competitive Advantage: Creating and sustaining superior performance*, Free Press, New York

Porter, M E and Kramer, M R (2002) The competitive advantage of corporate philanthropy, *Harvard Business Review*, 80 (12), 56–69.

Posner, E (2014) The case against human rights, *The Guardian*, 4 December www.theguardian.com/news/2014/dec/04/-sp-case-against-human-rights (archived at https://perma.cc/8RK3-HPAE)

References

Rangamani, P (2012) How people collaborate – a tribute to Elinor Ostrom, American Association for the Advancement of Science, 10 August, www.aaas.org/how-people-collaborate-tribute-elinor-ostrom (archived at https://perma.cc/7R7H-YM24)

Rich, N (2016) The lawyer who became DuPont's worst nightmare, *New York Times Magazine*, 6 January, www.nytimes.com/2016/01/10/magazine/the-lawyer-who-became-duponts-worst-nightmare.html (archived at https://perma.cc/V5RZ-3FDW)

Ritchie, H (2017) How much of the world's land would we need in order to feed the global population with the average diet of a given country?, Our World in Data, 3 September, https://ourworldindata.org/agricultural-land-by-global-diets (archived at https://perma.cc/Z73X-H73E)

Ritchie, H and Roser, M (2018) Plastic pollution, Our World in Data, September, https://ourworldindata.org/plastic-pollution (archived at https://perma.cc/F3LF-NYQL)

Ritchie, H, Roser, M and Rosado, P (2020) CO_2 and greenhouse gas emissions, Our World in Data, August, https://ourworldindata.org/co2-and-other-greenhouse-gas-emissions (archived at https://perma.cc/N27Q-W4SN)

Robertson, L (2022) How ethical is Nike?, Good On You, 29 June, https://goodonyou.eco/how-ethical-is-nike/ (archived at https://perma.cc/9CBD-7F2G)

Rockström, J and Klum, M (2015) *Big World Small Planet*, Yale University Press, New Haven, CT

Rollet, C (2021) Uyghur Tribunal PRC Verdict: 'Invasive Surveillance' are 'Crimes Against Humanity', IVPM, 9 December, https://ipvm.com/reports/uyghur-xinjiang-ruling (archived at https://perma.cc/R8UH-8HC2)

Roser, M, Ritchie, H, Ortiz-Ospina, E and Rodés-Guiraco, L (2019) World population growth, Our World in Data, https://ourworldindata.org/world-population-growth (archived at https://perma.cc/2SK8-BCH4)

Rowlatt, J (2021) Bill Gates: Solving Covid easy compared with climate, BBC News, 15 February, www.bbc.co.uk/news/science-environment-56042029 (archived at https://perma.cc/T5UY-FZE9)

Ruz, C (2011) The six natural resources most drained by our 7 billion people, *The Guardian*, 31 October, www.theguardian.com/environment/blog/2011/oct/31/six-natural-resources-population (archived at https://perma.cc/3CYG-V9KE)

Sedex (nd) Key legislation driving responsible business, www.sedex.com/blog/key-legislation-driving-responsible-business/ (archived at https://perma.cc/HA7F-CHB8)

Sensoneo (2019) Global Waste Index, https://sensoneo.com/global-waste-index-2019/ (archived at https://perma.cc/T8HS-UJTQ)

Sensoneo (2022) Global Waste Index, https://sensoneo.com/global-waste-index/ (archived at https://perma.cc/B2XT-DGDW)

Shaheed, A and Richter, R P (2018) Is 'human rights' a Western concept? IPI Global Observatory, 17 October, https://theglobalobservatory.org/2018/10/are-human-rights-a-western-concept/ (archived at https://perma.cc/S8GC-VBZT)

Spreckley, F (1981) *Social Audit: A management tool for co-operative working*, Beechwood College

Staal, A (2021) The business case is positive – evaluating ten procurement strategies for implementing sustainable procurement in New Zealand organisations, working paper, Auckland University of Technology, New Zealand

Statista (2022) Share of sustainable shopping behaviors among UK shoppers in 2022, www.statista.com/statistics/1056522/sustainable-shopping-behavior-of-uk-shoppers/ (archived at https://perma.cc/B4VJ-D3N7)

Steele, P T and Court, B H (1996) *Profitable Purchasing Strategies: A manager's guide for improving organizational competitiveness through the skills of purchasing*, McGraw Hill, London

Steffen, W et al (2015) Planetary boundaries: Guiding human development on a changing planet, *Science*, 347 (6223), www.science.org/doi/epdf/10.1126/science.1259855 (archived at https://perma.cc/NR6V-U8BQ)

Stockholm Resilience Centre (2022) Planetary Boundaries www.stockholmresilience.org/research/planetary-boundaries.html (archived at https://perma.cc/55S9-XQ7G)

Stronberg, J (2017) Sand mining part 2: the story of a conflict mineral, Resilience, 17 April, www.resilience.org/stories/2017-04-17/sand-mining-part-2-the-story-of-a-conflict-mineral/ (archived at https://perma.cc/8QLS-L8DA)

SwissRe Institute (2020) Biodiversity and Ecosystem Services – A business case for re/insurance, www.swissre.com/dam/jcr:a7fe3dca-c4d6-403b-961c-9fab1b2f0455/swiss-re-institute-expertise-publication-biodiversity-and-ecosystem-services.pdf (archived at https://perma.cc/S2Q8-987F)

Symrise Vanilla (nd) https://vanilla.symrise.com (archived at https://perma.cc/57TA-TWZA)

The Economist (2009) Triple bottom line – it consists of three Ps: profit, people and planet, 17 November, www.economist.com/news/2009/11/17/triple-bottom-line (archived at https://perma.cc/FL7Y-WU77)

The Economist (2022) The green boom – hot air, 22–28 May, 12

The World Counts (2021a) World population, www.theworldcounts.com/populations/world/effects-of-overpopulation (archived at https://perma.cc/VL86-2MKF)

The World Counts (2021b) Tons of hazardous waste thrown out, www.theworldcounts.com/challenges/planet-earth/waste (archived at https://perma.cc/WQ3L-TFGC)

Thunberg, G (2019) *No One is Too Small to Make a Difference*, Penguin Books, London

Top Glove (nd) Continuous improvement report, www.topglove.com/continuous-improvement-report/Transparency (archived at https://perma.cc/88MX-FP4H)

Transparency nternational (2017) People and Corruption: Citizens' voices from around the world, Global Corruption Barometer, 14 November, www.transparency.org/en/publications/people-and-corruption-citizens-voices-from-around-the-world (archived at https://perma.cc/682S-9HTL)

References

Transparency International (2020) Corruption perception index, www.transparency.org/en/cpi/2020 (archived at https://perma.cc/844N-ZNK9)

UN (2011) Guiding Principles on Business and Human Rights, United Nations, www.ohchr.org/sites/default/files/documents/publications/guidingprinciplesbusinesshr_en.pdf (archived at https://perma.cc/B2XV-QVU6)

UN (2016) The First Global Integrated Marine Assessment: World Ocean Assessment I, Division for Ocean Affairs and the Law of the Sea, www.un.org/regularprocess/content/first-world-ocean-assessment (archived at https://perma.cc/7SHQ-DURT)

UN (2021) The Second World Ocean Assessment: World Ocean Assessment II, Division for Ocean Affairs and the Law of the Sea, www.un.org/regularprocess/woa2 (archived at https://perma.cc/HB78-3MGN)

UN (2022a) The 17 goals, United Nations, Department of Economic and Social Affairs, Sustainable Development, https://sdgs.un.org/goals (archived at https://perma.cc/T8MT-ZM3K)

UN (2022b) For a liveable climate: Net-zero commitments must be backed by credible action, United Nations, www.un.org/en/climatechange/net-zero-coalition (archived at https://perma.cc/F3A5-XQUV)

UN (nd) Human rights, www.un.org/en/global-issues/human-rights (archived at https://perma.cc/MJ73-VFBP)

UN Global Compact (2022a) Living wage, www.unglobalcompact.org/what-is-gc/our-work/livingwages (archived at https://perma.cc/879U-88MT)

UN Global Compact (2022b) The ten principles of the UN Global Compact, www.unglobalcompact.org/what-is-gc/mission/principles (archived at https://perma.cc/G2TU-74VJ)

UNEP (2015) Global Waste Management Outlook, UN Environment Programme, www.unep.org/resources/report/global-waste-management-outlook (archived at https://perma.cc/4QD5-67KV)

UNEP (2018) Single-use plastics: A roadmap for sustainability, UN Environment Programme, 5 June, www.unep.org/resources/report/single-use-plastics-roadmap-sustainability (archived at https://perma.cc/KC47-B3TD)

UNEP (2022) Our planet is choking on plastic, UN Environment Programme, www.unep.org/interactives/beat-plastic-pollution/ (archived at https://perma.cc/Q59W-MK5G)

US Geological Survey (nd) How much gold has been found in the world? www.usgs.gov/faqs/how-much-gold-has-been-found-world? (archived at https://perma.cc/JJV8-UNQM)

US News & World Report (2022) Best countries for racial equality, www.usnews.com/news/best-countries/best-countries-for-racial-equality (archived at https://perma.cc/HYN6-WUEG)

US SIF Foundation (2020) Sustainable and impact investing – overview, www.ussif.org//Files/Trends/2020%20Trends%20Report%20Info%20Graphic%20-%20Overview.pdf (archived at https://perma.cc/M6KS-N3HW)

USDOL (2022) 2022 List of Goods Produced by Child Labor or Forced Labor, US Department of Labor, www.dol.gov/sites/dolgov/files/ILAB/child_labor_reports/tda2021/2022-TVPRA-List-of-Goods-v3.pdf (archived at https://perma.cc/5VPM-LC29)

Utrecht University (2021) Half of global waste water treated, rates in developing countries still lagging, EurekAlert! 8 May, www.eurekalert.org/news-releases/711446 (archived at https://perma.cc/3XUZ-YRVR)

Vignesh, K S, Rajadesingu, S and Arunachalam, K D (2021) Challenges, issues, and problems with zero-waste tools, in *Concepts of Advanced Zero Waste Tools: Present and emerging waste management practices*, ed C M Hussain, 69–90, Elsevier, www.sciencedirect.com/topics/earth-and-planetary-sciences/industrial-waste (archived at https://perma.cc/L7VP-VM3X)

Villena, V H and Gioia, D A (2020) A more sustainable supply chain, *Harvard Business Review*, march–April, https://hbr.org/2020/03/a-more-sustainable-supply-chain (archived at https://perma.cc/A4Y6-A6PW)

Visram, T (2021) ESG investing continued to soar in 2021. The government could boost it even more, *Fast Company*, 28 December, www.fastcompany.com/90706552/esg-investing-continued-to-soar-in-2021-the-government-could-boost-it-even-more (archived at https://perma.cc/A45J-4TLP)

Wakefield, J (2021) AI emotion-detection software tested on Uyghurs, BBC News, 26 May, www.bbc.co.uk/news/technology-57101248 (archived at https://perma.cc/XK8W-XGHF)

Walker, H and Brammer, S (2009) Sustainable procurement in the United Kingdom public sector, *Supply Chain Management*, 14 (2),128–37

Whelan, T and Fink, C (2016) The comprehensive business case for sustainability, *Harvard Business Review*, 21 October

WHO (2021) WHO/ILO: almost 2 million people die from work-related causes each year, World Health Organization, 17 September, www.who.int/news/item/16-09-2021-who-ilo-almost-2-million-people-die-from-work-related-causes-each-year (archived at https://perma.cc/7MS6-G27Y)

Wight, A (2019) Scientists around the world are turning agricultural waste into food, packaging and skincare products, GreenBiz, 17 May, www.greenbiz.com/article/scientists-around-world-are-turning-agricultural-waste-food-packaging-and-skincare-products (archived at https://perma.cc/ED2L-JBM9)

Wikipedia (nda) Agbogbloshie, https://en.wikipedia.org/wiki/Agbogbloshie (archived at https://perma.cc/GP9P-B8AV)

Wikipedia (ndb) *Dark Waters* (2019 film), https://en.wikipedia.org/wiki/Dark_Waters_(2019_film) (archived at https://perma.cc/W6VY-HS9V)

Wolfe, I (2022) How ethical is Patagonia? Good On You, 23 February, https://goodonyou.eco/how-ethical-is-patagonia/ (archived at https://perma.cc/ARJ4-6R35)

References

World Bank (2018) Global waste to grow by 70 percent unless urgent action is taken: World Bank Report, 20 September, www.worldbank.org/en/news/press-release/2018/09/20/global-waste-to-grow-by-70-percent-by-2050-unless-urgent-action-is-taken-world-bank-report (archived at https://perma.cc/R6L7-EUR3)

World Economic Forum (2021) Global Gender Gap Report: Insight report, March, www3.weforum.org/docs/WEF_GGGR_2021.pdf (archived at https://perma.cc/69AT-K4A7)

World Health Organization (2016) *Ambient air pollution: A global assessment of exposure and burden of disease*, WHO Press

World Health Organization (2018) Health-care waste, 8 February, www.who.int/news-room/fact-sheets/detail/health-care-waste (archived at https://perma.cc/RWT2-FVH8)

World Meteorological Organization (2022) United in Science 2022: A multi-organization high-level compilation of the latest climate science information, https://public.wmo.int/en/resources/united_in_science (archived at https://perma.cc/W5PZ-9HA6)

World Population Review (2022a) Average workweek by country 2022, https://worldpopulationreview.com/country-rankings/average-work-week-by-country (archived at https://perma.cc/KDT7-5724)

World Population Review (2022b) Most corrupt countries 2022, https://worldpopulationreview.com/country-rankings/most-corrupt-countries (archived at https://perma.cc/PV5V-PX8Q)

World Population Review (2022c) Most racist countries 2022, https://worldpopulationreview.com/country-rankings/most-racist-countries (archived at https://perma.cc/9J3E-6EA8)

World Population Review (2022d) Freedom index by country 2022 https://worldpopulationreview.com/country-rankings/freedom-index-by-country (archived at https://perma.cc/FXW3-LRBZ)

Worldometer (2022) CO2 Emissions by country, www.worldometers.info/co2-emissions/co2-emissions-by-country/WWF (archived at https://perma.cc/4VEB-3PC9) (nd) Deforestation and forest degradation, www.worldwildlife.org/threats/deforestation-and-forest-degradation (archived at https://perma.cc/YM26-K6DP)

Yang, Y and Murgia, M (2019) Data leak reveals China is tracking almost 2.6m people in Xinjiang, *Financial Times*, 17 February, www.ft.com/content/9ed9362e-31f7-11e9-bb0c-42459962a812 (archived at https://perma.cc/99RB-KDRF)

INDEX

Page numbers in *italic* indicate figures or tables.

3R approach (Reduce, Reuse, Recycle) 183
3S model 308
5A SRM methodology 120
5P governance framework 209–10,
    439–50, *440*
  Payoff 450
  People 439
  Plan 442, 444
  Proficiency 444, 447
  Promote 444, 467
5S SRM methodology 120, 122
1984 87

AA1000 180
AccountAbility 180
Agbogbloshie Waste Dump 43
air pollution 21, 473
Amazon 84
American Convention on Human Rights
    1969 50
animal welfare 45–46
antimoney 33, 43
asbestos 68
Assessing low-Carbon Transition (ACT)
    178
assessment, of suppliers 366–400, 413
  accreditation 383–84
  areas to assess 367
  assessment, defining 368
  auditing 384–400
    arrival, your 392–93
    audit checklist 387–88, *388–92*
    audit, defining 368
    child / forced labour 397–98
    cooperation of supplier 386, 394–95
    findings, categories of 396
    local reps, using 398–400
    mini-audits 384
    preparation for 393
    safety 393–94
  code of conduct 371–72, 467
  'inside-out' assessment 375, 377–80
    qualitative vs quantitative data 377
    success factors 379–80
  minimum requirements 370–71, *372–74*
  'outside-in' assessment 375, *376*

prioritization heat cube, the 368
quality management systems 367
skills for 385–86, 449
third-party providers, using 380–83
  benefits of 381
  drawbacks of 381–82
types of *369*
assessment, sustainability 215–68
  GHG emissions, analysing 257–68, 272
    CO_2 equivalent (CO_2e) 190, 258,
        409
    'down on the ground' assessment
        264–65
    emissions factor, determining an 260
    example analysis 266, *267*
    Global Warming Potential (GWP)
        258
    'helicopter hot spot view' assessment
        263
    mass, measuring 259–60
    net zero, reaching 267–68, 472
    throughout the SVCN 261–63, *265*
  hot spot analysis 224, 226–57, 272, 415
    biodiversity loss 237, 255, *256*
    geography hot spots 226, 236–37,
        238–55
    information, sources of 226–29
    process hot spots 224, 233–34,
        233–34, 235–36
    process of 255, *257*
    product hot spots 224, 229–30,
        230–32
  measurement, importance of 216–17
  PESTLE analysis 219, 221–24, 272,
    415–16
    areas to consider *222–24*
    example PESTLE analysis *225*
    process of 221
  remote assessment 217
  SSTP tool (Sustainability Situation,
    Target, Proposal) 217, 219, *220*,
    270, 272
AT&T 154
Attenborough, David 97, 98, 476
attribute analysis 325–30, *322, 461*
  applications for 326

Index

comparability 327–28
possible attributes *330–31*
process of 329
tangible vs intangible attributes 326

B&Q 230
baby boomers 144
Balanced Scorecard 189
Ballinger, Jeff 138
Basel Convention 1992 42, 43
Bekasi 43
biodiversity, loss of 10–13, 99
   biodiversity hot spots 237, 255, *256*
   causes of *11*
   climate change, impact of 12, 18, 26, 92
   defining 10
   deforestation 10, 12
   impacts of 12–13
Black Lives Matter (BLM) movement 61
blockchain 433–34
blood diamonds 54, 231
Bloomberg 380
'boiling the ocean' 271
bonded labour 51
bottom trawling 15
BP Deepwater Horizon oil spill 138
Branson, Richard 188
Brexit 95
bribery / corruption 71–76
   and culture 72
   forms of 74–76
   impact on sustainability 72–73
Brundtland Commission 115
built-in obsolescence 41–42
business case, making a 123–60, *146*, 445–47
   compliance, regulatory 127, 129–37
      organizational level, the 129–30
      supply chain level, the 130–37, *131–35*
   cost of sustainability 126–27
   growth / advantage 145, 147–48
      B2B businesses 147–48
      B2C businesses 147
      corporate philanthropy 155
      innovation 148
      unique selling proposition (USP), your 147
   hierarchy of sustainability 127, *128*
   investment, securing 156–57
      costs 157
   logic, inarguable 447, *448*
   motivational hierarchy, the *128*, 273
   risk management 137–40
      reputational damage 138–39
      supply failure 137–38
      supply-side risk areas 139, *140*
   shareholder demands 141–45
      public companies 145
      socially responsible investments (SRIs) 112, 142–45, *143*
   stakeholder expectations 125, 148–51
      communities 151
      consumers 150
      employees 150–51
   sustainability initiatives *158*, 158–60
      non-financial benefits 158–59
      positive impact stories 159–60
   sustainability vs profit 123–24
   value creation 151–56
      altruism, 'true' 155
      'corporate philanthropy' 151, 154–55
      Patagonia 153–54
'wobble', preventing 446
business requirements, and procurement 316–21
   process for defining 320–21
   RAQSCI model (Regulatory, Assurance of supply, Quality, Service, Cost, Innovation) 316–17, *319*, 325, 329, 347, 352, 460
   stakeholder questions *321–22*
Business Responsibility and Sustainability Reporting 133
Buyer's Toolkit, The 2

capability, building for sustainability 447, 449
capitalism 103, 104
carbon dioxide (CO2) 19, 39, 258, 259
   carbon capture 268, 474
   CO2 equivalent (CO2e) 190, 258, 409
   and deforestation 12
   Global Warming Potential (GWP) 258
   measuring emissions of 167, 170, 258–61, 378
      life cycle emissions 262
      supply-side 387, 429, 466
   net zero, reaching 23, 170, 267, 429
   and oceans 15–16
   and permafrost 25
   phosphorus mining 37
   top emitters by percentage 21, *22*
   Volkswagen scandal 138
carbon tax 471
Carbon Trust 228
Carnegie, Andrew 154
Carney, Mark 471
category management 119, 402

Index

5i® Category Management 119, 310–12, *313*
    and competitive position 311–12
    vs relationship-based procurement 312
Category Management in Purchasing 2, 119, 298, 310, 314, 322
CDP 180, 381
    CDP Climate 380
challenges, of sustainable procurement 113–14
change management 449–50
chemicals, toxic 68
Chernobyl 17
child labour 1, 43, 55–59, 93
    addressing 57–58
    auditing for 397–98
    Child Labour Due Diligence Act 133
    child slavery 51
    Minimum Age Convention 1973 (ILO Convention 138) 55
    types of 57
    Worst Forms of Child Labour Convention (ILO Convention 182) 55
circular economy, the 45, 112, 177, 182–86, *184*
    3R approach (Reduce, Reuse, Recycle) 183
    guiding principles 183, 185
    New Circular Economy Action Plan 183
climate change 8, 19–26, 99, 166
    and animal welfare 46
    and biodiversity loss 12, 18, 26, 92
    causes of 20
    climate change migrants 25–26
    commitments, meeting 23–24
    defining 19
    financial impact of 470
    global agenda, the 170
    global warming 19
    net zero, reaching 267–68
    and ocean degradation 15, 18, 92
    Paris Agreement 19, 23, 170
    renewable energy 21
    water cycle, impact on 25
Climate Disclosure Standards Board (CDSB) 144, 180
Climate Reporting and Performance (CRP) 144
CO2 Everything 228
cobalt 30
    and child labour 58–59
code of conduct, supplier 371–72, 467
communication, planning 467–69
    annual report 468–69
    stakeholders, determining 467
communities 76–79
    business impacts on 78
    First Nations people 79
competitors, working with 429
compliance, regulatory 127, 129–37
    organizational level, the 129–30
    supply chain level, the 130–37, *131–35*
conflict minerals 53–54
    Conflict Minerals Regulation 134
contracts, supplier 352–55, 430–32
    sustainability improvements, incentivizing 354–55, 423, 435–36
    wording, importance of 353–54
COP21 *see* UN Climate Change Conference 2015 (COP21)
COP26 *see* UN Climate Change Conference 2021 (COP26)
COP27 *see* UN Climate Change Conference 2022 (COP27)
copper 35
Corporate Due Diligence and Corporate Accountability Directive 136
Corporate Duty of Vigilance Law 134, 136
corporate responsibility (CR) 112
corporate social irresponsibility (CSI) 138–39
corporate social responsibility (CSR) 112
Corporate Sustainability and Reporting Directive (CSDR) 135, 192
Corporate Sustainability Due Diligence (CSDD) 135, 192
cost, of sustainability 126–27
Countering America's Adversaries Through Sanctions Act 2017 (CAATSA) 132
Covid-19 pandemic 12–13, 137
    corporate philanthropy 154
    emissions, impact on 19, 473–74
    global workforce size, impact on 63
    and racism 60–61
    and SRIs 142
    working conditions, impact on 70
cronyism 74
cryptocurrency 433–34
cybercrime 83–84

Dark Waters 76–77
data exploitation 97
data privacy / protection 84–88
    data collection, invisible 84–85
    profiling, intelligent 87–88
    'programmatic advertising' 85–87

Index

data science 447
Day One analysis 314, *315*
digital world, the *80*, 81–88, 95–97
    cybercrime 83–84
    data exploitation 97
    data privacy / protection 84–88
        data collection, invisible 84–85
        profiling, intelligent 87–88
        'programmatic advertising' 85–87
    internet censorship 82–83, 94
    overseas, risk from 96
    personal data, value of 81–82
direct discrimination 59
discrimination 59–61
    gender inequality 60, 66
    racism 60–61
Dodd-Frank Act 54
Dow Jones Sustainability Index (DJSI) 180
drag net fishing 15
DuPont 76–77

EBITDA (earnings before interest, taxes, depreciation, and amortization) 186
EcoVadis 178, 381
electric vehicles (EVs) 30
    cobalt supply for 58–59
Elkington, John 186
Ellen MacArthur Foundation 183
'embeddedness' 104
embezzlement 76
Energy Savings Opportunity Scheme (ESOS) 131
environmental, social and governance (ESG) 112, 142, 144
ESG Book 380
ESG Sustainalytics 380
ethical business 112
European Convention on Human Rights (ECHR) 50
European Green Taxonomy 180
Eurostat 227
e-waste 42–44
exhaust gases 8
extortion 76

Facebook 84, 87
Fair Labor Association (FLA) 153
fast fashion 41
FedCenter 226
First Nations people 79, 145
fishbone diagrams 358
'five whys', the 358
Floyd, George 60, 61
food waste 38

forced labour 51, 229, 237
    auditing for 397–98
Ford 154
fossil fuels 21, 32, 145, 185
frameworks, for sustainability
    AA1000 180
    Assessing low-Carbon Transition (ACT) 178
    CDP 180, 381
    circular economy, the 112, 177, 182–86, *184*
        3R approach (Reduce, Reuse, Recycle) 183
        guiding principles 183, 185
        New Circular Economy Action Plan 183
    Climate Disclosure Standards Board (CDSB) 144, 180
    Declaration on Fundamental Principles and Rights at Work 1998 (updated 2022) 179, 190, 380
    Dow Jones Sustainability Index (DJSI) 180
    EcoVadis 178, 381
    European Green Taxonomy 180
    FTSE4Good 180
    GHG Protocol, the 177, 178, *195*, *196*, 228
    global destination sustainability index 178
    Global Reporting Initiative (GRI) 144, 178
    Global Standard Index 180, 380, 381
    GRESB 178
    Guidelines for Multinational Enterprises 179
    Integrated Reporting (IR) 180
    ISO 14001 181, 383–84
    ISO 14064 181, 195
    ISO 20400 177, 181, 195, 197, 383
    ISO 26000 177, 181, 194, 383
    ISO 50001 182
    PAS 2050 182
    PAS 2060 182
    Science Based Targets initiative (SBTi) 170, 178
    Stakeholder Capitalism Metrics 144, 179
    Sustainability Accounting Standards Board (SASB) 144, 181
    sustainable procurement
        framework 197–204, *198*
        expanded goals *199–204*
    Task Force on Climate-related Financial Disclosures (TCFD) 181

triple bottom line (profit / people / planet) 186–90, *187*
   Balanced Scorecard 189
   metrics 189–90
UN Declaration on the Rights of Indigenous Peoples 179
UN Global Compact 177, 179, 190–91, 373
UN Guiding Principles 177, 179, 191–92, 373
UN Principles for Responsible Investment (PRI) 144, 181
UN Sustainable Development Goals (SDGs) 169, 177, 179, 190, 192–94, *193*, 197
Fraser Institute 227
Freedom House 228
Friedman, Milton 123, 152, 155, 186
FTSE4Good 180
FTSE Russell 380
Fukushima 17
'functional awareness' 422

G7 summit 98
gallium 35
Gellert, Ryan 153
Generation X 144
Generation Z 144
genetic modification of crops 475
global agenda, the 169–71
   global targets 170
Global Atlas of Environmental Justice 227
Global Corruption Barometer 227
global destination sustainability index 178
Global Reporting Initiative (GRI) 144, 178
Global Rights Index 229
Global Warming Potential (GWP) 258
goals for sustainable procurement, setting 206, *207*
Good On You 229
Google 84, 87
graft 76
Granovetter's continuum 104, *105*
green capitalism 112
greenhouse gases (GHGs) 19, 206
   Covid-19, impact of 473–74
   emissions, analysing 257–68, 272
      CO2 equivalent (CO2e) 190, 258, 409
      'down on the ground' assessment 264–65
      emissions factor, determining an 260
      example analysis 266, 267
      Global Warming Potential (GWP) 258
      'helicopter hot spot view' assessment 263
      mass, measuring 259–60
      net zero, reaching 267–68, 472
      throughout the SVCN 261–63, 265
   GHG Protocol, the 177, 178, 195, *196*, 228
   hydrofluorocarbons (HFCs) 259
   methane 19, 25, 39, 44, 258, 259
   nitrogen trifluoride (NF3) 259
   nitrogen, impact on 99
   nitrous oxide (N2O4) 19, 259
   Paris Agreement 19, 23, 170
   perfluorocarbons (PFCs) 259
   process hot spots 233–34
   sulfur hexafluoride (SF6) 259
   supply chain, contribution of 113
   top emitters by percentage 21, *22*
GRESB 178
Guiyu dump 43–44

helium 33
help, hurt, heroes approach 342
hierarchy of sustainability 127, *128*
hot spot analysis 224, 226–57, 272, 415
   biodiversity loss 237, 255, *256*
   geography hot spots 226, 236–37, *238–55*
   information, sources of 226–29
   process hot spots 224, 233–34, *233–34*, *235–36*
   process of 255, 257
   product hot spots 224, 229–30, *230–32*
hours, long 68–69
humanity, future of 91–92
human rights 49, 50–76, 103
   blood diamonds 54, 231
   bribery / corruption 71–76
      and culture 72
      forms of 74–76
      impact on sustainability 72–73
   child labour 1, 43, 55–59, 93
      addressing 57–58
      auditing for 397–98
      Minimum Age Convention 1973 (ILO Convention 138) 55
      types of 57
      Worst Forms of Child Labour Convention (ILO Convention 182) 55
   conflict minerals 53–54
   discrimination 59–61
      gender inequality 60, 66
      racism 60–61
   European Convention on Human Rights (ECHR) 50

Index

future of 92–95
    autocracies, rise in 94–95, 98
Human Rights Act 1998 50
investor focus on 144
modern slavery 51–53
    forms of 51
    signs of 52
sand mafia, the 54–55
Universal Declaration of Human Rights (UDHR) 50, 93–94, 190, 373
working conditions 61–71, 62, 235–36
    job quality 66–67, 70–71
    physical hazards 63–65, 67–69
    wages 66, 69–70
    workers' rights 65, 69
    working environment 65–66, 67–69
Human Rights Act 1998 50
Human Rights Environmental Due Diligence (HREDD) 134
human trafficking 51, 52
hydrofluorocarbons (HFCs) 259

impact assessment 277–79
    impact assessment and prioritization matrix 278, *280*
    process of 279
incineration 44
indirect discrimination 59
indium 34
infographics 468
'injelititus' 446
'inside-out' assessment 375, 377–80
    qualitative vs quantitative data 377
    success factors 379–80
Integrated Reporting (IR) 180
intergenerational responsibility 112
Intergovernmental Science-Policy Platform on Biodiversity and Ecosystem Services (IPBES) 227
intermediaries 424–26
    types of 424–25
International Labour Organization (ILO) 228
    Declaration on Fundamental Principles and Rights at Work 1998 (updated 2022) 179, 190, 380
    Minimum Age Convention 1973 (Convention 138) 55
    Worst Forms of Child Labour Convention (Convention 182) 55
International Organization for Standardization (ISO)
    ISO 9001 367, 383
    ISO 14001 181, 383–84
    ISO 14064 181, 195

ISO 20400 177, 181, 195, 197, 383
ISO 26000 177, 181, 194, 383
ISO 50001 182
internet censorship 82–83, 94
intersectional discrimination 59
investment, securing 156–57
    costs 157
Ishikawa diagrams 358
ISS-oekom 381
ISS Ratings and Rankings 380

keiretsu 428
key performance indicators (KPIs) 456, 459, 464
kickbacks 74
Kneese, Allen 183
Kyoto Protocol 258

landfill 44
lead, in exhaust fumes 7–8
Lean 120
Legislative Decree No 254 133
Lieferkettensorgfaltspflichtengesetz (Supply Chain Due Diligence Act) 133, 136
lithium 30
lobbying 75
logic, inarguable 447, *448*

Mandatory Greenhouse Gas Reporting (MGHGR) 131
Mazars 192
measurement, of sustainability 450–66
    benefit types 457–58
    components of 455
    importance of 216–17
    key performance indicators (KPIs) 456, 459, 464
    measuring system, process of designing a 453–54
    performance indicators 456
    positive impact stories 456, 458–59
    products / services 460–63
        total cost of ownership (TCO) 461, 462
        total impact of ownership (TIO) 333, 461–63, 462
    purpose of 450–51
    qualitative measures 454, 456
    quantitative measures 456
    suppliers 463–64, 465
    supply chain 466
methane 19, 25, 39, 44, 258, 259
Microsoft 84, 370
Millennials 144

Index

modern slavery 51–53
   forms of 51
   signs of 52
Modern Slavery Act 2015 (UK) 131
Modern Slavery Act 2018 (Australia) 135
molybdenum 34
Moody ESG Solutions Group 380
Morgan Stanley Capital International (MSCI)
   Global Standard Index 180, 380, 381
motivational hierarchy, the *128*, 273
Myers, Norman 255

nachhaltiger Ertrag 110
Negotiation for Procurement and Supply Chain Professionals 2
nepotism 75
net zero, reaching 23, 170, 267, 429
New Circular Economy Action Plan 183
Nike 138
'nine planetary boundaries' 99
nitrogen trifluoride (NF3) 259
nitrous oxide (N2O4) 19, 259
Non-Financial Reporting Directive (NFRD) 134
No One is Too Small to Make a Difference 149

ocean degradation 13–18
   acidity levels 16, 18
   causes of *14*
   climate change, impact of 15, 18, 92
   impacts of 13
   noise, impact of 18
   overfishing 13, 15
   pollution and litter 16–18
OMEIA® methodology, the 117–18, 163, 169, 209, 219, 270, 285, 307, 310, 338, 366, 402, 438
   full process *121*
   prioritization of projects *271*
   Stage 1 *164*
   Stage 2 *218*
   Stage 3 *286*
open dumping 44–45
opportunity analysis 279–81
   opportunity analysis matrix 281, *281*
   process of 281
Orchestra of SRM® 120, 340, *341*
Organisation for Economic Co-operation and Development (OECD) 179
   Guidelines for Multinational Enterprises 179
Orwell, George 87
Ostrom, Elinor 470, 472

'outside-in' assessment 375, *376*
'outward-in' thinking 114

palm oil 224, 231, 427
Paris Agreement 19, 23, 170
Parkinson, Cyril Northcote 446
PAS 2050 182
PAS 2060 182
Patagonia 153–54
perfluorocarbons (PFCs) 259
permafrost 25
Perrier 138
persistent organic pollutants (POPs) 16–17
personal data, value of 81–82
PESTLE analysis 219, 221–24, 272, 415–16
   areas to consider *222–24*
   example PESTLE analysis *225*
   process of 221
Philip Morris 154
phosphorus 33, 37
plastics 17–18, 38, 39, 99
   e-waste 43
   microparticles 18
   in the ocean 17–18, 40
   single-use plastics 18, 38, 170, 262
Porter, Michael 115
positive impact stories 159–60, 456, 458–59
precious metals 33, 35, 43, 231
predictive modelling 120
prioritization 270–82, *274*
   impact assessment 277–79
      impact assessment and prioritization matrix 278, *280*
      process of 279
   opportunity analysis 279–81
      opportunity analysis matrix 281, *281*
      process of 281
   prioritization heat cube, the 282, *283*, 368
   risk assessment 273, 275–77
      example risk assessment *276*
      process of 275, 277
      risk prioritization matrix 275, *277*
   and targets 282
product breakdowns 322–25, *324*
profiling, intelligent 87–88
programmatic advertising 85–87
projects, choosing potential 285–305
   fact-finding
      data sources *293–94*
      markets 294–97, *296*
      planning for 289–91, *292*

Index

suppliers 294, *295*
supply chains 297, *297*
scoping 286–87
  process of 287, *288*
stakeholder management 287, 289
  RACI analysis 289
value levers, sustainable 297–300, *300*
  in full 301–05
Public Services (Social Value) Act 2012 131
purchase price cost analysis (PPCA) 265, 322–25
  vs product breakdown for sustainability *324*

Quakers, the 154
quality management systems 367

RACI model (Responsible, Accountable, Consult or Inform) 171, 172, 289
RAQSCI model (Regulatory, Assurance of supply, Quality, Service, Cost, Innovation) 316–17, *319*, 325, 329, 347, 352, 460
rare earth metals 34, 232
Refinitiv 380
remote assessment 217
RepRisk 380
request for information (RFI) 175
resource depletion / waste mismanagement 26–45
  causes of 28
  circular economy, the 45
  disposability 37–39, 40–42
  e-waste 42–44
  non-biodegradability 39–40
  overconsumption 29–30
  population growth 27, *29*
  recycling 36, 44
  scarcity of resources 31–36, *31–35*
  waste streams 39
Rio Declaration on Environment and Development 190
risk assessment 273, 275–77
  example risk assessment 276
  process of 275, *277*
  risk prioritization matrix 275, *277*
risk management 137–40
  reputational damage 138–39
  supply failure 137–38
  supply-side risk areas 139, *140*
road map, your 271–72, 442–45, *443*
  process for building 444–45
RobecoSAM 381
Roosevelt, Eleanor 50

Royal Society of Chemistry 228
Russian invasion of Ukraine, 2022 94, 137, 219

S&P Global ESG Scores 380
sand 32, 232
  sand mafia, the 54–55
Science Based Targets initiative (SBTi) 170, 178
scorecard, supplier 463–64, *465*
Sedex 227
service-level agreements (SLAs) 461, 463
shareholder consultation 165
shareholder demands 141–45
  public companies 145
  socially responsible investments (SRIs) 112, 142–45, *143*
Shift 192
should-cost analysis *see* purchase price cost analysis (PPCA)
Six Sigma 120
smartphones 42
SMART targets 216, 359–60
socially responsible investments (SRIs) 112, 142–45, *143*, 472
  greenwashing in 144–45
social responsibility (SR) 112
Social Value Act 145
Spreckley, Freer 186
SRI BES index 227
SSTP tool (Sustainability Situation, Target, Proposal) 217, 219, 220, 270, 272
stakeholder expectations 125, 148–51
  communities 151
  consumers 150
  employees 150–51
STPDR process, the 355–62, *357*, 422, 430
  do 361
  plan 360
  review 361–62
  study 356, 358
  target 358–60
'strategic purchasing trilogy' 2
strategy, for sustainable procurement
  mobilizing 209–10
  setting 204–05, *207*
Streamlined Energy and Carbon Reporting (SECR) 131
'strong sustainability' 101
sulfur hexafluoride (SF6) 259
Supplier Relationship Management 2, 116, 120, 122, 261, 340
supplier relationship management (SRM) 119–20, 340–47, 208, 402
  Orchestra of SRM® 120, 340, *341*

segmentation of suppliers 342–47, *344*
   criteria for sustainability 343, 345, *346*
supply and value chain network, the (SVCN) 116
   improvement projects 420, 422–36
      flows 423, 432–34
      goods / services 423, 434–35
      incentivization 423, 435–36
      relationships 423, 427–32
      structure 422, 423–27
   structure and flow, understanding 406–08, *407*
   supply and value chain network management (SVCNM) 120, 122
   sustainability in
      challenges of 404
      elements of *403*
      information flows, effective 408–10
   SVCN mapping 410–20
      environment and context 415–16
      lenses, sustainability 416, *417–19*
      refining 419–20, *421*
      structure and linkages 411–13, *414*
supply chain management (SCM) 120, 122, 208, 405
   pillars of 405–06
Sustainability Accounting Standards Board (SASB) 144, 181
sustainability, defining 8, 112
sustainability, history of 110–12, *111*
sustainability initiatives *158*, 158–60
   non-financial benefits 158–59
   positive impact stories 159–60
sustainability, key themes of 9, *9*
sustainability vs profit 123–24
'sustainability zeitgeist', the 1
Sustainable Finance Disclosure Regulation (SFDR) 134
sustainable procurement, defining 115–17
   areas of focus *117*
sustainable procurement framework 197–204, *198*
   expanded goals 199–204
sustainable value engineering 331–35, *336*, *461*
   process of 225
   total impact of ownership (TIO) 333–35, *334*, 461–63, *462*
   value engineering, defining 332–33
Sustainalytics 381
Swiss Responsible Business initiative 132

tantalum 34, 232
targets for sustainable procurement, setting 206–07, *207*
Tariff Act (1930) 131
Task Force on Climate-related Financial Disclosures (TCFD) 181
Taylor, Breonna 60
team, your 439, *441*, 441–42
Thunberg, Greta 23, 149, 469
Timber Regulations 135
Top Glove 52–53
topsoil 32, 99
total impact of ownership (TIO) 333–35, *334*, 461–63, *462*
'toxic colonialism' 42
Transparency Act 133
Transparency in Supply Chains Act 132, 133
triple bottom line (profit / people / planet) 177, 186–90, *187*, 470
   Balanced Scorecard 189
   metrics 189–90

UN Climate Action Summit 2019 469
UN Climate Change Conference 2015 (COP21) 170
UN Climate Change Conference 2021 (COP26) 19, 23, 24, 137, 170, 267
   David Attenborough at 97
UN Climate Change Conference 2022 (COP27) 19, 23, 267
UN Conference on Trade and Development (UNCTAD) 229
UN Convention Against Corruption 190
UN Declaration on the Rights of Indigenous Peoples 179
UN Environment Programme 226
UN Framework Convention on Climate Change 170
UN Global Compact 177, 179, 190–91, 373
UN Guiding Principles 177, 179, 191–92, 373
Universal Declaration of Human Rights (UDHR) 50, 93–94, 190, 373
UN Principles for Responsible Investment (PRI) 144, 181
UN Sustainable Development Goals (SDGs) 169, 177, 179, 190, 192–94, *193*, 197
   synergies in 193–94
US Department of Labor 229
US Geological Survey 228
US presidential elections 2016 95
Uyghur Forced Labour Prevention Act UFLPA 132

value chain, the 115–16
value creation 151–56
  altruism, 'true' 155
  'corporate philanthropy' 151, 154–55
  Patagonia 153–54
vertical integration 424
Vienna Declaration and Programme of Action 50
VIPER model 347–52, *348, 349, 370, 460*
  effectiveness of operations 350
  innovation 351
  performance 350–51
  risk 349–50
  value 351
Virgin Atlantic 188
vision for sustainability, setting the 163–76, *164*
  global agenda, the 169–71
    global targets 170
  impacts, primary 165–69
    assessment tool 167, *167, 168*
    steps for assessing 169
  shareholder demands 164–65
  stakeholder expectations 171–76
    engagement methods 174–76
    expectation mapping 172–74, *173*
  RACI model (Responsible, Accountable, Consult or Inform) 171, 172
voice of the customer (VOC) 175
Volkswagen CO2 emissions scandal 138
von Carlowitz, Hans Carl 110

'weak sustainability' 101
willingness, supplier 362–64
  preferencing tool 362, *363*
working conditions 61–71, *62*, 235–36
  job quality 66–67, 70–71
  physical hazards 63–65, 67–69
  wages 66, 69–70
  workers' rights 65, 69
  working environment 65–66, 67–69
World Bank 226
World Business Council for Sustainable Development 195, 227
World Economic Forum 228
  Stakeholder Capitalism Metrics 144, 179
World Health Organization 21
Worldometers 227
World Resources Institute 195, 227

zinc 34